FUNDAMENTALS OF FRANCHISING

Canada

Second Edition

PETER V. SNELL AND LARRY WEINBERG, EDITORS

AMERICAN BAR ASSOCIATION
Forum on Franchising

Cover design by Jill Tedhams/ABA Publishing.

Printed in the United States of America.

21 20 19 18 17 5 4 3 2 1

Library of Congress Cataloging-in-Publication Data

Names: Snell, Peter, 1968- editor. | Weinberg, Larry, 1963- editor. | American Bar Association. Forum on Franchising, sponsoring body.
Title: Fundamentals of franchising, Canada / edited by Peter Snell and Larry Weinberg ; Forum on Franchising, American Bar Association.
Description: 2nd edition. | Chicago, Illinois : American Bar Association, 2017. | Includes bibliographical references and index.
Identifiers: LCCN 2017010874 (print) | LCCN 2017011719 (ebook) |
ISBN 9781634256995 (ebook) | ISBN 9781634256988 (alk. paper)
Subjects: LCSH: Franchises (Retail trade)—Law and legislation—Canada.
Classification: LCC KE1973 (ebook) | LCC KE1973 .F86 2017 (print)
| DDC 346.7104/8—dc23
LC record available at https://lccn.loc.gov/2017010874

Contents

About the Editors

Peter V. Snell is a partner at Gowling WLG. He is based in Gowling WLG's Vancouver office and also works out of the firm's Calgary and Toronto offices. Peter is the national co-chair of Gowling WLG's franchise practice. He specializes in Canadian franchise law, international, and Canadian business transactions, licensing, product distribution, and intellectual property. He devotes his practice to assisting franchise systems with their expansion plans in Canada and overseas. Peter's focus on business and intellectual property issues led to his being appointed as the Chair of the Intellectual Property Committee of American Bar Association Business Law Section from 2013 to 2016. In 2016 he was appointed as a member of the ABA Business Law Section Council of Governors. He was the Chair of the Canadian Franchise Association's Legal and Legislative Committee from 2011 to 2015 and has been on the Board of Directors of the CFA since 2011. In 2015 Peter was appointed as General Counsel to the CFA. Peter is on the Executive of the Ontario Bar Association's Franchise Law Section.

In 2004, he co-edited and co-authored the first edition of the ABA Forum on Franchising's *Fundamentals of Franchising—Canada*. In 2013 he co-authored the chapter "Intellectual Property Issues in Franchising" in the ABA publication *Intellectual Property Deskbook for the Business Lawyer (3d Edition)*. Peter co-authored the chapter on Canada in the ABA publication *International Franchise Sales Laws*. In 2015 Peter authored the chapter on Canada in the *Franchise Law Review (2d Edition)*, and in 2016 he was the author of the Canada chapter for the *3d Edition*. He is recognized as a leading lawyer in Canadian franchise law in *Chambers, The Best Lawyers in Canada, Canadian Legal Lexpert Directory, Who's Who Legal: Canada, Who's Who Legal: The International Who's Who of Business Lawyers, Who's Who Legal: Thought Leaders 2017, Franchise Times* Legal Eagles (as one of the top franchise lawyers in Canada and the United States), and the Expert Guides, *World's Leading Franchise Practitioners*. Peter was appointed as a special advisor to the government of British Columbia in the drafting of British Columbia's franchise legislation.

Larry Weinberg is a partner in the Toronto office of Cassels Brock & Blackwell LLP and chair of the firm's Franchise Law Group. Since 1989 he has had a practice that specializes in franchise law and providing all necessary legal services to both domestic and foreign franchisors. He currently serves as Chair of the IFA's Supplier Forum Advisory Board and is the only Canadian lawyer on the IFA Board of Directors. He also currently serves as Chair of the Canadian

Franchise Association's Legal and Legislative Committee and on the CFA Board of Directors. He is also currently Co-Chair of the International Bar Association's International Franchising Committee and a Past Chair of the Ontario Bar Association's Franchise Law Section. Larry was the founder of, and to date has organised and chaired, four Ontario Bar Association annual franchise law conferences. In 2006, he was the first Canadian lawyer to be appointed a Director of the ABA Forum's International Division and to a leadership role as a member of its Governing Committee. In 2009 he had the honor of being Co-chair of the ABA's 32nd Annual Forum on Franchising conference. In 2004 he acted as co-editor of the first edition of the ABA Forum on Franchising's book *Fundamentals of Franchising-Canada*. As well, he was co-editor and co-author of the Canadian Franchise Association's first and only official book publication, *How to Franchise Your Business*. He is a co-author of the chapter on Canada for the ABA Forum's book *International Franchise Sales Laws*. In 2004, 2005, and each year from 2009 to 2017, Larry was named by *Franchise Times* to its "Legal Eagles" list of the top franchise lawyers in the United States and Canada. He and Cassels Brock are each listed in the *Canadian Legal Lexpert Directory* as being among the leaders in Canada in franchise law. In 2014, 2015, and 2016, Larry received U.K.-based Who's Who Legal's one and only worldwide Lawyer of the Year award for Franchise law, and in 2014 the *Lexpert*® Zenith Award. Larry was called to the Bar of the Province of Ontario in 1989.

About the Authors

Joseph Adler is a partner at Hoffer Adler LLP in Toronto, a senior franchise lawyer and a registered trademark agent. Joseph serves as legal counsel for Canadian and U.S. (and other foreign) franchisors doing business in Canada and Canadian franchisors doing business in the U.S. and abroad. He also acts and has acted for various multi-unit franchisees and franchisee associations as well. Joseph is the immediate past Secretary and General Counsel to the CFA (2011–2015) and a former Director and Executive Member of the CFA's Board of Directors (2007–2015). Joseph has published and has been quoted in numerous articles and has spoken on various franchising topics at venues organized by the CFA, the OBA, the ABA Forum on Franchising, and the IFA. Recognized by his peers, Joseph is consistently listed as a leading practitioner in franchise law in the *International Who's Who of Franchise Lawyers*, *Canadian Legal Lexpert Directory*, *Franchise Times* as a "Legal Eagle"—one of the top franchise lawyers in the U.S. and Canada—and *The National Post*'s Best Lawyers in Canada (Franchising).

Pascale Cloutier is a partner in Miller Thomson LLP and is one of very few lawyers whose call to both the Quebec and Ontario Bars qualifies her as a "national" practitioner by virtue of her in-depth knowledge of Canada's two unique legal systems. Fluent in French and English, she is a commercial litigator with specialized expertise in franchising. Pascale has appeared before all levels of court, including the Supreme Court of Canada and the Court of Appeal, as well as trial courts. Pascale has spoken on various franchising issues at venues organized by the Ontario Bar Association, the Barreau du Québec, the Conseil Québécois de la franchise and Multilaw. She is also co-editor and regularly contributes to the journal *Franchise and Distribution*. Pascale is listed in *Best Lawyers in Canada©*, *Canadian Legal Lexpert Directory* and *The International Who's Who of Business Lawyers*.

Edith Dover is Associate General Counsel at Cara Operations Limited, Canada's oldest and largest full-service restaurant company. Edith provides strategic legal advice to Cara's business groups with a specialization in all aspects of franchise law and regulation. She manages franchise agreements and related documentation, disclosure documents, franchise transfers, disputes and terminations, and is involved in Cara's franchise system acquisitions and integration. Prior to joining Cara, Edith practiced commercial litigation at Osler, Hoskin & Harcourt

LLP. Edith is a member of the Law Society of Upper Canada (called to the Bar in 1992) and the Canadian and Ontario Bar Associations, and she sits on the Ontario Bar Association's Franchise Law Executive Committee.

Bruno Floriani is a senior partner who co-chairs Lapointe Rosenstein Marchand Melançon, L.L.P.'s Franchising, Licensing and Distribution Department. He is a leading practitioner in business law, with a particular focus on franchise, distribution, license, and technology law. For over 30 years, Bruno has advised a wide range of business clients, from large corporations and public companies to SMEs, in various industries, including the food and beverage, manufacturing, franchise, retail and IT industries. Bruno has extensive experience in structuring hybrid franchising, licensing and joint-venture arrangements to ensure the international expansion of the franchising and licensing networks of clients in over 40 countries. His experience with general commercial matters, combined with his expertise in the fields of domestic and international distribution, franchising, licensing and technology transfer, allow him to provide clients with a broad and invaluable perspective. Given his proficiency in these areas, Bruno has frequently been solicited to lecture at various conferences on domestic and international distribution, franchising, licensing and joint ventures, as well as intellectual property issues and privacy law. He has also written extensively on these topics in various national and international legal journals and trade periodicals, and currently writes quarterly for the International Law Office, an Internet newsletter, as its exclusive contributor in the area of Canadian franchise law. Bruno has been the editor of the multinational annual practical guide *Getting the Deal Through: Licensing* since 2009, the Canadian contributor to *Getting the Deal Through: Franchising* since 2008, and the Canadian contributor to *Getting the Deal Through: Distribution & Agency* since 2016. Bruno is recognized in Canada and abroad as a leading practitioner in the franchise field by *Chambers*, *Lexpert*, *The International Who's Who of Franchise Lawyers* and *Who's Who Legal: Canada*; in the license field by *Global Law Expert*; in business law by *The International Who's Who of Business Lawyers*; and in the technology field by *Best Lawyers.*

Andraya Frith is a senior partner at Osler, Hoskin & Harcourt LLP and Chair of the Firm's National Franchise and Distribution Practice Group, one of the most frequently recommended law firms for franchise law in Canada. She practises business law with an emphasis on franchising, distribution, privacy, and e-commerce law. Andraya has extensive experience advising Canadian and international franchisors of all sizes operating in a broad range of industries, including quick-service restaurants, retail, pharmacy, automotive, real estate and hospitality. She counsels franchisors on structuring international and domestic franchise transactions and preparing "best in class" franchise agreements and franchise disclosure documents for use in Canada's increasingly complex franchise regulatory environment. Andraya has developed particular expertise on advising foreign franchisors and retailers who are expanding their operations to Canada. She helps them manoeuvre through significant judicial, statutory and cultural differences between their home jurisdiction and Canada to help ensure a smooth and successful entry into the Canadian market. She also regularly advises franchisors, retailers and on-line businesses on Canadian distribution and trade practice law, including privacy, anti-spam, consumer protection, Internet sales, advertising, and telemarketing. Andraya provides franchising, intellectual property and privacy support on business transactions. She is a frequent author and speaker on franchising in both Canada and the United States. She is actively involved in various trade and bar associations, including as an Executive Member of the Ontario Bar Association's Franchise Law Section, and a member of the Legal and Legislative Committee and the Annual Law Day Planning Committee of the Canadian Franchise Association, the Legal Symposium Task Force (2016–2017) of the International Franchise Association, and the Publications Committee of the American Bar Association. She is the co-editor of the *Canadian Franchise Guide* (2d Edition), a comprehensive loose-leaf service published by Carswell. Andraya is consistently recognized as a leading franchise lawyer in Canada and internationally by *Chambers Canada, Franchising* (Band 1) (with sources praising her "listening skills, relationship building, strategic thinking, and ability to simplify information for various audiences"), *Chambers Global, Franchising*, the *Canadian Legal Lexpert Directory*, *Lexpert Guide to the Leading US/Canada Cross-Border Corporate Lawyers: Franchising Law, The Best Lawyers in Canada (2017 Franchise Lawyer of the Year)*, *Who's Who Legal: Canada* (noted for her "know-how and skill" and "excellent reputation"), and the *International Who's Who of Franchise Lawyers*. In 2009, Andraya was the recipient of *Lexpert's* Top 40 Under 40 Award.

Clark Harrop is a senior franchising and corporate lawyer with in-house expertise representing leading foodservice brands. Clark obtained his BA (1993) from York University and his LLB (1996) from Osgoode Hall Law School. He was called to the Ontario Bar in 1998. Clark is Senior Legal Counsel to McDonald's Restaurants of Canada and advises McDonald's on a wide range of franchising, corporate and commercial matters. He was previously Director of International Support and Senior Corporate Counsel for Tim Hortons. Clark is a member of the CBA, OBA and ABA and is a frequent speaker on legal and business issues, including franchising, joint ventures, negotiating business agreements and international expansion.

Jeffrey Hoffman is a partner and Co-chair of Dale & Lessmann's Franchise Law Group. Jeffrey's practice includes all areas of commercial litigation with an emphasis on franchise and distribution law disputes, real estate disputes, employment disputes, and matters involving allegations of professional negligence. Jeffrey has over 29 years of experience in commercial litigation, including appearances before the Superior Court of Justice and the Court of Appeal for Ontario, as well as domestic and international commercial arbitration. He also acts as a mediator. Jeffrey has been recognized in a number of legal publications for his work in franchise law, including Chambers Canada 2016, Who's Who Legal: Canada and Lexpert (Most Frequently Recommended). He was named "Best Lawyers in Canada—2014 Toronto Franchise Lawyer of the Year," and was once again selected by his peers for inclusion in The Best Lawyers in Canada 2017. He is the immediate past chair of the Ontario Bar Association Franchise Law Section and is a member of the Commercial List User's Committee of the Commercial Court, Superior Court of Justice (Ontario). He is a regular instructor at the Advocates' Society of Ontario. Jeffrey is a frequent author on litigation and franchise matters. He has presented to numerous conferences and seminars, including those conducted by the Ontario Bar Association and the Canadian Franchise Association.

Darrell Jarvis is a partner at Fasken Martineau DuMoulin LLP and practises business law with a focus on franchising, leasing, construction, and mergers and acquisitions. Darrell is a frequent speaker and author in the franchising area and is recognized by *Lexpert*, *Best Lawyers in Canada*, *Who's Who Legal* and *Chambers*. Darrell is a member of the Ontario Bar Association Franchise Law Section and is Vice Chair of the Canadian Franchise Association Legal and Legislative Affairs Committee. Darrell has extensive experience in drafting and reviewing franchise agreements, master franchise agreements and disclosure documents, and in default enforcement, dealing with insolvent franchisees, workouts, and the purchase and sale of franchised businesses. Darrell has been involved in the co-branding of franchised businesses, the franchise of products within another business, the establishment of franchised businesses within big-box stores, and the conversion of company-operated units to franchised businesses. Prior to joining Fasken Martineau in 2009, Darrell held a number of executive positions at Cara Operations Limited, where he led the Legal, Franchising, Real Estate Development, Construction and Design Departments. Cara is the operator and franchisor of Swiss Chalet, Montana's, Kelsey's, Harvey's, Milestones, and, formerly, Second Cup, and was a multi-unit franchisee of several national brands, including Tim Horton's and Outback Steakhouse.

Edward (Ned) Levitt is a partner in the Corporate Commercial Group of Dickinson Wright LLP and Co-chair of its Franchise and Distribution Law Group. Ned provides legal services to Canadian and international clients on all aspects of Canadian franchise, licensing and distribution law and has represented some of the world's foremost franchises. He is recognized in *Who's Who Legal*, *The Best Lawyers in Canada*, and the *Canadian Legal Lexpert® Directory* as one of Canada's leading authorities in franchising and distribution law. Ned is a noted lecturer and a prolific writer, having published numerous books, papers and articles on franchise and distribution law, including the leading text, *Canadian Franchise Legislation* (2001, LexisNexis). He received the Canadian Franchise Association Lifetime Achievement Award (2010) and was General Counsel to the Canadian Franchise Association from 2000 to 2007. Ned is a member of the International Franchise Association, where he sits on its International Committee, and is also a member of the Canadian Franchise Association, the American Bar Association Forum on Franchising, the International Bar Association, and is a Certified Franchise Executive (2010). Called to the Ontario Bar in 1975.

Mike Melvin is recognized as a leading practitioner in the area of franchise law in the *Canadian Legal Lexpert® Directory* and is a member of the Canadian Franchise Association's Legal and Legislative Affairs Committee. Mike regularly writes and speaks on issues affecting franchising. He advises both Canadian and U.S. franchisors on Canadian franchise legislation and franchise documentation, cross-border structures, franchise transactions and franchisee compliance matters. Mike enjoys an active practice as a partner with McInnes Cooper. The firm is among the 20 largest business law firms in Canada.

John Rogers is Senior Associate Counsel to the Vancouver, BC law firm of Clark Wilson LLP, where he is Chair of its Franchise Law Group and a member of its Corporate & Commercial Group. He is a leading lawyer in the fields of franchising, licensing and distribution law and is also knowledgeable in the preparation and implementation of a wide range of commercial contracts. John practiced law in Toronto, Ontario, for eight years. While there, he served a four-year term as General Counsel, Director and Secretary of the Canadian Franchise Association. He is currently a member of the CFA's Legal & Legislative Affairs Committee. Mr. Rogers is recommended by the *International Who's Who of Franchise Lawyers*, by *Franchise Times* as a "Legal Eagle" and is "repeatedly recommended" in franchising, according to *Canadian Legal Lexpert® Directory*. His practice takes him throughout North America. John speaks Spanish at an intermediate level and is a director of the Mexican Franchise Business Association of Canada. John has acted as an author and lecturer for the International Franchise Association, American Bar Association, Canadian Franchise Association, The

Canadian Institute, Ontario Bar Association, British Columbia Bar Association and the Continuing Legal Education Society. Mr. Rogers received his Bachelor of Laws degree from the University of British Columbia in 1976. He was called to the British Columbia Bar in 1977 and to the Ontario Bar in 2005.

Judy Rost is a partner with Alexander Holburn Beaudin + Lang LLP in Vancouver, British Columbia, Canada. She leads the firm's commercial litigation group and has a very strong reputation for her franchise dispute work for both Canadian and international clients. She has been recognized by *Lexpert* as a leading Canadian lawyer in franchising law and has been ranked in both *International Who's Who of Franchise Lawyers* and *Who's Who Legal Canada*. Judy has written for many publications, including the *Franchise Law Journal* on international arbitrations and a chapter on British Columbia in the ABA publication *Covenants Against Competition in Franchise Agreements* (Third Edition). She has also presented and published for the IFA/IBA Joint Conference on News from Around the World in relation to Canadian Franchising. Judy has successfully built her practice by being a skilled litigator who is responsive to her clients' needs, and by finding creative solutions to resolve their disputes.

David Shaw is a partner at Blake, Cassels & Graydon LLP, practicing in the Corporate & Commercial group. He regularly advises clients in a wide range of industries on franchise law matters, including the preparation of master and individual franchise agreements, area development agreements, disclosure documents and related documentation, as well as advising and assisting clients with respect to system rebranding, regulatory compliance, franchise acquisitions and divestitures, and terminations. David was named as a *Franchise Times* Legal Eagle for 2016 and 2017 and selected in the practice area of Franchise Law for inclusion in the 2013 to 2017 editions of *The Best Lawyers in Canada*, *Who's Who Legal 2015* and *2016*, *The Canadian Legal Lexpert Directory* for 2014 through 2017 and *Chambers Canada: Canada's Leading Lawyers for Business 2016*. David is a long-standing member of the Executive of the Ontario Bar Association's Franchise Law Section and currently serves as its Program Coordinator. He is also a member of the Canadian Franchise Association's Legal & Legislative Affairs Committee and its Legislation and Regulations Subcommittee, the American Bar Association's Forum on Franchising, and the International Franchise Association. In addition, he has chaired, presented and facilitated roundtables at many franchising conferences and has written numerous articles relating to franchising, including co-chairing the 2009 Canadian Franchise Association Legal Day and the 2014 Ontario Bar Association Franchise Law Conference.

Geoff Shaw is a partner in the Toronto office of Cassels Brock & Blackwell LLP, with significant experience in the resolution of franchise law disputes through trial, appeal, mediation or arbitration. He has over 40 reported decisions and is regularly retained to defend franchisors in class actions. Geoff is a frequent author for industry publications and regularly speaks at international franchise law seminars. He is an active member of the Canadian Franchise Association (Government Relations Committee), the American Bar Association's Forum on Franchising, and the Advocates' Society. Geoff has completed two terms as a member of the International Franchise Association's Legal Symposium Task Force. He is also recognized as a leading lawyer in the *Lexpert® Guide to the Leading U.S./Canada Cross-Border Corporate Lawyers in Canada, Chambers Canada, The Best Lawyers in Canada,* and *Who's Who Legal*, and he was named a "Legal Eagle" by *Franchise Times* in 2014, 2015 and 2016. Geoff completed his Masters in Law Specialty in ADR in 2011. He is an adjunct professor in franchise law at Queen's University Law School. He was called to the Ontario Bar in 1986.

Stephane Teasdale has practised law for almost 30 years and is a partner in the Franchise Law Group of Cassels Brock & lackwell LLP in Toronto. Stephane is renowned across the country for his unique expertise in franchise faw. Stephane provides legal and strategic counsel in transactional and litigation matters dealing with franchising, distribution, and intellectual property, as well as in corporate, commercial and business law. He advises prominent Canadian franchise systems domestically, as well as those wishing to expand internationally. In fact, Stephane has advised Canadian systems having expanded internationally to markets such as Europe, Africa, Australia and China. Stephane also regularly advises American and foreign franchise systems wishing to establish themselves or expand into Canada, particularly in Quebec. Stephane is actively involved in Canadian, American and international franchise associations, and is a member of the Quebec Franchise Council. He is frequently invited to lecture and has authored articles in Canada and abroad on franchise and distribution matters related to local, national and international markets. He has been recognized for many years by *The Canadian Legal Lexpert Directory, The Best Lawyers in Canada, Who's Who Legal, Martindale-Hubell* and most recently by Chambers Canada as one of the premier specialists in franchising in Canada.

Peter Viitre is a corporate and commercial partner at Sotos LLP. For over 20 years, Peter has advised Canadian domestic and international clients on a wide range of complex business law issues and transactions, with a particular emphasis on franchise aw and mergers & acquisitions. Peter's franchise practice is focused primarily on serving franchisors in a myriad of industries and encompasses all aspects of franchise law and other retail and distribution matters, including the preparation of franchise agreements and disclosure documents, regulatory compliance, fair dealing and franchisee relations, supply arrangements, advertising programs and funds, dispute resolution, enforcement and termination. Peter frequently speaks and writes on franchise issues and is currently the Vice-Chair of the Ontario Bar Association's Franchise Law Section. He has been recognized as a leading Canadian franchise lawyer in various peer review rankings, including *Lexpert®*, *Chambers*, *Franchise Times* (Legal Eagles), and *Best Lawyers*, which named him Franchise Lawyer of the Year for Toronto in 2015. In March 2016, Peter was appointed as a member of the Ontario Government's Business Law Advisory Council, whose mandate is to recommend changes to the province's corporate and commercial laws to strengthen Ontario's competitive advantage in the global economy, solidify its position as a jurisdiction of choice for business, encourage innovation and investment, and support a responsive and flexible regulatory framework. He is the Chair of the Council's Franchise Law Working Group. On the M&A side, Peter regularly advises business owners and investors on the investigation, structuring, negotiation, completion and implementation of purchase and sale transactions and has played a leading role in both Canadian and international deals involving companies in the franchise, general retail, consumer credit, information technology, natural resource, and sports and entertainment industries, among others. In addition to franchise and M&A matters, Peter also routinely advises clients on general commercial issues, including corporate governance, finance and marketing initiatives.

Daniel Zalmanowitz is a judge in the provincial court of Alberta, Canada. Before his appointment, he was partner in the Edmonton, Alberta, law firm of Witten LLP. He is a graduate with Bachelor of Arts and Bachelor of Laws degrees from the University of Alberta. He was admitted to the Bar of Alberta in 1979 and appointed Queen's Counsel in 2010. He has authored numerous papers and articles on franchising for the Canadian Bar Association, the Canadian Franchise Association, the *Franchise and Distribution Law Journal*, *The Lawyers Weekly* and other publications. He was on the editorial board of *The Franchise and Distribution Law Journal*. He was past chair and a member of the Legal & Legislative Affairs Committee of the Canadian Franchise Association for many years. He was a member of Uniform Franchise Law Committee of the Uniform Law Conference of Canada, which developed the model franchise legislation that is used for provincial franchise legislation in Canada. He was recognized in the *International Who's Who of Franchise Lawyers*, the *Canadian Legal Lexpert Directory*, and *The Best Lawyers in Canada* as a leading practitioner in the area of franchising.

Foreword to the First Edition

Fundamentals of Franchising®—Canada is a truly exciting accomplishment for the Forum on Franchising. For years, many of the Forum's most active and professional members have been our associate members from Canada. Having the 2004 Annual Forum on Franchising in Vancouver, Canada, gave us the opportunity to present an Intensive Program on Canadian franchise law, and it quickly became apparent that the work that was going into this Intensive Program would make an excellent monograph.

All of this may sound obvious, but in fact this publication was developed, written, and published in record time and is a testament to the hard work and organizational skills of the authors and editors. I would like to join the editors in their thanks to each of the authors. The entire team has shown tremendous professionalism and focus to complete this monograph. I would especially like to thank Peter Snell and his co-editor, Larry Weinberg—their ideas originally led to the program and the monograph—and John Baer, the Forum's Publications Officer, who took the lead in shepherding this book to completion.

Thank you.

Steven M. Goldman
Chair, Forum on Franchising
2004

Foreword to the Second Edition

The ABA Forum on Franchising is extremely pleased to publish *Fundamentals of Franchising®—Canada, Second Edition*, a must-have resource not only for Canadian practitioners, but for every international attorney seeking to understand franchising in the Canadian provinces. This book greatly expands the material in the first edition of this book, adding commentary and analysis for the four new provinces enacting franchise laws since our original publication in 2004.

I would like to thank Peter V. Snell and Larry Weinberg for taking the initiative to recommend that a second edition of *Fundamentals of Franchising®—Canada* be published at this time and graciously agreeing to continue to serve as co-editors. I would also like to thank Rebekah Prince for serving as Peter and Larry's liaison to the Publications Committee. Of course, this book would not have been possible but for each of our chapter authors. I would like to express my deep gratitude to each chapter author: John Rogers and David Shaw (Chapter 1—Structuring and Expansion to Canada); Pascale Cloutier and Stéphane Teasdale (Chapter 2—Franchising in the Province of Québec); Clark Harrop and Edward (Ned) Levitt (Chapter 3—Other Laws Affecting Franchising in Canada (including Privacy); Bruno Floriani and Judy Rost (Chapter 4—Trademark and Other Intellectual Property Issues); Edith Dover and Darrell Jarvis (Chapter 5—The Canadian Franchise Agreement); Andraya Frith and Daniel Zalmanowitz (Chapter 6—Franchise Disclosure Issues in Canada); Jeffrey Hoffman and Geoff Shaw (Chapter 7—Dispute Resolution and Franchise Litigation in Canada); Joseph Adler and Peter Viitre (Chapter 8—Acting for the Canadian Franchisee); and Mike Melvin (Appendices).

I would also like to thank Publications Officer Jim Goniea for his continued leadership of the Forum on Franchising's Publications Committee. Finally, I would like to thank the other members of the Forum's Publications Committee and the ABA professional staff for making this publication possible.

Karen Satterlee
Chair, Forum on Franchising
2015–2017

Acknowledgments

A book such as this requires the effort of many hands. The editors would like to take this opportunity to thank the many people who contributed to both the First and Second Editions of this work. Firstly, we would like to thank Chuck Modell, who, as chair of the ABA Forum on Franchising's 2004 Annual Meeting in Vancouver, was instrumental in the creation of the Canadian intensive program that originally gave rise to the First Edition. Steve Goldman, then chair of the ABA Forum on Franchising, deserves much credit for being a champion in the creation of this monograph to add to the series of already successful ABA publications.

The individual authors from both editions were all pressed into doing double duty, if not more, in order to prepare chapters appropriate for publication in this work. We thank each of them for their extraordinary efforts.

The Second Edition of this book has been in the making for some years. At the time of the First Edition, in 2004, only two provinces in Canada had a franchise law. As of today there are six. The problem in completing a Second Edition was that each time we thought we were finished, another province announced plans to introduce a franchise law. So we got used to putting the project aside, revising the book to make it current, and then having the situation repeat itself. But enough is enough already! So we have now completed this Second Edition, which is current up until April 2017 and incorporates the new franchise law in the province of British Columbia. British Columbia is the sixth province to bring in a franchise law, alongside those that now exist in Alberta, Manitoba, New Brunswick, Ontario and Prince Edward Island. As of this writing, no other unregulated provinces have indicated any plans to bring in a franchise law.

Thank you to the members of the ABA Forum for their patience in awaiting this Second Edition. And a similar thank you to the lawyers on the ABA Forum's Publications Committee who have worked with us patiently over the last few years, and in particular Rebekah Prince, our immediate liaison, and Jim Goniea, current Chair of the ABA Forum's Publications Committee, and John Baer (whom we miss dearly) and Kathy Kotel, who assisted us with the First Edition. As well, we would like to thank the lawyers and staff within our respective firms who supported and assisted us on this project.

Finally, and especially, we need to thank our families for continuing to put up with us, and our commitments at work, year after year. For Peter, this means thanking my wife, Cari, who was pregnant with our first child when the First Edition was being published. Our son Taylor arrived just in time for the 2004

Forum and the launch of the First Edition. Our second son, Trevor, arrived just after the 2006 Forum, and both are quickly growing up and eagerly anticipating new adventures. For Larry, this means thanking my wife, Debbie, and children Jesse, Ariel and Rebecca. Since 2004, the kids have all but grown up, and I am so happy to see them become young adults to be proud of.

Thank you.

Larry Weinberg (Toronto)
and Peter Snell (Vancouver)
April, 2017

Introduction to the First Edition

A large number of American franchise systems have, over the last 40 years, made Canada one of their chosen international expansion targets. Many of these have thrived in the Canadian marketplace. They have joined the various home-grown franchise and other retail or service chains in a climate that readily accepts franchising as a method of doing business. Geographic proximity, together with a common language, history and culture, are cited often as the reasons why Canada is the first stop on the road to international markets for U.S. franchisors. In fact, experience tells us that many franchise systems did not historically consider Canada an "international market" at all, but instead simply an extension of their domestic one.

Just as the rest of the world has become a more complicated place to do business, however, so too has entry into this "sort of" international market directly north of the 49th parallel (the geographic line that forms a large part of the border between the two countries). This book is, in part, recognition of that fact. It has been developed as part of the Intensive Program on "Fundamentals of Franchising—Canada" being held at the ABA's Annual Forum in Vancouver, British Columbia, Canada, on October 6, 2004. The intention is to educate those readers who are, or who have, clients intent on expanding into the Canadian marketplace. In many ways, Canada is very familiar to American companies as a place to franchise their business. But in many crucial aspects, it is a different place to franchise and to conduct business.[1]

Canada has a well-educated, highly-skilled workforce, with disposable incomes and spending patterns generally seen as being on par with American consumers. Canada also has available retail locations and undeveloped land, an abundance of natural resources, and an extensive infrastructure of highways, railways, shipping lines and telecommunications. Canada is also seen as receptive to foreign investment. Canadian cities are generally considered safe, and Canadian business practices and legislative developments tend to follow those in the United States (except, notably, in the area of litigation), giving American business the opportunity to succeed in the Canadian marketplace. The vast majority of Canada's population lives within one hundred miles of the American border.[2]

---

1. This Introduction is, in part, reprinted from an article by Larry Weinberg and Geoffrey Shaw in the Fall 2004 ABA Forum's *Franchise Law Journal*, titled "A Practical Road Map to Entering the Canadian Market," and is reprinted with permission.

2. "Canadian Statistics—Population of census metropolitan areas," online: 2001 Census boundaries, http://www.statcan.ca/english/Pgdb/demo05a.htm.

So, as a result of many factors, Canada becomes the natural place to grow for an American franchisor lured to foreign markets and concerned about saturating its own local market.

Some of these considerations will typically factor into a well-reasoned decision and execution of a plan to expand or push into Canada. Experience dictates, however, that there are probably just as many examples of franchisors that have not devised any real plan at all and are instead pulled into Canada. This usually occurs because of interests expressed from prospective franchisees or area developers located in Canada. Now, however, and in particular because of the regulation of the franchise sales process in Ontario, Canada's most populated province, a spur-of-the-moment decision to be pulled into Canada will less likely be acted upon. That is probably good news for all potential stakeholders (franchisors and franchisees). Most franchisors and franchise professionals would generally counsel that a franchisor should first be ready with a plan to push into a new country on its own terms, as opposed to being pulled into a new market by the lure of a single-unit franchise.

Throughout this book the reader will likely learn more about Canada's political structure and constitutional division of powers than they care to know about. To avoid too much confusion, this Introduction will provide a short primer on the topic. Canada, like the United States, is rooted in a system of federalism. All aspects of governmental power are divided between the federal (national) and provincial levels of government. While there is but one federal government, there are ten provinces. In addition, there are now three territories, comprising much of Canada's uninhabited north. Territories enjoy a certain degree of autonomy and have their own territorial governments, but otherwise rely to a great extent on the federal government.

The *Constitution Act, 1867*[3] s. 91 grants the federal government exclusive jurisdiction over such areas as trade and commerce, banking and bills of exchange, bankruptcy and insolvency, trademarks, patents and copyrights. Section 92 grants provincial governments exclusive jurisdiction over such areas as property and civil rights, as well as the administration of justice in the province. Of relevance to franchisors, therefore, is the fact that intellectual property law (patents, trademarks and copyright), as well as competition (antitrust) law, is within the federal jurisdiction with statutes that apply nationally, while private contractual matters fall within the purview of the provincial governments with their jurisdiction over "property and civil rights . . ." Hence, any franchise legislation in Canada will only ever likely arise at the provincial level, and to date, only the provinces of Alberta and Ontario have passed such laws.

3. (U.K.), 30 & 31 Vict., c. 3, reprinted on R.S.C. 1985, App. II. No. 5.

While this book will outline a host of important differences when comparing the business, law and practice of franchising in Canada and the United States, it will also reveal numerous similarities between the culture and law of both societies. The most successful franchise systems doing business in Canada will invariably be those that recognize and respect the differences, while fully exploiting the similarities.

We hope you gain much from this work.

Larry Weinberg and Peter Snell, 2004

Introduction to the Second Edition

The First Edition of this book was published in 2004. Since that edition was published, a lot has changed, both in the world and in the franchise laws and practices in Canada.

But upon reflection, a lot has stayed the same. For instance, the Introduction to the First Edition is still almost entirely as correct and relevant in 2017 as it was back in 2004. It still accurately provides an overview of the Canadian marketplace and legal system. As a result, we have decided to leave it in the book in its original form and commend you to read it. Recent information provided by the United States Department of Commerce confirms that Canada ranks as the number-one market for franchisors based in the United States looking to expand internationally.[1]

That being said, some things have changed in Canadian franchise law, and those things are what gave rise to the need for a second edition of this book. Most notably, in 2004 there were only two Canadian provinces with a franchise law. There are now six of the ten Canadian provinces with a franchise law that is in force.

Back in 2004 only the provinces of Alberta and Ontario had franchise laws. Today, Alberta, British Columbia, Manitoba, New Brunswick, Ontario, and Prince Edward Island have franchise laws. As well, since 2004 there has been a flurry of litigation involving franchise systems that has led to new conclusions on the interpretation of the franchise statutes in Canada. Accordingly, this Second Edition was needed so that the reader has up-to-date information on all of the provincial franchise laws.

A number of other points should be made in regard to this Second Edition. Firstly, we have reorganized the chapters to some degree. While most chapters are similar in title and coverage compared to the First Edition, their scope has been expanded. For instance, the chapter on Canadian franchise litigation has been expanded to correspond to the much greater frequency of reported case law in this area since the First Edition. Meanwhile, in 2004 we had a whole chapter devoted to Canada's then-new privacy laws. For this Second Edition, we have incorporated the discussion on privacy laws into an expanded chapter titled "Other Laws Affecting Franchising in Canada."

---

1. *2016 Top Markets Report – Franchising, A Market Assessment Tool for U.S. Exporters*, U.S. Department of Commerce, International Trade Administration, May 2016.

Second, we have changed and added some new chapter authors. In part this is on account of the growing number of franchise lawyers in Canada, and also takes into account some retirements from the profession.

Third, this edition takes into account the electronic world in which we now all live. So instead of including copies of each provincial franchise law, we have included a Table of Concordance that provides a list of the electronic links to where you may find the statutes and their regulations.

It is very likely that another 13 years will not have to pass until there is a third edition of this book. The pace at which provinces are adding franchise laws has increased, and there are still four provinces in this country that have no franchise laws whatsoever. While there is no hint at the time of publication that any of those four provinces will add legislation, it is perhaps inevitable. As well, the amount of litigation and reported case law has increased relatively because these franchise laws now exist, and provide, as will be discussed, a number of important rights if the disclosure rules are not complied with in full. So we expect more litigation and reported case law that will assist in the interpretation of these laws.

In the meantime, we hope you find the Second Edition of *Fundamentals of Franchising—Canada* a valuable tool.

Larry Weinberg and Peter Snell
April 2017

CHAPTER 1

Structuring an Expansion to Canada

John L. Rogers and David M. Shaw

Contents

I. Introduction[1]

A non-Canadian franchisor planning to expand its franchise system to Canada must make important decisions on the type of legal entity to use for the expansion and the method by which the expansion will be implemented. In addition, important tax issues must be dealt with: income tax, withholding tax, sales tax, harmonized sales tax, goods and services tax, and custom duties are all potentially relevant.

At the outset, it is important to understand the division of powers in Canada between the federal and provincial levels of government. This division is set forth in Canada's *Constitution Act*, a federal statute. Powers given to each level of government in Canada are similar to those in the U.S., but with important differences. For example, there is only one federal trademark statute in Canada. Residual power resides with the federal authority in each country, but residual federal power is invoked much less in Canada. Canadian courts have given a broad interpretation to key provincial powers: in particular, power to govern over "property and civil rights." In the result, Canadian provinces sometimes enjoy greater autonomy than U.S. states, for example, in the fields of trade and commerce.

In Canada, regulation of franchises and consumer protection are matters of provincial jurisdiction and often vary significantly between individual provinces. Canada has no federal enactment equivalent to the FTC Rule in the United States.

Practice Note

At present, six out of ten Canadian provinces—Alberta, Manitoba, Ontario, New Brunswick, Prince Edward Island and British Columbia—have franchise legislation. None of them require franchisors to register. Canada has no federal franchise legislation. British Columbia's *Franchises Act* is the newest franchise legislation, having come into force on February 1, 2017.

1. The authors, John L. Rogers of Clark Wilson LLP (jlr@cwilson.com) and David Shaw of Blake, Cassels & Graydon LLP (david.shaw@blakes.com), wish to thank Adam M. Dlin, Lawyer, Morgan Daniels Slager LLP, for his prior contribution to this chapter. The authors would also like to thank the following tax lawyers for their invaluable contributions: Richard T. Weiland, Partner, Clark Wilson LLP, Paul Stepak, Partner, Blake, Cassels & Graydon LLP, and Robert J. Kreklewich, Partner, Blake, Cassels & Graydon LLP.

II. Options for Expansion to Canada

A. Branch or Subsidiary

Initially, a non-Canadian franchisor may decide to maintain direct control over a Canadian expansion by opening and operating one or more franchise units in Canada on its own. This "direct franchising" may use a branch or subsidiary structure. Once the franchisor has established itself in Canada, it may find it easier to expand further by contracting with one or more Canadian master franchisees or area developers.

While tax considerations will be critical in deciding between a branch or subsidiary structure, non-tax factors are important as well.

In considering expansion options, a non-resident franchisor may wish to engage one or more experts, including a Canadian franchise lawyer, accountant and consultant, to assist with various aspects of the following:

- penetrating the Canadian market and reducing "rookie mistakes" in a cost-effective manner;
- facilitating incorporation of a subsidiary, Canadian trademark application and preparation of legal documentation (including, where required, a franchise Disclosure Document);
- "Canadianizing" the franchisor's concept, marketing materials, franchise agreement, operations manual and related documents;
- using a consultant's premises as an initial Canadian sales office and the consultant's sales team to locate and qualify potential Canadian franchisees;
- franchise site selection, lease negotiation and financing of franchisees; and
- recruiting, training and supporting new Canadian franchisees.

Practice Note

When a non-resident franchisor decides to maintain direct control over its Canadian expansion by opening and operating franchise units on its own, it will generally need to choose between a branch or subsidiary structure. Both tax and non-tax factors should be considered in making this decision.

1. Branch

(a) Structure

Rather than forming a separate corporate entity through which to operate, a non-resident franchisor may decide to develop its system in the Canadian market by operating from its home office or by establishing a branch office in Canada to provide a local base from which to administer the expansion. In either case, the franchisor will maintain direct control over the selection, training and administration of franchisees in Canada.

Practice Note

Establishing a branch operation in Canada does not require the formation of a separate subsidiary or other legal entity.

(b) Tax considerations of a branch

Income tax considerations of operating from a home office outside of Canada as opposed to setting up a branch office in Canada must be considered carefully. On the one hand, if the new Canadian operation is to be run by an arm's-length entity that is granted master franchise rights or area development rights, with the franchisor having little involvement in day-to-day operations, then income earned by the franchisor through initial franchise fees and royalties would likely be treated as 'passive.' In that case, gross franchise payments made by Canadian resident franchisees will only be subject to a withholding tax. Canada's general withholding tax on royalty payments is 25% but, by the Canada-U.S. Tax Treaty, is reduced to 10% for U.S. franchisors entitled to treaty benefits.

If, on the other hand, the franchisor actively administers the Canadian operation, its compensation would be treated as business income which would not be subject to withholding tax. Instead, the franchisor would be taxable in Canada on a net income basis at rates varying from 25% to 30%, depending on the province or territory of Canada in which the income is earned.

In addition, the Canadian government imposes a "branch tax" on a non-resident operating company equal to 25% of its net after-tax income in Canada that is not reinvested in the Canadian branch operation. The branch tax is designed to provide the Canadian tax authorities with revenue similar to what they would receive when a franchisor operates in Canada through a subsidiary. However, this rate is reduced by tax treaty to just 5% for U.S. resident corporations, with the first c$500,000 of after-tax Canadian income of the U.S. corporation being exempt from the branch tax.

Canadian income tax of a branch operation, including withholding tax and branch tax, will normally qualify for a foreign tax credit for the non-resident franchisor in the computation of its income tax liability at home.

When income derived in Canada is business income instead of passive royalty-type income and is not earned through an office or other permanent establishment in Canada (which may occur if all business locations in Canada are operated by independent franchisees), the provisions of most of Canada's tax treaties, including its tax treaty with the U.S., will provide an exemption from Canadian income tax, including branch tax. However, the absence of an office in Canada will likely suggest to the Canadian tax authorities that fees earned by the franchisor from Canadian operations are passive and therefore should be subject to withholding tax. The franchisor must be prepared to deal with this issue with the Canadian tax authorities; it will need to demonstrate that it has actively participated in the Canadian franchise operation to avoid paying withholding tax.

(c) Tax advantages of a branch

Some of the tax advantages of a non-resident franchisor operating through a branch in Canada are:

- if the non-resident franchisor has no permanent establishment in Canada, there will be no Canadian income tax liability, provided the income is determined to be "active";
- if the non-resident franchisor does have a permanent establishment in Canada, then, by treaty, Canadian income tax paid by it will usually qualify for a foreign tax credit when computing its home income tax liability;
- in the case of a U.S. corporation, the first c$500,000 of after-tax income earned in Canada is exempt from Canadian branch tax;
- losses from a Canadian branch operation will typically reduce taxable income in the franchisor's home jurisdiction; and
- if Canadian income is determined to be passive and subject to Canadian withholding tax, then non-resident franchisors in most jurisdictions will receive a foreign tax credit for such tax paid in Canada when calculating their home jurisdiction tax liability. If the Canadian operation has limited expenses, then the amount of the withholding tax payable may be substantially less than the Canadian tax that would have been payable by a subsidiary.

(d) Tax disadvantages of a branch

There are some tax-related disadvantages of using a branch in Canada, namely:

- at the point when the non-resident franchisor becomes subject to the branch tax, it will be payable annually as income is earned (accrual basis), rather than when income is paid to the foreign jurisdiction. On the other hand, withholding tax on a dividend distribution by a Canadian subsidiary to its parent will not be payable until the dividend is actually paid (cash basis); and
- there is a risk that tax authorities will assert that payments to the non-resident franchisor are passive income subject to a withholding tax on gross income paid (rather than tax at regular corporate rates and potential branch tax on the net income payment). If expenses are significant and the tax rate is not reduced by a tax treaty with Canada, a flat withholding tax on the gross payment (even though it might be reduced) could eliminate all profit. Additional withholding tax will apply if any portion of the payments to the non-resident franchisor is in respect of services performed by it in Canada. If a Canadian subsidiary is used, however, tax will only be payable on its net Canadian income.

Practice Note

The tax consequences of establishing a branch operation in Canada should be carefully considered before proceeding with the branch.

(e) Registrations required for a branch

A franchisor establishing a branch operation in Canada must register with a number of authorities, including:

- the corporate registry in each province and territory of Canada where the franchisor will "carry on business," generally interpreted as any place where the franchisor has a place of business, resident agent, is listed in a telephone directory, conducts advertising, or in some other way carries on business. Registration is effected by reservation of the franchisor's name, registration of an information form (which differs from province to province or territory) and, in some cases, filing of certified copies of the franchisor's charter documents. In the province of Québec, where French is the official language, a foreign corporation must choose a French name to be used in carrying on its business activities;

- Canada Revenue Agency (Canada's federal tax authority) for a "business number" for remittances of corporate income tax, employee payroll deductions, goods and services tax, or harmonized sales tax and import/export authorization (as applicable);
- authorities in each city and province or territory where the branch carries on business for a business licence and for licences related to sales tax and workers' compensation insurance (as applicable) and possibly other matters; and
- employees of the non-resident franchisor moving to Canada to work for the franchisor will need to obtain Canadian work permit visas.

Practice Note

Several registrations at various governmental levels are required to be obtained by a franchisor when establishing a branch operation in Canada.

2. Subsidiary

(a) Structure

As an alternative to the branch structure, a non-resident franchisor may choose to establish a wholly-owned Canadian subsidiary to operate its franchise system in Canada. In this case, the franchisor will have full operating control of the subsidiary as a separate corporate entity through ownership of the subsidiary's shares and appointment of its board of directors and managers. This structure may provide an effective shield against creditors for a non-resident franchisor seeking to avoid liability for potential start-up losses and other liabilities that may arise in a new Canadian operation. In deciding whether to operate through a subsidiary, some additional costs will need to be taken into account—for example, the costs associated with the incorporation and maintenance of a separate legal entity and annual preparation and filing of financial statements and Canadian income tax returns for the Canadian subsidiary.

Practice Note

Establishing a subsidiary requires the formation and maintenance of a separate Canadian legal entity having its own actual and potential liabilities.

(b) Jurisdiction of incorporation of a subsidiary in Canada

A subsidiary may be incorporated federally or in any province or territory of Canada. Some considerations in making a decision where to incorporate are:

- federal incorporation offers stronger name protection in that a franchisor will have the right to use its incorporation name in all ten provinces and three territories of Canada, even if another entity is using the same or a similar name in a province or territory;
- the federal jurisdiction and some of the provinces and territories have requirements that a certain number of directors be Canadian residents. Jurisdictions that do not have director residency requirements include the provinces of British Columbia, New Brunswick, Nova Scotia, Prince Edward Island and Québec, as well as the Nunavut Territory, the Northwest Territories and the Yukon Territory; and
- the initial and ongoing costs of federal incorporation and corporate maintenance generally exceed those of incorporating provincially.

A special category of incorporation known as an "unlimited liability company" (ULC) is available in the provinces of Nova Scotia, Alberta and British Columbia. ULCs are treated in the same way as other corporate entities for Canadian tax purposes, but as flow through entities for U.S. tax purposes. Unlike normal federal and provincial corporations where the liability of shareholders is limited to their payment for shares, the liability of shareholders of ULCs is unlimited; for this reason, in a typical ULC structure, the ultimate U.S. shareholder may establish a "liability blocker," such as an intermediate subsidiary, to be the ULC's sole shareholder. Due to their treatment under the Canada-U.S. Tax Treaty, distribution of profits from a ULC to a U.S. parent corporation requires a two-step distribution process in order to avoid adverse tax consequences. This two-step process involves a stated increase in the paid-up capital of the shares of the ULC, followed by a payment that reduces the paid-up capital. Note that the two-step process does not provide relief where the ULC's shareholder is a U.S. limited liability company (LLC) that is a flow-through entity for U.S. tax purposes.

Practice Note

A franchisor seeking to form a Canadian subsidiary will need to decide between incorporating the subsidiary federally or in a particular province or territory. A U.S. franchisor may wish to consider incorporating a ULC in Nova Scotia, Alberta or British Columbia for U.S. tax-planning purposes.

(c) Tax considerations of a subsidiary

No distinction is made between passive and active income in the case of subsidiaries; income tax on all net income is calculated at corporate rates which would be applicable if the non-resident parent carried on business directly in Canada (i.e., tax at 25% to 30%). Furthermore, no branch tax would be payable on the subsidiary's income.

Dividends paid by a subsidiary would be subject to withholding tax of 25% (or any lower rate established by an applicable tax treaty, such as 5% for a U.S. franchisor parent that qualifies for benefits under the Canada-U.S. Tax Treaty). The Canadian tax liability of a subsidiary does not usually qualify for a tax credit in the foreign jurisdiction. However, a U.S. parent would receive a foreign tax credit in computing its home tax liability for the 5% withholding tax payable on dividends (percentage reduced from 25% by the Canada-U.S. Tax Treaty) but again, not for regular Canadian income tax paid by the subsidiary.

A non-resident parent is entitled to charge a fee for providing assistance to its Canadian subsidiary to carry out its business activities. The fee, if reasonable, will be a deductible expense in calculating the Canadian subsidiary's income. If the franchisor is resident in a country that has a tax treaty with Canada, such fee payment will be exempt from Canadian income tax if the parent does not have a permanent establishment in Canada. It is important to deductibility that the fee not exceed the amount that would be payable if the subsidiary and parent were unrelated and were dealing on an arm's-length basis.

It may be possible for a subsidiary to carry on business solely from a foreign country and therefore not "carry on business" in Canada at all. In this case, some Canadian registrations may be avoided.

(d) Tax advantages of a subsidiary

The tax advantages of a non-resident franchisor operating through a subsidiary include the following:

- The risk of withholding tax on passive income is avoided. This is an advantage if taxation of gross revenue would result in a higher level of tax than the Canadian income tax payable (25% to 30% of net income).
- Dividends are not taxed until paid, whereas a branch tax would be payable when earned.

(e) Tax disadvantages of a subsidiary

Tax disadvantages associated with a non-resident franchisor parent carrying on business through a subsidiary include:

- any losses incurred by a Canadian subsidiary may not be used to reduce the parent's home income tax liability;
- Canadian income tax usually does not qualify for a foreign tax credit in computing the parent's income tax liability in its home jurisdiction—only withholding tax on dividends paid to the foreign parent will qualify; and
- no withholding tax option is available if income is passive (the flat withholding tax on gross income might have resulted in less tax).

Practice Note

As in the case of operating through a branch, the tax consequences of establishing a Canadian subsidiary should be considered and reviewed with a tax advisor prior to implementing such a structure.

(f) Potential shareholders' agreement for a subsidiary

If at any time a franchisor allows a third party to acquire shares in its subsidiary (for example, in exchange for the transfer of business outlets owned by the third party that are converted to units in the franchisor's system), then preparation of a shareholders' agreement is strongly recommended. A shareholders' agreement may (among other things):

- describe what types of shares each shareholder owns and any shareholder loan(s) each is to make;
- set out the expectations and obligations of the parties in a wide variety of circumstances;
- provide a means of dispute resolution;
- provide protection to a minority shareholder and minimize any inequality of key voting positions caused by differing percentages of voting shares held;
- set out the agreement of the parties on the percentages of votes required to approve major matters when a particular resolution or set of circumstances is presented;
- control who might become an additional shareholder of the subsidiary;
- provide for what will happen when one or more of the shareholders (or a principal of a corporate shareholder) dies, divorces, becomes disabled, becomes inactive in the franchise business, or becomes in some other way unable or unwilling to contribute to the business;
- set out circumstances when a shareholder in default may be removed; and

- provide a method for the shares of a shareholder to be repurchased by the subsidiary upon his/her retirement, disability or death (or that of a principal of a corporate shareholder).

> **Practice Note**
>
> **If there are one or more arm's-length shareholders of a subsidiary, then a shareholders' agreement is strongly recommended. It may cover many important matters.**

(g) Registrations required for a subsidiary

If a subsidiary (including a federally incorporated subsidiary) intends to carry on business in several Canadian jurisdictions, it must register with the corporate registries in all of those jurisdictions (except for its jurisdiction of incorporation) in order to carry on business in such jurisdictions. A subsidiary is required to complete the same registrations as a non-resident franchisor setting up a branch operation (see earlier discussion).

> **Practice Note**
>
> **As in the case of a branch, a subsidiary will be required to complete a number of regulatory registrations in Canada.**

B. Special Rules for an Unlimited Liability Company (ULC)

Special tax benefits applicable to a ULC generally apply only when the ULC is owned directly or indirectly by a U.S. parent.

1. Tax Considerations of a ULC

A ULC is treated as an ordinary Canadian company for Canadian income tax purposes, so it must pay tax at normal corporate rates in Canada. As with an ordinary Canadian company, a ULC does not pay branch tax. Due to a ULC's unlimited liability, U.S. tax rules generally treat the ULC as a flow-through legal entity and will treat Canadian tax payable as a debt owing by its U.S. parent. The income of a ULC is taxable in the U.S., where Canadian income tax paid by the ULC qualifies for a foreign tax credit. Tax benefits of a ULC are generally restricted to the U.S. and are not available in other countries.

2. Tax Advantages of a ULC

The tax advantages of a ULC (in contrast to a conventional branch or subsidiary) include:

- a ULC avoids the question of whether franchise agreement payments are passive income (and subject to withholding tax) or business income taxable on a net income basis—as is the case for Canadian resident taxpayers. Payments to a ULC will be taxed on a net income basis;
- there is a U.S. foreign tax credit for a ULC for Canadian income tax paid that is not available when a conventional subsidiary is used; and
- there is no Canadian branch tax payable by a ULC.

3. Disadvantages of a ULC

The disadvantages of a ULC are:

- the exemption of a branch from Canadian tax based on the absence of a permanent establishment in Canada is not available. As a ULC is treated as a Canadian resident for Canadian income tax purposes, it does not qualify for relief from Canadian tax available to a branch under the Canada-U.S. Tax Treaty;
- in some provinces, a ULC is more expensive to incorporate and maintain than a conventional limited liability business corporation; and
- making distributions from a ULC to a U.S. parent without adverse tax consequences requires additional planning steps involving a stated increase in the paid-up capital of the shares of the ULC, followed by a payment that reduces the paid-up capital. This relief is not available where the direct parent is a U.S. LLC that is itself a flow-through corporation for U.S. tax purposes.

Practice Note

A U.S. franchisor may wish to consider establishing a subsidiary as a ULC rather than a conventional limited liability corporation.

C. Joint Venture

Another alternative for the non-resident franchisor is to enter into a joint venture to establish and develop the Canadian market for its franchise system. Two or more parties may engage in a joint venture whereby they agree to collaborate in a business venture. The term "joint venture" has no precise meaning, but generally denotes an association of two or more parties, typically governed by a written contract, pursuant to which such parties agree to combine their resources in furtherance of a desired venture with a goal of maximizing profits.

The elements of a joint venture often include: (i) a contribution of money, property, effort, knowledge, skill or other assets to a common undertaking; (ii) a joint property interest in the subject matter of the venture; (iii) mutual control or management of the enterprise; (iv) an expectation of profit; and (v) a right to participate in those profits. Joint ventures are attractive, as they enable parties to combine resources in a synergistic manner that creates value from the venturers' working together which may exceed the value that they could realize independently as stand-alone businesses. Joint ventures are also useful for acquiring and sharing knowledge and experience and diversifying risk.

While joint venture formation is similar to an acquisition transaction in many ways, there is at least one fundamental difference: a joint venture marks the beginning rather than the end of the relationship between the parties. As a result, a sense of balance and a long-term perspective is crucial, with collaboration and cooperation between the parties being paramount. Accordingly, effective governance and dispute-resolution procedures play an important role in any joint venture agreement. In addition, the arrangement must be mutually beneficial to all venturers to enjoy a prospect of long-term viability.

A non-resident franchisor contemplating a joint venture will usually want to select a Canadian co-venturer that can contribute local franchise knowledge, operating experience, human resources and industry contacts, together with a reasonable amount of capital. One commonly identified source of joint venture failure is poor partner selection. Without the right co-venturer and an alignment of interests and objectives between the parties, no amount of legal contract drafting can solve irreconcilable differences between the parties that may arise. This is particularly true with respect to a joint venture that will operate for an indefinite term, as a longer term increases the risk that unforeseen problems may arise as markets evolve or the strengths and weaknesses of the parties and the brand of the venture change over time.

Practice Note

While joint venture formation is similar to an acquisition transaction in many ways, there is one fundamental difference: a joint venture marks the beginning rather than the end of the relationship between the parties.

Various legal forms may be utilized to form joint ventures. Generally, the formation of a joint venture may take one of three forms:

- equity joint venture;
- co-ownership; and
- contractual joint venture.

Each form will determine the nature of the joint venture agreement to govern the parties' relationship and the manner in which the joint venture will be operated, as described in further detail below. Tax considerations will often determine which form the joint venture will take (as discussed above and below).

Practice Note

The tax consequences associated with a joint venture should be reviewed with a tax advisor; they will often determine the type of structure to be used by the joint venturers.

1. Equity Joint Ventures

An equity joint venture typically has the following attributes:

- contribution of capital by each party; and
- each party having an ownership interest entitling it to participate in control of the joint venture and to share in its profits or losses.

The forms of equity joint ventures include general partnerships, limited partnerships, limited liability corporations and ULCs, as described below.

(a) Partnership

A common definition of a partnership is ". . . the relation which subsists between two or more persons carrying on business in common with a view of profit." Similar wording is used in various provincial partnership statutes in Canada. There are generally only two kinds of partnership that a franchisor and co-venturer may use—namely, "general" or "limited" partnerships. The legal relationship between partners is typically governed by a partnership agreement, which addresses, among other things, their respective rights and obligations, their intended management and operation of the joint venture business, the allocation of profits and losses among the partners, and the mechanism and requirements relating to bringing on a new partner or an existing partner leaving the partnership.

Because of its flow-through nature, a partnership might be appropriate if a joint venture business is expected to generate disproportionately large expenses in its early years, as the partnership structure would allow the individual co-venturers to take advantage of the tax write-offs arising from these expenses. In the case of a limited partner, the amount of losses that may be available is limited by the amount that the limited partner is considered to have "at risk" in the partnership.

> **Practice Note**
>
> **A franchisor and co-venturer may form either a general or limited partnership instead of a corporation, and may use a partnership agreement to establish their respective rights and obligations and their intended management and operation of the joint venture business.**

(i) General Partnership

A general partnership is a relationship between two or more persons carrying on business in common with a view to profit. At its core, a general partnership creates an agency relationship, where each partner acts as an agent of the general partnership as well as the other partner(s). A general partnership is not a separate legal entity and, absent the desire to carry on business under a different name, there is no requirement to register a general partnership. However, non-registration is not sufficient to avoid being found to be operating as a partnership, as a partnership can be found to exist based solely on the conduct of the parties.

A general partnership is an appealing form of joint venture because it involves few formalities. It is simple and inexpensive to establish and dissolve. Moreover, a general partnership is not subject to the mandatory rules imposed on corporations, including any director residency requirements.

However, general partnerships expose their partners to significant commercial risk, as the partners are jointly and severally liable for the debts and obligations of the general partnership, and each partner has unlimited liability with respect to the full amount of the general partnership's liabilities. Further, circumstances affecting a partner, such as death, bankruptcy, withdrawal or retirement, may result in the automatic termination of the partnership. While general partnerships provide parties with significant flexibility, without the benefit of business corporations legislation providing a robust statutory framework, careful drafting of the partnership agreement is imperative to properly establish the significant rights and obligations of the partners.

> **Practice Note**
>
> **In considering a general partnership structure, the parties should weigh the efficiency of the structure against the exposure to unlimited liability with respect to the general partnership's liabilities.**

(ii) Limited Partnership

A limited partnership represents a middle ground between a corporation and a general partnership with respect to liability of shareholders or partners. A limited partnership consists of one or more general partners, whose liability is unlimited, and one or more limited partners, whose liability is limited to the amount of money or property they agree to contribute to the limited partnership. While a limited partnership is not a separate legal entity, it is still formed in compliance with specific legislation, such as the *Limited Partnerships Act* of Ontario. As with a general partnership, a limited partnership has no statutory requirements for directors. Nevertheless, any partner that is itself a corporation must comply with its own corporate compliance requirements.

Limited partners of a limited partnership will not be liable for more than the payment of their agreed capital contributions to the limited partnership, provided they refrain from participating in the management of the limited partnership. Instead, liability to third-party creditors will accrue to the general partner that manages the limited partnership business. A general partner may limit its liability significantly if it is incorporated by the limited partners for the sole purpose of managing the limited partnership, is given few assets to manage, and capitalization of the general partner is limited in amount.

The disadvantages of a limited partnership, as compared to a general partnership, include greater expense and formality in its creation, maintenance and dissolution. In particular, unlike a general partnership, a limited partnership must be registered with a governmental authority to be duly formed.

Practice Note

In considering a limited partnership structure, co-venturers should weigh the benefits of limited liability against the higher cost associated with its formation and the inability of any limited partner to participate in the management of the business (without risking the loss of its limited liability status).

(iii) Tax Considerations of a Partnership

A partnership is not a separate legal entity and, as such, is not a separate taxpayer. The partnership determines its profits or losses for any period and then allocates them to the partners in accordance with the terms of the partnership agreement, and each partner then pays income tax directly. Deductions and expenses (including discretionary deductions) are taken at the partnership level in determining profit or loss. Limited partners are subject to rules that generally impact the tax treatment of losses and partnership distributions allocated to them in excess of their investment.

The tax treatment of a partner that is a franchisor will depend on whether it participates in the partnership through a subsidiary or a branch, and is generally as described above in Part II (A) (and (B) for a ULC).

Practice Note

From the perspective of a person making payments to a partnership, the partnership is generally treated as a "see-through." This means that where a partnership has one or more non-resident partners, payments of fees to it may be subject to withholding tax, as well as withholding on payments for services it may perform in Canada.

(b) Corporation

(i) Limited Liability Corporation

To avoid the risk of being or being deemed to be a partnership, and thereby potentially attracting joint and several liability, joint venturers may decide to form a corporation rather than simply establishing an unincorporated joint venture or partnership. If they do form a corporation, the parties will define their respective rights and obligations through charter documents, such as articles of incorporation and bylaws and a shareholders' agreement. The charter documents and shareholders' agreement will establish a corporate name, share structure and share terms (including voting rights, rights to receive dividends, the right to receive property of the corporation on its dissolution, and the requirements for governance and management of the corporation (including the election of directors and approval requirements)). A corporation is a legal entity separate and apart from its shareholders. It has the rights, powers and privileges of a natural person. It can enter into contracts, sue and be sued in its own name, and is obligated to prepare annual financial statements and corporate tax returns.

If the joint venture sets itself up as a Canadian corporation, the tax consequences will be the same as those already described for a Canadian subsidiary.

A corporation is well-understood and commonly used as a joint venture vehicle. While the legal consequences of a joint venture may not always be clear, a joint venture established using a corporation provides certainty and clarity with regard to many legal issues involved. As a result, use of a corporation enhances acceptance of the venture and overall certainty in the marketplace.

Corporate joint ventures have several appealing traits. They are easily formed and can offer the parties flexibility in terms of financing through debt or equity. Once created, a corporation exists perpetually, which enhances market acceptance and certainty. Tax treatment of corporations may lead to advantages including tax-deferred rollovers and, in some circumstances (subject to a specific anti-avoidance rule in the Income Tax Act), tax-free flow of intercorporate dividends between Canadian corporations.

In a corporation, the shareholders have limited liability for the corporation's debts up to the amount of the price they have paid for their shares of the corporation. The personal assets of the shareholders are generally not at risk for satisfying corporate debts and liabilities. While the limited liability aspect of a corporation is attractive, it may be illusory, as lenders often require guarantees from shareholders as a condition of advancing funds. In addition, a significant range of matters attracting potential personal liability of directors under various pieces of legislation also renders the limited liability somewhat illusory, as corporations and shareholders will often indemnify directors and nominee directors of their subsidiaries.

Notwithstanding the numerous advantages offered by using a corporation as the vehicle for operating a joint venture, some disadvantages remain. Corporations must adhere to statutory compliance and regulations, which include mandatory annual filings and the requirement to hold meetings of directors and shareholders. This is in addition to other regulatory and disclosure obligations if the corporation offers its shares to the public, all of which will result in increased maintenance and compliance costs.

Moreover, corporations in some Canadian jurisdictions are subject to director residency requirements.

Québec's *Business Corporations Act* includes many modern, progressive and even innovative concepts, including the ability to have no directors at all if a corporation has only one shareholder.

Practice Note

Using a corporation as the vehicle for a joint venture offers the advantages of limited liability for shareholders, flexibility of financing, and market certainty, but corporations and their directors must comply with statutory requirements.

(ii) ULC

As described in greater detail above, as an alternative to a limited liability corporation, joint venturers may incorporate a ULC in Alberta, British Columbia or Nova Scotia for use as a joint venture vehicle. Similar to an ordinary limited liability corporation, a ULC is a separate legal entity from its shareholders and has perpetual existence. Of course, as described above, the critical difference between a ULC and the more conventional limited liability corporation is the unlimited joint and several liability of a ULC's shareholders for corporate debts and liabilities. In some provinces, ULCs are more expensive to form and maintain than a conventional limited liability corporation. While there are no Canadian tax or corporate reasons to utilize a ULC as a joint venture vehicle, there are potential U.S. tax benefits that might warrant its use.

> **Practice Note**
>
> **In evaluating the advisability of a ULC as a joint venture vehicle, the U.S. tax efficiencies must be weighed against the effects of the "anti-hybrid" rule in the Canada–U.S. Tax Treaty, which restricts the availability of treaty benefits on certain payments from a ULC to its U.S. shareholders.**

2. Co-ownership

In a co-ownership situation, each owner holds an undivided interest in the assets of the joint venture. Co-ownership is a popular form for joint ventures involved in mining, oil and gas exploration, and major real estate developments (including shopping malls), but it is not commonly used in franchising.

Similar to contractual joint ventures, a co-ownership joint venture may have an uncertain legal status, create joint liability and be recharacterized as a general partnership if the parties act like partners with respect to joint venture activities. Though it may be a desirable form, a co-ownership may be complicated by the fact that the relationship must be addressed in its entirety in contractual documentation between the parties involved (as it does not benefit from a corporate statute governing its formation and operation).

When this form of venture is used, a tax advantage may derive from the fact that income or loss is calculated at the level of each joint venturer rather than in one common entity, such as a corporation, which may allow for flexible division of profits and losses. Each joint venturer may, within reason, claim differing levels of discretionary deductions, such as capital cost allowance (depreciation) on its interest in particular joint venture assets. Tax treatment for a franchisor will depend on whether its participation in the joint venture is through a subsidiary or a branch.

> **Practice Note**
>
> **A co-ownership presents opportunities for profit and loss offsets, but must be carefully considered in light of the fact that the relationship must be entirely governed by a comprehensive contract.**

3. Contractual Joint Venture

In a contractual joint venture, the co-venturers each agree to provide particular services or assets of their own for the joint benefit of all co-venturers. This form typically appeals to relationships involving long-term commitments such as outsourcing, licensing, distribution, and franchising arrangements (including master licence and area development arrangements).

A separate legal entity is not created by contract. This may provide for flexibility in the formation and operation of the joint venture and also be conducive to individual tax and succession planning by each party. The tax consequences of a contractual joint venture are generally the same as for a co-ownership that can be maintained as such (i.e., that will not be characterized as a partnership by tax authorities).

Notwithstanding the convenience and other advantages of a contractual joint venture, this type of arrangement also possesses unique challenges. The contract between joint venturers must be skillfully drafted to address the entirety of the relationship, as there is no robust statutory framework to fill in any gaps, as exists for corporations and, to a lesser extent, partnerships. Further, contractual joint ventures have uncertain legal status, and there is a risk that a joint venture of this type might be characterized as a general partnership, which could lead to unlimited liability for the parties involved and unintended tax treatment.

To help avoid the possible presumption that a partnership has been formed, the joint venture agreement should expressly declare that a partnership is not intended and that the venturers are independent contractors. The contract should also set out the scope of the venture and the methods of control and decision-making. It will need to stipulate the rights and obligations of the participants and provide mechanisms for settlement of disputes. Again, unlike a corporation, a joint venture is not a distinct legal entity. It cannot sue or be sued.

Master franchise agreements and area development agreements are examples of contractual joint ventures in which the franchisor licenses its franchise system, trademarks and branding to a master franchisee or area developer to develop and expand into their local market. The master franchisee or area developer, in turn, typically invests its own capital and resources in the establishment and development of the franchise system in a designated area (or all) of Canada and commits to developmental goals or quotas relating thereto.

Practice Note

A contractual joint venture can offer considerable flexibility; however, the uncertainty of its legal status can make contracting complex and create the risk of potential additional liability.

D. Master Franchise or Area Development

1. Master Franchise Agreement

A popular option available to a franchisor wishing to expand into Canada is the master franchise arrangement. It involves the granting of rights by the franchisor to one or more master franchisees (subfranchisors) to develop units in particular areas through subfranchisees. The rights granted to the master franchisee will normally be exclusive within a designated territory (which can be one or more provinces or even all of Canada) and will include the right to grant subfranchises to use the franchisor's trademarks and system within such territory. This differs from the standard franchise relationship in which a franchisor directly grants a franchisee the right to operate one branded business at a particular location.

In a master franchise structure, the franchisor relies on the experience and financial and human resources of the master franchisee to expand in the granted territory. It is vital that the franchisor choose a master franchisee that has experience in franchising, good character references, financial resources, well-trained staff, broad industry contacts, and working knowledge of the laws applicable to franchising and commercial practices of the territory. Also, good administrative skills are important. Sometimes the master franchisee will be required to open and operate one or more pilot locations itself or through a subsidiary in order to test and adapt the system to Canada. The master franchisee should bring valuable industry contacts, for example, in commercial leasing, banking and relevant types of suppliers. The franchisor must provide thorough training in the operation of its system to the master franchisee. The franchisor's training must enable the master franchisee in turn to provide training to new unit franchisees. In effect, the franchisor must "train the trainer."

The franchisor's revenue typically comes from three streams: (1) initial franchise, renewal and transfer fees; (2) periodic royalties typically based on a percentage of the franchisees' gross sales; and (3) in certain systems, sales of products and supplies to franchisees. In interposing a master franchisee to do most of the work, the franchisor must expect to share reasonable portions of these revenue streams with the master franchisee.

Most important, a formula for sharing initial franchise fees and ongoing royalties with the master franchisee must be established in the master franchise agreement. In the sharing formula, the franchisor must ensure that the master franchisee will receive enough income to support its provision of services to franchisees and to enable the master franchisee to continue to operate in Canada at a reasonable profit level.

In a master franchise arrangement, the franchisor must still supervise the master franchisee and, ideally, should make regular visits to some subfranchised locations, but much of the responsibility for running the system in the territory is transferred to the master franchisee. The saying is that "the master franchisee stands in the shoes of the franchisor" in the territory granted. This can result in substantial cost and time savings, although of course less revenue, to the franchisor. The franchisor must be prepared to place a great deal of faith in the master franchisee to properly maintain and develop the system in the territory granted, while at the same time protecting and enhancing the franchisor's brand there. A well-placed master franchisee can open doors in a market that is unfamiliar to the franchisor. However, choosing the wrong master franchisee can cause significant harm to the system very quickly, in terms of both operational efficiency and success and the reputation and value of the franchisor's brand. Also, while there is typically no privity of contract between the franchisor and the individual franchisees or their customers, the franchisor will often be viewed as having "deep pockets" that a plaintiff in either group may attempt to access if something goes wrong.

Practice Note

In a master franchise structure, the franchisor relies on the experience, contacts, financial and human resources of the master franchisee to expand in the granted territory. The master franchisee is said to "stand in the shoes" of the franchisor within the territory granted.

Other items to be covered in the master franchise agreement include the franchisor's ability to change its branding or franchise system to adapt to changing markets and technology, withholding tax on remittances to a non-Canadian resident franchisor, establishment of an advertising program, consequences of default of a unit franchise agreement, choice of law, and a dispute resolution mechanism. A master franchise agreement may also attach the form of subfranchisor "unit" agreement that the master franchisee must use and address the preparation and approval rights and requirements relating thereto. In doing so, the master franchisee must comply with the requirements of all applicable local laws, including provincial franchise legislation.

While the master franchisee will be required to comply with all applicable franchise legislation with respect to individual franchisees (since the master franchisee is the "franchisor" in that relationship for statutory compliance purposes), the franchisor itself will still be required to comply with applicable franchise legislation, including disclosure and good faith/fair dealing requirements, with regard to its relationship with the master franchisee.

In addition, the franchisor will want to ensure that the master franchisee discharges its obligations properly and that each franchise agreement is assignable to the franchisor upon the expiration or termination of the Master Franchise relationship.

Practice Note

There is often a strong business case for a franchisor to contract with a master franchisee in a foreign territory, as opposed to franchising individual units there directly. Interposing a master franchisee, however, is not inexpensive or without risk. As with any business relationship, finding the right master franchisee will be critical to the success of the master franchise relationship.

A variation on the master franchise relationship, sometimes called an "area representative" arrangement, involves finding a local candidate or entity that fulfills many of the functions of a master franchisee (e.g., franchisee recruitment, site selection, training and ongoing assistance). An area representative arrangement differs, however, in that the area representative does not have the right to sublicense to unit franchisees; the franchisor will directly franchise to them. Often, the franchisor pays the area representative a share of the fees the franchisor receives from unit franchisees. If appropriately structured, the area representative arrangement is not a franchise relationship at all, but rather an agency or marketing relationship.

2. Area Development Agreement

Establishing one or more area development agreements is another option for entry into Canada due to the large size of the country and prevalent regional differences. The franchisor will usually grant the area developer the right to develop the franchise system within an exclusive territory and, pursuant to such grant, to enter into unit franchise agreements with the franchisor. A Canadian area developer will need to possess the financial and human resources to establish an agreed number of franchise units in the exclusive territory granted. The area developer may be allowed to use its own subsidiaries as franchisees provided it maintains control of them through share-voting rights. The franchisor will want to receive and review charter documents and shareholders' agreements for such subsidiaries to confirm adequate control and governance by the area developer.

The area development agreement will typically have an initial fee for the right to open a specified number of units (possibly with an option for more units if the developer achieves its quota of openings over the initial term). The developer will sometimes be given a progressive partial discount against initial fees payable for its subsidiaries' units being opened. Some other provisions to be found in the area development agreement are: exclusivity of territory, the "shrinking" of territory (or, possibly, loss of exclusivity) if the developer fails to meet any quota, transfer rights, and a "cross-default" provision between the area development agreement and any franchise agreement held by the developer or its subsidiary.

Practice Note

Area development agreements with developers possessing "local knowledge" and other resources/attributes may be used to address regional differences in the Canadian market.

3. Tax Considerations

Generally, Canadian tax treatment of a non-resident franchisor will depend on whether it has established a Canadian subsidiary to contract with the master franchisee or area developer (in which case the tax consequences applicable to a Canadian subsidiary will apply) or the contract has been made directly by the non-resident franchisor (in which case the rules applicable to a branch operation will apply).

III. Goods and Services Tax (GST) and Harmonized Sales Tax (HST)

A. Overview

The Canadian government imposes a federal tax on goods and services supplied or imported into Canada. It is called the GST, which is similar to the value-added taxes (or VAT) that are imposed in Europe. The retail sales tax imposed by three Canadian provinces (see below) is in addition to the federal GST.

Generally speaking, GST is imposed on goods and services at all business levels: manufacturing, importing, wholesaling and retailing. The *Excise Tax Act,* which is the legislation that imposes GST, requires the supplier of goods and services in Canada to collect a tax equal to 5% of the value of the supply. The 5% tax is also applied on all goods imported into Canada (though there are exemptions for visitors' personal goods). However, if a party paying the tax is involved in commercial activity and is therefore charging GST on the goods and services that it provides to its customers, then such payor will be entitled to a refund (or credit) of all GST it has paid to provide such services or products. As a result, most manufacturers, wholesalers, retailers and importers obtain a full refund of the GST they have paid. The ultimate consumer absorbs the GST and is not entitled to a refund. In the end, the GST system is a multi-leveled structure for collecting a 5% tax on a value-added basis from the ultimate consumer.

Some types of businesses are not required to charge GST on their services but are still required to pay GST themselves. These businesses include banking, insurance and securities outlets, medical and dental services, and landlords of used residential accommodation (sales and rentals). The suppliers of these types of services do not receive a refund of GST they pay. They are referred to as "exempt suppliers." An exempt supplier, therefore, is in the same GST position as a consumer.

There is another group of businesses that are not required to charge GST to their customers but are nonetheless entitled to a refund of the GST paid by them to provide their services. Such suppliers are referred to as "zero-rated suppliers." The principal zero-rated suppliers sell basic groceries, medical supplies, agricultural supplies and exports.

The Provinces of Nova Scotia, Prince Edward Island, Newfoundland, New Brunswick and Ontario, in cooperation with the federal government, have replaced their formerly existing single-stage, retail sales tax with a multi-stage sales tax which uses a broader base of goods and services and the same operating structure as the federal GST (i.e., persons involved in supplying taxable goods and services to others obtain a full refund of GST paid). In these cases, the tax rate is a combined rate of GST and provincial sales tax and is referred to as the HST. The rate in Ontario, New Brunswick and Newfoundland is 13%, consisting of the 5% federal GST component and an 8% provincial component. The rate in Nova Scotia is 15%, consisting of the 5% federal GST and a 10% provincial rate. The rate in Prince Edward Island is 14%, consisting of the 5% federal GST and a 9% provincial rate.

Practice Note

The Canadian government levies taxes on goods and services supplied or imported into Canada which are combined, or "harmonized," with retail sales taxes in some provinces.

B. Application of GST/HST to Franchises

The grant or supply of franchise rights is taxable, and a registrant franchisor must charge GST/HST on all types of fees it collects from a Canadian franchisee (including initial franchise fees, royalties, advertising contributions, any rents or other charges). GST or HST will apply depending on the application of place of supply rules to determine the province in which the supply is considered to have been made.

However, the grant or supply of franchise rights in Canada by a non-resident franchisor will be deemed to be made outside of Canada and therefore not subject to GST/HST, unless:

- the supply was made in the course of a business carried on by such franchisor in Canada; or
- the non-resident franchisor was registered with the Canada Revenue Agency for GST/HST purposes.

The Canadian franchisee would still need to consider whether GST/HST is required to be self-assessed on reporting forms by the franchisee as a recipient of an "imported taxable supply." This self-assessment obligation would be required only for franchisees that are not exclusively involved in GST commercial activity (i.e., are involved in making exempt supplies for GST/HST purposes and thus do not claim full input tax credits).

Practice Note

Canadian franchisees will generally be required to pay GST/HST on all fees (initial franchise fees, royalties and marketing fund contributions) charged by franchisors, other than to non-resident franchisors that have not registered in Canada for GST/HST purposes and are not carrying on business in Canada.

C. Registration Requirements

1. Branch Operation

(a) Mandatory registration

A non-resident franchisor that directly grants franchise rights for a particular geographic area in Canada but does not actively participate in soliciting franchisees or assisting in franchise operations in Canada will not be considered to be carrying on business in Canada. Accordingly, such a franchisor need not register for GST/HST purposes and need not report to the Canada Revenue Agency on GST/HST collection.

However, a reasonably high level of business activity in Canada, including actively soliciting franchisees, likely means that the non-resident franchisor is carrying on business in Canada. If a non-resident franchisor opens a business office in Canada, this will be a clear indication to the Canada Revenue Agency that the franchisor is carrying on business in Canada. Under these circumstances, the non-resident franchisor will be required to register for GST/HST purposes. If a non-resident franchisor has set up a subsidiary in Canada, and representatives of the non-resident franchisor visit Canada as part of its administration of the franchise system in Canada, this alone will not cause the non-resident to be "carrying on business" in Canada. However, if such representatives bill the subsidiary or subfranchisees for services provided during such visits, then the representatives will be carrying on business in Canada in respect of those activities, which will, in turn, require the franchisor to register for GST/HST purposes.

Practice Note

A non-resident franchisor will not be required to register for GST/HST purposes if it does not actively participate in soliciting Canadian franchisees or assist in the operations of the Canadian franchise system.

(b) Voluntary registration

A non-resident franchisor may wish to voluntarily register for GST/HST purposes even if it is not considered to be carrying on business in Canada. Such registration will generally require that it collect GST/HST from its franchisees. The Canadian franchisee will necessarily be a GST/HST registrant and will generally get a full refund of the GST/HST it pays in the course of operating its business, except to the extent that the franchise is an exempt supplier (e.g., an insurance broker). Registration will also mean that the non-resident franchisor will get a full refund of the GST/HST that it incurs in Canada. For example, representatives of a non-resident franchisor taking business travel in Canada often pay GST/HST for airfare, hotel rooms, meals and car rentals. GST/HST might also be paid on equipment and supplies that are brought into Canada in the course of franchise operations. This GST/HST paid will be refunded only if the franchisor has become a GST/HST registrant.

Compliance with the GST/HST system by a registrant is less complex and less costly than income tax compliance.

Practice Note

Voluntary registration for GST/HST purposes by a non-resident franchisor may be advantageous for a non-resident from a tax recovery perspective.

(c) Security

A limitation of GST/HST registration by a non-resident franchisor is that a non-resident must post security (whether registration is voluntary or mandatory) with the Canada Revenue Agency for one-half of its estimated net GST/HST remittances (i.e., GST/HST collected minus GST/HST paid) for the following year. Such security is reviewed from time to time by the Canada Revenue Agency to ensure that it continues to represent one-half of the net GST/HST in the preceding year. The security can be by way of an insurance bond; however, another common practice is to pledge a Government of Canada bond (the interest would be received by the non-resident franchisor). When the estimated net GST/HST liability of the non-resident is less than c$3,000 per year and the taxable supplies are less than c$100,000 per year, security will be waived.

Practice Note

Non-resident franchisors may be required to post security for GST/HST purposes with the Canada Revenue Agency.

2. Canadian Subsidiary

If a non-resident franchisor establishes a Canadian subsidiary (including a ULC) to own or manage its Canadian franchise operation, the subsidiary must become a GST/HST registrant and must collect GST/HST from Canadian franchisees on all types of fees paid. Unlike its parent, the Canadian incorporated subsidiary will automatically be considered a resident of Canada. Only the Canadian subsidiary (and not the parent franchisor) will be subject to GST/HST requirements. The initial fee for the grant (supply) of master franchise rights by the non-resident franchisor to a Canadian subsidiary pursuant to a master franchise agreement will not be subject to GST/HST unless the non-resident franchisor has elected to register for GST/HST purposes.

Note, however, that a Canadian subsidiary of a non-resident franchisor is not required to post security for GST/HST even though it may not have an office or other permanent establishment in Canada.

Practice Note

The Canadian subsidiary of a parent non-resident franchisor carrying on business in Canada must become a GST/HST registrant, but as the subsidiary is deemed a Canadian resident, it is not required to post security.

IV. Provincial Sales Tax

A. Overview

The province of Alberta and the three Canadian territories (Yukon, Northwest Territories, and Nunavut), being four out of the 13 Canadian provinces and territories, do not charge HST or impose a retail sales tax on the sale of goods and services.

B. Retail Sales Tax

Three provinces impose a single-stage sales tax similar to the retail sales tax in most U.S. states. The tax is payable by a buyer on retail sales in such provinces and by a person who imports goods into such provinces.

The rates of tax in the single-stage sales tax jurisdictions are:

Province	Rate
British Columbia	7%
Saskatchewan	5%
Manitoba	8%

Additionally, federal GST of 5% will be charged in these three provinces.

Higher sales tax rates apply to certain products in various jurisdictions. British Columbia, for example, charges 8% to 10% sales tax on luxury cars and 10% on liquor.

Sales tax was initially only levied on the purchase of tangible personal property but in more recent years has been expanded to include some intangibles (e.g., software) and some services (e.g., legal services in British Columbia).

Practice Note

In addition to federal GST, the provinces of British Columbia, Saskatchewan and Manitoba each apply sales tax to retail sales made in the province and imports into each province. Also, in British Columbia, certain services attract sales tax.

C. Québec Sales Tax (QST)

In 1992, the Province of Québec replaced its single-stage retail sales tax with a multi-stage tax. It initially was similar to the federal GST, though not identical. The Province of Québec has subsequently fully harmonized the QST with the federal GST but still separately administers the QST. As a result, the two taxes are assessed separately. Persons involved in the supply of taxable goods and services get a full refund of QST paid. As of April, 2017, the QST rate is 9.975% and is no longer calculated on a GST-included price. Consequently, the combined GST/QST rate in Québec is now 14.975% (5% GST plus 9.975% QST).

Practice Note

The Québec sales tax is harmonized with the federal GST, but is administered separately by the Province of Québec.

CHAPTER 2

Franchising in the Province of Québec

Pascale Cloutier and Stéphane Teasdale

Contents

I. Introduction of the Province of Québec

With a population of 8 million, the Province of Québec is the second largest in Canada after Ontario. Québec has a unique status, as it is the only province in Canada where the official language is French—Canada has two official languages, English and French. Québec's legal system is based on a Civil Code, similar to the one in force in most of the Western European countries. Since the Canadian Constitution divides the powers to adopt legislation between the federal legislature and the provincial legislatures, Québec is also governed by federal laws and regulations.

The courts in Québec are established by the Canadian Constitution, and the rules of evidence and administration of justice are very much influenced by the British common-law system, with some distinction. Therefore, while the process of a trial is very similar to the one in the other Canadian provinces, Québec has its own unique Code of Civil Procedure, which makes the process of getting a file ready for trial different from the other provinces. As an example, Québec has no discovery of documents.

The Province of Québec has no specific laws or regulations governing franchising. Therefore, franchise agreements are governed by the general rules of contracts stipulated in the Québec Civil Code.

This chapter will provide an overview of the principal differences in franchising between Québec and the other provinces in Canada.

Practice Note

Unlike the rest of Canada, the Province of Québec is a civil-law jurisdiction, with a Civil Code that regulates the law of contract. Québec does not have any specific law that regulates franchising.

II. Disclosure

As mentioned, Québec has no specific laws or regulations governing franchising. Therefore, there is no mandatory disclosure process in Québec, and the Civil Code of Québec general provisions governing contracts apply to franchise agreements. The franchisor has a general obligation to divulge the information in its possession that could have an effect on the decision of the franchisee to enter into the franchise agreement. As a corollary obligation, the prospective franchisee has the obligation to ask for all information relevant to his decision to enter into the franchise agreement.

If the franchisor fails to provide relevant information to the prospective franchisee, the latter will have the onus of proving that the failure to communicate this specific information affected his or her decision to enter into the franchise agreement, and that the franchisee would not have contracted or would not have contracted on the same conditions if he or she had known this information.

The Supreme Court of Canada decision in *Banque de Montréal c. Bail Ltée,* [1992] 2 RCS 554 was not rendered in a franchise context, but is always referred to when determining the criteria governing the obligation to inform. The obligation to provide relevant information under the Québec Civil Code is summarized as follows:

- knowledge of the information, whether actual or presumed, by the party that owes the obligation to inform;
- the fact the information in question is of decisive importance; and
- the fact that it is impossible for the party to whom the duty to inform is owed to inform itself, or that the creditor is legitimately relying on the debtor of the obligation.

In the context of a franchise agreement, the obligation of the franchisor to inform the potential franchisee and the corollary obligation of the prospective franchisee to inform himself or herself have often been interpreted in favor of the franchisor in the absence of bad faith and false representations.

The most litigated aspect of the obligation to inform is related to financial projections. In the absence of false representations, most of the claims of franchisees about financial projections have been dismissed. The courts will review the language used by the franchisor when remitting the financial projections to the franchisee, the language of the franchise agreement in the absence of a guaranty on profits given by the franchisor, and, more important, the conduct of the franchisee when receiving the financial projections. (See *9069-7384 Québec Inc. c. Superclub Vidéotron ltée,* J.E. 2004-473 (Superior Court); *Guertin c. Entreprises J.J.P. Inc.,* J.E. 98-887 (Québec Court of Appeal); *Voncorp Inc. c. 147013 Canada Inc.,* J.E. 97-1474 (Superior Court)). Since the financial projections are often seen as one of the most important aspects of the decision of a prospective franchisee to enter a franchise agreement, the courts put a higher standard of onus on the franchisee to review the financial projections carefully.

If the franchisor does not communicate important information, the courts will often rule in favor of the franchisor if said information was otherwise easily verifiable and accessible by the franchisee. (See *Investissements Stanislas et Patricia Bricka Inc. c. Groupe C.D.R.E.M. Inc.,* J.E. 2001-1448 (C.A.)).

The duty of the franchisee to inform itself is considered by the courts under the norm of prudence and diligence of a reasonable person. (See *Guertin c.*

Entreprises J.J.P. Inc., J.E. 98-887 (Québec Court of Appeal), *Superclub Vidéotron ltée*, J.E. 2004-473 (Superior Court), and *175060 Canada Inc. c. Alimentations Robin's Québec Inc.*, J.E. 2002-949 (C.S.) and B.E. 2005 BE-100 (C.A.)).

In a recent decision, the Québec Court of Appeal ruled that a franchisor's omission to communicate the franchisee's poor performance on a psychometric exam performed at the request of the franchisor prior to the signing of the franchise agreement was a breach of the duty to inform. However, in this particular situation, the Court of Appeal ruled that this omission had no effect on the decision of the franchisee to enter the franchise agreement, and the franchisee's action was dismissed (*9150-0595 Québec Inc. c. franchises Cora Inc.*, 2013 QCCA 531 (Québec Court of Appeal)).

The remedies available to the franchisee for a breach of the obligation to inform are the rescission of the contract, a reduction of the obligations, and damages.

In all situations, both parties have the positive obligation to act in good faith (section 1375 *Civil Code of Québec*). Any voluntary communication of false information or communication of information in a way to falsely reassure a franchisee is prohibited and can give ground to an action in rescission of the franchise agreement and damages, provided that it was material to the decision of the franchisee to enter the franchise agreement. (See *Treats Inc. c. Sachian Inc.*, J.E. 98-1163 (Québec Court of Appeal).)

III. The Franchise Agreement

A. Nature of Agreement

The Civil Code of Québec (CCQ, S.Q., 1991, c.64) (the Civil Code) governs contract law in the Province of Québec and contains no specific provisions dealing with franchise agreements. The Civil Code thus lays the general contract law principles governing the rights and obligations of both the parties to the franchise agreement.

The franchisor-franchisee relationship is commercial in nature, and as a result, the agreement setting out the respective obligations of each party will also be of a commercial nature and will be subject to the general rules of contract under the Civil Code. The franchise agreement is an unnamed contract (J.-L. Baudouin and P.-G. Jobin, *Les Obligations*, 6th ed., Cowansville, Editions Yvon Blais, 2005, p. 70, pm.50) that some have described as being performed at several different times or without interruption, for a defined period of time that is not subject to any kind of formalism (*Id.*).

It is also considered to be a bilateral contract where the parties obligate themselves each to the other, so that the obligation of one party is correlative to the obligation of the other (CCQ, S.Q., 1991, c.64, art. 1380). Finally, the franchise agreement will also be considered onerous because each party obtains an advantage in return for his obligation (CCQ, S.Q., 1991, c.64, art. 1381).

B. Adhesion Contract

Franchise agreements are often characterized as contracts of adhesion, as the franchisee is in a more vulnerable position because the franchise agreement is not generally open to negotiation. Because of this real or perceived economic imbalance between the parties, the Civil Code contains certain provisions to protect the adhering party against abusive acts of the stipulating party.

Article 1379 of the Civil Code defines the contract of adhesion as follows:

> ART. 1379 A contract of adhesion is a contract in which the essential stipulations were imposed or drawn up by one of the parties, on his behalf, or upon his instructions, and were not negotiable.
>
> Any contract that is not a contract of adhesion is a contract by mutual agreement (CCQ, S.Q., 1991, c.64, art. 379).

In their book on obligations, authors J.-L. Baudouin and P.-G. Jobin suggest that "in a contract of adhesion [. . .], one of the parties loses the ability to negotiate freely the conditions of his undertaking, by being imposed in advance, the essential elements of the contract and retaining only the choice, which is purely theoretical, to enter or not into the contract" (translated from French). (J.-L. Baudouin and P.-G. Jobin, *Les Obligations*, 6th ed., Cowansville, editions Yvon Blais, 2005, p. 77, para. 55).

Clearly, franchise agreements are generally contracts prepared in advance by franchisors and proposed to franchisees in a form that appears final. However, this does not necessarily signify that all the terms, even the essential ones, of these agreements are not likely to be negotiated in certain circumstances.

In a decision of the Superior Court of Québec, the court stated that "authors Jean Pineau and Serge Gaudet in their book *Théorie des obligations* considered that courts are likely not to be wrong in characterizing insurance contracts, leasing contracts, franchise contracts or factoring contracts as contracts of adhesion" (*Distribution Stéréo Plus Inc. v. Télévision G.M. Beaudouin Inc. et al.* (November 13, 2007), Sherbrooke, 450-17-001320-044 (C.S.)). With respect to the authors cited by the court, this presumption appears incompatible with the interpretation of the terms of Article 1379 of the Civil Code.

In another decision of the Superior Court, the matter of *Le Super Club Vidéotron Ltée*, the Honorable Justice Joel A. Silkoff, J.S.C., analyzed, inter alia, Article 1379 of the Civil Code and comments of certain authors on the subject. He concluded as follows:

> [. . .] [102] [. . .] the Court is of the opinion that the franchise agreement is neither a contract of adhesion nor a contract subject to the provisions of the Consumer Protection Act.
>
> [103] Article 1379 of the Civil Code defines the contract of adhesion. The definition puts the condition to the effect that "[. . .] the essential stipulations could not be freely negotiated.
>
> [104] In the area of franchising, each contract is unique. In the present case, the plaintiffs should have called upon the advice of qualified professionals in order to study and inform themselves on the rights and obligations resulting from the franchise agreement. Referring to Richard Sully, they were even encouraged to do so but they did not deem it necessary to do so. Following the advice of professionals, they could have discussed with S.C.V. the aspects of the agreement that were possibly inacceptable. Nothing in the evidence allows the court to conclude that they could not "freely discuss" and possibly modify the essential stipulations of the agreement. (See *9069-7384 Québec Inc. c. Superclub Vidéotron ltée,* J.E. 2004-473 (Superior Court)) (Ibid., page 20 of the Vidéotron Decision) (translated from the French).

In another decision of *Gestion Jeroden Inc. v. Choice Hotels Canada Inc.*, the Superior Court analyzed the facts in order to determine whether the franchise agreement executed between the parties was in fact a contract of adhesion. The court concluded as follows:

> The contradicted evidence in the present file relating to the payment of the sum of $40,000 and its possible recovery were at the center of negotiations. [. . .] It appears to the Court that this termination provision, as well as the deposit of $40,000 and the conditions to which the deposit were subject, constituted essential considerations of the contract. These considerations termed essential were freely discussed and agreed to by the two parties. [. . .] The Court therefore concludes that we are not here in the presence of a contract of adhesion but a contract of mutual agreement. (AZ-00022119 (C.S.), page 12 of the entire Decision) (translated from the French).

Finally, it is also useful to recall the conclusions of the Court of Appeal of Québec in the *Provigo* case (*Provigo Distribution Inc. v. Supermarché A.R.G. Inc.,* [1998] R.J.Q. 47 (C.A.)) where the court defined a franchise agreement by establishing its applicable characteristics: "it is also, *sometimes*, a contract of adhesion" (Judgment, page 23) (emphasis added) (translated from the French).

So it now appears clear from the jurisprudence and doctrine that a franchise agreement is not always a contract of adhesion. Each case is specific, and the characterization of the franchise agreement as being a contract of adhesion (or not) will rest on the preponderant evidence made by the adherent that he was not able to freely discuss the agreement's essential terms. Failing such evidence, one could hardly conclude that the franchise agreement is automatically a contract of adhesion. Each case will necessarily be different, and each will be a question of fact, not of law. Franchise practitioners should therefore be familiar with the laws in Québec regarding contracts of adhesion in order to advise their clients accordingly.

Practice Note

Under the Québec Civil Code, contracts of adhesion are subject to special rules. While some have argued that a franchise agreement is a contract of adhesion, it is now clear from the jurisprudence that a franchise agreement is not always a contract of adhesion. Each case is specific, and the characterization of the franchise agreement as being a contract of adhesion or not will rest on the evidence.

C. Good Faith

Good faith and equity are cornerstones of civil law in Québec and more particularly in contract law. They are general principles that govern all contractual relations.

The provisions of the Civil Code dealing with good faith are the following:

> [6] Every person is bound to exercise his civil rights in good faith.
>
> [7] No right may be exercised with the intent of injuring another or in an excessive and unreasonable manner which is contrary to the requirements of good faith.
>
> [1375] The parties shall conduct themselves in good faith both at the time the obligation is created and at the time it is performed or extinguished.

To say that much has been written on the concept of good faith in Québec civil law would be less than an understatement, but we shall nonetheless attempt to summarize the concept as follows.

Good faith is not defined per se in the Civil Code. It is a vast concept that calls upon one's conscience in order to apply it to justice. It is a form of contractual morality (commentaries of the Minister of Justice on section 6 of the Civil Code (1991)). The duty of good faith has been well summarized in a recent decision of the Supreme Court of Canada in *Bhasin* (*Bhasin v. Hrynew,* [2014] 3 S.R.C. 494, par. 83):

> The Civil Code of Québec recognizes a broad duty of good faith which extends to the formation, performance and termination of a contract and includes the notion of the abuse of contractual rights: see arts. 6, 7 and 1375. While this is not the place to expound in detail on good faith in the Québec civil law, it is worth noting that good faith is seen as having two main aspects. The first is the subjective aspect, which is concerned with the state of mind of the actor, and addresses conduct that is, for example, malicious or intentional. The second is the objective aspect which is concerned with whether conduct is unacceptable according to the standards of reasonable people. As J.-L. Baudouin and P.-G. Jobin explain, [TRANSLATION] "a person can be in good faith (in the subjective sense), that is, act without malicious intent or without knowledge of certain facts, yet his or her conduct may nevertheless be contrary to the requirements of good faith in that it violates objective standards of conduct that are generally accepted in society": *Les Obligations* (7th ed. 2013), by P.-G. Jobin and N. Vézina, at para. 132. The notion of good faith includes (but is not limited to) the requirement of honesty in performing the contract: *ibid.*, at para. 161; *Bank of Montreal v. Kuet Leong Ng*, 1989 CanLII 30 (SCC), [1989] 2 S.C.R. 429, at p. 436.

In short, good faith has been used to examine the circumstances of exception of a contract, including the negotiations leading up to its conclusion. It has also been applied in the context of the execution of a contract and the circumstances in which the contract was terminated.

D. External Provisions

External clauses are clauses that refer to and incorporate provisions not expressly included in the contract itself or in its schedules. Article 1435 of the Civil Code provides:

> In a consumer contract or a contract of adhesion . . . an external clause is null if, at the time of formation of the contract, it was not expressly brought to the attention of the consumer or adhering party, unless the other party proves that the consumer or adhering party otherwise knew of it.

So, if the franchise agreement is a contract of adhesion, the franchisor has the burden of proving that the franchisee had knowledge of the external clauses at the time of formation of the contract.

Accordingly, there exists a presumption of nullity that may be rebutted by the franchisor with proof that:

- the clause has been expressly brought to the attention of the franchisee at the time of formation of the contract;
- the franchisee otherwise had knowledge of the external clause; or
- the external clause is of such common usage that it may be presumed to be known by the franchisee.

The provisions of the typical franchise agreement relating to an operations manual are a good example of external clauses. The avowed purpose of the Québec legislature is to prevent an adhering party, such as a franchisee, from being bound by the provisions of a document that it has not read or understood prior to signing the main contract. Therefore, it is advisable for the franchisor to provide a copy of the operations manual when the franchise agreement is executed, if not earlier. If the operations manual is particularly lengthy, it may be difficult to convince a court that the franchisee had the opportunity to read the entire manual at the time of execution of the franchise agreement. Thus, the franchisor may allow the franchisee to review the operations manual before the execution of the franchise agreement, subject to the franchisee's execution of a confidentiality agreement if the franchisor wishes.

If should be emphasized that the courts are not given the power to rewrite external clauses; they can only be upheld entirely or declared null. The consequence is severe, as the nullity of an external clause relating to an operations manual would mean that the franchisee is no longer bound by the offending provisions of the manual. In these circumstances, one cannot overstate the importance of being cautious.

E. Abusive Provisions

The rules of interpretation for adhesion contracts examined above relate to the formation of the contract; they were enacted to ensure that the adhering party's consent to certain questionable clauses is clearly obtained. The rule of interpretation relating to abusive clauses in adhesion contracts is different. Even if fully consented to by the adhering party, abusive clauses remain objectionable in principle, and the courts are given substantial powers to deal with them.

Under Article 1437 of the Civil Code:

> An abusive clause in a consumer contract or contract of adhesion is null, or the obligation arising from it may be reduced. An abusive clause is a clause which is excessively and unreasonably detrimental to the consumer or the adhering party and is therefore not in good faith; in particular, a clause which so departs from the fundamental obligations arising from the rules normally governing the contract that it changes the nature of the contract is an abusive clause.

Article 1437 thus gives the courts the power to declare abusive clauses null, or to rewrite such clauses to any degree deemed appropriate to establish contractual fairness.

It would seem that the "excessively and unreasonably detrimental" nature of a clause is to be determined objectively, without considering the particular circumstances. While it is clearly not required that the agreement in its entirety be unconscionable, it would also seem that the detrimental nature of the clause must be viewed in light of the entire agreement. Given the vagueness of the legislative definition of an abusive clause, it will be difficult to predict with any degree of certainty which provisions of a franchise agreement are likely to be considered abusive by Québec courts. One suspects, for example, that the following provisions would be subjected to careful scrutiny: provisions requiring the franchisee to continue paying royalties regardless of any breach by the franchisor; an absolute prohibition against the franchisee assigning its rights under the franchise agreement or transferring its business or permitting a transfer of its shares (if corporate); prohibitive transfer fees; or a waiver of liability provision. (For examples of abusive clauses, see *Slush Puppie Montreal Inc. v. 153226 Canada Inc. and Ouazzani Chadi*, J.E. 1994-1422 (Q.C.) and *Automobiles Duclos Inc. v. Ford du Canada Ltée*, J.E. 2002-1859 (S.C.)).

F. Covenants Against Competition

In Canada, and in Québec in particular, restrictive covenants will generally be enforced if they contain reasonable restrictions on trade and if their geographic scope and duration are reasonable. Franchisors would be well advised to be more conservative in setting out the terms of the covenants contained in their agreements or they risk court challenges.

In general, in-term non-competition covenants will tend to be farther-reaching, although where the geographic scope of the covenant extends beyond the province, it will likely be more often scrutinized by Québec courts. Post-term non-competition covenants (upon expiration or termination of the agreement) must be reasonable, and the courts in Québec will take a very strict approach in enforcing them.

Covenants against competition in Québec will generally lie somewhere between covenants in employment agreements (which are often very limited in order to allow employees to earn their living) and similar covenants found in the sale of businesses (where such covenants will be farther-reaching and of longer duration). The nature of the franchised business, the duration of the franchise agreement, and the presence of actual competition will often influence the scope of restrictive covenants in franchise agreements. Franchise practitioners should therefore give these provisions due consideration.

Finally, Québec courts will not rewrite or reduce the scope of covenants against competition. Plainly said, they are either valid or not—and in the latter case, unenforceable.

G. Termination

Franchise agreements generally set out the grounds upon which the franchisor may terminate the franchise agreement. Some of these grounds can result in immediate termination (such as in the event of the bankruptcy of the franchisee), while others require giving a franchisee notice and time to cure the default prior to the termination coming into effect. In any event, the reasonableness of such default and termination will be measured against the Civil Code provisions of good faith and abusive clauses, as previously discussed.

IV. Charter of the French Language (CQLR c C-11)

The Charter of the French Language (hereafter the Charter) became law in 1977. The objective of the Charter is to protect the quality and influence of the French language in the Province of Québec while making French the official language of government and law, as well as the everyday language of work, instruction, communication, commerce, and business (Preamble of the Charter of the French Language). Among other things, the Charter applies to different sectors of activities of businesses in Québec and is mainly focused on consumers and workers.

Compliance with the Charter may be onerous for a franchisor. Therefore, when using a master franchisee or an area developer, it is advisable to determine in advance who will be responsible for the cost of translating the materials.

Practice Note

The objective of the Québec Charter of the French Language is to protect the quality and influence of the French language in the Province of Québec while making French the official language of government and law, as well as the everyday language of work, instruction, communication, commerce, and business.

A. Office Québécois de la Langue Française

The Office Québécois de la Langue Française (hereafter the Office) is a public body responsible for defining and conducting Québec's policy on language. It is also responsible for ensuring compliance with the Charter. The Office has power to conduct enquiries and issue notices of non-compliance with the Charter. It is often referred as the "language police" outside the Province of Québec.

B. Use of Trademarks and Name

As a general rule (some exceptions apply), the name of a company doing business in the Province of Québec must be in French (section 63 Charter of the French Language). It can also be in another language, provided that a French version of the name exists. To register a business in Québec, a company needs a French name or a French version of a name in another language (sections 64 and 65 Charter of the French Language and 17 of An Act Respecting the Legal Publicity of Enterprises CQLR c P-44.1). If a company's name is in another language, the French version of the name must be used in Québec in a prominent manner (section 68, Charter of the French Language).

Trademarks are governed by federal laws in Canada. A trademark can be registered in a language other than French. Discussed below are the specifications on the use of trademarks in other languages in the sections "Signs and Advertising" and "Products and Labels."

C. Signs and Advertising

As a general rule, public signs, posters, and commercial advertising must be in French (section 58, Charter of the French Language). They can be in French and another language provided that French is markedly predominant (section 58, Charter of the French Language). The Office considers that the French language is markedly predominant when, on a signage, the French language is twice as visible as any other language. Exceptions where signage can be exclusively in another language or where they must be exclusively in French, are provided in the regulations (see sections 15-26, regulation respecting the language of commerce and business, CQLR c C-11, r9). The regulations also provide exceptions for health or public safety signage, international conventions, museums, news media, etc.

One of the most important exceptions is for registered trademarks. A registered trademark within the meaning of the *Trade-Marks Act* in a language other than French can be used in public signage, unless a French version of the trademark has been registered (section 25(4), Regulation respecting the language of commerce and business). For a long time, the Office considered that a trademark that has been applied for but not yet registered could benefit from this exception. The Office has changed its interpretation of section 25(4) of the regulations in the last few years. As a result, it is no longer clear if a trademark in a language other than French waiting for its registration would benefit from the exception.

A few years ago, the Office took a different approach on the use of trademarks in another language on exterior signs. They sent letters to retailers using a trademark in a language other than French on exterior signs requesting that these retailers add a French generic to their trademarks. Several retailers took a joint action for declaratory judgment against the Québec government to challenge the policy of the Office. The retailers have been successful in having the Superior Court declare that the use of a trademark on a sign can be exclusively in a language other than French, provided that the trademark is registered in Canada and no French version exists (*Magasins Best Buy ltée c. Québec,* 2014 QCCS 1427). The Court of Appeal confirmed the Superior Court judgment (*Québec (Procureure Générale) c. Magasins Best Buy Ltée,* 2015 QCCA 747).

All computer software, whether installed or not, must be available in French unless no French version exists (section 52.1, Charter of the French Language). Software can also be available in other languages provided that the French version can be obtained on terms that are no less favorable, except price, where it reflects higher production costs and has technical characteristics that are at least equivalent (section 52.1, Charter of the French Language).

Practice Note

A trademark registered under the Canadian federal *Trade-Marks Act* in a language other than French can be used in public signage, unless a French version of the trademark has been registered.

D. Translation of Agreements and Other Materials

The adhesion contracts and contract containing printed standard clauses must be drafted in French (section 55, Charter of the French Language). The parties may agree to execute a contract in another language. It is considered a good practice, when a franchise agreement is drafted in another language other than French, to add a section to the effect that the parties expressly requested that the contract be drafted in another language. As discussed earlier in this chapter (Section III. B.), franchise agreements are not always considered "adhesion contracts."

Documents "related to" an adhesion contract also have to be drafted in French unless the parties expressly requested that the documents be drafted in another language (section 55, Charter of the French Language).

Purchase orders, invoices, and receipts must be in French (Charter of the French Language, section 570).

Many franchisors decide to develop the Québec market with a local master franchisee or an area developer who has knowledge of the French language. It is important to determine in advance whether the Master franchisee/area developer or franchisor will incur the costs related to the translation of the materials for Québec use.

Practice Note

A franchise agreement can be drafted in a language other than French at the request of the parties. When requested, it is advisable to add following sentence at the end of the contract: "The parties expressly required that this contract be drafted in the English language [or in another language as the case may be]. Les parties ont expressément demandé que ce contrat soit rédigé en langue anglaise."

E. Products and Labels

In Canada, labels on products are mainly governed by federal laws. While federal laws contain minimum specifications in terms of language on labels, every inscription on a product, its container or wrapping, sold in the Province of Québec, must be drafted in French (Charter of the French Language, section 51). The labels can also have inscriptions in one or more other languages, but none of the other languages must be given greater prominence than French (section 51, Charter of the French Language). This rule applies to menus, wine lists, directions for use, and warranty certificates (Charter of the French Language, section 51). Some exceptions apply to an inscription embossed on a tire (Regulation respecting the language of commerce and business CQLR c C-11, r 9, section

4); cultural and educational products, such as books, magazines, disks, films or tapes, non-promotional greeting cards, appointment books, and calendars (Regulation respecting the language of commerce and business, section 2); inscriptions on products that are intended for a market outside Québec (Regulation respecting the language of commerce and business, section 3(1)); inscription on a product intended for incorporation into a finished product and is not offered for retail sale, etc. (Regulation respecting the language of commerce and business, section 3(4)).

If a product is from outside Québec and the inscription is engraved, baked or inlaid in the product itself, riveted or welded to it, or embossed on it on a permanent manner, the inscription can be exclusively in a language other than French. This exception does not apply to safety inscriptions, which have to be written in French on the product or attached to the product in a permanent manner (Regulation respecting the language of commerce and business, section 3(6)).

Exceptions also apply to inscriptions of the name of firms established exclusively outside Québec, the name of origin of an exotic product, a place name, and a recognized trademark within the meaning of the *Trade-Marks Act* (Regulation respecting the language of commerce and business, section 7).

These exceptions should be carefully reviewed in order to confirm that they apply to a specific situation.

The inscription on a product of artificial combination of letters, syllables, figures pictographs, figures, or initials are allowed (Regulation respecting the language of commerce and business, section 9).

Catalogues, brochures, folders, commercial directories, and similar publications must also be in French (section 52, Charter of the French Language). They can be available in a multitude of separate versions, provided that the material presentation of the French version is available under no less favorable conditions of accessibility and quality than the others. Exceptions apply for catalogues, brochures folders, commercial directories, and other similar publications in another language that are inserted in a news publication exclusively in this other language. Exceptions also apply to these publications intended for the same ethnic group (Regulation respecting the language of commerce and business, section 10). An individual can also request to receive a catalogue, brochure, folder commercial directory in another language than French

Restrictive language requirements also apply to toys and games (section 54, Charter of the French Language, and Regulation respecting the language of commerce and business, section 8).

F. Websites

Publicity on a website is governed by section 52 of the Charter (*Reid v. Court of Québec,* 2003 CanLII 17980 (QC CS); *Québec (Procureur Général) c. Hyperinfo Canada Inc.,* 2001 CanLII 16493 (QC CQ); *Québec (Procureur Général) c. Aroyan,* 2006 QCCQ 6922 (CanLII)). Therefore, commercial publicity on a website has to be in French.

G. Labour Relations

In Québec, the language of labour relations is French (section 41, Charter of the French Language). It is important to note that all documents that will be used by the employees of the franchisees or the employees of the franchisor in Québec must be translated into French. This general rule also applies to application forms for employees (Charter of the French Language, section 57). All communications with the employees of the franchisee or the franchisor must also be in French. It is also prohibited to dismiss, lay off, demote, or transfer an employee for the sole reason that he or she is exclusively French-speaking (section 45, Charter of the French Language). It is also prohibited for an employer to make the obtaining of employment or office dependent on the specific level of knowledge of a language other than French, unless it is specifically required for the position (section 46, Charter of the French Language).

H. Penalties and Other Sanctions

For individuals, the penalties for breach of the Charter are between $600 and $6,000 For corporations, the penalties are between $1,500 and $20,000. For a second offence, the penalties are doubled (Charter of the French Language, section 205(1)). A judge may also impose on the offender, in addition to other penalties, a further fine equal to the financial gain the offender realized or derived from the offence. This other fine may be above the maximum penalty stated by law (Charter of the French Language, section 205(3)).

Under certain circumstances, the distributor, seller or marketer of a product can also be convicted for a breach of the Charter (Charter of the French Language, section 205.1).

In determining the amount of the fine, a judge will take into account, among other things, the revenues and other benefits the offender derived from the offence and any damages and economic damages resulting from it (Charter of the French Language, section 205 (2)).

V. Consumer Laws

In Québec, the *Consumer Protection Act* (*Consumer Protection Act*, CQLR c. P-40) (hereafter CPA) applies to every contract for goods or services entered into between a consumer and a merchant in the course of its business (CPA, section 2). A consumer is defined as an individual (CPA, section 1 (e)). It excludes a merchant who is obtaining goods for the purpose of its business (*Consumer Protection Act*, section 1(e)). We are of the opinion that a franchisee is not a "consumer" as defined by the CPA, and to our knowledge, no courts have ever considered a franchisee as a "consumer."

Franchisors should nonetheless be aware of the basic obligations of a merchant under the CPA as their franchisees are merchants and they may themselves end up selling goods directly on the Internet or through corporate stores. When a franchisor is manufacturing or distributing goods, it may also be liable for latent defects and be sued directly by a consumer. The franchisor can also be liable for its false publicity or misleading advertising.

A. Rules Governing Consumer Contract

It is advisable to have any consumer contract reviewed before it is used in Québec. The CPA provides for specification for some type of contracts—contracts of credits (CPA sections 66-150 and Regulations Respecting the Application of the CPA, CQLR c P-40.1, r 3 sections 51-69 (Regulations)); contracts entered into by an itinerant merchant (CPA sections 55-65); contracts for services provided at distance, (CPA sections 54.1-54.16 and Regulations, sections 25.7 and 79.7-79.12); contracts for long-term lease of goods (CPA sections 150.1-150.32 and Regulations sections 69.1-69.7); contracts related to the sale, long-term lease, and repairs of automobiles and motorcycles (CPA sections 151-181, Regulations sections 69.1-69.7 and 70-78 and Order in Council respecting the Application of Rules of Conduct to used vehicle merchants, CQLR c P-40.1, r 3); contracts for the sale of prepaid cards (CPA sections 187.1-187.5); contracts for successive services for schooling, training (including fitness studios), or any other type of assistance services (CPA sections 188-214); contracts for pre-funeral arrangements (decree respecting to the Adoption of Rules of Conduct concerning the sale of prearranged funeral services and sepulchres by itinerant merchants, CQLR c P-40.1, r 1); and contracts for the repair of household appliances (CPA sections 182-187 and Regulations section 79). The Regulations also provide compulsory clauses for some of these contracts (Regulations sections 29-50).

In 2009, the CPA was amended to enact rules governing the sale of prepaid cards. "Prepaid cards" as defined by the CPA, include certificates, cards, or other medium of exchange that are paid for in advance and allow the consumer to acquire goods or services from one or more merchants (CPA section 187.1). Among other things, before selling a prepaid card, the merchant must inform the consumer in writing of the conditions of utilization of the card and how to check the balance on the card (CPA section 187.2). Any stipulation providing for an expiration date on a prepaid card is forbidden, unless the card is for an unlimited use of a service (CPA section 187.3. Section 187.3 does not apply to prepaid cards for mobile telephone services (Regulations, section 79.1). Other rules and exceptions are provided by the CPA (CPA sections 187.1-187.5) and the Regulations (Regulations, CQLR C P-40.1, r 3, sections 79.1-79.6).

The CPA provides that a consumer may ask for the rescission of a consumer contract when his or her obligations and the merchant's obligations are disproportionate or when the consumer's obligations are excessive, abusive or exorbitant (CPA section 8). In case of doubt or ambiguity, the contract entered with a consumer will be interpreted in favor of the consumer (CPA Section 17). All costs charged to a consumer have to be specified in the contract and it is forbidden to claim other costs (CPA section 12).

It is prohibited in a consumer contract to oblige a consumer to refer a dispute to arbitration unless the consumer agrees to refer an actual dispute to arbitration *after* the contract has been entered into (CPA section 11.1). It is also forbidden to restrict the consumer's right to court and more particularly to limit the consumer's right to bring a class action or to be a member in a class action (CPA section 11.1). The CPA prohibits a stipulation in a consumer contract that provides that the contract will be partially or entirely governed by a law other than the laws of Canada or the Province of Québec (CPA section 19). It also prohibits a clause of election of domicile, except if made by notarial act and stipulations obliging a Consumer to submit a dispute to a court outside the Province of Québec (CPA section 22.1).

The CPA edicts many other rules for consumer contracts, such as the interpretation of the contracts (CPA section 17), amendments to the contracts (CPA section 11.2), cancelation of the contracts (CPA sections 11.3 and 11.4), and others. It is important to keep in mind that the CPA's first objective is to protect consumers and most of the rules are enacted to achieve this goal.

These contracts have to be evidenced in writing (CPA sections 23-33). Such contracts include contracts entered with an itinerant merchant (CPA section 58); contracts of credit (CPA section 80); long-term lease contracts containing an option to purchase or a guaranteed residual value (CPA section 150.40); contracts of sale of an automobile or a motorcycle (CPA section 158); service contracts involving sequential performance for instruction, training or assistance services (CPA section 190) and their accessory contracts for the sale of goods

(CPA section 208); contracts for physical fitness studios (CPA section 199) and their accessory contracts for the sale of goods (CPA section 208); and contracts involving sequential performance for a service provided at distance (CPA section 214.2). After signing the contract, the merchant must tender it to the consumer and give the latter sufficient time to become aware of its terms and conditions (CPA section 27). The contract must be signed on each copy of the contract, at the end, after the conditions (CPA section 28). The contract is concluded when the merchant and the consumer have signed it (CPA section 30). After the signature, the merchant must remit a duplicate of the contract to the consumer (CPA section 32). The contract is only binding upon the consumer after he or she has remitted a copy of the contract (CPA section 33). The Regulations provides specifications for written contracts, such as type and size of the paper and the font (Regulations sections 26-28.1).

Some merchants are required to hold a permit (CPA sections 321-338 and Regulations sections 168-178). The permit requirements (CPA section 321) apply to itinerant merchants, merchants who make a contract to loan money, merchants who operate fitness studios and merchants who offer an additional warranty. Some exceptions apply to this enumeration.

B. Warranties

The CPA provides language for legal, conventional, and additional warranties for the sale of goods.

The legal warranty is the warranty that is provided by law. Without entering into the details, one should note that the Civil Code provides rules governing legal warranties (section 1726 et seq.). The CPA also specifies rules governing legal warranty. While the language is slightly different, the scope of the legal warranty is similar in both the Civil Code and the CPA. The Civil Code has a larger application since it not only applies to consumer contracts but any sale of products. Another distinction is the presumption of malfunction provided by the Civil Code. This distinction has no practical effect for a consumer since he can rely on both the Civil Code and the CPA in legal proceedings against a merchant.

The legal warranty provided by the CPA stipulates that goods sold must fit the purpose for which similar goods are usually used (CPA section 37). It also provides that the goods must be durable in normal use for a reasonable length of time, having regard to their price, the terms of the contract and the conditions of their use (CPA section 38). It is forbidden to exclude or restrict the application of the legal warranty (Regulations section 25.4). A consumer may institute legal proceedings directly against the merchant and the manufacturer for a breach of section 37 or 38 (CPA section 54).

A consumer has a right of action for latent defect against the merchant and the manufacturer, unless the consumer could have discovered the defect by an ordinary examination of the goods (CPA section 53). The manufacturer and the merchant are also liable for lack of instructions for the use of the goods resulting in injuries (CPA section 53). The manufacturer and the merchant cannot argue that they were not aware of the defect or the lack of instructions (CPA section 53). These recourses are also available for a subsequent purchaser (CPA section 53). It is forbidden for a merchant or a manufacturer to exclude or limit the right of action of the consumer for latent defect (Regulations section 25.6).

A merchant may also provide a conventional warranty for the goods sold. The CPA provides rules governing the conventional warranties. Among other things, exclusions to conventional warranties are forbidden unless clearly indicated in separate and successive clauses (CPA section 44), mandatory language must be drafted in the warranty certificate (CPA section 45), and the time of the warranty must be stipulated clearly (CPA section 46). It is also forbidden for a merchant or manufacturer to request from the consumer evidence that the previous owner of the goods complied with the terms of the warranty (CPA section 52.1).

The CPA also governs the sale of additional warranties. Additional warranties are usually offered by retailers to extend the time of the conventional warranty or cover situations excluded from the conventional warranty.

Since 2010, it is mandatory for a merchant to give oral and written notice of the existence of the legal warranty before selling an additional warranty (CPA section 228.1). The merchant must also inform the consumer of the existence and duration of the conventional warranty, if any (CPA section 228.1).

The oral notice that must be given before proposing an additional warranty is the following:

> *The law provides a warranty on the goods you purchase or lease: they must be usable for normal use for a reasonable length of time (Regulations section 91.10b) and 91.11).*

The written notice that must be given before the conclusion of a contract for additional warranty is the following (Regulations section 91.9 and 91.10):

NOTICE CONCERNING THE LEGAL WARRANTY

The Consumer Protection Act gives a warranty on all goods you purchase or lease from a merchant.

The goods must be usable

- *for the purposes for which they are ordinarily used (section 37 of the Act) and*

- *in normal use for a reasonable length of time, which may vary according to the price paid, the terms of the contract and the conditions of use (section 38 of the Act).*

For more information on this legal warranty, go to the website of the Office de la protection du consommateur at www.opc.gouv.qc.ca."

Some exceptions apply for contracts made in writing or orally from a distance (Regulations sections 91.12 and 91.13).

C. Language

When a written contract is required (*supra* section A), the contract must be drafted in French (CPA section 26). It can also be drafted in another language at the request of the parties (CPA section 26). When requested, it is advisable to add the following sentence at the end of the contract: "The parties expressly required that this contract be drafted in the English language [or in another language as the case may be]. Les parties ont expressément demandé que ce contrat soit rédigé en langue anglaise."

When a consumer contract is drafted in French and in another language, in the case of divergence of interpretation, the interpretation most favourable to the consumer prevails (CPA section 26).

D. Representations and Advertising

Merchants are bound by the written representations made to a consumer in advertising, written documents, or verbally by its representatives or salespersons. It is forbidden to exclude or limit the obligations of a merchant resulting from representations made by one of its employees (Regulations section 25.5).

The CPA enacts rules for false or misleading representations made by a merchant, manufacturer, or advertisers (CPA sections 215 and seq.). It is forbidden to make false or misleading representations to a consumer (CPA section 219). To determine if a representation constitutes a prohibited practice, the general impression it gives and, as the case may be, the literal meaning of the words used must be taken into account (CPA section 218). The general impression has been ruled by the Supreme Court of Canada (*Richard vs. Time Magazine Inc.* 2012 1 S.C.R. 265) as a two-step analysis that involves (1) describing the general impression that the representation is likely to convey to a credulous and inexperienced consumer and (2) determining whether that general impression is true to reality.

The CPA enacts very specific rules governing the representations made to consumers. A thorough review of these rules is recommended before advertising goods or services to consumers.

Among other things, the CPA enacts rules prohibiting ascribing certain advantages to a product (CPA section 220(A)) or to falsely represent certain characteristic of goods or services (CPA section 221), or discredit the goods or services offered by others (CPA section 222(b)).

As a general rule, advertising directed to children under 13 years of age is prohibited (CPA sections 248 and 249). Some exceptions are provided by the Regulations (Regulations sections 87-91).

E. Penalties and Other Sanctions

The CPA provides for penalties for breach of the CPA and Regulations (CPA sections 277 et seq.). The fines for an offence to the CPA are between $300 and $6,000 for an individual and $1,000 and $40,000 for a corporation (CPA sections 278 and 279). For a second or subsequent conviction, the fines can be doubled (CPA sections 278 and 279). When a company is convicted of an offence, its directors and representatives who had knowledge that the offence was perpetrated are deemed to be party to the offence, unless they can establish that they did not acquiesce to the perpetration of the offence (CPA section 282).

The CPA also provides civil recourses. The civil recourses include, among other things, rescission of the contract, specific performance, reduction of the obligation of the consumer, and damages (CPA sections 271 and 272). Punitive damages can also be granted to a consumer (CPA section 272). The Supreme Court of Canada in *Richard* (CPA section 220(A)) affirmed that punitive damages can be granted in the absence of another remedy. It also stated that for punitive damages to be granted, the behaviour of the defendant must have been intentional, malicious or vexatious and its conduct displayed ignorance, carelessness or serious negligence with respect to its obligations under the CPA.

VI. Security

Security instruments in the Province of Québec are not altogether different than in the rest of the other Canadian provinces although their designation may differ.

A. Personal Guarantees

Where franchisees are corporate entities, franchisors will generally require that the franchisee's principals, such as shareholders or officers of the corporate entity, personally guarantee the obligations of the franchisee. Personal guarantees are not attached to specific property but rather serve to guarantee the entire debt of the debtor in case of default.

Guarantors can enjoy the benefit of division and discussion towards other guarantors unless they have specifically renounced to same (which lenders typically require). The benefit of division allows the guarantor to require the creditor to divide its claim and reduce it to the amount of its share and portion of the debt. The benefit of discussion allows the guarantor to require the creditor to first enforce its rights on the assets of the principal debtor before enforcing the guarantee against the guarantor, where guarantors bind themselves jointly and severally with the principal debtor or other debtors, they may not invoke such benefits toward the other debtors.

Article 2355 of the Civil Code (CPA section 220(A)) prohibits a renunciation by a guarantor to his right to obtain information from the creditor with respect to the scope and terms of the principal obligation and the status of its performance by the principal debtor.

Article 2363 of the Civil Code (CPA section 220(A)) provides that a guarantee attached to the performance of special duties (such as positions as directors and officers of a corporation) terminates upon cessation of the duties (it is to be noted that the status of "shareholder" does not fall within the meaning of "special duties"). As a result, in order to avoid the application of Article 2363, where a guarantee is granted by directors or officers of the franchisee, the guarantee should contain a provision specifying that it is not attached to their position as directors or officers.

Article 2362 of the Civil Code (CPA section 220(A)) provides that where the guarantee is contracted with a view to covering future or indeterminate debts (such as royalties or rent), or for an indeterminate period, the guarantor may terminate it after three years, as long as the debt has not become due, by giving prior and sufficient notice to the debtor, the creditor and the other guarantors. Such provision obviously creates a concern for franchisors, and it is still unclear whether franchisees can simply waive the benefit of this provision. Nevertheless, it is important to revise all guarantees to include a renunciation, together with a renunciation of the benefits of division and discussion. It is also recommended to include an undertaking by the guarantor to provide a written renewal of his guarantee upon request. One may also include, in the franchise agreement, an obligation of the franchisee to cause any guarantor to renew his personal guarantee upon its termination or to substitute it with a guarantor that is as solvent as the previous one, failing which the franchisee will be deemed in default under the franchise agreement.

Article 2361 provides that the death of the guarantor terminates the guarantee for debts that have not accrued at the time of death. This provision is made in favour of public order and thus may not be waived by a guarantor.

B. Movable Hypothecs

1. Creation

The movable hypothec in the Province of Québec is the equivalent of the security interest governed by the various Personal Property Security Acts (or PPSA) in the Canadian common-law provinces, or the Uniform Commercial Code in the United States. The movable hypothec confers real security on specific movable assets. In the case of a default of the grantor of the movable hypothec, the creditors may enforce their rights on the asset(s) covered by the hypothec in a variety of ways set out hereafter. The hypothec may be legal or conventional. The legal hypothec can be created either by law or following a judgment rendered against the debtor. The conventional hypothec is that which is created by mutual agreement.

The conventional hypothec is created by way of a written hypothec agreement setting out the terms upon which the hypothec is granted including the obligations secured by hypothec and the assets covered. Anyone having the capacity to alienate property may grant a hypothec on said property. Except where the debtor operates an enterprise and the hypothec is charged on the property of that enterprise, an individual person may grant a movable hypothec without delivery only on road vehicles or other movable property determined by regulation and subject to the conditions determined by regulation.

2. Registration

A movable hypothec may only be enforced against third parties, particularly holders of other hypothecs on the same property, if the hypothec has been registered in the Register of Real and Personal Rights of the Province of Québec. The registration involves the filing of a specifically designated form that contains information regarding the grantor of the hypothec, the holder, the general terms of the hypothec, and the assets covered by same. The form must also refer specifically to the written hypothec agreement. Finally, the movable property covered by the hypothec can be specific or can also consist of all of the personal property (the universality of movables) owned by the grantor.

3. Enforcement

The movable hypothec confers upon the holder the right to follow the property and the right of priority in the event of the sale of such property (Art. 2663 CCQ). The holder of the hypothec can enforce its rights in the event of a default of the grantor under the terms of the hypothec agreement. They are:

- Taking in payment:
  The creditor exercises its right to take the property in full and complete payment of its debt in capital, interest, and costs.
- Sale under judicial control:
  The creditor will seek the court-controlled sale of the property. In this case, the debt is not extinguished. Rather, the proceeds of the judicial sale of the property will serve to reduce the amount of the debt. The creditor can claim the difference owing.
- Taking of possession for purposes of administration:
  More often used where the property generates revenue, the creditor may use the revenue to reduce the amount of the debt. This method of enforcement does, however, create an obligation on the part of the creditor to render an account of sums collected.
- Direct sale by the creditor (Art. 2784 CCQ):
  The property is sold by the creditor directly without court intervention. However, the creditor may expose itself to scrutiny regarding the sale price.

In each case, the creditor will be required to deliver a prior notice of the exercise of a hypothecary right, which is 20 days.

These enforcement rights are in addition to the common claims of creditors against the debtors. Furthermore, as an accessory real right, the hypothec will be extinguished if the principal obligation, which it is made to secure, is itself extinguished. In addition to being an accessory right, it is also indivisible. The hypothec therefore subsists "in whole on all the secured property, on each one and every part of each despite the divisibility of the property or the obligation" (Art. 2662 CCQ). As a result, it has been decided that the taking in payment of certain property can extinguish the entire obligation in spite of the value of the property in question (*Prêts Relais Capital Inc. c. Carrier*, 2012, QCCA 1295, J.E. 2012-1486, [2012] R.J.Q. 1266 par 48 to 51). That indivisibility may however be limited by law or by contract.

C. Immovable Hypothecs

Immovable hypothecs relate to real estate and are like mortgages. They are governed by provisions under the Civil Code similar to those relating to moveable hypothecs. However, the immovable hypothec must be created by agreement before a notary authorized to practice in the Province of Québec, failing which it is null. It can only affect immovable property or a universality of immovables. The immovable hypothec must be registered at the Land Registry Office, which is the sole mode of registration accepted.

VII. Recent Developments and Case Law

One of the most talked-about court cases of the last years has been the lawsuit involving Dunkin' Donuts and a number of franchisees in the Province of Québec. The facts and resulting judgments are somewhat unique and discussed below in more detail.

In May 2003, a group of 21 Dunkin' Donuts franchisees operating 32 stores in the Province of Québec sued Dunkin' Brands Canada Ltd. alleging that it had failed to protect and enhance the brand in Québec. They further alleged that this constituted a contractual fault that caused them lost profits and lost investments. In addition, the franchisees alleged a host of other contractual and civil faults, including poor management practices, failure to provide proper support to the franchisees, an absence of a proper marketing plan, bad faith in the performance of the franchise agreements, and violation of the general obligation of loyalty owed to the franchisees.

On June 21, 2012, the trial court, the Superior Court of Québec, rendered judgment in the case of *Bertico Inc. et al v. Dunkin' Brands Canada, Ltd.* (trial judgment in *Bertico Inc. et al. v. Dunkin' Brands Canada Ltd.* (formerly *Allied Domecq Retailing International (Canada) Ltd.*, 2012 QCCS 2809, June 21, 2012 (S.C.)) concluding that Dunkin' Donuts was in fact liable on the basis of the alleged breaches of contract and civil faults and awarded the amount of C$16,407,143 claimed by the franchisee plaintiffs, calculated on the basis of $7.4 million for lost profits and $9 million for lost investments, plus interest and costs. In addition, the trial judge denied all offsets in unpaid royalties and ad fund contributions, thereby dismissing Dunkin' Donuts' counterclaims, and nullified releases signed by some franchisees in the context of their undertaking to accept financial incentives pursuant to a remodel program.

Dunkin' Donuts subsequently appealed the Superior Court judgment, and on April 15, 2015, the Court of Appeal of the Province of Québec rendered its decision on appeal.

In short, the Court of Appeal confirmed the trial court's finding on liability, but reduced the damages and granted Dunkin' Donuts' counterclaims.

On the issue of liability, the Court of Appeal stated that the case was not "unprecedented" and summarized its view in the following terms:

> **[8]** In describing the case as one that is "unprecedented" in the annals of franchise law, the franchisor has, in my respectful view, wrongly characterized aspects of franchise arrangements widely understood by courts and legal scholars in this province as uncontroversial, in particular in respect of duties that may be inferred from the nature of agreements such as the ones

> in the case at bar. The collapse of the Dunkin' Donuts chain may well have no match as a financial misfortune in the annals of the quick-service restaurant business in Québec—that is not an issue for this Court to decide—but nothing in the judge's account of the franchisor's obligations was "unprecedented" or even demonstrably wrong-headed; in point of fact, he was expressly careful to follow precedent, namely the doctrine of implied obligations under article 1434 C.C.Q. and the duty of good faith set forth in *Provigo Distribution Inc. v. Supermaché A.R.G. Inc.*, decided by this Court eighteen years ago and generally recognized as the leading authority in Québec law since that time (Appeal Judgment, Paragraph 8).

Of particular note is the Court of Appeal's reliance on Article 1434 of the *Civil Code of Québec* (CCQ), which reads as follows:

> **Article 1434**. A contract validly formed binds the parties who have entered into it not only as to what they have expressed in it but also as to what is incident to it according to its nature and in conformity with usage, equity or law (CCQ, S.Q. 1991, c.64).

The Court of Appeal also relied on its own decision in the case of *Provigo*, a landmark decision in the Québec franchise law landscape rendered in 1997 (*Provigo Distribution Inc.* v. *Supermarché A.R.G. Inc.,* [1998] R. J. Q. 47 (C.A)), which essentially extended and, to a certain extent, defined some implicit obligations that flow from the explicit provisions of franchise agreements essentially based on the concept of good faith, enshrined in the CCQ as follows:

> **Art. 6**. Every person is bound to exercise his civil rights in good faith. (CCQ, S.Q., 1991, c.64)

> **Art. 7**. No right may be exercised with the intent of injuring another or in an excessive and unreasonable manner, and therefore contrary to the requirements of good faith. (CCQ, S.Q., 1991, c.64)

A. Liability

In its analysis of the trial court decision, the Court of Appeal found that the trial judge had failed to show a reversible error, and more specifically, regarding the following issues:

B. The Obligations Contained in the Franchise Agreements

The interpretation of the terms of the franchise agreements was the focus of considerable debate particularly regarding the franchisor's principal obligation to "protect and enhance the brand." On this issue, the Court of Appeal found that the franchisor had failed to show an error committed by the trial judge in his interpretation of the contract. In arguing that the judge's "entire reasoning" was based on paragraph 3.C of the 1992 contract and the recital of the standard form of 2002, the franchisor has misread the judgment to suit its argument. The obligation of means to protect and enhance the brand imposed on the franchisor was not incompatible with explicit terms of the contracts. But, just as importantly, the judge's interpretation of the duties owed to the franchisees rested on the whole of the agreements, including the implicit obligations based on the nature of the franchise arrangement and, in particular, the implied obligation of good faith incumbent on both parties. The court found no palpable and overriding error in the trial judge's conclusion that the franchisor had promised to take reasonable measures to protect and enhance the brand. The court added that even if one was to consider the inference of obligations based on the nature of the contract under article 1434 C.C.Q. or the obligation of good faith as raising a question of law, it was of the view that no error of law had been shown either (Appeal Judgment, Paragraph 48).

Regarding implied obligations incidental to the nature of the franchise agreements, the Court of Appeal reaffirmed the trial judge's reliance on Article 1434 C.C.Q, which it stated was well founded, (CCQ, S.Q. 1991, c.64) and held that the franchise agreements established a relationship of cooperation and collaboration between the franchisor and its franchisees, reflecting both common and divergent interests, over a long period of time. Unlike in other arrangements where a franchisor might merely provide a licence and some modest start-up advice, the Dunkin' Donuts franchisees were by no means left to their own devices after their launch in the quick-service restaurant business. Protecting the brand was no doubt too important to the franchisor not to take an active hand in the arrangement over the course of its term. Sustaining the "system" as a flourishing restaurant chain required, as the terms of the agreement made plain, an ongoing interaction between the franchisor and each of its franchisees. The franchisor took on a role in choosing appropriate franchisees and approving new acquirers of existing franchises, of advising franchisees at the start of the venture, and of offering assistance to them along the way to be sure that each franchisee respected the system upon which the reputation of the brand rested. The franchisee relied on the franchisor assuming this role to justify its investment. Not only would each franchisee receive assistance and benefit from the collaboration of the franchisor, but the franchisees were entitled to count on the franchisor to see that the system would be supervised and that the weaker links in the chain of franchisees be corrected or excised. This relationship was required to continue over the life of the agreement. In this sense, the agreement was a "relational" one that, as is often the case in such long-term arrangements, did not spell out all of its terms (Appeal Judgment, Paragraph 62).

In addition, the court held that these implicit obligations formed part of a long-term collaborative relationship between the franchisor and each individual franchisee, within an established network in which service and quality of experience were imagined as nearly identical from restaurant to restaurant. The court found important that the trial judge held as important the recognition that the character of these specific franchise arrangements was an "ongoing" one in respect of a "system" that the parties agreed to sustain as critical to the success of the brand. As a result, the trial judge found that the obligations the franchisor has in respect of the brand were necessarily "continuing" and "successive" (para. [59]). The collaborative nature of these quick-service restaurant franchising agreements that extended upwards of 20 years was central to explaining why article 1434 C.C.Q. served to import the obligations it did (Appeal Judgment, Paragraph 63).

Moreover, given the role the franchisor assigned to itself in overseeing the ongoing operation of the network and the uniform system of standards, the court held that it was fair to characterize the obligation of means to protect and enhance the brand as a "*complément nécessaire*" [necessary complement] of the contracts due to their nature. It was thus appropriate, in the court's view, for the trial judge to infer that the franchisor had implicitly agreed to undertake reasonable measures to help the franchisees, over the life of the arrangement, to support the brand. This included a duty to assist them in staving off competition in order to promote the ongoing prosperity of the network as an inherent feature of the relational franchise contract (Appeal Judgment, Paragraph 64). This necessary complement to the express terms rested on the presumed intention of the parties to these particular agreements. The trial judge inferred the franchisor's obligations flowing from the nature of the agreements not from a body of suppletive or public order rules, but from his sense of the unstated intention of the parties, consonant with articles 1425 and 1426 C.C.Q. In light of the theory of implied obligations, this was a principal justification for obligations inferred from the nature of the agreement under article 1434 C.C.Q. In other words, in characterizing the essential obligation of the franchisor as a duty to protect and enhance the brand, the trial judge did not assign a new and unintended obligation on the franchisor, but he drew on the explicit terms, supplemented by implicit obligations flowing from the nature of the agreement that, in both cases, reflected the intention of the parties. The "*élargissement du cercle contractuel*" [increase of the contractual circle] in this case was based on the trial judge's finding of fact as to parties' intent. The court also noted that the franchisor pointed to no express term that would have ousted the implied obligations that came with the nature of this long-term agreement (Appeal Judgment, Paragraph 66).

The Court of Appeal revisited the notion of implied obligation of good faith analysed at length in *Provigo* (*Provigo Distribution Inc. v. Supermarché A.R.G. Inc.*, [1998] R.J.Q. 47 (C.A.)) and found that "[t]he judge was correct to rely on

Provigo as support for an implicit obligation of good faith which, in connection with the present franchising arrangement, buttressed the obligation to protect and enhance the brand based on the parties presumed intent. The judge rightly decided that the duty outlined in *Provigo* is not confined to the circumstances of franchisors who compete unfairly with their franchisees [. . .]" (Appeal Judgment, Paragraph 69).

The Court of Appeal also found that, where the parties must work together to achieve the object of the franchise arrangement over a long period of time, the *Provigo* case recognized that both the nature of the agreement and equity allowed a "duty to cooperate" to be inferred as a contractual obligation for the franchisor. Accordingly, in the *Dunkin'* case, the nature of the agreement, on one hand, and equity, on the other, provided two distinct normative justifications for this implied obligation of good faith under article 1434 C.C.Q. Thus, where the nature of the agreement justified the inference, the implied obligation is best viewed as a reflection of the presumed intention of the parties. Parties to a long-term franchise agreement like the ones in the case at bar can typically be presumed to have intended reasonable standards of cooperation based on the relational nature of the arrangement. Equity does not depend on presumed intention, but is more closely connected to the law's concerns for fairness in contract. In this particular case, the court found that equity mandated the franchisor's due regard for the franchisees' interests, taking into account what the court called in *Provigo* the franchisor's superior know-how and expertise, without which long-term common objectives of both parties could not be met. Thus the implied duty of good faith under article 1434 C.C.Q. acts to reinforce and confirm the duties of assistance and cooperation for the franchisor associated with the nature of the contract. In sum, good faith brings with it, as an implied obligation based on both equity and the long-term nature of these franchise agreements, an intensification of the cooperation which remains the fundamental characteristic of any relational contract (Appeal Judgment, Paragraph 71).

The Court of Appeal found, in addition, that beyond the duty not to take actions that would wrongfully cause the franchisees harm, the franchisor assumed, on the basis of this implied duty of good faith in the 1992 and 2002 franchise agreements, a duty "to assist and cooperate with the franchisees by taking certain active measures in support of the brand" (Appeal Judgment, Paragraph 72). This meant that the franchisees were entitled to rely on the franchisor, as a matter of contractual fairness and as a reflection of their own presumed intentions, to take reasonable measures to protect them from the market challenge presented by the Tim Hortons chain of restaurants. The court found that the trial judge correctly identified these two sources of implied obligations such that where a violation of these implied obligations incident to the nature of the contract and in conforming to equity was established, the judge was entitled to conclude that there was a contractual fault as the court held in *Provigo* (Appeal Judgment, Paragraph 72).

The court also held that it was important not to exaggerate the content of the implied obligation of good faith and its attendant "duty to collaborate." Thus, despite some shared objectives, franchisors and franchisees also have divergent interests but are no less in a relationship of collaboration. The pursuit of these divergent interests was possible, but only within the parameters of the terms of the contract and the implied obligation of good faith (Appeal Judgment, Paragraph 72). The Court of Appeal found that in this light, it was fair to see the parties, despite the aspirational language of "partnership" sometimes used in connection with the arrangement, as having some different goals. The parties were thus entitled, within the bounds of the execution of the contract in good faith (article 1375 C.C.Q.) (CCQ, S.Q., 1991, c.64) and the content of the obligation of good faith that is implicit in their agreement (article 1434 C.C.Q.) to pursue those divergent interests. As the Supreme Court held in a comparable context, the obligation of good faith does not displace the "legitimate pursuit of economic self-interest" that is at the core of freedom of contract (Appeal Judgment, Paragraph 74).

The Court of Appeal found that the judge had not imposed on the franchisor, through the duty of good faith, an unfair standard of disinterested behaviour or required it to confer a liberality on the franchisees. It was in the franchisor's interest, broadly speaking, to assist its franchisees, to supervise the network and to collaborate with them by proposing reasonable measures to combat a competitor who, in the longer term, threatens the value of the brand for both parties. When established, the failure to do so was a contractual fault that gave rise to damages not as an arbitrary measure of redistribution of wealth but as an ordinary contractual remedy based on corrective justice. In any event, the court found that it was enough to observe that the trial judge had made no error in identifying an implicit obligation for the franchisor to take reasonable measures to promote and enhance the brand and that this conclusion found justification both in the nature of the agreement and in equity. Thus, whether the doctrine of the implied obligation of good faith might have a more robust or more expansive content, including the question as to whether "good faith" and "loyalty" are qualitatively different sources of contractual duty, was a matter best left to another day (Appeal Judgment, Paragraph 75).

The Court of Appeal found that, beyond the obligation to allow individual franchisees to use the Dunkin' Donuts system, the contracts created, through express language and by necessary implication, a duty owed to the franchisees, collectively to take reasonable measures to support and enhance the brand. This included the duty to respond with reasonable measures to help the franchisees as a group to meet the market challenges of the moment and to assist the network of franchisees by enforcing the uniform standards of quality and cleanliness it holds out as critical to the success of the franchise (Appeal Judgment, Paragraph 77). This would also suggest that it is up to the franchisor to police the network by taking reasonable means to root out the free-riders. With respect to the word "enhance," the franchisor did not guarantee that the reputation of the brand would be enhanced but undertook to take reasonable means to that end, and the trial judge did not say otherwise.

In sum, the trial judge made no reversible error in his identification of the franchisor's obligations in the franchise agreements.

C. The "Intensity" of the Franchisor's Contractual Obligations

The Court of Appeal found that the trial judge both said and clearly meant that the obligation imposed on the franchisor was one of means, not of result. The trial judge was therefore entitled to find that the franchisor's violation of a contractual obligation of means caused 100% of the damages claimed if the evidence supported that view, without necessarily following that he imposed an obligation of result. As stated by the Court of Appeal, "The franchisor is right to say that the contract did not impose an obligation on it to guarantee the franchisees' success or insulate them from competition. There is no disputing the fact that the franchisor's obligation was limited to taking reasonable measures to protect and enhance the brand. But the judge rightly recognized this. In paragraph [62] of his reasons, he made plain his sense of the extent of the franchisor's duty to protect and enhance the brand: Although not the insurer of the franchisees nor the guarantor of their successes, ADRIC [the franchisor] is nevertheless responsible to them for the harm caused by its civil faults. The judge both said, and clearly meant, that the obligation imposed on the franchisor was one of means, not of result" (Appeal Judgment, Paragraph 94).

D. The Application of the Business Judgment Rule

The Court of Appeal rejected the application of the Business Judgment Rule and found that it applied to matters relating to the personal responsibility of directors and officers and to shareholders and not as a means of exculpating a corporate contracting party from liability for fault under a contract with third parties.

E. Evidence of the Franchisor's Fault

On the evidence of the franchisor's fault, the Court of Appeal found that it was based on two principal findings. First, the judge observed the relative inaction of the franchisor between 1995 and 2000 when faced with the newfound competition, delinquent franchisees, the need for consultants in a position to assist the respondents, and the like, and found that the effects continued into the period relevant to the cause of action. Second, the judge found that the franchisor's response, from 2000 onwards, came too late and was insufficient. It is important to note that these findings are linked. The response in 2000 might have proved adequate, measured against the standard of the franchisor's obligation of means, but for the accumulated difficulties that the franchisees and the brand were feeling after what the judge described as years of relative neglect leading up to the response. The view he took of the insufficient measures taken between 1995 and 2000 is an essential feature of the judge's finding of fault for the whole of the period (Appeal Judgment, Paragraph 113).

F. Causation

On the issue of causation, the trial judge found that there was evidence to support the argument that Dunkin' Donuts' failure to meet the competition head on and in a timely fashion caused the losses claimed. None of the externalities served to break the chain of causation and the franchisees were not negligent in the day-to-day management of their stores. Furthermore, the same causation analysis could apply across the network to all the franchisees.

The Court of Appeal found that the conclusion on causation is a finding of fact and that the trial judge had committed no palpable and overriding error that would allow the finding of causation to be set aside.

G. The Releases

On ancillary issues, the trial judge ruled that, under the circumstances, the execution of certain releases had been obtained by the misrepresentation that the minimum critical mass of 75 remodeled stores would be or had been obtained, which vitiated consent and the releases given on this basis were thus null. The question as to whether a party provided valid consent to a contract is a finding of fact and the trial judge had committed no palpable and overriding error that would allow the Court of Appeal to intervene on this point.

VIII. Damages

A. Damages for Lost Profits

Where the evaluation of damages depends on the appreciation by the trial judge of conflicting expert reports, an appellate court will generally not intervene in the absence of a palpable and overriding error of fact or an error of law.

The Court of Appeal was nonetheless convinced that the trial judge made two errors of calculation that called for a reduction in the amount of damages. He made a first error in calculating the relevant dates for determining lost profits and made a second error of calculation when he relieved the franchisees from paying the royalties and other payments owed by them under the franchise agreements (Appeal Judgment, Paragraphs 172, 173, 174, 175, 176, 177, and 178). Beyond these two errors, the Court of Appeal found that the trial judge had made no overriding error in preferring the comparable method for evaluating lost profits. It was reasonable for the trial judge to adopt the comparable method using Tim Horton's as the comparable business for calculating lost profits.

However, in choosing the figure of 100% of Tim Hortons' growth as the factor for determining the franchisees' lost profits, the trial judge failed to take into account certain imponderables that potentially affect all businesses. The Court of Appeal agreed with the franchisor that the 100% figure failed to allow for the competition that Dunkin' Donuts would have faced from Tim Hortons, even if the franchisor had not committed a fault. Not taking this into account was deemed to be a reviewable error.

The Court of Appeal ultimately discounted the 100% growth rate used by the trial judge by reducing it to 75% in order to allow for the competition factor from Tim Hortons in the calculation of profits of the franchisees, including the competitive advantage of the drive-thru service. The Court of Appeal therefore revised the amount of lost profits from $7,360,000 to $4,372,472.

B. Damages for Lost Investments

The trial judge's view of the evidence was that certain damages had been shown with respect to lost investments on the basis of evidence given by an ordinary witness. Given that the franchisees had suffered lost investments, according to the trial judge, it was his duty to settle on an amount based on the evidence adduced. The Court of Appeal found that Dunkin' Donuts had failed to demonstrate that the trial judge committed a palpable and overriding error on this point. The Court of Appeal recognized that the method used for fixing the quantum of damages lacked in precision. However, given that no effort has been made by Dunkin' Donuts to show exactly where, in his reading of the financial statements, the trial judge went astray in his conclusion, the franchisor failed to convince the Court of Appeal that the trial judge had committed a reviewable error.

Dunkin' Donuts also failed to convince the Court of Appeal that the lost profits and lost investment amounted to double compensation. Nevertheless, two adjustments needed to be made: given the Court of Appeal's conclusion that the amount of lost profits should be based on 75% rather than 100% of Tim Hortons growth, the amount used by the trial judge to determine lost investments should be reduced accordingly. Rather than using Tim Horton's 2005 results with a factor of 100%, the calculation should proceed using a factor of 75%. The lost investments were therefore reduced by the Court of Appeal by 25%.

Furthermore, the franchisees who renovated their stores and who received a contribution from the franchisor under the renovation plan should reimburse the franchisor for its contribution from the money they received as damages. Because the trial judge annulled the releases, the parties needed to be returned to the situation they were in prior to that arrangement. The franchisees having been awarded the full amount for the lost investment of a renovated store, the trial judge should have deducted the amount that the franchisor contributed to the cost of renovations for those franchisees who had signed releases to avoid a double payment for that latter amount.

The Court of Appeal thus reduced the amount of damages for lost profits from $9,047,143 to $6,536,041.25, allowing for the franchisor's contribution to renovation of $249,316 to be refunded and calculating the total using 75% of the increase in sales in 2005.

Beyond these two adjustments, the franchisor had not convinced the Court of Appeal that the trial judge had committed a reviewable error.

C. Significance of the Case

On June 15, 2015, Dunkin' Donuts filed an application for leave to appeal to the Supreme Court of Canada (*Dunkin' Brands Canada Ltd.* v. *Bertico Inc. et al.*, File number 36475). In May 2016, the Supreme Court dismissed the application.

There is no doubt that the Dunkin' case has created some uncertainty as to the duties owed by franchisors to their franchisees in Québec. Unfortunately, the Court of Appeal judgment provides no guidance as to what is meant by such obligations as "enhancing the brand" or "staving off competition," as well as what actions franchisors should take to fulfill those obligations. Conversely, franchisor obligations are now clearly of means and not of result. Finally the Court of Appeal recognized a Franchisor's implied obligation owed to the Network of franchisees, i.e. to the franchisees collectively to take reasonable measures to support and enhance the brand. This included the duty to respond with reasonable measures to help the franchisees as a group to meet the market challenges of the moment and to assist the network of franchisees by enforcing the uniform standards [...] it holds out as critical to the success of the franchise. It remains to be seen what impact the case will have and how courts in Québec, and perhaps elsewhere, will interpret this judgment.

Practice Note

Franchisors should be proactive in all aspects of the assistance, support, and guidance they provide their franchisees regarding such issues as brand development, responding to new market trends and mounting competition, as well as product or service innovation. Furthermore, they would be well advised to use all reasonable means necessary to carry out those obligations.

CHAPTER 3

Other Laws Affecting Franchising in Canada

Edward Levitt and Clark Harrop

Contents

I. Introduction

Expanding into a foreign jurisdiction, done properly, requires an attention to the detail of many laws in the target territory, not just the franchise laws. There is no exception to this when the system is expanding into Canada.

Given the vast array of businesses that adopt franchising as their distribution method of choice, it would be impossible to outline all of the laws and regulations that will have to be considered in this single publication, and it is incumbent upon each franchisor to retain the appropriate advisors to research the laws that affect them.

However, this chapter will review some of the federal, provincial, territorial and municipal laws that are most commonly encountered by franchisors expanding their systems into Canada.

II. Laws Affecting the Movement of People and Goods Across the Border

In Canada, immigration is the responsibility of several federal governmental agencies, including Citizenship and Immigration Canada (CIC), Canada Border Services Agency at ports of entry (i.e., Canadian international airports and Canada-U.S. land border crossings), and the Department of Foreign Affairs and International Trade at visa offices located outside Canada. Immigration laws and policies are contained in the *Immigration and Refugee Protection Regulations Act* (SC 2001, c. 27), along with related regulations, policy manuals and operations memoranda.

Persons who are neither Canadian citizens nor Canadian permanent residents are referred to as "foreign nationals" in Canadian immigration law and do not have the right to work in Canada unless properly authorized. Described below are the requirements most applicable to foreign franchisors establishing Canadian operations.

A. Bringing Your Executives and Employees into Canada

Employees who are foreign nationals must, unless exempted, obtain work permits to work in Canada. "Work" is defined as "an activity for which wages are paid or a commission is earned, or that is in direct competition with the activities of Canadian citizens or permanent residents in the Canadian labour market" (*Immigration and Refugee Protection Regulations*, S.O.R./2002-227, s. 2). Note that the duration of the work is not a factor, so even if an employee will be working in Canada for a very short period of time, a work permit may be required. Only if a foreign national qualifies under a work permit-exempt category will a work permit not be required. The legislation provides that if an employee is found to have worked illegally in Canada without a work permit, he or she may be held inadmissible to Canada for a period of two years.

Employees of franchisors who are carrying out pre-operational activities in Canada may be allowed to enter Canada as temporary "business visitors." Later, when business operations in Canada are commenced, however, work permits must be obtained.

Practice Note

Key employees of a franchisor may often obtain Canadian work permits under the "intra-company transferee-senior manager" or "intra-company transferee-specialist" categories. The latter requires a demonstration of special knowledge of the products or services or related processes and procedures related to the business concerned.

1. Temporary Work Permits

Before determining whether a work permit is required, it must be determined whether a foreign national employee needs to obtain an underlying visa, called a "temporary resident visa," before traveling to Canada. If an employee attempts to enter Canada at a port of entry without the requisite visa, the immigration officer will not permit entry. A visa must be applied for at a visa office outside Canada so that an immigration officer can adjudicate whether the person involved is admissible to Canada (health, non-criminality, security and other requirements are examined) and has the ability to leave the other country (normally as evidenced by a valid passport or other travel document) prior to entering Canada.

If it is determined that a work permit and a temporary resident visa are needed, the employee must apply for a work permit at a visa office. The visa office will issue a temporary resident visa which will usually enable the person to receive a work permit at the port of entry. If it is determined that an employee is eligible for entry to Canada under a work permit-exempt category, then the person will apply under the exempt category at a visa office. The visa office will issue a temporary resident visa which will enable the person to enter Canada as a visitor.

Practice Note

Obtaining a temporary resident visa can include a processing time of up to several weeks, depending on the visa office and the nationality of the applicant. For applications submitted inside Canada, the processing time for a paper application is approximately 16 days, and for an online application, approximately 11 days (plus mailing time). For applications submitted outside Canada, the processing time varies but can be anywhere between two and seven months. A visa is issued for a fixed period of time and will allow for either a single or multiple entries to Canada.

Practice Note

If there is a reasonable chance that the employee may need to leave Canada during the period of stay applied for, a multiple-entry visa should be sought. Otherwise, another visa will have to be obtained prior to the employee re-entering Canada (unless the employee only visited the United States of America (U.S.) and holds a Canadian work permit valid beyond the return date).

(a) Temporary resident visa exemptions

Certain nationalities are exempted from the need to obtain a temporary resident visa to travel to Canada. For example, persons who are citizens or permanent residents of the United States are exempted. A listing of the nationalities is available from CIC. A visa-exempt foreign national can apply to enter Canada at a port of entry. If a work permit was applied for outside of Canada, the person will be referred to the immigration office where the work permit will be issued upon presentation of a work permit approval letter. If the person is applying for a work permit at the port of entry, he or she will be referred to the immigration office to make the application.

(b) Work permit exemptions

Business visitors and other specific categories of foreign nationals are authorized to work in Canada without a work permit. A "business visitor" is defined as a foreign national "who seeks to engage in international business activities in Canada without directly entering the Canadian labour market" (*Ibid.* at s. 187(1)). To be considered a business visitor, the following requirements must be met:

- the primary source of remuneration for the business activities is outside of Canada; and

- the principal place of business and actual place of accrual of profits by the employer remain predominantly outside Canada. In practice, if there are Canadian operations as well as the foreign operations, it may be difficult to enter as a business visitor because the immigration officer may consider the business activities to be benefiting the Canadian operations primarily.

Employees of a foreign franchisor who will be carrying out the following types of activities in Canada are permitted to do so without a work permit:

- key employees (e.g., senior management or specialists) assisting in establishing the Canadian operation, until such time as the Canadian operation is up and running;
- employees providing training to other employees of a Canadian branch or subsidiary so long as any production of goods or services that results from the training is merely incidental; and
- commercial speakers and leaders of seminars that last a maximum of five days, as well as guest speakers making a speech or delivering a paper at a dinner, convention or similar function.

Employees of an American franchisor who are either Unites States or Mexican citizens are permitted to enter Canada without a work permit under NAFTA provided they are planning to carry out activities in Canada under one of the categories of "Research and Design," "Growth, Manufacture and Production," "Marketing," "Sales," "Distribution," "After-Sales Service," or "General Service." "General Service" includes such things as discussions and negotiations respecting the sale, purchase, marketing, distribution, advertisement, procurement, transmission, transportation or packaging of goods or services, public relations, and advertising and tourism.

(c) Work permit categories

There are several different categories under which a work permit may be obtained. Each category will dictate the requirements and procedures for applying and the location at which the application can be made, which in turn will affect the processing time, the length of the work permit, and whether the work permit is extendable. Generally, a foreign national employer must obtain a positive Labour Market Impact Assessment (LMIA) from Human Resources Skills and Development Canada (HRSDC) before a work permit application is submitted. A positive LMIA will provide that the employment of a foreign national is likely to have a neutral or positive economic effect on the labour market in Canada. Normally, a foreign franchisor can maintain successfully that expanding its franchise system to Canada will result in new jobs being created in Canada.

When assessing whether the employment of a foreign national is likely to have a neutral or positive economic effect on the labour market in Canada, HRSDC will take into account the following factors:

- whether the employer has made reasonable efforts to hire or train qualified Canadian citizens or permanent residents;
- whether the employment is likely to fill a labour shortage;
- whether the employment is likely to result in direct job creation or job retention for Canadian citizens or permanent residents;
- whether the employment is likely to result in the creation or transfer of skills and knowledge for the benefit of Canadian citizens or permanent residents; and
- whether the wages offered are consistent with the prevailing wage rate for the occupation and whether the working conditions meet generally accepted Canadian standards.

(d) Work permit conditions

A work permit is issued for up to three years but generally may be extended. The work permit will likely be issued only until the expiry date of the passport, so the employee should seek a new passport before applying for a work permit.

A work permit is both employer-specific and occupation-specific according to specific occupations based on a National Occupational Classification (NOC). For example, the president of a Franchise System may be classified as a "Senior Manager—Trade," NOC 0015. As well, a work permit is location-specific. If an employee will be spending significant time working in more than one location, a separate work permit for each location may be necessary, especially if the locations are in different provinces or territories of Canada.

Practice Note

Canadian work permits are specific to an employer, to an occupation and to a specific location. Multiple work permits for different locations may be obtained, if required.

(e) Hiring temporary foreign workers

The Government of Canada lists four basic steps employers must take to hire a temporary foreign worker:

1. Determine if you need to apply for an LMIA.
2. Apply for an LMIA from Service Canada, if required.
3. Have the foreign worker complete the work permit application.

4. If the worker is eligible, a Canadian Border Services Agency officer will issue the work permit at the point of entry when the foreign worker arrives in Canada.

For more information, visit www.cic.gc.ca.

2. Permanent Residency Requirements

A permanent resident is someone who has been given permanent resident status by immigrating to Canada, but is not a Canadian citizen. Permanent residents are citizens of other countries. If an employee is expected to work in Canada for several years, obtaining permanent resident status may be beneficial. A permanent resident is not constrained by the conditions regarding employment as a foreign worker holding a work permit (i.e., conditions regarding length of authorization, employer, occupation and location). There can also be non-immigration benefits to being a permanent resident. For example, dependent children who have become permanent residents can attend Canadian universities and colleges without paying higher international student tuition rates.

There are several different categories under which permanent resident status can be obtained. Each category has different requirements, with some categories being more appropriate for persons who work for arm's-length employers and other categories more appropriate for entrepreneurs or persons who have strong business and management backgrounds. As well, all provinces and territories (except the Province of Quebec) have established immigration programs to implement federal immigration programs and to promote highly skilled workers and businesspeople immigrating to those places. The main advantage of gaining provincial or territorial support (called a "nomination") for a permanent residence application is that the visa office will then, subject to any admissibility issues, expedite the processing of the application, substantially decreasing the processing time from several years to one year or less.

Practice Note

To maintain permanent resident status, a person must normally have resided in Canada for at least two years out of the last five. This allows flexibility for persons required to spend periods of time working in other countries.

Canada recognizes multiple citizenships, meaning that it does not require a person to give up citizenship of another country to become a citizen of Canada. Since the U.S., for example, also recognizes multiple citizenships, a U.S. citizen can also be a Canadian citizen and vice-versa. Permanent resident status confers many rights of Canadian citizenship, but can be lost if residency requirements are not maintained (e.g., residing in Canada at least two years during the last five-year period), while citizenship may generally not be lost unless the person voluntarily renounces it. A person with Canadian citizenship may live abroad for extended periods and maintain the right to return to Canada.

To apply for Canadian citizenship, a person must normally have permanent resident status and have resided in Canada for at least three of the four years prior to the date of the application. Note that this residency requirement is more stringent than the requirement to maintain permanent resident status.

B. Bringing Your Existing Supply Chain into Canada

In situations where a foreign franchisor or its foreign affiliates supply their Canadian systems, there are several legal restrictions to be aware of. The following regulatory barriers control the importation of goods into Canada: (1) import restrictions, (2) import duties, and (3) technical standards.

Under s.8 of the *Export and Import Permits Act* (R.S.C., 1985, c. E-19, s.8) certain goods may require import permits to cross the Canadian border. Such permits are part of a quota system used to protect certain Canadian industries by limiting the quantity of certain goods imported into Canada. The Trade Controls and Technical Barriers Bureau is responsible for administering the *Export and Import Permits Act* through the *Import Control List* (ICL), the *Export Control List* (ECL), and the *Area Control List* (ACL). The ICL generally comprises a list of goods, some of which are only controlled for certain countries of origin; all goods contained in this list require an import permit. The ECL is a list of goods only; all goods contained on this list also require an export permit. The ACL is a list of countries for which export permits are required to export any and all goods.

Import duties attempt to protect Canadian businesses by imposing a fee at the border on certain goods, affecting the competitiveness of imported products. Duties in Canada normally range between 0% and 35%. Some goods are not subject to duty (e.g., certain electronic products, antiques, and toys).

Technical standards serve to guard local industries from competition by setting certain technical standards that can be complied with more easily or cost-effectively by domestic manufacturers. Such standards are created by several levels of government and private organizations, such as the Canadian Standards Association in Canada.

Practice Note

Franchisors entering Canada must be aware of regulatory barriers on goods at the Canadian border—in particular, import restrictions, import duties and technical barriers.

1. Consumer Packaging and Labelling Act

American and overseas franchisors need to be aware of specific Canadian packaging and labeling issues that must be complied with in relation to consumer products. It is unlikely that the standard packaging utilized in the franchisor's American operations will be in compliance with Canadian packaging and labeling requirements. Specifically, consumer products for sale in Canada (with limited exceptions) must abide by the federal *Consumer Packaging and Labelling Act* (R.S.C. 1985, c. C-38). The Consumer Packaging and Labelling Act requires products imported into Canada or advertised in Canada to have a label stating the net quantity of the product. The Act prohibits labels from containing any false or misleading representation relating to the product. The label must include the following information: the identity and principal place of business of the person by or for whom the product was manufactured or produced for resale, the identity of the packaged product (both its generic name and its function), and information relating to the nature, quality, age, size, material content, composition, geographic origin, performance, use or method of manufacture.

The *Consumer Packaging and Labelling Regulations* (C.R.C., c. 417) provide that all information required to appear on a product label must be shown in both English and French, not only in Québec, but throughout all jurisdictions in Canada. The label must be applied to the container in which the product is displayed for sale to the consumer. Labels on edible products must include the number of servings and the net quantity of each serving.

The regulations also standardize containers to prevent consumers from being misled or confused by the undue proliferation of container shapes and sizes. Certain products that must be in standardized containers include peanut butter, wine, glucose syrup and refined sugar syrup (see s. 36 of the regulation for full details of the standard packaging requirements).

All numerical information must appear in Canadian units of measurement, as set out in Schedule 2 of the federal *Weights and Measures Act* (R.S.C. 1985, c. W-6) (for example, pounds, ounces, cubic feet and cubic inches must be converted into kilograms, grams, cubic metres and cubic centimetres).

Practice Note

Franchisors must ensure that packaging and labeling complies with Canadian requirements, including the federal Consumer Packaging and Labelling Act and the Weights and Measures Act.

2. Food and Drugs Act

Many franchise systems operate in the food industry and must be aware of applicable sections of the federal *Food and Drugs Act* (R.S.C. 1985, c F-27). The Food and Drugs Act regulates the advertising, sale and importation of foods, drugs, cosmetics and medical devices. “Food” is defined to include any article manufactured, sold or represented for use as food or drink for human consumption, including chewing gum and any ingredient that may be mixed with food for any purpose. “Drugs” are defined to include substances or mixtures of substances manufactured, sold or represented for use in diagnosing, preventing or treating a disease in man or animal; restoring or modifying organic functions in man or animal; or disinfecting premises in which food is manufactured or kept. Any product may become a drug for the purpose of the Food and Drugs Act if therapeutic claims are made by a manufacturer through labeling or advertising.

With regard to pre-market control, foods and drugs are treated differently by the Food and Drugs Act. There are no pre-marketing approvals required for foods, although certain foods require pre-marketing notification. Drugs, on the other hand, must be approved for importation and sale by the Health Promotion Board and be given a Drug Identification Number signifying the drug’s compliance with federal regulations. The sale of certain foods is prohibited under the Act, unless they have been prepared according to very detailed Canadian standards, and such foods may be subject to inspection by the Canadian Food Inspection Agency (CFIA).

Since 2015, Canada’s food safety regime has seen a number of important changes that impact franchisors involved in importing food products into Canada from other countries, as well as those that manufacture food products in Canada. Pursuant to the *Safe Food for Canadians Act* (S.C. 2012, c. 24), the CFIA has received new regulatory powers to enable traceability and improve the effectiveness of food recalls. Importers of certain foods require a valid import license to bring into Canada. Examples of such foods include dairy, eggs, meat, processed (canned) food, fish and seafood, fresh fruits, and vegetables. In order to obtain such a licence, importers will need to develop, implement and maintain a Preventive Food Safety Control Plan, which outlines actions and measures taken to keep their food safe and compliant with Canadian regulations. CFIA’s inspections of food processors have been streamlined to improve consistency, including permitting inspectors to inspect all food commodities, make warrant requests on-site, and issue penalties on the spot.

(a) Food labeling and advertising

In Canada, the law on labeling food is extensive and includes lengthy legislation and regulations. Under the *Food and Drug Regulations* (C.R.C., c. 870) nutrition labeling is mandatory for most foods. The regulation governs nutrient content claim requirements, and the use of diet-related health claims. The CFIA provides a guide to food labeling and advertising, which can be found on their website at www.inspection.gc.ca.

Mandatory nutrition labels help give consumers information about edible products, including calories, serving size, and percentage of fat, saturated fat, trans fat, cholesterol, sodium, carbohydrate, fiber, sugars, protein, vitamin A, vitamin C, calcium, and iron. Certain categories of foods qualify for an exemption from these requirements. These exempt food categories include fruit, vegetables, raw meat, alcoholic beverages, foods served or sold in restaurants, individual servings sold for immediate consumption, and milk or cream sold in a refillable glass container. Although the format for nutrition labeling appears to be similar to American requirements, companies should not use a United States label to satisfy Canadian requirements. There are varying requirements between the two countries; for example, a listing of calories from fat is mandatory in the United States, but is not required in Canada.

Advertising for foods and alcoholic beverages are subject to review by the Food and Drugs Act and related regulations and the Consumer Packaging and Labelling Act and related regulations. The CFIA guide to food labeling and advertising makes it clear that mandatory information or claims that are acceptable on a food label may also be used to advertise that food. Unacceptable label information is generally also not acceptable in advertising. Therefore, manufacturers and advertisers should ensure that their labels comply with federal statutes before developing advertisements for the foods. Food manufacturers wishing an opinion on a label may request government officials to review a specific label; however, a label review does not constitute a review of the advertising script.

Practice Note

Companies should not rely upon the use a U.S. label to satisfy Canadian labeling requirements. Great care should go into the labeling and advertising of all food products to ensure compliance with Canadian standards.

3. Customs Tariffs

In addition to the various applicable taxes (as discussed below), the importation of goods into Canada may be subject to customs duties. Customs law in Canada is primarily governed by two enactments: (1) the *Customs Act* (R.S.C. 1985, c.1 (2nd Supp.)) sets out the procedures for importing goods into Canada and the rules for calculating value for duty; and (2) the *Customs Tariff Act* (S.C. 1997, c.36) includes a schedule enumerating various categories of goods or products and the applicable tariff rates.

Canada and most other countries (including the U.S.) use the same tariff schedule (referred to as a "harmonized tariff"), so generally a particular product will come within the same tariff category wherever it is shipped in the world. The applicable rate of duty on individual products will, however, often be different.

Customs duties apply to goods, but not to intangibles such as franchise rights.

(a) North American Free Trade Agreement

In 1989, Canada and the United States entered into a bilateral free trade agreement (FTA) which contemplated that customs duties on almost all goods would be phased out between the two countries over a period of ten years. The ten-year period has been completed and, with the exception of a very limited number of products, American- and Canadian-sourced goods enter each country on a duty-free basis.

In 1994, Mexico also became a party to the FTA, and its name was changed to the North American Free Trade Agreement (NAFTA). NAFTA superseded the bilateral FTA between Canada and the United States and extended FTA-like provisions to bilateral trade between Canada and Mexico (and the United States and Mexico) in goods and services that are North American. While NAFTA requires the member countries to negotiate a level of conformity among their laws governing weights, measures, production, consumer standards and health/sanitary issues, Canada still imposes its own (comparatively stringent) requirements.

Franchisors importing goods into Canada must not assume that products purchased from an American supplier originate from the United States and therefore qualify as duty-free. To qualify as a product originating from a NAFTA country, the good must meet the "rules of origin test."

While NAFTA exempts customs duties, this does not affect the imposition of the federal goods and services tax (GST) on goods imported into Canada.

(b) Other trade agreements

As noted above, goods will qualify for NAFTA only if they are made in United States, Canada or Mexico. The NAFTA Agreement sets out detailed rules for determining whether a particular product qualifies for NAFTA exemption. A certificate of origin signed by the exporter/manufacturer confirming compliance with NAFTA requirements is required.

If goods do not qualify for NAFTA, they may still qualify for one of the other bilateral treaties that Canada has negotiated with its various trading partners. The most common tariff categories are as follows:

- General Tariff—This is the rate for countries with whom no special agreement has been negotiated. There are very few countries in this category (one example is North Korea). The rate is generally 35%.
- Most-Favoured-Nations Tariff (MFN)—An MFN tariff will normally reduce but not necessarily eliminate custom duties. The MFN tariff applies to goods of almost all countries. Notwithstanding its description as "most

favourite nations," it usually provides the least favourable reduction in tariffs other than the general tariff.
- General Preferential Tariff—These are special rates (usually more favourable than MFN rates) to third-world developing nations on specific goods as a method of promoting development in those countries. A specified percentage of the cost of production of the goods to be imported must have been sourced in the country entitled to the tariff or in Canada.

There is also no credit in computing Canadian customs, nor any reduced rate of duty, if the product from a foreign country has entered Canada through the United States. Any United States customs duty paid when the goods entered the United States would require a separate refund claim to United States tax authorities. Direct shipment to Canada from the country of manufacture is usually more beneficial, as the direct transportation costs are deductible in computing value for duty. Indirect shipping costs (costs incurred to initially ship the goods to the United States) are not deductible.

In recent years, Canada has negotiated the Comprehensive Economic and Trade Agreement with the European Union and the Canada-Korea Free Trade Agreement with South Korea. In addition, Canada is a signatory to the Trans-Pacific Partnership. Canada is currently conducting consultations in connection with the Comprehensive Economic and Trade Agreement and the Trans-Pacific Partnership. Neither trade agreement will come into force until they have been ratified by all signatories. For more information, visit the Global Affairs Canada website at www.international.gc.ca.

Practice Note

Franchisors importing goods into Canada should not assume that all goods purchased from a supplier in a NAFTA country necessarily originate in that country and therefore qualify as duty-free under NAFTA.

4. Taxes on Imports into Canada

In addition to any duties, goods imported into Canada are subject to GST, or the federal part of the harmonized sales tax (HST), unless items are specified as non-taxable importations. The GST/HST is calculated on the Canadian dollar value of the goods, including duty and excise tax, and is collected at the border at the same time as these duties and taxes. The owner or importer of record is responsible for paying the GST/HST on imported goods. If a party is registered for the GST/HST and is the importer (the person who caused the goods to be imported into Canada), he may claim an input tax credit (ITC) for the tax paid on the imported goods, as long as the party meets the requirement for claiming ITCs.

On its website, the Canada Revenue Agency lists examples of non-taxable importations:

- certain zero-rated goods (goods that are specifically taxed at 0% in Canada, such as prescription drugs);
- medals, trophies, and other prizes won outside Canada in competition (but not saleable goods, such as an automobile);
- tourist literature imported by governments or specified organizations for public distribution free of charge;
- goods imported by a charity or public institution that have been donated to the charity or institution;
- goods imported for the sole purpose of maintenance, overhaul, or repairs, if the title or use to those goods does not pass while they are in Canada, and the goods are exported as soon as the services are completed;
- goods imported by manufacturing service companies where the goods are processed for non-residents and later exported without being used in Canada. Any parts to be used in or attached to, and materials directly consumed or expended in the processing of, those goods are also non-taxable. The manufacturing service companies must apply in writing for an import certificate to be able to import goods on a non-taxable basis;
- warranty replacement property and replacement parts supplied by a non-resident at no charge other than for shipping and handling; and
- goods valued at $20 or less sent to a person by mail or courier at an address in Canada, except for the following prescribed goods:
- excisable goods (such as beer, tobacco, and wine);
- books, newspapers, magazines, periodicals, or other similar publications, where the vendor was required to register for the GST/HST but did not do so; and
- goods bought from a retailer in Canada and mailed or transported from outside Canada directly to the purchaser.

In most cases, the HST applies at the border to taxable importations of non-commercial goods imported by a resident of a participating province, regardless of the point of entry into Canada or customs clearance. Taxable non-commercial goods imported into a participating province by a resident of such a province are subject to the HST on importation, except for motor vehicles required to be registered in a participating province, or a mobile home or floating home that has been used or occupied in Canada by an individual.

Although the provincial part of the HST is not payable when a party imports commercial goods that are destined for the participating provinces, the goods may be subject to the self-assessment rules discussed under Goods, intangible personal properties (IPP) and services brought into a participating province. Generally, the value on which tax is required to be self-assessed is the lesser of the amount paid for the good and the fair-market value of the property.

The self-assessment rule for goods will also apply when goods are brought into a particular participating province from another participating province for which the provincial part of the HST is lower. If a person is required to self-assess under this rule, the amount of tax will be determined by multiplying the difference between the provincial part of the HST for the destination participating province and the provincial part of the HST for the origin province by either the amount paid for the property or the fair-market value of the good at the time of bringing it in.

Sales tax rates vary by province. The table below outlines sales tax estimates in the different provinces and territories:

Province	*Sales tax type*	*PST (%)*	*GST (%)*	*HST (%)*	*Combined effective rate (%)*
Alberta	GST		5		5
British Columbia	GST + PST	7	5		12
Manitoba	GST + PST	8	5		13
New Brunswick	HST			13	13
Newfoundland & Labrador	HST			15	15
Northwest Territories	GST		5		5
Nova Scotia	HST			15	15
Nunavut	GST		5		5
Ontario	HST			13	13
Prince Edward Island	HST			14	14
Quebec	GST + QST	9.975	5		14.975
Saskatchewan	GST + PST	5	5		10
Yukon	GST		5		5

For more information, visit the Canada Revenue Agency website at www.cra-arc.gc.ca.

(a) Mandatory GST/HST registration

A non-resident franchisor that sells franchise rights for a particular geographic area but does not actively participate in soliciting franchisees or assisting in franchise operations in Canada will not be considered to be carrying on business in Canada. Accordingly, the franchisor could avoid becoming a registrant and avoid reporting to Canada Revenue Agency on GST/HST collection.

However, a high level of business activity in Canada, including actively soliciting franchisees, would often indicate that the foreign franchisor is carrying on business in the province(s) involved. If the franchisor sets up a business office in Canada, this will be a clear indication to the Canada Revenue Agency that it is carrying on business here. Under those circumstances, the foreign franchisor will be required to register. If a non-resident franchisor has set up a subsidiary in Canada, and representatives of the non-resident franchisor visit Canada as part of administration of the franchise system here, this alone will not cause the non-resident to be "carrying on business" in Canada. However, if the representatives separately bill the subsidiary or sub-franchisees for services provided during such visits, the representatives will be carrying on business in respect of those activities and the franchisor will be required to register.

(b) Voluntary GST/HST registration

A foreign franchisor may want to voluntarily become a registrant even if it is not considered to be carrying on business in Canada. Registration would require it to collect GST/HST from its franchisees, except to the extent the franchisor is an exempt supplier (e.g., an insurance broker). The Canadian franchisee will necessarily be a GST registrant and will get a full refund of the GST/HST it pays in the course of operating its business. Registration would also mean that the non-resident franchisor would get a full refund of the GST/HST that it incurs in purchasing goods and services in Canada. For example, representatives of a foreign franchisor on business travel in Canada often pay GST/HST for hotel rooms, restaurant meals, car rentals and airline tickets. GST/HST might also be paid on equipment and supplies that are brought into Canada in the course of franchise operations. This GST/HST will be refunded only if the franchisor has become a registrant.

Management of the GST/HST system by a registrant is much less complex and less costly than income tax compliance.

5. Supply Management in Canada—Marketing Boards in Canada

A franchisor may also find that it cannot, or the restrictions are economically prohibitive to, import certain food items into Canada. Franchisors in the food and beverage industry should be aware of restrictions imposed by marketing boards (such as poultry and dairy) prior to expansion into Canada. The Canadian Government has intervened in certain industries to raise the income of farmers through price and income support programs and supply management programs. Another category of government intervention concerns the approval of programs establishing "self-regulated" institutions, such as cooperatives and marketing boards.

Every province in Canada has industry-specific marketing boards to regulate and control things such as the promotion, production, transportation, packaging, storage and marketing of certain products. In British Columbia (B.C.) these marketing boards include the: B.C. Chicken Marketing Board, B.C. Cranberry Marketing Board, B.C. Egg Marketing Board, B.C. Milk Marketing Board and B.C. Vegetable Marketing Board.

In Ontario, marketing boards have been established to set standards for certain products, including the price that will be paid to producers, conditions of sale and the issue of licenses. These boards include the Ontario Asparagus Growers' Marketing Board, Ontario Bean Producers' Marketing Board, Ontario Greenhouse Vegetable Producers' Marketing Board and Ontario Tender Fruit Producers' Marketing Board. There are also marketing boards that regulate how much a farmer can produce and market, such as the Chicken Farmers of Ontario, Dairy Farmers of Ontario, Ontario Broiler Hatching Egg and Chick Commission, and Ontario Turkey Producers' Marketing Board.

The above listings are just a few of many examples. A franchisor wishing to start or expand a business in Canada should first determine whether a marketing board exists for the particular products that are required for use as inventory or in production of finished products, and then determine what restrictions exist under the appropriate marketing board.

(a) Milk and dairy-based products—Canadian Dairy Commission

The Canadian Dairy Commission (CDC) was established under the *Canadian Dairy Commission Act* (R.S.C. 1985, c.C-15) as a Crown corporation with a mandate to manage dairy policies and control milk production in an attempt to stabilize revenues and avoid surpluses. The CDC plays a large role in influencing dairy policy, a jurisdiction shared by provincial and federal governments. Once a year the CDC establishes support prices for butter and skim milk powder. These prices are used by provincial milk marketing boards to establish prices in each province.

Franchisors entering into the Canadian market should take note of Canada's high tariffs on dairy products:

Tariffs as of June, 2016, for Selected Canadian Dairy	
Products	**Tariff* (%)**
Fluid milk	241
Yogurt	237.5
Butter	298.5
Cheese	245.5
Ice cream	277
Skim milk powder	270

*Tariff applied to quantities that exceed import quota.
Import quota is equal to less than 5% of Canadian dairy consumption.
Source: World Trade Organization

(b) Chicken—Chicken Farmers of Canada

Meat and poultry products are among the most stringently controlled food products. The Chicken Farmers of Canada (CFC) is a national organization formed under the *Farm Products Agencies Act* (R.S.C. 1985, c. F-4) and is funded through farmer levies paid according to the amount of chicken produced. The CFC operates within the regulatory environment in accordance with the Federal-Provincial Agreement for Chicken, signed by provincial and federal governments as well as provincial chicken boards. The CFC also monitors compliance with provincial quota allocations and the inter-provincial or market development trade of chicken.

Canada's poultry and egg industry operates under a marketing system designed to match the supply with the demand. An effective supply management system requires the ability to determine supply from all sources, domestic as well as international. Under the World Trade Organization (WTO) Agreement on Agriculture, Canada was obliged to convert its existing agricultural quantitative import controls to a system of Tariff Rate Quotas (TRQ). TRQs determine the quantity and the tariff at which a specific agricultural product is imported into a country. Canada's market access level for a given year is the greater of its commitment under the WTO or under the NAFTA.

(c) Eggs—Canadian Egg Marketing Agency

The Canadian Egg Marketing Agency (CEMA) is formed under the *Farm Products Agencies Act* and charged with the responsibility of regulating the interprovincial trade in eggs and allocating federal egg quotas to each province. Under the federal part of the egg-marketing scheme, a federal quota and licence are needed to produce and market eggs for interprovincial trade.

For more information, visit the Agriculture and Agri-Food Canada website at www.agr.gc.ca.

Practice Note

A franchisor should always check to see if a marketing board regulates the product or service the company sells or provides to ensure compliance with applicable regulations.

6. Importation and Sourcing/Sale of Alcohol

Moving alcohol across provincial, state or international borders can be a difficult task. In Canada, alcohol is controlled at the provincial level and is overseen by provincial liquor commissions. It is illegal to sell alcohol without a valid license or authorization from the appropriate liquor authority. Each province has its own unique set of rules, restrictions, and duties applied to the importation of alcoholic beverages. In Ontario, for example, the Alcohol and Gaming Commission is responsible for the implementation of the *Liquor License Act* (R.S.O. 1990, c.L.19) and the *Alcohol and Gaming Regulation and Public Protection Act* (R.S.O. 1996, c.26). The Registrar of Alcohol and Gaming is responsible for the regulation of liquor sales licenses. Franchisors in the bar, restaurant and hotel business must apply for and obtain a liquor license in order to legally sell alcohol. In British Columbia, Alberta, Manitoba, Ontario and Prince Edward Island, all servers selling alcohol within a bar, restaurant or hotel (or persons with management responsibility over alcohol servers) must complete a program of alcohol service education and be certified to serve alcohol. In British Columbia the program is "Serving It Right"; in Alberta, "ProServe"; in Manitoba, "Serving It Safe Responsible Service and Safety Program"; in Ontario, "Smart Serve"; in Prince Edward Island, "It's Our Business." Other provinces have alcohol service training programs that are not mandatory but are recommended for alcohol servers, including: Saskatchewan ("Serve It Right Saskatchewan"); Quebec ("Service in Action"); New Brunswick ("It's Good Business: Responsible Beverage Service"); Nova Scotia ("It's Good Business"); and Newfoundland and Labrador ("It's Good Business").

Franchisors should also be aware that in some provinces, the ability to collect royalties that are in whole or in part calculated on the sale of liquor may be restricted. In Ontario, a liquor license holder is required to provide the Ontario Alcohol and Gaming Commission with a copy of any agreement that entitles another party to 15% or more of the gross revenue from alcohol sales. Were the royalty rate in a franchise agreement 15% or higher, this would require the franchisee to provide a copy of the franchise agreement. Certain other provinces, notably British Columbia, Quebec and Prince Edward Island, have regulations which provide that a license to sell alcohol may not be "used" by a person other than the license holder. It would be for the alcohol and gaming commission in each province to determine whether the collection of a royalty by a franchisor amounts to "use" of the franchisee's license.

III. Laws Affecting How Products and Services Are Advertised

A. Trademarks, Trade Names and Trade Dress

Upon entering the Canadian market, one of the first things a foreign franchisor should do is apply for registration of its trademarks under the federal *Trade-marks Act* (R.S.C. 1985, c.T-13). Although registration provides a superior form of protection, unregistered rights may be protected under the common-law action of passing off.

See Chapter 4 and www.cipo.ic.gc.ca for further discussion on Canada's trademark regime.

B. Pricing and Advertising in Canada

The federal *Competition Act* (R.S.C. 1985, c. C-34 [Act]) applies to individuals carrying on business in Canada, including franchisors, franchisees and suppliers. The Act sets out substantive competition rules, including a framework for administration and enforcement. (In addition, the *Competition Tribunal Act*, R.S.C. 1985, c.19 (2nd Supp.) constitutes the Competition Tribunal, an adjudicative body comprising judicial members drawn from the Federal Court and lay members who typically have a background in economics or business fields. The tribunal has jurisdiction to hear applications in non-criminal matters brought under Part VII.1 (deceptive marketing practices) and Part VIII (reviewable matters) of the Act. The Competition Bureau is authorized under the Competition Act to operate as an independent law enforcement agency, responsible for the enforcement of its provisions. Although competition laws are under federal jurisdiction, many provinces have enacted complementary consumer protection and trade practice legislation.

On March 12, 2009, the Federal Government introduced the most significant amendments to the Competition Act in the last 20 years. These amendments introduce new provisions that have fundamentally changed the way franchisors can do business in Canada.

Practice Note

Franchisors operating their systems in Canada should review their master franchise agreements, unit franchise agreements, operations manuals and operating policies for compliance with Canada's *Competition Act.*

1. Competition Act and Resale Price Maintenance in Canada

The amendments to the Competition Act have effectively decriminalized resale price maintenance in Canada. Resale price maintenance allows manufacturers and distributors to agree to sell goods at certain prices or within a certain range (between a price floor and a price ceiling). In its *Guide to Amendments to the Competition Act*, the Competition Bureau explains: (a) the criminal pricing provisions concerning price discrimination, predatory pricing, geographic price discrimination and promotional allowances have been repealed; (b) pricing practices are now subject to review under a civil provision, but a remedy is only available where there is evidence of substantial anti-competitive effect; and (c) the removal of these offences promotes innovative pricing programs and increases certainty for Canadian businesses. (*A Guide to Amendments to the Competition Act*, online at Competition Bureau, www.competitionbureau.gc.ca).

Franchise agreements have routinely been drafted to allow franchisors the ability to suggest the prices of menu items. Prior to the amendments, if a franchisor was a producer or supplier of products, it would suggest retail resale prices and often fix a maximum price to franchisees. The franchisor would make clear that franchisees were under no obligation to accept such suggested prices and could sell for less than the suggested or maximum pricing and would in no way suffer in their business relations with the franchisor by failing to accept them. The penalties associated with this under the old Competition Act are no longer in effect. In its place the new provisions now make price maintenance a reviewable practice, subject to the administrative review by the Competition Tribunal. The new provisions allow the tribunal to issue a cease-and-desist order, prohibiting a business from engaging in certain practices, but there is no threat of criminal sanctions. Parties that are directly affected can apply to the tribunal for a remedial order; however, the tribunal may not make an award for damages. (*Competition Act*, at s. 77). There is a presumption that price maintenance is legal until it is proven to have an "adverse effect on competition." (*Competition Act*, at s. 75).

Certain franchisors that have significant market influence must be aware of the abuse of dominance provisions in sections 78 and 79 of the Competition Act. Under section 79 of the Competition Act, the elements required to establish abuse of dominance are: (a) one or more persons substantially or completely control, throughout Canada or any area thereof; (b) engaging in a practice of anti-competitive acts; and (c) the practice has had, is having or is likely to have the effect of preventing or lessening competition substantially in a market.

The amendments to the Competition Act may allow franchisors to mandate uniform pricing, permitting greater harmonization across the franchise system.

For more information on resale price maintenance in Canada, visit www.competitionbureau.gc.ca.

2. Advertising Sale Prices in Canada

The Competition Act includes five provisions regarding price representations:

- Bait-and-switch selling (Section 74.04);
- False or misleading ordinary selling price representations (Section 52 and subsections 74.01(2) and 74.01(3));
- Sale above advertised price (Section 74.05); and
- Double ticketing (Section 54) (*Price-related Representations*, online at Competition Bureau, www.competitionbureau.gc.ca).

(a) Bait-and-switch selling

Section 74.04 of the Competition Act is of particular importance to franchisors. The bait-and-switch scenario arises when goods are advertised at a "bargain price" but are not supplied in reasonable quantities. Subject to certain exemptions, a person who advertises a product for sale in a market and then supplies the product during the period at a higher price engages in reviewable conduct.

According to the Competition Bureau, the provision was drafted for situations where the supplier of the product is the same entity conducting the advertising (*Ibid.*). In a franchise system, stores are operated by franchisees, while franchisors or advertising cooperatives handle advertising. Bait-and-switch selling above an advertised price has significant implications for franchisors who fail to take sufficient precautions to ensure their franchisees act in accordance with advertisements. It may be insufficient for a franchisor to simply insist as a term of its franchise agreement that franchisees stock reasonable quantities of certain goods and sell goods at advertised prices. Franchisors should instead monitor compliance and include limitations in advertisements that products are available only at participating stores, and, preferably, identify stores where they know the products or sale terms will not be available.

If a franchisee or franchisor is found to be liable under section 74.04 of the Competition Act, it may: (a) be ordered to stop engaging in certain conduct; (b) have to publish a corrective notice; (c) pay an administrative penalty to a maximum of $750,000 if an individual or $10 million if a corporation for a first-time occurrence; (d) pay an administrative penalty to a maximum of $1 million if an individual or $15 million if a corporation for a subsequent occurrence.

For more information on price representations in Canada, visit www.competitionbureau.gc.ca.

(b) False and misleading advertising

False or misleading advertising operates under a dual track in the Competition Act. The Competition Bureau has the choice between pursuing criminal or civil remedies in relation to misleading advertising. The most egregious acts will be pursued as criminal offences—for example, knowingly or recklessly making representations to the public that are false or misleading in a material respect for the purposes of promoting a product or business interest. Imprisonment and fines are among the possible criminal sanctions. The representation need not be limited to advertising, but could include a misrepresentation made on or in association with a product, or a misrepresentation made by a franchisor to induce a person to become a franchisee. A general impression test is used to assess whether a statement is materially misleading, even if it is technically true.

The Competition Bureau normally pursues civil remedies over criminal offences with respect to misleading advertising. Under civil provisions, the penalties imposed have a wide range. As in the case of bait-and-switch selling, if a franchisor is found liable under 74.01, it may: (a) be ordered to stop engaging in certain conduct; (b) have to publish a corrective notice; (c) pay an administrative penalty to a maximum of $750,000 if an individual or $10 million if a corporation for a first time occurrence; (d) pay an administrative penalty to a maximum of $1 million if an individual or $15 million if a corporation for a subsequent occurrence. In pursuing these remedies, the Competition Bureau does not need to prove the advertising was deliberate.

Practice Note

Franchisors must be cautious when making price representations in order to avoid large administrative penalties imposed by the Competition Act.

3. Voluntary Codes

Corporations advertising in Canada follow a number of voluntary codes, including the Canadian Code of Advertising Standards (Code) and the Broadcast Code for Advertising to Children (Children's Code). Both codes are meant to supplement existing federal and provincial advertising laws. It should be noted that advertising to children is prohibited in Québec under the *Consumer Protection Act* (C.Q.L.R. c. P-40.1).

Advertising Standards Canada (ASC) is Canada's nonprofit, self-regulating body responsible for administering and handling complaints under these voluntary codes. The ASC is composed of industry leaders in the field of advertising, including agencies and media organizations.

(a) Canadian Code of Advertising Standards

The Code establishes the standards of acceptable advertising in Canada. It has 14 provisions, which must be complied with in both letter and spirit. These provisions address the following topics: (a) accuracy and clarity; (b) disguised advertising techniques; (c) price claims; (d) bait and switch; (e) guarantees; (f) comparative advertising; (g) testimonials; (h) professional or scientific claims; (i) imitation; (j) safety; (k) superstition and fears; (l) advertising to children; (m) advertising to minors; and (n) unacceptable depictions and portrayals.

The Code creates an avenue for the ASC to conduct a review of any consumer, advertiser or special interest group complaints or trade disputes. The ASC accepts complaints submitted by email, mail or fax. Customer complaints to the ASC regarding advertising contraventions are handled by one of the two councils: (a) le Conseil des normes handles complaints in Québec; and (b) the Standards Council handles complaints in all other provinces. Complaints from advertisers are administered under the ASC's Advertising Dispute Procedure. Special interest group complaints have their own Special Interest Group Complaint Procedure. For more information on the Canadian Code of Advertising Standards, visit www.adstandards.com.

(b) Broadcast Code for Advertising to Children

Advertisements targeting children under the age of 12 are regulated by a separate set of voluntary guidelines called the Broadcast Code for Advertising to Children. The Children's Code is administered by the ASC and its Children's Clearance Committee. The goal of the Children's Code is to prevent the exploitation of the gullible and innocent nature of children, recognizing the unique characteristics of a younger audience. Adhering to the Children's Code is a necessary condition to obtain a Canadian Radio-television and Telecommunications Commission licence.

For more information on the Canadian Code of Advertising Standards and the Broadcast Code for Advertising to Children, visit www.adstandards.com.

Practice Note

Franchisors should comply with the Canadian Code of Advertising Standards and the Broadcast Code for Advertising to Children in both letter and spirit.

4. Language Laws in Québec

The *Charter of the French Language* provides residents of Québec certain rights.

Franchisors conducting business in the province must ensure that all corporate entities carry out their business in French. (*Charter of the French Language*, C.Q.L.R. c. C-11). In particular, all advertising and product packaging must be drawn up in French. Franchisors can provide an English translation of their advertising materials and websites as long as the French version is no less prominent.

More information on the laws of Québec can be found in Chapter 2.

C. Canada's Anti-Spam Law

Canada has enacted what may be the strictest spam law in the world. Canada's Anti-Spam Law (CASL) came into force on July 1, 2014, with certain provisions to be phased in over a three-year transition period. The reach of the CASL extends to organizations located outside of Canada that send commercial electronic messages (CEMs) to or install computer programs on computers located in Canada.

The legislation does more than just simply regulate unsolicited emails. Subject to limited exceptions, the CASL prohibits a business from sending CEMs for a business purpose unless it complies with the following three rules: (a) the business must have expressed or implied consent to send the message; (b) the business must clearly identify itself, including prescribed contact information; and (c) every message must have an "unsubscribe" mechanism. More specifically, when in force, the law will generally prohibit:

- sending of commercial electronic messages without the recipient's consent, including messages to email addresses, social networking accounts and text messages sent to a cell phone;
- alteration of transmission data in an electronic message which results in the message being delivered to a different destination without express consent;
- installation of computer programs without the express consent of the owner of the computer system or its agent;
- use of false or misleading representations online in the promotion of products or services;
- collection of personal information through accessing a computer system in violation of federal law; and
- collection of electronic addresses by the use of computer programs or the use of such addresses without permission (address harvesting) (*Fast Facts*, online at Government of Canada, fightspam.gc.ca).

While the United States *Controlling the Assault of Non-Solicited Pornography and Marketing Act* provides for an opt-out consent regime, the CASL requires express "opt-in" or implied consent (15 U.S. Code Chapter 103). Implied consent is allowable in certain circumstances, most notably when an existing business relationship exists. The CASL defines an "existing business relationship" to include situations where the recipient has purchased goods and services in the last two years or made an inquiry regarding the sender's business in the last six months.

Three federal bodies are responsible for the enforcement of the CASL: (a) Canadian Radio-television and Telecommunications Commission; (b) Competition Bureau; and (c) Office of the Privacy Commissioner of Canada. These federal bodies have the authority to impose a wide variety of penalties. Contravention of the CASL can lead to severe administrative fines ($10 million for a first-time occurrence and $15 million for subsequent violations). Beginning July 1, 2017, the CASL will also allow for a private right of action. In certain situations, individuals will be able to seek statutory damages.

For more information on Canada's Anti-Spam Law, visit fightspam.gc.ca.

Practice Note

Given the wide-reaching nature of the CASL along with its significant enforcement provisions, franchisors must be careful to ensure compliance with the law. Canadian practitioners expect class actions to follow the private right of action coming into force July 1, 2017.

D. Contests in Canada

The Competition Act imposes disclosure and other requirements on promotional contests undertaken for the purposes of promoting a product or business interest. Since the requirements apply to a contest, lottery, game of chance or skill, or mixed chance and skill, many franchise systems are affected. In addition to compliance with the Competition Act, contests launched in Canada must not violate the *Criminal Code of Canada* (R.S.C. 1985, c. C-46). Franchisors must be careful to prevent poorly structured marketing contests in order to avoid significant penalties imposed for noncompliance with these statutes.

For a contest to be legitimate, franchisees or sellers must provide adequate and fair disclosure of a number of important details. If franchisors fail to do so, they will have engaged in reviewable conduct and may be subject to prohibition orders and/or monetary penalties.

The Province of Québec imposes its own registration requirements for contests run in that province. These are considered more onerous than the requirements elsewhere in Canada, resulting in many franchisors excluding participation from residents of Québec.

Practice Note

Contest administrators must provide adequate and fair disclosure in compliance with the provisions of the federal Competition Act and Criminal Code.

1. Competition Act

Section 74.06 of the Competition Act is the civil provision relating to contests. Specifically, it requires contest promoters to disclose the number and approximate value of the prizes, the areas to which the prizes relate, the contest closing date, and information regarding the chances of winning (*Promotional Contests*, online, at Competition Bureau, www.competitionbureau.gc.ca). Participants must be selected randomly or on the basis of skill. Franchisors must also eliminate payment required to enter the contest. The Competition Act requires a free method of entry that does not inconvenience or dissuade potential participants from entering.

Adequate and fair disclosure must be made by the franchisor in a conspicuous manner. The contest should not require participants to visit a particular franchise location in order to obtain further details regarding the contest. To meet the standard of adequate and fair disclosure, franchisors should abide by the following guidelines:

- Approximate value: franchisors must disclose the approximate market value of the prize or a range of possible values of the prize.
- Regional allocation: franchisors must clearly disclose if prizes are allocated on a regional basis.
- Chances of winning: if the total number of prizes is known, it is considered to be a fact that "materially affects the chances of winning" and must be disclosed.
- Series of prizes: franchisors must not imply in promotional material and advertisements that prizes remain to be won when they have already been claimed.
- Early bird prizes: franchisors must disclose any early bird prizes to be awarded at the contest starting date.
- Disclosure at point of sale: franchisors must disclose contest rules wherever specially-marked packages are sold (usually in the form of a list on the package of the products).

If franchisors are found to be engaged in reviewable conduct under section 74.06, they may be ordered to publish a corrective notice or pay a fine of up to $10 million for a first-time occurrence and $15 million for subsequent violations. For more information on contest rules under the Competition Act, visit www.competitionbureau.gc.ca.

2. Criminal Code Provisions Governing Illegal Lotteries

Under paragraph 206(1)(f) of the Criminal Code, if a contest qualifies as a gambling operation or a game of chance in which the contestant or competitor pays money or other valuable consideration, such contest is prohibited unless it is run by the provincial government. A violation of this section of the Criminal Code can result in fines and/or imprisonment. This section effectively prohibits potential contestants from having to purchase a product or service as the sole condition of entering a contest. If a franchisor's contest involves an element of chance, then an element of skill must be introduced, and contestants must not be required to purchase a product or service to enter.

For more information, visit www.competitionbureau.gc.ca.

3. Contest Registration in Québec

Franchisors operating contests in Canada often exclude participants in Québec due to the extra regulatory requirements of that province. If the total prize value is more than $2,000, franchisors must register their contest with the Quebec provincial regulator, the *Régie des alcools des courses et des jeux* (*Régie*), and comply with the Rules Respecting Publicity Contests (C.Q.L.R. c. L-6, r. 6 [Rules]) enacted under the *Lotteries Act* (*An Act respecting lotteries, publicity contests and amusement machines*, C.Q.L.R. c. L-6). In addition to contest registration, the *Régie* and the Rules require franchisors to: (a) file all rules, advertising and promotional material at least 10 days before the contest begins; (b) post security if any single prize is worth more than $5,000 or the total prize value is worth more than $20,000; and (c) pay taxes based on total prize value.

More information on the laws of Québec can be found in Chapter 2.

Practice Note

Before launching a contest in the province of Québec, franchisors must comply with additional regulatory requirements.

E. Nutrition Claims

Obesity has been identified as a significant contributing factor to several chronic conditions, such as heart disease and diabetes. According to Statistics Canada, heart disease is the second leading cause of death in Canada, accounting for 20% of total deaths; diabetes is the sixth-leading killer (*The 10 leading causes of death, 2012*, online at Statistics Canada, www.statcan.gc.ca). Children in particular are at risk of suffering the long-term effects of being overweight. As obesity has become a growing concern, Canadian policymakers have taken notice.

The Public Health Agency of Canada and the Canadian Institute for Health Information released a report in 2011, titled *Obesity in Canada*, highlighting several shocking statistics (*Obesity in Canada*, online at Public Health Agency of Canada, www.phac-aspc.gc.ca). According to the report: (a) approximately one in four Canadian adults are obese, and 8.6% of children and youth aged six to 17 are obese; (b) between 1981 and 2007-2009, obesity rates roughly doubled among both males and females in most age groups in the adult and youth categories; (c) across Canada, adult obesity rates vary from 5.3% in Richmond, British Columbia, to 35.9% in the Athabasca region of Saskatchewan; and (d) the economic costs of obesity are estimated at $4.6 billion in 2008, up approximately 19% from $3.9 billion in 2000. Following these findings, Canadian policymakers have attempted to implement a multifaceted, long-term approach to tackle this problem.

1. Voluntary Codes

In July 2008 New York City became the first jurisdiction in the U.S. to require large restaurant and coffee chains to list calorie amounts on their menus. Since 2008 a number of states, counties and cities have passed laws requiring menu board labeling, including California, Maine, Massachusetts, New Jersey, Oregon, Philadelphia, Nashville and Seattle, although not all have been implemented. The federal Food and Drug Administration published its final rule on menu board labeling in December 2014 and is expected to commence enforcement in May 2017. The Canadian government is experiencing growing pressure to mandate menu labeling legislation. Currently, Canadian franchisors may disclose nutritional information on a voluntary basis. Such disclosure is not standardized or conspicuous.

(a) Restaurants Canada—voluntary guidelines to providing nutrition information to consumers

In 2005, the Nutrition and Fitness Roundtable of the Canadian Restaurant and Foodservices Association (renamed Restaurants Canada in February 2014) developed voluntary guidelines for restaurants to disclose nutritional information to consumers. These guidelines have developed a standardized manner in which such information is presented, allowing customers to make consistent comparisons.

In these guidelines, Restaurants Canada establishes the following minimum requirements:

- Nutrient values will be provided for core or standard menu items self-selected by chains depending on the complexity of the menu.
- Nutrient values will be as consistent as possible with the core nutrition label information required for packaged goods and will include:

Calories
Fat *Saturated Fat* *Trans Fat*
Cholesterol
Sodium
Carbohydrate *Fibre* *Sugars*
Protein
Vitamin A
Vitamin C
Calcium
Iron

- This information will be made available to restaurant consumers through in-store brochures, pamphlets or posters, which will be consistently and readily available to customers at each unit location.
- The availability of the nutrition brochures or pamphlets will be prominently displayed on menus, menu boards and vehicles such as take-out and home delivery packaging.
- The nutritional information will also be made available on participating company websites, and the online availability of the information will be prominently identified.
- These are minimum standards, and companies may wish to exceed these guidelines.
- Companies are encouraged to use the same pamphlets or brochures to provide allergen information for standard or core menu items (*CRFA Nutrition Information User's Guide*, online at Canadian Restaurant and Foodservices Association, www.crfa.ca).

To access the Voluntary Guidelines for Providing Nutrition Information to Consumers and more information on this topic, visit www.restaurantscanada.org.

(b) British Columbia Informed Dining Program

In 2011, British Columbia introduced its Informed Dining Program in partnership with the Canadian Restaurant and Foodservices Association and other industry participants. Restaurants participating in the Informed Dining Program are required to: (a) display the program logo and a statement on the menu board advising guests that nutrition information is available; (b) provide calories and the 13 core nutrients for all standard menu items upon request before or at the point of ordering; and (c) highlight and provide information regarding daily calorie and sodium requirements. (*Informed Dining for Restaurants,* online at Healthy Families BC, www.healthyfamiliesbc.ca).

British Columbia is the first province to introduce this program. In response, Manitoba has signed on to support the rollout of the Informed Dining Program, and other provincial governments have indicated they are interested in developing a similar regime. For more information on British Columbia's Informed Dining Program, visit www.healthyfamiliesbc.ca.

2. Non-voluntary Requirements

(a) Ontario

On May 28, 2015, the *Healthy Menu Choices Act* (Healthy Menu Choices Act, 2015, S.O. 2015, c. 7 [Act]) received royal assent. The Act and regulations came into force on January 1, 2017.

The Act developed from discussions between Canadian consumer groups and food and healthcare industry officials. Its aim is to help citizens make healthy decisions when eating outside the home. It require franchisors in the food industry to: (a) list calories for food and beverages, including alcohol, to be posted on menus and menu boards in restaurants, convenience stores, grocery stores, and other food service premises with 20 or more locations in Ontario; (b) post a contextual statement that would help to educate patrons about their daily caloric requirements; and (c) authorize public health inspectors to enforce menu labeling requirements (*Helping Families Make Healthy Food Choices*, online at Ministry of Health and Long-Term Care, news.ontario.ca)

The Act impacts franchisors with more than 20 locations in Ontario by requiring them to update their menus and menu boards to display calorie information for every standard food and beverage item (and size) in order to become compliant. For more information on the Act, visit www.ontla.on.ca and www.health.gov.on.ca/.

IV. Privacy Law

Knowledge about customer preferences and habits is very valuable information. The dramatic rise of e-commerce and the Internet and the increased use of computers have transformed concepts of customer goodwill and the ability of retailers to collect, store and analyze information about customer preferences and habits. As such, privacy has become an increasingly important issue in Canadian law.

In Canada, there are two significant federal laws: Canada's federal public-sector privacy law, the *Privacy Act* (R.S.C. 1985, c. P-21), and Canada's federal private-sector privacy law, the *Personal Information Protection and Electronic Documents Act* (S.C. 2000, c. 5 [*PIPEDA*]).

The Privacy Act came into effect in 1983, introducing obligations on federal government departments and agencies by limiting the collection, use and disclosure of personal information. This legislation also allows individuals to access and correct personal information about themselves held by federal government organizations.

As of January 1, 2004, PIPEDA came into effect to protect all personal information collected, used or disclosed by private-sector organizations during the course of commercial activities. As it was first introduced, PIPEDA applied to commercial activities undertaken by federally regulated private-sector organizations, but it has since been extended to include other industries, such as retail, service and manufacturing companies, and other provincially regulated organizations.

A. Collection of Customer Data

A franchise system is not a single entity in the eyes of the law. Rather it consists of a number of legal entities, bound together by contracts that require that all of these individual entities act in a somewhat coordinated way when selling a product or service under a single trademark or brand owned by the franchisor. The application of privacy laws to the franchise structure results in two significant problems that do not arise for other retailers.

In a franchise system, it is the franchisees that have the day-to-day customer contact and thus accumulate knowledge about customer preferences and habits. Franchisors have traditionally dealt with this problem by, among other things, inserting provisions in franchise agreements outlining that it is the franchisor who owns the customer list, or at least requiring transfer of the list or other customer information to the franchisor. After the introduction of PIPEDA in Canada, notwithstanding such contractual provisions, such information cannot be transferred without customer consent. Franchisees and dealers have used privacy laws to resist demands for such transfers (Connie Gugliemo, "Ransom: Customer Data" *ZDNet.com*, October 8, 2000). When Motorola required its independent dealers in the U.S. to enter into a new form of agreement requiring them to collect and transfer to Motorola "valid end-user customer information," the dealers resisted, citing privacy concerns.

The second significant problem for franchisors considering the effect of Canadian privacy laws on their systems is whether privacy compliance standards will be set systemwide and perhaps vigorously enforced by the franchisor, or whether franchisees will simply be required to comply with all relevant laws, and otherwise left to their own devices.

There are a variety of factors that will need to be taken into account in making this decision, including:

- the nature of the product and/or services;
- the way marketing is currently carried out;
- the way marketing will need to be carried out in the future with growing Internet usage;
- who owns the customer lists; and
- the risks of noncompliance.

There may also be employment issues and implications from the cross-border application of privacy laws.

For a franchisor considering how to comply with privacy laws, one of the first steps will be to consider to what extent customers and/or the public see privacy compliance as part of the franchisor's goods and/or services, and therefore to consider the extent to which a common privacy compliance standard is expected for goods and services bearing the franchisor's trademark. The franchisor can then go on to consider other issues, such as the best way to market the goods and/or services through the system and how that is affected by privacy compliance.

Franchisors will have to examine their compliance options in light of the balance struck between the benefits achieved through uniform marketing on the one hand and the costs of both systemwide implementation and maintenance, and the risk to the franchisor of liability for franchisee conduct on the other.

1. Federal—PIPEDA

Like most developed countries in the world, Canada has implemented a general private-sector personal information protection law. In introducing PIPEDA, the federal government aimed to strengthen e-commerce in Canada by providing a legal framework that would comply with the E.U. Data Directive. Prior to PIPEDA, Canadian companies did not appear to have the same concerns as their American counterparts regarding restrictions on use of consumer information, possibly because many already adhered to a voluntary code developed by the Canadian Standards Association known as the Model Code for the Protection of Personal Information, or the CSA Model Code.

PIPEDA applies to information collected, used or disclosed in the course of commercial activity that takes place across Canada, between provinces, and within a province that has not enacted "substantially similar" legislation. Paragraph 26(2)(b) of PIPEDA allows the Governor in Council to exempt an organization, a class of organizations, an activity or a class of activities from the application of PIPEDA within any province that has passed legislation deemed to be substantially similar to PIPEDA. The following provincial laws qualify as such (*Office of the Privacy Commissioner of Canada, "Substantially Similar Provincial Legislation,"* www.priv.gc.ca): Alberta's *Personal Information Protection Act* (S.A., Ch. P-6.5 [Alberta Act]; British Columbia's *Personal Information Protection Act* (S.B.C. 2003, c. 63 [B.C. Act]; Québec's *An Act Respecting the Protection of Personal Information in the Private Sector* (L.R.Q., c. P-39.1 [Québec Private Sector Law]; Ontario's *Personal Health Information Protection Act* (S.O. 2004, c. 3, Sch. A), with respect to health information custodians; New Brunswick's *Personal Health Information Privacy and Access Act* (S.N.B. 2009, c. P-7.05), with respect to personal health information custodians; and Newfoundland and Labrador's *Personal Health Information Act* (S.N.L. 2008, c. P-7.01), with respect to health information custodians.

Globalization has created a business world where the free flow of personal information is vital to the economy. Any restriction on the movement of information creates barriers to commerce. The Organization for Economic Co-operation and Development and its member countries addressed this issue in its OECD *Guidelines Governing the Protection of Privacy and Transborder Flows of Personal Data* (OECD Guidelines). Although they are not legally binding, the OECD Guidelines attempt to harmonize privacy standards across member countries. See www.oecd.org for more information on the OECD Guidelines.

Franchisors that collect personal information during the course of franchising activities must be aware of the provisions of PIPEDA, substantially similar provincial privacy legislation, and the OECD Guidelines, as applicable.

(a) Canada's ten privacy principles

In 1996, the Canadian Standards Association released the CSA Model Code. It established the first voluntary, national standard for personal information protection. The ten privacy principles set out in Schedule 1 to PIPEDA emerged from the CSA Model Code and contain the substantive provisions of PIPEDA. The statute itself provides exceptions to these substantive requirements and must be referred to when reading the provisions of the schedule.

Practice Note

Because of PIPEDA's unusual structure, it is best to read Schedule 1 first before turning to the actual statute.

The result has been that PIPEDA is unusually difficult to interpret. The language of the CSA Model Code, as a voluntary industry standard, is inherently vague. While some provisions—most notably the exceptions for obtaining consent—have been clarified, other important concepts, such as what is "sensitive" information, are left to the courts to determine. Even the process for seeking remedies is not clear, making it difficult to assess the risks of noncompliance. To add to the confusion, different lawyers often give differing opinions when interpreting PIPEDA. Ultimately, clients will have to determine their own comfort level in difficult areas.

One of the more interesting provisions of PIPEDA is a limitation on the purposes for which an organization may collect, use or disclose personal information (*PIPEDA*, at s. 5(3)). Such purposes must be ones that ". . . a reasonable person would consider appropriate in the circumstances." This restriction has been frequently cited by the federal Privacy Commissioners in their findings.

The following is a brief discussion on Canada's ten privacy principles.

Principle 1—Accountability

This principle generally requires the designation of an individual or individuals who are accountable for the organization's compliance with PIPEDA. The organization is specifically held responsible for information that has been transferred to a third party for processing, which must be protected by contractual means. Organizations are required to implement policies and practices to give effect to the principles, including training staff. This principle remains as set out in the CSA Model Code and has not been modified by PIPEDA.

Principle 2—Identifying Purposes

The purposes for which personal information is collected must be identified to the individual at or before the time that it is collected. Once this has been done, the information cannot be used for a new or further purpose without the additional consent of the individual.

Section 5(3) of PIPEDA provides that "[A]n organization may collect, use or disclose personal information only for purposes that a reasonable person would consider are appropriate in the circumstances." This section provides an outer limit on the purposes that may be used by an organization to justify data collection, use or disclosure. Obtaining the consent of the individual for the collection of personal information outside of these limits may be insufficient for compliance.

This principle is also modified by principles 4 and 5 regarding limiting collection, use, disclosure and retention.

Principle 3—Consent

This principle is generally regarded as the cornerstone of PIPEDA protection. Generally speaking, personal information cannot be collected, used or disclosed without the knowledge or consent of the individual, unless there is a specific exemption provided for in section 7 of PIPEDA. An organization may not, as a condition of the supply of a product or service, require such consent beyond what is required for a legitimate fulfillment of the transaction. The form of consent may be explicit or implicit, or "opt-in" or "opt-out," depending upon the sensitivity of the information. It is always prudent to try to obtain written consent. Consent can be withdrawn at any time, subject to legal or contractual restrictions and reasonable notice.

Care must be taken in reading the specific sections of this principle in the schedule because it is extensively revised by section 7 of PIPEDA, which provides the specific and only exceptions from obtaining consent for the collection, use, and disclosure of personal information.

Principle 4—Limiting Collection

This principle provides that the collection of personal information shall be limited to that which is necessary for the purposes identified by the organization. Purposes need to be reasonably specific. Information must be collected by fair and lawful means.

This principle is not modified by PIPEDA.

Principle 5—Limiting Use, Disclosure and Retention

This principle provides that personal information shall not be used or disclosed for purposes other than those for which it was collected, except with the consent of the individual or as required by law. Personal information shall be retained only as long as is necessary for the fulfillment of those purposes. Organizations must develop guidelines with maximum and minimum retention periods.

This principle is also modified by section 7 of PIPEDA.

Principle 6—Accuracy

Personal information shall be as accurate, complete and up-to-date as is necessary for the purposes for which it is to be used. However, the extent to which this must be implemented depends on the use of the information, taking account of the interests of the individual. While this principle is vaguely worded, it is relevant mainly to organizations that collect information to make decisions that may affect the subject individual adversely.

This principle is not modified by PIPEDA.

Principle 7—Safeguards

Personal information is to be protected by security safeguards appropriate to the sensitivity of the information. As with Principle 3—Consent, "sensitivity" is a key concept. The purpose of the safeguards is not just to protect against theft, but also to protect against unauthorized access, disclosure, copying or use. The methods of protection should include physical measures, such as locked filing cabinets and restricted access; organizational measures, such as security clearances and access on a "need-to-know" basis; and technological measures, such as passwords and encryptions.

Practice Note

Franchisors should pay particular attention to the security that they provide to customers' personal information.

Principle 8—Openness

An organization shall make readily available specific information about its policies and practices relating to the management of personal information. This principle effectively requires the use of privacy statements by organizations operating in Canada, on websites, or on other material, including printed material, through which they collect personal information. It also requires that the privacy policy developed pursuant to Principle 1 be made available to individuals. Specifically, the information to be made available shall include:

- the name or title and the address of the person who is accountable pursuant to Principle 1;
- the means of gaining access to personal information held by the organization;
- a description of the type of personal information held by the organization, including a general account of its use;
- a copy of any brochures or other information that explain the organization's policies, standards or codes; and
- what personal information is made available to related organizations, such as subsidiaries.

Principle 9—Individual Access

Upon request, an individual shall be informed of the existence, use and disclosure of his or her personal information and shall be given access to that information. An individual shall be able to challenge the accuracy and completeness of the information and have it amended as appropriate. This right of access is limited by the provisions of sections 8 and 9 of PIPEDA, which set the terms for requesting access and prescribe when access is prohibited (*PIPEDA*, at s. 9(1)) or may be refused by the organization holding the information (*Ibid.* at s. 9(3)).

Under PIPEDA, such disclosure includes an account of the use that has been made of the information and an account of the third parties to which the information has been disclosed. Such disclosure can be expensive to make if the files containing such information have not been properly structured in advance to record and summarize such information as use occurs.

The full cost of making such disclosure cannot be recovered from the person making the request. Paragraph 4.9.4 of this principle provides that responses are to be at minimal or no cost to the individual. Section 8(6) further specifies that the individual may be required to pay only if he or she is notified in advance of the approximate cost and agrees to pay.

Principle 10—Challenging Compliance
An individual shall be able to address a challenge concerning compliance to the individual accountable for the organization's personal information.

2. Alberta

Ontario was the first province to commence a consultation process for its own privacy law after the coming into force of PIPEDA, but the law was never introduced in the legislature. Only British Columbia and Alberta have passed laws to specifically take advantage of the provincial exemption provisions of PIPEDA. Both the Alberta Act and B.C. Act came into effect on January 1, 2004. The two provinces collaborated closely on the drafting of their laws, with the intent of establishing a model law that other provinces could use.

On November 15, 2013, the Supreme Court of Canada released its unanimous decision in *Alberta (Information and Privacy Commissioner) v. United Food and Commercial Workers, Local 401* (2013 SCC 62 (United Food)), ruling that the rights protected by the Alberta Act infringe on a union's right to freedom of expression enshrined in section 2(b) of the *Canadian Charter of Rights and Freedoms (S 2, Part I of the Constitution Act, 1982, being Schedule B to the Canada Act 1982 (UK)*, 1982, c. 11).

Agreeing with the government of Alberta and the Information and Privacy Commissioner of Alberta, the SCC declared the entirety of the Alberta Act to be invalid, giving Alberta's legislature 12 months to become compliant. The SCC stated: "[. . .] like privacy, freedom of expression is not an absolute value and both the nature of the privacy interests implicated and the nature of the expression must be considered in striking an appropriate balance" (*United Food*, at ¶ 38). Limited changes to the Alberta Act were enacted in December 2014 to clarify that a trade union could collect, use, and disclose personal information without consent in limited circumstances concerning a matter of significant public interest or importance relating to a labour relations dispute (sections 14.1(1), 17.1(1), and 20.1(1)) if the collection, use, and disclosure of personal information is reasonably necessary for that purpose (section 14.1(1)(a), 17.1(1)(a), and 20.1(1)(a)), and it is reasonable to collect, use and disclose the personal information without consent for that purpose, taking into consideration all relevant circumstances, including the nature and sensitivity of the information (sections 14.1(1)(b), 17.1(1)(b), and 20.1(1)(b)). However, the provisions do not affect or restrict a trade union's ability to collect, use, or disclose personal information without consent in the specific circumstances outlined in the Act in sections 14, 17, and 20. Of importance to franchisors, particularly franchisors based outside of Canada, section 13.1 of the Alberta Act requires notification to be provided to individuals where personal information is being collected by service providers located outside of Canada. This could impact franchisors who utilize the software and services of a parent corporation or affiliate based outside of Canada, or whose data servers are located outside Canada. In light of the decision in United Food, PIPEDA and similar legislation may be open to similar constitutional challenges.

Further, section 62(1)(e.1) was added so that the Lieutenant Governor in Council may make regulations respecting the collection, use, and disclosure of personal information by trade unions under sections 14.1, 17.1, and 20.1 of the Act. Section 62(1)(k) was changed so that the Lieutenant Governor in Council may make regulations for prescribing or determining whether personal information or that of a specific type comes within the meaning of the new provision, and if so, how it should be treated as prescribed by the Act (section 62(2)(b)).

3. British Columbia

The principles embodied in the design of the B.C. Act are the same as PIPEDA; however, unlike PIPEDA, the law does not use the CSA Model Code as a schedule. Rather, the principles in the CSA Model Code have been integrated directly into one overall law. In this regard, it is easier to read than PIPEDA. The B.C. Act also differs from PIPEDA in a number of other ways, motivated primarily by an effort to avoid errors in PIPEDA, or areas where PIPEDA is not regarded as particularly workable. The main differences (apart from the provisions for remedies) may be summarized as follows:

- Implicit Consent—the concept is defined in section 8 of the B.C. Act. PIPEDA does not explicitly set standards with respect to consent.
- Existing Databases—the B.C. Act provides that information collected before the laws came into force may continue to be used for the purposes for which it was originally collected (B.C. Act, at ss. 3(2)(i), 14(b) and 17(b); Alberta Act, at s. 4(4)). PIPEDA makes no special provisions for existing databases, which has led to some significant compliance concerns. (The Office of the Privacy Commissioner of Canada responded to these concerns by issuing a Fact Sheet on July 27, 2004, titled "Best Practices for dealing with pre-PIPEDA personal information (grandfathering)). It is available from the Privacy Commissioners website at www.privcom.gc.ca/fs-fi/02_05_d_22_e.asp.

- Employees—the B.C. Act defines "employee personal information" and provides that consent is not required for the collection, use or disclosure of such information provided that it is ". . . reasonable for the purposes of establishing, managing or terminating an employment relationship between the organization and the individual," and the employee is notified of the practice in advance. PIPEDA requires the consent of the employee.
- Unincorporated Associations—the B.C. Act provides that unincorporated associations may be considered "organizations" for the purpose of the law. PIPEDA simply states that an "organization" includes an association, a partnership, a person and trade union. In practice, the Privacy Commissioner of Canada has regarded separate legal entities as separate organizations. A franchise system is an unincorporated organization.
- Exceptions with Respect to Investigations—the B.C. Act provides for the collection, use and disclosure of personal information without consent for a broader range of investigatory purposes than is allowed under PIPEDA.
- Sale of Business Assets—the B.C. Act allows for the disclosure without consent of the personal information of customers, employees, offices, directors and shareholders as part of the transfer of the assets of the business under certain conditions. It is considered that these provisions were omitted from PIPEDA in error.

These differences between the B.C. Act and PIPEDA may be important for franchisors if franchisees are left to develop their own privacy policies.

4. Québec

To expand upon the provisions of the Civil Code, Québec's Private Sector Law was introduced in 1993 and came into force January 1, 1994. Under this law, the province set standards with respect to the collection and use of personal information, including having a defined purpose or object; collecting only the necessary information; informing the person from whom the file is established; and obtaining consent for transferring such file to a third party.

On November 19, 2003, the federal Government of Canada declared that Québec's Private Sector Law is substantially similar to PIPEDA in terms of the extent to which it protects personal information (S.O.R./2003-374). However, there are a few critical differences that franchisors should take note of.

Québec's Private Sector Law contains notice requirements in Article 8 that are broader than those under PIPEDA's Principle 8. Individuals must be advised of the categories of persons within the organization who will have access to the information and the place where the file will be kept. Article 20 explicitly limits the access of employees and agents of a corporation to that which is needed in the performance of their duties.

Franchisors considered to be carrying on business in Québec and wishing to transfer information relating to Québec out of the province will have obligations under Article 17 to take all reasonable steps to ensure that either the information will not be used for purposes not relevant to the object of the file or disclosed to third persons without consent, or, in the case of nominative lists, that the individuals have a valid opportunity to have their name deleted from the list.

The consent obligations under Québec's Private Sector Law are very strict in comparison to PIPEDA. When conducting business in Québec, franchisors must pay particular attention to these differences. More information on the laws of Québec can be found in Chapter 2.

Practice Note

To view the Office of the Privacy Commissioner of Canada's *Privacy Handbook for Lawyers,* visit www.priv.gc.ca.

V. Securing Payment

In order to secure performance of a franchisee's obligations, a franchisor may want to obtain a security interest over the franchisee's assets. In Canada, most provinces have a *Personal Property Security Act* (PPSA) which deals with taking, registering and enforcing security on personal property (B.C.: R.S.B.C. 1996, c. 359; Alberta: R.S.A. 2000, c. P-7; Saskatchewan: S.S. 1993, c. P-6.2; Manitoba: C.C.S.M., c. P-35; Ontario: R.S.O. 1990, c. P-10; Nova Scotia: S.N.S. 1995-96, c. 13; New Brunswick: S.N.B. 1993, c. P-7.1; Prince Edward Island: S.P.E.I. 1997, c. 33; Newfoundland: S.N.L. 1998, c. P-7.1; Yukon: R.S.Y. 2002, c. 169; Northwest Territories and Nunavut: S.N.W.T. 1994, c. 8). Québec is the one exception, and its "hypothec" system is discussed later in this chapter. Under Canada's constitution, provinces have jurisdiction over property matters. The legislation is very similar in principle and in general execution to Article 9 of the American *Uniform Commercial Code* (U.C.C. Article 9 [UCC]). Within Canada, there are differences in the PPSA of each province, but the legislation is similar in basic principles. The following overview of the PPSA regime therefore applies generally to all of the PPSAs, but the legislation in each province must be reviewed to confirm that the mandatory requirements of that province are met.

In addition to obtaining a security interest in the franchisee's assets, franchisors will normally require personal guarantees of officers and directors of the franchisee to gain further comfort.

Practice Note

Franchisors in Canada make it a practice to secure payment and performance of all obligations under franchise agreements through use of the PPSA and personal guarantees.

A. Taking Security in a Franchisee's Assets

Franchisors will often supply franchisees with products and equipment in order to run their business in a manner that is consistent with the brand. As suppliers of equipment and inventory, franchisors should consider taking a security interest under the PPSA to secure payment of monies owing to the franchisor.

The PPSA applies to most security interests in personal property, and in particular applies to any agreement that in substance creates a "security interest." The PPSA defines a "security interest" as an interest in personal property that secures payment or performance of an obligation and also includes certain "deemed" security interests. In a franchise situation, a franchisor may take a security interest in personal property from a franchisee to secure the franchisee's obligations in or pursuant to the franchise agreement. The actual grant of the security interest may be contained within the franchise agreement or in a separate document, such as a supply agreement or general security agreement.

There are certain interests a franchisor may take which are not security interests, and therefore are not governed by the PPSA. These include a promissory note, which is only evidence of indebtedness, and personal guarantees, which are merely a secondary covenant to pay.

A franchisor or affiliate supplier may be well advised to take a registered security interest over chattels used by the franchisee in operation of the franchised business in priority to the franchisee's other creditors who have not registered a security interest or have registered one subsequent to that of the franchisor or affiliate supplier. In practice, the franchisee's bank lender will usually demand first priority, and while this would leave the franchisor's security in a second position, it would still rank ahead of other third parties' interests. Where the franchisor or its affiliates is supplying the majority of the franchisee's inventory, it should attempt to obtain first position as against inventory, with any bank with security yielding priority to that extent.

1. Provincial PPSA Legislation

(a) Attachment

Each PPSA deals with the concept of "attachment" in the taking of a security interest. In simple terms, attachment means the creation of the security interest between the secured party (franchisor) and the debtor (franchisee). Attachment occurs when value has been given, the debtor has rights in the collateral (property to be secured), and the secured party obtains a signed security agreement from the debtor.

Whatever the form of security agreement, the PPSA requires words creating a security interest, such as "the debtor grants to the secured party a security interest in . . . ," a complete description of the particular collateral being charged, or a general description of the collateral, such as "all of the debtor's present and after-acquired personal property," and the signature of the debtor on the security agreement.

(b) Online registry system

In addition to "attachment," a security interest must be "perfected" to be enforceable against third parties. Perfection is achieved either by the secured party taking possession of the collateral or, more usually, by registering a financing statement. All of the PPSA jurisdictions in Canada have an online Personal Property Registry (PPR) for searches of debtors' names to identify existing security interests registered against them and for registration of financing statements. Like Article 9 of the UCC, the PPR provides a notice filing system in which a financing statement giving notice of the security interest, not the security agreement itself, is registered. As it is an online registration system, the debtor does not have to sign a financing statement, and in fact a financing statement can be registered before the security agreement itself is signed. However, "perfection" (i.e., making the security interest effective against third parties) does not occur until the time that both the security agreement has been signed and the financing statement has been registered. In general, priority is determined from the date of registration.

The Ontario PPSA still requires that the financing statement be completed by a "check the box" system, which requires the secured party to classify the collateral as "consumer goods," "inventory," "equipment," "accounts," or "other." This system requires that the secured party understand the nature of the goods being supplied to the debtor and how they are considered under the Ontario PPSA. Additional descriptive language may also be provided. In most other provinces the equipment, inventory and any other assets are described by the insertion of descriptive language on the financing statement.

Practice Note

All provinces maintain systems for registration of security interests. Although they appear to be similar, there are nuances in the systems of certain provinces that should be noted when registering a financing statement.

(c) Place of registration

To successfully take security from a franchisee in Canada, a franchisor or third-party supplier must not only obtain a signed security agreement and file a financing statement, but must determine the correct jurisdiction to file the financing statement. In PPSA, the general rule for place of registration of a financing statement is:

- for most goods (other than certain mobile goods), register where the collateral is located; and
- for intangibles, mobile goods that are equipment or leased inventory, and non-possessory security interests in securities, instruments, negotiable documents of title, money or chattel paper, register where the debtor is located.

Obviously, if both the collateral and the franchisee debtor are located in the same jurisdiction, then a financing statement only has to be filed in that jurisdiction. However, if the collateral is located in one place and the franchisee is in another, the safest practice is to register a financing statement in both places.

If a franchisee debtor does business in more than one province, the best practice is to register in the PPR of all provinces in which the franchisee does business.

Practice Note

A financing statement "perfecting" the security interest must be registered in the province where the collateral is located or where the franchisee carries on business (both registrations are advisable for the purpose of giving broader notice).

(d) Priority

Under the PPSA, the residual priority rule provides in general that the first secured party to register a financing statement (or to take possession of collateral if perfection is by way of possession) has priority over later secured parties or other third parties, such as purchasers or trustees in bankruptcy. However, there are numerous exceptions to this residual priority rule, which may apply to franchisors or their designated suppliers:

- A registered secured party has no priority over a buyer or lessee of goods sold or leased by the debtor in the ordinary course of business. For example, if a franchisor held a perfected security interest in the inventory of an automobile franchise, a consumer purchasing an automobile from that franchisee would take free and clear of the prior registered security interest.
- Later-registered "purchase money security interests" (PMSI) take priority over prior registered security interests in the same collateral. A PMSI is a defined term and includes:

(i) a security interest in favour of a vendor that advances credit to a debtor to pay the purchase price of the collateral being acquired (e.g., a franchisor extending credit to a franchisee to acquire its opening inventory of goods and perhaps ongoing inventory); or
(ii) a secured party that extends credit to allow the debtor to acquire personal property (e.g., a supplier that lends money to a debtor to acquire items of equipment), and the credit is in fact used to acquire that equipment.

- To obtain priority by perfection of a PMSI, the secured party must register a financing statement within the following time periods for collateral other than inventory:
  (i) for collateral other than intangibles, within 15 days of the debtor obtaining possession of the collateral; and
  (ii) for intangibles (e.g., accounts receivable), within 15 days after the security interest in the intangibles attaches.

It is important to note that there are additional requirements to obtain a PMSI in inventory.

2. Québec—the Hypothec

In the Province of Québec, security interests are governed by the *Civil Code of Québec* (L.R.Q., c. C-1991 [Code]). The Code creates one type of security: the *hypothec*. A hypothec is a charge on one or more specific corporeal or incorporeal properties or on the universality of the properties of the debtor, including, without limitation, inventory, equipment and accounts receivable. It confers on the hypothecary creditor the right to follow the secured property into whoever's hands it may come into in order to exercise one of its remedies. The hypothec must be registered at the Québec Register of Personal and Movable Rights (RPMR) to be enforceable against third parties and will rank according to the date and time it is registered in the RPMR.

More information on the laws of Québec can be found in Chapter 2.

Practice Note

In the Province of Québec, security interests are governed by the Civil Code, which creates one type of security: the hypothec. The hypothec can be taken as a charge against all of the personal property of the debtor, but must be registered in Québec in order to be enforceable against third parties.

B. Personal Guarantees from Franchisees

Although franchisors and franchisees enter into a business relationship together with the expectations of mutual success, in some situations the business fails. Both parties have a lot riding on the viability of the business—for the franchisee, often their entire livelihood; for the franchisor, the risk of deteriorating brand value. Virtually all franchisors will require a personal guarantee. Where the franchisee is a corporation, it is common practice for a franchisor to require the shareholders, officers and directors of the franchisee to personally guarantee the obligations of the franchisee to the franchisor. Guarantees act as a source of comfort for the franchisor, allowing them to look to the guarantor upon default.

Personal guarantees in a franchise agreement need to comply with Canadian practice and common law.

1. Alberta—Guarantees Acknowledgement Act

Alberta is the only province in Canada to legislate a guarantees acknowledgment act. The *Alberta Guarantees Acknowledgement Act* (RSA 2000, c G-11 [AGAA]) was enacted to protect unsophisticated franchisees from unknowingly taking on oppressive liabilities. The AGAA requires individual guarantors to appear before a lawyer who will complete a certificate in the prescribed form certifying that the guarantor is aware of and understands the terms of the guarantee. The *Alberta Guarantees Acknowledgement Forms Regulation* (Alta Reg 66/2003) provides a standard form of certificate).

Courts have generally applied these requirements strictly. Failure to obtain a properly executed notarial certificate will generally render the guarantee unenforceable, resulting in some guarantors using technicalities to avoid obligations under their guarantee.

> **Practice Note**
>
> **Franchisors should make special note of the Alberta Guarantees Acknowledgement Act. Failure to comply with the AGAA will likely render a guarantee unenforceable.**

2. Québec—Implications of the Civil Code

In Québec, personal guarantees are governed by the Code.

Article 2355 of the Code prohibits a renunciation by a guarantor to his right to obtain from the creditor information with respect to the scope and terms of the principal obligation and the status of its performance by the principal debtor.

Article 2363 of the Code provides that a guarantee attaches to the performance of special duties (such as positions as directors and officers of a corporation) and terminates upon cessation of the duties (it is to be noted that the status of "shareholder" does not fall within the meaning of "special duties"). As a result, to avoid the application of that article, a guarantee that is granted by directors or officers of the franchisee should contain a provision specifying that it is not attached to their position as directors or officers.

Article 2362 of the Code provides that any guarantor of future debts (for example, royalties or rents) or of existing debts but for an undetermined period of time may, after three years, terminate his or her guarantee as to the future by providing a reasonable written notice. Such provision obviously creates a concern for franchisors. It is important to revise all guarantees to include a renunciation, together with a renunciation of the benefits of division and discussion; it is also recommended to include an undertaking by the guarantor to provide a written renewal of his guarantee upon request. One may also include in the franchise agreement an obligation of the franchisee to cause any guarantor to renew his or her personal guarantee upon its termination or to substitute it with a guarantor as solvent as the previous one, failing which the franchisee will be deemed in default under the franchise agreement.

Article 2361 provides that the death of the guarantor terminates the guarantee for debts that have not accrued at the time of death. This provision is made in favour of public order and thus may not be waived by a guarantor.

More information on the laws of Québec can be found in Chapter 2.

Practice Note

In Québec, personal guarantees are subject to certain rules not applicable to the rest of Canada. Accordingly, if a guarantee is to be taken from a resident of Québec, both the franchise agreement and normal form of guarantee may need to be revised.

CHAPTER 4

Trademark and Other Intellectual Property Issues

Judy Rost and Bruno Floriani*

Contents

* Mr. Floriani acknowledges with gratitude the invaluable and extensive assistance of his colleague, Catherine Daigle (formerly at Lapointe Rosenstein Marchand Melançon, LLP at the time of writing), in the preparation of this chapter.

I. Trademarks

In Canada, rights in a trademark arise either statutorily, from registration under the *Trade-Marks Act*, R.S.C. 1985, c. T-13 (TMA), or as a result of the use of the trademark in the marketplace, otherwise known as common-law rights. Although there are significant advantages to registration, the owner of an unregistered trademark (or in certain cases, trade name or other signs) may not only assert its rights over others based on the use of its trademark, but may also rely on these rights to prevent the registration by third parties of confusingly similar trademarks.

Practice Note

The TMA has undergone two extensive amendments since December 2014 that will have a major impact on trademark owners and practitioners in Canada. These amendments have been effected through Bill C-31, *Economic Action Plan Act 2014, No. 1* (Bill C-31), and Bill C-8, *Combating Counterfeit Products* Act (Bill C-8).

Bill C-31 introduces the most significant changes to the TMA in 50 years. However, given that full implementation of the provisions of Bill C-31 is subject to the adoption of suitable regulations (which are not anticipated prior to 2018) at the earliest, the current registration system remains in effect.

Bill C-8, which is currently in full effect, adds new prohibitions and offences intended to address the issues relating to the distribution of counterfeit products in Canada.

Detailed information on these changes to the TMA is contained in sections 4(d) and 7 of this chapter.

A. Common-Law Protection of Trademarks

1. Common-Law Passing-Off

The tort of "passing-off" under common law attempts to address concerns in the marketplace that consumers should be able to rely upon the quality of goods they purchase under, and associate with, certain names and labels. This body of common law was originally developed to prevent unauthorized use of a trademark or trade name owned by a competitor in a manner that would wrongly lead consumers to believe that the unauthorized user's products or services were those of the trademark or trade-name owner.

Over time, the concept of passing-off was extended not only to trademarks or trade names, but also to trade-dress copying, unfair advertising, or misappropriation of rights in names and personality.

For a passing-off action to be successful, three requirements must be established by the plaintiff, as stated by the Supreme Court of Canada in *Ciba-Geigy Canada Ltd. v. Apotex, Inc.* (1992), 44 C.P.R. (3d) 289 at 301:

- the existence of goodwill or reputation in the plaintiff's trademark;
- a misrepresentation, whether intentional or not, that leads or is likely to lead the public to believe that the defendant's products, services or business are associated with or authorised by the plaintiff; and
- actual or potential damages to the plaintiff.

The onus in a passing-off action is on the plaintiff to demonstrate that its trademark has acquired, to some extent, reputation or goodwill in the geographical area where it seeks to enforce its rights. This is because an unregistered trademark is only enforceable where it has become known. The relevant date for showing the acquisition of reputation or goodwill is the date when the defendant first started to use its trademark.

In some cases, a successful passing-off claim can be made even without actual use in Canada. This requires supporting evidence demonstrating substantial spillover advertising or promotion in Canada. Such a demonstration, which is not easily made, will usually require significant efforts and investment from the plaintiff.

Once the reputation or goodwill attached to the plaintiff's trademark is established, the plaintiff will then have to demonstrate that there has been a misrepresentation by the defendant resulting in a likelihood of confusion with the plaintiff trademark. Confusion stems from an inaccurate conclusion that the defendant's products, services or business are those of the plaintiff, or that there is an affiliation between the parties, where there is in fact none. The assessment of confusion in passing-off claims is similar to that involving a registered trademark [see Section B(4)].

The third and final requirement of a successful passing-off claim concerns damages, which can be established through lost profits or market share, or even loss of control over the use of a trademark. Damages or potential damages must not be speculative, but rather be clearly identifiable.

The tort of passing-off is not a static concept. Its use is ever-expanding and includes not only a name, but also the look of a particular retail business—what is referred to as its "trade dress." This is of particular interest and usefulness in the franchising context.

Trade dress, also referred to as "get-up" in relation to service facilities and premises, refers to the unique look and overall appearance of the business (this concept is also used with respect to products). It includes layout of the premises, colour schemes, interior and exterior design, specially designed furniture and other similar distinguishing features. A more modern definition of "get-up" was quoted with approval by the Supreme Court of Canada in *Ciba-Geigy Canada Ltd. v. Apotex, Inc.*, (1992), 44 C.P.R. (3d) 289 at 301:

> The term "get-up" is normally used in passing-off to mean the whole visible external appearance of the goods in the form which they are likely to be seen by the public before purchase. If the goods are sold in packages, then their get-up means the appearance of the pack taken as a whole. If they are sold or displayed unpackaged, then the get-up relied on can only be that inherent in the goods themselves.

In the Province of Québec, a civil law jurisdiction, an action in passing-off would be instituted on the basis of Article 1457 of the *Civil Code of Québec*, R.S.Q., c. C-64, which states the general principle of extra-contractual liability, the equivalent of tort, and reads as follows: "Every person has a duty to abide by the rules of conduct which lie upon him, according to the circumstances, usage or law, so as not to cause injury to another . . . ."

B. *Trade-Marks Act*

In Canada, the registration of trademarks is governed by the TMA.

As mentioned above, trademark owners have common-law rights which may be exercised in the form of an action for passing-off. However, obtaining a registration pursuant to the TMA is the greatest protection that can be achieved to establish a claim to ownership of a trademark. First, registration is evidence of the claim to prior ownership. Second, if ever challenged, registration is the best evidence available that the registrant is the owner of the trademark, and places an onus on a non-registrant to prove otherwise. Third, from a practical perspective, registration provides public notice to others of an owner's claim, which is often sufficient to protect against infringers and conflicting trademarks. Finally, registration expands the trademark protection on a Canada-wide basis, whereas a common-law trademark affords protection only in the geographic areas where it has acquired goodwill.

> **Practice Note**
>
> **The registration of a trademark is governed by Canadian federal law. Accordingly, a registered owner's rights can be asserted all across Canada.**

1. Types of Trademarks

Under the TMA, a "trademark" includes four types of trademarks:

- a trademark that is *used* by a person for the purpose of *distinguishing* wares or services manufactured, sold, leased, hired or performed by him from those manufactured, sold, leased, hired or performed by others;
- a certification trademark;
- a distinguishing guise; or
- a proposed trademark.

As the definitions of "used trademark" and "proposed trademark" are similar, they will both be treated below as trademarks. Moreover, although not included in the definition of a trademark per se, we will also address the notion of official trademarks in this section, as they constitute a unique feature of Canadian trademark law.

(a) Trademarks

A trademark in Canada consists of any trademark, sign, logo, symbol, design, acronym, single word or sentence, or any combination of these elements that is used or proposed to be used in Canada for the purposes of distinguishing the wares, services or business of a person or entity from those of others. Sounds have also been recognized as valid trademarks by the Federal Court of Canada in *Metro-Goldwyn-Mayer Lion Corp. v. Canada (A-G),* rendered on March 3, 2012, T-1650-10.

(b) Certification trademarks

Certification trademarks are used in a particular trade to identify wares or services that are of a defined standard with respect to (i) the character or quality of such wares or services; (ii) the conditions under which the wares have been produced or the services performed; (iii) the category of persons by whom these wares have been produced or the services rendered; and (iv) the area where the wares have been produced or the services rendered (Section 2).

Although the owner of a certification trademark is responsible for establishing the standard that designates the trademark, it cannot itself be engaged in the manufacture, sale, hire or lease of the wares, or perform the services associated with the certification trademark. Rather, Section 23 TMA specifies that a certification trademark may only be used under license by third parties provided that the wares sold or services rendered by them meet the standard established by the owner of the trademark.

(c) Distinguishing guises

Protection of trade dress (or get-up) by registration is possible in Canada, although it is still considered a non-traditional trademark. Under the TMA, such a trademark is defined as a "distinguishing guise," and means either (i) the shaping of wares or their containers or (ii) a mode of wrapping or packaging wares, the appearance of which is used by a person to distinguish the wares or services manufactured, sold, leased, hired or performed by him from those of others.

A distinguishing guise is only registrable by its owner if it has acquired distinctiveness through use at the date of the filing of the application. Thus, it is not possible to apply for registration of a distinguishing guise based on proposed use. The owner of the distinguishing guise will have to demonstrate through an affidavit that consumers have come to recognize it as designating the source of the product with which it is associated. The evidence must show acquired distinctiveness in each of the provinces and territories, otherwise the registration will be limited geographically.

(d) Official trademarks

Official trademarks are not considered trademarks as properly understood under the TMA. Section 9 TMA offers extraordinary protection to the owners of official trademarks, which are unique to Canadian law.

Official trademarks may be granted to royalty, governments, universities or other public authorities in Canada. There is no examination process attached to the advertisement of official trademarks, nor does the Registrar have discretion to refuse them unless the body sanctioning the trademark does not fall under the established requirements for public authorities (see the Intellectual Property Office's Practice Notice dated 22-08-2007 on the subject). As official trademarks are not required to satisfy any of the registrability requirements as would ordinary trademarks (Section 12), they may, for example, be descriptive or confusingly similar to trademarks that were previously filed or registered.

Once granted, an official trademark appears on the register without any renewal deadline, and thus will not be revoked or expunged from the register without a formal abandonment filed by its owner. It will not be possible for a third party to adopt a trademark that is similar to the official trademark unless consent is granted by its owner.

Finally, it should be noted that the TMA does not provide for the concept of "service mark" as a type or category of trademark. Accordingly, all references to that term contained in a non-Canadian franchise agreement or trademark license agreement adapted for use in Canada should be deleted.

Practice Note

Canada's law does not recognize a service mark, as the concept is included in the meaning of the term trademark. While the term is generally understood, "trademark" should be used in place of "service mark" wherever possible.

2. Registrability

(a) Use and Distinctiveness as Key Features

As previously mentioned, trademarks are defined in the TMA as trademarks *used or proposed to be used* by a person or entity for the purpose of *distinguishing* or to *distinguish* its wares or services from those of others. Thus, the concepts of use and distinctiveness are both key features of the Canadian system.

Distinctiveness can be described under Canadian trademark law as the capacity for a trademark to function as a connection between wares or services and their source or origin. This connection has to be perceived by consumers, so that the wares sold or services performed under a given trademark may only be associated with a single source, as explained in *Kirkbi AG* v. *Ritvik Holdings Inc.,* [2005] 3 S.C.R. 302.

However, distinctiveness alone is not sufficient for a trademark to be registrable, since trademark rights in Canada are acquired, perfected, maintained and violated through *use* for the purpose of distinguishing the source of wares or services. As such, the concept of use is also fundamental. Section 4 TMA defines the key elements constituting use of a trademark:

> 4. (1) A trademark is deemed to be used in association with *wares* if, *at the time of the transfer of the property in or possession of the wares*, in the normal course of trade, it is marked on the wares themselves or on the packages in which they are distributed or it is in any other manner so associated with the wares that notice of the association is then given to the person to whom the property or possession is transferred.
>
> (2) A trademark is deemed to be used in association with *services* if it is *used or displayed* in the *performance* or *advertising* of those services.

(3) A trademark that is trademarked in Canada on wares or on the packages in which they are contained is, when the wares are exported from Canada, deemed to be used in Canada in association with those wares. [Emphasis added.]

In order to satisfy the statutory criteria for use, the courts have determined, as exemplified in *Plough (Canada) Ltd.* v. *Aerosol Fillers Inc.* (1980), 53 C.P.R. (2d) 62 (F.C.A.), that a trademark must be used visually, although this requirement is not set out in the TMA. Until recently, the Trade-marks Office persistently refused the registration of non-traditional trademarks based on the jurisprudence and the TMA requirement that a trademark application contain a drawing accurately representing the trademark. Only in 2012 were sound trademarks accepted in Canada. However, the Trade-marks Office still requires that an application for a sound trademark contain a drawing graphically representing the sound.

What qualifies as use in association with wares under the TMA does not necessarily coincide with the common commercial understanding of use of the trademark. In order to constitute use in Canada in relation to wares, four conditions must be satisfied. The trademark must:

1. in the normal course of trade;
2. (a) be trademarked on the wares themselves or on the packages in which they are distributed, or
   (b) in any other way be so associated with the wares that notice of the association is then given to the person to whom the property or possession is transferred,
3. at the time of the transfer of the property in or possession of the wares,
4. in Canada.
   [See Burshtein, Sheldon. *The Basics of Trademark Use in Canada: The Who, What, Where, When, Why and How*, Twelfth Annual Trade-mark Institute, Intellectual Property Institute of Canada, August 2006, for a detailed analysis of the concept of use in Canada.]

For example, free distribution of goods bearing a trademark to create goodwill and to generate sales of such goods does not constitute use of a trademark with such goods, unless this is a regular practice in the industry for dealing in the goods to acquire goodwill and profits, or unless followed within a reasonable period of time by normal commercial sales.

The manner in which the association may be made is not limited to a display on the wares or their packaging. However, there must be an association with the wares at the time of transfer of possession or title. References in letters, publications, product bulletins or conference papers do not constitute trademark use. The appearance of a trademark in magazine and newspaper advertisements, news releases and the like normally does not provide sufficient association with the trademark. The appearance of a trademark on a chart that is not affixed to the wares, where the chart compares wares of various competitors, is not considered use.

Use with respect to services requires actual performance or the capacity to perform the services in Canada. Menus, menuboards and restaurant signage raise interesting issues. While in *McDonald's Corporation* v. *Phil's Industries of Canada Ltd.* (1984), 81 C.P.R. (2d) 260 (Opposition Board), the display of a trademark on a fast-food menuboard for a particular item was held not to be use in association with restaurant services, the reference to a trademark on a menu has been found to be use with such services, such as in *Gowling & Henderson v. Phillfoods Ltd.* (1989), 22 C.P.R. (3d) 419 (Trade-marks Office Hearing Officer). In one case, *Oyen, Wiggs, Green & Mutala v. Aimer* (1999), 86 C.P.R. (3d) 90 (Trade-marks Hearing Officer), a trademark displayed on an interior sign, which was clearly visible when the customers ordered, constituted use in association with foods that were not prepared in the restaurant, such as beverages. The trademark was held to be used with restaurant services. In another case, *Goudreau, Gage, Dubuc & Martineau Walker v. Cinnabon, Inc.* (1987), 81 C.P.R. (3d) 281 (T.M. Senior Hearing Officer), the display of a trademark on a wall-mounted sign outside a bakery constituted use of the trademark in association with bakery goods, such as rolls, because when the rolls are consumed on the premises, the trademark cannot be applied to them, and because every customer would see the sign upon entering. However, use of the same trademark on beverage cups was not use of the trademark with the rolls, but was rather only a use of the trademark in association with the services of operating a retail bakery store.

Practice Note

In order to avoid jeopardising ownership rights in its trademarks, a franchisor should make sure that there is proper use of the trademarks within the meaning of the TMA.

(b) Registrable trademarks

Setting aside various technical limits on what may be used and registered as a trademark (such as the prohibition on the use and registration of any trademark which would be mistaken for items that were sold under governmental authority (or lead a person to so believe) (Section 9), subsection 12(1) sets forth the basic requirements as to the registrability of a trademark:

(. . .) a trademark is registrable *if it is not* (a) a word that is primarily merely *the name or the surname of an individual* who is living or has died within the preceding 30 years; (b) whether depicted, written or sounded, either *clearly descriptive or deceptively misdescriptive* in the English or French language of the character or quality of the wares or services in association with which it is used or proposed to be used or of the conditions of or the persons employed in their production or of their place of origin; (c) the name in any language of any of the wares or services in connection with which it is used or proposed to be used; (d) *confusing* with a registered trademark . . . . [Emphasis added.]

(c) Filing basis for registration

Pursuant to section 30, a person may secure a registration in the following situations:

- *Actual use*: if the trademark is in actual use in Canada, then the application for registration should claim priority from the date that usage in Canada began. Under this category, the right to registration and ownership arises from being the first to have used the trademark.
- *Making known in Canada*: it is possible to obtain a registration despite a trademark not being actually used in Canada if, through reputation, it has become known in Canada.
- *Intention to use*: an applicant may apply for registration of a trademark on the basis of future use, in circumstances where it is not then being used by the applicant. If the application for registration on the basis of a proposed use is allowed, the applicant must file with the Registrar of Trade-marks, no more than three years after the date of filing of the original application, a declaration attesting that the use of the trademark in Canada has commenced, failing which the application will be deemed to have been abandoned (Section 40).
- *Use and registration abroad*: registration may be obtained based on the applicant's registration (or eventual registration) of the trademark in its country of origin combined with use of said trademark anywhere in the world. In *Reitmans (Canada) Ltd. v. Thymes Ltd.*, 2013 FC 127, the Federal Court of Canada created some uncertainty as to when the foreign trademark must be used in order to rely on this filing basis. Pursuant to this decision, care should be exercised so as to confirm the existence of foreign use as of the filing date of the Canadian application, regardless of when this filing basis is included in the application (i.e., it may be added subsequent to the initial filing on another basis provided it is added prior to the advertisement of the trademark for registration purposes).

In addition, when an application for registration of a trademark in Canada is filed, and a similar application for registration has been filed in and for any country that is a member of the Union for the Protection of Intellectual Property (which includes the United States) in the previous six months, the date of filing of the application in or for the other country will be deemed to be the date of filing of the application in Canada, such that the applicant will be entitled to priority in Canada accordingly (Section 34).

Any trademark registered in such other country will be registrable with respect to the wares or services in association with which it has been used and is registered in that other country, provided that it is not (1) confusingly similar to a trademark which had been previously used or made known in Canada or in respect of which an application had been previously filed in Canada by any other person, or (2) a trade name previously used in Canada by any other person (Subsection 16(2)). Furthermore, if any such trademark is registrable pursuant to subsection 16(2) but fails to meet the requirements for registrability set forth in subsection 12(1) and described above, such trademark registered abroad may nevertheless be registrable under an exception available to trademarks registered abroad, namely if (a) it is not confusing with a registered trademark, (b) it is not without distinctive character, (c) it is not contrary to morality or public order or of such a nature as to deceive the public, or (d) it is not prohibited under section 9 described above (Section 14).

Practice Note

It is possible to file a trademark application on the basis of an intention to use, which effectively serves as a trademark reservation system. However, in order to obtain a registration, actual use of the trademark must be shown within three years of the original filing.

3. Registration Process

Prior to filing an application for the registration of a trademark, it is common practice to conduct searches in order to determine the availability of that trademark. As is the case in the United States, those searches will include registrability searches in the records maintained by the Trade-marks Office to determine whether there could be potential confusion with a previously registered trademark or another pending application. The searches will also include a review of secondary sources to determine if there are any similar trademarks or trade names in use in the marketplace. Among these sources are trade directories, telephone directories, corporate name databases, magazine and newspaper articles, and the Internet.

However, franchisors and their counsel should be mindful of the inherent limitations of these availability searches. Records maintained by the Trademarks Office are subject to the usual "errors and omissions" caused by inaccurate or incomplete database input. Corporate name databases may not have been updated and are incomplete, inasmuch as the nature of the business is not identified. Secondary sources are by no means conclusive and cannot be relied upon as providing an absolute (or even reliable) assurance with respect to the adoption and use of a trademark. They nevertheless serve a very valuable purpose in informing the applicant of the possibility of an infringement claim by a third party.

Practice Note

Regardless of whether an application for registration of a trademark is to be filed in Canada, a comprehensive search is recommended so as to identify potential claims of infringement by a third party with a similar trademark.

A trademark examiner will review the application to determine if the trademark meets the requirements of the TMA and is otherwise registrable. If the examiner believes that the proposed trademark does not meet the registration requirements, the applicant will be so advised and may amend certain aspects of the application or submit arguments to overcome any objection. If changes are not possible, the application may be abandoned by the applicant or refused by the Registrar of Trade-marks. Where an application is refused, the applicant may appeal the decision to the courts. Failure to respond to the examiner's report and reminders may result in automatic abandonment. The first examiner's report or approval notice is normally made available to the applicant within 18 months of the filing of an application.

If the Registrar of Trade-marks approves an application for registration of a trademark, an advertisement of the application will be published in the *Trade-marks Journal*. Within two months of such advertisement, any interested person may file a statement of opposition to the registration with the Registrar of Trade-marks. If the Registrar considers that the opposition raises a substantial issue (which is usually the case), the Trade-marks Opposition Board will invite both parties to submit evidence and argument (Section 19). If no opposition is filed, it is possible that the registration process may be completed within 36 months from the application date.

Registration of a trademark is subject to renewal within a period of 15 years from the date of issuance or the date of the most recent renewal.

Registration of a trademark in association with any wares or services, unless shown to be invalid, gives the owner of a trademark, in respect of those wares or services, the exclusive right to the use of the trademark throughout Canada (Section 38) and, if used as registered, is an absolute defence to an action in passing-off or in infringement [see *Jonathan, Boutique pour Hommes Inc.* v. *Jay-Gur International Inc.*, (2003) 23 C.P.R. (4th) 292 (F.C.T.D.); *Molson Canada v. Oland Breweries Ltd.* (2002), 19 C.P.R. (4th) 201 (Ont. C.A.)].

Canada is in the process of, but has not yet implemented the *Protocol Relating to the Madrid Agreement Concerning the International Registration of Trademarks* (Madrid Protocol), concluded on June 27, 1989 (and amended on October 3, 2006, and on November 12, 2007), nor the *Nice Agreement Concerning the International Classification of Goods and Services for the Purposes of the Registration of Trademarks* (Nice Agreement), concluded on June 15, 1957 (and revised on July 14, 1967, and on May 13, 1977; and amended on September 28, 1979). Consequently, the international system of classes of goods and services is not currently obligatory in Canada. Until implementation of the Madrid Protocol, which is not currently expected in 2018 at the earliest, the wares or services applied for in an application for registration of a trademark should be set out in specific, ordinary commercial terms (Subsection 30(a)). The Trade-marks Office began to accept trademark applications with wares and services voluntarily grouped according to the international classifications on September 28, 2015, but maintains that the wares or services appearing in the class headings are merely general indications relating to the class to which the wares or services belong to and that the application must contain a description compliant with subsection 30(a) of the TMA.

Practice Note

Canada does not currently adhere to the international class system, instead requiring that all wares and services be described in a trademark application in ordinary commercial terms.

4. Prohibited Use and Remedies

(a) Statutory passing-off

Subsections 7(b) to (d) create the statutory offence of passing-off. Subsection 7(b) is properly understood as a codification of the common law and provides the trademark owner with statutory protection.

Pursuant to that subsection, no person shall direct public attention to its wares, services or business in such a way as to cause or be likely to cause confusion in Canada, at the time the action is commenced, between his wares, services or business and the wares, services or business of another.

The Federal Court of Appeal recently summarized what constitutes statutory passing-off under the TMA in *PharmaCommunications Holdings Inc.* v. *Avencia International Inc.*, 2009 FCA 144:

> [. . .] Paragraph 7(b) of the Act is a codification of the common law of passing-off, and there are no longer any "significant differences" between the statute and the common law [Kelly Gill and R. Scott Joliffe, eds., *Fox on Canadian Law of Trademarks and Unfair Competition,* 4th ed., looseleaf (Toronto: Thomson Carswell, 2002) at § 4.1 and § 4.2(e)].
>
> [9] In *Ciba-Geigy v. Apotex Inc.*, 1992 CanLII 33 (SCC), [1992] 3 S.C.R. 120 at 132, the Supreme Court established a tripartite test for establishing passing-off: 1) the existence of goodwill; 2) the deception of the public due to a misrepresentation; and 3) actual or potential damage to the plaintiff. Although *Ciba-Geigy* was a common-law passing-off case, this test has been applied by the Federal Court in numerous statutory claims [see, for example, *Prince Edward Island Mutual Insurance v. Insurance Co. of Prince Edward Island,* 1999 CanLII 7462 (FC) (1999), 159 F.T.R. 112 at para. 26 (T.D.), *aff'd,* (2000) 9 C.P.R. (4th) 520 (F.C.A.)].
>
> [10] More recently, in *Kirkbi AG v. Ritvik Holdings Inc.*, 2005 SCC 65 (CanLII), 2005 SCC 65, [2005] 3 S.C.R. 302 at para. 66, the Supreme Court affirmed the tripartite test, including the requirement of actual or potential damage (at para. 66). It also confirmed that the same principles inform both the common law and the statute (at para. 63).

(b) Infringement

Infringement actions may be initiated with respect to registered trademarks pursuant to sections 19 and 20 of the TMA.

Section 19 provides the owner of a registered trademark associated with certain wares or services with an exclusive right to use it across Canada. [See *Bacardi & Co.* v. *Havana Club Holdings S.A.,* (2003) 32 C.P.R. (4th) 366 (F.C.); *aff'd,* (2004) 32 C.P.R. (4th) 306 (F.C.A.).]

However, section 19 is limited to infringing use of an identical trademark, whereas section 20 broadens protection to encompass trade names and trademarks used by a defendant that are confusingly similar to those of the plaintiff.

Pursuant to the expanded definition of infringement set forth in section 20 revised pursuant to Bill C-8, the right of a registered trademark owner to its exclusive use is deemed to be infringed by any person who is not entitled to its use under the Act and who, inter alia, (a) sells, distributes, or advertises wares or services in association with a confusing trademark or trade name; or (b) manufactures, causes to be manufactured, possesses, imports, exports, or attempts to export any goods in association with a confusing trademark or trade name for the purpose of their sale or distribution (Subsection 20(1)).

In order to successfully claim infringement in accordance with either section 19 or section 20, the plaintiff must demonstrate that the defendant uses its trademark or trade name for the purpose of indicating the origin of the wares or services. The use for purposes of an infringement action must be in accordance with the requirements of section 4, and use as a trademark must fall within the definition of trademark included in section 2. The infringing use must also relate to wares or services available to Canadian consumers.

As noted above, a claim of infringement under section 20 requires a plaintiff to demonstrate confusion. The test to determine if confusion exists, as set out in *Mattel, Inc. v. 3894207 Canada Inc.*, [2006] 1 S.C.R. 772, is whether the use of the plaintiff's and defendant's trademarks in the same area would likely cause an average consumer, having an imperfect recollection, to infer as a matter of first impression that the goods or services with which the trademarks are associated are manufactured, sold, leased, hired or performed by the same person, regardless of whether the goods or services are of the same general class. To assist this inquiry, subsection 6(5) TMA provides that in determining whether trademarks or trade names are confusing, the court or the Registrar, as the case may be, shall have regard to all the surrounding circumstances, including:

- the inherent distinctiveness of the trademarks or trade names and the extent to which they have become known;
- the length of time the trademarks or trade names have been in use;
- the nature of the wares, services or business;
- the nature of the trade; and
- the degree of resemblance between the trademarks or trade names in appearance or sound or in the ideas suggested by them (Section 6(5)).

It is important to note that the foregoing surrounding circumstances are not exhaustive, and different circumstances will be given different weight in a context-specific assessment.

(c) Depreciation of goodwill

Section 22 TMA prohibits the use of a registered trademark by anyone in a manner that is likely to cause depreciation of the goodwill attaching to such trademark. This section has been relied on, for example, in the case of comparative advertisement.

The Supreme Court of Canada in *Veuve Clicquot Ponsardin* v. *Boutique Cliquot,* [2006] 1 S.C.R. 824, identified as follows the requirements for a successful action based on section 22:

> "Section 22 has four elements. Firstly, that a claimant's registered trademark was used by the defendant in connection with wares or services – whether or not such wares and services are competitive with those of the claimant. Secondly, that the claimant's registered trademark is sufficiently well known to have significant goodwill attached to it. Section 22 does not require the trademark to be well known or famous (in contrast to the analogous European and U.S. laws), but a defendant cannot depreciate the value of the goodwill that does not exist. Thirdly, the claimant's trademark was used in a manner *likely* to have an effect on that goodwill (i.e. linkage) and fourthly that the *likely* effect would be to depreciate the value of its goodwill (i.e. damage)."

(d) Other remedies

Substantial changes to the TMA have been introduced with the adoption of the *Combating Counterfeit Products Act*, S.C. 2014, c. 32 (Counterfeit Products Act), which received royal assent on December 9, 2014. The Counterfeit Products Act has as its main objective the reduction of the trade of counterfeit goods in Canada, as well as providing registered trademark owners with new civil and criminal remedies. Additional border protection measures have also been made available to registered trademark owners, who may now file a Request for Assistance from customs authorities to take action against counterfeit trademark goods before they enter or leave the Canadian market.

5. Expungement

(a) Cancellation for non-use

Section 45 TMA provides for a summary proceeding for removing from the register trademarks that are no longer used by their owners. Traditionally, cancellation proceedings have been referred to as a tool for removing "deadwood" from the register, as explained in *BCF S.E.N.C.R.L. v. Spirits International B.V.*, 2012 FCA 131.

Trademarks that have been registered for at least three years are exposed to the possibility of cancellation proceedings. Although the Registrar itself has the independent authority to request evidence of use by the trademark's owner, cancellation proceedings are usually initiated at the request of third parties.

Once the Registrar has notified the owner of the cited trademark that a cancellation proceeding has been initiated, the owner must demonstrate either (i) use of its trademark within the three-year period preceding the issuance of the Registrar's notice, or (ii) special circumstances excusing the absence of use in the same period.

Evidence of use (or reasons excusing the absence thereof) is established by the owner by way of affidavit or statutory declaration. The owner need only file some evidence of use beyond a bald statement; thus the burden on the registrant is not a heavy one. However, it is nevertheless the responsibility of the trademark owner to describe use of its trademark, in the normal course of trade, in accordance with the requirements of sections 2 and 4. For example, an application for a sound trademark must contain a drawing graphically representing the sound. [See also *Guido Berlucchi & C. S.r.l. v. Brouillette Kosie Prince*, 2007 FC 245.]

Once the evidence of use is filed, the requesting party is limited to the filing of arguments, as it cannot itself file evidence or proceed with a cross-examination of the affiant. If no evidence of use is filed, or if the evidence fails to demonstrate use or to justify the absence of use in the relevant period, the trademark will either be expunged from the register or, alternatively, the scope of the existing trademark registration could be restricted to certain wares or services for which the evidence of use has been held sufficient by the Registrar.

Proceedings initiated under section 45 TMA are not intended to provide an alternative for invalidity proceedings under section 57.

(b) Invalidity

Pursuant to section 18 TMA, a registration is invalid if the trademark (i) was not registrable at the date of registration; (ii) is not distinctive at the time proceedings bringing the validity of the registration into question are commenced; or (iii) has been abandoned. A trademark is also invalid if the applicant for registration was not the person entitled to secure the registration. However, pursuant to subsection 17(2) and in proceedings initiated after the expiration of five years from the date of registration, no registration shall be expunged or held invalid on the ground of previous use or making-known, unless it is established that the person who adopted the registered trademark did so with the knowledge of that previous use or making-known.

In addition to the invalidity grounds set forth in section 18 TMA, other non-statutory grounds have been recognized by the courts, such as fraudulent or material misrepresentation made for the purpose of registration [see *Andres Wines Ltd. v. E. & J. Gallo Winery* (1975), 25 C.P.R. (2d) 126 (F.C.A.)] or invalidity based on the functional character of a trademark [see *Remington Rand Corp. v. Philips Electronics N.V.*, (1995) 64 C.P.R. (3d) 467 (F.C.A.)].

In accordance with section 57, the Federal Court has exclusive jurisdiction to order that an invalid registration be struck from the register. However, no person is entitled to initiate proceedings that would question any decision from the Registrar or from which a right to appeal would lie.

Proceedings initiated pursuant to section 57 are brought by application before the Federal Court either by filing of a notice of motion, by counterclaim in an infringement proceeding, or by statement of claim in an action claiming additional relief under section 58. For such an application to be successful, the registration at issue must be in good standing at the time of the hearing. Once a registration is voluntarily abandoned by its owner or expunged, the Federal Court no longer has the jurisdiction to declare the registration invalid. The burden is on the applicant to demonstrate that the registration is invalid. In accordance with subsection 17(1), the applicant requesting a declaration of invalidity based on its prior rights must also demonstrate that it had not abandoned its own trademark at the date of advertisement of the respondent's application for registration of a trademark.

6. Licensing

(a) What constitutes use under license

Most franchisors will readily admit that one of the most important and valuable assets of the franchise system is the name or other trademarks used to distinguish their business from others. Part of the value attributable to these trademarks is, of course, the ability to trade under these words and symbols without fear that others can use the same or a similar name or design, the effect of which would tend to confuse the public and diminish goodwill.

Under Canadian law, the validity of a trademark is partially based on distinctiveness, and thus a given trademark should direct the consumers to a single source. However, it is common for a trademark owner to capitalize on the goodwill attached to its trademark by licensing its use to third parties.

In accordance with section 50, the use, advertisement or display of a trademark by a licensee is deemed to have the same effect as such use, advertisement or display of said trademark by its owner, provided that:

- the licensee is licensed by or under the authority of the owner of the trademark; and
- the owner maintains, under the license, direct or indirect control of the character or quality of the wares or services associated with the trademark.

Contractual control "on paper"—i.e., the right to exercise control pursuant to the franchise agreement—is not sufficient to meet the control requirement set forth above. The owner must actually exercise control over quality or character of the wares or services associated with the trademarks and take steps to do so.

Standards should be established and their compliance must be enforced. If proceedings are instituted to dispute the exercise of actual control, proper records of the various control mechanisms and inspections to ensure compliance with the standards would prove helpful, if not essential.

Unless proven otherwise, if public notice is given of (i) the fact that the trademark is used under license and (ii) the identity of the owner, a presumption arises that the trademark is used under license from the owner and that the latter has control over the character or quality of the wares or services associated with the trademark (Subsection 50(2)).

Interestingly, the TMA does not require that the license be in writing. However, prudent practice dictates that such licenses should always be in writing, and a franchise agreement is probably one of the most complex and extensive manifestations of such a license. It is also possible for franchisors to use a separate trademark license agreement in conjunction with their franchise documentation. This approach is, however, generally used only where the trademark owner is a distinct and separate entity from the franchisor.

Most franchise agreements should, when properly drafted, comply with all of the requirements for licensing under the TMA, thereby ensuring continued maintenance of the owner's trademark registrations.

For example, franchise agreements used in Canada should require the franchisee to give notice to the public of the franchisor's ownership of the licensed trademarks with a provision in their franchise agreement, such as the following:

> Affixing of Notice—Whenever the franchisee uses any of the licensed trademarks, the franchisee will, as requested by the franchisor, place such notices, mentions, or inscriptions as are determined by the franchisor to the effect that the licensed trademarks are the property of the franchisor and the franchisee uses the licensed trademarks strictly under license and only in its capacity as licensee.

Typically, a well-drafted franchise agreement will provide the franchisor with direct or indirect control of the character and quality of the wares or services offered by the franchisee/licensee in association with the trademarks. While these provisions can be of varying complexity and deal with a number of other related issues, the following is an example of a basic provision establishing the required control:

> The franchisee agrees to sell such products and items, and only such products and items, as meet the franchisor's uniform standards of quality and quantity, that have been prepared in accordance with the franchisor's methods and techniques for product preparation, and as are expressly approved in writing by the franchisor for sale by the franchisee.

When drafting trademark-licensing provisions, franchisors should also be aware of the rule set out in subsection 50(3) TMA: In the absence of an agreement to the contrary between the owner and the licensee, the licensee may force the owner to take proceedings for infringement of the licensed trademarks. If the owner refuses or neglects to do so within two months after being so requested, the licensee is authorized to institute proceedings for infringement in the licensee's own name as if the licensee were the owner, making the owner a defendant.

As a result, it is common to include a waiver by the franchisee of this statutory right, so as to reserve to the franchisor the decision as to whether it is advisable to institute proceedings for infringement.

Practice Note

Inspection reports relating to a franchised business should contain a specific reference to control of the quality or characters of the wares or services offered by the franchisee.

(b) Marking requirements

Unlike in the United States, no statutory provision in Canada expressly requires the use of trademark notices such as ® or TM. However, for a number of reasons, the use of such notices is highly recommended, especially when trademarks are used under license.

As mentioned earlier, where public notice is given of the identity of the trademark owner and of the fact that the trademark is used under license, then the use is deemed to be under the control of the trademark owner. For the owner to benefit from this presumption, proper marking of the wares or services associated with the trademark is required.

Proper marking is also helpful in informing consumers of the use of words or design elements, for example, as a trademark.

As there are no specific marking requirements in Canada, trademark owners or licensees may choose various forms of trademark notices depending on the nature of the use, aesthetic concerns, or packaging sizes and modes, per example. This being said, care should be exercised so that proper marking symbols, such as ®, TM, or *, with a suitable notice identifying the owner of the trademark, and, as the case may be, the licensee information, appear at least once on labels, packaging, or in advertising material on which the trademark is displayed.

In case of licensed use, language such as "used under license," "used with permission," "licensed use" or "licensed user" are commonly used and accepted.

Practice Note

In order to give notice to the public regarding trademark ownership, it is highly advisable to include a notification, which can include the symbol ™ (if the trademark is not registered) or ® (if the trademark is registered), or their French equivalents, ᴹᶜ or ᴹᴰ.

(c) Intercompany licenses

Many franchisors have chosen, either upon their creation or subsequently, to "isolate" their valuable trademarks from their franchise operations by assigning them to a distinct entity, often a holding company with no other assets or activities. In this case, it would be highly advisable for the owner of the trademarks to enter into a license agreement with the franchisor, despite the fact that the two companies are related. In fact, the absence of a valid license to use the trademark may jeopardize its validity.

As mentioned earlier, section 50 does not expressly require a written license; however, recent doctrine and case law establish that it is, in fact, highly advisable to reduce the license to writing. Firstly, in order for the use by another person to be deemed in compliance with the TMA, the owner of the trademarks has to prove the existence of a license. Secondly, the owner must prove that it has complied with the control requirement.

Absent a written agreement, providing satisfactory evidence of the existence of a license may be extremely difficult. For example, the mere fact that the licensee is a wholly-owned subsidiary of the owner was determined in *MCI Communications Corp. v. MCI Multinet Communications Inc.*, (1995) 61 C.P.R. (3d) 245 (T.M.O.B.), to be insufficient to establish the existence of a valid license and of control. Also, neither share ownership nor the fact that the president of both the owner of the trademarks and the licensee is the same individual will satisfy the control requirements of the TMA. The mere fact that the registrant can control the use by the licensee would similarly not appear to be sufficient to establish validity. [See *Dynatech Automation Systems Inc. v. Dynatech Corp.*, (1995) 64 C.P.R. (3d) 101 (T.M.O.B.). See also Rowden, Cynthia and Bereskin, Daniel, "Control Remains Vital in Trademark Licensing," *Intellectual*

Property, Volume II, No. 2, 1995, p.66. For a decision to the contrary, see *Petro-Canada v. 2946661 Canada Inc. et al.*, (1998) 83 C.P.R. (3d) 129 (F.C.T.D.).]

In *Unitel Communications v. Bell Canada,* (1995) 61 C.P.R. (3d) 12 (F.C.T.D.), the Federal Court found that Bell was not in a position to control the quality of the services rendered in association with its trademark. As a result of Bell's inability to prove the existence of a license in the absence of a written agreement, and given the lack of control by Bell over the use of its trademark, its trademark was expunged.

Practice Note

Licensing arrangements between related entities should be in writing, otherwise the validity of the trademark may be jeopardized.

The importance of control has been strongly emphasized. However, this rule may raise vicarious liability issues, as we have recently seen in the United States in the labour and employment context. At some point, one could attempt to claim that enforcing standards and requirements with respect to the quality of wares and services is tantamount to controlling the business itself. Franchisors should be careful not to cross this fine line, which could trigger product and civil liability for the acts of the franchisee.

7. Upcoming Changes to the Trade-marks Act

In addition to the changes implemented by the Counterfeit Products Act with respect to counterfeiting and the international trade in counterfeit products, the major amendments to the TMA introduced through Bill C-31 will result in a fundamental change to Canadian trademark law and practice.

On June 19, 2014, Bill C-31 received royal assent to become law. However, full implementation of the bill is subject to the adoption of accompanying regulations, which is expected to occur by 2018 at the earliest. Until then, the current TMA and current Canadian practice will remain in effect.

Among the various amendments of note introduced by Bill C-31, the following changes are expected to have a significant impact on trademark owners:

- *Important changes to use requirements*: Under the current regime, a trademark registration can only be obtained if the applied-for trademark has been used in Canada or otherwise used and registered abroad. Bill C-31 provides that use will no longer be a requirement for registration in Canada. When filing an application for registration of a trademark, it will no longer be necessary to state whether the trademark has been used or is proposed to be used and to indicate the date of first use of the trademark in Canada when applicable. No declarations of use will be required prior to registration.

- *Implementation of the Nice classification system*: Although applicants will still provide a statement of wares and services in ordinary commercial terms, they will also be required to classify these wares and services according to the Nice classification. Practitioners believe that the adoption of the Nice classification will most likely translate into pay-per-class filing fees, although this will only be known with certainty once the Regulations under Bill C-31 are adopted.
- *New and broadened definition of trademark*: In addition to a change to the statutory spelling of the word "trademark" (which has lost its hyphen), the new and improved definition will include any "*sign or combination of signs* that is used *or proposed to be used* by a person for the purpose of distinguishing or so as to distinguish *their goods* or services from those *of* others." A "Sign" is defined in the bill as including "*a word, a personal name, a design, a letter, a numeral, a colour, a figurative element, a three-dimensional shape, a hologram, a moving image, a mode of packaging goods, a sound, a scent, a taste, a texture and the positioning of a sign.*" This will eliminate some uncertainty surrounding the ability to register some of these items as trademarks in Canada.
- *Reduced term of registration*: The renewal term will be shortened to 10 years (whereas the current TMA provides for a renewal term of 15 years).
- *Divisional applications*: Applicants will be able to divide an application in order to obtain registration for certain wares and/or services while leaving others pending, which could be helpful when facing objections at the examination stage or during opposition proceedings.

Public consultation on regulations and proposed changes to fees will be held before Bill C-31 is fully implemented. The publication of the draft regulations is being closely monitored by trademark practitioners throughout Canada but is not expected before the end of 2017 at the earliest.

8. International Treaties

Since June 29, 1951, Canada has been a member of the International Union for the Protection of Industrial Property (Paris Union). This Union was formed under the *International Convention for the Protection of Industrial Property* (Convention) in order to protect industrial property, such as trademarks, trade names, service marks, industrial designs, indications of source or appellation of origin, and the repression of unfair competition. In essence, the Convention provides for equal treatment of nationals and residents of the signatory countries and a certain priority of registration.

The Canadian Government's stated intent in adopting the recent amendments to the TMA introduced by Bill C-31 is to align Canada's regime with international best practices and to ensure consistency with the provisions of the Madrid Protocol, the *Singapore Treaty on the Law of Trademarks* concluded on March 27, 2006, and the Nice Agreement. Implementation of these treaties will be enacted by the upcoming regulations.

The TMA acknowledges the Paris Union in the definition section of the Act; however, it does not form part of the law in Canada. [See *PharmaCommunications Holdings Inc. v. Avenicia International Inc.,* 2009 FCA 144 at 167–172, and *P. Jadow and Sons Inc. v. Gruppo Cyanomex* SA, unreported, October 27, 1992, Fed. CT. T-2729-89 at 25.]

On January 1, 1996, Canada enacted the *World Trade Organization Agreement Implementation Act*, S.C. 1994, c. 47, which extends reciprocal protection under the TMA and the *Copyright Act,* R.S.C. 1985, c. C-42 (discussed below) to member countries of the World Trade Organization.

C. Domain Names

1. Registration of .ca Domain Names

The Canadian Internet Registration Authority (CIRA) is the organization responsible for the management, control and operation of the .ca registry.

In order to register a .ca domain name, the registrant must comply with the Canadian Presence Requirements for Registrants, Version 1.3 (CPR). Although the CPR includes a connection to Canada, it nevertheless enables a broad group of persons or entities to register a .ca domain name.

Amongst others, Canadian citizens, permanent residents and corporations under the laws of Canada (or any province or territory) are entitled to register a .ca domain name.

The owner of a trademark registered under the TMA is also entitled to register a .ca domain name provided, however, that the domain name consists of or includes the exact word component of that registered trademark (Subsection 2(q)).

The registration of domain names by trademark owners constitutes a useful tool to protect the goodwill associated with said trademark and will be of assistance in preventing infringing use by third parties. As such, trademark owners should verify the availability of .ca domain names consisting of, or including, any component of their trademark once it is registered.

2. Domain Name Disputes and Resolution

CIRA provides .ca domain name owners with a forum where clear cases of bad-faith registrations can be dealt with quickly and inexpensively. The Domain

Name Dispute Resolution Policy (CIRA DR Policy) set forth the terms and conditions relating to dispute resolution. Any complaint filed under the CIRA DR Policy is also subject to the application of the CIRA Dispute Resolution Rules. As such, the CIRA DR Policy is not intended to cover disputes relating to competing rights and is not meant to deal with trademark infringement or passing-off, per example.

Eligible complainants must meet the CPR requirements (including being owners of a trademark registered under the TMA).

Several grounds are available to a complainant alleging the registration in bad faith of a .ca domain name. One of the grounds referred to at par. 3.1 of the CIRA DR Policy is the registration of a .ca domain name by a registrant that is confusingly similar to a trademark owned by the complainant. To support such an allegation, the complainant's trademark must have been registered under the TMA prior to the date of registration of the contested domain name, and the complainant must continue to have rights in the trademark.

For a domain name to be held confusingly similar, it has to so nearly resemble the complainant's trademark in appearance, sound or suggested ideas as to be likely to be mistaken for the trademark (par. 3.3, CIRA DR Policy). The onus is on the complainant to demonstrate that the domain name is confusingly similar to a registered trademark and that such domain was registered in bad faith in accordance with the requirements of paragraph 3.5 CIRA DR Policy. The complainant must also provide some evidence that the registrant had no legitimate interest in the domain name.

If the complaint is allowed by the panel in charge of rendering a decision, the .ca registration will either be deleted from the register or else transferred to the complainant. However, if the complaint is dismissed and the registrant demonstrates, on a balance of probabilities, that said complaint was filed in bad faith by the complainant, then the panel has the authority to order the complainant to pay up to $5,000 to the registrant in respect of the registrant's costs of responding to the proceeding.

II. Copyright

A. Copyright Act

Copyright law is a statutory creation within the exclusive jurisdiction of the federal government of Canada and is governed by the *Copyright Act*, R.S.C., 1985 c. C-42 (Copyright Act). The purpose of copyright law is to protect authors, in the broad sense, who create original works, whether they be literary, artistic, dramatic or musical.

1. Scope and Term of the Right

(a) Definition of copyright

The Copyright Act provides that "copyright" in relation to a work means the sole right to (a) produce or reproduce the work or any substantial part thereof in any material form whatever, (b) to perform the work or any substantial part thereof in public, or (c) if the work is unpublished, to publish the work or any substantial part thereof. It also includes the sole right (a) to produce, reproduce, perform or publish any translation of the work, and (b) in the case of a computer program that can be reproduced in the ordinary course of its use, other than by a reproduction during its execution in conjunction with a machine, device or computer, to license the computer program, as well as to authorize any such acts (Subsection 3(1)).

(b) Types of works

For the purposes of the Copyright Act, in addition to sounds, choreographic and cinematographic works, the definition of "work" includes books, magazines and other similar written materials, drawings, plans, computer programs, musical compositions and photographs. In order for a given work to benefit from copyright protection, it must be original (Subsection 5(1)).

In the franchising context, operations manuals, standard plans and specifications, menus, advertising materials, catalogues, proprietary software and websites would in most cases qualify as a "work" under the Copyright Act.

(c) Criteria of originality

In *CCH Canadian Ltd. v. Law Society of Upper Canada*, 2004 SCC 13, the Supreme Court of Canada determined what constitutes an "original" work within the meaning of the Copyright Act. According to the Court:

> For a work to be 'original' within the meaning of the *Copyright Act*, it must be more than a mere copy of another work. At the same time, it need not be creative, in the sense of being novel or unique. What is required to attract copyright protection in the expression of an idea is an exercise of skill and judgement. By skill, I mean the use of one's knowledge, developed aptitude or practised ability in producing the work. By judgement, I mean the use of one's capacity for discernment or ability to form an opinion or evaluation by comparing different possible options in producing the work. This exercise of skill and judgement will necessarily involve intellectual effort. The exercise of skill and judgement required to produce the work must not be so trivial that it could be characterized as a purely mechanical exercise.

In this decision, the Court states that copyright protects only the expression or form of ideas, and that originality applies only to that expression or form and not to the idea itself. For example, in the franchising context, two quick-service restaurant manuals can discuss the same concepts—service, speed and quality—but there is no copyright infringement, even if the concepts are quite novel, unless a substantial portion of the author's work is copied.

Finally, in coming to its decision in *CCH Canadian Ltd.,* the Court cited with approval another decision that commented on the policy underlying the Copyright Act:

> The Copyright Act is usually presented as a balance between promoting the public interest in the encouragement and dissemination of works of the arts and intellect and obtaining a just reward for the creator.
>
> The proper balance among these and other public policy objectives lies not only in recognizing the creator's rights but in giving due weight to their limited nature.
>
> As a consequence, "in interpreting the Copyright Act, courts should strive to maintain an appropriate balance between these two goals." [See *Théberge v. Galerie d'Art du Petit Champlain Inc.*, [2002] 2 S.C.R. 336.]

(d) Conditions for subsistence of copyright

The Copyright Act lists certain criteria that must be met in order for copyright to subsist in a work. Specifically, the Act requires that an author, at the time the work is made, must be a citizen or subject of, or a person ordinarily resident in, a "treaty country," or that the work was first published in a "treaty country" (see *Copyright Act,* Section 5. Under the Act, a treaty country is defined as a Berne Convention country, UCC country or WTO member.).

Canada adheres to the Berne Convention (see *Berne Convention for the Protection of Literary and Artistic Works*, signed on the 9th of September 1886, Completed at Paris on the 4th of May 1896, Revised at Berlin on the 13th of November 1908, Completed at Berne on the 20th of March 1914, Revised at Rome on the 2nd of June 1928 and Revised, C.T.S. 1948/22), which essentially attempts to ensure that member countries offer the same protection to authors from other member countries as they would to their own authors.

Canada also adheres to the provisions of the *Universal Copyright Convention* (see Universal Copyright Convention as Revised at Paris on 24 July 1971). This Convention eliminates the requirement for Canadians to register or give notice of their copyright in order to benefit from copyright protection. However, for the reasons described below, it is preferable that the symbol © or the word "copyright," with the name of the copyright owner and year of first publication of the work, appear on the work at an appropriate place. The terms of the Universal Copyright Convention have not been incorporated into the Copyright Act; however, countries that adhere to the Convention enjoy the benefits of the Copyright Act.

(e) Term

Pursuant to section 6 of the Copyright Act, the copyright subsists for a term equal to the life of the author, the remainder of the calendar year in which the author dies, and a period of 50 years following the end of that calendar year.

2. Ownership of Copyright

(a) Ownership and author of a work

In subsection 13(1), the Copyright Act provides that, as a general rule, the author of a work is the first owner of the copyright in such work.

An important exception, discussed below, is where the author made the work in the course of employment. Another exception applies to any photograph, engraving or painting commissioned before the Copyright Modernization Act came into force. Where a painting, plate or photograph was ordered by a third party for valuable consideration before June 29, 2012, the person who ordered this work will be deemed the owner of the copyright, unless otherwise agreed (Subsection 13(2)).

(b) Employees vs. independent contractors

Where the author of a work was in the employment of another person *and* the work was made in the course of employment by that person, in the absence of any agreement to the contrary, the employer will be deemed the first owner of the copyright (Subsection 13(3)). In contrast, an independent contractor retains ownership in the copyright unless a written assignment is given.

The Copyright Act provides that the owner of the copyright in any work may assign the right, in whole or in part, or any interest in the right, by assignment or grant of license. However, to be valid, any assignment or grant must be *in writing* and signed by the owner of the right being assigned or licensed (Subsection 13(4)).

A franchisor who retains the services of another person (other than an employee) should be alert to the need for a written assignment of any copyright. If, pursuant to a service contract or otherwise, an independent contractor develops plans and specifications, an operation manual, proprietary software, a website, menus, or advertising materials, or performs any other work for a franchisor, that franchisor should insist on entering into a written agreement with such person that contains a specific assignment provision, in the franchisor's favour, of any copyright in such work.

In order to avoid any dispute with respect to the status of a person as an "employee" or as to whether the work was created in the course of employment under subsection 13(3), it is common practice to have employees who, by the nature of their job description may create a "work," execute an assignment of copyright as part of their employment contract or on a separate document.

Practice Note

Where an independent contractor creates a work for a franchisor, the contractor retains ownership of the copyright, unless a written assignment is provided by the contractor to the franchisor. Further, employees are also often asked, as a precaution, to sign assignments of the copyright ownership in any work they author or create as part of their employment arrangements.

(c) Assignments and licenses

A copyright owner can assign some or all of its rights. As a result, the owner can limit use to a particular territory or medium (such as print, sound recording or film) and limit the duration. An assignment transfers complete control in the use of the work, subject to moral rights and any limits imposed by the terms of the assignment. In contrast, a license is granted where the owner wants to retain control and is only permitting the licensee to perform certain acts. A franchisor will frequently license the use of its software to franchisees, for example.

(d) Translation and creation of independent work

A franchisor expanding its activities in Canada, and especially in the Province of Québec where French is the dominant language, will eventually either want or be required to translate some of its standard franchise documents, as well as other materials used in its system.

Although the right to translate a work subject to the Copyright Act is a component of the copyright, if the translation is performed by a third party (as is commonly the case), the copyright in the translation would be owned by that third party. Accordingly, the prudent franchisor should enter into a written agreement with the translator containing specific assignment provisions as described above or, if the franchisor entered into a master franchise agreement or an area development agreement with a developer and allocated responsibility for translation to such developer, the franchisor should cause the master franchisee or developer to obtain assignment of the copyright in the translation in favour of the franchisor.

Unless these steps are taken, the franchisor will not be entitled to use the translated work without a license, or after-the-fact assignment from the author, which could turn out to be a very costly outcome.

3. Moral Rights

(a) Right to integrity and association

The Copyright Act creates the concept of "moral rights" (Subsection 14.1(1)). In essence, "moral rights" are the right of an author to the integrity of its work, the right to be associated with the work as its author by name or under a pseudonym, and the right to remain anonymous. The failure to obtain a waiver of such rights means that the author of a work can retain certain rights in regard to the work, and this can negatively affect the copyright owner's ability to exploit the work as they choose.

(b) Assignments and waivers

Moral rights may not be assigned, but may be waived in whole or in part. The mere assignment of copyright does not imply a waiver of moral rights—any such waiver must be explicit and in writing. From a practical standpoint, such waiver will in most cases be included in the copyright assignment provisions described above.

Practice Note

To avoid any dispute as to the future use of a copyrighted work, prudent franchisors will obtain a written copyright assignment with a waiver of moral rights in their favour from anyone involved in the development or translation of a "work."

(c) Term

Moral rights in a work extend for the same term as the copyright. The result is that moral rights exist after the death of the author and can be specifically bequeathed (Subsection 14.2(2)).

4. Registration Process

As previously noted, registration of a copyright in Canada is not a condition precedent to its creation or validity. However, registration is an inexpensive and simple process which may be accomplished by filing the prescribed form with the Copyright Office, and does provide some important advantages. It should be noted that in Canada, the item being copyrighted does not have to be filed. In fact, the Register of Copyrights is evidence of the particulars entered in it, and a certificate of registration is evidence that the copyright subsists and that the person registered is owner of the copyright. This is a useful evidentiary tool.

In addition, in proceedings for infringement of copyright, the plaintiff is not entitled to any remedy other than an injunction if the defendant proves that, at the date of the infringement, the defendant was not aware and had no reasonable ground to suspect that copyright subsisted in the work under review, *unless* the copyright was duly registered at the date of the infringement (Section 53 and subsection 39(1)). In view of these advantages, it would be advisable for a franchisor to register copyright in those documents and other materials that qualify as a "work" under the Copyright Act and that are essential to its system.

5. Prohibited Use and Remedies

(a) Infringement of copyright

A person cannot produce or reproduce a copyrighted work without the owner's permission, unless a specific statutory exception applies. It does not matter if the person is unaware of the copyright in the work and innocently copies it; the act is still an infringement. However, the absence of any wrongful intent may reduce the amount of any damages awarded by a court for infringement.

An infringement occurs only if a "substantial part" of a work is copied. In *Cinar Corporation* v. *Robinson*, 2013 SCC 73, the Supreme Court of Canada considered the best approach to assess whether a "substantial part" had been copied. The plaintiff claimed that the defendant had copied the characters, graphics and story line that the plaintiff developed, in a children's television program. The Court considered the "abstraction-filtration-comparison" approach used in the United States and concluded that while that approach might be useful for some works, it did not lend itself readily to an assessment relating to a television show. Instead, the assessment should focus on whether there has been substantial copying of the plaintiff's work considering the cumulative effect of the copied features.

(b) Exceptions to infringement

As opposed to the law in the United States, where exceptions to a claim of infringement are at the discretion of the courts in the context of fair dealing, in Canada the list of exceptions is found in the relevant statutes. Historically, the fair-dealing exceptions included, among other things, criticism and news reporting where the source of the work is named. In 2012, the Copyright Modernization Act significantly broadened the exceptions to include research, private study and other private uses, education, parody and even mashups, often referred to as the "YouTube exception."

(c) Remedies

The owner of a copyright whose copyright or moral rights have been infringed is entitled to a range of remedies by way of injunction, damages, an accounting of profits, delivery of the infringing items, and other remedies that are or may be conferred by law for the infringement of a right (Subsections 34(1) and (2)). Directors and officers of a corporation can be personally liable for infringement where they knew that the conduct was likely to constitute an infringement (Section 4, Counterfeit Products Act).

Indicating the name of the author on a work may prove very helpful in a copyright infringement case, as it would trigger a presumption that the person whose name is so indicated is the author of such work (Subsection 34.1(1)).

Subsection 38(1) of the Copyright Act creates an interesting remedy in favour of a copyright owner by allowing the owner to recover possession of all infringing copies of his work and of all plates used or intended to be used for the production of infringing copies, as well as to bring proceedings for seizure of those copies or plates before judgment, as if those copies or plates were the property of the copyright owner.

6. Changes to Copyright Law

A significant piece of legislation was assented to on June 29, 2012—namely, the *Copyright Modernization Act*, S.C. 2012, c. 20 (Copyright Modernization Act)—in order to bring Canadian copyright laws up to date.

It expands the activities that are allowable uses of copyrighted works, mostly in relation to personal use and education. However, it prohibits the bypassing of digital locks found on DVDs, software and electronic books, with a few limited exceptions.

Additional modifications to the Copyright Act were introduced in 2014 through the Counterfeit Products Act, as discussed earlier with respect to the TMA (mostly dealing with copyright infringement and the export of pirated copies for specific commercial purposes) and remaining carry-over effects of the Copyright Modernization Act. For example, the Copyright Act, pursuant to the Counterfeit Products Act, provides that "every person commits an offence who knowingly (a) makes for sale or rental an infringing copy of a work or other subject-matter in which copyright subsists; (b) sells or rents out, or by way of trade exposes or offers for sale or rental, an infringing copy of a work or other subject-matter in which copyright subsists; (c) distributes infringing copies of a work or other subject-matter in which copyright subsists, either for the purpose of trade or to such an extent as to affect prejudicially the owner of the copyright; (d) by way of trade exhibits in public an infringing copy of a work or other subject-matter in which copyright subsists; (e) possesses, for sale, rental, distribution for the purpose of trade or exhibition in public by way of trade, an infringing copy of a work or other subject-matter in which copyright subsists; (f) imports, for sale or rental, into Canada any infringing copy of a work or other subject-matter in which copyright subsists; or (g) exports or attempts to export, for sale or rental, an infringing copy of a work or other subject-matter in which copyright subsists" (Section 4, Counterfeit Products Act, amending subsection 42(1) of the Copyright Act by striking out "or" at the end of paragraph (d) and replacing the portion of the subsection after paragraph (d) with paragraphs (e), (f) and (g)).

In addition, section 4 of the Counterfeit Products Act added subsection 42(2.1) of the Copyright Act, which outlines certain criminal remedies for the foregoing offences: "every person who commits an offence under subsection (1) or (2) is liable (a) on conviction on indictment, to a fine of not more than $1 million or to imprisonment for a term of not more than five years or to both; or (b) on summary conviction, to a fine of not more than $25,000 or to imprisonment for a term of not more than six months or to both." Since January 1, 2015, new border enforcement provisions (contained in the Counterfeit Products Act) "allow rights holders to take action against pirated copyright goods before the goods enter into Canada" and ". . . allow Canada to implement its border enforcement obligations under the Canada-Korea Free Trade Agreement and the Canada and European Union (EU) Comprehensive Economic and Trade Agreement" [see Sookman, Barry. *Sookman: Computer, Internet and Electronic Commerce Law* (Toronto: Thomson Reuters Canada Limited) (loose-leaf updated 2015, release 8), Chapter 3.9].

In addition, the Supreme Court of Canada released a decision in 2013 that deals with many facets of copyright law [see *Cinar Corporation* v. *Robinson*, 2013 SCC 73].

III. Other Intellectual Property Rights

A. Industrial Designs

Under Canadian law (see *Industrial Design Act*, R.S.C. 1985, c. I-9), an industrial design consists of any visual feature (shape, configuration, pattern or ornament) which, when applied to a product, gives it a specific appearance. Features that are limited to a utilitarian function cannot be protected. Exclusive right in an industrial design is acquired through registration. Industrial designs are the Canadian equivalent of design patents under the law of the United States.

Industrial designs are valuable assets to their owners insofar as they make manufactured articles appear attractive or distinctive to consumers. Franchisors may be interested in protecting, for example, unique design features of restaurant or store layouts, which would in turn provide them with statutory remedies in case of unauthorized use (*Id.*, s. 11) or infringement (*Id.*, s. 15) by third parties.

B. Patents

Patents are not commonly an issue in franchise agreements, and unlike the Copyright Act, the Canadian *Patent Act*, R.S.C. 1985, c. P-4, requires registration by the inventor in order to grant a statutory monopoly over any new and useful inventions. As patents are issued on a country-by-country basis, an invention that is patented or admissible to being patented in a foreign country (for example, in the United States) is not necessarily deemed to be proper subject matter for protection in Canada, and vice versa.

Business method patents were, for many years, not accepted in Canada. However, in a 2010 matter involving the well-known Amazon "one-click" method to purchase goods online, the Federal Court of Canada (see *Amazon.com, Inc. v. Canada (Attorney General)*, 2010 FC 1011) ordered the patent commissioner to reconsider her rejection of the patent application in light of the claimed invention as a substantive whole. The decision was affirmed on appeal to the Federal Court of Appeal (FCA) [see *Canada (Attorney General) v. Amazon.com, Inc.*, 2011 FCA 328].

The FCA decision was much anticipated by the legal community, as the prevailing view had previously been that business processes or methods were not patentable in Canada, unlike the United States. The FCA held that there was no basis to determine conclusively that a business method should not be patentable subject matter in Canada, and clarified that it is the language of the claim that is important, rather than the underlying concept behind the invention, in making a determination as to patentability. The FCA held that if the claim, which must be read purposively, defines "new, useful and non-obvious subject matter that falls within one of the categories of the statutory definition of 'invention'" (art, process, machine, manufacture or composition of matter), then the claim describes patentable subject matter.

The FCA thus confirmed that business methods can be patentable subject matter and that business methods should be evaluated, in terms of their patentability, in the same manner as inventions. This marked a notable shift in tone from the previous focus on an invention's tangible embodiment. Regrettably, when the Canadian Intellectual Property Office reconsidered and admitted this business process as patentable subject matter, it did not provide reasons. As a result, future decisions of Canadian courts may be required to shed light on the criteria to be used by the patent office for patentable business methods. Nevertheless, franchisors may now give greater consideration to the patentability of their business methods in Canada.

IV. Confidential Information Protection

In Canada, there is no specific statute governing confidential information. The protection of confidential information, including trade secrets, is governed by provincial common law (or civil law, in the case of the Province of Québec).

All types of business information, if confidential, can be protected from unauthorized use and disclosure in Canada, including customer lists, data, business, financial or marketing plans, formulas, recipes, processes, plans and drawings. There are three requirements that must be met in order to establish a breach of confidence [see *Lac Minerals Ltd. v. International Corona Resources Ltd.*, [1989] 2 S.C.R. 574]:

- the information conveyed was confidential;
- it was communicated in confidence; and
- it was misused by the party to whom it was communicated.

The courts will consider whether reasonable measures were taken to maintain the confidentiality (which may include, for example, an obligation by the recipient party to cause its employees to execute a confidentiality undertaking). An action for breach of confidence will not succeed if the information has been shared outside of the organization.

Interestingly, under Article 2088 of the *Civil Code of Québec*, R.S.Q., c. C-64, employees in the Province of Québec are bound not to *use* any confidential information they may obtain in carrying on or in the course of their work; these obligations continue for a reasonable time after termination of employment, and permanently where the information concerns the reputation and private life of another person.

A typical franchise agreement should contain a confidentiality undertaking, as well as an obligation of the corporate franchisee to cause its directors, officers and key employees to execute and deliver the franchisor's standard form of confidentiality undertaking.

CHAPTER 5

The Canadian Franchise Agreement

Darrell Jarvis and Edith Dover

Contents

I. Introduction

With a large majority of Canada's population living close to the border of the United States and given the two countries' similar cultural backgrounds, it is not surprising that Canada is frequently a popular destination for American-based franchise systems. Being part of the North American marketplace also makes Canada an attractive location for franchise systems that have their roots in other parts of the world.

There are a number of differences between the Canadian and the United States marketplace, and a franchisor looking to start up or expand into Canada cannot assume that what works elsewhere will also work in Canada. For example, Canada's population base tends to be spread out, impacting distribution costs. Tax laws are different, and the supply of products can be affected by marketing boards in Canada for such things as poultry and dairy. With this in mind, a franchisor commencing business in Canada must approach expansion with a careful eye to what is unique about Canada.

The backbone of any franchise relationship, wherever the franchise system is located, is the franchise agreement. Franchisors from outside of Canada, as well as franchisors starting up systems in Canada, need to focus attention on the franchise agreement they intend to use in Canada. In preparing for expansion in or to Canada, the franchisor should address some unique issues relating to the laws and practices of franchising in Canada. Whether it is because of the Canadian legal system or simply due to the evolution of different conventions, the reality is that franchise agreements used in Canada differ in some ways from those used in the United States. No matter where the franchise system originated, a franchisor needs to be careful not to adopt, in a wholesale fashion for use in Canada, a franchise agreement drafted for use in the United States or other parts of the world without first considering what changes are necessary or recommended. The advantages of these recommended changes will be weighed against the franchisor's desire to use a standard uniform agreement wherever they franchise. Many franchisors, as they gain in experience in international franchising, learn the dangers of trying to adopt a worldwide precedent franchise agreement. Accordingly, it will always be the case that a foreign franchisor entering the Canadian marketplace should first consider what unique "Canadianization" of the agreement is recommended.

A franchise relationship is often referred to as being similar to a marriage. As in marriage, many unforeseen challenges can arise. Any good franchise agreement will anticipate major events in the relationship and provide solutions in advance to prevent problems from becoming relationship-ending issues. Franchisors want to see their franchisees succeed and flourish. The success of the franchisees will ultimately determine the success and profitability of the system as a whole.

It is not sufficient to focus on the franchise agreement alone. It is important to realize that a series of other documents may be incorporated by reference and are integral parts of the arrangements between the franchisor and the franchisee. Due to some unique ways of carrying on business in Canada, other aspects of the relationship between the franchisor and franchisee need to be considered. For example, because Canadian franchisors have, at least historically, often sought to control the franchised business premises by leasing the premises directly from the landlord and then subleasing to the franchisee, a lease or sub-lease, or an agreement relating to the development and construction of the premises, are important elements in the relationship. In addition, and particularly where the franchisor is the ongoing supplier of inventory to the franchisee, it is common in Canada for the franchisor to take a security interest from its franchisees. Therefore, a security agreement, often called a General Security Agreement, will be included in the standard package of documents that form part of the franchise relationship.

In addition to the franchise agreement, other documents that might form part of a standard package of documents in Canada include:

1. a lease or sublease;
2. a facility development agreement;
3. a general security agreement;
4. a secrecy agreement; and
5. an Independent Legal Advice certificate (mandatory in Alberta).

The franchise agreement will also reflect the business system chosen by the franchisor in its expansion plans. Whether a franchisor chooses to sell franchises directly from its American (or overseas) base, enter into a master franchise or area development agreement, or utilize a Canadian entity (as a wholly-owned subsidiary of the foreign-based franchisor), this will be reflected in how the franchisor contracts with the franchisees.

The structuring of the franchise system is important because, first and foremost, the franchise relationship in Canada is governed by contract. The agreement itself creates a licence for franchisees to market products and/or services utilizing the franchisor's business methods (including the use of the business name, licensing of trademarks and copyright, trade dress, operations manuals, etc.). In addition to the contractual relationship between the franchisor and the franchisee, in six provinces (referred to below) franchise legislation will also impact this relationship. Unlike the United States, Canada does not have a federal law specifically regulating or governing franchising, and any such regulation comes from the provinces, in part as a result of the constitutional division of powers between the federal government and the provinces. While franchise agreements have as an essential component the licensing of the right to use a trademark (which is a matter within the federal jurisdiction), contracts are considered matters of provincial jurisdiction.

When entering into a franchise relationship and drafting a franchise agreement for use in Canada, it is imperative that franchisors comply with applicable provincial franchise legislation. Six provinces currently have franchise legislation: Alberta, British Columbia, Manitoba, New Brunswick, Ontario and Prince Edward Island (these provinces will hereinafter be referred to as the Franchise Law Provinces).

The franchise legislation in the Franchise Law Provinces—specifically, the *Franchises Act, R.S.A. 2000, Chapter F-23* (Alberta), the *Arthur Wishart Act, S.O. 2000, Chapter 3* (Ontario), *The Franchises Act* (Bill 15) (Manitoba), *Franchises Act, Chapter F-23.5* (New Brunswick), *Franchises Act, Chapter F-14.1* (Prince Edward Island) and *Franchises Act*, S.B.C. 2015, Chapter 35 (British Columbia) (collectively, together with all regulations to such Acts, the Canadian Franchise Acts), is similar, including in respect of requirements related to franchise disclosure.

In the Franchise Law Provinces, key considerations include the disclosure obligations and rights of rescission in the event that pre-sale disclosure is not provided (or not provided in the time frame or manner required under the Canadian Franchise Acts), as well as the statutory obligation of good faith and fair dealing. The statutory rescission rights are of greater implication to proper disclosure than to drafting the franchise agreement; however, the duty of good faith and fair dealing is an important consideration in the performance and enforcement of the agreement. More information about the general provisions of the Canadian Franchise Acts can be found in Chapter 4.

What needs to be addressed in the "Canadianization" of the franchise agreement? This is a question often asked of a Canadian franchise lawyer. The answer is, frankly, that it depends on the factual circumstances of the franchise system. This chapter will explore the answers to that question on an issue-by-issue basis.

A. Term and Renewal

The grant of franchise rights is normally for a specific term. It is common in Canada to see an initial term of anywhere from five to ten years, with a longer initial term (e.g., 20 years) seen on occasion, but infrequently. It is almost unheard of for the franchise agreement to be of an indefinite or perpetual term.

Quite often, but not always, a franchisor will offer at least one right of renewal to the franchisee. There is, however, no legal obligation to offer a renewal unless provided for in the franchise agreement. Renewal terms do not have to be for the same length of time as the initial term (nor, for that matter, the same length of time as other renewal terms). In many cases, a franchisee will be required to pay a renewal fee to the franchisor at the time of renewal.

The length of the term should reflect the commercial reality of the franchise relationship. Too short a term and a potential franchisee will not be given the opportunity to amortize the cost of the investment in the business or obtain a reasonable return.

As mentioned previously, the franchisor in Canada has often also been the franchisee's sub-landlord. Therefore, the length of the term is often tied to the term of the lease for the premises from which the franchise will be operated, which also historically has been from five to ten years. Over the past decade, there has been a trend in franchising in Canada away from the practice of the franchisor leasing the premises directly. While franchisors leasing the premises directly still occurs frequently, most of the American franchisors that have expanded into Canada in the past decade have not adopted this practice and instead insist on the franchisee leasing the premises. The main perceived advantage to the franchisor leasing the premises directly is the ability to control the premises and take over the location (under the rights granted to a sub-landlord).

Practice Note

While many Canadian franchisors will lease the business premises and sublease them to the franchisee, there is a trend toward the predominantly American practice of requiring the franchisee to lease the premises directly.

If a renewal provision is to be granted, the franchisor should consider whether performance criteria will need to be met by the franchisee prior to being granted the right to renew. The franchisor may also want the franchisee to sign a new franchise agreement at the time of the renewal. This allows the franchisor to present its franchisees with its then-current standard form of franchise agreement, which has likely evolved since the initial agreement was signed by the franchisee.

If provided for in the original franchise agreement, renewals give franchisors the opportunity to increase royalties and/or advertising fund fees. However, it should be noted that changing the business terms of a franchise relationship is often a controversial topic. A dramatic change in the business terms could be argued as offending the statutory duty of good faith (in the Franchise Law Provinces) and/or the common-law duty of good faith (more discussion on the common-law duty of good faith is covered in Chapter 6). It is foreseeable that in Canada a franchisee will at some point challenge a franchisor's attempt to substantially alter the business terms of the franchise relationship on renewal, on the basis that this is a violation of the franchisor's duty of good faith to the franchisee.

Renewal is often also seen as the chance to require franchisees to update or renovate the franchise location with the franchisor's latest system modifications. Franchisors should note that in Canada, and especially in the Franchise Law Provinces, these requirements may need to be reasonable to accommodate the franchisor's duty of good faith. Renewals being granted by the franchisor can be tied to the franchisee's ability to maintain its lease in the current location.

It continues to be the practice of many franchisors to require a general release of all claims from the franchisee for the period of time up to the date of the renewal, notwithstanding the questionable enforceability of such releases or the ability of franchisors to require them. Such all-encompassing broad and general releases, when given simply as a condition of the consent to assignment of the franchise agreement or the exercise of a right of renewal are now unenforceable, at least with respect to franchises operated in the province of Ontario or under franchise agreements that have adopted the law of Ontario as the governing law of the agreement (*405341 Ontario Limited v. Midas Canada Inc.*, 2010 ONCA 478, 264 O.A.C. 111 (*Midas*), aff'g [2009] O.J. No. 1279, 176 A.C.W.S. (3d) 38 (Ont. Sup. Ct.) and [2009] O.J. No. 4354, 181 A.C.W.S. (3d) 467 (Ont. Sup. Ct.). See also *2176693 Ontario Ltd. v. Cora Franchise Group Inc.*, [2014] O.J. No. 550, 2014 ONSC 600). In *Midas*, one of the conditions of renewing or assigning the franchise agreement was a "general release of any claims and causes of action" against the franchisor. The plaintiffs were members of a class proceeding who objected to the insistence on the releases to the extent that they would, by their terms, cover the claims asserted in their class action. The court held that a release which would have the effect of releasing a franchisee's right to fair dealing under the Arthur Wishart Act or its right to damages for a breach of the franchisor's obligations under the statute would be void. The court distinguished this from an earlier case, *1518628 Ontario Inc. v. Tutor Time Learning Centres, LLC* (*1518628 Ontario Inc. v. Tutor Time Learning Centres, LLC*, [2006] O.J. No. 3011, 2006 CanLII 25276 (Ont. Sup. Ct.), aff'd (12 April 2007) 598/06 (Div. Ct.)), where a true release given in settlement of a dispute for existing, known breaches of the Act, where the parties were represented by counsel in the settlement, was upheld. In this case, the question was whether the franchisee could be compelled contractually to release rights that it has under the Arthur Wishart Act in order to obtain benefits under its franchise agreement. The court held that if the exercise of a franchisee's rights under a franchise agreement requires a release of rights given by the Arthur Wishart Act, the release will, *prima facie*, be void by virtue of Section 11 of the Act, which provides that any purported waiver or release by a franchisee of a right given under the Arthur Wishart Act or of an obligation or requirement imposed on a franchisor by or under the Act is void.

In recent years, many franchisors of the Franchise Law Provinces have continued to require releases as a condition of granting consent to the assignment or renewal of a franchise agreement, perhaps hoping that *Midas* will someday be overturned. Other franchisors continue to require releases, but carve out any claims relating to the breach of obligations under the respective Canadian Franchise Act. In such cases, the release may be characterized as being "to the extent permitted by law."

Before the franchise agreement is renewed, the agreement will often provide that the franchisee satisfy certain preconditions. These can include the following:

- the franchisee is in compliance (and has complied) with the franchise agreement during the initial term (or the immediately preceding renewal term);
- the franchisee agrees to upgrade and modernize the premises to fit current system design requirements;
- the lease for the premises is renewed, or the franchisee agrees to relocate to a new site acceptable to the franchisor;
- the franchisee accepts and agrees to sign the franchisor's then current form of franchise agreement;
- the franchisee agrees to reimburse the franchisor for all reasonable legal fees and other costs and expenses incurred as a result of the franchisee exercising its right of renewal; and
- the franchisee will have executed a release (to the extent permitted by law) of any and all claims against the franchisor as of the date of execution of the renewal agreement (see discussion above).

Unlike the attention that has been paid in state legislation in the United States to renewal provisions, and the obligations of franchisors who choose not to renew a franchise agreement, Canada has no such statutory obligations. In Ontario, with its legislated good faith requirements, it has been decided by the courts, as discussed below, that the duty of good faith does not impose an obligation to renew where there is no contractual right.

In Ontario, the extent of the statutory duty of good faith in negotiating an extension of a franchise relationship was put to the test in *TDL Group Ltd. v. 1060284 Ontario Ltd.* ([2000] O.J. No. 1239 (S.C.J.)), a case involving a Tim

Horton's franchisee. In the *Tim Horton's* case, the franchisor sought an order declaring that the license and sublease agreement it had with the defendant franchisee for a term of ten years would expire in 2000. The agreement had no provision for an automatic renewal, but instead provided the franchisor with an option to offer a renewal. The franchisee argued that the franchisor had an obligation to act in good faith and was therefore required to exercise its right to make a renewal offer.

The court held that the franchisor was under no duty to renew the agreement. The court stated that the principle of good faith prevents a party from exercising in bad faith a right or obligation it already has. However, the principle cannot be used to convert a right into an obligation, that is, to convert an option to renew an agreement into an obligation to do so. Another Ontario court decision, *530888 Ontario Ltd. v. Sobeys, Inc.* ((2001), 12 B.L.R. (3d) 267 (Ont. S.C.J.)), came to a similar decision in concluding that there was no inherent right to require the franchisor to renew.

Historically, under Alberta's initial franchise legislation, a franchisor could not unilaterally terminate a franchise except for "good cause." This same standard of "good cause" also applied to the non-renewal of a franchise. When Alberta's franchise legislation was amended in 1995, this "good cause" requirement for termination and non-renewal was eliminated. Since the amendment of Alberta's franchise legislation in 1995, the Alberta courts have not specifically addressed the duty of good faith in the context of a renewal of a franchise agreement. However, it can be anticipated that the precedent set by the Ontario courts would be given considerable weight in any determination by the Alberta courts.

The result is, if a franchisor determines it does not wish to allow a franchisee the right to exercise a renewal of the franchise agreement that has been contractually granted, this refusal must be looked at carefully in the context of the rights under the franchise agreement itself, the statutory duty of good faith in the Franchise Law Provinces, and the common-law duty of good faith, to the extent it exists in the other provinces and territories of Canada.

B. Territory and Reservation of Rights

Franchise systems in Canada frequently grant exclusive rights to specific geographical territories. Another less common approach is to grant the franchisee the right of first refusal to acquire additional locations within a set territory. If the franchisee does not exercise the right of first refusal, then the franchisor is free to offer such franchises to third parties within that territory. The less a franchisor needs to tie up a territory with one particular franchisee, the more flexibility the franchisor will have in the future to expand the franchise system and exploit a market.

Maintenance of exclusive territorial rights may be based on meeting certain performance targets, such as minimum sales thresholds or other criteria. This is particularly common in franchises for the sale of services or other non–"bricks and mortar" franchise systems where market penetration requires ongoing efforts from the franchisee beyond the operation of a physical location. Without a minimum performance obligation, a franchisee could tie up a significant territory without exploiting it. The franchisor, as a result, would earn no royalties or other ongoing fees and would have no recourse. Therefore, in some cases, the failure to meet performance targets could lead to a default of the franchise agreement or, less severely, the conversion of the territory to non-exclusive status, allowing the franchisor to license other franchisees to operate in the territory or conduct business itself. Performance criteria can also, in some cases, impact the franchisee's right to renew.

It is now typical for the franchisor to reserve the right to exploit alternative channels of distribution, such as Internet sales. A franchisor should be careful to provide for a reservation of such right in its franchise agreement.

The Internet is just one example of a potential territorial issue the franchisor may encounter when granting exclusive territorial rights to a franchisee. Other alternate channels of distribution that the franchisor wishes to explore can also create overlaps. For example, a franchisor may at some point wish to have its products distributed through supermarkets. Without reserving the right to do so, this could conflict with the exclusive territory granted to a franchisee. Another example would be a franchisor's desire to open outlets in non-traditional locations or "captive markets" within the franchisee's exclusive territory. Captive markets are markets that service a defined population, such as a hospital, university or public attraction (for example, a zoo, casino, home improvement store or amusement park). The franchisor may also exclude from the exclusive territory sales to particular customers, such as national accounts supported directly by the franchisor.

Even where exclusivity of a territory has not been granted to a franchisee, alternate channels can still be an issue of good faith and disputed by franchisees as being an encroachment of their market, leading to a reduction of sales. This may arise even if the franchise agreement has reserved to the franchisor the right to exploit such alternate channels. For example, if a franchisor starts to exploit a channel of distribution that is new to the system, and the franchisee in fact suffers a loss of sales, this could be argued as a breach of good faith and fair dealing under the Canadian Franchise Acts, as well as potentially under the common law. It is therefore important in Canada to try to prevent the possibility of a good faith claim of encroachment by reserving as many identifiable channels of alternate distribution as possible, as well as describing other channels that may develop in the future. Even with a carefully drafted provision in the franchise agreement, claims could still arise. One solution in such a situation can be a sharing of the benefits of such additional sales by the franchisor and franchisee.

> **Practice Note**
>
> **The franchise agreement should attempt to anticipate possible alternate channels of distribution and, where appropriate, allocate these rights between the franchisor and the franchisee. Even if addressed, facts could give rise to a claim of encroachment based on the duty of good faith and fair dealing.**

C. Non-competition Covenants

Generally speaking, most franchise agreements will include covenants that restrict competition both during the term of the franchise agreement and following its termination. Public policy concerns with respect to covenants in restraint of trade play an important part in the interpretation of these covenants in Canada. Only reasonable restrictions on trade are permitted, and factors such as geographical restriction, duration of restriction, and degree of restraint will be considered. It is important in Canada to not try to be too far-reaching in these covenants, or the courts may refuse to enforce them.

> **Practice Note**
>
> **Enforcement in Canada of non-competition covenants found in many franchise agreements drafted for use in foreign jurisdictions can be a problem, as they may be found to be too long, too far-reaching, or cover too broad a territory to be enforceable.**

Non-competition provisions that are "in-term" (during the term of the franchise agreement) can be broad and have application potentially worldwide, except in Québec, where there must be a reasonable geographic limitation (this geographic limitation in Québec can be broader in an "in-term" provision than a "post-term" one). Non-competition provisions that arise "post-term" (after expiration or termination of the franchise agreement) must be reasonable, and the courts will take a very strict approach to enforcing them.

A detailed analysis of litigation arising from post-term non-competition provisions as well as a useful practice note on the drafting of non-competition provisions is contained in Chapter 6. Three key elements must be addressed in a non-competition covenant: geography, duration, and scope of the activity to be restricted. The geography element usually requires a consideration of the areas of where the franchisee carries on business, where the franchisor carries on business, and (maybe, but perhaps not in all cases) the areas where expansion is targeted. The duration of the non-competition covenant is also an important consideration, as are the activities being restricted. Generally speaking, non-competition provisions should be drafted so that they will survive for only one or two years following expiration or termination of the franchise relationship. As for the scope of the activities being restricted, a statement of it being "any competing business" may be too broad, so it is better to use ordinary commercial terms relevant to that type of business wherever possible. For example, if the franchise system is a quick-service hamburger restaurant, the restriction should explicitly state if the restricted activity is limited to the sale of hamburgers, as opposed to all fast foods, as opposed to all restaurants. In this example, the narrower the scope, the greater the possibility of enforcement.

Courts are more likely to enforce a non-competition provision if the covenant was negotiated as part of a sale of a business, instead of as a term of a person's employment. Public policy considerations are against unreasonably interfering with a person's ability to make a living; however, when the restriction was agreed upon in the context of receiving a benefit, such as in the sale of a business, the courts are less likely to interfere. Whether the granting of a franchise to a franchisee is more akin to a sale of a business or an employment relationship would be determined by the courts in Canada on the specific facts of each case.

Canadian courts will generally not rewrite a non-competition covenant to make it reasonable and therefore enforceable. However, in some cases a court may delete a section of a non-competition covenant, based on a proper severance clause included in the franchise agreement, as long as the remainder of the non-competition covenant still makes sense. Generally, Canadian courts will not rewrite restrictive covenants (*Attwood v. Lamont*, [1920] 2 K.B. 146 (Div. Ct.), reversed [1920] 3 K.B. 571 (C.A.); *TMI Turf Management Inc. v. R. DeNoble Enterprises Ltd.*, (1994) 54 C.C.E.L. (2d) 165 (B.C.S.C.); *Sterling Fence Co. Ltd. and Chu Wu v. Steelguard Fence Ltd. and Robert Earl Fry*, 1992 CarswellBC 1771 (S.C.) [*Sterling Fence*]; and *Rapid-Med Plus Franchise Corp. v. Elliott* (1992), 44 C.P.R. (3d) 25 (Man. Q.B.)). Chapter 6 explores in detail the leading cases in Canada regarding the enforcement of non-competition covenants.

Accordingly, franchise agreements created for jurisdictions other than Canada may not provide enforceable restrictions on competition and should be reviewed carefully by a knowledgeable Canadian franchise lawyer before use. Franchisors should also keep in mind that as the franchise system changes and evolves over time, the form of the various non-competition covenants to be granted by franchisees may need to be revisited.

Practice Note

Franchisors should have all parties who are to be restricted by non-competition covenants sign the franchise agreement or a separate non-competition agreement. While there have been instances of courts enforcing non-competition covenants against the principal owners of a franchise, or persons relating to a franchisee, it is safer to bind them through contract.

It is important to have all of the parties who are to be restricted by the non-competition covenant sign the franchise agreement or, depending on how the documentation is structured, a separate non-competition agreement ancillary to the franchise agreement. The courts in Canada will generally not allow franchisors to enforce non-competition covenants in franchise agreements where the franchisor is named as a third party beneficiary, but the franchisor is not a party to the agreement (*International Airport Industrial Park Ltd. v. Tanenbaum* (1976), 69 D.L.R. (3d) 1 (S.C.C.); *Datile Financial Corp. v. Royal Trust Corp. of Can.* (1991), 5 O.R. (3d) 358 (Ont. Gen. Div.), reversed in part on other grounds (1992), 11 O.R. (3d) 224 (Ont. C.A.); *Iampen v. Royal Bank* (1987), 79 A.R. 305 (Alta. Master)). For example, say the franchisor wishes to develop its franchise system in Canada using a master franchisee, who then in turn signs franchise agreements with unit-level franchisees. If the franchisor is not a party to these various unit-level franchise agreements, then no privity of contract exists to allow the enforcement of non-competition covenants that might exist in these agreements naming the franchisor as a third-party beneficiary.

To avoid this situation, the franchisor should either be a signatory to each of the unit-level franchise agreements or provide for an assignment of the master franchisee's position under the franchise agreement upon termination, which would then allow the franchisor to enforce the agreements, including the non-competition covenants. Neither is a perfect solution, as being an additional party to the unit level franchise agreement could potentially obligate the franchisor to comply with disclosure obligations under the Canadian Franchise Acts (depending on the location of the unit franchisees), and obtaining an assignment could take several days or weeks to complete and will not assist the franchisor prior to such assignment taking effect.

Practice Note

If the franchisor is not a party to a franchise agreement, such as where there is a master franchisee that signs franchise agreements with unit-level franchisees, and the franchisor wishes to enforce a non-competition covenant against the unit-level franchisee, then the franchisor needs to establish privity of contract with that unit-level franchisee. This can be done either by being a party to the franchise agreement or in some way obtaining an assignment of the master franchisee's position (for example, on termination). It is important to keep in mind that the concept of third-party beneficiaries has not found favor in Canada, and the franchisor cannot expect to enforce such covenants by being named as a third-party beneficiary in a franchise agreement to which it is not a party.

Along with non-competition covenants, the franchise agreement will normally contain covenants restricting the solicitation of employees, contractors, suppliers, other franchisees, and customers. These covenants may be more broadly drafted than restrictions on the franchisee's ability to do business, as these are seen as less of a restraint on a person's ability to earn a living. However, recent employment case law in this area has applied the same concepts as those seen with non-competition covenants: the scope of the non-solicitation of customer or supplier provisions must be reasonable. It is therefore recommended that non-solicitation provisions as they relate to customers or suppliers be reasonable in terms of duration and geography. It is quite usual to see non-solicitation provisions of one to two years depending on the business. Generally speaking, non-solicitation of customers and supplier provisions should focus on those customers or suppliers that the person had material contact with or knowledge of by virtue of the franchise agreement. Where non-solicitation of customers or suppliers are applied on a worldwide basis, courts in Canada are more reluctant to enforce these restrictive provisions, as the individual would not have had dealings with all customers or suppliers across the world. Courts are more inclined to enforce non-solicitation of employee provisions to protect the knowledge base of the business for a reasonable period of time—usually in the one- to two-year period post-employment, in employment law cases. It is also recommended that the persons (customers, suppliers or employees) who are not to be solicited need to be clearly identifiable in the covenant. Without clarity, the courts may not enforce these non-solicitation provisions. Generally speaking, however, courts in Canada are willing to enforce these covenants because they protect the goodwill and the business interests of the franchisor as well as the other franchisees that are part of the franchised system. The theory that underpins enforcement of these covenants is that the franchisee only obtained access to this information and these contacts as a result of his or her previous involvement in the franchise system.

> **Practice Note**
>
> **You can protect your customers, suppliers and employees from being solicited as long as your non-solicitation provision is drafted reasonably, taking into account the duration of the franchise system's business cycle and limited to those individuals the person would have had dealings with during the term of the agreement.**

Obtaining non-competition and non-solicitation covenants is in many ways as important as obtaining financial guarantees from all of the franchisee's principals. Without specifically signing the franchise agreement or separate non-competition agreements, these individuals can argue that there is no privity of contract between themselves and the franchisor, and therefore the non-competition and non-solicitation provisions are likely to be found by Canadian courts to be unenforceable.

D. Initial Fees and Royalty Payments

One of the main provisions that a franchisor will focus on in the franchise agreement is the initial fee and the amount of ongoing royalty fee obligations. The Canadian franchise agreement needs to address what the initial franchise fee will be and when it is payable. New franchisors may be willing to accept that the initial franchise fee be paid over a set period of time. However, other than in the context of new franchise systems, it would be extremely unusual to see the initial franchise fee being paid over a period of time. In some cases, the franchise agreement may provide that the initial franchise fee is refundable in certain limited situations (as discussed below). Generally speaking, the initial fees are meant to compensate the franchisor for the cost of selling franchises and training franchisees, but usually the franchisor will end up charging no more than what the market will bear. In other words, it is difficult to charge a higher initial franchise fee for one pizza franchise if a competing pizza franchise system of similar size and strength in the market charges less.

Normally, the initial franchise fee will be specified as a one-time, non-refundable (in whole or in part) fee that is fully earned upon execution of the franchise agreement for the opportunity granted to the franchisee to establish the franchised business. The initial franchise fee (along with all other amounts owing under the franchise agreement) should state if it is in Canadian or U.S. dollars. A fee stated in U.S. dollars can be problematic for Canadian franchisees whose sales will most likely be made in Canadian dollars. An American-based franchisor will need to decide if charging its standard initial franchise fee in U.S. dollars will be feasible, and if so, who will be responsible for exchanging the funds. More discussion of currency issues is contained in the "Boilerplate Provisions" section of this chapter.

The most common reasons for allowing a full or partial refund of the initial franchise fee are failure to secure a location, failure to complete the training course, or failure to secure adequate financing. It will be up to the franchisor to set out in the franchise agreement how to determine if the franchisee has failed to complete these tasks, and whether the franchisee is entitled to additional attempts to overcome the failure (such as providing a substitute designated manager for training); however, the determination is usually to be made by the franchisor acting reasonably.

Royalty payments are almost always based upon a percentage of gross sales, net of sales taxes (the federal Goods and Services Tax (GST) and any applicable Provincial Sales Tax (PST) or, in the provinces where the two are combined, the Harmonized Sales Tax (HST)). For more discussion of provincial and federal sales tax considerations, see Chapter 1. It is also possible that they will be calculated as a flat fee. Of particular note in Canada is that GST (or HST, as applicable) is payable in most cases on royalty fees, and therefore the franchise agreement should state that GST or HST is to be added on top of the royalty fee. The applicability of GST and HST to royalty payments will depend upon the residency of the franchisor (along with potential withholding tax issues). The tax considerations that surround royalty payments and the charging of initial franchise fees is discussed in more detail in Chapter 1.

The frequency of the payment obligation, whether it is weekly or monthly, along with the date that the payment must be made needs to be specified in the franchise agreement. The trend is toward more frequent payments, and these payments being made by electronic fund transfers. In some cases, the royalty fee calculation, particularly if it is a flat fee, will include a cost of living, or inflation, escalator. If this escalator relates to the Consumer Price Index (CPI), then revisions may be needed to the franchise agreement to reflect that it relates to the CPI in Canada.

The sale of alcohol is regulated in Canada at the provincial or territorial level (British Columbia: *Liquor Control and Licensing Act*, R.S.B.C. 1996, c. 267; Alberta: *Gaming and Liquor Act*, R.S.A. 2000, c. G-1; Saskatchewan: *Alcohol and Gaming Regulation Act*, 1997, S.S. 1997, c. A-18.011; Manitoba: *The Liquor and Gaming Control Act*, S.M. 2013, c. 51, Sch. B.; Ontario: *Liquor License Act*, R.S.O. 1990, c. L.19; Quebec: *An Act Respecting Liquor Permits*, R.S.Q. c. P-9.1; Nova Scotia: *Liquor Control Act*, R.S.N.S. 1989, c. 260; New

Brunswick: *Liquor Control Act*, R.S.N.B. 1973, c. L-10; Prince Edward Island: *Liquor Control Act*, R.S.P.E.I. 1974, c. L-17; Newfoundland and Labrador: *Liquor Control Act*, R.S.N.L. 1990, c. L-18; Yukon: *Liquor Act*, R.S.Y. 2002, c. 140; *Liquor Act*; Northwest Territories: S.N.W.T. 2007, c. 15; Nunavut: *Liquor Act* (*Nunavut*), R.S.N.W.T. 1988, c. L-9). Legislation regulating the sale of alcohol in each province and territory limits the sale of alcohol except by those individuals and entities that have been issued a liquor licence by the provincial/territorial commission responsible for regulating the sale of alcohol in the province or territory. For instance, section 17(1) of the *Liquor Control and Licensing Act* of British Columbia (R.S.B.C. 1996, c. 267) provides that a licensee cannot allow another person to use its licence without first obtaining the approval of the general manager of the Liquor Control and Licensing Branch appointed under that Act.

Franchisors should note that legislation in certain provinces contains restrictions that affect the collection of royalties by franchisors on the sale of liquor by franchisees. For example, section 62 of *The Liquor and Gaming Control Act* of Manitoba (S.M. 2013, c. 51, Sch. B) provides that every licence is only valid if used by the person, and at the premises, named in the licence and "[. . .] shall remain valid only as long as the person [named in the licence] continues to be [. . .] *the only person entitled to at least 80% of the profits from the sale of liquor* [of the premises named in the licence]" [*emphasis added*]. Similarly, section 93(1) and Regulation 719 to the *Liquor Licence Act* of Ontario (RSO 1990, c L.19) provides that if another person other than the licence holder is entitled to receive 15% or more of the gross revenues from the sale of liquor under the licence, the licence holder shall provide the Registrar with a copy of the agreement or details of the arrangement entitling the non-licence holder to proceeds of liquor sales under the licence. However, unlike Section 62 of The Liquor and Gaming Control Act in Manitoba, which states that the licence becomes invalid if the licence holder is not entitled to at least 80% of the profits from the sale of liquor, Regulation 719 to Ontario's Liquor Licence Act appears only to impose a notification requirement where the licence holder is not entitled to at least 85% of the profits from the sale of liquor (so that the licence does not become invalid on account of such fact).

Franchisors should also keep in mind, particularly in granting their approval to a transfer of a franchise, that the sale of a business by a franchisee—in whole or in part, whether by way of an asset sale or share sale, typically triggers requirements under provincial and territorial liquor legislation to notify or obtain the consent of the responsible commission for such sale. Similar requirements often apply in respect of the issuance of shares by a corporate licence holder. The legislation varies quite significantly from jurisdiction to jurisdiction, however, with respect to what level of action triggers the notification or consent requirements. For example, section 15(1) of the *Liquor Act* of the Northwest Territories (S.N.W.T. 2007, c.15) requires that the licence holder obtain approval "[. . .] for any issue or transfer of shares that would result in a shareholder beneficially owning or controlling more than 10% of the voting rights attached to all outstanding shares" of the corporate licence holder. Section 66(2.1) of the Liquor Control Act of New Brunswick stipulates that "where a licensee by sale of shares or otherwise, sells, transfers, assigns or conveys more than fifty per cent interest of the business in respect of which the licence was issued, that licensee and the person who acquires more than fifty percent interest in the business" to provide notification of such in accordance with that Act.

E. Interest Rates

Often franchise agreements will specify rates of interest charged on overdue fees and royalty payments. Franchisors in Canada need to be aware of the fact that s. 347 of the federal *Criminal Code*, R.S.C. 1985, c. C-46, makes usury an offence by providing that anyone who enters into an agreement that extracts an effective annual interest rate exceeding 60% on the credit advanced is committing an offence. While the interest rates charged by franchisors on overdue amounts do tend to be high (often in a similar range to credit cards, from 18% to 30%), in order to discourage the use of the franchisor as an alternative to bank financing, usury laws are not normally issues that need to be of practical concern.

In accordance with section 347(1)(a) and (b) of the Criminal Code, depending on how the offence is prosecuted, the punishment for violation of this provision can be up to five years' imprisonment or can involve a fine of up to $25,000 and/or an imprisonment of up to six months.

Included in the calculation of the annual interest rate are penalties or charges for late payment (*Garland v. Consumers' Gas Co.*, [1998] 3 S.C.R. 112), royalty payments (*Boyd v. International Utility Structures Inc.*, [2001] B.C.J. No. 739 (B.C.S.C.)), administrative or other fees, fines, commission, or any other similar charge or expense for the advance of credit under the agreement.

Where an agreement provides that interest is payable but neither the agreement nor the law fixes the rate of interest, then s. 3 of the *Interest Act*, R.S.C. 1985, c. I-15, provides that the rate will be 5% per annum. Section 4 of the Interest Act provides that an interest rate exceeding 5% per annum cannot be charged unless the agreement expressly states the *yearly* rate or percentage of interest. This contrasts with most American franchise agreements, which provide for monthly interest rates, and therefore requires adjustment to be enforceable in Canada. The primary exception to section 4 of the Interest Act is mortgages on real property.

F. Location, Design and Construction

In the case of retail franchise systems, the success of a business is often significantly affected by its location and the development of its physical premises (for some service-oriented franchise systems, this is obviously less of a consideration if there are no special premises from which the business is to be conducted). The responsibility for finding a commercial lease, entering into that agreement, and renovating or developing the appropriate business premises should be allocated in the franchise agreement. In many cases, especially those agreements that involve a "turnkey operation," the franchisor bears the responsibility for this type of development. This is perhaps more common in Canada, where the franchisor frequently will lease the premises directly and sublease them to the franchisee. American retailers and other franchisors are often surprised, however, at the increased bargaining power of major Canadian landlords and rethink their approach to leasing, including use of landlords' forms of agreements. It is common in Canada for tenants to enter into binding offers to lease with an obligation to further negotiate and execute the landlord's form of lease. This approach strikes American tenants as peculiar, as it further reduces the bargaining power of the tenant. The logical alternative is to insist on proceeding "straight to lease," which not all major landlords will accept.

The prime reason why Canadian franchisors lease the premises directly is so that they can retain better control of the premises. As the rights of landlords in Canada are better established than the rights of franchisors, franchisor/sub-landlords are in a stronger position to default and terminate a franchisee acting as landlord under a sublease than as franchisor under the franchise agreement. The franchisor may then rely upon cross-default provisions in the sublease and franchise agreement to terminate the franchise agreement. Further, in the event the franchise relationship comes to an end, either as a result of the expiry of the term or in the event of a default by the franchisee, the franchisor maintains control of the premises as tenant. Sometimes a Canadian franchisor will utilize a separate holding company to act as the lessee to attempt to reduce the franchisor's exposure under the lease, while still having control over the real estate. The utility in such a strategy can dissipate, however, as the franchisor accumulates more and more leases in the holding company, providing a substantial pool of assets in the event of a claim by a landlord.

Where a sublease is used, a specific standard form is usually prepared by the franchisor as a separate stand-alone agreement while "working with" the franchise agreement. The terms of the sublease must be carefully drafted to protect the interests of the franchisor, with an eye to provisions where default in rent would result in a default of the entire franchise agreement. In addition, both the franchise agreement and sublease would contain "cross-default" provisions for the reasons set out above. A key aspect of the sublease agreement is to deem, or characterize, all payments under the franchise agreement as being "rent," thus providing the franchisor with the remedies available to landlords to seize or sue in the event that the franchisee is in breach of its obligations under the franchise agreement to pay royalties (or any other payment obligation).

Practice Note

Franchisors should include appropriate cross-default provisions in all contracts that are part of the franchise relationship. This will allow for terminating the franchise relationship in the event of a material default under one of the other agreements.

If the franchisor's property strategy involves having the franchisee lease directly from a landlord, the franchisor can seek a covenant from the landlord that if there is a default by the franchisee under the lease or the franchise agreement, then the franchisor has the right to take over the leased premises. In addition, such a default should give the franchisor the ability to terminate the franchise agreement. To achieve this, the franchisor will enter into a tripartite agreement with the landlord and the franchisee. This can require negotiations, and, practically speaking, only some franchisors will invest the time and expense to extract such a covenant from the landlord.

If responsibility for the design and construction of the franchisee's location is the obligation of the franchisee, then specifications typically need to be provided. If the franchisor is responsible for the design and construction, but it is at the franchisee's cost, then the payment terms need to be incorporated into the franchise agreement.

Site selection should also be within the control or approval of the franchisor. Franchisees will often have a specific location in mind, but this must match the franchisor's system criteria, and therefore the franchisor should retain veto power over site selection. Assisting the franchisee in obtaining building permits and authorizations may increase the franchisor's goodwill and help to ensure compliance with the franchisor's plans and specifications for the location; however, unless it is a turnkey location, it is less likely that the franchisor will get involved, and the franchise agreement will specify that the franchisee must obtain all necessary permits and approvals.

The franchisor will often want the franchisee to use suppliers designated by the franchisor for fixtures, furnishings, equipment and signage. For a franchisor new to Canada, its existing suppliers may not be cost-effective, and the franchisor may wish to seek out local suppliers. This may become a necessity if the franchisor cannot import certain items into Canada. For example, any inventory or equipment that is electrical may require Canadian Standards Association (CSA) or Underwriters Laboratories of Canada (ULC) approval. A list of the products for which CSA has developed standards can be found at www.csa.ca.

The CSA develops standards in the following areas: business/management systems, communications/information, construction, electrical and electronics, environment, gas equipment, health care, materials technology, and transportation/distribution. A list of the products for which ULC has developed standards can be found at www.ulc.ca/standards/catalogue_standards.asp. The standards are developed by various ULC committees, including the Committee on Fire Tests (for building materials, assemblies and furnishings), the Committee on Security and Burglar Alarm Equipment and Systems, the Committee on Physical Security Equipment and the Committee on Fittings for Flammable Fuels.

G. Pricing Provisions

Prior to March 2010, section 61 of the *Competition Act*, R.S.C. 1985, c. C-34, made it a "per se" criminal offence in Canada for anyone to attempt by agreement, threat, promise or any like means to influence upward, or to discourage the reduction of the price at which any other person sold a product. This is referred to as "price maintenance." Any policy by a franchisor requiring franchisees to sell products at a particular price, or setting minimum levels that franchisees could not sell below, would certainly have constituted price maintenance under the Competition Act, exposing the franchisor to substantial penalties. It was also illegal to refuse to supply a product to a franchisee because of a franchisee's low-pricing policy or to otherwise discriminate against a franchisee for that reason. A "per se" offence is one in which simply engaging in the conduct is sufficient to commit the offence; the resulting competitive effect of the conduct is irrelevant.

Changes to the Competition Act came into force in March 2010, and as price maintenance is no longer a criminal offence, the penalties formerly associated with price maintenance are now gone. Rather, section 76 of the Competition Act makes price maintenance subject to civil administrative review by the Competition Tribunal based on a competitive effects test. The Competition Tribunal can issue an order to prohibit a company from continuing to engage in the conduct, but has no power to award damages or levy penalties. Private parties that are "directly affected" by the conduct covered by the price maintenance provision can, with leave of the Competition Tribunal, also apply for a remedial order, but they can no longer sue for damages in relation to price maintenance. For more discussion about the Competition Act, see Chapter 3.

1. Unfair Business Practices

Eight of Canada's ten provinces (including Quebec, Saskatchewan, Alberta, Ontario, Manitoba, Newfoundland and Labrador, Prince Edward Island, and British Columbia) have enacted legislation in an attempt to control unfair business practices (Quebec: *Consumer Protection Act*, R.S.Q., c. P-40.1; Saskatchewan: *Consumer Protection Act*, S.S. 1996, c. C-30.1; Alberta: *Fair Trading Act*, R.S.A. 2000, c. F-2; Ontario: *Consumer Protection Act*, 2002 S.O. 2002, c. 30; Manitoba: *The Business Practices Act*, C.C.S.M. 1990, c. B-120; Newfoundland and Labrador: *Consumer Protection and Business Practices Act*, S.N.L. 2009, c. C-31.1; PEI: *Business Practices Act*, R.S.P.E.I. 1988, c. B-7; BC: *Business Practice and Consumer Protection Act*, S.B.C. 2004, c. 2). Generally speaking, the provincial unfair business practices legislation provides the power to provincial authorities to investigate or prosecute unfair business practices and, in some cases, creates a private right of action for an aggrieved consumer. Although the definition of what is considered to be an unfair practice is similar from province to province, the remedies available may vary. For example, under the British Columbia *Business Practices and Consumer Protection Act*, S.B.C. 2004, c. 2, s. 4, there are two types of practices that are prohibited as unfair. First, suppliers are prohibited from engaging in deceptive acts; that is, any conduct or representation that misleads a consumer or guarantor. Second, section 8 of the Act prohibits unconscionable practices by a supplier, which includes exerting undue pressure on the consumer; taking advantage of the consumer's incapacities, infirmities or similar limitations; offering a price that grossly exceeds the price offered in similar consumer transactions; entering into the transaction where there is no reasonable probability of full payment by the consumer; and providing terms to the consumer that are inequitably harsh or adverse to the consumer.

Section 10 of the British Columbia legislation provides that if an unconscionable practice is entered into, the transaction is not binding on the consumer or guarantor. In addition, an action may be brought against a supplier in the Supreme Court for an injunction preventing the transaction. Sections 172, 190 and 192 of the Business Practices and Consumer Protection Act allows the court to grant remedies to the consumer ranging from the restoration of money or property to a fine of up to $10,000 for an individual and C$100,000 for a corporation, with the possibility of an additional payment as compensation to the consumer.

Franchisors need to ensure that their franchisees strictly comply with the provisions of the unfair business practices legislation. This is normally accomplished in the franchise agreement by requiring the franchisee to comply with all applicable laws as well as with the franchisor's system requirements and manuals. Effective field support by the franchisor will also assist in ensuring full compliance.

H. Training and Operating Assistance

In almost every franchise system, a training program for franchisees is an essential element. The franchise agreement should specify how many people from the franchisee's operation will be receiving the training in the central elements of the operation of the franchise system. To protect the quality and consistency of the franchise system products, the agreement should include a provision that the franchisee must complete the training program prior to beginning the business. This is a good place for an escape clause; if the franchisee is unable to complete the program to the franchisor's satisfaction, the franchisor should have the ability to have the franchise agreement "unwound." In some cases, this will result in the franchisor refunding some or all of the franchise fee previously paid by the franchisee. If this is to be the case, it should be specified in the franchise agreement. Usually the refund would be provided in consideration of the franchisee giving a release of all claims to the franchisor.

If training is to take place in a location remote from the franchised business (for example, some systems require training to occur at a centralized facility in Canada, or the franchisor's home jurisdiction outside of the country), then the cost of travel and accommodation should be allocated in the franchise agreement. This is usually specified as an expense of the franchisee.

The franchise agreement should state if the system training is an extra cost to the franchisee. While initial training is often included in the upfront initial franchise fee (although it is not uncommon for an extra fee to be charged), extraordinary training or retraining is usually an extra cost. Practically speaking, the franchisor's right to require the franchisee to retrain is an important method to help police the conduct of the franchisees. The actual cost of the retraining or assistance is usually left to the discretion of the franchisor.

Refresher training is also commonly found in Canadian franchise systems (in some cases, "refresher" and "retraining" are used interchangeably). These programs are usually mandatory, but in some cases franchisors will implement a voluntary refresher training program. These would normally be at the franchisee's cost and be conducted at the location specified by the franchisor.

As well, the level and content of ongoing support from the franchisor should be set out in the franchise agreement, although it is often necessarily left vague and to the discretion of the franchisor as to how much support is required. One of franchisees' chief complaints is a lack of support from "head office." Complaints of this nature can be avoided by adhering to the terms of the contract and, even more important, providing valuable support to the franchisees.

It is in the best interests of the franchise system for the franchisor to provide assistance to the franchisee to keep the system healthy and viable. Items that would often be covered in a franchise agreement with respect to ongoing operational assistance may include:

1. selection, purchasing, stocking, preparation and display of products;
2. training of employees;
3. formulation and implementation of advertising and promotional programs;
4. establishment and maintenance of administrative, bookkeeping, accounting, inventory control and general operating procedures;
5. improvements to the franchise system, including new product and service development;
6. financial advice and consultation; and
7. overall system compliance.

A properly drafted operating assistance clause in the franchise agreement together within an effective field support program can achieve the objective of enforcing system compliance.

I. Advertising Fund

A successful advertising program can elevate a franchise system's brand awareness, increase traffic and sales to its franchisees, and improve the profitability of the organization. A poor campaign can leave franchisees upset and can hurt bottom-line profits. Marketing and advertising have a subjective component, and not every franchisee will agree with every advertising campaign. It is important for the strength of the brand that the franchise system maintains consistency in its marketing and advertising. What issues need to be considered, and which provisions should the franchisor consider including in its franchise agreement in regard to franchising?

A fundamental benefit of doing business in a franchise format is the ability of individual units to join forces in marketing their products and services through a combined advertising fund. However, there are pitfalls and hazards to be avoided in joint advertising and marketing programs, and franchisors must be careful in how they set up their system's advertising fund and advertising programs and how these are provided for in their franchise agreement.

1. Establishment of Advertising Funds

It is generally recognized that franchise systems evolve in three different stages through their advertising activities. This evolution often mirrors the franchise system's development from infancy to a fully mature system. In its infancy, the franchisor will often rely upon each of its franchisees to plan and implement local marketing, often with little control by the franchisor. At this stage the franchisor may produce some promotional materials for use by the franchisee and will establish its website. However, the franchisor is generally less involved with the local advertising materials produced by the individual franchisees. The franchisor may temporarily suspend the franchisee's requirement to contribute to the marketing fund in exchange for increased expenditure on local advertising.

As the fledgling franchise system grows, franchisees geographically linked will pool their resources in the form of local advertising cooperatives so that they can collectively buy advertising time and space more efficiently. Often franchisors will insist upon this and may even be involved in its administration. The intention is that by combining resources, franchisees can broaden the scope of their advertising for the same cost, or they can continue to reach the same number of potential customers at a lower cost per franchise unit. For this to be effective, the market must contain a minimum number of franchised units that will be able to benefit from such cooperative activity. Without a critical mass within a defined territory, it will not be seen by individual franchisees as being efficient to pursue cooperative advertising in certain media, such as television, where the costs can be prohibitive. This critical mass may be even harder to achieve in Canada due to its relatively small population being spread out across a large geographic area.

The third stage sees the franchise system creating a centralized advertising fund. This is generally engaged in by more mature systems that want to achieve efficiencies by pooling the resources of the franchisees on a much larger scale and often through the use of more expensive media, such as television. This requires the formal establishment of an advertising fund, which is normally administered by the franchisor with either formal or informal input (but not control) from franchisees. In the event that the franchisor establishes and administers an advertising fund, the franchise agreement should enable the franchisor to make reasonable charges against the fund, such as for a portion of the salary or salaries of the person or people administering the fund and managing or implementing the marketing.

It is important to realize that while three stages are identified, these are not mutually exclusive. Often, (1) a franchise system will utilize a centralized advertising fund for systemwide marketing campaigns, while at the same time (2) local cooperatives will utilize their buying power to produce targeted campaigns within their own territory, and (3) individual franchisees may be required to do their own direct advertising within their community. Some franchise systems, especially mature ones from other countries, may skip stage two entirely and focus primarily on local and national campaigns.

No matter what stage a franchise system may be at, it is important that the franchise agreement anticipate all three of these stages to provide the franchisor with sufficient flexibility and control to effectively run advertising campaigns and utilize centralized advertising funds and/or local advertising cooperatives.

2. Advertising Provisions in the Franchise Agreement

When a franchisor first starts a franchise system, it may have no idea of when it will start using cooperative advertising or when it will establish a centralized advertising fund. While dreaming big, the reality is that even though the franchisor may not know when national or international advertising campaigns will become part and parcel of its operations, it is critically important that the franchise agreement address the issue of advertising and advertising funds.

If the first generation of the franchise agreement does not lay the framework upon which a concrete structure of advertising cooperatives and advertising funds can be built, then the franchisor may find that it lacks the contractual ability to move its franchise system into a more advanced marketing approach in the future. Control and consistency are two fundamental considerations in looking at the provisions of the franchise agreement. It is not unusual for franchisors to later regret the concessions they granted to the "pioneers" of the system, particularly if they relate to unequal contributions to the advertising fund.

U.S. and overseas franchisors need to consider whether they will operate a separate fund for Canadian franchisees and whether advertising fund revenues are to stay in Canada. If they are to be removed from Canada, withholding tax issues may apply (see Chapter 1 for more details on withholding tax issues), and franchisees may be concerned that their contributions are not being focused on their own domestic market.

With respect to local marketing materials created by the franchisee, the franchise agreement should specify that the franchisee assigns all copyright and waives any moral rights to the materials created. The waiver of moral rights is a concept found under Canadian law and is discussed in more detail in Chapter 2. In brief, under the *Copyright Act*, R.S.C. 1985, c. C-42, as amended, S.C. 1997, c. 24, the author of a work retains "moral" rights to the copyrighted work, even after it has been sold or assigned to another person, and even if the author was completing the work under contract. In accordance with section 14.1(1) of the *Copyright Act*, the moral rights of an author relate to the integrity of the work and the right, where reasonable in the circumstances, to be associated with the work as author.

With respect to developing the local marketing provisions of the franchise agreement, the franchisor should consider the answers to the following questions:

- What is the required expenditure on local marketing going to be?
- Will the amount of the local marketing expenditure decrease when a marketing fund, to which the franchisee must contribute, is established?
- Will the franchisor be developing content for local marketing campaigns?
- What level of approval over local marketing will the franchisor engage in, and what is its capacity to do so?
- Will the franchisee be permitted to establish a website? To what extent will the franchisee be permitted or encouraged to engage in social media?

It may be that the franchisor will want ultimate veto over any marketing run by a franchisee, but does not necessarily want to have to make all the decisions about developing local marketing campaigns. In the case of local advertising funds, the franchisor will usually establish a minimum amount to be spent by the franchisee on local advertising. Often the franchisee has the right to conduct the advertising campaign at its reasonable discretion, subject to the franchisor's right to approve all advertisements and marketing material. Franchisors need to keep in mind that many franchisees are by nature entrepreneurial, and to keep them happy, franchisors may wish to give them some control over the running of local marketing campaigns. Advertising funds are a different matter, and the franchisor will exert control over the development, form and content of advertising programs that use an advertising fund. Normally, franchisees contribute a percentage of their gross sales per annum to the advertising fund. It is quite common in Canada for the franchise agreement to dictate the exact percentage or a range (often 2% to 4%), with the franchisor having the discretion to decide from time to time how much to collect. This is a significant expense for franchisees, and it is not uncommon for franchisees to want to have some say over how those advertising dollars are spent.

Each of the Canadian Franchise Acts requires that the disclosure document set out any fees that must be paid by the franchisee, including fees that must be submitted to an advertising fund or "advertising co-operative." Franchise legislation in Ontario, New Brunswick, Manitoba Prince Edward Island and British Columbia prescribes additional information that must be disclosed as part of the disclosure process in respect of the advertising fund (see: O. Reg. 199/05, s. 6; N.B. Reg. 2010-92, Sch. A, Part 3, s. 9; Man. Reg. 29/2012, Sch. A, s. 15; P.E.I. Reg. EC 232/06, Sch. I, Part 3, s. 8; and B.C. Reg. 238/2016, Sch. s. 15). The Ontario, New Brunswick and Manitoba Regulations require franchisors to specify the percentage of the advertising fund that has been spent on national campaigns and local advertising in the two years immediately preceding the date of disclosure. Prince Edward Island's and British Columbia's regulations do not provide for this disclosure requirement. A franchisor therefore must ensure that it can track and account for advertising fund monies collected and spent.

The legislation in Ontario, New Brunswick, Manitoba and British Columbia require the franchisor to disclose whether it will provide reports to the franchisee on the franchisor's use of the advertising funds. Franchisors may commit in the franchise agreement to prepare statements accounting for the use of advertising funds in any given year, but there is no legal obligation to do so. Franchisors should always maintain the advertising fund as a separate account from their general operating accounts. This will enable them to track the funds and provide a proper accounting to the franchisees. Sometimes the franchisor will explicitly disclaim that the funds are held in trust, and invariably the franchisor will not want to be found to have fiduciary responsibilities regarding these funds.

While a fledgling franchisor often feels that it wants to maintain full control over marketing in its system, a wise franchisor will also listen to its franchisees. Even with extensive marketing departments and expert advice from outside advertising agencies, franchisees will have unique observations and perspectives on their local market conditions. Franchisors should seek the advice from their franchisees, and many franchisors will appoint a franchisee advisory panel to help advise on the expenditure of marketing fees. These franchisee advisory panels will normally only be able to make recommendations, and the final decision on expenditure of marketing funds will be that of the franchisor.

Frequently franchisees will complain that they are not being treated equally in advertising campaigns instituted by the franchisor. This can happen especially when there is a much smaller number of franchisees in one part of the country versus another. For example, if a franchise system has 50 units in Ontario, 10 in Alberta and 4 in British Columbia (with both Alberta and British Columbia being in the west), the franchisees in Western Canada may not agree with a franchisor's decision to spend most of its advertising dollars in Ontario. The exact opposite can also occur: it could be the Ontario franchisees that are upset that a lion's share of the advertising fund is spent in Western Canada by the franchisor trying to grow that part of the franchise system. Ultimately, it is impossible to satisfy everyone. This is frequently an issue in Canada due to the way the population is spread out geographically.

The franchise agreement usually attempts to address this by stating that the advertising fund is intended to maximize the general public recognition and patronage of the franchise system for the benefit of all units and the system, and that the franchisor has no obligation to ensure that any particular franchisee benefits directly or pro rata from the placement or conduct of such advertising and promotion. Even with this provision, it is not uncommon for a franchisee to complain about the direction of the marketing campaign or that the advertising fund is not being spent in an efficient or effective manner.

Practice Note

Complaints about how a centralized advertising fund is spent is a frequent issue for Canadian franchisees particularly as a result of Canada's population base being spread far apart, with distinct larger pockets of population. Franchisors should insert in their franchise agreements a statement that the advertising fund is intended to maximize the general public recognition and patronage of the franchise system for the benefit of all units and franchisees in the system and that the franchisor has no obligation to ensure that any particular franchisee benefits directly or pro rata from the placement or conduct of such advertising and promotion.

Many franchisors choose to compensate themselves for advertising-related overhead expenses at the head office. This right must be provided for in the franchise agreement, and the percentage retained for this purpose must be disclosed to prospective franchisees in disclosure documents required in Manitoba, Ontario and New Brunswick (see: O. Reg. 199/05, s. 6; N.B. Reg. 2010-92, Sch. A, Part 3, s. 9; and Man. Reg. 29/2012, Sch. A, s. 15).

J. Intellectual Property Protection and Confidentiality

At the core of all franchising is the licensing of a brand name and trademark. It is not surprising, then, that the provisions of a franchise agreement that relate to intellectual property protection are critically important. An analysis of Canadian trademark, trade secret, patent and copyright law is contained in Chapter 2, but some key points need to be understood when considering what provisions should be included in the franchise agreement.

A franchise system includes a variety of intellectual property rights, bundled together. These can include: copyrighted materials (i.e., training manuals), products, the appearance of retail sales premises (trade dress), trade secrets, trademarked names, and patented processes or equipment. Intangible property rights are some of the most valuable aspects of a franchise.

A non-disclosure and confidentiality clause should be included in the franchise agreement relating to the franchisor's intellectual property. This will bind the franchisee and, if properly drafted, will further bind any guarantors or principal owners of the franchisee. In addition, though, any key or critical information which employees are privy to as a result of their work with the franchise must also be protected by a confidentiality agreement. As employees will generally not be parties to the franchise agreement, the franchisor should include a covenant that the franchisee will obtain signed confidentiality agreements from all employees (in the form provided by the franchisor) prior to the disclosure of any confidential information.

On account of the confidential information that a franchisor will be disclosing to a prospective franchisee pursuant to the disclosure document, franchisors are often eager to protect such information by way of having the prospective franchisee execute a non-disclosure or confidentiality agreement. Each of the Franchise Law Provinces other than Ontario has recognized the value of such an agreement at the disclosure stage through their applicable franchise legislation.

Section 5(1) of the *Arthur Wishart Act* in Ontario states that the "[. . .] franchisor shall provide a prospective franchisee with a disclosure document and the prospective franchisee shall receive the disclosure document not less than 14 days before the earlier of the signing by the prospective franchisee of the franchise agreement or *any other agreement relating to the franchise* . . ." [*emphasis added*]. The same section also restricts payments relating to the franchise from the prospective franchisee (or anyone on behalf of the prospective franchisee) to the franchisor or the franchisor's associate during this 14-day period. Franchise lawyers in Canada have typically interpreted this provision to include confidentiality and non-disclosure agreements, meaning that prospective franchisees are prohibited from entering into any such agreements prior to the expiry of the 14-day period referenced at Section 5(1) of the Arthur Wishart Act.

As mentioned above and subject to the restrictions in this paragraph, the Franchise Acts in each of Prince Edward Island, Alberta, New Brunswick, Manitoba and British Columbia specifically permit franchisees to enter into confidentiality or non-disclosure agreements at any time, including during the initial period following disclosure. Each of these Franchise Acts contain a carve-out from the provisions restricting franchisees from executing a franchise agreement or related agreements prior to or during the disclosure period; this carve-out applies to agreements that relate solely to "keeping confidential, or prohibiting the use of, any information or material that may be provided to the prospective franchisee." Each of the Franchise Acts also includes a carve-out for agreements that only have terms designating a location or territory for a prospective franchisee (Section 5(12)(a) of the Franchises Act (Manitoba), Section 5(9)(a) of the Franchises Act (Prince Edward Island), Section 4(7)(b) of the Franchises Act (Alberta), Section 5(11)(a) of the Franchises Act (New Brunswick) and (Section 5(11) of the Franchises Act (British Columbia)). However, in order to rely on the exemption that allows these types of agreements to be executed prior to and during disclosure, the confidentiality or non-disclosure agreement must not: (A) prohibit the disclosure of information to: (i) an organization of franchisees; (ii) the franchisor's other franchisees of the same system; or (iii) the franchisee's professional advisors, or (B) require that information be kept confidential or prohibit the use of information: (i) that is in or comes into the public domain without breaching the agreement; (ii) that is disclosed to any person without breaching the agreement; or (iii) that is disclosed with the consent of each of the parties to the agreement (Section 5(13) of the Franchises Act (Manitoba)). In the event that the agreement's terms violate either (A) or (B), the agreement will be deemed by the franchise legislation in Manitoba, Prince Edward Island, New Brunswick and British Columbia (but not Alberta) to be a franchise agreement or any other agreement relating to the franchise (Section 5(13) of the Franchises Act (Manitoba); Section 5(12) of the Franchises Act (New Brunswick); Section 5(10) of the Franchises Act (PEI) and Section 5(12) of the Franchises Act (British Columbia)).

Operation and system manuals setting out standards and procedures are protected by copyright and may also need to be protected as a trade secret. The franchise agreement should state that the franchisee acknowledges that the manuals are the property of the franchisor (often a franchise agreement will characterize them as being "on loan" to the franchisee) and are to be returned to the franchisor (together with any copies made) immediately upon termination or expiry of the term of the agreement. The franchisee should also be required to keep the manuals confidential. The franchisor may add, modify or replace the manuals at any time at in its sole discretion. Typically, the cost of implementing any such system changes will be covered by the franchisees.

U.S. and overseas franchisors should realize that the contents of the manuals may need to be amended in order for the contents to be appropriate for operating the franchise business in Canada. For example, measurements may need to be converted to the metric system for recipes, and Canadian sales taxes may need to be taken into consideration in accounting requirements. These are but two examples, and there can be many more depending on the franchise system.

K. License to Use Trademarks

As trademarks are such a fundamental aspect of the franchised business, the provisions relating to them in the franchise agreement are normally non-negotiable and also normally not controversial from a franchisee's perspective. The grant of a right to utilize the trademark(s) should be restricted to their use in connection with the franchised business. The trademarks should be identified in the agreement, but they can also include any additional trademarks owned by the franchisor and designated by it during the term of the franchise agreement.

It is important for franchisors expanding to Canada not to assume that their trademarks are available for use in Canada. Checking and securing trademarks is a critical first step to take before expanding to Canada. For more discussion of securing trademarks for use in Canada, see Chapter 4.

From the franchisor's perspective, controlling its trademarks by way of license preserves the value of the franchise system itself. Control is also a requirement under the *Trade-marks Act*, R.S.C. 1985, c. T-13, s. 40(2); otherwise, an owner can lose its rights to its trademarks. From the franchisee's perspective, the right to use a trademark under license will be an essential component of its business success. The customer's ability to distinguish it from other similar businesses, or the trademarked characteristics of the franchise system, adds value to the franchisee's business.

The concept of "service marks" does not exist under Canadian trademark law. The equivalent is referred to only as a "trademark.". While many American franchise agreements will routinely refer to "trademarks" and "service marks" references in a Canadian franchise agreement should only be to "trademarks." A trademark in Canada may be registered for use in association with wares and/or services.

Generally, the rights granted under the franchise agreement to use the trademark will be subject to the following restrictions:

1. The right to use the trademark is subject to continued compliance with the terms of the provisions of the trademark sections of the franchise agreement.
2. Any unauthorized use will be deemed an infringement of the franchisor's rights of ownership to the trademarks.
3. The franchisee acquires no right, title or interest in and to the trademarks, and all goodwill arising from the use of the trademarks inures to the benefit of and will belong to the franchisor.
4. During the term of the franchise agreement and thereafter, the franchisee agrees not to, directly or indirectly, dispute, contest, attack, call into question or cause to be called into question the validity or enforceability of the trademarks, the franchisor's ownership of the trademarks, or the ability of the franchisor to grant the rights or attempt to depreciate or otherwise attempt to negatively affect the value of the goodwill attaching to the trademarks.
5. The franchisee will give prompt notice of any illegal use or any unauthorized use of the trademarks or any confusingly similar trademarks or trade names by third parties of which the franchisee becomes aware, and will notify the franchisor if it is aware of any action or threatened action by any person against the trademarks.

6. The franchisee will execute such applications or agreements to protect the interests of the franchisor in the trademarks.
7. The franchisee will not use the trademarks as any part of its corporate name or for any other purpose except in accordance with the franchise agreement or as agreed to in writing by the franchisor.
8. If the business, partnership or corporate statutes require the franchisee to make an application to use the trademarks, such application will specify that the franchisee's use of the trademarks is subject to and limited by the provisions of the franchise agreement.
9. Upon a transfer or termination of the franchise agreement, the franchisee will cease all use of the trademarks.

Section 50(2) of the Trade-marks Act deems a proper license to have been granted if proper public notice is given of the fact that the use of the trademark is a licensed use. The notice must also identify the owner of the trademark. For this reason, franchise agreements for use in Canada should require the franchisee to post a notice in its premises and potentially on its letterhead and other relevant places that it is operating under license and identifying the owner of the trademark(s). An example of this notice would be: "This business is owned and operated independently by [name of franchisee] who is an authorized licensed user of the trademark "[owner's trademark is inserted here]," which is owned by [franchisor]."

Another consideration is whether to include an indemnification from the franchisor to the franchisee in the event the franchisee is sued by a third party for infringement of a trademark. This is sometimes included, but not always. In any event, if a franchisee is sued, it would likely commence a claim against the franchisor regardless of whether there was an explicit indemnity provided for in the franchise agreement.

The franchisor should maintain the right in the franchise agreement to require the franchisee to modify or discontinue the use of any trademark at the direction of the franchisor, but at the sole cost and expense of the franchisee.

An issue that arises on occasion is, if a third party infringes one or more trademarks of the franchise system, who has the right to sue? Section 50(3) of the Trade-marks Act gives a licensee the right to sue in the event of an infringement under certain circumstances. For this right to arise, the franchisee would have to call on the franchisor to take proceedings for infringement of the trademark, and if the franchisor refuses or neglects to do so within two months after being so called upon, the franchisee may institute proceedings for infringement in the franchisee's own name as if the franchisee were the owner, making the franchisor a defendant. This right of the franchisee is subject to any agreement between the franchisor, as owner of the trademark, and the franchisee. Therefore, the franchise agreement should specify that the franchisor has the sole discretion to take any action it deems appropriate. This would effectively prevent the franchisee from instituting an action for infringement of any of the franchisor's trademarks.

L. Accounting Records, Audits and Inspections

To assist in compliance with the provisions of the franchise agreement, franchisors will require strict auditing and reporting provisions. A typical franchise agreement will include specific directions as to the method of bookkeeping and handling of finances, and may even dictate the type of point-of-sale machine or software program used to track funds.

Financial reporting by the franchisee should be required throughout the year on a continuing basis (often tied to the royalty fee payment frequency), combined with an annual obligation for the franchisee to provide financial statements to the franchisor (in the case of many small retail or service franchises, these statements are usually unaudited; in other franchise systems, the requirement will be for the financial statements to be audited). This will assist the franchisor in ensuring that royalty payments are calculated accurately. The franchisor should also reserve the right to audit the financial statements, sales reports, tax returns and other information that the franchisee is required to submit to the franchisor. The cost of this audit would normally be at the expense of the franchisor, unless the results of the audit determine an underpayment by the franchisee, in which case the franchisee would be required to pay for the cost of the audit.

The franchise agreement should provide that the franchisor and/or its representative should have the right at all times to inspect the franchised location, to take inventory of product and to examine the manner in which the franchisee is conducting its business. In the event of such inspection the franchisee and its staff will be required by the franchise agreement to co-operate fully with the franchisor. Since consistency of service and product between different franchises is always a concern, this right to inspect is important in allowing the franchisor to determine if a particular franchisee is not complying with the franchisor's system standards.

The franchise agreement should contain the franchisee's acknowledgment and consent to the franchisor's use and disclosure where necessary of any financial information provided. Under the Canadian Franchise Acts, a franchisor who intends to make any earning projections needs to base it on reasonable information and, in Franchise Law Provinces other than Alberta, make the supporting information available for inspection. Therefore, if this information comes from the franchisees in the system, the franchisor needs to be able to disclose this information.

M. Insurance

Typically, a franchise agreement will require a franchisee to maintain a basic level of insurance. This is intended to protect both parties.

A typical franchise agreement requires that the franchisee purchase the level and type of insurance mandated by the franchisor and name the franchisor as an additional insured. Often the franchisor will mandate the insurance broker or the insurer to be used so that group rates can be negotiated. This would normally result in a cost savings to the franchisee unless the franchisor does not pass along the savings, in which case the franchisor should reserve the right to collect rebates under the franchise agreement and properly disclose this right in its disclosure document. If insurance is not sufficient to cover a loss, this would normally be the responsibility of the franchisee.

There are two basic types of insurance that are normally covered in the franchise agreement.

1. Liability Insurance

The most basic and common form of commercial insurance policy is the Comprehensive General Liability Policy (sometimes referred to as a Commercial General Liability Policy). It is most often referred to as a "CGL." The CGL policy was devised so that companies could have a relative level of confidence that certain basic risks were covered by one insurance policy (rather than several policies insuring against specific risks). In the most general terms, the CGL policy contains two types of protection: (a) bodily injury and property damage liability (including medical payments) for damage caused by the insured's products or employees, and (b) bodily injury or property damage caused by events on the insured's premises (primarily slip and fall and flooding of other businesses from the insured's premises).

CGL policies often exclude any liability for damage caused by pollution. Thus, if the franchised business includes a risk of spilling any product that could contaminate property, the franchisor should require the franchisee to maintain separate insurance to cover this risk.

If the franchised business is licensed to sell alcohol, the franchisor should require the franchisee to carry commercial host liability insurance (if not covered under the CGL).

Practice Note

Franchise operations that are licensed to sell alcohol should require franchisees to carry commercial host liability insurance.

2. Property Insurance

Depending on the type of business, franchisors should consider requiring franchisees to carry policies to protect the business from property losses. Some examples are:

1. **Fire Insurance and Tenant's or Owner's Insurance**—It is important that franchisees maintain this insurance and have the franchisor named as an additional insured.
2. **Inventory Insurance**—Both franchisees and franchisors who have significant inventory should maintain this insurance.
3. **Burglary/Employee Dishonesty Insurance**—This can be important to franchisees and franchisors where there is a possibility that they could be defrauded by an employee or employees.
4. **Business Interruption Insurance**—If the operations of the franchisor or a franchisee are interrupted, there are certain expenses and payments that continue to come due. If a fire or flood damages the premises and the insured cannot conduct business, the business interruption insurance covers the ongoing expenses until the business is operating again. Franchisors will want to require the franchisees to have the franchisors named as additional insureds to protect them from potential losses.

N. Assignment, Transfer and Sale

As a preamble to an assignment or transfer provision in a Canadian franchise agreement, it is typical to see a statement to the effect that: "The franchisee acknowledges that the franchisor, in granting this franchise and the rights and interests under this agreement, has relied upon, amongst other things, the character, background, qualifications and financial ability of the franchisee and, where applicable, its partners, officers, directors, shareholders, managers and guarantors." This justifies what is to invariably follow, namely, restrictions on the franchisee's right to assign, transfer, or sell its rights and interests under the franchise agreement.

A franchisee may lose enthusiasm for the business and decide that it wishes to assign the interest remaining in the franchise agreement to another person. Alternatively, a franchisee may discover that its business is producing sufficient profits and it wishes to sell to realize a gain on its investment. Either way, at some stage the franchisee may want to sell the franchised business to someone else.

From a franchisor's perspective, it is important to have the authority to decide to whom a franchise can be transferred or assigned. A substantial amount of time and expense is incurred by a franchisor when a franchise is transferred—especially considering the costs for training, orientation, legal expenses and, where applicable, obtaining the landlord's approval—so it is reasonable that a franchisor will require that strict conditions be met for the assignment of a franchise agreement.

Often the franchise agreement will require that, prior to the franchisee seeking the franchisor's consent to an assignment or transfer, it must provide the franchisor with a right of first refusal to acquire the franchisee's business operations on the same terms as offered to the third party. If the franchisor declines to purchase the franchisee's business and approves the transfer (and the franchisee and transferee meet the conditions specified by the franchise agreement), then the franchisee would be free to complete the sale to the third party within a set period of time (often 30 to 60 days). If the sale does not complete within that time frame, then the right of first refusal would apply again with respect to any proposed transfer or assignment.

The franchise agreement should state that the franchisor's consent to the transfer or assignment "shall not be unreasonably withheld," but it should also provide some of the grounds upon which its rejection of the proposed transfer or assignment will not be considered "unreasonable. A franchise agreement will often include the following conditions:

1. The proposed assignee or an affiliate of the proposed assignee is not a competitor of the franchisor.
2. The franchisor is provided with a copy of the agreement of purchase and sale between the franchisee and the proposed assignee and all documents referred to therein as relied upon by the parties.
3. As of the date of the franchisee's request for consent, and as of the effective date of transfer, there shall be no default in the performance or observance of any of the franchisee's obligations under the franchise agreement or any other agreement between the franchisee and the franchisor.
4. The franchisee has obtained the consent of all necessary parties to the assignment of any licenses, and the lease or sublease (depending on if the premises are subleased from the franchisor or leased directly from the landlord), to the proposed transferee.
5. The franchisee shall have settled all outstanding accounts with the franchisor up to the date of closing of the proposed transfer.
6. The franchisee shall have delivered to the franchisor a release (to the

extent permitted by law) of the franchisor, its directors and officers, their affiliates, and the directors and officers thereof, from all obligations under the franchise agreement of any such persons, in a form satisfactory to the franchisor.

7. The proposed transferee shall have entered into a written assignment in a form prescribed by the franchisor or, at the option of the franchisor, shall have executed a new franchise agreement in the form then being used by the franchisor, which may provide for a higher royalty and for greater expenditures for advertising and promotion than under the original franchise agreement, and shall have executed such other documents and agreements as are then customarily used by the franchisor in the granting of franchises.
8. The proposed transferee shall have provided guarantees from anyone whom the franchisor may request, guaranteeing the proposed transferee's performance of its obligations under the agreements to be entered into.
9. The proposed transferee shall have completed, to the satisfaction of the franchisor, such training in the operations of the franchised business, at the proposed transferee's or the franchisee's sole expense, as the franchisor may require.
10. The proposed transferee shall have provided, to the satisfaction of the franchisor, a business plan indicating that the proposed transferee possesses the required level of business experience and acumen necessary in the operation of the franchised business.
11. The purchase price to be paid to the franchisee by the proposed transferee or, if applicable, the proposed encumbrance and debt associated therewith is reasonable in the circumstances taking into account the debt and interest charges being acquired or already in existence.
12. The franchisee shall pay to the franchisor any fees and/or expenses that may be incurred by the franchisor in dealing with the franchisee's application for approval and the franchisor's then-existing transfer fee.

The franchise agreement should state that the refusal of the franchisor to consent to the proposed transfer based upon noncompliance with any of the above conditions will not be deemed to be an unreasonable withholding of consent. Sometimes counsel to franchisors will attempt to state that the consent to transfer may be arbitrarily withheld or, in "its sole discretion" denied. As noted above, given the good faith obligations under the Canadian Franchise Acts, along with a growing recognition of good faith under the common law in Canada (see Chapter 2 for more discussion on this point), this approach may be problematic.

Generally speaking, franchise agreements will be freely assignable by a franchisor, and to the extent that a purchaser or assignee assumes the covenants and obligations of the franchisor under the franchise agreement, the franchisor is freed of further liability to the franchisee.

Under Canadian law, an assignment does not release the assignor unless there is a specific release given. Therefore, it is important that a release be obtained by the franchisor from the franchisee at the time of assignment.

O. Termination

Not all terminations, of course, are a result of a default. Some terminations are natural—for example, when the term of the agreement has expired. For terminations other than the natural effluxion of time, the franchise agreement must spell out clearly when and how a franchisor may terminate the franchise rights granted and make reference to any specific restrictions (i.e., restrictive covenants) that are to remain in place.

The franchise agreement will set out the grounds upon which the franchisor may terminate the franchise agreement. Some of these grounds can result in immediate termination, while others require giving the franchisee notice and time to cure the default prior to a termination coming into effect. Unlike some jurisdictions in the United States, there is no statutory definition in Canada of "good cause" to mandate what constitutes a default, or what is acceptable grounds for denying a renewal or transfer. In Canada, absent specific provisions in the franchise agreement, this would be predominantly guided by the duty of good faith and fair dealing under the Canadian Franchise Acts, where applicable, and under the common law in Canada.

It is common for a franchisor in Canada to have a provision allowing it to terminate the franchise relationship at its inception if, in the franchisor's opinion, acting reasonably, the franchisee's participation in the franchisor's initial training program discloses the franchisee's or the franchisee's key employees' inability to adequately manage and operate the franchised business. In the event of such termination, the franchisor would often refund to the franchisee all, or a portion of, the money received by it from the franchisee, less the franchisor's reasonable costs. The amount of the refund can vary greatly depending upon the individual arrangements provided for in the franchise agreement.

The franchisor should reserve the right to terminate if the franchisee is in default of its obligation to make a payment on time of any amount payable under the franchise agreement. Normally, the franchisor will give the franchisee notice of such default and a set period of time to make payment. Along with the cross-default provision (where the default of an obligation under one agreement, such as the sub-lease, is deemed to be a default under the franchise agreement), franchisors will usually list a franchisee's failure to observe or perform any part of the agreement, the manuals or operating guidelines provided by the franchisor as being an event of default.

A concern for every franchise system is having a location go "dark" and cease operating for even a short period of time. The franchise agreement's termination provisions should address this by providing that the agreement can be terminated if the franchisee fails to conduct business for a set period of time (usually in the range of three to five business days) without the prior written consent of the franchisor, or if the premises are used by any person other than those properly entitled to use them. The franchisor should also be able to terminate the franchise agreement if the franchisee ceases or threatens to cease to carry on business, or takes or threatens to take any action to liquidate its assets, or stops making payments in the usual course of business.

Any act of bankruptcy, insolvency, a general assignment for the benefit of creditors or a bulk sale of assets by the franchisee or any of the guarantors should be specified in the franchise agreement as giving the franchisor the right to terminate. This is also the case if a custodian, receiver, manager, or any other person with like powers shall be appointed to take charge of all or any part of the franchisee's or guarantor's undertaking, business, property or asset. If the franchisee or the guarantor is a corporation, then certain other events should be specified in the franchise agreement as giving the franchisor the right to terminate, including:

1. if an order shall be made or a resolution passed for the winding up or liquidation of either the franchisee or the guarantor;
2. if either the franchisee or the guarantor passes or purports to pass, or takes or purports to take, any corporate proceedings toward its dissolution, liquidation or amalgamation;
3. if either the franchisee or the guarantor shall lose its charter by expiration, forfeiture or otherwise; or
4. if any proceedings with respect to either the franchisee or the guarantor are commenced under Canadian insolvency legislation (either under the liquidation provisions or those provisions similar to "Chapter 11" in the United States): the *Bankruptcy and Insolvency Act*, R.S.C. 1985, c. B-3, and the *Companies' Creditors Arrangement Act* (Canada), R.S.C. 1985, c. C-36.

Other potential defaults that should be considered for inclusion in the Canadian franchise agreement might be:

- if the franchisee or any agent or representative of the franchisee:
  (i) fails to submit any report required to be furnished to the franchisor within a set period of time from the date such report was due;

(ii) understates gross sales (for the calculation of royalty payments) by more than a set percent; or

(iii) materially distorts any other material information pertaining to the franchised business, or fails to maintain its records in a manner which permits a determination of gross sales, unless the franchisee proves to the satisfaction of the franchisor that it had no knowledge of such distortion (these gross sales provisions are, of course, only necessary where gross sales are important to the franchise relationship);

- if the franchisee fails to strictly comply with the performance criteria established by the franchisor (if there are any); or
- if the franchisee shall fail to observe or perform any of the terms and conditions of any applicable license necessary for the operation of the franchised business.

All of these rights of termination necessitate an understanding and a setting out of the franchisee's and the franchisor's rights and obligations upon termination in the franchise agreement.

1. Franchisee's Obligations upon Termination or Expiration

As would be expected, the franchisee has numerous obligations upon expiration or termination of the franchise agreement. These should be set out in the franchise agreement itself to avoid ambiguity about the franchisee's obligations. These obligations all have at their heart the protection of the franchise system, its trademarks, and the goodwill relating to the system. As litigation may otherwise result from the termination of a franchise agreement, it is important that the rights and obligations of the franchisee and franchisor are clearly stated.

It is common to find the franchisee being obligated to permit the franchisor or its representatives to enter the franchise location and, at the franchisor's option, to cure any default by the franchisee, to operate the franchised business for the franchisor's account, or to secure the franchisee's complete and timely compliance with the other obligations of the franchisee upon termination. As well, the franchisee will be required to pay to the franchisor, within a set period of time after the effective date of termination or expiration, all royalties, advertising fees and other charges then due and unpaid by the franchisee, including, but not limited to, the franchisor's costs and expenses in reentering the franchised location.

The franchisee must be obligated to immediately discontinue the operation of the franchised business, use of the system, and use of the trademarks, copyright and other intellectual property of the franchisor licensed under the franchise agreement. The franchisee will typically be obligated to cease displaying and using all signs, stationery, letterhead, packaging, forms, containers, operating guidelines, bulletins, instruction sheets, printed matter, advertising and other physical objects used from time to time in connection with the franchise system, or containing or bearing any of the trademarks or other names, marks or designations of the franchisor.

If the franchisee is to retain possession of the leased location post-termination, then the franchise agreement should obligate the franchisee to promptly and, at its expense, make such modifications to the interior and/or exterior decor of the leased location as the franchisor requires to remove all identification that it is a location of the franchise system. It is important that the franchisee abandons all connections to the franchise system, and therefore the franchisor may wish to require that the franchisee remove all listings from all telephone directories and all other trade or business directories and to assign to the franchisor, or any other party designated by the franchisor, all of the franchisee's telephone numbers, listings, domain names, and email addresses in connection with the franchised business.

To protect the franchisor's copyrighted materials, the franchisee should be required to return to the franchisor all manuals and all other proprietary and confidential material provided to the franchisee by the franchisor, along with any copies the franchisee may have made.

2. Franchisor's Rights and Obligations upon Termination

The franchise agreement will not contain many provisions dealing with the franchisor's obligations upon termination. More commonly, the franchise agreement will provide the franchisor with the right, but not the obligation, to purchase from the franchisee all or any portion of the inventory and items bearing the franchise system's trademarked logos held by the franchisee and/or all or any part of the fixtures, equipment, furniture or other assets located on, in, or at the leased location or otherwise used in connection with the franchised business. There are no provisions in federal or provincial legislation in Canada imposing any additional obligations upon a franchisor upon termination of the franchise agreement.

P. Guarantor's Covenants

Personal guarantees of the franchise agreement need to comply with Canadian practice and common law. This includes provisions relating to waivers of defences, jurisdiction clauses, and enforcement covenants.

Virtually all franchisors will require a personal guarantee by the principals of an incorporated franchisee. This is seen as being an important requirement not solely for monetary reasons, but also for the purposes of obtaining the principals' personal commitment to the success of the business, and to bind them personally to the non-competition and confidentiality provisions.

In the Province of Alberta, a guarantee is not enforceable against the guarantor unless a specific form of certificate mandated by law is completed by the guarantor and is sworn before a lawyer, as required under the Alberta *Guarantees Acknowledgement Act*, R.S.A. 2000, c. G-11.

There are several unique considerations to keep in mind when obtaining personal guarantees from franchisees in the province of Québec. The *Civil Code of Québec*, S.Q. 1991, c. 64 gives any guarantor the right to require the franchisor to first seize the assets of the principal debtor before looking to enforce the guarantee provided by such guarantor. As well, where there is more than one guarantor, each guarantor is granted the benefit of "division," which requires the franchisor to divide its action amongst all the guarantors that have provided a guarantee (see: S.Q. 1991, c. 64 Art. 2347, Art. 2349, and Art. 2352). This reduces the proportionate amount of the debt sought from each guarantor. To avoid these provisions, the franchisor should require each party providing a personal guarantee to waive and renounce the benefits of these articles of the Civil Code of Québec.

In addition, Article 2362 of the Civil Code of Québec provides the surety (guarantor) with a unilateral right to terminate the guarantee in certain situations:

> Where the suretyship is contracted with a view to covering future or indeterminate debts, or for an indeterminate period, the surety may terminate it after three years, so long as the debt has not become exigible, by giving prior and sufficient notice to the debtor, the creditor and the other sureties.

This article of the Civil Code of Québec has prompted discussion amongst practitioners in Québec as to whether a guarantor can waive the benefit of this provision. As this has not been tested by the courts in Québec, the best practice is to have the personal guarantors waive the benefit of this article. For more discussion of personal guarantees in Québec, see Chapter 1.

Practice Note

Alberta and Québec have unique requirements regarding guarantees. In Alberta, a special independent legal advice form must be completed and sworn before a lawyer. In Québec, the guarantor should be required to expressly renounce the benefit of specific articles of the Civil Code of Québec. This will assist the franchisor in the enforcement of the personal guarantee.

The franchise agreement or guarantee will usually also contain a form of further assurances provision requiring the guarantor to execute and deliver, under separate agreement, such form of guarantee or indemnity evidencing the guarantor's continuing obligations under the franchise agreement as the franchisor may in its discretion determine.

Q. Security to Franchisor

A majority of Canadian-based franchisors will require a security interest from their franchisees, and especially if the franchisor is the primary supplier of goods and services to the franchisee. In the United States, it is less common for the franchisor to take security unless it is financing the purchase of the business.

Security is usually taken by way of a general security agreement (GSA). Registration and perfection of security interests is a provincial matter. If the franchisor is taking a security interest against real property (land), this can be registered as a mortgage in the applicable provincial land title office. For security taken against personal property, registrations are filed and perfected under each province's personal property registry system (similar to a Uniform Commercial Code (UCC) filing in the U.S.). The franchisor should ensure that it completes filing in each provincial registry where the franchisee has operations. These filings are completed electronically and are relatively straightforward. Chapter 1 has further discussion of the personal property registry system in Canada.

There is little difference between the provinces in personal property security registrations, except for Québec, where the GSA is referred to as a hypothec, and there are specific rules governing the registration and enforcement of the hypothec. This is discussed in the Personal Property Security section of Chapter 1.

If a security interest is to be granted, then the termination provisions of the franchise agreement and GSA should include a cross-default provision.

Maintaining secured creditor status will also give rise to the right to appoint a receiver in the franchisee's business, should a default occur. In Canada, the GSA may provide for the private appointment of a receiver (and manager) without having to apply to the courts. Alternatively, a secured creditor may seek judicial appointment of a receiver by the courts. In most franchise default situations, where the business is relatively small and the franchisor may already hold the lease, the private appointment "self-help" process is particularly advantageous, and judicial appointments are rare.

The taking of security by the franchisor will in almost all situations be subordinate to the franchisee's bank financing, but it still has value. One of the reasons it can have value is that even if the franchisor is not on the lease, it can get the right to take over possession of the business as a secured creditor. This is of great significance to franchisors who want to prevent a location from going "dark" and ceasing to operate for even a short period of time.

Those franchisors that do not take a security interest usually cite the cost and administrative burden as the two reasons to not bother. However, with up-to-date lease or franchise administration software in place, the average franchisor should be able to institute a system to keep track of registrations and relevant dates, such as upcoming renewals of registrations.

R. Boilerplate Provisions

1. Canadian Spelling and Language Issues

The course of Canada's history has led to some interesting historical developments in its language and culture. There are a number of differences in spelling and use of language between what is in common usage in Canada and other parts of the world. Generally speaking, Canadian spelling follows British spelling, but there are many times where that is not the case. As well, Canada has two official languages, French and English. For franchisors doing business outside of Québec, this may not have a great impact, although consideration must be given to this when registering trademarks and/or if incorporating federally.

The language differences are important in regard to the packaging of goods for the Canadian marketplace, as well as in advertising the franchise system's products and services to the Canadian public. They do not have a large impact on the drafting of franchise agreements. In many cases, spelling and language issues in Canada are more of a curiosity for foreign franchisors, and really only important to the most staunch of Canadian nationalists. Arguably, with the predominance of "spellcheck" using American spelling, more Canadians are adopting American spelling. Throughout this book Canadian spelling and terminology are used and many non-Canadian readers will, at first glance, see these as mistakes. However, they are perfectly accurate in a Canadian context. There are many examples of "Canadian" spelling, a few of which are set out in the following chart:

Canadian Spelling	U.S. Spelling
Colour	Color
Cancelled	Canceled
Catalogue	Catalog
Cheque	Check
Labour	Labor
Fulfil	Fulfill
Licence (n)	License (n)
License (v)	License (v)
Offence	Offense
Trade-mark	Trademark

There are other unique aspects to the usage of words in Canada that will affect the drafting of the franchise agreement. In Canada the term "attorney" is not used to describe lawyers, and therefore references to "attorney's fees" should be changed to "legal fees." The terms "shareholders" and "shares" are used in Canada in place of "stockholders" and "stock." References to "temporary restraining orders" should be replaced with "interim or interlocutory injunctions." As well, in Canada there is no criminal offence known as a "felony"; "indictable offence" would normally be an appropriate substitution. In addition, there is no concept in Canada of the plea of "no contest."

Often Canadian franchise agreements will be drafted to include what is commonly referred to as the "Québec English language provision." This clause is required to be in franchise agreements utilized in Québec if the language of choice for the agreement is English. Many franchisors include it in all their franchise agreements signed in Canada. An example of the Québec clause is the following:

The parties hereto confirm that it is their desire that this Agreement, as well as all other documents relating hereto, including all notices, have been and shall be drawn up in the English language only. *Les parties aux presentes conferment leur volente que cette convention, de meme que tous les documents, y compris tout avis, s'y rattachant, soient rediges en langue anglaise seulement.*

The Québec English language provision is required in the Province of Québec as a result of the *Charter of the French Language*, R.S.Q., c. C-11 [Charter]. The Charter provides that French is the official language of Québec. Further, section

55 of the Charter states that contracts predetermined by one party, contracts containing printed standard clauses, and the related documents must be drawn up in French. Agreements may be drawn up in another language as long as it is at the express wish of the parties, and therefore franchisors looking to utilize an English-language franchise agreement will insert the Québec clause above. Franchisors that intend to grow in Québec should seriously consider translating their documents into French. Further discussion of the unique aspect of doing business in Québec is covered in Chapter 1 and should be consulted by franchisors looking to expand their business there.

2. Currency Selection

The Canadian franchise agreement should specifically state in what currency payments are to be made. It is common to see a clause that states:

Except where otherwise expressly provided, all monetary amounts in this Agreement are stated and shall be paid in Canadian currency.

The exchange rate between the Canadian and American dollar has fluctuated widely over the years, and a franchisor should very carefully think about the impact on its franchisees before requiring any fees to be paid by Canadian franchisees in American dollars. The Canadian franchisees will presumably be earning revenues and paying expenses in Canadian dollars, and if the Canadian dollar is significantly weaker than the American dollar, this can unfairly prejudice the Canadian franchisee. Even so, in some situations it is preferable to have payments in a currency other than the Canadian dollar. In those cases, the mechanics of currency exchange should be specified (including the date of calculation of the exchange rate). If the franchisor is a non-resident of Canada, then withholding tax issues will arise (see Chapter 1 for more details of withholding tax issues).

3. Penalty Clauses and Equitable Remedies

Clauses in commercial agreements in Canada that contain financial penalties in lieu of damages are generally not enforceable in Canadian courts. For example, a failure by a franchisee to meet monthly reporting requirements leading to a fine of $1,000 for each day it is late in reporting would not be enforceable.

> **Practice Note**
>
> **Financial penalty provisions in lieu of damages in franchise agreements are not enforceable in Canada.**

In *Dunlop Pneumatic Tyre Co., Ltd. v. New Garage and Motor Co., Ltd.*, [1915] A.C. 79 (H.L.), the court created a test to determine what constitutes a penalty as opposed to liquidated damages. The following key points are taken from this case:

1. The use of the words "penalty" or "liquidated damages" in a contract prima facie have that meaning. However, use of these words is not conclusive.
2. "The essence of a penalty is a payment of money stipulated as in terrorem [by way of threat] of the offending party; the essence of liquidated damages is a genuine covenanted pre-estimate of damage" (citing *Clydebank Engineering Company v. Yzquierdo y Castaneda (Don Jose Ramos)*, [1905] A.C. 6 (H.L.)).
3. Whether a sum is a penalty or a liquidated damage is a question of construction that is determined on a case-by-case basis at the time of making the contract, not at the time of breach (citing *Public Works Comr. v. Hills*, [1906] A.C. 368 (P.C.) and *Webster v. Bosanquet*, [1912] A.C. 394 (P.C.)).
4. Tests that have been developed include the following:
   (a) A sum payable will be held to be a penalty if it is extravagant and unconscionable in comparison to the greatest loss conceivable from a breach of contract (citing *Clydebank Engineering Company v. Yzquierdo y Castaneda (Don Jose Ramos)*, [1905] A.C. 6 (H.L.)).
   (b) A sum payable will be held to be a penalty if the only breach consists of not paying a sum of money and the sum stipulated is greater than the sum owed (citing *Kemble v. Farren* (1829), 130 E.R. 1234).
   (c) There is a presumption that a sum payable is a penalty when it consists of compensation on the occurrence of certain events (citing *Lord Elphinstone v. Monkland Iron and Coal Co.* (1886), 35 W.R. 17 (H.L.)).

No reference should therefore be made to specific financial remedies for failures to perform that are designed as penalties. Instead, any financial remedy should be stated to be a genuine pre-estimate of liquidated damages. This will increase the likelihood of such a clause being enforced. For example, it is common to see a $25 administrative charge for any cheques returned for insufficient funds.

Before inserting a pre-estimate of liquidated damages into a franchise agreement, the franchisor should be aware that this could negatively affect its ability to get an interlocutory injunction, as it significantly weakens the argument that the franchisor will suffer irreparable harm if it is unable to get the injunction. (This is one of the key elements required to get an interlocutory injunction. See Chapter 6 for more discussion on the elements needed to obtain an interlocutory injunction.)

Practice Note

Utilizing a pre-estimate of liquidated damages clause may restrict the franchisor's ability to obtain an interlocutory injunction.

4. Waiver of Jury

In American franchise agreements, it is common to see a provision stating that the franchisee waives its ability to request a jury trial. In Canada this is seen as largely unnecessary, although including such a provision will not be harmful. Civil disputes are tried before a single judge with no jury except in very limited and rare situations. Non-pecuniary and punitive damage awards are not as prevalent an issue as they are in the United States, which is presumably one of the reasons that the waiver of jury trial provision has become so common. Further discussion of this point is contained in Chapter 6.

5. Severability

It is common to have a clause in a Canadian franchise agreement stating that:

> [E]ach of the provisions contained in this Agreement is distinct and severable and a determination of illegality, invalidity or unenforceability of any such provision or part hereof by a court of competent jurisdiction shall not affect the validity or enforceability of any other provision hereof, unless as a result of such determination this Agreement would fail in its essential purposes.

Some franchise agreements from other jurisdictions (including some United States franchise agreements) will attempt to substitute provisions in case the ones found in the agreement are invalid or unenforceable. It is unlikely that these provisions will be enforced under Canadian common law (*Sterling Fence*). This is especially important in relation to non-competition clauses. For more discussion of drafting and the interpretation of non-competition clauses, see the discussion earlier in this chapter and in Chapter 6.

6. Entire Agreement Clause

Generally, a contact's "entire agreement" clause will be enforceable in Canada. However, in some fact situations, Canadian courts have found remedies for franchisees under a number of theories in which promises made external to the written contract are given contractual effect, such as by way of pre-contractual representations, negligent misrepresentations, collateral contracts, and the doctrine of unconscionability.

In 2014, the Supreme Court of Canada created a general duty of honesty in contractual performance, in the decision in *Bhasin v. Hrynew*, 2014 SCC 71. Simply put, the duty requires that the parties to a contract not lie or otherwise knowingly mislead each other about matters directly linked to the performance of the contract. The Court said that the new duty of honest performance should not be thought of as an implied term but rather as a general doctrine of contract law that imposes as a contractual duty a minimum standard of honest contractual performance. The duty operates irrespective of the intentions of the parties and is to this extent analogous to equitable doctrines that impose limits on the freedom of contract, such as the doctrine of unconscionability. Because the duty is a general doctrine of contract law that applies to all contracts, like unconscionability, the parties are not free to exclude it. The Court said that it would not rule out the parties' relaxing the requirements of the doctrine as long as they respected its minimum core requirements. Any modification of the duty of honest performance would need to be in express terms, but a generically worded entire agreement clause would not suffice to modify or "relax" the duty.

Canadian courts have therefore found ways around entire agreement clauses in some instances, as was the case in *Atlas Supply Co. of Canada v. Yarmouth Equipment Ltd.*, [1991] N.S.J. No. 178 (N.S.C.A.). In this case, the defendant franchisee entered into a franchise agreement with the plaintiff franchisor corporation. The franchisor concealed from the franchisee projections showing that the franchise was not viable and instead showed the franchisee different projections showing profitability. The court found that the franchisor intended the wrong projections to induce the franchisee and other potential franchisees and knew that the defendant was relying on the projections. The defendant had no source of questioning the projections, and the franchisor reassured the defendant concerning its sources. The franchise failed and the franchisor sued the defendant for damages, claiming the defendant defaulted in its obligations to pay under the franchise agreement.

Although there was an exclusionary clause in the franchise agreement that precluded reference to warranties and representations not set out in the agreement, both the trial judge and the court of appeal found that the franchisor's projections constituted a warranty that was meant to induce, and did in fact induce, the defendant to enter into the contract. The franchisor had therefore breached its warranty. The franchisor had exhibited unconscionable conduct, and there was an unequal bargaining power between the parties. The court therefore found it would be inequitable to enforce the franchise agreement.

In *Ronald Elwin Lister Ltd. v. Dunlop Canada Ltd.*, (1982), 135 D.L.R. (3d) 1 (S.C.C.), the Supreme Court of Canada set aside a guarantee in a franchise agreement as a result of a collateral warranty given by the franchisor to the franchisee in respect of statements regarding past and future performance. The entire agreement clause in the *Dunlop* case did not include a statement that collateral warranties were not part of the agreement. It is therefore important to have a properly drafted entire agreement clause. This clause needs to address the issues of collateral warranty along the lines of:

This Agreement, any documents incorporated by reference in this Agreement, and the Schedules to this Agreement, constitute the entire agreement between the parties pertaining to the subject matter of this Agreement and supersedes all prior agreements, understandings, negotiations and discussions with respect to the subject matter of this Agreement whether oral or written. Except as provided in this Agreement, there are no conditions, representations, warranties, undertakings, promises, inducements or agreements whether direct, indirect, collateral, express or implied made by the Franchisor to the Franchisee. No supplement, modification, amendment or waiver of this Agreement shall be binding unless executed in writing by both parties.

7. Governing Law and Jurisdiction

It is normally advisable to have the laws of the Canadian province or territory in which the franchisee is located govern the franchise agreement. It is also advisable to avoid requiring the parties to bring any action exclusively in a jurisdiction other than where the franchisee is located. It is not unusual for franchise systems located in other jurisdictions to want to have their home jurisdiction's laws govern and insist upon all matters being tried in that jurisdiction. This can be problematic for a number of reasons.

First of all, the franchise legislation in each of the six Franchise Law Provinces contains a provision that any provision of a franchise agreement that purports to restrict the application of the law of that province, or to restrict jurisdiction or venue, is void with respect to a claim otherwise enforceable under that franchise act. Arguably, this still leaves the door open to pursuing claims that do not constitute "claims otherwise enforceable" under the respective franchise act in a venue outside the province in which the franchise is located, but most likely this would result in a "split claim," where suits are being pursued in two jurisdictions.

Secondly, while Canadian courts in the common-law jurisdictions will generally recognize and enforce a foreign judgment, this judgment must be final and conclusive on the merits and for a definite sum of money. Since injunctive relief is an important tool to the franchisor for enforcement of the franchisee's obligations under the franchise agreement and related documents, a foreign choice of laws and jurisdiction provision may cause complications.

Foreign courts may not be willing to grant injunctive relief with respect to a franchise operation in Canada, and it is equally unlikely that a Canadian court would recognize and enforce any injunctive relief granted by a foreign jurisdiction. If the franchise agreement names a foreign jurisdiction as having exclusive jurisdiction, and the franchisor attempts to ignore this provision and applies to a Canadian court for relief, the court may stay the action. This potentially could cause considerable delay and create uncertainty for the franchisor.

A further consideration is whether the franchisor would truly be better off under the laws of its home jurisdiction. Often this is selected out of perceived convenience rather than on the merits of the laws applicable in its home state. For example, many jurisdictions in the United States have specific state franchise laws (along with the federal law), antitrust laws, common-law principles, and other applicable statutes that are more onerous on the franchisor than the equivalent laws in Canada. In this case, it would not make sense for the franchisor to want to have the laws of its home state apply.

Note that if the franchised business is located in a province other than one of the Franchise Law Provinces, it would be inadvisable to select the law of any of the Franchise Law Provinces to apply to the franchise agreement, in order to avoid the application of that province's franchise legislation to the franchise agreement.

8. Mediation and Arbitration

In some provincial jurisdictions in Canada, once an action has been commenced, mediation is mandatory prior to the trial of a civil action. The Code of Ethics of the Canadian Franchise Association also states:

> A franchisor should make reasonable efforts to resolve complaints, grievances and disputes with its franchisees through fair and reasonable direct communication and where reasonably appropriate under the circumstances, mediation or other alternative dispute resolution mechanisms" (see: CFA—"Code of Ethics" online at Canadian Franchise Association, http://www.cfa.ca/ethics.html).

It is increasingly the case in Canada that arbitrations do not necessarily have advantages over the judicial process. If arbitration is still preferred by the franchisor, the franchise agreement utilized in Canada should set out the rules, forum and jurisdiction for the arbitration (Ontario and British Columbia have two, one for domestic arbitrations and the other for international disputes). Each province has arbitration legislation with its own specific set of rules. In addition, there are numerous industry-specific regulations that govern the arbitration of accounts in Quebec (for example, the *Regulation Respecting the Conciliation and Arbitration Procedure for the Accounts of Physicians*, R.Q. M-9, r.12.1 and the *Regulation Respecting the Conciliation and Arbitration Procedure for the*

Accounts of Notaries, R.Q. N-3, r.3.1.) (also see: British Columbia: *Commercial Arbitration Act*, R.S.B.C. 1996, c. 55; *International Commercial Arbitration Act*, R.S.B.C. 1996, c. 223; *Alberta: Arbitration Act*, R.S.A. 2000, c. A-43; *Saskatchewan: Arbitration Act*, 1992, S.S. 1992, c. A-24.1; *Manitoba: Arbitration Act*, C.C.S.M., c. A120; *Ontario: Arbitration Act*, 1991, S.O. 1991, c. 17; *International Commercial Arbitration Act*, R.S.O. 1990, c. I.9; Nova Scotia: *Arbitration Act*, R.S.N.S. 1989, c. 19; New Brunswick: *Arbitration Act*, S.N.B. 1992, c. A-10.1; *Prince Edward Island Arbitration Act*, P.E.I., c. A-16; Yukon: *Arbitration Act*, R.S.Y. 2002, c. 8; *Northwest Territories and Nunavut: Arbitration Act*, R.S.N.W.T. (Nu) 1988, c. A-5. In Québec, the *Civil Code of Québec*, S.Q. 1991, c. 64, Chapter XVIII governs arbitrations.).

Some American franchisors like to use the American Arbitration Association (AAA) rules and procedures; however, there is currently no office of the AAA in Canada, and therefore this is often not practical.

Some American franchisors like to specify that resolution of disputes will be subject to mandatory mediation in their home jurisdiction in the U.S. As discussed above, however, this would be problematic in any of the Franchise Law Provinces where legislation provides that the jurisdiction of respective courts cannot be precluded in relation to any claim under the respective franchise act.

Alternative dispute resolution clauses are still generally uncommon in a Canadian franchise context. This is in part because franchisors see them as adding complication to the process of enforcing the franchisee's obligations under the franchise agreement. Even if there is specific mention in the franchise agreement that, notwithstanding the arbitration or mediation provisions, the parties can seek injunctive relief from a court of competent jurisdiction without first submitting to arbitration or mediation, it is still possible that the franchisee will attempt to defend against the matter by arguing that the dispute must first be heard by an arbitrator/mediator. This can cause delay in the enforcement of the franchise agreement, as well as potentially increase the franchisor's legal costs. For more discussion of alternative dispute resolution, see Chapter 6.

It is important to keep in mind that the parties can always choose to have a dispute mediated or heard by an arbitrator without agreeing to this ahead of time in the franchise agreement. This approach would fit entirely with the Code of Ethics of the Canadian Franchise Association without necessarily obligating the franchisor to submit to alternative dispute resolution.

If arbitration is to be included as a clause in the franchise agreement, it would be customary in Canada for that clause to provide for the specific rules to be followed in the arbitration, as well as the forum, jurisdiction and language of the arbitration. Particularly in respect of the Province of Québec, it should be specified as to whether the arbitration is to be conducted in English or French.

The arbitration clause would also customarily provide that arbitration is final and binding between the parties and is not subject to appeal. The parties can also specify that the award is to be confidential; however, this confidentiality may be hampered somewhat by the disclosure requirements of the Canadian Franchise Acts.

II. Conclusions

Lawyers from outside of Canada who are familiar with franchise agreements can see that a lot of provisions that would ordinarily be contained in a Canadian franchise agreement are indeed very similar to provisions that would appear in agreements elsewhere. However, there are unique differences in the Canadian laws and practices, so a franchisor needs to be careful not to adopt wholesale a franchise agreement drafted for use in the United States or other parts of the world without first considering what unique "Canadianization" of the agreement is required.

CHAPTER 6

Franchise Disclosure Issues in Canada

Andraya Frith and Daniel Zalmanowitz*

Contents

* Frank Zaid, retired partner of Osler, Hoskin & Harcourt LLP, is the original author of this chapter in the First Edition of this book. The authors would also like to thank Paul Kotschorek, counsel at Osler, Hoskin & Harcourt LLP, for his contribution to this chapter.

I. History of Franchise Legislation in Canada

A. Introduction

Under Canada's constitution, franchise legislation is a matter delegated to the Canadian provinces rather than the federal government. Accordingly, apart from federal legislation that has a direct impact on franchising, such as intellectual property and competition legislation, franchise registration, disclosure and relationship legislation is within the exclusive mandate of the provinces of Canada.

Six provinces (Alberta, Ontario, Prince Edward Island, New Brunswick, Manitoba and British Columbia) have enacted stand-alone franchise legislation. Alberta was the first province to do so in 1971, followed by replacement franchise legislation in 1995. Ontario followed with franchise legislation in 2000. In 2005, the Uniform Law Conference of Canada (ULCC) developed a Franchises Act and regulations based on the Ontario legislation as a starting reference. The ULCC Franchises Act and regulations were developed for use by provinces as model toward harmonizing provincial franchise legislation. Between 2006 and 2012, Prince Edward Island, New Brunswick and Manitoba enacted legislation that follow the ULCC model Franchises Act and regulations with some variations. In 2015, British Columbia passed its own franchise legislation, which is also based on the ULCC model. Regulations were approved in October 2016 and the British Columbia legislation came into force on February 1, 2017. The remaining provinces and territories in Canada have no legislation that specifically governs franchises.

The six provincial acts share many of the same features. All of them have similar but not identical franchise legislation that requires disclosure. None require registration with any government agency or commission. Where the acts are distinguishable, the differences will be referred to specifically. The current versions of the acts and regulations can be accessed using the Internet links listed in the appendices to this book.

B. Alberta

The Province of Alberta was the first province in Canada to enact legislation dealing directly with franchising, in 1971 (*The Franchises Act,* S.A. 1971, c. 38 (Can.)). The original Franchises Act was modeled after counterpart legislation in California. The act was a disclosure-registration statute rather than a disclosure-relationship statute. The legislation was administered by the Alberta Securities Commission and designed to provide protection to the public by requiring full, plain and true disclosure of all material facts relating to the franchise being offered. Pursuant to the act, no person, unless exempt, could trade in a franchise in Alberta until an application for registration of the franchise and prescribed ancillary documents had been filed with the Alberta Securities Commission and a receipt was obtained from the Registrar.

From 1987 onwards, the Alberta government undertook a number of initiatives to amend the Franchises Act as a result of its general desire to deregulate government legislation. Various position papers, surveys and draft legislation were brought forward until February 14, 1995, when the Alberta Securities Commission issued a letter, together with a proposed new Franchises Act, requesting comments from the industry at large. The proposal addressed three main concerns:

1. Eliminating the cost and time delays caused by the necessity of registration with and review by the Alberta Securities Commission;
2. Ensuring that prospective franchisees have the information necessary to make informed decisions; and
3. Promoting industry self-management.

Ultimately, the Alberta legislature passed its new Franchises Act on May 16, 1995 (S.A. 1995, c. F-17 (Can.)) (the Alberta Act). The revised act was the product of a cooperative effort between representatives of the Alberta government and a committee composed of representatives of the Canadian Franchise Association, the former Alberta Franchisors Institute and the Franchisee Association of Alberta. The new statute completely overhauled the regulatory mechanism of the previous Franchises Act by eliminating registration requirements and all relationship and other policies enforced by the Alberta Securities Commission in its review of franchise filings.

Many of the operative provisions of the Alberta Act, including the disclosure requirements, are contained in the regulations. The Alberta Securities Commission released draft regulations on August 23, 1995, and final regulations were approved by the Alberta Securities Commission on September 22, 1995, after receipt of comments on the draft regulations (*Franchises Regulation,* Alta. Reg. 240/1995 (Can.)).

In order to simplify the process for franchisors whose registrations expired prior to proclamation of the Alberta Act, the Director of the Alberta Securities Commission issued a blanket exemption order on June 27, 1995, automatically extending all current registrations and exemptions to the date on which the Alberta Act took effect.

C. Ontario

In August 1970, a committee was formed by the Ontario Minister of Financial and Commercial Affairs "to review and report upon what are commonly described as referral, pyramiding or multi-level sales practices, arrangements and franchises and to consider all aspects of the relationship of franchisors and franchisees and the implications of these arrangements to the consumer and the investor and generally to recommend what, if any, changes in the law are desirable" (*Report of the Minister's Committee on Franchising* (Toronto: Department of Financial and Commercial Affairs, 1971). The report was issued in July 1971 and is commonly known as the "Grange Report" after the Committee Chairman, S.G.M. Grange.

Notwithstanding the Grange Report's recommendations for franchise regulation, many years of government and industry consideration, debate and discussion followed with no conclusive legislative action. Finally, all of the activity culminated with the introduction of Bill 33, which was introduced into the Ontario legislature on December 14, 1999. Bill 33, known as the *Arthur Wishart Act (Franchise Disclosure), 2000*, was passed by the Ontario legislature on May 17, 2000, and received Royal Assent on June 8, 2000 (S.O. 2000, c.3 (Can.)) (the Ontario Act). All provisions of the Ontario Act except those dealing with disclosure were proclaimed in force on July 1, 2000. A regulation made under the Ontario Act setting forth disclosure requirements was first published on October 31, 2000, amended on November 23, 2000, and came into force on January 31, 2001, with the provisions of the Ontario Act dealing with disclosure (O. Reg. 581/00, as amended by O. Reg. 611/00 (Can.)). In a Government of Ontario press release issued with the introduction of Bill 33, the Minister of Consumer and Commercial Relations stated that "franchising is an important economic activity in this province accounting for almost 40% of all retail sales. We are helping to improve the operation of business activities vital to the economy of Ontario."

D. Prince Edward Island

Prince Edward Island was the next province to enact franchise disclosure legislation after Ontario. Franchise legislation was first tabled in the Prince Edward Island legislature in 2001. The draft legislation introduced was prepared by a group called Islanders for Fair Franchise Law. The legislature's Standing Committee on Community Affairs and Economic Development held public hearings and consultations. Among the Committee's recommendations was that the Attorney General implement legislation based on disclosure legislation in Alberta and Ontario and that it be consistent with other Canadian provinces. The resulting legislation, the Franchises Act (R.S.PEI 1988, c. F-14.1 (Can.)) (the PEI Act), was passed by the Prince Edward Island legislature and given royal assent on June 7, 2005. The obligation to disclose under the PEI Act came into effect on January 1, 2007. The regulation containing the substantive details of the disclosure obligations are contained in the Franchises Act Regulations (PEI Reg. EC 232/06 (Can.)) (the PEI Regulation).

The PEI Act and the PEI Regulation were based on Ontario's legislation but also adopted a number of the provisions contained in the ULCC Model Franchises Act and regulations that were being considered at the time.

E. New Brunswick

The New Brunswick Legislature enacted the Franchises Act on June 27, 2007 (S.NB. 2007, c F-23.5 (Can.)) (the NB Act). As in the preceding provinces' franchise legislation, the substantive details of the disclosure obligations are in the regulations (Disclosure Document Regulation, N.B. Reg. 2010-92 (Can)) (the NB Regulation). The obligation to disclose in New Brunswick commenced on February 1, 2011.

The New Brunswick Act and the NB Regulation are, for the most part, based on the ULCC Model Franchises Act and Model Regulations, but there are some important differences. One major difference is New Brunswick's inclusion of a detailed dispute resolution mechanism that is set out in the Mediation Regulation (N.B. Reg. 2010–93 (Can.)) (the NB Mediation Regulation).

F. Manitoba

Although franchise legislation was first introduced in the Manitoba Legislature by way of a private member's bill, Bill 18, in 1992, it was not passed into law. It was not until after the Manitoba Law Reform Commission undertook a report on Franchise Law that legislation was considered by the Manitoba Legislature (*Franchise Law* (Winnipeg: Manitoba Law Reform Commission, 2008). Manitoba's The Franchises Act was assented to in 2010 and came into force on October 1, 2012 (C.C.S.M., c. F156 (Can.)). The substantive details of the disclosure requirement are contained in the Franchises Regulation (Man. Reg. 29/2012 (Can.)) (the Manitoba Regulation). The obligation to provide a disclosure document to prospective franchisees commenced in Manitoba on October 1, 2012, with the enactment of the act. The Manitoba Act and its Manitoba Regulation were modelled on the ULCC Model Franchises Act and Model Regulations but contain some provisions that are unique to Manitoba. One unique feature is that the Manitoba legislation specifically permits disclosure in different parts at different times subject to complying with certain formal requirements (C.C.S.M., c. F156, s. 5(3) (Can.)).

G. British Columbia

The Province of British Columbia began considering franchise legislation in the late 1970s. However, it was not until after the British Columbia Law Institute issued its *Report on a Franchises Act for British Columbia* in March of 2014 that the government took steps to implement franchise legislation. The report recommended that the province enact franchise legislation based generally on the ULCC Model Franhises Act, and on October 5, 2015, the government introduced a bill to enact a franchises act for British Columbia. The bill received royal assent on November 17, 2015 (S.B.C., c.35 (Can.) (the BC Act)), and the regulation was released (the BC Regulation) by Order in Council dated October 3, 2016. The BC Regulation is based on the ULCC's Model Regulations. The Order in Council also set February 1, 2017 as the date on which the BC Act and the BC Regulation came into force.

H. Other Provinces and Territories

The other jurisdictions in Canada (provinces of Saskatchewan, Quebec, Newfoundland and Labrador, and Nova Scotia and the territories of the Northwest Territories, Yukon and Nunavut) have no specific franchise legislation.

I. Uniform Law Conference of Canada (ULCC)

The ULCC is devoted to harmonizing the Canadian statute law where it would be beneficial. It does so by preparing legislation that it recommends for enactment by the provinces, territories, and sometimes the federal government as well. The ULCC voting membership is made up of lawyers representing the federal, provincial and territorial governments. These lawyers come from the private sector, departments of justice, law reform bodies, and the academic community.

While there had been previous attempts by the ULCC to deal with the regulation of franchising through the 1980s, its recommendations were never adopted as legislation in any Canadian provinces or territories. In 2002, the ULCC established "a new project to consider and make recommendations for the adoption of uniform franchise legislation (the Model Act) throughout Canada (Uniform Franchises Act Report of the Working Committee (Fredericton: Uniform Law Conference of Canada), para. 1 (Can.)). The project was directed by a working committee established by the ULCC as part of its Commercial Law Strategy, the aim of which is to modernize and harmonize commercial law in Canada with a view to creating a comprehensive framework of commercial statute law, which will make it easier to do business in Canada that will directly benefit Canadians and the economy as a whole.

The reports of the committee and the ULCC Model Franchises Act and Model Regulations can be accessed on the ULCC's website at www.ulcc.ca. The committee used as its model the Ontario Act and the Ontario Regulations and made changes, additions, and modifications considered necessary or appropriate. The ULCC Model Franchises Act and Model regulations were adopted by the ULCC at its annual meetings in 2004 and 2005.

As previously mentioned, the ULCC Model Act and its Model regulations were used as the framework for the Prince Edward Island, New Brunswick, Manitoba, and British Columbia franchise legislation and are likely to influence the other provinces and territories, which have not yet enacted their own. It may also serve as the basis for harmonization of the Ontario and Alberta franchise legislation should those provinces consider amendments with a view to adopting a uniform framework.

II. Overview of the Requirements under Canadian Provincial Franchise Legislation

A. Introduction

At the present time, only six provinces (Alberta, Manitoba, Ontario, New Brunswick, Prince Edward Island, and British Columbia) have enacted franchise legislation. Unless an exemption is available, all six statutes require the preparation and delivery of a disclosure document with prescribed content requirements to prospective franchisees. All of the statutes also regulate the franchise relationship to a certain degree through provisions dealing with the rights of franchisees to associate, a statutory duty of fair dealing, and applicable law, venue and jurisdiction. The statutes contain prescribed forms for the preparation of a disclosure document in the regulations to the legislation. Furthermore, there are prescribed standards for financial statement inclusion in and as part of the disclosure document and franchisor certification, with varying degrees of personal liability for directors and officers.

Notwithstanding the similarities of the legislation, there are noticeable differences in the application of the statutes, including the contents of disclosure documents, mandatory statements and risk warnings, financial statement reporting, exemptions from financial statement inclusion in a disclosure document, and forms of franchisor certificates. The legislation in Alberta, PEI, New Brunswick, Manitoba and British Columbia gives a franchisor the ability to utilize a form of disclosure document prepared in accordance with the laws of another jurisdiction, as long as supplementary information is provided. See Part IV.A. (Matters of Special Interest to Foreign Franchisors) below in this chapter for details of what is needed.

For purposes of comparison, the discussion below will use Ontario's *Arthur Wishart Act* (Franchise Disclosure), 2000 as a basis of comparison to the application and contents of the Alberta Act, Manitoba Act, PEI Act, NB Act, and BC Act. The statutes will be collectively referred to as the "Provincial Acts," the regulations as the "Ontario Regulations," the "Alberta Regulations," the "Manitoba Regulations," the "PEI Regulations", the "NB Regulations" and the "BC Regulations", respectively, and collectively as the "Provincial Regulations."

As mentioned earlier, access to the Provincial Acts and Provincial Regulations are available through the links included in the Appendices to this book.

B. Highlights of the Provincial Acts

The following is a description of the highlights of the Provincial Acts:

1. A duty of fair dealing is imposed on each party in respect of the performance and enforcement of a franchise agreement. In the PEI Act, the NB Act, the Manitoba Act and the BC Act, the duty further extends to the exercising of a right contained in a franchise agreement.
2. The duty of fair dealing is not defined in the Alberta Act but is defined in each of the other Provincial Acts as including the duty to act in good faith and in accordance with reasonable commercial standards.
3. Franchisees are given the right to associate with one another and to form an organization of franchisees.
4. Franchisors are required to provide franchisees with a disclosure document containing prescribed information not less than 14 days before execution of a franchise agreement or the payment of any consideration. There are some exceptions for the taking of limited, fully refundable deposits in the Alberta Act, the Manitoba Act and the BC Act and for signing confidentiality and territory or site reservations in all of the Provincial Acts except the Ontario Act.
5. The disclosure documents must contain specified information, financial statements as prescribed by the Provincial Regulations (unless exemptions, which differ among the Provincial Acts, apply), copies of the franchise agreement and ancillary documents, and other mandatory statements prescribed by the regulations. The specific items to be contained in disclosure documents and the mandatory statements to be included differ among the provinces.
6. A two-year right of rescission by the franchisee is allowed for failure to provide a disclosure document. A shorter 60-day right of rescission is provided for a deficient disclosure document or where the franchise agreement was signed before the mandatory 14-day waiting period.

7. A franchisee is entitled to damages for misrepresentation in a disclosure document or failure of the franchisor to deliver a disclosure document.
8. Liability is imposed on persons who breach the duty of fair dealing, interfere with the freedom of franchisees to associate, and for misrepresentation in a disclosure document, though the extent and scope of the liability differs between the Alberta Act and the other Provincial Acts.
9. Franchise agreements cannot restrict the application of local laws, venue or jurisdiction outside of the respective provinces with respect to a claim otherwise enforceable under the applicable Provincial Act.
10. Exemptions from the application of the legislation and disclosure document requirements are found in all of the Provincial Acts, although they differ in application and definition from province to province.

C. Important Definitions under the Provincial Acts

1. Franchise

The definition of a "franchise" in the Ontario Act means a right to engage in a business for which the franchisee is required by contract or otherwise to make a payment or continuing payments, whether direct or indirect, or a commitment to make such payment or payments to the franchisor, or the franchisor's associate, in the course of operating the business or as a condition of acquiring the franchise or commencing operations, and (a) in which (i) the franchisor grants the franchisee the right to sell goods or services substantially associated with the franchisor's trademark, service mark, trade name, logo or advertising or other commercial symbol, and (ii) the franchisor exercises significant control over or offers significant assistance in the franchisee's method of operation, or (b) in which (i) the franchisor grants the franchisee the representational or distribution rights, whether or not a trademark, service mark, trade name, logo or advertising or other commercial symbol is involved, to sell or distribute goods or services supplied by the franchisor or a supplier designated by the franchisor, and (ii) the franchisor or a third person designated by the franchisor provides location assistance, including securing retail outlets or accounts or securing locations or sites for vending machines, display racks or other product sales displays. The definitions of "franchise" in the PEI Act, the NB Act, the Manitoba Act and the BC Act are substantially the same (R.S. PEI 1988, c. F-14.1. s. 1(1)(b); S.N.B. 2007, c. F-23.5, s. 1(1); C.C.S.M., c. F156, s. 1(1); S.B.C., c.35, s. 1(1), (Can.)). These definitions are somewhat more detailed than those of the Alberta Act (R.S.A. 2000, c. F-23, s. 1(1)(d) (Can.)). A "franchise" also includes a master franchise and a subfranchise in all of the Provincial Acts (R.S.A. 2000, c. F-23, s. 1(1)(d); S.O. 2000, c.3, s. 1(1); R.S.PEI 1988, c. F-14.1. s. 1(1)(b); S.N.B. 2007, c. F-23.5, s. 1(2); C.C.S.M., c. F156, s. 1(1); S.B.C., c.35, s. 1(1), (Can.)).

The comprehensive definitions of a "franchise" in the Ontario Act, PEI Act, NB Act, Manitoba Act and BC Act capture a number of business relationships other than traditional business format franchises, and includes what are commonly referred to as business opportunities in the United States. The following illustrates the potential scope of the definitions:

1. The initial portion of the definition requires the franchisee to make payments in the course of operating the business. The payments need not be related to sales, be periodic or be for intellectual property or other intangible rights. In fact, the payments may simply be made in the course of operating the business or for products or services supplied by the franchisor or the franchisor's associate.
2. There is no definition of a "franchise fee" in any of the Provincial Acts other than the Alberta Act, and payment of a "franchise fee" is not an element of a "franchise" in those provinces as it is in Alberta.
3. Subject to the exemption referred to below in number 5 regarding pure wholesale arrangements, traditional product distribution or dealer arrangements may fall within subsection (a) of the definition. Where a manufacturer grants a distributor or dealer the right to sell goods associated with the manufacturer's trademark and offers significant assistance in the distributor or dealer's method of operation (including building design and furnishings, locations, business organization, marketing techniques or training), the arrangement may constitute a "franchise." As a result, motor vehicle dealers, farm implement dealers, gasoline retailers, petroleum resellers and product distributors may be considered franchises within the scope of the definition.
4. Subsection (b) of the definitions only requires that the franchisor grant the franchisee distribution rights to sell goods or services supplied by the franchisor or a supplier designated by the franchisor, and that the franchisor or a third person designated by the franchisor provides location assistance. Location assistance includes securing retail outlets or accounts or securing sites for vending machines, display racks or other product sales displays. Thus, this branch of the definition may include arrangements where a supplier typically arranges customer accounts for its dealers, and they may also include arrangements where a supplier services sites for its dealers' vending machines, display racks or other product displays. Soft drink manufacturers, warehouse jobbers, cosmetic manufacturers and video disk suppliers may find that their arrangements inadvertently fall within this branch of the definition of a franchise. These definitions may therefore extend to what are often referred to in the United States as "business opportunities."

5. The PEI Act, NB Act, Manitoba Act, and the BC Act each exclude arrangements arising out of an agreement to purchase a reasonable amount of goods or services at a reasonable wholesale price (R.S.PEI 1988, c. F-14.1., s. 2(3)(g), S.N.B. 2007, c. F-23.5, s. 2(4)(g) and C.C.S.M., c. F156, s. 2(3)(j); S.B.C., c.35, s. 2(3)(g) (Can.)). This excludes pure wholesale and distribution arrangements which do not have a franchise fee or significant operating controls from the application of the acts in those four provinces.

Practice Note

The extended definition of the term "franchise" means that many distribution-type relationships and business opportunities may fall within the definition in the Ontario Act, PEI Act, NB Act, the Manitoba Act and the BC Act, though the latter four include some relief from this through their wholesale arrangement exclusions.

Each relationship should be examined on its own facts in the context of the definition. The payment of a franchise fee is not an essential ingredient of the definitions given the remainder of the definition, which includes a continuing financial obligation to the franchisor by the franchisee and significant continuing operational controls or assistance by the franchisor on the operations of the franchised business.

The definition of "franchise" in the Alberta Act means a right to engage in a business:

(i) in which goods or services are sold or offered for sale or are distributed under a marketing or business plan prescribed in substantial part by the franchisor;
(ii) that is substantially associated with the trademark, trade name, logotype or advertising of the franchisor or designating the franchisor; and
(iii) that involves:
  (a) a continuing financial obligation to the franchisor by the franchisee and significant continuing operational controls by the franchisor on the operation of the franchised business, or
  (b) the payment of a franchise fee (R.S.A. 2000, c. F-23, s. 1(1)(d) (Can.)).

The term "franchise fee" in the Alberta Act is defined as a direct or indirect payment to purchase a franchise or to operate a franchise business (R.S.A. 2000, c. F-23, s. 1(1)(f) (Can.)). However, the following payments are excluded from the definition of a franchise fee under the Alberta Act:

(i) a purchase of or an agreement to purchase a reasonable amount of goods at a reasonable bona fide wholesale price;
(ii) a purchase of or an agreement to purchase a reasonable amount of services at a reasonable bona fide wholesale price; or
(iii) the payment of a reasonable service charge to the issuer of a credit or debit card by the establishment accepting the credit or debit card as the case may be (R.S.A. 2000, c. F-23, s. 1(1)(f) (Can.)).

2. Franchise Agreement

The definition of a "franchise agreement" in each of the Provincial Acts includes any agreement (not just the franchise agreement) that relates to the franchise between a franchisor (or the franchisor's associate) and a franchisee (R.S.A. 2000, c. F-23, s. 1(1)(e); S.O. 2000, c.3, s. 1(1); R.S.PEI 1988, c. F-14.1. s. 1(1)(c); S.N.B. 2007, c. F-23.5, s. 1(1); C.C.S.M., c. F156, s. 1(1); S.B.C., c.35, s. 1(1) (Can.)). Therefore, typical ancillary documents like applications or deposit agreements, subleases, trademark licenses, software licenses, Internet or intranet access agreements, equipment or sign leases, reservation systems agreements, security documents, guarantees and assignments may all be subject to the provisions of the Provincial Acts dealing with a franchise agreement.

The following are examples of how the courts have interpreted and applied the Provincial Acts. The cases cited in this chapter are intended to be examples of the applicable case law.

In *Khachikian v. Williams*, [2003] O.J. No. 5876 (Can. Ont. Sup. Ct.), the payment of a license fee in exchange for assistance with business plans, without an agreement having been reached through negotiations, was found to be a franchise agreement, although no written agreement was entered into. The cheque for the license fee was considered to be sufficient evidence in writing so that the oral agreement exclusion in the Ontario Act did not apply.

In *Bekah v. Three for One Pizza*, 67 O.R. (3d) 305, [2003] O.J. No. 4002, 2003 CanLII 64302 (Can. Ont. Sup. Ct.), a deposit agreement was found to be a franchise agreement even though the purchase of the franchise had not been completed. See also *1368741 Ontario Inc. v. Triple Pizza (Holdings) Inc.*, [2004] O.J. No. 297, 2004 CanLII 60163 (Can. Ont. Sup. Ct.), affirmed [2004] O.J. No. 3562, 2004 CanLII 60163 (Can. Ont. C.A.).

In *2130489 Ontario Inc. v. Philthy McNasty's Enterprises Inc.*, 2012 ONCA 381, 2012 ONCA 381 (CanLII), [2001] O.J. No. 6561 (Can.), the term "franchise agreement" was held to include a new agreement that was entered into subsequent to the signing of a franchise agreement to resolve financial issues. The court held that the term should be interpreted broadly, and a second franchise agreement entered into subsequent to and with the intention of replacing the original franchise agreement without a new disclosure document gave rise to a right to rescind for up to two years.

In *Marshall v. Little Mac Enterprises Ltd.*, 295 AR 177, 2000 CanLII 28251 (ABQB) (Can.), decided under the Alberta Act, an agreement pursuant to which the plaintiff would receive the right to use the franchisor company's name, training package, and the disclosure of the company's program was found to be a franchise under the Alberta Act. The court found that the fact that the defendant did not have substantial control over all aspects of the business did not exclude the operation of the act. Therefore, the franchisee was entitled to rescind and to damages under the Alberta Act as a result of the franchisor's failure to provide a disclosure document.

In *1706228 Ontario Ltd. v. Grill It Up Holdings Inc.*, 2011 ONSC 2735, 2011 ONSC 2735 (CanLII) (Can.), it was held that even though there was no express franchise agreement, the relationship between parties met the definition of "franchise." The franchisee had paid for the development of a fast-food restaurant location, and an asset purchase agreement, sublease and license agreement were signed. The franchisee refused to sign the franchise agreement that was presented and was entitled to rescind its agreements because no disclosure document was given, and the franchisee was entitled to damages under the Ontario Act.

In *Distefano v. Energy Automated Systems Inc.*, 2011 ONSC 2735, 2011 ONSC 2735 (CanLII) (Can.), a plaintiff sought to have the forum selection clause in an agreement be declared void pursuant to the Ontario Act on the basis that the arrangement was a "franchise." The court found that a five-day training program required as a condition precedent to obtaining a dealership was not "significant assistance" to satisfy the requirement of "significant assistance in the franchisee's method of operation" in the definition of franchise.

Practice Note

All of the Canadian Provincial Statutes define a "franchise agreement" to include not just the agreement, but also many of the typical ancillary documents.

3. Franchisor's Associate

The definitions of "franchisor's associate" in acts other than the Alberta Act are substantially the same. "Franchisor's associate" means a person: (a) who, directly or indirectly, (i) controls or is controlled by the franchisor, or (ii) is controlled by another person who also controls the franchisor, and (b) who (i) is directly involved in the grant of the franchise (A) by being involved in reviewing or approving the grant of the franchise, or (B) by making representations to the prospective franchisee on behalf of the franchisor for the purpose of granting the franchise, marketing the franchise or otherwise offering to grant the franchise, or (ii) exercises significant operational control of the franchisee, and to whom the franchisee has a continuing financial obligation in respect of the franchise (S.O. 2000, c.3, s. 1(1); R.S.PEI 1988, c. F-14.1. s. 1(1)(g); S.N.B. 2007, c. F-23.5, s. 1(1); C.C.S.M., c. F156, s. 1(1); S.B.C., c.35, s. 1(1) (Can.)). The expansive definitions of a franchisor's associate therefore include principal owners or controlling shareholders of a franchisor who are personally involved in the granting or marketing of franchises and parent companies of Canadian subsidiaries established to conduct franchise operations in Canada where the parent company is involved in reviewing or approving the grant of the franchise.

There is no specific definition of a "franchisor's associate" in the Alberta Act. However, an "associate of a franchisor" is defined as a person who is directly involved in the granting of the franchise or, if there are continuing financial obligations by the franchisee to that person, significant operational controls by that person on the franchisee, and the person controls the franchisor, the person is controlled by the franchisor, or the person and the franchisor are under the common control of another person (R.S.A. 2000, c. F-23, s. 1(2) (Can.)).

In *Zwaniga v. John Vince Foods Distribution L.P.*, 2012 ONSC 3848, 2012 ONSC 3848 (CanLII) (Can.), there was a distribution agreement between the franchisee and Revolution Foods Technology Inc. as a vending machine distributor. The defendant, John Vince Foods Distribution L.P., was found not to be an associate of the franchisor. John Vince Foods had contracted with the franchisor to supply peanut products through a sponsorship and supply agreement. The court held that the contractual arrangement between John Vince Foods and the franchisor did not amount to control from a corporate perspective for the purposes of the definition of franchisor's associate in the Ontario Act.

In *Simpson v. First Choice Hair Cutters Ltd.*, ([2003] O.J. No. 2884 (Can. Ont. Sup. Ct.), appeal to Ontario Court of Appeal dismissed, 2004 CanLII 10245 (ONCA) (Can.), a parent company of a franchisor was held not to be a "franchisor's associate" as defined by the Ontario Act.

In *1490664 Ontario Ltd. v. Dig this Garden Retailers Ltd.*, 2005 CanLII 25181 (ONCA) (Can.), ownership of 50% (as opposed to more than 50%) of a franchisor was found to be sufficient for an individual to be a "franchisor's associate" under the Ontario Act.

In *Sovereignty Investment Holdings Inc. v. 9127-6907 Quebec Inc.*, 2008 CanLII 57450 (ONSC) (Can.), directors and officers of a franchisor who also owned the franchisor and were involved in all major decisions affecting the grant of the franchise were found to be franchisor's associates under the Ontario

Act. Additionally, a sublandlord that was related to the franchisor was held to be a franchisor's associate as a result of the provisions of the sublease, which the court held constituted a continuing financial obligation and gave the sublandlord significant operational control over the franchisee. See also *6792341 Canada Inc. v. Dollar It Limited*, 2009 ONCA 385 (CanLII); 95 O.R. (3d) 291 (Can.).

Following are three other decisions in which principals of a corporate franchisor have been found to be franchisor's associates and thus jointly and severally liable for the obligations of the franchisor in an action for damages on statutory rescission of the franchise agreement:

- *6862829 Canada Ltd. v. Dollar It*, 2010 ONCA 34 (CanLII) (Can.)
- *MBCO Summer Hill Inc. v. MBCO Associates Ontario Inc.*, 2001 ONSC 5432 (CanLII) (Can.), varied 2011 ONCA 236 (CanLII) (Can.)
- *Adlakha v. Meehan*, 2011 ONSC 444 (CanLII) (Can.)

Practice Note

Each of the Provincial Acts contains an expansive definition of a "franchisor's associate," which can include principal owners and controlling shareholders. A franchisor's associate can be liable to a franchisee in certain instances for breaches of those acts.

III. Application of the Provincial Acts

Each of the Provincial Acts applies to a franchise agreement or renewal or extension of the franchise agreement entered into on or after the coming into force of those acts and to a business operated under such an agreement, renewal or extension if it is to be operated partly or wholly in any of those Provinces (R.S.A. 2000, c. F-23, s. 3; S.O. 2000, c.3, s. 2; R.S.PEI 1988, c. F-14.1. s. 2; S.N.B. 2007, c. F-23.5, s. 2(2); C.C.S.M., c. F156, s. 2; S.B.C., c.35, s. 2 (Can.)). Other than the Alberta Act, there is no residency requirement for the franchisee. The Alberta Act applies to the sale of a franchise made on or after the coming into force of the Alberta Act if the franchised business is to be operated either partly or wholly in Alberta and the purchaser of the franchise is an Alberta resident or has a permanent establishment in Alberta (R.S.A. 2000, c. F-23, s. 3; S.O. 2000, c.3, s. 3(1)(b) (Can.)).

As an example, if a U.S.-based franchisor sells a franchise to a franchisee located in the United States, and the business is to be operated in Ontario, Prince Edward Island, New Brunswick, Manitoba, British Columbia and Alberta, it will be required to comply with each of those acts other than the Alberta Act. In effect, the franchise agreement and ancillary documents would have to conform to the requirements, and a compliant disclosure document must be delivered to the franchisee in accordance with all the Provincial Acts other than the Alberta Act. The law that governs the franchise agreement and ancillary documents would be subject to interprovincial conflicts of laws principles, but the Alberta Act would not likely apply if the franchisee does not meet the Alberta residency requirements.

In *Ellis v. Subway Franchise Systems of Canada Ltd.*, 2000 CanLII 22770 (ONSC) (Can.), it was held that the Ontario Act was not retroactive except for certain sections as specifically enumerated.

In *Katotikidis v. Mr. Submarine Ltd.*, 2002 CanLII 49646 (ONSC) (Can.), it was held that although the duty of fair dealing would apply to franchise agreements entered into before the coming into force of the Ontario Act, the duty of good faith would not apply to events occurring before the date when the Ontario Act came into force.

In *Machias v. Mr. Submarine Ltd.*, 2002 CanLII 49643 (ONSC) (Can.), the Ontario Act was held not to apply to a franchise that was operated outside of Ontario.

In *Esplanade Irish Pubs Inc. v. Greey Realty Holdings Ltd.*, 2003 CanLII 1817 (ONSC) (Can.), affirmed *Prime Restaurants of Canada Inc. v. Greey Realty Holdings Ltd.*, 2004 CanLII 22795 (ONCA) (Can.), the definition of "franchisee" under the Ontario Act was held not to apply, since the lease was entered into before the Ontario Act came into force.

Practice Note

The Alberta Act applies only to purchasers who are residents of Alberta or have permanent establishments already in Alberta.

Exemptions from the application of the entirety of each of the Provincial Acts other than the Alberta Act are available for the following continuing commercial relationships or arrangements:

1. employer-employee relationships;
2. partnerships;
3. membership in a co-operative association;
4. an arrangement arising from an agreement to use a trademark or other commercial symbol designating a person who offers on a general basis, for consideration, a service for the evaluation, testing or certification of goods or services;
5. an arrangement arising from an agreement between a licensor and a single licensee to license a specific trademark or other commercial symbol where the license is the only one of the general nature and type to be

granted by the licensor with respect to that trademark or other commercial symbol; and

6. a relationship or arrangement arising out of an oral agreement where there is no writing to evidence any material term or aspect of the relationship or arrangement (S.O. 2000, c.3, s. 2(3); R.S.PEI 1988, c. F-14.1. s. 2(3); S.N.B. 2007, c. F-23.5, s. 2(4); C.C.S.M., c. F156, s. 2(4); S.B.C., c.35, s. 2(3) (Can.)).

The Ontario Act and the PEI Act also do not apply to a service contract or franchise-like arrangement with the Crown (i.e., the federal, provincial or territorial governments) (S.O. 2000, c.3, s. 2(3)8.; R.S.PEI 1988, c. F-14.1. s. 2(3)(h) (Can.)).

The Manitoba Act, the PEI Act, the NB Act and the BC Act also contain exclusions of arrangements arising out of agreements for the purchase and sale of a reasonable amount of goods or services at a reasonable wholesale price or for the purchase of a reasonable amount of services at a reasonable price (R.S.PEI 1988, c. F-14.1., s. 2(3)(g), S.N.B. 2007, c. F-23.5, s. 2(4)(g) and C.C.S.M., c. F156, s. 2(3)(j); S.B.C., c.35, s. 2(3)(g) (Can.)).

The Alberta Act does not provide for exemptions from the application of the entire Alberta Act, other than in the transitional provisions. Since the application of the Alberta Act depends on the concept of a sale of the "franchise," the definition of a "franchise" becomes the determinate factor as to whether the Alberta Act applies. Also incumbent to the definition of a franchise in the Alberta Act is the concept of a "franchise fee." As indicated earlier, the definition of "franchise fee" in the Alberta Act is specifically stated to not include a purchase of or an agreement to purchase a reasonable amount of goods at a reasonable bona fide wholesale price, a purchase of or an agreement to purchase a reasonable amount of services at a reasonable bona fide wholesale price, or a payment of a reasonable service charge to the issuer of a credit or debit card by an establishment accepting the credit or debit card, as the case may be. As previously mentioned, while there are blanket exclusions of such agreements for the wholesale purchases of goods or services in each of the PEI Act, the NB Act, the Manitoba Act and the BC Act, there are no similar exemptions under the Ontario Act.

In *MGDC Management Group v. Marilyn Monroe Estate*, 2014 CANLII 4584 (ONSC) (Can.), the arrangement arising from an agreement between a licensor and a single licensee exemption referred to in Section 2(3) 5 of the Ontario Act was applied to exempt a license arrangement. Even though the agreement being considered contained elements beyond a simple trademark license, the court found that not all of the essential elements from the definition of a franchise were present, so the exemption applied.

A. Obligation to Disclose

As of the dates of the enactment of the obligation to disclose (see History of Franchise Legislation in Canada at the beginning of the chapter for dates), under all of the Provincial Acts, a franchisor is required to provide a prospective franchisee with a disclosure document not less than 14 days before the earlier of: (a) the signing by the Franchisee of the franchise agreement or any other agreement relating to the franchise; or (b) the payment of any consideration relating to the franchise under all of the Provincial Acts (S.A. 1995 c.F-17 s.4(2); S.O. 2000, c.3, s.5(1); R.S. PEI 1988, C.F-14.1 s. 5(1); S.N.B. 2007, c.F-23.5, s. 5(1); C.C.S.M., c.F156, s. 5(2); S.B.C., c.35, s. 5(1), (Can.)). In each of the Alberta, Manitoba, PEI, NB and BC Acts, an agreement that provides only for one or more of the following is not a franchise agreement, thereby not requiring the delivery of a disclosure document:

(i) the keeping confidential or prohibiting the use of any information or material that may be provided to the prospective franchisee; and
(ii) the designation of a location or territory of the prospective franchised business.

In each of the PEI, NB, Manitoba and BC Acts, there are further definitions as to what is considered confidential information. An agreement that prohibits the disclosure of information to an organization of franchisees, other franchisees of the same system or to a franchisee's professional advisors would not be exempt from the disclosure requirement. There is no similar limitation on confidentiality agreements in the Alberta Act. The Ontario Act does not contain any exemption for a confidentiality agreement or a location or territory designation agreement.

The Alberta, Manitoba and BC Acts provide that the payment by a prospective franchisee of a fully refundable deposit prior to the disclosure period elapsing does not constitute a breach of the disclosure obligation. The Alberta, Manitoba and British Columbia Acts provide that a fully refundable deposit is one that does not exceed 20% of the initial franchise fee that is refundable without any deductions and that is given under an agreement that does not bind the prospective franchisee to enter into any franchise agreement (Alta. Reg. 240/95, s. 5; Man. Reg. 29/2012, s. 11; B.C. Reg. 238/2016, s. 11 (Can.)). In the Manitoba Regulations, the maximum amount of a deposit is C$100,000 (Man. Reg. 29/2012, s. 11 (Can.)). The BC Act also contains a provision requiring that the deposit be "refundable without any deductions, if a prospective franchisee does not enter into a franchise agreement . . ." (S.B.C., c.35, s. 5(13)(b) (Can.)).

> **Practice Note**
>
> **Unlike the Alberta Act, the Manitoba Act and the BC Act, the other Provincial Acts do not contain any exemption from the disclosure obligation for a deposit agreement. The Ontario Act is the only one that does not contain any exemption from the disclosure obligation for a confidentiality agreement or a location or a territory designation agreement.**

Under each of the Provincial Acts, a disclosure document must contain any and all material facts including, without limitation, financial statements as prescribed by the respective regulations, copies of all agreements relating to the franchise, certification by the franchisor, and other information as prescribed under each of the Provincial Regulations (R.S.A. 2000, c. F-23, s. 4(3); S.O. 2000, c.3, s. 5(4); R.S.PEI 1988, c. F-14.1. s. 5(4); S.N.B. 2007, c. F-23.5, s. 5(4); C.C.S.M., c. F156, s. 5(5); S.B.C., c.35, s. 5(4)(5) (Can.)).

Under the Provincial Acts, other than the Alberta Act, there are specific prescribed statements that must be used to assist the prospective franchisee in making informed investment decisions. Under the Alberta Regulations, there is a specific requirement to quote the sections of the Alberta Act relating to the rescission rights in the event of failure to disclose and rights to damages for misrepresentation (Alta. Reg. 240/95, Schedule 1, 19-20 (Can.)). It is critical that the disclosure documents in each of the provinces contain all material facts in addition to the prescribed information. In each case, franchisors will have to consider carefully what constitutes a material fact (a defined term) at the time of disclosure apart from and in addition to the specific material fact items outlined in the Provincial Regulations.

Each of the Provincial Acts contains similar definitions of "material fact" with some minor variation. Under the Provincial Acts, a "material fact" is defined to mean (in Ontario, it is defined more broadly to "include") any information about the business, operations, capital or control of the franchisor, the franchisor's associate, or the franchise system that would reasonably be expected to have a significant effect on the value or price of the franchise to be granted or the decision to acquire the franchise (R.S.A. 2000, c. F-23, s. 1(1)(o); S.O. 2000, c.3, s. 1(1); R.S.PEI 1988, c. F-14.1. s. 1(1)(l); S.N.B. 2007, c. F-23.5, s. 1(1); C.C.S.M., c. F156, s. 1(1); S.B.C., c.35, s. 1(1) (Can.)).

In *6792341 Canada Inc. v. Dollar It Limited*, 95 O.R. (3d) 291; 2009 ONCA 385 (CanLII) (Can.), it was held that where the franchisor requires a franchisee to enter into a sublease for the premises, the disclosure document must also include a copy of the head lease if the form of sublease incorporated by reference the terms of the head lease. In *6862829 Canada Ltd. v. Dollar It Limited*,

2010 ONCA 34 (CanLII) (Can.), financial statements that failed to disclose a pending lawsuit against the franchisor were determined to have omitted a material fact. Ultimately, in both of these cases the disclosure document was held to be so defective that it was determined not to meet the threshold for required disclosure at all, and the franchisees were given the right to rescind the franchise agreements and to be compensated as required by the Ontario Act.

In *2240802 Ontario Inc. v. Springdale Pizza Depot Ltd.*, 2013 ONSC 7288, aff'd 2015 ONCA 236 (CanLII) (Can.), Springdale's disclosure document did not mention the ongoing litigation by a former franchisee against Springdale for rescission based on deficient disclosure. The court held that this information was a material fact that had to be disclosed. However, in *Caffe Demetre Franchising Corp. v. 2249027 Ontario Inc.*, 2015 ONCA 258 (CanLII) (Can.), the court noted that there is no specific provision in the Ontario Act or the regulations that requires all franchisor-initiated litigation to be disclosed in a disclosure document. The court stated that *2240802 Ontario Inc. v. Springdale Pizza Depot Ltd.* does not stand for the proposition that any litigation involving a franchisor amounts to a material fact requiring disclosure. Rather, section 2(5) of O. Reg. 581/00 specifically provides identified categories of litigation that must be disclosed. According to the court, litigation must be disclosed if it falls within the description contemplated by s. 2(5) of the regulation, but if it does not, whether or not the litigation is a material fact will be a question of fact determined on a case-by-case basis.

In *Trillium Motor World Ltd. v. General Motors of Canada Ltd.*, 2015 ONSC 3824 (CanLII) (Can.), the court held that General Motors was not required to disclose the facts relating to its restructuring at the time it was attempting to get dealers to sign agreements to exit the system. The court found that General Motors was not required to deliver a disclosure document under s. 5 of the Ontario Act because the documentation referred to in this section relates to any document that has the effect of changing a prospective franchisee into a franchisee. The agreements that the dealers were entering into effectively changed a franchisee's status such that it was no longer a franchisee. The court also held that the duty to disclose important and material facts under section 3 of the Ontario Act does not extend so far as to require General Motors to keep the dealers abreast of every development or to share details of the restructuring plan on an ongoing basis. At the time of publication, this case is being appealed.

In *1250264 Ontario Inc. v Pet Valu Canada Inc.*, 2016 ONCA 24 (CanLII) (Can.), the court stated that a misrepresentation in a disclosure document (or a failure to disclose material facts in a disclosure document) cannot amount to a breach of the statutory duty of good faith and fair dealing in section 3 of the Ontario Act because such a misrepresentation does not occur in the "performance and enforcement" of the franchise agreement, as required by the clear wording of section 3.

In *Raibex Canada Ltd. v. ASWR Franchising Corp.*, 2016 ONSC 5575 (CanLII) (Can.), the court granted a two-year rescission remedy primarily because the disclosure document did not contain a copy of the head lease and associated site-specific cost information, despite there being no site identified at the time of disclosure or when the franchise agreement was executed (a practice the court recognized is not uncommon in the franchise industry). The court found that the franchisor must delay delivering a disclosure document until all material facts (not just facts about the head lease) are known. At the time of publication, this case is being appealed by the franchisor defendants.

B. Exemptions from the Obligation to Disclose

Exemptions from disclosure under the Provincial Acts (RSA 2000, c. F-23, s. 5(1); S.O. 2000, c.3 s. 5(7); R.S. PEI 1998, c. F-14.1 s. 5(7); S.N.B. 2007, c. F-23.5, s. 5(8); C.C.S.M. c. F-156, s. 5(11); S.B.C., c.35, s. 5(8) (Can.)) include the following:

(a) The grant of a franchise by a franchisee if, among other things, the grant is for the franchisee's own account and the grant is not effected by or through the franchisor. A grant is not effected by or through the franchisor merely because the franchisor has a right, exercisable on reasonable grounds, to approve or disapprove the grant or a transfer fee to be paid in an amount set out in the franchise agreement or in an amount that does not exceed the reasonable actual costs incurred by the franchisor to process the grant.

(b) The grant of a franchise to a person who has been an officer or director of the franchisor or the franchisor's associate for at least six months for that person's own account. In the Manitoba Act, the PEI Act, the NB Act and the BC Act the six-month period has to be immediately before the grant of the franchise.

(c) The grant of an additional franchise to an existing franchisee if that additional franchise is substantially the same as the existing franchise that the franchisee is operating and, in each of the Provincial Acts other than the Alberta Act, if there has been no material change since the existing franchise agreement or latest renewal or extension of the existing franchise agreement was entered into.

(d) The grant of a franchise by an executor, receiver, trustee or guardian on behalf of a person other than the franchisor or the estate of the franchisor.

(e) The grant of a franchise to a person to sell goods or services within a business in which that person has an interest if the sales arising from those goods or services as anticipated by the parties at the time the agreement was entered into, do not exceed, in relation to the total sales of the business, 20% in all of the Provincial Acts (generally known as a "fractional franchise"). In each of the Manitoba, PEI, NB and BC Acts, the percentage is stated in the respective section of those acts, and they specify that the relevant time period for assessing the percentage of total sales is "during the first year of operation of the franchise"; in Ontario and Alberta, the percentage is prescribed in the regulations and the legislation does not specify a relevant time period (Alta. Reg. 240/95, s. 4; O. Reg. 581/00, s. 8; R.S.PEI 1988, c. F-14.1. s. 5(7)(e); S.N.B. 2007, c. F-23.5, s. 5(8)(e); C.C.S.M., c. F156, s. 5(11)(e); S.B.C., c.35, s. 5(8)(e) (Can.)).

(f) The renewal or extension of a franchise agreement, where there has been no interruption in the operation of the business and no material change since the franchise agreement or latest renewal or extension of the agreement was entered into (the Alberta Act does not impose the requirement that there has been no material change).

(g) The grant of a franchise if the prospective franchisee is required to make a total annual investment to acquire and operate the franchise in an amount that does not exceed C$5,000 (Alta. Reg. 240/95, s. 6; O. Reg. 581/00, s. 9; PEI Reg. EC 232/106. s. 7; N.B. Reg., 2010-92, s. 10; Man. Reg. 29/2012, s. 10 (Can.)).

(h) In PEI, New Brunswick and Manitoba, if the franchise agreement is not valid for longer than one year and does not involve the payment of a non-refundable franchise fee, and the franchisor or its associate provides location assistance, including securing retail outlets or accounts or locations or sites for vending machines, display racks, or other product sales displays.

(i) In Ontario and BC, there is a similar exemption for franchise agreements not valid for longer than one year which do not involve the payment of a non-refundable fee, but there is no additional requirement for location assistance. The BC Act contains some language that is not found in the Ontario Act in that it specifies that all renewals or extensions of the agreement must comprise a period of less than one year, and in addition to there being no non-refundable initial franchise fee, there must also be no non-refundable renewal or extension fees.

(j) In Ontario only, the grant of a franchise where the prospective franchisee is investing in the acquisition and operation of the franchise over a period of one year, in an amount greater than C$5,000,000 (the "sophisticated franchisee" exemption) (O. Reg. 581/00, s. 10 (Can.)). The BC Act contains a similar exemption: where the franchisee "is investing an amount greater than a prescribed amount in the acquisition of the franchise" (S.B.C., c.35, s. 5(8)(i) (Can.)). Note, however, that in BC only investments in the *acquisition* of the franchise qualify (as opposed to investments in the acquisition *and operation* of the franchise). Like in Ontario, the prescribed amount is C$5,000,000 (B.C. Reg. 238/2016, s. 10); and

(k) In Alberta only, the sale of a right to a person to sell goods or services within or adjacent to a retail establishment as a department or division of the establishment, if the person is not required to purchase goods or services from the operation of the retail establishment (R.S.A. 2000, c. F-23, s. 5(1)(g) (Can.)).

In *1518628 Ontario Inc. v. Tutor Time Learning Centres LLC*, 2006 CanLII 25276 (ONSC) (Can.) ("Tutor Time"), the imposition by the franchisor of a condition that the guarantee of the spouse of the franchisee also be signed was held to make the sale "effected by or through the franchisor" and not subject to the sale effected by a franchisee for its own account exemption. Therefore, disclosure was required. In *917246 Alberta Ltd. v. Panda Flowers (1999) Ltd.*, 2004 ABQB 234, 2004 ABQB 234 (CanLII) (Can.), the court considered a specific fact situation and found that the sale was for the franchisee's own account without having been "effected by or through" the franchisor, so there was no requirement to disclose.

In *MAA Diners Inc. v. 3 for 1 Pizza & Wings (Canada) Inc.*, 2003 CanLII 10615 (ONSC), aff'd 2004 CanLII 19240 (ONCA) (Can.), the court pierced the corporate veil to find that a vendor of a franchise, although not the franchisor's associate, was the same entity as the franchisor and therefore not exempt from providing disclosure, as the sale was effected by or through the franchisor.

In *TA & K Enterprises Inc. v. Suncor Energy Products Inc.*, 2011 ONCA 613, 2011 ONCA 613 (CanLII) (Can.), the Ontario Court of Appeal upheld a judge's decision that a franchisor of gas stations did not have to provide a disclosure document because the new one-year agreements were renewals or extensions as exempted by Section 5(7)(f) of the Ontario Act or franchise agreements for less than one year without the payment of a franchise fee as exempted by Section 5(7)(g)(ii).

C. Material Changes

Under all of the Provincial Acts, a franchisor is required to provide a prospective franchisee with a written statement of any material change as soon as practicable after the change has occurred and before the earlier of (a) the signing of the agreement, and (b) the payment of any consideration relating to the franchise (R.S.A. 2000, c. F-23, s. 4(4); S.O. 2000, c.3, s. 5(5); R.S.PEI 1988, c. F-14.1. s. 5(5); S.N.B. 2007, c. F-23.5, s. 5(6); C.C.S.M., c. F156, s. 5(8); S.B.C., c.35, s. 5(6) (Can.)).

In determining whether delivery of a statement of a material change is required, it is necessary to consider the definition of "material change." In each of the Provincial Acts, "material change" is defined to mean a change in the business, operations, capital or control of the franchisor or the franchisor's associate, a change in the franchise system or, under the Ontario Act, a change prescribed by regulation that would reasonably be expected to have a significant adverse effect on the value or price of the franchise to be granted or on the decision to acquire the franchise (R.S.A. 2000, c. F-23, s. 1(1)(n); S.O. 2000, c.3, s. 1(1); R.S.PEI 1988, c. F-14.1. s. 1(1)(k); S.N.B. 2007, c. F-23.5, s. 1(1); C.C.S.M., c. F156, s. 1(1); S.B.C., c.35, s. 1(1) (Can.)). If the decision to implement the change has been made by senior management of the franchisor, disclosure may also be required if senior management believes that confirmation of the decision by the board of directors is probable even though the board has not considered the change. In each of the PEI, NB, Manitoba and BC Acts, the definitions also refer to a change in the franchise rather than just a change in the franchise system, and there are no references to any prescribed change.

In *MDG Kingston Inc. v. MDG Computers Canada Inc.*, 2008 ONCA 656 (CanLII) (Can.)), changes in costs and expenses to franchisees and other fundamental changes to the business in the context of a renewal of a franchise agreement were held to be material changes. The court of appeal clarified that material changes need to be adverse changes.

Practice Note

For franchisors whose securities are listed for trading on a stock exchange or who otherwise distribute their securities to the public, this obligation might conflict with respect to the timing of disclosure under securities commission or stock exchange regulations or policies.

D. Delivery Mechanics

Under each of the Provincial Acts, other than Alberta and BC, a disclosure document may be delivered personally, by registered mail, or by any other prescribed method (S.O. 2000, c.3, s. 5(2); R.S.PEI 1988, c. F-14.1. s. 5(2); S.N.B. 2007, c. F-23.5, s. 5(2); C.C.S.M., c. F156, s. 5(4); S.B.C., c.35, s. 5(2) (Can.)). The BC Act provides that a disclosure document may be delivered personally, by email, or by any other prescribed method (S.B.C., c.35, s. 5(2) (Can.)). The Manitoba

Act also permits delivery by fax. The regulations under the PEI Act, the NB Act, the Manitoba Act, the Ontario Act and the BC Act state that delivery is permitted by courier and electronically (PEI Reg. EC 232/106. s. 2; N.B. Reg., 2010-92, s. 3; Man. Reg. 29/2012, s. 5; O. Reg. 581/00, s. 12 (Can.); B.C. Reg. 238/2016, s. 8(1)). There are some differences among the requirements of those provinces. In New Brunswick, Manitoba, Ontario and BC, the courier must be prepaid. In BC the prepaid courier or equivalent must permit tracking and confirmation of receipt of the delivery. In PEI, Manitoba, Ontario and BC there must be an acknowledgment of receipt by the franchisee. There are also some technical differences as to what qualifies as proper electronic delivery of a disclosure document in PEI, New Brunswick, Manitoba, Ontario and BC so care must be taken to follow those requirements.

The Manitoba Regulation and the BC Regulation provide that a statement of material change is to be given in the same manner as a disclosure document (Man. Reg. 29/2012, s. 6; BC Reg. 238/2016, s.8(2)) (Can.)). While not specified in Ontario, Prince Edward Island and New Brunswick, presumably a statement of material change may be provided in the same manner as a disclosure document.

The Alberta Act does not specify any method of delivery for either document. The act requires only that a franchisor must give every prospective franchisee a disclosure document and provide a description of the material change (R.S.A. 2000, c. F-23, s. 4 (Can.)).

The Ontario Act, the PEI Act, the NB Act and the BC Act all require that a disclosure document be delivered as one document at one time (S.O. 2000, c.3, s. 5(3); R.S.PEI 1988, c. F-14.1. s. 5(3); S.N.B. 2007, c. F-23.5, s. 5(3) (Can.)). The Manitoba Act contains no such specification, and it specifically contemplates disclosure in more than one part (C.C.S.M., c. F156, s. 5(3) (Can.)).

Under the Manitoba Act, the disclosure document is considered not to have been given until the last document has been delivered. The Manitoba Regulation prescribes rules that apply if disclosure is given in more than one document (Man. Reg. 29/2012, s. 4 (Can.)). There are mandatory statements that need to be repeated for each part that is given, and prescribed wording must be prominently displayed. Further, there are certain parts of the prescribed information that need to be given together.

For practical purposes, it is strongly recommended that all disclosure documents and statements of material change be delivered in a manner that can be substantiated by written proof of delivery. Further, a proper form of receipt executed by the franchisee and any other person who may be asked to sign the franchise and related agreements (i.e., guarantor) should be completed and returned to the franchisor whenever possible.

> **Practice Note**
>
> **For practical purposes, it is strongly recommended that all disclosure documents and statements of material change be delivered in a manner that can be substantiated by written proof of delivery, and that a signed receipt is obtained.**

E. Rescission

Franchisees are given a right of rescission under each of the Provincial Acts if the franchisor has not provided a disclosure document as required by the Provincial Legislation. In each of the Provincial Acts other than the Alberta Act, a franchisee may rescind the franchise agreement no later than 60 days after receiving the disclosure document if the franchisor fails to provide the disclosure document or statement of material change within the time requirements of the applicable Provincial Act or if the contents do not meet the requirements of the applicable Provincial Act (S.O. 2000, c.3, s. 6(1); R.S.PEI 1988, c. F-14.1. s. 6(1); S.N.B. 2007, c. F-23.5, s. 6(1); C.C.S.M., c. F156, s. 6(1); S.B.C., c.35, s. 6(1) (Can.)). Further, under those Provincial Acts, the franchisee may rescind the franchise agreement without penalty or obligation within two years of entering into the agreement if the franchisor never provided a disclosure document (S.O. 2000, c.3, s. 6(2); R.S.PEI 1988, c. F-14.1. s. 6(2); S.N.B. 2007, c. F-23.5, s. 6(2); C.C.S.M., c. F156, s. 6(2); S.B.C., c.35, s. 6(2) (Can.)). Notice of rescission must be in writing and must be delivered to the franchisor personally, by registered mail, fax, or any other method prescribed by regulation (S.O. 2000, c.3, s. 6(4); R.S.PEI 1988, c. F-14.1. s. 6(4); S.N.B. 2007, c. F-23.5, s. 6(4); C.C.S.M., c. F156, s. 6(4) (Can.)). No other methods have yet been prescribed under the PEI Act and the New Brunswick Act. The BC Act provides for personal delivery or by other prescribed methods but does not include registered mail. The Manitoba, Ontario Regulation and the BC Regulation provide that notice of rescission may be delivered by prepaid courier with the BC Regulation requiring that the courier or equivalent provide tracking and confirmation of receipt of delivery (Man. Reg. 29/2012, s. 9; O. Reg. 581/00, s. 13; B.C. Reg. 238/2016, s. 9 (Can.)). Under the Alberta Act, if a franchisor fails to give a franchisee the prescribed disclosure document in accordance with the time requirements of the Act, the prospective franchisee may rescind the franchise agreement by giving notice of cancellation no later than 60 days after receiving the disclosure document or no later than two years after the granting of the franchise, whichever occurs first (R.S.A. 2000, c. F-23, s. 1(13) (Can.)). Under each of the Provincial Acts other than Alberta, a franchisor, within 60 days of the effective date of rescission, must refund to the franchisee any money received from or on behalf of the franchisee, other than money for inventory, supplies or equipment; purchase from the franchisee any inventory purchased pursuant to the franchise agreement at a price equal to the purchase price paid by the franchisee; purchase any supplies and equipment that the franchisee had purchased pursuant to the agreement at a price equal to the purchase price paid by the franchisee; and compensate the franchisee for any losses incurred in acquiring, setting up and operating the franchise less the amounts expended on the repurchase requirements (S.O. 2000, c.3, s. 6(6); R.S.PEI 1988, c. F-14.1. s. 6(6); S.N.B. 2007, c. F-23.5, s. 6(6); C.C.S.M., c. F156, s. 6(6); S.B.C., c.35, s. 6(5) (Can.)). The financial exposure to a franchisor on rescission can be substantial, as all direct and indirect losses incurred by the franchisee must be compensated. Under the Alberta Act, a franchisor, within 30 days of receiving a notice of cancellation, must compensate the franchisee for any net losses the franchisee has occurred in acquiring, setting up and operating the franchised business (R.S.A. 2000, c. F-23, s. 14(2) (Can.)).

There are many court cases in which the rescission rights under the Alberta Act and the Ontario Act have been considered. It is settled that, where no disclosure document has been given, the two-year right to rescind and be compensated for losses will apply. However, in addition to that right of rescission, the Alberta Act, the Ontario Act, and the other Provincial Acts include a right to rescind within a 60-day period if the disclosure is merely defective. For defective disclosure, the court will consider whether a deficient disclosure document is so deficient that it is as if no disclosure document had been given at all. The advantage to a franchisee in making such a claim is the ability to increase the time to rescind from 60 days to two years.

In *Hi Hotel Limited Partnership v. Holiday Hospitality Franchising Inc.*, 2007 ABQB 686, 2007 ABQB 686 (CanLII) (Can), affirmed 2008 ABCA 276, 2008 ABCA 276 (CanLII) (Can), it was held that the failure to attach a signed certificate of the franchisor was a defect that rendered the disclosure document so defective it was as if no disclosure document had been given at all. The franchisee, who was a sophisticated hotel operator, was entitled to rescission under the Alberta Act.

The case was followed in *144824 Alberta Inc. v. Asian Concepts Franchising Corporation*, 2013 ABQB 221, 2013 ABQB 221 (CanLII) (Can.). In that case, a franchisor's certificate was signed by only one director or officer rather than the two that were required where the franchisor has more than one director or officer. The defect was found to be fatal, and the franchisee was entitled to rescission for up to two years.

There are numerous other decisions under the Ontario Act in which one or more deficiencies have either individually or cumulatively been found fatal to it being considered a disclosure document. The *Dollar It* cases mentioned earlier, *6792341 Canada Inc. v. Dollar It Limited*, 95 O.R. (3d) 291; 2009 ONCA 385 (CanLII) (Can.), and *6862829 Canada Ltd. v. Dollar It Limited*, 2010 ONCA 34 (CanLII) (Can.), are examples of courts analyzing deficiencies and finding deficient disclosure documents to not be disclosure documents at all. In *Caffe Demetre Franchising Corp. v. 2249027 Ontario Inc.*, 2015 ONCA 258 (CanLII) (Can.), the court considered *6792341 Canada Inc. v Dollar It Limited* (2009 ONCA 385) and held that there must be "stark and material deficiencies" in a disclosure document before the court finds that effectively no disclosure was ever provided. In this case, the franchisor's failure to disclose litigation commenced by the franchisor against the previous franchisee was not such a deficiency.

Another example of fatal deficiencies is *2337310 Ontario Inc. v 2264145 Ontario Inc.*, 2014 ONSC 4370, where the disclosure document did not contain any of the franchisor's financial statements, information about the franchise lease, nor various agreements that the defendants had entered into between themselves. Similarly, in *2240802 Ontario Inc. v. Springdale Pizza Depot Ltd.*, 2013 ONSC 7288, aff'd 2015 ONCA 236 (CanLII) (Can.), the court held that the requirement to provide a franchisee with independently verified financial information is not a mere technicality but is instead a foundational part of disclosure.

Raibex Canada Ltd. v. ASWR Franchising Corp., 2016 ONSC 5575 (CanLII) (Can.), mentioned above, found that there were multiple deficiencies leading to a two year rescission remedy. As noted above the court found that the disclosure document should have included the head lease and associated site-specific costs (despite there being no lease in existence at the time of disclosure or execution of the franchise agreement). The court also found the disclosure document to be deficient for failing to disclose the costs associated with the mode of development employed by the franchisee. The disclosure document provided costs estimates for building a new restaurant but not for converting an existing restaurant. Despite the franchisee's actual conversion costs being less than the upper range of the disclosed cost of a new build, the court found the disclosure did not meet the requirements. Instead of estimating the costs of conversion, the franchisor provided a disclaimer stating that the costs were impossible to predict. The court equated the use of the disclaimer with an admission that the franchisor could not meet its disclosure requirements. At the time of publication, this case is being appealed by the franchisor defendants.

Apblouin Imports Ltd. v. Global Diaper Services Inc., 2013 ONSC 2592, 2013 ONSC 2592 (CanLII) (Can.), is an example under the Ontario Act where a deficiency was found not to be enough to extend the 60-day rescission period to two years. In this case, the delivery of a disclosure document was made by email rather than by a prescribed method.

It should also be noted that under each of the Provincial Acts there is an express statement that rights conferred under those acts are in addition to any other right or remedy that a franchisee or franchisor may have at law (R.S.A. 2000, c. F-23, s. 15; S.O. 2000, c. 3, s. 9; R.S.PEI 1988, c. F-14.1. s. 10; S.N.B. 2007, c. F-23.5, s. 10 C.C.S.M., c. F156, s. 0 (Can.), S.B.C., c. 35, s. 11).

F. Damages for Misrepresentation

Under the Provincial Acts other than the Alberta Act, if a franchisee suffers a loss because of a misrepresentation contained in the disclosure document, a statement of material change, or as a result of the franchisor's failure to comply with the disclosure document requirements of the applicable act, the franchisee has a right of action for damages against the franchisor, the franchisor's broker, the franchisor's associate, and every person who signed the disclosure document or statement of material change (S.O. 2000, c.3, s. 7(1); R.S.PEI 1988, c. F-14.1. s. 7(1); S.N.B. 2007, c. F-23.5, s. 7(1); C.C.S.M., c. F156, s. 7(1); S.B.C., c.35, s. 7(1) (Can.)). A franchisor's broker is a person other than the franchisor, franchisor's associate, franchisor's agent or franchisee, who grants, markets or otherwise offers to grant a franchise, or who arranges for the grant of a franchise. Under the Ontario Act, there is also a right of action against the franchisor's agent, defined as "a sales agent of the franchisor who is engaged by the franchisor's broker and who is directly involved in granting the franchise" (O. Reg. 581/00, s. 0.1 (Can.)). This greatly expands the classes of persons who are subject to liability beyond those that would otherwise be liable under common law.

Under the Alberta Act, if a franchisee suffers a loss because of a misrepresentation contained in a disclosure document, the franchisee has a right of action for damages against the franchisor and every person who signed the disclosure document (R.S.A. 2000, c. F-23, s. 9 (Can.)).

A "misrepresentation" is defined to include an untrue statement of a material fact, or an omission to state a material fact to make a statement not misleading (R.S.A. 2000, c. F-23, s. 1(1)(q); S.O. 2000, c.3, s. 1(1); R.S.PEI 1988, c. F-14.1. s. 1(1)(n); S.N.B. 2007, c. F-23.5, s. 1(1); C.C.S.M., c. F156, s. 1(1); S.B.C., c.35, s. 1(1) (Can.)). The definition of "misrepresentation" is inclusive in all of the Provincial Acts, with the result that other forms of misrepresentation may be applicable as well. If a disclosure document contains a misrepresentation, each of the Provincial Acts provides that the franchisee is deemed to have relied on the misrepresentation. In the BC Act only, the legislation states that the franchisee is "conclusively" deemed to have relied on the misrepresentation.

The incorporation of liability for misrepresentations in a disclosure document on a broker, agent or associate of a franchisor will likely result in liability being extended to a much broader class of persons than those who would otherwise be liable under common law, particularly given the extended meaning of a "franchisor's associate" under the Ontario Act and an "associate of a franchisor" under the Alberta Act.

G. Liability

The Provincial Acts impose joint and several liability on all persons found liable or who accept liability for breaching the duty of fair dealing, and for interfering with the freedom of the franchisees to associate. Directors and officers who sign a disclosure document or statement of material change are also subject to personal liability for misrepresentations in the disclosure document or statement of material change and, in each of the Provincial Acts other than Alberta, for failure to comply with the disclosure obligations (S.O. 2000, c.3, s.8; RSA 2000, c F-23, ss.11-12; R.S.PEI 1988, c. F-14.1, s.9; S.N.B. 2007, c. F-23.5, s.9; C.C.S.M., c. F156, s.8; S.B.C., c.35, s. 10 (Can.))

All the statutes contain a number of exemptions from liability for misrepresentations. The first exemption occurs where the person proves the franchisee purchased the franchise with knowledge of the misrepresentation (S.O. 2000, c.3, s.7(4); RSA 2000, c F-23, s.10(1); R.S.PEI 1988, c. F-14.1, s.7(4); S.N.B. 2007, c. F-23.5, s.7(4); C.C.S.M., c. F156, s.7(4); S.B.C., c.35, s.8(1) (Can.)).

Secondly, a person other than the franchisor is not liable in an action for misrepresentation if the person proves that the disclosure document was given without that person's knowledge or consent and that on becoming aware of its having been given, the person promptly gave notice that it was given without that person's knowledge and consent (S.O. 2000, c.3, s.7(5)(a); RSA 2000, c F-23, s.10(2)(a); R.S.PEI 1988, c. F-14.1, s.7(5); S.N.B. 2007, c. F-23.5, s.7(5); C.C.S.M., c. F156, s.7(5); S.B.C., c.35, s.8(2)(a) (Can.)). There are also a number of exemptions in each of the Provincial Acts from liability relating to experts whose reports, opinions or statements are made part of the disclosure document (S.O. 2000, c.3, s.7(5)(c); RSA 2000, c F-23, s.10(3); R.S.PEI 1988, c. F-14.1, s.7(5)(c) and s.7(5)(e); S.N.B. 2007, c. F-23.5, s.7(5)(c); C.C.S.M., c. F156, s.7(5)(c) and s.7(5)(e); S.B.C., c.35, s.8(2)(c) and s.8(2)(e) (Can.)).

H. Waivers, Jurisdiction, Venue and Forum

The rights conferred by the statutes are in addition to and do not derogate from any other right or remedy a franchisee may have at law (S.O. 2000, c.3, s.9; RSA 2000, c F-23, s.15; R.S.PEI 1988, c. F-14.1, s.10; S.N.B. 2007, c. F-23.5, s.10; C.C.S.M., c. F156, s.9; S.B.C., c.35, s. 11(1) (Can.)).

Any provision in the franchise agreement attempting to restrict the application of the particular provincial franchise law or to restrict jurisdiction or venue to a forum outside of the particular province is void with respect to a claim otherwise enforceable under the relevant Act (S.O. 2000, c.3, s.10; RSA 2000, c F-23, s.17; R.S.PEI 1988, c. F-14.1, s.11; S.N.B. 2007, c. F-23.5, s.11; C.C.S.M., c. F156, s.10; S.B.C., c.35, s.12(1) (Can.)). Therefore, it is common practice for franchise agreements (including all ancillary documents) for franchises being operated in one of the six provinces to be governed by the law of the province in which the franchise is located, and such agreements should not restrict claims from being resolved in that particular province. Litigation, arbitration, and other alternative dispute resolution proceedings should therefore be conducted in the province in which the franchise is located in accordance with the local law. Foreign franchisors should ensure that all relevant documents are reviewed and amended for compliance with the applicable provincial law.

Practice Note

No franchise agreement can restrict the application of the applicable provincial franchise law in regard to a claim otherwise enforceable under the relevant statute. Foreign franchisors should ensure that all relevant documents are reviewed and amended for compliance with the applicable provincial law.

Any waiver or release by the franchisee of a right given under the Acts or of an obligation or requirement imposed on a franchisor under the Acts is void (S.O. 2000, c.3, s.11; RSA 2000, c F-23, s.18; R.S.PEI 1988, c. F-14.1, s.12; S.N.B. 2007, c. F-23.5, s.12; C.C.S.M., c. F156, s.11; S.B.C., c.35, s.13(1) (Can.)). In 2006, the court in *Tutor Time* provided guidance regarding general releases. The court concluded that Section 11 of the Ontario Act could not operate to invalidate a release of statutory claims given by a franchisee, with independent legal advice, in the course of the settlement of a dispute of existing, known breaches of the Ontario Act. The BC Act contains an exception for waivers or releases provided in accordance with the settlement of an action, claim or dispute (S.B.C., c.35, s.13(2) (Can.)). Therefore, waiver provisions that attempt to avoid the general application of franchise laws, such as those commonly found in United States franchise agreements, for example, should be deleted from Canadian franchise agreements given the fact that such provisions will be deemed to be void.

> **Practice Note**
>
> **Any general waiver or release by the franchisee of a right given under the Acts, or of an obligation or requirement imposed on a franchisor under the Acts, is void. Courts may, however, enforce releases of these statutory claims given by a franchisee, with independent legal advice, in the course of the settlement of a dispute of existing, known breaches of the Acts.**

In any proceeding under the Acts, the burden of proving an exemption or an exclusion is on the person claiming it (S.O. 2000, c.3, s.12; RSA 2000, c F-23, s.19; R.S.PEI 1988, c. F-14.1, s.13; S.N.B. 2007, c. F-23.5, s.13; C.C.S.M., c. F156, s.12; S.B.C., c.35, s.14 (Can.)).

I. Financial Information Exemptions

If a disclosure document is being used across Canada, the franchisor must meet the criteria for exemption in each of the Provincial Acts in order for financial statements to be excluded. Where the franchisor is relying on these exemptions, each of the Provincial Acts requires that the disclosure document include a statement that the franchisor qualifies for the applicable exemption. Note that the exemption is only from disclosing the franchisor's financial statements. The franchisor must still prepare its financial statements in accordance with the standards set out in the Acts, as the franchisor's net worth must be assessed based on such financial statements. The exemptions in each of the Provincial Acts are summarized on the following pages.

	Ontario (O. Reg. 581/00, s.11 (1) (Can.))	**Alberta** (Franchises Act Exemption Regulation, Alta Reg. 312/2000, s.1 (Can.))	**PEI** (Franchises Act Regulation, P.E.I. Reg. EC232/06, s.6 (Can.))	**New Brunswick** (Disclosure Document Regulation, N.B. Reg, 2010-92, s.8 (Can.))	**Manitoba** (Man. Reg. 29/2012, s.8 (Can.))	**British Columbia** (B.C. Reg. 238/2016, s.6 (Can.))
	Under the Ontario Act, a franchisor is exempt from the obligation to disclose financial statements if: (i) the franchisor's net worth on a consolidated basis according to its most recent financial statements that have been audited or for which a review engagement report has been prepared is at least $5,000,000 or is at least $1,000,000 if the franchisor is	Under the Alberta Franchises Act, a franchisor is exempt from the obligation to disclose financial statements if: (i) the franchisor's net worth on a consolidated basis according to its most recent financial statements that have been audited or for which a review engagement report has been prepared is not less than $5,000,000 or not less than $1,000,000 if the franchisor is controlled by	Under the PEI Franchises Act, a franchisor is exempt from the obligation to disclose financial statements if: (i) the franchisor's net worth on a consolidated basis according to its most recent financial statements, which have been audited or for which a review engagement report has been prepared, is at least $2,000,000 or is at least $1,000,000 if the franchisor is controlled by a	Under the New Brunswick Franchises Act, a franchisor is exempt from the obligation to disclose financial statements if: (i) the franchisor's net worth on a consolidated basis according to its most recent financial statements, which have been audited or for which a review engagement report has been prepared, is at least $2,000,000 or is at	Under Manitoba's The Franchises Act, a franchisor is not required to provide the financial statements required under section 7 if: (a) the franchisor has a net worth on a consolidated basis according to its most recent financial statements, which have been audited or for which a review engagement report has been prepared, which (i) is at least $5,000,000, or (ii) is at least $1,000,000, if the franchisor is controlled by a corporation whose net	A franchisor is not required to include financial statements in a disclosure document under section 5 if all of the following conditions are met: (a) the franchisor has a net worth on a consolidated basis according to its most recent financial statements, which have been audited or for which a review engagement report has been prepared, which (i) is at least $5 million, or (ii) is at least $1 million, if the franchisor is controlled by a corporation whose net worth on a consolidated basis according to

	Ontario (O. Reg. 581/00, s.11 (1) (Can.))	**Alberta** (Franchises Act Exemption Regulation, Alta Reg. 312/2000, s.1 (Can.))	**PEI** (Franchises Act Regulation, P.E.I. Reg. EC232/06, s.6 (Can.))	**New Brunswick** (Disclosure Document Regulation, N.B. Reg, 2010-92, s.8 (Can.))	**Manitoba** (Man. Reg. 29/2012, s.8 (Can.))	**British Columbia** (B.C. Reg. 238/2016, s.6 (Can.))
	Under the Ontario Act, a franchisor is exempt from the obligation to disclose financial statements if: (i) the franchisor's net worth on a consolidated basis according to its most recent financial statements that have been audited or for which a review engagement report has been prepared is at least $5,000,000 or is at least $1,000,000 if the franchisor is	Under the Alberta Franchises Act, a franchisor is exempt from the obligation to disclose financial statements if: (i) the franchisor's net worth on a consolidated basis according to its most recent financial statements that have been audited or for which a review engagement report has been prepared is not less than $5,000,000 or not less than $1,000,000 if the franchisor is controlled by	Under the PEI Franchises Act, a franchisor is exempt from the obligation to disclose financial statements if: (i) the franchisor's net worth on a consolidated basis according to its most recent financial statements, which have been audited or for which a review engagement report has been prepared, is at least $2,000,000 or is at least $1,000,000 if the franchisor is controlled by a	Under the New Brunswick Franchises Act, a franchisor is exempt from the obligation to disclose financial statements if: (i) the franchisor's net worth on a consolidated basis according to its most recent financial statements, which have been audited or for which a review engagement report has been prepared, is at least $2,000,000 or is at	Under Manitoba's The Franchises Act, a franchisor is not required to provide the financial statements required under section 7 if: (a) the franchisor has a net worth on a consolidated basis according to its most recent financial statements, which have been audited or for which a review engagement report has been prepared, which (i) is at least $5,000,000, or (ii) is at least $1,000,000, if the franchisor is controlled by a corporation whose net	A franchisor is not required to include financial statements in a disclosure document under section 5 if all of the following conditions are met: (a) the franchisor has a net worth on a consolidated basis according to its most recent financial statements, which have been audited or for which a review engagement report has been prepared, which (i) is at least $5 million, or (ii) is at least $1 million, if the franchisor is controlled by a corporation whose net worth on a consolidated basis according to

	Ontario (O. Reg. 581/00, s.11 (1) (Can.))	**Alberta** (Franchises Act Exemption Regulation, Alta Reg. 312/2000, s.1 (Can.))	**PEI** (Franchises Act Regulation, P.E.I. Reg. EC232/06, s.6 (Can.))	**New Brunswick** (Disclosure Document Regulation, N.B. Reg, 2010-92, s.8 (Can.))	**Manitoba** (Man. Reg. 29/2012, s.8 (Can.))	**British Columbia** (B.C. Reg. 238/2016, s.6 (Can.))
	has at least 25 franchisees in Canada or in a single jurisdiction other than Canada engaging in business at all times; (iii) the franchisor or the corporation which controls the franchisor has engaged in the line of business associated with the franchise for at least five years immediately preceding the date of the disclosure document; *and*	business at all times during the five-year period immediately preceding the date of the disclosure document, *or* (b) the franchisor or the corporation which controls the franchisor has conducted business that is the subject of the franchise continuously for at least five years immediately preceding the date of the disclosure document. If the franchisor meets *each* of the above criteria	than Canada at all times in the five years immediately preceding the date of the disclosure document; (iii) the franchisor or the corporation which controls the franchisor has engaged in the line of business associated with the franchise in the five years immediately preceding the date of the disclosure document; *and* (iv) in the five years	(a) has had at least 25 franchisees engaged in business in Canada or 25 franchisees engaged in business in a single jurisdiction other than Canada, at all times in the five years immediately preceding the date of the disclosure document or (b) has had at least 25 franchisees engaged in business in Canada at all times during a portion of the five-year period immediately	disclosure document, (ii) has had at least 25 franchisees engaged in business in a single jurisdiction other than Canada at all times during the five-year period immediately preceding the date of the disclosure document, (iii) is controlled by a corporation that meets the requirements of subclause (i),	Canada at all times during the 5-year period immediately preceding the date of the disclosure document, (iii) is controlled by a corporation that meets the requirements of subparagraph (i), (iv) is controlled by a corporation that meets the requirements of subparagraph (ii), (v) has had at least 25 franchisees engaged in business in Canada at all

	Ontario (O. Reg. 581/00, s.11 (1) (Can.))	**Alberta** (Franchises Act Exemption Regulation, Alta Reg. 312/2000, s.1 (Can.))	**PEI** (Franchises Act Regulation, P.E.I. Reg. EC232/06, s.5 (Can.))	**New Brunswick** (Disclosure Document Regulation, N.B. Reg, 2010-92, s.8 (Can.))	**Manitoba** (Man. Reg. 29/2012, s.8 (Can.))	**British Columbia** (B.C. Reg. 238/2016, s.6 (Can.))
	(iv) for the past five years immediately preceding the date of the disclosure document, the franchisor, the franchisor's associates, and the directors, general partners and officers of the franchisor have not had any judgment, order or award in Canada or (if applicable) in the other jurisdiction against any of them relating to fraud, unfair or deceptive practices or a law regulating franchises.	((i) and (ii)), the financial statements do not need to be included in the disclosure document used in Alberta.	immediately preceding the date of the disclosure document, the franchisor, the franchisor's associates, and the directors, general partners and officers of the franchisor have not had any judgment, order or award in Canada or (if applicable) in the other jurisdiction against any of them relating to fraud, unfair or deceptive practices or a law regulating franchises including the Act. If the franchisor meets each	preceding the date of the disclosure document and is controlled by a corporation that had at least 25 franchisees engaged in business in Canada at all times during the remainder of that five-year period or (c) has had least 25 franchisees engaged in business in a single jurisdiction other than Canada at all times during a portion of the five year period immediately preceding	(iv) is controlled by a corporation that meets the requirements of subclause (ii), (v) has had at least 25 franchisees engaged in business in Canada at all times during a portion of the five-year period immediately preceding the date of the disclosure document and is controlled by a corporation that had at least 25 franchisees engaged in business in Canada at all times during the remainder	times during a portion of the 5-year period immediately preceding the date of the disclosure document and is controlled by a corporation that had at least 25 franchisees engaged in business in Canada at all times during the remainder of that 5-year period, or (vi) has had at least 25 franchisees engaged in business in a single jurisdiction other than Canada at all times during a

	Ontario (O. Reg. 581/00, s.11 (1) (Can.))	**Alberta** (Franchises Act Exemption Regulation, Alta Reg. 312/2000, s.1 (Can.))	**PEI** (Franchises Act Regulation, P.E.I. Reg. EC232/06, s.6 (Can.))	**New Brunswick** (Disclosure Document Regulation, N.B. Reg, 2010-92, s.8 (Can.))	**Manitoba** (Man. Reg. 29/2012, s.8 (Can.))	**British Columbia** (B.C. Reg. 238/2016, s.6 (Can.))
	If the franchisor meets each of the above criteria, the financial statements do not need to be included in the disclosure document used in Ontario.		of the above criteria, the financial statements do not need to be included in the disclosure document used in PEI.	the date of the disclosure document and is controlled by a corporation that had at least 25 franchisees engaged in business in that jurisdiction at all times during the remainder of that five year period; (iii) the franchisor or the corporation which controls the franchisor has engaged in the line of business associated with the franchise	of that five-year period, or (vi) has had at least 25 franchisees engaged in business in a single jurisdiction other than Canada at all times during a portion of the five-year period immediately preceding the date of the disclosure document and is controlled by a corporation that had at least 25 franchisees engaged in business in that jurisdiction at all times during the remainder of that five-year	portion of the 5-year period immediately preceding the date of the disclosure document and is controlled by a corporation that had at least 25 franchisees engaged in business in that jurisdiction at all times during the remainder of that 5-year period; (c) the franchisor or a corporation controlling the franchisor (i) has engaged in the line of business associated with the

	Ontario (O. Reg. 581/00, s.11 (1) (Can.))	**Alberta** (Franchises Act Exemption Regulation, Alta Reg. 312/2000, s.1 (Can.))	**PEI** (Franchises Act Regulation, P.E.I. Reg. EC232/06, s.6 (Can.))	**New Brunswick** (Disclosure Document Regulation, N.B. Reg, 2010-92, s.8 (Can.))	**Manitoba** (Man. Reg. 29/2012, s.8 (Can.))	**British Columbia** (B.C. Reg. 238/2016, s.6 (Can.))
				during the remainder of that five-year period; *and* (iv) in the five years immediately preceding the date of the disclosure document, the franchisor, the franchisor's associates, and the directors, general partners and officers of the franchisor have not had any conviction, judgment, order or award in Canada or (if	requirements of subclause (i), or (iii) has engaged in the line of business associated with the franchise continuously during a portion of the five-year period immediately preceding the date of the disclosure document and is controlled by a corporation that engaged continuously in that line of business during the remainder of that five-year period; and (d)	disclosure document and is controlled by a corporation that engaged continuously in that line of business during the remainder of that 5-year period; (d) during the 5-year period immediately preceding the date of the disclosure document, (i) in the case of a franchisor described in paragraph (b) (i), (iii) or (v), the franchisor, the franchisor's associates and the directors, officers and

	Ontario (O. Reg. 581/00, s.11 (1) (Can.))	**Alberta** (Franchises Act Exemption Regulation, Alta Reg. 312/2000, s.1 (Can.))	**PEI** (Franchises Act Regulation, P.E.I. Reg. EC232/06, s.6 (Can.))	**New Brunswick** (Disclosure Document Regulation, N.B. Reg, 2010-92, s.8 (Can.))	**Manitoba** (Man. Reg. 29/2012, s.8 (Can.))	**British Columbia** (B.C. Reg. 238/2016, s.6 (Can.))
				applicable) in the other jurisdiction against any of them relating to fraud, unfair or deceptive business practices. If the franchisor meets each of the above criteria, the financial statements do not need to be included in the disclosure document used in New Brunswick.	during the five-year period immediately preceding the date of the disclosure document, (i) in the case of a franchisor described in subclause (b)(i), (iii) or (v), the franchisor, the franchisor's associates and the directors, general partners and officers of the franchisor have not had any conviction, judgment, order or award relating to fraud or unfair or deceptive business practices made against any	general partners of the franchisor have not had a conviction, judgment, order or award relating to fraud or unfair or deceptive business practices made against any of them in Canada, and (ii) in the case of a franchisor described in paragraph (b) (ii), (iv) or (vi), the franchisor, the franchisor's associates and the directors, officers and general partners of the franchisor have not had a

	Ontario (O. Reg. 581/00, s.11 (1) (Can.))	**Alberta** (Franchises Act Exemption Regulation, Alta Reg. 312/2000, s.1 (Can.))	**PEI** (Franchises Act Regulation, P.E.I. Reg. EC232/06, s.6 (Can.))	**New Brunswick** (Disclosure Document Regulation, N.B. Reg. 2010-92, s.8 (Can.))	**Manitoba** (Man. Reg. 29/2012, s.8 (Can.))	**British Columbia** (B.C. Reg. 238/2016, s.6 (Can.))
					of them in Canada, and (ii) in the case of a franchisor described in subclause (b)(ii), (iv) or (vi), the franchisor, the franchisor's associates and the directors, general partners and officers of the franchisor have not had any conviction, judgment, order or award relating to fraud or unfair or deceptive business practices made against any of them in Canada or in the jurisdiction referred to in subclause (b)(ii) or (vi).	conviction, judgment, order or award relating to fraud or unfair or deceptive business practices made against any of them in Canada or in the jurisdiction referred to in paragraph (b) (ii) or (vi).

	Ontario (O. Reg. 581/00, s.11 (1) (Can.))	**Alberta** (Franchises Act Exemption Regulation, Alta Reg. 312/2000, s.1 (Can.))	**PEI** (Franchises Act Regulation, P.E.I. Reg. EC232/06, s.6 (Can.))	**New Brunswick** (Disclosure Document Regulation, N.B. Reg, 2010-92, s.8 (Can.))	**Manitoba** (Man. Reg. 29/2012, s.8 (Can.))	**British Columbia** (B.C. Reg. 238/2016, s.6 (Can.))
					If the franchisor meets each of the above criteria, the financial statements do not need to be included in the disclosure document used in Manitoba.	

Practice Note

A franchisor may be exempt from having to include its financial statements in a disclosure document if it is in compliance with the regulations of the province in which the franchise is located regarding net worth, operating history, number of franchised businesses, and judgments against the business. The exemption, however, is not indefinite, and the franchisor should revisit the exemption criteria annually to confirm it remains exempt from the requirement to provide its financial statements. If relying on an exemption, the disclosure document must include a statement to the effect that financial statements are not being provided because the franchisor qualifies for the exemption. This exemption does not exempt the franchisor from preparing compliant financial statements on an annual basis. A franchisor must still prepare compliant financial statements in order to assess whether it meets the net-worth exemption criteria to validly claim the exemption.

J. Financial Statements

Following is a summary of the disclosure requirements related to a franchisor's financial statements.

Unless the franchisor meets the exemption criteria set out in the regulations for each of the Provincial Acts, the disclosure document must include financial statements for the most recently completed fiscal year of the franchisor's operations. If 180 days have not yet passed since the end of the most recently completed fiscal year and financial statements have not been prepared and reported for that year, the disclosure document may include financial statements for the previous fiscal year.

If the franchisor has operated for less than one fiscal year or if 180 days have not yet passed since the end of the first fiscal year of operations and financial statements for that year have not been prepared, the disclosure document shall include the opening balance sheet for the franchisor. The BC Regulation requires that the opening balance sheet be prepared and reported on in the same manner required of financial statements (BC Reg. 238/2016, s.5(6) (Can.)).

In Ontario, financial statements must be in the form of (i) audited financial statements prepared in accordance with generally accepted auditing standards that are at least equivalent to those set out in the *Canadian Institute of Chartered Accountants Handbook*, or (ii) financial statements prepared on a review engagement basis in accordance with generally accepted accounting principles that are at least equivalent to the review and reporting standards applicable to review engagements also set out in the *Canadian Institute of Chartered Accountants Handbook* (O. Reg. 581/00, s.3(1) (Can)).

Practice Note

The Ontario Act requires that the financial statements included in a disclosure document comply with generally accepted auditing standards that are at least equivalent to those set out in the *Canadian Institute of Chartered Accountants Handbook* or that have been prepared on a review engagement basis in accordance with generally accepted accounting principles that are at least equivalent to the review and reporting standards applicable to review engagements also set out in the *Canadian Institute of Chartered Accountants Handbook.* Failure to comply will mean that the disclosure document does not meet the requirements of the Ontario Act.

Subject to the exemption in Alberta, P.E.I., New Brunswick or British Columbia, financial statements of the franchisor for the most recently completed fiscal year prepared in accordance with generally accepted accounting principles for the jurisdiction in which the franchisor is based must be included (Alta. Reg. 240/95, s.3; PEI Reg. EC 232/106. s.5; N.B. Reg., 2010-92, s.7; Man. Reg. 29/2012, s.7 B.C. Reg. 238/2016, s.5 (Can.)). The minimum standard of review and reporting is a review engagement standard, and the audit and review standards of other jurisdictions are acceptable so long as they are at least equivalent to Canadian standards. If 180 days have not passed since the end of the most recently completed fiscal year, statements in the previous year may be used. For new franchisors who have not completed one fiscal year of operation or 180 days has not passed since the end of the first fiscal year, the disclosure document must include the franchisor's opening balance sheet. As noted above, in BC the opening balance sheet must be reviewed and reported in the same manner as required for financial statements (BC Reg. 238/2016, s.5(6) (Can.)).

Practice Note

Note that, unlike in Ontario, financial statements meeting the required standards but prepared in accordance with the accounting principles of the franchisor's home jurisdiction are acceptable in Alberta, P.E.I., New Brunswick, Manitoba and British Columbia.

In Manitoba, the franchisor's financial statements must be prepared in accordance with (a) Canadian generally accepted accounting principles as set out in the *CICA Handbook*, or (b) in accordance with generally accepted accounting principles of the jurisdiction in which the franchisor is based, *if the statements are supplemented by information that sets out any changes necessary to make the presentation and content of such statements equivalent to Canadian generally accepted accounting principles as set out in the CICA Handbook.* This italicized portion is a disclosure requirement imposed by the Manitoba regulations that is not currently imposed in Ontario, Alberta, P.E.I., New Brunswick, or British Columbia.

Practice Note

If the franchisor's financial statements are not prepared in accordance with Canadian generally accepted accounting principles, the franchisor should consult with its local accountant to determine whether any supplemental information must be disclosed in Manitoba to make the presentation and content of the financial statements equivalent to Canadian generally accepted accounting principles.

The Alberta Regulation and the BC Regulation both make reference to the standards of the new professional oversight body for accountants in Canada, Chartered Professional Accountants Canada ("CPA"). On a province by province basis the CPA is replacing the Canadian Institute of Chartered Accountants. At the date of publication, Alberta and BC are the only provinces which have recognized this change in their franchise regulations (Alta. Reg. 240/95, s. 3(2); B.C. Reg. 238/2016, s. 5(2) (Can.)). Local accounting advice should be obtained to determine how best to comply with the requirements in Manitoba, Ontario, New Brunswick and Prince Edward Island.

K. Certificate of Disclosure

In each of the Provincial Acts, every disclosure document delivered in the particular province must contain a certificate in the prescribed form certifying that the document contains no untrue information, representations or statements, and includes every material fact, financial statement and other information required by the Acts and Regulations (O. Reg. 581/00, s.7(1); Alta. Reg. 240/95, s.2(3); PEI Reg. EC 232/106. s.4(3); N.B. Reg., 2010-92, s.6(2); Man. Reg. 29/2012, s.2(4); B.C. Reg. 238/2016, s.7(3) (Can.)). The term "material fact" is defined in each of the Provincial Acts, and all material facts must be disclosed in the disclosure document in addition to the specific material facts itemized in the particular province's regulations.

The certificate of disclosure must be signed and dated by the franchisor. If the franchisor is incorporated and has only one director or officer, it must be dated and signed by that person (O. Reg. 581/00, s.7(1); Alta. Reg. 240/95, s.2(3); PEI Reg. EC 232/106. s.4(3); N.B. Reg., 2010-92, s.6(2); Man. Reg. 29/2012, s.2(4); B.C. Reg. 238/2016, s.7(3) (Can.)). If the franchisor is incorporated and has more than one director or officer, it must be dated and signed by at least two persons who are directors or officers (O. Reg. 581/00, s.7(1); Alta. Reg. 240/95, s.2(3); PEI Reg. EC 232/106. s.4(3); N.B. Reg., 2010-92, s.6(2); Man. Reg. 29/2012, s.2(4); B.C. Reg. 238/2016, s.7(3) (Can.)). It should be noted that the Ontario, PEI, and New Brunswick Acts do not define director or officer. Therefore, it is possible that individuals other than those formally appointed by the franchisor entity may be found to be directors and/or officers. In the Alberta Act, the Manitoba Act and the BC Regulation, there is a definition of officer that includes individuals who perform functions or act in a capacity similar to the functions of an officer (RSA 2000, c F-23, s.1(r); C.C.S.M., c. F156, s.1(1); B.C. Reg. 238/2016, s.1(1))).

Failure to have the certificate properly signed will give rise to a two-year rescission remedy.

L. Risk Statements

The Ontario Regulations (O. Reg. 581/00, s.4 (Can.)) require that every disclosure document contain the following specific statements in one section at the beginning of the document:

1. A commercial credit report is a report which may include information on the franchisor's business background, banking information, credit history and trade references. Such reports may be obtained from private credit-reporting companies and may provide information useful in making an investment decision.
2. Independent legal and financial advice in relation to the franchise agreement should be sought prior to entering into the franchise agreement.
3. A prospective franchisee is strongly encouraged to contact any current or previous franchisees prior to entering into the franchise agreement.
4. The cost of goods and services acquired under the franchise agreement may not correspond to the lowest cost of the goods and services available in the marketplace.

Similarly, the following paragraphs are required by the P.E.I. Act and the New Brunswick, B.C. and Manitoba Regulations to be included in the disclosure document:

1. A prospective franchisee should seek information on the franchisor and on the franchisor's business background, banking affairs, credit history and trade references.

2. A prospective franchisee should seek expert independent legal and financial advice in relation to franchising and the franchise agreement prior to entering into the franchise agreement.
3. A prospective franchisee should contact current and previous franchisees prior to entering into the franchise agreement.
4. Lists of current and previous franchisees and their contact information can be found in this disclosure document (PEI Reg. EC 232/106. Schedule 1, s.1; N.B. Reg., 2010-92, Schedule 1, s.1; Man. Reg. 29/2012, s.3(1); ; B.C. Reg. 238/2016, s. 3 (Can.)).

The PEI, Manitoba and BC Regulations require the risk statements to be at the beginning of the disclosure document, and the PEI and BC Regulations require that they be presented together (PEI Reg. EC232/06, s.3(1); Manitoba Reg. 29/2012, s.3; BC Reg. 238/2016, s.3 (Can.)).

The Alberta Regulations do not mandate any specific risk warnings, but require that section 13 of the Alberta Act, which gives franchisees the right to rescind all franchise agreements, and section 14 of the Alberta Act, which provides a statement regarding the effect of cancellation, and a copy of section 9 of the Alberta Act, which provides for a franchisee's right of action for damages, all be quoted in the disclosure document (Alta. Reg. 240/95, ss.19-20 under Schedule 1 (Can.)).

M. Alternative Dispute Resolution

The Ontario, Manitoba, P.E.I. and BC Regulations (O. Reg. 581/00, s.5; Man. Reg. 29/2012, s.24; PEI Reg. EC 232/106. s.3(16) to Schedule 1; B.C. Reg. 238/2016, s.4 (Can.)) require a description of mediation or other alternative dispute resolution and the circumstances under which the process may be initiated, if an internal or external mediation or other alternative dispute resolution process is used. Regardless of whether an alternative dispute resolution process is used, an Ontario and Manitoba disclosure document must contain a statement in prescribed language with respect to the possibility of utilizing mediation as a voluntary dispute resolution process.

The New Brunswick Act and Mediation Regulation (Mediation Regulation, N.B. Reg., 2010-93 (Can.)) provide a detailed statutory scheme that governs dispute resolution between parties to a franchise agreement where the process, time lines, and formalities required when engaging in dispute resolution are described (S.N.B. 2007, c. F-23.5, s.8; N.B. Reg., 2010-93 (Can.)). Any party to a franchise agreement who has a dispute with another party(ies) may deliver to the party(ies) a notice of dispute outlining the nature of the dispute and the desired outcome. Within 15 days after delivery of the notice of dispute, the parties shall attempt to resolve the dispute, failing which, any party may deliver a notice to mediate to all parties to the franchise agreement within 30 days after delivery of the notice of dispute. A party who receives the notice of mediation and is of the opinion that the dispute is not suitable for mediation may deliver a notice declining mediation to the other party(ies). If no party submits a notice declining mediation, the parties shall jointly appoint a mediator within 14 days (if there are four or fewer parties) or within 21 days (if there are five or more parties). While pre-mediation conferences are optional, the actual mediation of the dispute must begin within 45 days after a mediator is appointed unless another date is specified by the mediator with the agreement of all parties. Upon conclusion of mediation, the mediator shall complete a certificate of completed mediation and deliver a copy to each of the parties.

N. General Information

Under the regulations of each of the Provincial Acts a disclosure document must include certain background information, including the following:

(a) identification of the franchisor;
(b) business history of the franchisor;
(c) business background of directors, general partners and officers;
(d) details of previous convictions of fraud, unfair or deceptive business practices, or violations of a law that regulates franchises or business, or charges pending against the franchisor, the franchisor's associate, or a director, general partner or officer of the franchisor;
(e) details regarding administrative orders or penalties imposed under a law of any jurisdiction regulating franchises or business, or pending administrative actions under any such laws against the franchisor, the franchisor's associate, or a director, general partner or officer of the franchisor;
(f) details regarding findings of liability in a civil action of misrepresentation, unfair or deceptive business practices, or violation of a law that regulates franchises or businesses, including a failure to provide proper disclosure to a franchisee, or any civil actions involving such allegations currently pending, against the franchisor, the franchisor's associate, or a director, general partner or officer of the franchisor; and
(g) details of any bankruptcy or insolvency proceedings which took place during the six years (five years in New Brunswick) immediately preceding the date of the disclosure document against the franchisor and its associates, or a company whose directors or officers have management responsibility relating to the franchise (in Alberta), or against a corpora-

tion whose directors or officers include a current director, officer or general partner of the franchisor, or included such a person at the time when the bankruptcy or insolvency proceeding was taking place (in Ontario, P.E.I., New Brunswick, Manitoba and British Columbia).

O. Material Facts

Each of the Provincial Acts outlines prescribed material facts that must be included in one part of the disclosure document dealing with the following matters:

1. A list of all costs associated with the establishment of the franchise, including:
   (i) the amount of any deposits or franchise fees, whether the deposits or fees are refundable, and if so, under what conditions,
   (ii) an estimate of the costs for inventory, leasehold improvements, equipment, leases, rentals and all other tangible and intangible property necessary to establish the franchise and an explanation of any assumptions underlying the estimate, and
   (iii) any other costs associated with the establishment of the franchise not listed in subparagraph i or ii, including any payment to the franchisor, whether direct or indirect, required by the franchise agreement, the nature and amount of the payment, and when the payment is due.

It must be noted that the matters itemized are not exhaustive. Any other costs associated with establishing the franchise must be disclosed. Other costs not specifically listed which could typically be incurred by a franchisee in establishing the franchise include real estate commissions, design fees, architect's fees, training fees, signage costs and professional fees. Prior to the 2004 amendments, the Ontario Regulations required that a disclosure document include an estimate of the costs of establishing and operating a franchise. There was considerable uncertainty as to how a franchisor could make adequate disclosure about the costs of operating a franchise. Additionally, there seemed to be a conflict between this disclosure item, which required mandatory disclosure of operating costs, and a subsequent disclosure item in the regulation, which clearly indicated that disclosure of an estimate of annual operating costs was voluntary. By deleting the reference to "operating" costs, the Ontario Regulations now clearly state that disclosure is only necessary in connection with the costs of establishing the franchise.

> **Practice Note**
>
> **The prescribed material facts that must be included in a disclosure document include a list of all costs of establishing the franchise. Providing an estimate of operating costs is optional in all six provinces.**

2. If an estimate of annual operating costs for the franchise is provided, a statement specifying the basis for the estimate, the underlying assumptions, and a location where information is available that substantiates the estimate.

Note that it is optional whether or not a franchisor provides an estimate of annual operating costs. However, if such an estimate is provided, then the specified items must be disclosed.

It is important that, if an estimate of annual operating costs is provided, the assumptions underlying the estimate be relevant to the franchisee, the franchisee's market and the specific location to be franchised (if known). It is also required under this item that information be made available for the franchisee to inspect in order to substantiate the estimate.

3. If an earnings projection is provided, a statement specifying the reasonable basis for the projection, the underlying assumptions, and where information is available that substantiates the projection.

It is important to note that an earnings projection for the franchise does not have to be provided. However, if the franchisor does provide an earnings projection, the statement specifying the basis for the projection must be on a "reasonable" basis, as contrasted to the statement of annual operating costs in item 2. Further, the assumptions underlying the projections should be relevant to the franchisee and the franchisee's market, and the franchisor must disclose a location where information is available for inspection by the franchisee to substantiate the projection.

Details of any earnings claims information (which must have a reasonable basis at the time it is prepared) used by the franchisor must include material assumptions underlying its preparation and presentation, whether it is based on actual results of existing outlets, and, in Alberta only, the percentage of outlets that meet or exceed each range of results. The disclosure document must also state the place where substantiating information is available for inspection by franchisees. If information is given in respect of a franchisor outlet, the franchisor must state that the information may differ in respect of a franchisee outlet. Earnings claims consist of information from which a specific level or range of actual or potential sales, costs, income or profit from franchisee or franchisor outlets can be ascertained. The regulations in P.E.I., New Brunswick, Manitoba and

British Columbia define an "earnings claim" to include any information given by or on behalf of the franchisor or, except in British Columbia, a franchisor's associate, directly or indirectly, from which a specific level or range of actual or potential sales, costs, income, revenue or profits can easily be ascertained. Alberta also adopts the same approach to what can constitute an "earnings claim." Accordingly, franchisors must carefully consider the nature of any financial information given to franchisees at any time before or during the disclosure process in order to avoid inadvertently providing an earnings claim. This situation can arise even if the franchisor has no intention of providing an earnings claim (e.g., reviewing and approving a proposed business plan). If so, the information must be included in the disclosure document and accompanied by all required assumptions and explanations. Failure to do so could lead to a rescission claim not only for a deficient disclosure document, but also for misrepresentation due to the missing information.

Practice Note

The regulations do not mandate that earnings projections be provided. If earnings projections are provided, they should, if at all possible, be based on actual operating results relevant to the franchisee, the franchisee's market, and the specific location to be franchised (if known). The reasonable basis for the projection must also be provided.

However, a franchisor must be certain to disclose any assumptions or notes with respect to earnings projections to ensure that the basis for the projections are not misleading, inaccurate or inapplicable to the franchise in question.

4. The terms and conditions of any financing arrangements that the franchisor or the franchisor's associate offers directly or indirectly to franchisees.

This item is somewhat difficult to interpret by reason of the fact that many franchisors do not directly offer financing arrangements to a franchisee, but may participate in such arrangements indirectly, for example, by guaranteeing loans or giving comfort letters to financial institutions that may provide financing to the franchisees.

5. In all of the Provincial Acts other than the Alberta Act, a description of any training or, except in Manitoba and BC, other assistance offered to franchisees and, if the training is mandatory, a statement specifying who bears the costs of the training. In BC the responsibility for costs must be specified regardless of whether the training is mandatory.

This item does not specifically require the description of the actual costs to be incurred by a franchisee with respect to training or other assistance. However, it is recommended that the costs be included in this item. In any event, they would be required to be included in item 1.

6. In all provinces except BC, if the franchisee is required to contribute to an advertising fund, a statement describing the percentage of the fund that has been spent on national campaigns and local advertising in the two fiscal years immediately preceding the date of the disclosure document, and the percentage of the fund that has been retained by the franchisor, the franchisor's parent or the franchisor's associate in the two fiscal years immediately preceding the date of the disclosure document. Further, another statement must be included describing the projected amount of the contribution, a projection of the percentage of the fund to be spent on national or local advertising campaigns for the current fiscal year, and a projection of the percentage of the fund to be retained by the franchisor, the franchisor's parent or the franchisor's associate in the current fiscal year.

   In BC, if the franchisee is required to contribute to an advertising fund, a statement describing the frequency with which franchisees will be required to make contributions to the fund, and the percentage or portion of the fund that may be spent primarily for the administration of the fund and the persons who will administer the fund.

In all provinces a franchisor must indicate whether reports on advertising activities financed by the fund will be made available to franchisees.

Practice Note

The regulations require detailed disclosure regarding the franchisor's advertising fund and related expenditures on a fiscal year-end basis. There is no grace period for providing updated information, which can present practical challenges.

Franchisors must ensure that their advertising expenditures for a fiscal year are known immediately upon completion of the fiscal year, since in all provinces except BC, the disclosure document requires a description of the percentage of the fund spent on national campaigns and local advertising in the two fiscal years immediately preceding the date of the disclosure document without any grace period.

The amount of funds "retained" by the franchisor likely includes funds paid to the franchisor for services or overhead allocations relating to the franchisor's administration of the fund. The projection of the percentage of the fund to be spent on national or local advertising campaigns for the current fiscal year will require difficult calculations, since the "current fiscal year" will undoubtedly include a period of time before and after delivery of the disclosure document. With respect to that period of time prior to the delivery, these figures will for the most part already be known to the franchisor. With respect to a projection of the percentage of the fund to be retained, a franchisor must make sure that it takes into account some reasonable projection of additional franchisees who will be paying advertising fees during the fiscal year after the date of the disclosure document.

Finally, with respect to disclosure of whether reports on advertising activities will be made available to the franchisee, it is recommended that the franchisor include how it will be accounting for the cost of preparing such reports.

7. A description of any restrictions or requirements imposed with respect to obligations to purchase or lease from the franchisor, the franchisor's associate or approved suppliers, the goods and services the franchisee may sell, and to whom the franchisee may sell goods or services.

This item will require details of exclusive, authorized or designated supplier arrangements.

8. A description of any policy of the franchisor regarding volume rebates, and whether or not the franchisor or the franchisor's associate receives rebates, commissions, payments or other benefits as a result of purchases of goods and services by the franchisee and, if so, whether they are shared with franchisees, directly or indirectly.

Note that disclosure is simply required of the franchisor's policy regarding volume rebates and whether such rebates or other benefits are shared with franchisees. There is no requirement to disclose the sources or amounts of such rebates or the projected percentage or absolute amount of rebates to be shared with franchisees.

Practice Note

A description of the franchisor's volume rebate policy must also be included in a disclosure document; however, the actual sources or amounts of rebates received do not have to be disclosed.

9. In all of the Provincial Acts other than the Alberta Act, a description of the rights the franchisor or the franchisor's associate has to trademarks, trade names, logos or other advertising, or other commercial symbols associated with the franchise.

A description (and listing) of all licensed trademarks is recommended for compliance with this item. Although this is not a requirement in Alberta, it is recommended that this disclosure be included, as it may be a material fact. In New Brunswick, a franchisor must also disclose any known or alleged material impediments to the use of its trademark, trade names, logos or advertising, or other commercial symbol associated with the franchise (N.B. Reg., 2010-92, s.15 (Can.)).

Practice Note

The franchisor is required to describe in a disclosure document its rights in and to the franchise system's trademarks and similar items. However, there is no disclosure required of other intellectual property rights, such as patents. If a franchisor is disclosing candidates in New Brunswick, it must also provide any known or alleged material impediments to the use of its trademark, trade names, logos or advertising, or other commercial symbol associated with the franchise.

10. In Ontario, New Brunswick, Manitoba and British Columbia only, a description of every license, registration, authorization or other permission the franchisee is required to obtain under any applicable federal or provincial law or municipal by-law to operate the franchise. In Ontario, municipal licences, permits and registrations also must be listed.

This disclosure item will require the franchisor to ensure that it has properly researched all licenses, registrations, authorizations or other permissions required under all local by-laws, which, in certain cases, may impose a considerable burden on the franchisor (e.g., municipal business licenses, signage by-laws, environmental permits, registration as a steward under waste diversion legislation if applicable, etc.).

11. A statement indicating whether the franchisee is required to participate personally and directly in the operation of the franchise or, if the franchisee is a corporation, whether the principals of the corporation are so required.
12. In Alberta, Ontario, New Brunswick and Manitoba only, a description of any exclusive territory granted to the franchisee. In New Brunswick and Manitoba, there is an alternative of disclosing the manner in which territory will be decided and the name of the person who will be making that decision if the exclusive territory is not known at the time of disclosure. In British Columbia only, if territorial rights are granted to the franchisee, a description of the franchisee's rights to the territory.
13. If the franchise agreement grants the franchisee rights to exclusive territory, a description of the franchisor's policy, if any, as to whether the continuation of such rights depends on the franchisee achieving a specific level of sales, market penetration or other condition, and under what circumstances these rights may be altered. In BC these requirements exist whether or not the territory granted is exclusive.

This item will require disclosure, for example, of quotas, minimum sales, population growth or other numerical criteria applicable for a franchisee to maintain exclusivity.

14. Except in BC, a description of the franchisor's policy, if any, on the proximity between an existing franchise and:
    (i) another franchise;
    (ii) any other distributor using the franchisor's trademark, trade name or logo, or advertising, or other commercial symbol;
    (iii) a franchise owned or operated by the franchisor that distributes similar products or services under a different trademark, trade name or logo; and
    (iv) a franchise granted by the franchisor that distributes similar products or services under a different trademark, trade name or logo.

This item will require disclosure, for example, of any impact policies utilized with respect to compensation for encroachment upon the franchisee's market, or other policies with respect to the ability of the franchisor to distribute products or services directly under the same trademarks or different trademarks than those associated with the franchise system, regardless of whether or not compensation to the franchisee is included in such policies.

15. In Ontario, the name, last-known address and telephone number of each franchisee in Ontario who operated a franchise of the type being offered that has been terminated, cancelled, not renewed or reacquired by the franchisor or otherwise left the system within the last fiscal year immediately preceding the date of the disclosure document. In Alberta, a list of the names, last-known addresses and telephone numbers of each franchisee in the franchisor's total operating area who operated a franchise of the type being offered that has been terminated, cancelled, not renewed, reacquired, or otherwise left the system within the previous fiscal year. In PEI, a list of the names, last-known addresses and telephone numbers of all franchisees of the franchisor, franchisor's associates or affiliates of the franchisor that operated a franchise of the type being offered in PEI, New Brunswick and Nova Scotia of the same type that has been terminated, cancelled, not renewed, reacquired, or otherwise left the system within the previous fiscal year. In New Brunswick, a list of the names, last-known addresses and telephone numbers of all franchisees of the franchisor, franchisor's associates or affiliates of the franchisor that operated a franchise of the type being offered in New Brunswick and, if applicable, in the jurisdictions from which the list of existing franchisees required to be disclosed in New Brunswick was drawn, of the same type that has been terminated, cancelled, not re-

newed, reacquired, or otherwise left the system within the previous fiscal year. In Manitoba, a list of the names, last-known addresses and telephone numbers of all franchisees of the franchisor, franchisor's associates or affiliates of the franchisor that operated a franchise of the type being offered in Manitoba and, if applicable, in the jurisdictions from which the list of existing franchisees required to be disclosed was drawn that has been terminated, cancelled, not renewed, reacquired, or otherwise left the system within the previous fiscal year. In British Columbia, a list of the names, last known addresses and telephone numbers of all franchisees of the franchisor or of the franchisor's affiliates that operated a franchise of the type being offered in Canada and, if applicable, in any foreign jurisdictions from which the list of existing franchisees required to be disclosed was drawn that has been terminated, cancelled, reacquired, not renewed or otherwise left the system within the previous fiscal year.

While it is uncertain whether franchisees that left the system because their franchise agreements expired without any further renewal rights must be included in the information to be disclosed under this item, it is recommended that such disclosure be made.

16. In Ontario, for each closure of a franchise (in any jurisdiction) within the previous three fiscal years immediately preceding the date of the disclosure document, the reasons for the closure, including whether the franchisor terminated or cancelled the agreement, the franchisor refused to renew the agreement, or the franchisee refused to renew the agreement or otherwise left the franchise system (O. Reg. 581/00, s.16 (Can.)). In Alberta, information about closures of franchisee or franchisor outlets of the same type of franchise being offered, including the total number of franchises in the franchisor's total operating territory that have within the last three fiscal years been terminated, cancelled, not renewed, reacquired by the franchisor, or otherwise left the system, and the name, last-known address and telephone number of every former franchisee in franchisor's total operating territory that has within the previous fiscal year been terminated, cancelled, not renewed, reacquired by the franchisor, or otherwise left the system and the reason for their termination, cancellation or non-renewal. In P.E.I., the names, last-known address and telephone numbers of each franchisee in Prince Edward Island, New Brunswick and Nova Scotia who operated a franchise of the type being offered that has been terminated, cancelled, not renewed, reacquired, or otherwise left the system within the previous fiscal year must be included. In New Brunswick and Manitoba, the names, last-known

address and telephone numbers of each franchisee in New Brunswick or Manitoba (or any other jurisdiction from which the franchisor draws its list of existing franchisees) who operated a franchise of the type being offered that has been terminated, cancelled, not renewed, reacquired, or otherwise left the system within the previous fiscal year immediately preceding the date of the disclosure document must be included. In British Columbia, the total number of franchises in Canada of the franchisor or of the franchisor's affiliates of the same type as the franchise being offered within the previous three fiscal years that have been terminated or cancelled, not renewed by the franchisee or the franchisor, reacquired or otherwise left the franchise system.

17. A list of the locations of all franchises in Ontario of the type being offered, including the business address, telephone number and name of each franchisee and, if there are fewer than 20 franchisees in Ontario, the list must include those franchises that are geographically closest to Ontario until information on 20 franchises has been provided (O. Reg. 581/00, s.18 (Can.)). A list of all existing franchisee and franchisor outlets in operation in Alberta, including their names, addresses and telephone numbers. If there are fewer than 20 locations in operation in Alberta, the disclosure document must also set out information for the remaining number of locations for outlets outside Alberta that are geographically closest to Alberta (Alta. Reg. 240/95, Sch. 1-14 (Can.)). In Prince Edward Island (PEI Reg. EC 232/106. s.1(1) of Part 4 (Can.)), the disclosure must include all franchisees in Prince Edward Island, New Brunswick and Nova Scotia. In New Brunswick (N.B. Reg., 2010-92, s.2 of Part 1 (Can.)), the disclosure must include all franchisees in New Brunswick and any other jurisdiction from which the franchisor draws the list of current franchisees. In Manitoba (Man. Reg. 29/2012, s.25 (Can.)), if there are fewer than 20 franchisees that currently operate franchises in Manitoba of the same type as the franchise being offered, the list shall also include information on the franchisees that currently operate franchises of the same type in Saskatchewan or Alberta until information is provided on 20 or all the franchisees, whichever is the lesser number. If there are fewer than 20 franchisees in Manitoba, Saskatchewan and Alberta, the list shall also include information on franchisees that operate franchises that are geographically closest to Manitoba until information on 20 or all franchisees is provided. In British Columbia, if there are fewer than 20 franchisees of the same type as the franchise being offered that currently operate in Canada, the list must include the

name, business address and telephone number of the franchisees that currently operate franchises of the same type as the franchise being offered, that are in the foreign jurisdiction closest to British Columbia, until 20 or all the franchisees are listed, whichever is the lesser number.

18. Except in BC, a description of all restrictions and conditions in the franchise agreement relating to the termination or renewal of the agreement and the transfer of the franchise. In Alberta only, the requirement is to state whether there are such restrictions and conditions, and if so, where in the franchise agreement they can be found, without the need to include a description of those restrictions and conditions. In BC the disclosure document must include a list of all provisions in the franchise agreement that deal with the termination of the franchise agreement, the renewal of the franchise agreement and the transfer of the franchise. There is no direction as to whether this must be a detailed list or simply a recitation of relevant section numbers.

Practice Note

Franchisors should note that in disclosing all restrictions and conditions related to termination, renewal or transfer, all that is required is a description, or, in BC, a list, but not a complete reproduction, of the relevant terms in all agreements relating to the franchise, not just the franchise agreement.

Practice Note

Franchisors should continue to take seriously the obligation to disclose and should ensure that their procedures for interacting with prospective franchisees comply with the remedial spirit driving the courts' interpretation of the Provincial Acts.

All Provincial Acts require, in addition to the specific disclosure items set forth in their respective regulations, that all "material facts" as defined in the statutes be included in the disclosure document. In considering specific material facts that should be included, franchisors must always be careful to recall the following relevant considerations:

19. The Acts require the disclosure of all "material facts," including those itemized in the regulations.
20. In many cases, the specific items described require disclosure with respect to the franchisor and the "franchisor's associate." The definition of the term "franchisor's associate" (or "associate" in Alberta) should be reviewed in each case to determine whether disclosure will extend to the

franchisor's associate (or "associate" in Alberta) in addition to the franchisor.

21. Since the disclosure document must in every case be current as of the date of disclosure, where disclosure is required for items for a fixed period of time immediately preceding the date of the disclosure document, the document must be updated for such items at the time of each disclosure.
22. Case law has demonstrated that courts expect disclosure documents to include specific material facts about the actual franchise being granted. Accordingly, the disclosure document must include that prospective franchisee's specific territory, initial fee, performance standards, and other information about his or her franchise, not just general descriptions of these disclosure items or formulas for their calculation.

IV. Matters of Special Interest to Foreign Franchisors

A. Can a Foreign Franchisor Use Its Domestic Disclosure Document in Canada?

1. Ontario

Pursuant to subsection 5(4) of the Ontario Act, a disclosure document is required to contain all material facts, including those prescribed by regulation, copies of all proposed agreements relating to the franchise, statements as prescribed by regulation for the purposes of assisting the prospective franchisee in making informed investment decisions, and other information and copies of documents as prescribed by regulation. Pursuant to subsection 5(6) of the Ontario Act, all information and disclosure documents must be accurately, clearly and concisely set out.

Pursuant to section 10 of the Ontario Act, any provision in a franchise agreement purporting to restrict the application of the law of Ontario or to restrict jurisdiction or venue to a forum outside Ontario is void with respect to a claim otherwise enforceable under the Act in Ontario. Further, under section 11 of the Ontario Act, any purported waiver or release by a franchisee of a right given under the Act or of an obligation or requirement imposed on a franchisor by or under the Ontario Act is void.

What does all of this mean to a United States franchisor with an existing U.S. franchise disclosure document (US FDD) who wishes to offer a franchise to a prospective franchisee in the Province of Ontario?

First, the Ontario Regulations require in section 4 that certain statements dealing with risk disclosure must be provided together in one section at the beginning of the disclosure document. The only practical way for this requirement to be satisfied would be for a wrap-around or addendum to be included at the beginning of a US FDD.

Second, the Ontario Regulations require in section 6 that every disclosure document must include specified disclosure items together in one part of the document. If the ordering of these items is not followed consecutively, or if the items are not grouped together, it is possible that the requirements of the regulation will not have been satisfied. Since a US FDD requires disclosure of prescribed items in a different order and must be responsive to differently worded questions, it is likely not possible to comply with this requirement by using a US FDD with a wrap-around or addendum.

Third, as aforementioned, the Ontario Act itself requires in section 5(6) that all information in a disclosure document must be accurately, clearly and concisely set out. By using a US FDD that contains disclosure items extraneous to or in addition to those required to be disclosed pursuant to the Ontario Regulations (unless they constitute "material facts"), it is possible that a franchisor may not have complied with the requirement to disclose accurately, clearly and concisely when the disclosure language of corresponding items under a US FDD is used.

It is also interesting to note that neither the Ontario Act nor the Ontario Regulations provide specifically for the right of a franchisor who has prepared a disclosure document under the laws of another jurisdiction to be able to use such a document with a wrap-around or addendum (as is specifically provided for under each of the Alberta, PEI, New Brunswick, Manitoba and British Columbia Acts). While it is not necessarily true that the absence of such a provision means one cannot utilize a document required under another jurisdiction, undoubtedly it would be argued that the fact the other Provincial Acts have specifically allowed such a procedure should be taken to mean that disclosure in Ontario was intended to follow the specific requirements of the Ontario Act and Regulations.

Practice Note

Because use of a wrap-around document is not expressly permitted by all of the Provincial Acts, the difficulty in preparing a compliant wrap-around, and given the similarities of each of the Provincial Acts, most franchisors choose to prepare a single national disclosure document that can easily be used in and complies with all of the Provincial Acts.

With respect to the form of disclosure document, if not for legal reasons, then certainly for practical reasons, it is recommended that an Ontario form of disclosure document be prepared and should follow the specific form set out in the Ontario Regulations. There are several reasons why the use of a US FDD with a wrap-around or addendum may not likely comply with the requirements of the Ontario Act.

In 2006, the court in *Tutor Time* (*1518628 Ontario Inc. et al v. Tutor Time Centres*, [2006] O.J. No. 3011 (Can.)) provided guidance regarding this matter. The court concluded that the franchisor had not properly disclosed by not providing a US FDD until a few days before the completion of the transaction, by failing to provide material facts, and by providing the US FDD for reasons other than disclosure. This gave the franchisee the right to rescind for two years rather than for late or incomplete disclosure, which only gives rise to a 60-day rescission. Similarly, the question of whether Ontario franchise law extends to franchisees in other provinces governed by a franchise agreement came up in the case of *Midas* (*405341 Ontario Limited and Midas Canada Inc*., [2010] O.N.C.A. 478 (Can.)) The franchise agreement in this case provided that it would be governed by the laws of Ontario. The franchisor argued that the Ontario Act would not apply to franchisees operated by class members in other provinces that had their own franchise legislation. The court disagreed and held that by agreeing that the laws of Ontario were to govern the validity, construction, performance and enforcement of the franchise agreement applicable to franchisees operating in another province, the intention of the parties was that Ontario law apply, irrespective of the particular location of the Midas franchises in Canada.

Practice Note

It is the widely accepted view of Canadian franchise lawyers that franchise disclosure documents prepared for compliance with domestic U.S. law cannot be used in Canada without significant risk. Further, without obtaining an unqualified opinion from a reputable and experienced Canadian franchise lawyer, lawyers from other jurisdictions might also be taking a significant (and perhaps unnecessary) risk in guiding or advising their clients otherwise.

2. Alberta, P.E.I., New Brunswick, Manitoba and British Columbia

The regulations in Alberta, P.E.I., New Brunswick, Manitoba and British Columbia also address the situation where a franchisor that is required to provide a disclosure document to a prospective franchisee in the particular province where the franchise is located has an approved disclosure document from another jurisdiction. In such a case, the franchisor may use that disclosure document provided that the franchisor also provides a supplementary addendum or wrap-around document setting out any material changes necessary for the document to comply with the disclosure requirements of the particular province where the franchise is located (Alta. Reg. 240/95, s.2(2); PEI Reg. EC 232/106. s.3(2); N.B. Reg., 2010-92, s.4; Man. Reg. 29/2012, s.2(2); B.C. Reg. 238/2016, s.2(3) (Can.)). Such a wrap-around document would include any additions or amendments to the foreign disclosure document necessary to make it compliant, such as the risk warning statements to franchisees ensuring the financial statements and any earnings claims meet the requirements of the applicable province's franchise legislation, the required information on existing and former franchisees, and the proper form of franchisor's certificate.

Practice Note

In many cases, it may require more time and cost to prepare a "wrap-around" document than preparing an appropriate disclosure document in the first place for a given province. Indeed, it is becoming a universal practice for franchisors in Canada to prepare a national form of franchise disclosure document that meets the requirements of all Provincial Acts and that can be used across the country.

B. Can a Foreign Franchisor Use Its Domestic Law to Govern Its Canadian Franchise Documents?

It is not uncommon for foreign franchisors and their professional advisors to insist upon the law of their domestic jurisdiction governing a Canadian franchise agreement. While the Acts do not specifically require that franchise agreements and related documents be expressly stated to be governed by the laws of the province in which the franchisee's particular franchise is located, they do state that any provision in a franchise agreement (which, by definition, includes any agreement relating to the franchise) purporting to restrict the application of such provincial law, or to restrict jurisdiction or venue to a forum outside the particular province, is void with respect to a claim otherwise enforceable under the applicable franchise statute. If, despite this provision in the Acts, a foreign franchisor attempts to have its domestic laws apply to its franchise agreements, apart from the difficulty of introducing expert evidence in a Canadian court to establish the principles of the domestic governing law, there is also the difficultly of enforcing a foreign judgment in Canada if a foreign forum is mandated for determination of disputes and remedies.

While the courts of most common-law jurisdictions in Canada may recognize a foreign governing-law clause, such a provision will often result in difficulties that will outweigh perceived advantages. For example, United States franchise laws, anti-trust laws, common-law principles and other applicable statutes are generally more onerous to a franchisor than those in Canada. One should question why it is of use to a franchisor to voluntarily insist upon the application of such principles.

Further, franchisors frequently need to seek injunctive relief against franchisees, particularly following termination of the relationship, in order to restrain a franchisee from breaching restrictive covenants respecting trademarks and the like, and from breaching non-competition covenants. Although it is open to a foreign court to grant an injunction against a Canadian franchisee, provided of course that the foreign court is willing to assume jurisdiction over a Canadian franchisee, and the test for an injunction is satisfied, the franchisor would still have to commence a separate proceeding in the superior court of the province in which the Canadian franchisee resides in order to enforce the injunction. Although the Canadian law may be evolving to allow for recognition of some non-monetary orders, these developments are in very early stages, and there is no clear guidance as to the circumstances in which a Canadian court will recognize a non-monetary order. Under the current state of the law, it is unlikely that a Canadian court would recognize and enforce injunctive or other non-monetary relief imposed by a foreign court with respect to the conduct of a franchisee in Canada. As such, where a Canadian franchisee is concerned, it is much easier for a franchisor to obtain an injunction from the court in the Canadian province in which the franchisee is resident.

In addition, this means of injunctive relief would unquestionably be more time-consuming than if an injunction was sought directly in a Canadian court. If, on the other hand, a franchisor were to ignore the exclusive jurisdiction provision and apply directly to a Canadian court when seeking an injunction, then it would be open to the franchisee to seek a stay of the action on the basis that the franchisor must bring its action in the state of jurisdiction, again resulting in delay and increased uncertainty.

Additional problems will arise with respect to the Province of Québec, which is a civil-law jurisdiction. Before a Québec court will enforce a foreign judgment, the defendant will be afforded an opportunity to raise any defence available in the initial action. In other words, if the franchisor had brought and won an action in its home jurisdiction, it could be faced with the expense and uncertainty of litigating the same issue twice.

Practice Note

It is generally suggested that foreign franchisors ensure that their franchise agreements and related documents are governed by the laws of the province in which the franchised business is located and the laws of Canada applicable therein, and that no choice of venue provision be included, or that the choice of venue be the province in which the franchised business is located.

CHAPTER 7

Dispute Resolution and Franchise Litigation in Canada

Geoff Shaw and Jeff Hoffman

Contents

I. Introduction

When this text was first published in 2004, there were only two provinces in Canada with franchise disclosure and relationship legislation, Alberta and Ontario. Franchise proceedings tended to be based on a blend of statutory and common-law causes of action. The Ontario franchise statute, the *Arthur Wishart Act (Franchise Disclosure), 2000*, S.O. 2000, c. 3 (the AWA or Ontario statute) was barely four years old, and cases decided under it were, for the most part, rescission claims based on the complete failure on the part of franchisors (many of which were not aware of existence of the statute) to provide prospective franchisees with a franchise disclosure document. See, for example, *MAA Diners Inc. v. 3 for 1 Pizza & Wings (Canada) Inc.*, [2003] O.J. No. 430 (S.C.J.); appeal dismissed, [2004] O.J. No. 297 (C.A.), and *1490664 Ontario Ltd. v. Dig This Garden Retailers Ltd.*, [2004] O.J. No. 3008 (S.C.J.), appeal dismissed, [2005] O.J. No. 3040 (C.A.).

Over the past 13 years, as franchisors became more aware of the nature and extent of their duty to disclose and as jurisprudence in the area of franchise law developed, the focus of claims shifted from common-law claims and statutory rescission claims to claims based on the quality of the disclosure provided (for example, whether material facts were omitted or misrepresentations made within a franchise disclosure document), and on breaches of the mutual statutory duty of fair dealing, though common-law claims and statutory rescission claims continued to be made.

Notably, though class proceedings have been permitted in Canada for some time, their use for the determination of franchise disputes has expanded dramatically over the past 13 years and included, for the first time, claims for infringement of the right of franchisees to associate. Franchise disputes often involve the interpretation of standard form agreements and the consideration of uniform methods of operation. It is not surprising, therefore, for the courts to find that franchise cases often have common issues that are ideally suited to determination through class proceedings. In certifying franchise claims as class actions, the courts in Canada recognized "the inherent vulnerability in the dependent ongoing nature of the relationship between franchisor and franchisee"—*1176560 Ontario Inc. v. Great Atlantic & Pacific Co. of Canada*, [2002] O.J. No. 4781 (S.C.J.), at para. 42; affirmed [2004] O.J. No. 865 (Div. Ct.), and the judicial economy that is served through collective action (*Ibid.*, S.C.J. at para. 52).

Historically, with respect to alternative dispute resolution, there was a reluctance on the part of franchisors doing business in Canada to include alternative dispute resolution provisions in their franchise agreements. Today, parties to franchise agreements are much more receptive to mediation and arbitration of their disputes, whether they arise from a contractual obligation to mediate and/or arbitrate or from the recognition by parties and their lawyers that mediation and arbitration can be a cost-effective and quick way to resolve their disputes. Like courts in the United States courts in Canada recognize and uphold the agreement of parties to resolve their disputes outside of the courts, including recognition of the competence-competence principle, under which an arbitrator determines his or her own jurisdiction to hear a particular dispute.

In this chapter, we will discuss litigation and alternative dispute resolution generally, and highlight issues that are unique to the determination of franchise disputes in Canada.

II. Legal System

Constitutionally, Canada's legal system is divided into two distinct legal jurisdictions, federal and provincial.

Federal legal jurisdiction includes matters that are national in scope and affect more than one province, such as trade and commerce, including intellectual property matters, such as trademarks, copyrights, patents and industrial designs (Canada's equivalent to design patents), and bankruptcy and insolvency.

Matters of contract, including franchises, are considered to be matters of "property and civil rights" and within exclusive provincial jurisdiction. (Larry Weinberg and Geoffrey B Shaw, "A Practical Road Map to Entering the Canadian Market" (2004), 24 *Franchise L.J.* 63 at 63). Not all provinces have chosen to enact franchise legislation. Franchise disclosure and relationship statutes exist in six of the ten provinces of Canada: Alberta, Ontario, New Brunswick, Prince Edward Island, Manitoba, and British Columbia. *Franchises Act*, R.S.A. 2000, c. F-23 (the Alberta statute), *Franchises Act*, R.S.P.E.I. 1988, c. F-14.1 (the PEI statute), *Franchises Act*, S.N.B. 2014, c. 111 (the New Brunswick statute), *the Franchises Act*, C.C.S.M. c. F156 (the Manitoba statute), and *Franchises Act*, S.B.C. 2015, c. 35 (the BC statute). These statutes may be viewed online at www.canlii.org.

The federal legal system and those of all provinces other than Québec are based upon English common law, while Québec's legal system is based upon French civil law. In the common-law provinces, decisions made by courts outside of a province are considered to be of "persuasive" as opposed to "binding" authority, though decisions by the courts of the United Kingdom and other Commonwealth countries, such as Australia and New Zealand, are generally given more weight than decisions made by courts in the United States, likely because of the historic connection between the judicial systems of Canada and the U.K. Indeed, until 1949, decisions of the Supreme Court of Canada could be appealed to the Judicial Committee of the British Privy Council. Due to the geographic proximity and substantial amount of trade and commerce that occurs between Canada and the United States, one might expect that American jurisprudence would have a greater impact upon Canadian courts than is actually the case.

Practice Note

Canadian common-law courts will be more likely to apply English and other Commonwealth countries' court decisions as precedents than those of courts in the United States. Though not binding on the courts of Canada, decisions made in the United States are seen as having some persuasive value.

III. Jurisdiction of Courts

The courts of Canada are divided into the Federal Court, which has limited jurisdiction to deal only with matters regulated under federal laws, and the courts of each province, which are courts of general jurisdiction. Each province has a series of lower courts and a superior or supreme court, as well as a Court of Appeal. Appeals from a provincial Court of Appeal are heard (if leave to appeal is granted) by the Supreme Court of Canada, the highest court in the country, from which there is no appeal. Leave to appeal is granted where the Supreme Court is of the opinion that there is a question of public importance or the importance of any issue of law or mixed fact and law is such that it ought to be decided by the Supreme Court. The Federal Court also has a Court of Appeal, with further appeals to the Supreme Court of Canada, if leave to appeal is granted.

Because the provincial courts have a general jurisdiction, they can hear matters that arise under both federal laws and provincial laws, whereas the Federal Court, with its limited jurisdiction, can only hear matters that arise under federal laws, and cannot hear matters that arise under provincial laws. This dichotomous court system often leads to the initial question of which court system to initiate an action in.

As a practical matter, if an action is to be taken for trademark infringement, a purely federal matter, the action would be taken in Federal Court. However, as is often the case, the action may also involve other issues, which may not all be matters of federal law. An example would be a case that includes passing off, which is a common-law right of action and as such is considered to fall within jurisdiction of the provincial courts as a matter of property and civil rights in the province. In such cases, due to the limited jurisdiction of the Federal Court, the action would be brought in the appropriate provincial court, which, because of its general jurisdiction, can hear both the non-federal and the federal law claims.

A further example would be a franchise termination case, which would likely involve contract issues, a matter of provincial jurisdiction, and may also involve trademark infringement issues, where the terminated franchisee is continuing to use the franchisor's trademarks and copyrights, but is doing so as an infringer post-termination. Such an action would also be brought in the appropriate provincial court.

Forum shopping can thus play a part in the initial strategy decisions regarding litigation.

The Federal Court has a number of regional offices that serve as registries for the geographic convenience of the parties, although all Federal Court matters are ultimately administered by the principal registry office in Ottawa. Cases in Federal Court can also be heard in various regions of the country.

IV. Litigation Differences Between Canada and the U.S.

In Canada, judges at the Federal Court and Supreme Court of Canada levels, as well as at the Superior or Supreme Court and Court of Appeal levels in the provinces, are appointed and paid by the federal government. For the courts of the provinces, the appointments will normally be made in consultation with the applicable provincial government. However, the important point to note is that these appointments are not public matters of process. There are no elections of judges and no confirmations of their appointment involving any public process. This private appointment process, and federal government payment of judges, is generally considered to create an independent judiciary. Canada's legal system is generally known for this element of independence, and thus has a strong reputation for being a fair hearing forum.

Each province determines its own rules of civil procedure. This chapter cannot survey all of the provincial rules of civil procedure, but it will point out a few matters of difference between Canadian and U.S. litigation, by way of general commentary.

While contingency fee litigation is now allowed in all provinces, it only became available in some provinces relatively recently. The general experience to date is that it is less prevalent in Canada than in the U.S., except perhaps for some limited fields, such as personal injury claims. That being said, the trend appears to be toward an increase in contingency fee litigation. This may in part result from the rise of class action litigation in Canada.

Canadian litigation usually involves less extensive discovery of witnesses than American litigation. There are differences among the respective rules of civil procedure in each province; however, generally speaking, it is not open to the parties to prolong the pre-trial process through the use of extensive discoveries. It is considered to be incumbent upon the parties to conduct their discoveries efficiently, so as not to add cost or take added time, unless the discovery process will involve a real and serious issue that the court will be expected to rule upon at the trial. The theory is that not all witnesses need to be discovered (deposed) before the trial of the action. Discovery may be limited to only the parties to an action unless the court, on application, grants leave to examine a non-party witness for discovery. Usually such leave is granted only where the party seeking the information cannot obtain it by or through a party to the proceeding and has requested the information directly from the non-party witness, who has refused to provide it. Recent rule changes and the consideration of the principle of proportionality have affected the scope of documentary discovery as well as the length of the oral examinations that may take place in a proceeding.

While this represents a difference in civil procedure between Canada and the United States, the economy of discoveries may not necessarily result in civil cases being heard faster in Canada than in the United States.

V. Judge-Made Law

The use of jury trials in civil matters in Canada is very limited. Trials by jury are available, but rare. Their most common use in civil trials is in tort claims, such as damages for personal injury. According to statistics cited in a November, 2007, Civil Justice Reform Project in Ontario, about 23% of that province's civil trials were held before a jury with the 74% of those cases involving personal injury (www.attorneygeneral.jus.gov.on.ca/english/about/pubs/cjrp). This tradition of judge-made law has evolved historically.

In matters of contract interpretation, or in cases involving matters of a complex legal nature, juries will not normally be used. Cases involving such matters will be heard by a judge alone. In most civil litigation of the types usually occurring in franchise disputes, the cases are heard by a judge, and the instances of jury trials are few and far between.

A case that illustrates this point in a franchise dispute is *Salem v. Priority Building Services Ltd.*, [2003] B.C.J. No. 2459 (B.C.S.C.). The franchisee sought a jury trial, and the franchisor sought to strike out the jury notice so that the trial could be heard by a judge alone. A prior proceeding in this action decided some of the issues regarding the franchise agreement, its interpretation, and its termination.

The parties then put forward their arguments regarding the suitability of this case for trial by a jury. The following excerpts from the decision of the court summarize their arguments on this point:

The defendant argues that the jury notice should be struck for any one of several reasons:

- the issue is principally concerned with the construction of a written agreement, and is therefore precluded by Rules 39(25) and 10(1)(b);
- the trial will involve a prolonged examination of documents, which cannot be conveniently made;
- matters are of an intricate or complex nature such that Rule 39(27) precludes a jury; and
- Justice Melnick has made findings of fact such that any contrary conclusions of fact by a jury may cause the court embarrassment.

The plaintiff submits that:

- the application is out of time under Rule 39(27)(a);
- the matter is not principally concerned with the construction of an agreement, that aspect of the case having been already done by Justice Melnick in the Rule 18A application;
- the issues are not as complex as alleged by the defence, but will turn rather on facts, and that credibility in respect of those alleged facts will be the key issue; and
- Justice Melnick's conclusions are in respect of a legal issue, not a factual issue, and will not significantly limit or constrain a jury's considerations.

In considering these points, the court commented that most contract disputes involve mixed questions of fact and law, but what is more important is the matter of degree. In other words, is the legal interpretation of those facts and their impact on the issues at hand (in this case, the franchise agreement between the parties) of greater or lesser importance to the decision-making process? The court commented that the issues were more law-related than fact-related, and that even once the facts were decided, there were significant issues involved as to the effect of those facts on the franchise agreement between the parties.

In response to the defendant franchisor's arguments that there were too many documents and too many transcripts involved for the case to be suitable for a jury trial, the court made the following points in rejecting this as a suitable argument against trial by jury:

> Juries in civil and criminal matters are, with respect, routinely asked to examine, understand, and correlate extensive documents and the sheer

> number of the documents in this case does not suggest sufficient complexity to warrant removing the matter from a jury. Moreover, Mr. Spence argues that most of the documents are relatively short and simple in their nature as, for example, letters between the parties or memos. All in all, I do not regard this as sufficient reason to strike the jury.
>
> . . .
>
> I should note that I do not accept that a jury will be unduly confused by the use at trial of transcripts from examinations for discovery or cross-examinations on affidavits. Even if the jury hears seven individuals confronted with their earlier evidence, I think the members of the jury would be capable of considering the evidence and coming to conclusions respecting credibility. Juries are asked, in my view, to do this regularly, and to do so where credibility may be tested in relatively complex ways.

However, of greater importance to this consideration is whether the case involves matters of an intricate or complex nature, which may go beyond what is suitable for trial by a jury. The franchisor's counsel argued that the franchisee's case posed multiple and complex causes of action. Damages were being sought in both contract and tort. In finding this to be the compelling and deciding argument for trial by a judge alone, the court stated the following:

> I accept Mr. Harney's argument respecting the complexity of the numerous causes of action as pleaded. The pleadings pose issues in equity (unconscionable agreements), fiduciary relationships (including, one supposes, the effects or limitations that contract may place upon such relationships), the duty of good faith and issues of negligent misrepresentation, as well as tortious interference with contractual relations. The jury would also be asked to decide the question of vicarious liability. Finally, a result will also have to consider the difference between contract and tort damages. Many of these individual issues have sub-issues and multiple tests. Individually, perhaps, a jury could consider and decide upon many if not all of these issues, but taken in their totality (or even in multiples) I regard the matter as being of such an intricate or complex matter as to be unsuitable for a jury.

Finally, the plaintiff franchisee's counsel tried to argue that the case was still suitable for a jury trial, despite the fact that some of the issues and findings of fact had been determined in a separate prior proceeding. The court disagreed and struck the jury notice:

> Judges instruct juries daily on legal issues and the rules of evidence, and how those might affect or constrain a jury's considerations of the facts.

> Nevertheless, excepting voir dires, such instructions rarely follow on another process of fact-finding that is already a fait accompli. I can easily credit the difficulty a jury might have, knowing it to be the finder of fact, but having been instructed as to what facts have already been considered and established by the court. Moreover, the deliberations of a jury being secret, a party will never realistically know whether the jury has, in fact, accepted certain conclusions already decided by a Judge. I do not regard the fact of a prior Rule 18A application as necessarily precluding a subsequent trial before a jury, but in this particular case the possibility of contrary findings offers potential embarrassment, and I conclude that such a potential would be significantly reduced or eliminated by a trial before a judge alone.

In *Dodd v. Prime Restaurants of Canada Inc.*, [2012] O.J. No. 1087 (S.C.J.), the defendant franchisor moved for summary judgment dismissing the plaintiff's claim and for an order striking out the plaintiff's jury notice. The motion for summary judgment was dismissed but the jury notice was struck.

Under the franchise agreement, the plaintiff had waived trial by jury. The plaintiff argued that the waiver was not valid as he had rescinded the franchise agreement that included the no jury clause. The relevant section of the franchise agreement read:

> The Franchisor and the Franchisee irrevocably waive trial by jury (should same be lawfully available) in any action, proceeding or counterclaim, whether at law or in equity, brought by either of them against the other, whether or not there are other parties in such action or proceeding.

The court held that the "No Jury Trial" provision of the franchise agreement was not rescinded with the rescission the franchise agreement. While the provincial statute gave the franchisee the right to rescind the franchise agreement, it did not void the agreement ab initio. The provision survived the rescission of the balance of the agreement (at para. 61). The waiver of a right to a jury was not contrary to public policy and was common in the context of commercial agreements dealing with matters likely outside of the expertise of most prospective jury members (at para. 61). Last, the claim for rescission fell within the category of claims prohibited by statute to be placed before a jury in Ontario (at para. 63).

Practice Note

Expect that most franchise cases, which involve multiple causes of action and complex legal issues, will be tried by a judge sitting without a jury.

A "No Jury" provision in a franchise agreement survives the rescission of the franchise agreement and has been held not to offend public policy.

VI. Damage Awards

A. Introduction

Canada is generally thought to be a less litigious jurisdiction than the United States. A general reluctance on behalf of Canadian courts to award harsh punitive damages (known as treble damages in the United States) coupled with the rarity of civil jury trials in Canada are meaningful contributors to this distinction.

Canadian civil trials generally fall into the following broad categories:

1. **General damages,** which are determined by the court generally, such as when there is no particular way to measure the actual damages suffered. General damages would include damages for breach of contract, negligence, or breach of a statutory duty; as well as damages for economic loss, normally being a monetary loss, and including a consequential loss caused as a result of the primary act giving rise to the cause of action, for example a negligent misrepresentation where, due to the special relationship between the parties, the loss was considered to be foreseeable; compensatory damages, which might include a party's consequential damages; and damages for other general causes of action;
2. **Special damages,** for losses capable of exact calculation, including specific losses or expenses incurred by the plaintiff;
3. **Aggravated damages**, where under the circumstances, the plaintiff has suffered greater harm than would have be expected; and
4. **Punitive damages,** sometimes referred to as exemplary damages, to punish a party for its egregious conduct.

B. Codified Damages in Franchise Law

The range and scope of remedies available to aggrieved franchisees are narrower in Canada than in the United States Canadian remedies are entirely civil in nature, with provincial legislation prescribing private rights of action. Conversely, in the United States, violating franchisors may be subject to civil action, administrative remedies, sanctions, and in some cases criminal fines and imprisonment.

In each of the six jurisdictions in Canada with franchise legislation (Ontario, Manitoba, Alberta, Prince Edward Island, New Brunswick, and BC), the respective statutes outline a statutory right of action for damages if a disclosure document contains a misrepresentation, or omits required information amounting to a misrepresentation. In all of the provinces with franchise legislation except Alberta, there is a statutory right of action for damages for a breach of the duty of fair dealing. In all of the provinces with franchise legislation, there is also a statutory right of action for damages for contravention of the right of a franchisee to associate.

In Ontario, the right of action for damages for breach of the duty of fair dealing is contained in s. 3(2) of the AWA. Section 4(5) of the AWA provides a right of action for damages against the franchisor if the franchisor contravenes the right to associate.

The operative provision for damages for misrepresentation or failure to disclose is s. 7 of the AWA. In order to recover damages under this section, a franchisee must establish that the loss was suffered because of a misrepresentation in a disclosure document or as a result of the franchisor's failure to comply, in any way, with its disclosure obligation. Importantly, the AWA deems reliance on the misrepresentation unless the defendant can prove knowledge of the misrepresentation on the part of the plaintiff. This is an important difference between the statutory right of action and that which is available at common law. A franchisee's right of action for damages extends beyond the franchisor to the franchisor's associates, brokers, and agents, as well as every person who signed the disclosure document containing the misrepresentation. From a practical perspective, a misrepresentation or failure to disclose might also activate the more direct remedy of rescission. Therefore, the right of action for damages is often pleaded in the alternative. In *1490664 Ontario Ltd. v. Dig This Garden Retailers Ltd.*, 2005 Can LII 25181, the Ontario Court of Appeal held that a claim for damages under s. 7 of the AWA could be sought in addition to a claim for rescission and compensation under s. 6(6) of the AWA.

In Alberta, the first Canadian jurisdiction to adopt franchise legislation, the statutory framework of the Alberta statute is substantially similar to the Ontario legislation with respect to damage awards. Section 9(1) sets out the right of action for damages in the event of an overt misrepresentation or misrepresentation by omission in a disclosure document, which a franchisee may enforce against the franchisor and every person who signed the disclosure document containing the misrepresentation. Section 11 of the Alberta statute contains a right of action for damages for contravention of the right to associate.

The damages that may be awarded under the Manitoba statute, the PEI statute, the New Brunswick statute, and the BC statute parallel those that may be awarded under the Ontario statute with the exception that damages are not available against a "franchisor's agent," defined in the regulation under the Ontario statute as "a sales agent of the franchisor who is engaged by the franchisor's broker and who is directly involved in the granting of a franchise" (s. 0.1, O. Reg. 580/00 under the AWA).

C. Punitive Damages

Punitive damage awards in franchise litigation are relatively rare in Canada. In *Katotikidis v. Mr. Submarine Ltd.*, [2002] O.J. No. 1959 and [2002] O.J. No. 4101 (S.C.J.) (*Mr. Submarine*), a franchisee operating in a shopping center faced difficulties when the mall's anchor tenant shut down. The franchisor agreed to assist the franchisee with a move to a new location nearby, but suddenly reneged and offered the new location to a third party. The franchisor's conduct was tantamount to total abandonment of the franchisee. Further exacerbating the franchisee's difficulties in this case was the existence of a non-competition provision in connection with the original location. The court condemned egregious conduct on the part of a franchisor by making a punitive damages award due to the franchisor's violation of the duty of good faith and fair dealing. In determining the amount of punitive damages to be paid, the court reviewed the seminal decision of *Whiten v. Pilot Insurance Co.*, [2002] S.C.J. No. 19, where the Supreme Court of Canada stated "that an award of punitive damages must be rationally related to the underlying purposes or objectives of punitive damages, which is to denounce and to deter the disregard for legal and equitable rights of others." The court went on to say that it has a duty to determine the lowest award that would serve that purpose. Taking this approach, punitive damages of $10,000 were awarded to the plaintiff, Katotikidis.

More recently, in *1159607 Ontario Inc. v. Country Style Food Services Inc.*, [2012] O.J. No. 1241 (S.C.J.), affirmed in 2013 ONCA 589, the plaintiffs sought punitive damages and damages for breach of the duty of good faith, in addition to rescission damages and damages for misrepresentation. The facts involved a franchisor willfully concealing from a franchisee specifics of a lease, specifically pertaining to the length of the term. When a dispute arose and the franchisee learned of the deficient disclosure on the part of the franchisor, the franchisee immediately sought rescission. The court held that a significant change to the term of a lease was clearly a material change and as such, it should have been disclosed to the plaintiffs. The franchisee was able to rescind the franchise agreement. In addition, placing great emphasis on the franchisor's deliberate concealment of vital information, the court awarded $25,000 for breach of the duty of good faith and fair dealing. The plaintiffs were entitled to damages for breach of the duty of good faith and fair dealing or for punitive damages, but not both.

Historically, Canadian courts have been reticent to award punitive damages unless particularly egregious or excessive conduct has taken place. This position is consistent with the current state of punitive damages in franchise law litigation, though a growing body of case law serves as a warning for franchisor behaviour.

The decision in *Richard v. Time Inc.*, 2012 SCC 8, should be noted because of its decision to award punitive damages in a commercial context under Quebec's *Consumer Protection Act*. This case involved a consumer who was misled by a letter received in the mail suggesting he had won a cash prize. When the consumer responded to the letter and never received the expected cheque, he brought a motion seeking compensatory and punitive damages. The publishers were ultimately ordered to pay punitive damages to the consumer based on these misleading representations and a failure to clearly indicate the contest rules. The conduct of the publishers constituted civil fault triggering extra-contractual liability. The Supreme Court of Canada upheld the trial judge's award of $1,000 compensatory damages and awarded $15,000 in punitive damages, a lower quantum than the $100,000 punitive damages awarded by the trial judge.

D. Recent Developments

Three decisions have given rise to considerable discussion amongst commentators of Canadian franchise law. In *2189205 Ontario Inc. et al. v. Springdale Pizza Depot Ltd. et al.*, [2012] O.J. No. 2641 and [2014] O.J. No. 347 (S.C.J.); motion to oppose reference dismissed, [2013] O.J. No. 1080 (S.C.J.); appeal dismissed, [2013] O.J. No. 4664 (C.A.); application for leave to appeal dismissed (S.C.C.) (*Springdale*), the court was confronted with the issue of whether any net profits of a franchisee could be set off against losses for which the franchisee was to be compensated pursuant to s. 6(6) of the Ontario statute. The fact situation in *Springdale* featured the unusual case of a rescinding franchisee who was also profitable at the time of rescission. Justice Lederman held that the franchisee was permitted to recover approximately $300,000 in rescission damages even though the franchisee was turning a modest profit at the time of rescission. In its decision, the court found that the franchisor could not set off the franchisee's profits against the rescission damages, thus allowing the franchisee to both keep its profits and obtain its full measure of rescission damages. The decision received some criticism upon its release, but was upheld by the Ontario Court of Appeal in the fall of 2013.

Franchisors doing business in the Province of Québec must take note of the recent affirmation by that province's Court of Appeal of the trial decision in *Dunkin' Brands Canada Ltd. v. Bertico Inc. et al.*, [2012] Q.J. No. 4996 (S.C.); appeal dismissed, 2015 QCCA 624 (*Dunkin' Donuts*); leave to appeal dismissed by the Supreme Court of Canada, 2016 CarswellQue 1813, which found that the franchisor owed a duty to its franchisees to protect the franchise's brand in the wake of increasing competition.

In this decision, the plaintiffs were 21 Dunkin' Donut franchisees operating in Québec. The defendant was the Canadian arm of a Massachusetts-based franchisor (Dunkin'). The Québec Superior Court found that the franchise agreement imposed an obligation on the franchisor to "protect and enhance both its reputation and the demand for the products of the Dunkin' Donuts System." During the years of 1995 to 2005, Tim Hortons grabbed considerable market share from Dunkin' Donuts, and the franchisee's alleged that the franchisor had failed to meet its obligation to protect the brand under the franchise agreement, along with several other civil faults. Although the franchisor had initiated a "remodel incentive program" to renovate and revamp stores, such initiatives did not stave off competition. There was a dramatic decline in the number of Dunkin' Donut stores in Québec, from 210 in 1998 to a mere 13 in 2012.

In its defence, Dunkin' submitted that the franchisees were poor operators, but the trial judge found such allegations were devoid of merit. The trial judge awarded damages for lost profits, as well as lost investment opportunities given the poor sales prospects for the locations, totaling over $16 million in damages.

On appeal, the Quebec Court of Appeal largely upheld the judgment, with the exception of three errors related to the calculation of damages. First, the trial judge awarded damages for lost profits that were calculated for a period longer than Quebec's three-year limitation period. Second, the Court of Appeal deducted from the franchisees' damages amounts due under the franchise agreements to Dunkin'. Third, the trial judge had awarded lost profits based on a model that the franchisees of Dunkin' could have achieved the same annual growth in sales as Tim Hortons franchisees but for Dunkin's breach [182]. While the Court of Appeal held that it was reasonable for the trial judge to adopt such a comparable method, he erred in ignoring imponderables or unanticipated factors that may have limited the success of the plaintiff franchisees. The Court of Appeal reduced the franchisees' lost profit claim by 10% to take into account these contingencies and by a further 15% to allow for the fact that Dunkin' franchisees would have faced competition from Tim Hortons even if Dunkin' had not committed a fault [188] and the fact that Tim Hortons had a competitive advantage over Dunkin' by reason of the prevalence of its drive thru service [189]. The damages for lost profits awarded at trial were thus reduced by 25%. This same reduction was applied to the damages awarded for lost investment. Where franchisees received funds from Dunkin' to renovate their stores, the Court of Appeal required them to reimburse Dunkin' for its contribution out of the money they received as damages [215].

The Court of Appeal held that the trial judge had correctly followed precedent in imposing the implied obligation under article 1434 of the Civil Code of Québec (which provides that parties are bound not only to what they have expressed in writing in a contract, but also as to what is incident to it according to its nature and in conformity with usage, equity, or law) and the duty of good faith in addition to those duties expressly provided for in the franchise agreement.

The Court of Appeal held that the contracts established "a relationship of cooperation and collaboration between the Franchisor and its franchisees, reflecting both common and divergent interests, over a long period of time" [62]. The agreement was a "relational" one which "did not spell out all of its terms."

The Court of Appeal held that the implied duty of good faith incorporates a duty to assist and cooperate with franchisees by taking active measures in support of the brand, and includes a collective duty owed to the network of franchisees, where any individual franchisee has a right of action in the event of a breach.

So, the franchisor had obligations to individual franchisees—technical assistance, for example [78]—but it also owed a duty to the whole network to take reasonable measures to maintain the health and prosperity of the network [80].

The franchisor held out to each franchisee that the brand was something of value as an inducement to join the network, [81] so by failing to fulfill its duty to protect and enhance the brand, the franchisor was "going back on its word in each individual contract by denying the existence of the very cause of the arrangement." [82]

The franchisor had a duty to "police the system" and root out delinquent franchisees or "free-riders" who cut corners and breached the franchise agreement for their own gain, but who harmed the system [83-85].

The Court of Appeal noted that the obligation was not to guarantee successful results, but to take reasonable means to protect and enhance the brand:

> . . . The Franchisor was not bound to guarantee that the fox did not enter the hen-house, but merely to take reasonable measures to protect the Dunkin' Donuts' system. Had the Franchisor taken proper measures to protect and enhance the brand and, notwithstanding those efforts, Tim Hortons or another competitor had encroached on some of the Franchisees' market share, the latter would have had no basis for complaint [93].

The Court of Appeal upheld the finding of liability but reduced the overall damages awarded at trial by some $6 million for the reasons discussed above. In 2016 the Supreme Court of Canada dismissed the franchisor's application for leave to appeal.

Some observers suggest that the application of the *Dunkin'* decision ought to be restricted to Quebec, given that the case was decided under the Quebec Civil Code. Others have suggested that duties discussed in the Dunkin' decision extend to franchise systems operated outside of Quebec. The authors are of the view that the decision in the *Dunkin'* case has limited if no application outside of Quebec, other than perhaps to inform franchisors operating outside of Quebec to both abide by their contractual obligations and their duties of fair dealing in the performance and enforcement of franchise agreements, the latter of which duties are also present in the Quebec Civil Code.

Finally, in *Salah v. Timothy's Coffees of the World Inc.*, [2009] O.J. No. 4444 (S.C.J.); appeal dismissed, 2010 ONCA 673 (*Salah*), the Court of Appeal for Ontario determined that damages for breach of the duty of fair dealing under the AWA, need not be limited to compensatory damages, but that general damages may be awarded and that such damages may include damages for mental distress. In the *Salah* case, the franchisee was led to believe that he would receive a new sublease when the existing head lease expired. When the head lease expired, the franchisor entered into a new lease for a different unit within the same mall and granted a franchise to a new franchisee. At trial, the judge held that the franchisor breached the franchise agreement by refusing to honour a term that obligated the franchisor grant a new sublease to the franchisee and that the manner in which the franchisor dealt with the franchisee was not fair and did not constitute good faith [118]. The trial judge held that the franchisor "actively misled" the franchisee as to what was going on with the lease that he expected to be renewed and that was renewed [122].

The Court of Appeal for Ontario agreed with the trial judge and her decision to award damages for the breach of the duty of good faith, separate and in addition to any award in compensation of pecuniary losses. Chief Justice Winkler wrote:

> The *Wishart Act* is *sui generis* remedial legislation. It deserves a broad and generous interpretation. The purpose of the statute is clear: it is intended to redress the imbalance of power as between franchisor and franchisee; it is also intended to provide a remedy for abuses stemming from this imbalance. An interpretation of the statute which restricts damages to compensatory damages related solely to proven pecuniary losses would fly in the face of this policy initiative [26].
>
> The right of action provided under s. 3(2) of the *Wishart Act* against a party that has breached the duty of good faith and fair dealing is meant to ensure that franchisors observe their obligations in dealing with franchisees. In that regard, the conduct that the trial judge found egregious in the present case is precisely the mischief that this legislation was enacted to remedy [27].
>
> . . . any such award must be commensurate with the degree of the breach or offending conduct in the particular circumstances. Taking the

conduct of the appellant as found by the trial judge into account, I see no error in her decision to award damages on a merged basis for the breach of duty of good faith and mental distress, either in principle or in respect of quantum. In my view, her findings as to the breach of duty of good faith alone would support the amount of the award [29].

Practice Note

Damages for breach of the duty of fair dealing need not be tied to a particular loss but may be awarded as general damages "commensurate with the degree of the breach or offending conduct in the particular circumstances."

VII. Costs and Legal Fees

Canadian courts generally award a successful party a portion of its legal costs, with such costs to be paid by the losing party, absent special circumstances. This long-held principle is codified in the various provincial statutes and rules of civil procedure. Generally, costs are fixed by the judge hearing a motion or trial, after a review of each party's costs outline or bill of costs. Costs are fixed, based on a consideration of what is fair and reasonable in the circumstances of the case and what each side's reasonable expectations were in terms of the costs to be incurred in a particular matter. The court considers such factors as (a) the amount claimed and the amount recovered in the proceeding; (b) the apportionment of liability; (c) the complexity of the proceeding; (d) the importance of the issues to the parties; (e) the conduct of any party that tended to shorten or to lengthen unnecessarily the duration of the proceeding; (f) whether any step in the proceeding was (i) improper, vexatious, or unnecessary or (ii) taken through negligence, mistake, or excessive caution; and (g) a party's denial of or refusal to admit anything that should have been admitted.

Costs are awarded in accordance with the prescribed tariffs though the scale of costs and the quantum of the costs to be awarded are in the discretion of the court. The prescribed tariffs of costs are generally appended to the specific court rules applicable to the court in which the case is heard. The tariffs of costs will vary with the particular province, the level of the court, and the scale of costs awarded by the court. When fixing costs, the court will also consider the seniority of the lawyers that argued the case and their respective hourly rates and whether time spent on a particular step was excessive or reasonable. The costs that can be recovered include a party's fees, disbursements, and expert's fees.

A clause in an agreement automatically awarding costs to one party, usually the franchisor, for example, may be pleaded, but the court has the inherent jurisdiction to award costs, and so at best such a clause will only be one of the factors the judge will look at when considering the award of costs. See, for example, the case of *R. v. Innocente* (2003), 214 N.S.R. (2d) 263, 2003 NSSC 75 (S.C.). Such clauses, if they are overly broad and general, will not normally be given much weight by a judge, but where the clause is more specific and refers to the actual situation at hand, it will be given greater weight by a judge in his or her determination of the costs to be awarded.

Cost awards will normally not be sufficient to fully compensate or reimburse the winning party for all of its legal fees and disbursements expended in the litigation, except in special circumstances. There are different scales of costs, as mandated by the court rules of each particular level of court, and in each province. The exact terminology for these scales will also vary from province to province. Generally speaking, the cost scales are:

1. party and party costs or partial indemnity costs, the lowest measure, which may only cover, on average about 50 to 60 percent of a party's actual costs; and
2. solicitor and client costs or substantial indemnity costs, a higher measure, which may cover up to 100 percent, but usually less of a party's actual costs.

A court may order costs of a motion within a proceeding or leave the determination of the costs of the motion to the trial judge. Where a motion addresses the substance of the case, for example on a motion for summary judgment, costs are usually fixed and made payable within 30 days of the date of the order or such other time period as the court may determine. Where a motion is procedural and does not determine the merits of the case, costs may be fixed, and either made payable (a) forthwith; (b) within a fixed period of time; (c) made payable to the successful party in the cause (to the successful party on the motion but only if the successful party on the motion succeeds at trial); (d) to the successful party in any event of the cause (to the successful party on the motion regardless of whether the successful party succeeds on at trial); or (e) in the cause (to whomever succeeds at trial).

In a complex matter, a judge may order that costs be assessed by a court assessment officer who will determine the issue of costs as directed by the judge.

Where a plaintiff makes an offer to settle and leaves it open for acceptance until after the commencement of a hearing, the plaintiff will recover its costs on a higher scale (from the date of the offer) if the judgment was greater than the offer that was made. If the judgement is less than the offer that was made, then the offer will have no effect on the costs ordered to be paid by the defendant. The successful plaintiff will still recover its costs, but on the lower scale of costs. Conversely, if a judgment is less than a defendant's offer to settle, the plaintiff may recover its costs to the date of the offer, but be responsible to pay the costs that the defendant incurred from the date of the offer to the date of judgment. In this way, the rules of civil procedure encourage the making of offers and the settlement of legal proceedings.

These costs rules and sanctions also deter the commencement of frivolous litigation and the taking of unnecessary steps within the litigation as the court can take into account the conduct of a party in the determination of which party is required to pay costs, the scale of costs, and the quantum of costs to be paid.

VIII. Class Actions in Canada

A. Introduction

Class actions are an emerging trend in Canadian franchise litigation. In simple terms, a class action is a lawsuit in which a large number of people or parties with similar legal claims unite together in a "class" to bring an action against a defendant. The procedural process for class actions is governed by provincial legislation. Ontario enacted legislation in the area in 1992 with the *Class Proceedings Act* (the Ontario Act), with British Columbia following in 1995. All other provinces except PEI and the Territories have class action legislation.

B. Procedure

For a group of plaintiffs to bring a class action, they first must be certified as a class. The certification stage serves as a gatekeeper, through which admittance is granted only to claims with sufficient commonality. In Canadian jurisdictions other than Quebec, class actions are commenced via complaint in the form of a statement of claim. In the statement of claim, the proposed representative plaintiff communicates the intention to proceed as a class action. For certification to occur, the representative plaintiff must meet the certification tests. In the Ontario Act, this test is broken down into five steps. The plaintiff must establish that:

1. "the pleadings disclose a cause of action";
2. "there is an identifiable class of [two] or more" people who would be represented by the representative plaintiff(s);
3. "the claims of the class raise common issues";

4. a class proceeding would be the preferable method for resolution of the common issues; and
5. a representative plaintiff has been identified that "fairly and adequately" represents the class, has no conflict of interest with other class members on the common issues, and has produced a plan of proceeding that is workable.

Plaintiff's counsel will request to schedule a hearing on a certification motion, but timelines can be prolonged in Canadian class action litigation. On the short end of the spectrum, there may be a four- to eight-month wait for a motion to be heard, but the wait may extend well beyond that for often-complex process of gathering affidavit evidence, expert opinions, and cross-examinations to run its course.

Franchisors that attempt to bring preliminary motions before certification motions should be advised that Canadian courts will likely only permit preliminary motions that might narrow or dispose of the litigation entirely.

C. Goals of Class Proceedings

In *Hollick v. Toronto (City),* the Supreme Court of Canada first articulated the policy rationale validating the existence of the class action lawsuit. The three goals of class actions were expressed as follows: (a) class actions provide judicial economy by allowing a court to address claims in a group rather than as individual claims; (b) class proceedings split the cost of expensive litigation, thereby facilitating access to justice; and (c) class proceedings are designed to cause positive behaviour modification amongst potential defendants who have the knowledge they could be subject to large class actions. As will be seen in the review of the jurisprudence to follow, these goals provide a lens through which courts interpret the procedural merits of a franchise class action.

D. Recent Developments

Franchise class action litigation is an area that has experienced significant development in recent years. A growing number of franchise class actions have been certified, and the body of law on the topic continues to grow, while only one case has gone to a full trial. The following section will provide an overview of some of the important cases that have emerged in the area.

1. Tim Hortons

Canadian franchisors greeted this decision with favour when it was handed down by the Ontario Superior Court of Justice in 2012. This claim resulted from a group of franchisees who were upset with the *Tim Hortons* (the franchisor) decision to adopt the Always Fresh (AF) menu, which obligated franchisees to sell certain lunchtime items at a loss, among other things. The plaintiffs alleged that the franchisor's conduct in modifying its franchise system constituted, inter alia, breach of express and implied terms of the franchise agreement and breach of the common-law duty of good faith and fair dealing. While the AF menu did bring significant changes to the Tim Hortons franchise system, the court strongly defended the right of the franchisor to make changes to its franchise system pursuant to the executed franchise agreement. The court viewed the actions of the franchisor as rational business decisions made for valid economic and strategic reasons. As a result, Justice Strathy took the bold step of dismissing the plaintiff's $2 billion claim on summary judgment. Strathy's decision was upheld at the Ontario Court of Appeal, and leave to appeal to the Supreme Court of Canada was denied.

Nevertheless, in Justice Strathy's dismissal of the action, he affirmed that franchise disputes are indeed frequently suitable for certification because of the "existence of a clearly identifiable class, a common standard form contract and a common business system, coupled with conduct of the franchisor that treats every franchisee in the same way." Justice Strathy did temper his remarks by observing: "this is not to say that a class action will be the preferable procedure for the resolution of every franchise case."

The *Tim Hortons* decision is significant in several ways. In light of Justice Strathy's comments regarding certification, the decision follows the trend of Ontario being a fertile ground for the certification of franchise class actions. At the same time, franchisors can note that despite the court's general reluctance to hear motions prior to a certification hearing, it is possible to succeed on a summary judgment motion brought during the certification hearing. Perhaps most important from a franchisor perspective, the decision upholds a franchisor's right to make commercially reasonable decisions with respect to change to its franchise system when it gives regard to both its own interests and the interest of its franchisees.

2.Midas Canada

The Midas Canada franchise class action was commenced in 2006. Similar to *Tim Hortons,* the impetus for the action was once again changes made by Midas Canada (the franchisor) to its franchise system. In particular, the franchisor's changes essentially discontinued all sales of products to the franchisees and set up a third-party supply chain system. The plaintiffs alleged breach by Midas Canada of its common-law duty to exercise its rights under the franchise agreement honestly, fairly and in good faith, and to uphold its duty of fair dealing under the Ontario Act. The court decided that, while certain changes to franchise systems are natural, and indeed necessary to adapt to dynamic market factors, there is an obligation to effect significant changes in good faith, in a commercially reasonable manner, and in a way that considers the franchisees' interests.

Midas Canada serves as example of the court's approach to certification decisions. The procedural nature of the steps in the Ontario Act reinforce that the case is not to be assessed on its legal merits at the time of certification. Firstly, the court was satisfied that a trial of the common issues would substantially advance the litigation of the claims linked to the causes of action. The court was convinced that judicial economy would be served by a class proceeding, making it a preferable procedure, and that the litigation plan presented was workable. As a result, the class was certified, albeit on more narrow grounds that the plaintiff initially sought.

In 2013, after six years of prolonged litigation, the court approved a settlement in *Midas Canada*. After having initially claimed for the amount of $75 million, the franchisees received $8.5 million from the franchisor under the terms of the settlement. Canadian franchisors might take some encouragement from the court's analysis in its settlement decision. The court noted the changing landscape of Canadian franchise litigation, particularly in respect of the *Tim Hortons* decision, in which the Ontario Court of Appeal outlined the difficulty of proving bad faith and the lack of fair dealing in respect of changes to a franchise system. Nevertheless, *Midas Canada* is a reminder that franchisors must continue to be cognizant of their good faith and fair dealing obligations, in addition to contractual duties imposed by the franchise agreement, particularly when significant changes to equipment and supply practices are contemplated.

3. Quizno's Canada

In this class action, the plaintiff franchisees' claims arose from the franchisor's vertical supply and pricing arrangements, and included a range of contractual and antitrust claims. In particular, the franchisees' argument was tied to a contractual provision in the franchise agreement that mandated they purchase food products and supplies from certain suppliers designated by the franchisor. The franchisees put forth that these designated suppliers were engaging in illegal price maintenance and, as a result, the plaintiffs were being overcharged for their supplies.

The motions judge who initially heard the certification motion refused to grant certification, stating that damages could not be determined on a class-wide basis and, as such, a class action was not the preferable procedural vehicle. The divisional court strongly disagreed, citing section 6 of the Ontario Act to establish that inability to prove damages on class-wide basis is not a bar to certification. While losses and damages may have varied by region or timeframe for different franchisees, it was systemic conduct on the part of the franchisor that gave rise to its liability. The Ontario Court of Appeal upheld this reasoning, firmly establishing that in a motion for certification the plaintiff must only prove that there is a reasonable likelihood that damages can be proved on an aggregate basis.

The court's support for this line of reasoning is beneficial for franchisees, who now face a lower threshold for the difficult issue of proving harm or damages as a component of liability. The court's attitude in *Quizno's Canada* and the relatively low threshold to achieve certification is clearly captured in the statement that "this case will satisfy at least two objectives of the *Class Proceedings Act* of judicial economy and access to justice . . . it seems to me that this case involving a dispute between a franchisor and several hundred franchisees is exactly the kind of case for a class proceeding." This decision also has important ramifications for competition class actions in Canada, the details of which are beyond the scope of this chapter.

In January 2015 the Quizno's class action was settled with approval from the court. However, an approval motion heard several months earlier to affirm settlement on similar terms failed to gain court approval. The settlement included a nominal cash payment to reimburse class counsel for some of the disbursements they had incurred and a release from class members. The release that was first agreed to included class members releasing all defendants not only from current matters but future ones as well.

In commenting on the terms of the first settlement, the approval judge noted that but for the matter of the release, the settlement would have been fair and in the best interests of the class members, notwithstanding that the settlement was "very poor for the Class Members, who [would] have gained nothing." Rather, the "future" aspects of the release was the fatal component to the approval of the settlement.

Ultimately, the action was settled and approved on similar terms, but with a less restrictive release being given.

4. Pet Valu Canada

In January of 2011, Justice Strathy certified a class action against a franchisor, Pet Valu Canada Inc. (*Pet Valu*) brought by a group of franchisees for a narrow set of claims based on allegations that the franchisor was obligated to pass on certain supplier volume rebates and discounts to franchisees, and failed to do so. The certification order approved notice to all class members and provided them with information regarding the opt-out period. The court also dictated that communications with potential class members during the opt-out period should be limited. The issue of opt-outs in this case became the subject of a drawn-out dispute that illustrates the challenges of placing limits on communication when many potential class members have an ongoing business relationship with the franchisor.

While the court made provisions to allow for the franchisor to communicate with class members in the context of its ongoing business relationships, the court failed to establish a framework to govern the communications of unnamed parties, specifically other franchisees, with class members during the opt-out period. In this case, an influential subgroup of franchisees undertook an aggressive campaign to persuade potential class members to opt out of the class action. Neither party to the actual class action was directly involved in the campaign, but this did not prevent Justice Strathy from taking the extraordinary step of judicial intervention in the opt-out process, setting aside approximately 100 opt-out forms that the judge found had been obtained under the spectre of the aggressive campaigning, and the misinformation about the proceedings that accompanied it.

In May 2013, on appeal by the franchisor, the Ontario Court of Appeal overturned Justice Strathy's decision. The court confirmed that class members have an "unassailable right to speak out in opposition to a class proceeding in an attempt to convince other class members to opt out" in the context of "acceptable intra-class debate." The court found that the campaign did not constitute coercion or misinformation or cause intimidation. Rather, class members were afforded access to objective information regarding the class action to counter the opinion of the campaigning subgroup in the form of the notice of certification and access to class counsel's website. Ultimately, the court was not satisfied that there was evidence that established that any decisions to opt out were involuntary or improperly influenced. Finally, the court commended the franchisor for staying above the fray, by not contributing directly or indirectly to the campaign, and by sending communications designed to assure class members that business relationships would not be compromised regardless of the decision to opt in or out.

While the Court of Appeal interpreted the evidence very differently than the motions judge, they agreed upon the general principle that courts should be highly vigilant in their efforts to protect the integrity of class proceedings, including the opt-out process. Both courts stressed the critical importance of ensuring the franchisees' decision is voluntarily made, regardless of the particular choice made. The court warned against the politicization of the opt-out process, and reiterated that certification motions are not determined through a referendum of the class members.

This decision regarding opt outs is important for franchisor defendants, class members, and class proceeding litigants generally. It provides guidance and insight into permissible conduct by class members who oppose a class action and seek to encourage fellow class members to opt out. It helps clarify expectations for all class proceeding litigations in a post-certification environment. Finally, it confirms that a decision to invalidate opt-out notices will only be made in the most extraordinary of circumstances, where the evidence of intimidation or coercion is especially egregious.

The franchisor moved for summary judgment on the seven common issues certified under the class proceeding and a 2014 decision found in favour of the franchisor. After the hearing of the summary judgment motion but before the decision was released, the plaintiff moved to amend its statement of claim and certify a new common issue that focused on purchasing power rather than volume rebates. This decision, 2015 ONSC 29, also addressed two further common issues that had been deferred at the summary judgment trial along with a determination of whether the franchisor's duty of good faith and fair dealing was breached, which is discussed in further detail under the ,Duty of Good Faith and Fair Dealing in Canada section below.

Regarding the motion to amend the pleadings, the court dismissed this motion on the ground of prejudice to the defendant franchisor. Although pleading amendments are routinely approved, the court found that there would be actual prejudice to the franchisor in respect of the proposed amendments and new common issue. The court noted that a motion that adds a new common issue at the end of a summary judgment hearing would tilt the class proceeding in the plaintiff's favour and quoted Justice Perell, who stated that, "courts should also be aware that the procedure of a class action is meant to level the playing field, not tip the field in the favour of plaintiffs." Regarding the two further common issues that had been deferred, Justice Belobaba read in certain language to the common issue to ultimately find in favour of the plaintiff.

The defendant franchisor appealed this decision to the Court of Appeal and the plaintiff franchisee cross-appealed. In the decision *1250264 Ontario Inc. v. Pet Valu Canada Inc.*, 2016 ONCA 24, the Court of Appeal denied the cross-appeal and upheld the trial judge's decision denying the last-minute amendment motion to add a new common issue. The court stated that allowing the addition of a new common issue at the end of the matter that was fundamentally different than the others would be "fundamentally unfair" to the defendant. The Court of Appeal went on to allow the franchisor's appeal, noting that the trial judge erred by adding material language to the common issue, which essentially recast the issue without advising the defendant or allowing the opportunity to make submissions. An application for leave to appeal the decision of the Court of Appeal to the Supreme Court of Canada was dismissed, 2016 CanLII 66262.

5. Other Cases

Trillium Motor World Ltd. v. General Motors of Canada Ltd., 2015 ONSC 3824, involved a class action brought by franchisee dealerships against GMC Ltd. The case was in the context of the global financial crisis and saw GMC Ltd. devise a plan to reduce its dealership network in an attempt to avoid creditor protection under Canada's insolvency legislation. After GMC Ltd. delivered Notices of Non-Renewal and Wind-Down Agreements to 240 dealers, giving them six days to consider, a class was formed to bring a claim against GMC Ltd. alleging a breach of both common-law and statutory obligations under the provincial franchise legislation. Justice T. McEwen held that there was no breach of any common-law or statutory obligation toward the class members in this case. Although GMC Ltd. was determined to be a franchisor within the meaning of the legislation and therefore owed a duty of fair dealing to the class members, the court did not find that there was a breach of such duty. The duty of good faith and fair dealing (which is discussed in more detail below), required GMC Ltd. to treat affected dealers with honesty and fairness and give due regard to their interests, among other things. Although the dealers were given only six days to consider the proposed agreements, based on the circumstances there was no dishonesty or unreasonableness found to justify a breach of good faith and fair dealing. This decision also determined that GMC Ltd. did not interfere with class members' right to association, which is discussed in more detail in the Right of Association section below. An appeal of this decision by the franchisees was heard in early 2017. A decision from the Court of Appeal for Ontario had not been released as of the date of publication.

TA & K Enterprise Inc. v. Suncor Energy Products Inc. was an appeal from franchisees' allegations that the franchisor failed to provide certain disclosure documents. The franchisees argued that they should be able to rescind their franchise agreements as a result. The claims arose from the large amalgamation of Suncor and Petro-Canada, the terms of which included the eventual termination of approximately 200 franchise agreements. The court held that the franchisor was not required to deliver disclosure documents to franchisees as it was entitled to rely on one of a number of disclosure exemptions under the Ontario Act. The Cout of Appeal for Ontario upheld the lower court's granting of summary judgment in favour of the franchisor. As in the aforementioned *Tim Hortons* case, the court relied heavily upon the terms of a carefully drafted franchise agreement to guide their analysis.

Another case involving franchisor disclosure obligations in a class actions context is *578115 Ontario Inc. v. Sears Canada Inc.* The plaintiff franchisees complained that Sears was withholding parts of rebates owed to them under the terms of the franchise agreement without their knowledge, and that Sears was keeping a "secret rebate" given by suppliers for itself. Justice Strathy certified the class by Sears franchisees in August 2010, citing that "no procedures, other than individual actions or single actions joining multiple plaintiffs, had been proposed as preferable to a class action." He also stated that "judicial economy and access to justice would be attained" through a class action, and reiterated than in certifying the class he was offering no opinion of the merits of the plaintiff's claim. Sears defended against the allegations and ultimately entered into a settlement agreement for $1,575,000 in December, 2013. This case highlights for franchisors the importance of following best practices for the disclosure of rebates and once again demonstrates the desire of Canadian courts to use class proceedings as a method of equalizing the bargaining power disparity between franchisor and franchisee.

E. Conclusion

Overall, the relatively low threshold for certification has made Canada a fertile ground for franchisee class actions in recent years. As demonstrated by several of the key decisions, Canadian courts are not shy to demonstrate their concern for access to justice, judicial economy, and behavioural modification. These class action policy goals seem to fit franchisee and franchisor disputes, in which the typical relationship includes a common franchise agreement and an inherent power imbalance favouring the franchisor over the franchisee. Class proceedings offer a tool for the resolution of disputes between the parties of the franchise relationship that is becoming increasingly relevant in Canadian jurisdictions. Prudent franchisors and franchisees should continue to monitor Canada's growing body of jurisprudence in the area.

IX. Right of Association

Franchisees have rights under the common law and by statute, to associate together, free from a franchisor's direct or indirect interference or threats of retribution or penalty for doing so. (See section 4 of each of the Ontario, P.E.I., New Brunswick, Manitoba, and BC statutes and s. 8 of the Alberta statute.)

The right to associate is codified in the *Canadian Charter of Rights and Freedoms* (Part I of the Constitution Act, 1982, being Schedule B to the Canada Act 1982 (U.K.), 1982, c. 11). Section 2 (d) of the *Charter* reads:

> "2. Fundamental freedoms.—Everyone has the following fundamental freedoms:

...

(d) freedom of association."

The Québec *Charter of Human Rights and Freedoms* (R.S.Q., c. C-12) provides for this right in Article 3, which reads:

> "3. Every person is the possessor of the fundamental freedoms, including freedom of conscience, freedom of religion, freedom of opinion, freedom of expression, freedom of peaceful assembly and freedom of association."

The Ontario, P.E.I., New Brunswick, Manitoba and BC statutes establish and protect the right to associate each with virtually identical wording. For example, section 4 of the Ontario statute reads:

> "Right to associate
>
> 4. (1) A franchisee may associate with other franchisees and may form or join an organization of franchisees.
>
> Franchisor may not prohibit association
>
> (2) A franchisor and a franchisor's associate shall not interfere with, prohibit or restrict, by contract or otherwise, a franchisee from forming or joining an organization of franchisees or from associating with other franchisees.
>
> Same
>
> (3) A franchisor and franchisor's associate shall not, directly or indirectly, penalize, attempt to penalize or threaten to penalize a franchisee for exercising any right under this section.
>
> Provisions void
>
> (4) Any provision in a franchise agreement or other agreement relating to a franchise which purports to interfere with, prohibit or restrict a franchisee from exercising any right under this section is void.
>
> Right of action
>
> (5) If a franchisor or franchisor's associate contravenes this section, the franchisee has a right of action for damages against the franchisor or franchisor's associate, as the case may be."

The Alberta statute protects franchisees' right to associate in section 8, which reads:

> "Franchisee's right to associate
>
> 8 (1) A franchisor or its associate must not prohibit or restrict a franchisee from forming an organization of franchisees or from associating with other franchisees in any organization of franchisees.

(2) A franchisor or its associate must not directly or indirectly penalize a franchisee for engaging in the activities described in subsection (1)."

Though the right to form an association of franchisees is protected, there is no obligation on the part of a franchisor to recognize such an association or to meet with or negotiate with such an association or a group of franchisees.

The right of franchisees to associate was first considered by the court in *405341 Ontario Inc. v. Midas Canada Inc.*, [2009] O.J. No. 4354 (S.C.J.); affirmed [2010] O.J. No. 2845 (CA) (*Midas*). In this class proceeding, the plaintiff made a post-certification motion to the court for a declaration that the requirement in the franchise agreement to sign a general release in favour of the franchisor, as a condition of the renewal or assignment of a franchise agreement, was void on the grounds that (a) it offended the non-waiver provision of the Ontario statute and (b) it violated the right of franchisees to associate. The motion was granted.

The requirement to sign a general release in favour of Midas had the practical effect of whittling down the size of the class as, over time, any franchisee that sought to renew or assign its franchise agreement would have to sign a release that had the effect of releasing all claims made or to be made against Midas, including the claims made in the class proceeding.

Justice Cullity held that the right to associate including the right to participate in a class action:

> Although defendant's counsel were critical of the plaintiff's reliance on cases under section 2(d) of the *Canadian Charter of Rights and Freedoms* for this purpose, I am of the opinion that, when read in its context in the AWA, the right of association in section 4 does encompass the right of franchisees to participate in a class action for the purpose of enforcing their rights against the franchisor under the statute or otherwise. Section 4 is not concerned with the right to associate socially or recreationally. Its inclusion in the statute would be inexplicable if it was not intended to permit franchisees to associate for the purpose of protecting their interests and enforcing their rights through collective action. (Midas S.C.J. at para. 17).

Justice Cullity wrote that the following quotation from *Dunmore v. Ontario (Attorney General), [2001] 3 S.C.R. 1016, at para. 16, a* case decided under the *Canadian Charter of Rights and Freedoms,* was equally applicable to the position of franchisees under the Ontario statute:

> [I]ndividuals associate not simply because there is strength in numbers, but because communities can embody objectives that individuals can-

> not. For example, a "majority view" cannot be expressed by a lone individual, but a group of individuals can form a constituency and distil their views into a single platform. Indeed, this is the essential purpose of joining a political party, participating in a class action or certifying a trade union.

The Court of Appeal for Ontario, in affirming the lower court's decision, wrote that the "motion judge was correct to hold that the requirement in the Agreement to provide a release upon extension or assignment violated rights of association under s. 4 of the Act" (Midas CA at para. 39).

Since the *Midas* decision was pronounced, there have been a number of attempts to certify and advance "right to associate" claims as common issues in class proceedings. Some of these attempts have been successful; one has not.

In *Spina v. Shoppers Drug Mart Inc.*, [2012] O.J. No. 4659 (SCJ) (*Spina*), a putative class proceeding, the franchisor moved to strike out a number of claims on the grounds that they did not disclose a reasonable cause of action.

In *Spina*, the plaintiffs alleged, among other things, that Shoppers pocketed money (rebates, professional allowances, overcharges for services) that ought to have been included in the revenue (gross sales) of the franchised stores where, after the payment of expenses, the money would be shared among the franchisees (called Associates) and Shoppers. The plaintiffs submitted that Shoppers breached its contracts and its statutory duties by not sharing the growing profits from its franchise system. Included in the claim was the allegation that Shoppers interfered with the Associates' right to organize or associate in an independent franchisee association. The associated cause of action was breach of statutory right to associate and/or common-law right to associate (see para. 52).

The plaintiffs alleged that in 2002, Shoppers began to interfere in the activities of the franchisee association and took control of its activities by taking control of its financing, requiring Shoppers' approval of the franchisee association agendas, denying it the right to vote on changes to Shoppers' policies and controlling the contents of minutes of the franchisee association meetings.

The plaintiffs also alleged that Shoppers routinely reprimanded, threatened, and intimidated the plaintiffs and Associates who raised concerns about Shoppers' administration of the franchise system at association meetings (see para. 99). Shoppers, it was alleged, also refused to recognize another association of franchisees formed after the commencement of litigation.

The plaintiffs sought:

(a) a declaration that the class was entitled to an independent and representative franchisee association free from control, interference, intimidation and reprisals by the defendants and

(b) an order enjoining the defendants from interfering with the franchisee organization referred to in paragraph (a) above.

Justice Perell used a baseball analogy to describe his role on the motion to strike out portions of the statement of claim:

> The court as the umpire charged with identifying which of these many pitches is in the legal strike zone has the enormous task of carefully scrutinizing and analyzing each pitch. However, I believe that the court's task can be simplified with some organization and remembering that under the plain and obvious test, there is a generous strike zone making it relatively easy for a Plaintiff to throw a strike (see para. 156).
>
> My general approach will be to organize the discussion by beginning with the claims where it is easiest to say that the Plaintiffs have thrown a pitch within the legal strike zone and then proceeding to the progressively more difficult pitches to call. The resulting analysis will have seven stages, or innings to continue the baseball metaphor (see para. 157).

After reviewing the statement of claim and the documents incorporated by reference in it, Justice Perell held that it was plain and obvious that the interference with association claim was not a genuine claim but was a matter of the plaintiffs adding colour to the statement of claim. The plaintiffs feared, but had not actually suffered, interference with their right to associate.

The allegations were struck out with leave to amend if "in the future there is real interference with their right under the *Arthur Wishart Act*" (see para. 202).

Contrast the decision in the *Spina* case with the decisions in *1146845 Ontario Inc. v. Pillar to Post Inc.*, [2013] O.J. No. 3106 (S.C.J.), and *Trillium Motor World Ltd. v. General Motors of Canada Ltd.*, [2011] O.J. No. 889 (S.C.J.); affirmed, [2012] O.J. No. 1579 (Div. Ct.). In the *Pillar to Post* case, the defendants to a class action sought to strike out portions of the statement of claim on the basis that the claim did not provide sufficient particulars of the allegations being made against them, including a claim for interference with the right to associate. Justice Perell dismissed the motion. He held that, though the pleading was lengthy, the plaintiffs pleaded sufficient material facts to support the claim, including the claim for interference with the right to associate under the Ontario statute. The allegations included the following:

> 69. At all material times, PTP was aware that franchisees were trying to organize a franchisee association in order to better protect the rights of PTP franchisees and to equalize the bargaining and economic power between PTP and franchisees. PTP employed its strategy to alter the PTP franchise system and to intimidate franchisees in order to ensure they

> did not form an association or otherwise join together in order to level the bargaining power between PTP and franchisees.
>
> 70. In addition, the defendants have undertaken a strategy to intimidate franchisees and ensure that this action is not commenced by, inter alia, threatening that they will lose their franchises if the action is commenced, that they will never be able to sell or market their franchise if the action proceeds, that the entire PTP franchise system will suffer and that the franchise system will lose its value if the proceeding is commenced.
>
> 71. The defendants' actions as set out above are an attempt to bully and to intimidate PTP franchisees from associating with each other. As a result, the defendants are liable for interference with the franchisees' right to associate pursuant to the Franchise Legislation.

In *Trillium Motor World Ltd. v. General Motors of Canada Ltd.*, [2011] O.J. No. 889 (S.C.J.); affirmed, [2012] O.J. No. 1579 (Div. Ct.) the court certified a class proceeding against GM and lawyers engaged by the Canadian Automobile Dealers' Association (CADA). The plaintiff dealer alleged, among other things, that GM interfered with the dealers' right to associate at a time when GM was undergoing a restructuring and had provided approximately 240 of its dealers with Wind-Down Agreements (see fn. 1 of the S.C.J. decision).

The plaintiff dealer alleged that GM adopted a strategy that was designed to divide the franchisees, give them no time to make a unified response to GM's offer, and keep them in the dark concerning GM's actual financial position.

At trial, 2015 ONSC 3824, Justice McEwan held that GM did not interfere with, prohibit, restrict, penalize, attempt to penalize or threaten to penalize the class members' exercise of their right to associate.

The plaintiffs argued that GM, by refusing to disclose a list of its dealers to the plaintiffs, prevented the plaintiffs from exercising their right to associate. GM argued that there was no positive obligation on its part to facilitate association. The trial judge agreed with GM. He held that s. 4 of the AWA did not impose positive obligations on the franchisor. Justice McEwan wrote:

> Even when one considers the remedial nature of the *Wishart Act*, the plain and ordinary meaning of the language in s. 4 does not support Trillium's position. Section 4 prevents franchisors from restricting, prohibiting and interfering with franchisees who exercise their right to associate. It also prevents franchisors from penalizing or threatening to penalize those who do. Section 4 does not require franchisors like GMCL to facilitate or encourage association or to do anything beyond refraining from activities that inhibit association. It is a negative duty in the fullest sense [277].

> Provided that GMCL did not meddle with or interpose in the dealers' attempts to organize, did not prevent the dealers from exercising their right to associate, and did not punish or threaten to punish the dealers for doing so, it acted in compliance with the negative duty created by s. 4 [278].

Justice McEwan explained that the court will examine the franchisor's actions in the context in which they took place in determining whether the franchisor's actions "amounted to interfering, restricting, prohibiting or penalizing in the circumstances of the case." *This decision is under appeal.*

In *1176560 Ontario Ltd. v. Great Atlantic & Pacific Co. of Canada*, [2002] O.J. No. 4781 (S.C.J.); affirmed [2004] O.J. No. 865 (Div. Ct.), Justice Winkler certified a class proceeding in which the members of the class alleged that the franchisor had, in breach of the franchise agreement, failed to share volume rebates that the franchisor received from suppliers.

The franchisees sought to invoke the remedial powers of the court under sections 12 and 19 of the *Class Proceedings Act*, 1992 (Ontario) in order to curb and regulate the conduct of the franchisor because, after the commencement of the proceeding:

(a) A&P monitored the franchisees' payments to their lawyers in respect of the proceeding, which the plaintiffs contended was misuse of the confidential information that A&P obtained by acting on behalf of the franchisees in accounting functions;
(b) franchisees who refused to execute releases in respect of the lawsuit were subjected to rent increases, implemented unilaterally by A&P in breach of the franchise agreements, and in any event, before they were due and owing;
(c) A&P caused each proposed class member to receive a copy of its statement of defence and counterclaim, without including the plaintiffs corresponding reply and defence to the counterclaim; and
(d) the president of A&P's franchise operations expressly stated his intention to personally deliver to each franchisee, and to have each of them execute, a new franchise agreement and a release from the claims asserted in this proceeding in favour of A&P, without regard to the fact that the matter came before the court for a determination of the certification motion.

After considering the totality of the evidence before him, Justice Winkler granted an order to require the franchisor to refrain from communicating with class members during the opt out period, other than communications sent in the ordinary course of business. The court drew from the evidence the inference that A&P intended to defeat the certification motion by improperly interfering with the class proceeding process. The court held that A&P engaged in a course of conduct that was intimidating, threatening, and coercive, and sufficiently misleading to vitiate any notion that the franchisees executing releases were doing so on an informed basis.

While not couched as a breach of the right to associate, the conduct of the franchisor was seen as having been taken in an effort to defeat the franchisees' collective action:

> The conduct evident in the action to date underscores the need for the court to maintain close supervision over class proceedings, even in the pre-certification stages. More importantly the court is, and must remain, the proper arena for disputes between litigants in a class proceeding. Certification motions are not decided by polls among the class. The battle cannot be taken to the individual class members. Conduct aimed at pitting one member of the class against another cannot be condoned. While legitimate defence tactics are acceptable in class proceedings, this court will not permit defendants to undermine the process in the pre-certification period in an effort to bring an end to the class proceeding. (*Ibid.*, at para. 93).

Practice Note

Franchisors must ensure that there are no provisions in their franchise agreements or other agreements relating to a franchise that purport to interfere with, prohibit, or restrict a franchisee from exercising the right to associate.

Interference with the right to associate is prohibited, as is penalizing, attempting to penalize, or threatening to penalize a franchisee, directly or indirectly, for exercising its right to associate and could lead to an action for damages against the franchisor or franchisor's associate(s), liability for which is joint and several.

> Once a class proceeding has been threatened or commenced, franchisors ought to be particularly careful not to take any step that may be seen as undermining the proceeding. Attempts to defeat the certification of the proceeding as a class action ought to be made through the courts.
>
> The right to associate does not impose positive obligations on a franchisor only a negative duty i.e., a duty not to interfere, etc.

X. Enforcement of Foreign Judgments in Canadian Courts

A. General

Canadian courts will enforce a foreign judgment where it can be shown that there was a "real and substantial connection" between the cause of action and the foreign jurisdiction. If the real and substantial connection is established, then Canadian courts will generally enforce a foreign judgment unless it can be shown that: (a) that the judgment was obtained by fraud; (b) the judgment was obtained without affording to the judgment debtor the opportunity to respond to the proceeding that gave rise to the judgment in accordance with the principles of fairness and natural justice; or (c) enforcement of the judgment would be contrary to public policy. The public policy defence requires more than simply pointing out a difference between the foreign law and the domestic law of Canada. It requires that the enforcement of the judgment be fundamentally at odds with the Canadian justice system. This is a narrow exception which is often pleaded but rarely successful. Cases where Canadian courts have declined to enforce a foreign judgment are rare.

The Supreme Court of Canada has held that the real and substantial connection test should apply not only to interprovincial judgments, but also to the recognition and enforcement of foreign judgments.

The "real and substantial connection" test requires that a significant connection exist between the cause of action and the foreign court. A defendant can be brought within the sphere of a foreign jurisdiction's law where he or she has participated in something of significance or was actively involved in that foreign jurisdiction. A fleeting or relatively unimportant connection will not be sufficient to give a foreign court jurisdiction. The connection to the foreign jurisdiction must be a substantial one (see *Beals v. Saldanha*, [2003] S.C.J. No. 77 at para. 32 (*Beals*)).

Where a real and substantial connection is established, the Canadian court will enforce the judgment, subject to any defences to enforcement raised by the defendant. The defence regarding a difference in the substantive law between the jurisdictions generally falls under the public policy analysis and requires that the foreign law be at odds with Canada's "view of basic morality" (*Beals*, at para. 71). This is a high standard to meet, as is discussed further below.

In the most recent ruling on the subject, the Supreme Court of Canada, in *Chevron Corp. v. Yaiguaje*, [2015] 3 S.C.R. 69, dismissed an appeal from the Court of Appeal for Ontario in which the Ontario court permitted the enforcement in Ontario of an Ecuadorean judgment against Chevron. Chevron did not own any assets in Ecuador and it refused to acknowledge the judgment or pay the debt. Chevron was served at its offices in California with respect to the action in Ontario to enforce the judgment in Canada. Chevron sought to set aside the service ex juris and a declaration that the court had no jurisdiction to hear the action. It also sought to stay or dismiss the action. At first instance, the motions court judge ruled in favour of the plaintiffs on the issue of jurisdiction but nonetheless stayed the action. The Court of Appeal overturned the stay. On the issue of jurisdiction, it held that as the foreign court had a real and substantial connection with the subject matter of the dispute or with the defendant, an Ontario court had jurisdiction to determine whether the foreign judgment should be recognized and enforced in Ontario against Chevron:

> Canadian courts, like many others, have adopted a generous and liberal approach to the recognition and enforcement of foreign judgments. To recognize and enforce such a judgment, the only prerequisite is that the foreign court had a real and substantial connection with the litigants or with the subject matter of the dispute, or that the traditional bases of jurisdiction were satisfied. It is true that in any case in which a Canadian court exercises authority over a party, some basis must exist for its doing so. It does not follow, however, that jurisdiction is and can only be established using the real and substantial connection test, whether that test is satisfied by the existence of assets alone or on another basis. In actions to recognize and enforce foreign judgments within the limits of the province, it is the act of service on the basis of a foreign judgment that grants an Ontario court jurisdiction over the defendant. I arrive at this conclusion for several reasons. First, this Court has rightly never imposed a requirement to prove a real and substantial connection between the defendant or the dispute and the province in actions to recognize and enforce foreign judgments. Second, the distinct principles that underlie actions for recognition and enforcement as opposed to actions at first instance support this position. Third, the experiences of other jurisdictions, convincing academic commentary, and the fact that comparable statutory provisions exist in provincial legislation reinforce this approach. Finally, practical considerations militate against adopting Chevron's submission [27], . . .

The Supreme Court held that first, there was nothing unfair about enforcing the judgment in Canada as Chevron had attorned to the jurisdiction of the Ecuadorean courts. Second, "no unfairness results to judgment debtors from having to defend against recognition and enforcement proceedings. In essence, through their own behaviour and legal noncompliance, the debtors have made themselves the subject of outstanding obligations" [55]. Third, requiring that the defendant have assets in the jurisdiction of the enforcing court would "undermine order and fairness" [56]. The Supreme Court wrote:

> In today's globalized world and electronic age, to require that a judgment creditor wait until the foreign debtor is present or has assets in the province before a court can find that it has jurisdiction in recognition and enforcement proceedings would be to turn a blind eye to current economic reality [57].

B. Defences to a Foreign Judgment

The principle of comity plays a role in governing international business transactions such that judgments from foreign jurisdictions will be respected by Canadian courts unless they are "egregious" and against public policy (*Beals*, [2001] O.J. No. 2586 (CA)).

The Ontario Court of Appeal has relied on the observation that:

> If foreign law is to be refused any effect on public policy grounds, it must violate some fundamental principle of justice, some prevalent conception of good morals, or some deep-rooted tradition of the forum . . . . In the common-law provinces of Canada very seldom has public policy been invoked in the courts with success, as this exception has been construed narrowly. (Castel in *Canadian Conflict of Laws*, 4th ed. (Toronto: Butterworths, 1997), cited in *Society of Lloyd's v. Meinzer* (2001), 210 D.L.R. (4th) 519 (Ont. CA).)

The public policy basis for refusing to enforce a foreign judgment is based on essential morality:

> This must be more than the morality of some persons and must run through the fabric of society to the extent that it is not consonant with our system of justice and general moral outlook to countenance the conduct, no matter how legal it may have been where it occurred (1992), 6 O.R. (3d) 737 (C.A.).

The leading case in Ontario on the meaning of "public policy" in this context is the decision of the Court of Appeal in *Boardwalk Regency v. Maalouf* (1992), 6 O.R. (3d) 737 (C.A.) (*Maalouf*) at paras. 7-8. In that case, the defendant had gambled on credit at the plaintiff's casino in New Jersey and had written and dishonoured a cheque for $43,000 in payment of the debt. Default judgment was granted against him in New York, and the creditor attempted to enforce this judgment in Ontario. The defendant argued that enforcing the foreign judgment would be contrary to public policy reflected in the provincial *Gaming Act*, which made wagering contracts void, consideration for gaming illegal, and contracts unenforceable. The issue at the Court of Appeal was:

> . . . whether the language of the *Gaming Act*, apart from its direct impact on domestic contracts, is to be taken as an expression by the legislature which bears the mantle of public policy to the point of making it offensive to participate in enforcement of the foreign judgment. It cannot be every statutory statement or prohibition which raises this defence or little would be left of the principle of comity underlying conflict of laws jurisprudence (*Maalouf*, at para. 6).

The majority of the Court of Appeal concluded that gambling under licence was not the type of morally repugnant activity that was tainted by immorality in such a way as to refuse enforcement of the judgment. Similarly, because gambling was legal and regulated in New Jersey, it would not offend the Canadian general public to enforce a debt legally incurred in such a jurisdiction.

C. Recognition of Final Money Judgments and Other Final Orders

The Supreme Court of Canada, in *Pro Swing Inc. v. Elta Golf Inc.*, [2006] S.C.J. 52, clarified the law as to the type of foreign judgments and orders that the courts in Canada will recognize and enforce. On the facts of the case, the Supreme Court dismissed an appeal from an order refusing to enforce an order for contempt of court made the United States District Court for the Northern District of Ohio Eastern Division in a trademark infringement claim. The court refused to enforce the contempt order on a number of grounds, including that it was quasi-criminal in nature. A Canadian court will not enforce a penal order, either directly or indirectly. The Court of Appeal held that the order could not be enforced as it lacked certainty of terms.

The Supreme Court restated the traditional common-law rule: "In order to be recognizable and enforceable, a foreign judgment must be '(a) for a debt, or definite sum of money (not being a sum payable in respect of taxes or other charges of a like nature or in respect of a fine or other penalty); and (b) final and conclusive, but not otherwise' (*Dicey and Morris on the Conflict of Laws* (13th ed. 2000), vol. 1, Rule 35, at pp. 474–75 (footnotes omitted))."

The ***foreign*** judgment is evidence of a debt. All the enforcing court needs is proof that the judgment was rendered by a court of competent jurisdiction and that it is final, and proof of its amount. The enforcing court then lends its judicial assistance to the ***foreign*** litigant by allowing him or her to use its ***enforcement*** mechanisms (at para. 11).

The Supreme Court held that "in an era of large-scale cross-border commerce, e-commerce and cross-border litigation," it was time to amend the common-law rule.

The Supreme Court extended the common-law rule to equitable orders provided that "the judgment must have been rendered by a court of competent jurisdiction and must be final, and it must be of a nature that the principle of comity requires the domestic court to enforce" (at para. 31):

> Comity does not require receiving courts to extend greater judicial assistance to foreign litigants than it does to its own litigants, and the discretion that underlies equitable orders can be exercised by Canadian courts when deciding whether or not to enforce one (at para. 31).

Practice Note

Interlocutory orders, such as temporary restraining orders or interim or interlocutory injunctions made outside of Canada will not be enforced by a Canadian court. Such relief ought to be sought against a Canadian defendant in the court of competent jurisdiction in the province in which the defendant resides or carries on business or the activity sought to be restrained took place.

A final order, both monetary and nonmonetary, will likely be enforced by a Canadian court, subject to the debtor raising narrow, limited defences.

D. Moving for Injunctive Relief

By way of example, in *Curves International Inc. v. Archibald*, [2011] N.S.J. No. 298 (S.C.), Curves commenced a proceeding before the Nova Scotia Supreme Court seeking, among other things, a declaration that a franchise agreement was terminated (but for terms that survived termination), a permanent injunction restraining the former franchisee from competing and from carrying on other activities, and an interim and interlocutory injunction to restrain the former franchisee from carry on certain actions.

The former franchisee made a motion to the court to dismiss the action for want of jurisdiction.

The franchise agreement provided that disputes be determined in Texas:

> Franchisee agrees that the relationship, rights and obligations of the parties of this Franchise Agreement shall be governed by the internal **laws of the state of Texas**, except to the extent governed by the U.S. Trademark Act of 1946 (Lanham Act, 15 U.S.C. Section 1051 *et seq.*) and *The*

> *Canadian Trade-Marks Act* (R.S.C. c. T-10), and any provincial or federal legislation governing franchising which now exists or which may becomc law. Franchisee agrees that any action arising out of or relating to the relationship, rights, or obligations of the parties herein shall be brought in the Province or in any State or U.S. Federal court of general jurisdiction *where Franchisor's principal business address is then located* and Franchisee irrevocably submits to the jurisdiction of such courts and waives any objection it may have to either the jurisdiction or venue of such court. (*Emphasis ours.*)

The court held that Curves had met the burden of demonstrating that there was "strong cause" why the action should not be stayed in favour of Texas. It established that the proceeding had a real and substantial connection to Nova Scotia. It was unlikely that a court in Nova Scotia would enforce an order for an injunction made in Texas.

E. Québec Considerations

A non-Canadian judgment that is final and conclusive on the merits of the case will be more likely to be enforced in Canada's common-law provinces. However, in Québec, the courts will generally allow the defendant to raise any defences that would have been available in the initial action, before ordering the enforcement of a foreign judgment. This being the case, suing in a foreign court for a judgment to be enforced in Québec will likely involve a duplication of litigation before achieving an enforceable order.

> **Practice Note**
>
> **For Québec franchises, it is preferable as a plaintiff franchisor to sue a Québec franchisee in the Québec courts, for greatest efficiency in enforcing the (favourable) judgment.**

XI. Choice of Law and Forum and Waivers

A. Choice of Law and Choice of Forum Provisions

Generally speaking, Canadian courts will uphold the agreements made by the parties, and this includes choice of law and choice of forum clauses.

Where parties have agreed to a particular forum to resolve their disputes, the onus will be on the party seeking to displace the forum chosen by the parties. The test is "strong cause." As the court wrote in *Momentous.ca Corp. v. Cana-*

dian American Ass'n of Professional Baseball Ltd. 2010 ONCA 722 at para. 39; appeal dismissed, [2012] S.C.R. 359:

> . . .[t]he plaintiff must show strong cause why the choice of forum clause should not prevail. And in exercising its discretion, the court is guided by the rationale that ordinarily parties should be held to the bargain they have made.

However, there are many differences between the laws of Canada and those of the United States, and these need to be considered carefully when considering choice of law and choice of forum clauses. In addition, each provincial franchise-specific statute limits the rights of the parties to choose both law and forum in relation to claims made under them.

The Ontario, P.E.I., Manitoba, New Brunswick, and BC statutes each provide that:

> Any provision in a franchise agreement purporting to restrict the application of the law of [name of province] or to restrict jurisdiction or venue to a forum outside [name of province] is void with respect to a claim otherwise enforceable under this Act in [name of province].

The Alberta statute has a similar provision. It reads:

> Any provision in a franchise agreement restricting the application of the law of Alberta or restricting jurisdiction or venue to any forum outside Alberta is void with respect to a claim otherwise enforceable under this Act in Alberta.

There have been two cases where plaintiffs sought unsuccessfully to oust choice of law and choice of forum clauses on the basis that the provisions were void under the Ontario statute. In both cases, the courts held that the agreements that governed the relationships between the parties were not franchise agreements and that the statutory provision that required the disputes to be determined in Ontario did not apply.

In *Di Stefano v. Energy Automated Systems Inc.*, [2010] O.J. No. 385 (S.C.J.), Justice Code stayed an action commenced in Ontario in favour of Tennessee because the contract between the parties provided that Tennessee was the forum in which any disputes regarding the agreement were to be determined. The plaintiffs, a group of ten dealers, argued that they were "franchises," and as a result, the dispute had to be determined in Ontario.

Justice Code held that they were not "franchises." The plaintiffs paid the defendant manufacturer for a five-day training course and planned to sell products associated with its trademarks. There was no evidence that the manufacturer exercised "significant control" over or offered "significant assistance" in the plaintiffs' method of operation (an element of the definition of "franchise" in Ontario). The only evidence of assistance was the five-day training program taken prior to obtaining a dealership. Justice Code held that this assistance was not "significant" and that this "slender thread" was not a "reasonable basis" to assert that the contracts were franchise agreements. The legislature did not intend that by merely teaching nascent distributors about sophisticated products, a manufacturer would become, in law, a "franchisor" (at paras. 26–28).

In *MGDC Management Group Inc. v. Marilyn Monroe Estate*, [2014] O.J. No. 3668 (S.C.J.), The Estate of Marilyn Monroe, LLC granted a license to use the "Marilyn Monroe" trademark to a licensee for the establishment of Marilyn Monroe–branded cafes. The licensee fell into arrears of fees and the license agreement was terminated. The licensee took the position that the license agreement under which the right to use the trademark was granted was, in fact, a franchise agreement. The licensee purported to rescind the license agreement and made an application to the Superior Court of Justice (Ontario) for rescission and compensation under the Ontario statute.

The estate's motion to dismiss the application was granted. First, the court held that the Ontario statute did not apply to the grant by a trademark owner of a single license to use the trademark.

Section 2 (3) 5 of the Ontario statute read:

> Non-application
>
> 2 (3) This Act does not apply to the following continuing commercial relationships or arrangements:
>
> > 5. An arrangement arising from an agreement between a licensor and a single licensee to license a specific trademark, service mark, trade name, logo or advertising or other commercial symbol where such licence is the only one of its general nature and type to be granted by the licensor with respect to that trademark, service mark, trade name, logo or advertising or other commercial symbol.

Second, the controls exercised by the estate over the use of the trademark were necessary to protect the integrity of the trademark but did not amount to significant control or significant assistance over the method of operating the business. The estate had none of the hallmarks of a franchisor.

Last, since the Act did not apply to the license agreement or the relationship of the parties to it, the forum selection and choice of law clause in the license agreement was enforceable. It provided that the legal relations among the parties be governed by and construed in accordance with the laws of the State of New York and that the venue of all litigation be exclusively in New York, New York.

Geographically speaking, each provincial franchise statute provides that it applies to a franchise agreement where the business to be operated by the franchisee under the franchise agreement is operated partly or wholly in that province (see, for example, s. 2 of the Ontario statute). In Alberta, the franchise statute applies where the business to be operated by the franchisee under the franchise agreement is operated partly or wholly in Alberta *and* the purchaser of the franchise is an Alberta resident or has a permanent establishment in Alberta for purposes of that province's corporate tax legislation.

However, the parties to a franchise agreement are free to contract into the laws of another jurisdiction in Canada with franchise legislation.

In *405341 Ontario Ltd. v. Midas Canada Inc.*, [2009] OJ No 4354 (SCJ), appeal dismissed, [2010] OJ No 2845 (CA), the franchise agreements of all franchisees across Canada provided that they were to be governed by the laws of the Province of Ontario, including all matters relating to their validity, construction, performance, and enforcement.

Midas argued that not all of its franchisees could take the benefit of the Ontario statute as many of them did not operate their business partly or wholly in Ontario. The court disagreed:

> I believe the most reasonable inference is that, by agreeing that the laws of Ontario are to govern the validity, construction, performance and enforcement of a franchise agreement applicable to franchises operating in another province, the intention of the parties was that their rights and obligations—including the reciprocal and inviolable rights and duties of fair dealing—are to be the same as if the business of the franchise was operated in Ontario. The territorial limitations in section 2 of the AWA have, in my opinion, no more effect for this purpose than that of the general presumption that statutes are not "intended to apply extraterritorially to persons, things or events outside the boundaries of the enacting jurisdiction" (*Sullivan on the Construction of Statutes* (5th edition), page 731).
>
> Accordingly, I find that the validity and enforceability of the impugned provisions of the franchise agreements are governed by the overriding provisions of sections 4 and 11 of the AWA irrespective of the location of the Midas franchises in Canada. (S.C.J. at para. 35 and 36)

Apart from the possible difficulties in enforcing foreign judgments against Canadian franchisees in Canadian courts as discussed above, there are usually other good reasons to consider choosing the Canadian law and the Canadian courts of the province in which the particular franchise or franchisee is located.

These include making it easier to obtain and enforce injunctive relief; making it easier and more effective to deal with matters of purely Canadian law, such as a registered trademark and a registered interest in Canadian land; making it more timely, less expensive, and easier to enforce a judgment won in the court action; and having the action tried and the judgment rendered where the franchisee and the franchisee's assets are located. In particular, Canadian trademark and real estate disputes would be best left to be resolved under local law and in local courts.

Another aspect of choice of foreign law that needs to be considered is that, should a dispute end up in a Canadian court, despite the existence of a clause in the franchise agreement stating that the laws of an American state (for example) are to apply, the Canadian court will require that expert evidence be introduced in order to prove the foreign law. This could add another level of complexity and another level of costs to the case.

Where an agreement is to be governed by a foreign law, but the foreign law is not pleaded or relied upon, the court in Canada may choose to apply the law of the province in which the case was commenced to the facts of the case. A franchise case that illustrates this point is *Ahsan* c. *The Second Cup Ltd.* [2001] Q.J. No. 1763 (Sup. Ct.), varied (2003), J.E. 2003-736, [2003] Q.J. No. 3007 (Sup. Ct.). This was a case brought before the court in Québec, where the franchise agreement stated that the governing law was to be that of Ontario. The Court of Appeal wrote:

> All the agreements entered into between the parties contain a provision to the effect that they shall be governed by the laws of the province of Ontario. However, these laws have not been pleaded. Therefore we must apply the provisions of the *Civil Code of Québec*, namely for the qualification of the agreements, the right to resiliate them and the damages that can be awarded, as prescribed by art. 2809 C.C.Q.:
>
> > 2809. Judicial notice may be taken of the law of other provinces or territories of Canada and of that of a foreign state, provided it has been pleaded. The court may also require that proof be made of such law; this may be done, among other means, by expert testimony or by the production of a certificate drawn up by a jurisconsult.

Where such law has not been pleaded or its content cannot be established, the court applies the law in force in Québec (emphasis added).

Although this case dealt with the Québec courts, the decision has equal application to the courts of the common-law provinces.

There are a number of cases to mention on the topic of choice of forum (forum selection) clauses. A franchise case of interest is *Clayton Systems 2001 Ltd. v. Quizno's Canada Corp,* 2003 BCSC 1573. In that case, the franchisees sued Quizno's Canadian sub-franchisor for misrepresentation. The sub-franchisor then entered into an asset purchase agreement with Quizno's Canada Corp. Both parties were from British Columbia.

The franchisees added Quizno's Canada Corp. as a defendant. The original defendant also sought to add Quizno's Canada Corp. as a third-party defendant for indemnification purposes, to which Quizno's Canada Corp. objected because the asset purchase agreement provided that it:

> . . . shall be governed by and interpreted in accordance with the laws of the State of Colorado . . . .

The British Columbia Supreme Court allowed Quizno's Canada Corp. to be added as a third-party defendant, and stated that the clause in the asset purchase agreement (the forum selection clause) should not determine the venue of the third-party proceedings, for the following reasons:

> The indemnity issue is a fairly straightforward issue involving matters of contractual interpretation. In all of the circumstances, I conclude that Ventures has satisfied the substantial burden of showing why the forum selection clause should not determine the venue of the third party proceedings. I consider the most important factors to be the following: (1) the main action is proceeding in B.C. in any event and there are no parallel proceedings extant in Colorado; (2) all of the issues have a distinctly Canadian 'flavour' in terms of the participants, the background to the dispute and the matters in issue; (3) there is no evidence that the law of Colorado regarding the enforcement of an indemnity differs from that of B.C.; and, most importantly, (4) the plaintiffs will be extremely prejudiced if they succeed against the defendants but cannot recover any judgment before third party proceedings are litigated in Colorado [28].
>
> To enforce the choice of forum clause in these circumstances could potentially deprive the plaintiffs of a remedy to which they would otherwise be entitled. Accordingly, it is just and equitable that all of the claims between the parties be resolved in one trial in B.C. [29].

The court relied on the leading Supreme Court of Canada case on choice of forum clauses to conclude that the parties shall be held to their bargain, and the party wishing another forum has the burden of establishing a strong reason.

The leading case in Canada on the topic of forum selection is *Z.I. Pompey Industries v. ECU-Line N.V.*, [2003] 1 S.C.R. 450. There, equipment was being delivered by ship from Belgium to Montréal and by rail from Montréal to Seattle. The plaintiffs sued in the Federal Court of Canada claiming damages in transit by rail between Montréal and Seattle. The bill of lading contained an exclusive forum selection clause that read as follows:

> Any claim or dispute arising hereunder or in connection herewith shall be determined by the courts in Antwerp and no other courts.

The defendants sought to stay the action in Canada on the grounds of the exclusive forum selection clause. The Supreme Court of Canada entered the stay of the action in a unanimous decision.

There is a presumption that forum selection clauses are valid and should bind the parties. The test of whether to grant a stay of the action is whether there is "strong cause" not to apply the forum selection clause.

Regarding "strong cause," the court quoted with approval from a leading English admiralty case, *The Eleftheria*, [1969] 2 W.L.R. 1073, [1969] 2 All E.R. 641, as follows:

> (1) Where plaintiffs sue in England in breach of an agreement to refer disputes to a foreign Court, and the defendants apply for a stay, the English Court, assuming the claim to be otherwise within the jurisdiction, is not bound to grant a stay but has a discretion whether to do so or not. (2) The discretion should be exercised by granting a stay unless strong cause for not doing so is shown. (3) The burden of proving such strong cause is on the plaintiffs. (4) In exercising its discretion the Court should take into account all the circumstances of the particular case. (5) In particular, but without prejudice to (4), the following matters, where they arise, may be properly regarded: (a) In what country the evidence on the issues of fact is situated, or more readily available, and the effect of that on the relative convenience and expense of trial as between the English and foreign Courts. (b) Whether the law of the foreign Court applies and, if so, whether it differs from English law in any material respects. (c) With what country either party is connected, and how closely. (d) Whether the defendants genuinely desire trial in the foreign country, or are only seeking procedural advantages. (e) Whether the plaintiffs would be prejudiced by having to sue in the foreign Court because they would (i) be deprived of security for that claim; (ii) be unable to enforce any judgment obtained; (iii) be faced with a time-bar not applicable in England; or (iv) for political, racial, religious or other reasons be unlikely to get a fair trial.

The Supreme Court of Canada also noted that gross inequality of bargaining power, and evidence of the same on a motion to stay the action, could invalidate a forum selection clause. However, in this case, although the bill of lading was a contract of adhesion, the court held that such contracts are usually entered into by sophisticated parties familiar with the type of transaction who should be held to their bargain absent abnormal circumstances. Argument was made in the case that there had been a fundamental breach of contract. However, the court felt that, in reaching its decision on the forum selection clause, it "must not delve into whether one party has deviated from, or fundamentally breached an otherwise validly formed contract."

The strong cause test means that an inquiry must be made into matters such as convenience of the parties, fairness between the parties, and the interests of justice. The substantive legal issues should be left for determination by the court hearing the merits of the case.

When the Supreme Court of Canada decision was released, it was generally felt that, despite the fact that the case dealt with a bill of lading, it was likely to be applied to commercial contracts in general with exclusive forum selection clauses. This came to pass very quickly. In the subsequent case of *B.C. Rail Partnership v. TrentonWorks Ltd.*, 2003 BCCA 597, 28 C.P.C. (5th) 51 (S.C.), rev'd (2003), 20 B.C.L.R. (4th) 1, 2003 BCCA 597 (C.A.), the following clause was considered:

> 19(g) This Agreement shall be governed in all respects, whether as to validity, construction, capacity, performance or otherwise, by and under the laws of Nova Scotia, Canada (without giving effect to principles of conflicts of laws). Lessee irrevocably and unconditionally submits to the jurisdiction of and venue in, federal and provincial courts located in Nova Scotia, Canada for any proceeding arising under this Agreement, and TO THE EXTENT PERMITTED BY APPLICABLE LAW, LESSOR AND LESSEE EACH WAIVES (sic) ALL RIGHTS TO TRIAL BY JURY IN ANY LITIGATION ARISING HEREFROM OR IN RELATION HERETO.

The above clause was interpreted as being an "exclusive" jurisdiction clause. It did not expressly state that this was so. The court said that there was no requirement to adopt a "literal construction" of such a clause, and further stated the following:

> Turning to the clause itself, I am of the opinion that objectively interpreted it was intended by the parties to be an exclusive jurisdiction clause and not simply an attornment clause.
>
> Clause 19(g) refers to Nova Scotia *venue* as well as jurisdiction and to *any proceeding arising under this agreement* [emphasis added]. Given their ordinary meaning, I think that "any proceeding" must be intended to mean proceedings commenced by either party to the lease and not merely those commenced by Greenbrier. There is no limiting reference

to attornment as in the Old North State clause. If clause 19(g) was not interpreted to extend to proceedings by either party, the clause would in effect be silent on proceedings commenced by BC Rail in British Columbia or any other jurisdiction having jurisdiction simpliciter. I do not think that it is commercially reasonable to conclude that the parties did not intend to bring proceedings by BC Rail as well as by Greenbrier within the express words of the agreement.

The clause did not say "exclusive." The findings in this case may mean that, as a matter of best practice, if the drafter wants to express non-exclusive jurisdiction, the wording of the clause should expressly say so.

Practice Note

In drafting a forum selection clause, the best practice is to explicitly state whether the forum selection is intended to be exclusive or non-exclusive.

B. Non-waiver Provisions

The PEI, New Brunswick, Manitoba, and BC statutes each have the following non-waiver provision:

> Any purported waiver or release by a franchisee or a prospective franchisee of a right conferred by or under this Act or of an obligation or requirement imposed on a franchisor or franchisor's associate by or under this Act is void.

The BC statute has a carve-out provision whereby a waiver or release by a franchisee, or by a prospective franchisee, made in accordance with a settlement of an action, claim or dispute is not void.

Section 18 of the Alberta statute reads:

> Any waiver or release by a franchisee of a right given by this Act or the regulations or of a requirement of this Act or the regulations is void.

Section 11 of the Ontario statute reads:

> Any purported waiver or release by a franchisee of a right given under this Act or of an obligation or requirement imposed on a franchisor or franchisor's associate by or under this Act is void.

In *405341 Ontario Ltd. v. Midas Canada Inc.*, [2009] OJ No 4354 (SCJ), appeal dismissed, [2010] OJ No 2845 (CA), Justice Cullity considered terms of the Midas standard form franchise agreement that required a franchisee, as a condition of renewal or assignment of the franchise agreement, to provide Midas with a general release.

For example, under section 7.4 of the franchise agreement, Midas was required to consent to the assignment if the franchisee met a number of conditions, including the delivery of a general release.

Subsection 7.4 (f) of the franchise agreement read:

> Franchisee and each of its shareholders, directors and officers shall have executed and delivered to Midas a general release of any and all claims and causes of action against Midas, its affiliated corporations, and their respective officers, agents and employees.

Justice Cullity declared the requirement to provide a general release void:

> In my judgment, if the exercise of a franchisee's rights under a franchise agreement requires a release of rights given by the AWA, the release will, at least prima facie, be void by virtue of section 11. I say "prima facie" in order to leave open the possibility of cases such as Tutor Time, or other circumstances in which it would be inequitable to permit a franchisee to rely on the provisions of section 11. In this case, the fact that the franchisee is under no obligation to exercise the rights under the agreement appears to me to be of no relevance. The case is one where the franchisor is attempting to require the execution of a release that would deprive the franchisees of their rights under the Act. In the absence of any circumstances that should exclude an application of section 11, I am satisfied that such a release would be void and that, in consequence, the agreement to provide it is unenforceable. (S.C.J. at para. 28).

Justice Cullity's order was affirmed by the Court of Appeal for Ontario, [2010] OJ No 2845 (CA). Justice MacFarland wrote the following for the court:

> The language of s. 11 could not be clearer. If you include a term in your franchise agreement that purports to be a waiver or release of any rights a franchisee has under the Act, it will be void (C.A. at para. 26).
>
> To permit the appellant to require the class members to release any claims they might have against the appellant in order to take advantage of any other rights they might have under the Agreement, in my view, is simply contrary to the spirit, intent and letter of the Act. Where a franchisor insists upon such waiver or release, s. 11 makes it clear that any such waiver or release will be void (C.A. at para. 29).

> The purpose of the Act is to protect franchisees. The provisions of the Act are to be interpreted in that light. Requiring franchisees to give up any claims they might have against a franchisor for purported breaches of the Act in order to renew their franchise agreement, unequivocally runs afoul of the Act. To suggest that by accepting the terms of the Agreement, the respondents have in effect "settled" their claims within the meaning of Tutor Time, in my view, misapprehends and misstates the ratio of that case. Here there has been no settlement of the respondent's rights; the respondent is merely trying to assert its rights through its claims. The assertion that it has waived or released those rights contravenes s. 11 of the Act (C.A. at para. 30).
>
> In my view, the motion judge was correct in concluding that under s. 11 of the Act the extension and assignment provisions of the Agreement were unenforceable and a release in accordance with those provisions would be void (C.A. at para. 31).
>
> . . .
>
> The franchisee is required to release existing claims it has under the Act as a condition of extending or assigning its Agreement. Unless it gives up any claims it has, its Agreement cannot be extended or assigned. It is nothing like a voluntarily negotiated settlement of existing claims as was the case in Tutor Time. It is quite simply the franchisor relying on a term of the franchise agreement—a standard form contract of adhesion—to defeat the rights its franchisees would otherwise have under the Act. To interpret the Agreement in any other way is to ignore reality and emasculate the very provisions that are in place in the Act to protect franchisees from this very sort of thing (C.A. at para. 38).

More recently, in *2176693 Ontario Ltd. v. Cora Franchise Group Inc.*, [2014] OJ No 550 (SCJ) (*Cora*), Justice Matheson declared void and unenforceable a provision of Cora's franchise agreement that required a franchisee and its directors, officers and shareholders to sign and deliver a general release of any claims against Cora and its officers, directors, shareholders, and employees as a condition precedent to the franchisor consenting to an assignment of the franchise agreement (at para. 41).

The franchisees in the *Cora* case sought to assign their franchise agreements in order to mitigate their damages pending the determination of their lawsuit against Cora. Cora refused to consent to the assignment of the franchise agreement in the absence of a general release. When the lawyers for the franchisees pointed out that the general release requirement offended s. 11 of the AWA, the franchisor responded by saying that it would not waive its contractual right to a release "with the exception of those [rights] addressed in section 11 of the *Arthur Wishart Act*" (at para. 9). The franchisor then provided the franchisees with a form of release that excluded rights prescribed by the AWA. In other words, the franchisor agreed to carve out of its release any rights or claims available to the franchisees under the AWA, but it still insisted on a form of release that waived or released any rights or claims that the franchisees had at common law.

Justice Matheson held that the provision of the franchise agreement that required a release to be signed and delivered as a condition of the franchisor's consent to the assignment of the franchise agreement was void and could not be read down to be compliant or otherwise enforceable in part (at para. 21). The qualification that Cora sought, namely to secure a release for claims other than those available to the franchisees under the AWA, was not available to Cora as it was not in the franchise agreement (at para. 13).

The Cora franchise agreement provided that the release to be signed by the franchisees was to be "in the form specified by the Franchisor" which is similar to the language used in paragraph 20 of the DSSA: "in a form provided by the Company." It was not open to Cora to change its form of release to avoid the effect of section 11 of the AWA:

> The ordinary meaning of "general release . . . of any claims" in section 22.6.4 includes rights under the AWA. The qualification that the Franchisor now attaches to its request for a release, excluding rights under the AWA, is not in the franchise agreement.

I reject the Franchisor's submission that by offering to accept a narrower release after the issue was raised it has saved the requirement for a general release from the operation of s. 11 of the AWA. This approach serves only to allow for abuse. It allows a franchisor to "wait and see" if an objection is raised, and potentially secure the full general release if the franchisee does not assert its rights under the AWA. Thus, the door is open for the franchisor to take advantage of the franchisee, who may be unaware of s. 11 of the AWA.

The words "in the form specified by the Franchisor" in section 22.6.4 also do not take the release provision outside of s. 11 of the AWA. Again, based upon an ordinary interpretation of those words, they relate to form, not substance. Those words do not narrow the substantive requirement for a general release.

> This is not a case whether the actual form of the release is a part of the agreement. It was not, for example, appended as a schedule to the franchise agreements at issue here. It was provided years later, only after the issue of s. 11 of the AWA was expressly raised by the Franchisee (at para. 13-16).

The decision in the *Cora* case drives home the point that a provision in a franchise agreement that calls for a general release of claims cannot be saved by drafting a release that excludes claims under the AWA:

> The words of s. 11 also do not expressly contemplate that a provision in an agreement can be void and unenforceable only in part. Even the narrower sections of the statute that are focused on provisions in franchise agreements, such as s. 10, contemplate rendering an offensive provision in a franchise agreement void, not finding the provision unenforceable only to the extent of the conflict.
>
> To interpret s. 11 to essentially allow a franchisor to read down its offensive release clause certainly fails to protect franchisees. It allows franchisors to take advantage of franchisees, as discussed above. This is directly contrary to the purpose of the AWA.

Further, in considering the scheme of the AWA, it must be recognized that some of the rights found in the AWA are codifications of common-law rights. The suggestion that the general release should be read down to release only non-statutory rights invites considerable debate and confusion about the status of all overlapping claims (at para. 21-23).

On appeal, the Court of Appeal for Ontario held that the release provision itself was not void, only unenforceable. It was not the provision calling for a release that was void, but the waiver or release itself that was void. Any clause calling for such a release was unenforceable because it would contravene s. 11 of the AWA, 2015 ONCA 152 paras. 28-31.

The appellant argued that the application judge erred because she refused to read down or sever that portion of the franchise agreement that called for a general release so that it only provided for a release of claims other than those under the AWA. The Court of Appeal rejected this argument. The Court of Appeal held that notional severance was not an appropriate remedy because it could undermine s. 11 of the AWA [40]. Justice van Rensburg of the Court of Appeal wrote:

> [57] Applying notional severance to clauses otherwise unenforceable under the *AWA* would similarly invite franchisors "to draft overly broad [provisions] with the prospect that the courts will only sever . . . or read [those provisions] down. It would provide no incentive to franchisors to ensure their franchise agreements are in compliance with the *AWA*. It would also increase the risk that a franchisee—having signed a waiver or release of all claims—would erroneously believe it is not entitled to pursue any claims against the franchisor, including its *AWA* claims. "Read-

ing down" contractual requirements that overreach would have a chilling effect on the exercise of franchisees' rights. Each of these possibilities suggests that notional severance would diminish the protection offered by *s. 11* of the *AWA* against franchisors who might seek to have franchisees contract out of their *AWA* rights.

[58] In my view, therefore, permitting notional severance of the overbroad clause in this case could subvert the policy and purpose of *s. 11* of the *AWA*.

...

[71] Accordingly, I would conclude that the impugned clause in the franchise agreement is not voided by s. 11 of the AWA, but rather it is unenforceable, as enforcement would result in a release which would be void by virtue of s. 11. In all the circumstances of this case and in light of the purpose of s. 11 and the other provisions of the AWA, the impugned clause should not be notionally severed and enforced in part to require the delivery of a release of non-AWA claims by the franchisee as a condition of the franchisor's consent to an assignment. I would therefore dismiss the appeal.

XII. Duty of Good Faith and Fair Dealing in Canada

A. What Does the Duty Entail?

The duty of fair dealing arises from an agreement between parties. Canadian courts have not recognized a stand-alone duty of good faith that is independent from the terms expressed in a contract or from the objectives that emerge from those provisions. The implication of a duty of good faith has not gone so far as to create new, unbargained-for rights and obligations. Nor has it been used to alter the express terms of the contract reached by the parties. Rather, courts have implied a duty of good faith with a view to securing the performance and enforcement of the contract made by the parties, or as it is sometimes put, to ensure that parties do not act in a way that eviscerates or defeats the objectives of the agreement that they have entered into.

In the recent decision of *Bhasin v. Hrynew,* 2014 SCC 73 (*Bhasin*), the Supreme Court made it clear that a breach of an alleged duty of good faith is not a cause of action in and of itself. Good faith is only recognized through already existing legal concepts: honest, candid, forthright, or reasonable contractual performance. Outside of these doctrines, claims of good faith will likely fail. Rather, the Supreme Court did recognize an "organizing principle of good faith" at common law. This principle requires parties to perform their contractual duties honestly and reasonably and not capriciously or arbitrarily and requires parties to have appropriate regard to the legitimate contractual interests of the contracting partner. Therefore, *Bhasin* created a new common-law duty that applies to all contracts as a manifestation of the general organizing principle of good faith: a duty of honest performance, requiring parties to be honest with each other in relation to the performance of their contractual obligations. Even where a party has the right to terminate an agreement on written notice, *Bhasin* suggests that the party giving notice cannot mislead or be dishonest with the recipient of the notice as to the reason(s) for the notice.

The duty of good faith requires that a party to a contract "act fairly and take all reasonable steps to achieve the objectives of the agreement." It cannot act in such a way as to undermine or defeat the objectives of the agreement.

The duty of good faith permits parties to act self-interestedly, but in doing so they must also have regard to the interests of the other party. Good faith is a two-way street. Whether a party under a duty of good faith has breached that duty will depend, in part, on whether the other party conducted itself fairly. Whenever a contract grants discretionary powers to a party, that discretion must be exercised in good faith. Discretion under a contract must be exercised reasonably, fairly and with regard to how the other party's interests are affected.

The statutory duty of fair dealing simply codified the duty of good faith at common law. "Fair dealing" was not a concept that existed at common law.

Because the duty of fair dealing arises from the franchise agreement, a party that conducts itself strictly in accordance with the agreement should not face a claim for breach of the duty of fair dealing. However, the duty addresses an issue that is different from a breach of a contractual term: it addresses whether the term was performed or enforced in a manner that was honest, reasonable, fair, and in good faith.

While the decision in the *Bhasin* case created a duty of honest contractual performance, the Supreme Court held that this duty did not extend to or should not be confused with a duty of disclosure, 2014 SCC 71, at paras. 73 and 86.

In the *Spina* case, the court struck the franchisee's claim for a common law or statutory duty of disclosure, holding that such a duty went beyond a duty of good faith or fair dealing and was not consistent with the franchisor and franchisee relationship. Both of these recent cases seemed to establish that the duty of good faith does not generally include a duty of disclosure of information during the course of the franchisor-franchisee relationship. However, in *1250264 Ontario Inc v. Pet Valu*, 2012 ONSC 29 (*Pet Valu*), it was held that section 3 of the *Wishart*

Act imposed a duty to disclose information that was material or "fundamental" to the franchise system, as described in the franchise agreement. The judgment specifically distinguished the facts of the case from the facts in *Spina*, and did not dispute the fact that section 3 does not impose disclosure obligations for "routine or non-material" information. *Pet Valu* is discussed in further detail later in this section.

The recent *Raibex Canada Ltd. v ASWR Franchising Corp.*, 2016 ONSC 5575, (*Raibex*) decision of the Ontario Superior Court of Justice will have drastic effects on the business of franchisors who follow the common practice of granting franchises for locations yet to be determined.

In *Raibex*, the defendant franchisor was found liable for rescission under section 6(2) of the AWA for failing to disclose a copy of the head lease and location-specific development costs for the franchise, despite the fact that the location was unknown at the time of disclosure and subsequent execution of the franchise agreement. Pursuant to the franchise agreement, the location was to be determined pursuant to a location selection process set out in the franchise agreement.

In her decision Justice Matheson stated:

> If it is simply impossible to make proper disclosure because material facts are not yet known, then the franchisor is not yet ready to deliver the statutorily required disclosure document. The franchisor must wait – it does not get excused from its statutory obligations.

This decision created an unprecedented expansion of disclosure obligations under the AWA. Justice Matheson found, essentially, that the delivery of a disclosure document and the execution of a franchise agreement prior to determining the location of the franchise is "premature" since all material facts are not yet known. This introduced a new timing requirement for disclosure and the execution of franchise agreements that is not set out in the AWA and has not been imposed by courts prior to this case.

In addition, Justice Matheson's decision did not differentiate between situations where the franchisor assumes the head lease and those where franchisees enter into leases directly.

In principle, the *Raibex* decision leads to the perplexing conclusion that a franchisee could choose to rescind when disclosure is made and the franchise agreement signed before other types of site-specific facts, which may not even be lease related, are known. Given the myriad variables that any particular site may have, this would leave franchisors with the never-ending question of determining at what point enough material facts are known that it is "ready to deliver" disclosure. An appeal of the *Raibex* decision by the franchisor was heard in early 2017. A decision from the Court of Appeals for Ontario had not been released as of the date of publication.

Prior to these cases, it was established law in Canada that the franchise relationship is not a fiduciary one (see *Jirna Ltd. v. Mister Donut of Canada Ltd.*, [1975] 1 S.C.R. 2, aff'g, [1972] 1 O.R. 251 (Ont. C.A.), rev'g, [1970] 3 O.R. 629 (H.C.), though that decision arguably left open the possibility of such a finding under the right circumstances. The issue of whether a franchisor owed a fiduciary duty to a franchisee was more recently canvassed and rejected by the Ontario Court of Appeal in *Shelanu Inc. v. Print Three Franchising Corp.*, (2006) 64 O.R. (3d) 533 (C.A.).

There is also recognition in Canadian contract law of entire agreement or integration clauses. These clauses have been upheld, and used to prevent application of external evidence that would vary the contract as written, in many cases, including franchise cases. This recognition was given by the Supreme Court of Canada in the case of *Ronald Elwyn Lister Ltd. v. Dunlop Canada Ltd.*, [1982] 1 S.C.R. 726. Not every case will uphold an entire agreement clause. The courts will override the entire agreement clause in favour of the franchisee when, for example, a franchisor makes untrue, inaccurate, or misleading statements to the franchisee in order to induce it to enter into an agreement. In such a circumstance, an entire agreement clause will not protect the franchisor from a claim for fraudulent or negligent misrepresentation. The leading case in Canada that establishes the test for negligent misrepresentation is *Queen v. Cognos Inc.*, [1993] 1 S.C.R. 87, 99 D.L.R. (4th) 626. Examples of where the courts have ignored entire agreement clauses in the face of pre-contractual misrepresentations include *Zippy Print Enterprises Ltd. v. Pawliuk*, [1993] 44 ACWS (3d) 692 (S.C.), aff'd, [1995] 3 W.W.R. 324, 100 B.C.L.R. (2d) 55 (C.A.); *Dean v. Rise 'N Bake Pastries Inc.* (2001), 13 B.L.R. (3d) 217 (Ont. S.C.J.), aff'd (2002), 29 B.L.R. (3d) 189 (Ont. C.A.); and *1005633 Ontario Inc. v. Winchester Arms Ltd.*, [2000] O.J. No. 2404, 2000), 8 B.L.R. (3d) 176 (Ont. S.C.J.), additional reasons, [2000] O.J. No. 4327; appeal dismissed, [2000] O.J. No. 4711.

B. Statutory Provisions

The franchise statutes that have been enacted in some Canadian provinces impose on each party to a franchise agreement a duty of fair dealing in the performance and enforcement of the franchise agreement.

The statutes in Ontario, Manitoba, PEI, New Brunswick, and BC provide that the duty of fair dealing includes the duty to act in good faith and in accordance with reasonable commercial standards. In Manitoba, PEI, New Brunswick, and BC this duty is expressly extended to include "the exercise of a right under the agreement."

A party to a franchise agreement in Ontario, Manitoba, PEI, New Brunswick, or BC has a right of action for damages against another party to the franchise agreement who breaches the duty of fair dealing. There is no such express right under the Alberta statute. A party to a franchise agreement anywhere else in Canada, where there is no franchise legislation, may still commence a proceeding at common law for breach of the implied contractual duty of good faith. The wording of the provincial statutes varies slightly one to the next:

Section 7 of the Alberta statute reads:

> Fair Dealing
> 7. Every franchise agreement imposes on each party a duty of fair dealing in its performance and enforcement.

Section 3 of the Ontario statute reads:

> Fair dealing
> 3. (1) Every franchise agreement imposes on each party a duty of fair dealing in its performance and enforcement.
>
> Right of action
> (2) A party to a franchise agreement has a right of action for damages against another party to the franchise agreement who breaches the duty of fair dealing in the performance or enforcement of the franchise agreement.
>
> Interpretation
> (3) For the purpose of this section, the duty of fair dealing includes the duty to act in good faith and in accordance with reasonable commercial standards.

Section 3 of the PEI and BC statutes read:

> 3. (1) Every franchise agreement imposes on each party a duty of fair dealing in the performance and enforcement of the agreement, including in the exercise of a right under the agreement.
>
> (2) A party to a franchise agreement has a right of action for damages against another party to the franchise agreement who breaches the duty of fair dealing.
>
> (3) For the purpose of this section, the duty of fair dealing includes the duty to act in good faith and in accordance with reasonable commercial standards.

Section 3 of the Manitoba statute reads:

Fair dealing
3(1) Every franchise agreement imposes on each party a duty of fair dealing in the performance and enforcement of the agreement.

Right of action
3(2) A party to a franchise agreement has a right of action for damages against another party to the franchise agreement who breaches the duty of fair dealing.

Interpretation
3(3) For the purpose of this section,

(a) the duty of fair dealing includes the duty to act in good faith and in accordance with reasonable commercial standards; and
(b) the performance and enforcement of a franchise agreement includes the exercise of a right under the agreement.

Section 3 of the New Brunswick statute reads:

Fair dealing

3(1) Every franchise agreement imposes on each party a duty of fair dealing in the performance and enforcement of the franchise agreement.

3(2) A party to a franchise agreement has a right of action for damages against another party to the franchise agreement who breaches the duty of fair dealing.

3(3) For the purposes of this section,

(a) the duty of fair dealing includes the duty to act in good faith and in accordance with reasonable commercial standards, and
(b) the performance and enforcement of the franchise agreement includes the exercise of a right under the agreement.

In Québec, franchise agreements are governed by the provisions of the Québec Civil Code as contracts of adhesion (*Civil Code of Québec*, S.Q. 1991, c. 64 at Arts. 1435, 1436).

The code has several provisions dealing with the concept of good faith. The main three articles that set out the applicable statutory duty of good faith are Articles 6 and 7, setting forth the general duty in civil matters, and Article 1375, setting forth the duty in contractual matters:

6. Every person is bound to exercise his civil rights in good faith.

7. No right may be exercised with the intent of injuring another or in an excessive and unreasonable manner which is contrary to the requirements of good faith.

1375. The parties shall conduct themselves in good faith both at the time the obligation is created and at the time it is performed or extinguished.

In Québec, the duty of good faith extends to pre-contractual negotiations, as set out in Article 1375 quoted above. This is not the same under common law, as determined by the Supreme Court of Canada in the case of *Martel Building Ltd. v. Canada*, [2000] 2 S.C.R. 860, 193 D.L.R. (4th) 1, 2000 SCC 60. The English case of *Walford v. Miles*, [1992] 2 A.C. 128, [1992] 2 W.L.R. 174, 1 All E.R. 453 (H.L.), a House of Lords decision not involving franchising, also stands for the principle that at common law, there is no pre-contractual duty to negotiate in good faith. This issue was also canvassed in the Canadian franchise case of *1402066 Ontario Ltd. (c.o.b. Cupps Coffee House) v. Cupps International*, [2002] O.J. No. 2493 (S.C.J.).

Further, the statutory duty of good faith is not extended to pre-contractual negotiations under the above-quoted sections of the franchise statutes of Ontario, Alberta, PEI, New Brunswick, and BC, which specifically refer to the duty as being applicable to the "performance and enforcement" of franchise agreements. Under the formation of contracts section of the Code there is a general provision that both parties have consented to contract with each other. This is set out in Article 1385 of the Code:

A contract is formed by the sole exchange of consents between persons having capacity to contract, unless, in addition, the law requires a particular form to be respected as a necessary condition of its formation, or unless the parties require the contract to take the form of a solemn agreement.

It is also of the essence of a contract that it have a cause and an object.

The concept is explored further in Articles 1399, 1400, 1401, 1404 and 1407 of the Code:

1399.
Consent may be given only in a free and enlightened manner.
It may be vitiated by error, fear or lesion.

1400.
Error vitiates consent of the parties or of one of them where it relates to the nature of the contract, the object of the prestation or anything that was essential in determining that consent.
An inexcusable error does not constitute a defect of consent.

1401.

Error on the part of one party induced by fraud committed by the other party or with his knowledge vitiates consent whenever, but for that error, the party would not have contracted, or would have contracted on different terms.

Fraud may result from silence or concealment.

1404.

Consent to a contract the object of which is to deliver the person making it from fear of serious injury is not vitiated where the other contracting party, although aware of the state of necessity, is acting in good faith.

1407.

A person whose consent is vitiated has the right to apply for annulment of the contract; in the case of error occasioned by fraud, of fear or of lesion, he may, in addition to annulment, also claim damages or, where he prefers that the contract be maintained, apply for a reduction of his obligation equivalent to the damages he would be justified in claiming.

The contract is formed by the agreement or consent of both parties. However, the "fraud" of one party can vitiate the consent of the other, as set out in Article 1401. This can result from misrepresentation, silence, or concealment. The result can be a repudiation of the contract, as set out in Article 1407. The court can grant an annulment, award damages, or award a reduction of the wronged party's obligation equivalent to its damages, as also set out in Article 1407. This vitiation may be alleviated where good faith can be shown, as seen in Article 1404.

In respect of pre-contractual negotiations, it is generally considered that, in order to properly gain consent, disclosure of material information is required where the information, if known to the contracting party, could have an important impact on its agreement to contract (Articles 1401 and 1435). As mentioned above, silence may amount to misrepresentation, or to a breach of the duty to disclose (see *1250264 Ontario Inc. v. Pet Valu Canada,* 2015 ONSC 29, discussed below). Pre-contractual disclosure, at least of material information that relates to the nature of the contract, and which would be considered to be essential in determining a contracting party's consent, should therefore be made.

Pre-contractual disclosure may be required when the facts indicate that but for the misrepresentation, or the omission to disclose the information, the party would not have contracted, or would only have contracted on different terms. It is important to note, however, that this pre-contractual disclosure obligation is qualified by a corresponding obligation on the other contracting party (in this example, the franchisee) to seek information and take precautionary measures, such as seeking independent legal and financial advice, to satisfy its doubts and answer its questions regarding the provisions of the proposed franchise agreement. See, for example, *Treats Inc. v. Sachian*, REJB 1998-06398 (Que. C.A.) aff'ing REJB 1997-03100 (CS) and *2328-4938 Quebec Inc. v. Le Naturiste J.M.B. Inc.* (2000), REJB 2000-20038, [2000] J.Q. no. 2962 (Que. Sup. Ct.); see also *9069-7384 Quebec Inc. v. Le Superclub Vidéotron Ltée.* (2004), REJB 2004-53205 (Que. Sup. Ct.).

C. Case Law: Interpretation of the Duty of Good Faith, and Examples of Good and Bad Faith Conduct

One of the important "stepping-stone" cases in the establishment of the common-law contractual obligation of good faith in Canada was the case of *Gateway Realty Ltd. v. Arton Holdings Ltd.* (1991), 106 N.S.R. (2d) 180 (T.D.), aff'd on other grounds (1992), 112 N.S.R. (2d) 180 (C.A.). There, the court stated:

> The law requires that parties to a contract exercise their rights under that agreement honestly, fairly and in good faith. This standard is breached when a party acts in a bad faith manner in the performance of its rights and obligations under the contract. 'Good faith' conduct is the guide to the manner in which the parties should pursue their mutual contractual objectives. Such conduct is breached when a party acts in 'bad faith'—a conduct that is contrary to community standards of honesty, reasonableness or fairness. The insistence on a good faith requirement in discretionary conduct in contractual formation, performance, and enforcement is only the fulfillment of the obligation of the courts to do justice in the resolution of disputes between contending parties.

Another early, important case in Canada regarding the duty of good faith in franchising, a case decided after the Ontario statute came into force but that dealt with events that pre-dated the Ontario statute, is *Shelanu Inc. v. Print Three Franchising Corp.* (2003), 64 O.R. (3d) 533, 226 D.L.R. (4th) 577, 38 B.L.R. (3d) 42 (C.A.), rev'g (2000), 11 B.L.R. (3d) 69 (S.C.J.), supp. reasons 11 B.L.R. (3d) 100 (Ont. S.C.J.). In the *Shelanu* case, the franchisor (Print Three) established a competing franchise (Le Print Express). No locations were established in the franchisee's exclusive territory. The franchise agreement was silent regarding the franchisor engaging in a similar business during the term. The competing franchise was generally a smaller operation, targeted at a different customer base.

The Ontario Court of Appeal ruled that in the circumstances of this case, this establishment of a competing franchised business did not amount to a breach of the franchisor's duty of good faith at common law.

The court further found that, although the franchisor had breached the common-law duty of good faith in respect of other issues, the franchisor was not in fundamental breach of the franchise agreement. The court commented that not every contractual breach breaches the duty of good faith, nor will every breach of the duty of good faith be considered a fundamental breach of the franchise agreement that would excuse the other party (in this case, the franchisee) from its future performance under the franchise agreement, or entitle the other party to treat the franchise agreement as at an end. As referenced earlier in this section, the court also found that the franchisor-franchisee relationship was not a fiduciary one. However, the ruling did state that the franchisor was obligated to act with regard to the legitimate interests of the franchisee, as well as its own; to deal with the franchisee promptly; and to deal with the franchisee honestly, fairly and reasonably (including in the exercise of its discretion). In this particular case, the franchisee did not demonstrate that it suffered any damages; there was no evidence that it lost income; and the franchisee only complained of the franchisor's actions almost seven years after they took place.

The decision of the Court of Appeal for Ontario in *Shelanu* represents a general affirmation of the common-law duty of good faith in franchising. *Shelanu* is a seminal decision regarding the duty of good faith in a franchise relationship:

> The relative position of the parties . . . in the typical franchisor-franchisee relationship. First, it is unusual for a franchisee to be in the position of being equal in bargaining power to the franchisor. . . . The second characteristic, inability to negotiate more favourable terms, is met by the fact that a franchise agreement is a contract of adhesion. As I have indicated, a contract of adhesion is a contract in which the essential clauses were not freely negotiated but were drawn up by one of the parties on its behalf and imposed on the other. Further, insofar as access to information is concerned, the franchisee is dependent on the franchisor for information about the franchise, its location and projected cash flow, and is typically required to take a training program devised by the franchisor. The third characteristic, namely that the relationship continues to be affected by the power imbalance, is also met by the fact that the franchisee is required to submit to inspections of its premises and audits of its books on demand, to comply with operation bulletins, and, often is dependent on, or required to buy, equipment or product from the franchisor. It is hardly surprising, therefore, that a number of courts . . . have recognized that a duty of good faith exists at common law in the context of a franchisor-franchisee relationship.

It is of interest to note the court's specific comments relating to the exercise of discretion, namely that even where the franchisor retains sole discretion, it must exercise it reasonably, honestly and in good faith:

> Even if . . . Print Three had an absolute discretion with respect to the use of the Air Miles (loyalty program), Print Three could not exercise that discretion without regard to Shelanu's interests; it was obliged to exercise the discretion in a reasonable manner. . . . Here, the trial judge found Print Three acted arbitrarily and unreasonably and not in conformity with the standards for exercising a discretion. On the evidence, it was open to him to make this finding.

Lastly, the following reasoning from the judgment regarding the finding that setting up a competing franchise did not amount to a breach of the duty of good faith in this case is informative:

> My reasons for [overturning the finding of a breach of good faith] may be summarized as follows: (1) the different nature of the business engaged in by Le Print Express; (2) Shelanu's delay in complaining about the establishment of that business; (3) the lack of evidence before the trial judge as to Shelanu's consequential loss of income; (4) the trial judge's findings that there had been no misrepresentation concerning what Print Three was to provide in exchange for royalty payments and that Print Three had done the minimum required to discharge those obligations; and (5) the trial judge's finding that the decline in Print Three franchises was primarily due to prevailing economic conditions. The finding that Print Three breached 'reasonable commercial standards' must also fail for the same reasons.
>
> Inasmuch as I have not upheld the trial judge's finding of fact in respect of Le Print Express, I would not uphold his conclusion that the establishment of Le Print Express was a breach of Print Three's duty of good faith.

In *1250264 Ontario Inc. v. Pet Valu Canada* 2014 ONSC 5056, the plaintiff franchisees argued that the duty of fair dealing included an ongoing duty to disclose what they described as material financial information regarding volume rebates received by the franchisor, such as the amounts received and the criteria for distribution. Justice Belobaba deferred his consideration of this common issue. At 2015 ONSC 29, Justice Belobaba dealt with the issue he deferred on the earlier motion for summary judgment, namely whether the failure to disclose details regarding volume rebates was a breach of the fair dealing section of the Ontario statute or a breach of common law. Justice Belobaba found on the evidence before him that:

> Pet Valu decided for its own purposes to keep the volume discount information to itself and not tell its franchisees. The case law is clear that keeping or hiding material information from franchisees could well be a violation of the s. 3 duty of good faith and fair dealing and could result in a significant damages award [55].

Justice Belobaba went on to find that Pet Valu received significant volume rebates; that it had a duty to disclose those rebates to its franchisees; and that it breached the duty of fair dealing when it failed to do so. He held that Pet Valu did not breach the duty of fair dealing by not disclosing its policy on the allocation of volume rebates but that it did breach that duty in not disclosing the amounts received, retained, and shared so that franchisees could draw their own conclusions and make further informed decisions. In terms of damages, the motions court judge sought further submissions as to what those damages ought to be, particularly in light of the fact that the class members were former franchisees that had sold their franchises.

The Court of Appeal for Ontario granted an appeal from Justice Belobaba's ruling (2016 ONCA 24).

The Court of Appeal held that it was an error for the lower court judge to invite the plaintiff to move to add a further common issue to this class proceeding, a motion that the lower court judge dismissed. It also held that it was wrong for the judge to recast a common issue on his own initiative "without advising Pet Valu that he proposed to make this change and affording Pet Valu the opportunity to make submissions. In effect, he gave judgment on an issue that was never certified. Doing so was fundamentally unfair to Pet Valu" [49]. One of the common issues asked whether Pet Valu breached a duty at common law or under s. 3 of the AWA to make disclosure regarding volume rebates to the franchisees, which the judge revised to read "significant volume discounts."

Last, the Court of Appeal held that the lower court judge "cast the net of s. 3 too widely." The duty of fair dealing, it clarified, was a duty to perform and enforce the franchise agreement in good faith and not a duty to disclose information during the course of the franchise agreement:

> [60] This case is more like *Spina*. In *Spina*, Perell J. found that it was plain and obvious that what he characterized as a "pre-litigation oriented duty of disclosure" went well beyond the scope of s. 3. The franchisee alleged that the franchisor breached s. 3 of the AWA by failing to disclose financial information necessary for the franchisees to verify

whether the franchisor was meeting its obligations under the franchise agreement. Perell J. wrote at para. 218:

> The Plaintiffs would require [the franchisor] to provide information to verify that it has not breached the [agreement], with the Plaintiffs themselves defining what is or is not a breach of the [agreement].

[61] Here, the motion judge effectively found that Pet Valu had breached s. 3 of the AWA by failing to disclose information necessary for the appellants to verify whether or not Pet Valu had breached a representation under the franchise agreement that Pet Valu received "significant volume discounts." It is akin to the pre-litigation-oriented duty of disclosure rejected in Spina.

Practice Note

The statutory duty of fair dealing is a duty to perform and enforce the franchise agreement in good faith. It is a duty owed by all parties to the franchise agreement. A party to a franchise agreement cannot act in such a way as to eviscerate the object of the agreement. In exercising discretion under a franchise agreement, a franchisor must give consideration to the impact that the decision will have on the franchisee. The duty does not require a franchisor to disclose information to a franchisee during the term of the agreement that it is not otherwise required to disclose by contract.

Another franchise case that expounds on the duty of good faith in franchising is *Country Style Food Services Inc. v. 1304271 Ontario Ltd.* (2003), 32 B.L.R. (3d) 207, 7 R.P.R. (4th) 184 (Ont. S.C.J.). Here, the landlord provided the franchisor, and ultimately the franchisee, with a site plan for further development of the property surrounding the franchised location. The franchisor signed the head lease, and the franchisee signed a sub-lease with the franchisor. The franchised location was open for approximately one year. The landlord then changed its site plan and constructed a new building on the property, in a different place, which hindered traffic flow and reduced access to the franchisee's location. This change had a serious detrimental effect on the franchisee's business.

After some initial objections were raised with the landlord by the franchisor on the franchisee's behalf, the franchisor subsequently abandoned the franchisee's cause, and sided with the landlord in the end. The court found that the franchisor's conduct breached its common-law duty of good faith and fair dealing toward its franchisee. The franchisor was found liable to the franchisee for its damages. Also of note is that the trial judge found that the landlord was jointly and severally liable to the franchisee, and that in a subsequent hearing of the claim over by the franchisor against the landlord (2003), 18 R.P.R. (4th) 20, [2003] O.J. No. 5171 (S.C.J.), the landlord was held liable to indemnify the franchisor for the amount of the award to the franchisee.

In the case of *530888 Ontario Ltd. v. Sobeys Inc.* (2001), 12 B.L.R. (3d) 267 (Ont. S.C.J.) and in the case of *TDL Group Ltd. v. 1060284 Ontario Ltd.* (2000), 6 B.L.R. (3d) 54 (Ont. S.C.J.) the courts held that it was not a breach of the duty of good faith to refuse to extend or renew an expired franchise agreement where there was no contractual right of renewal. The court in *Sobeys* found there was no inherent right to require the franchisor to renew, and the court in *TDL* found there was no good faith obligation of the franchisor to renew, even when there was no reason not to. These cases uphold the common-law principle of non-interference with the freedom of the parties to contract on agreed terms.

In the case of *Esmail v. Petro-Canada* (1995), 6 W.D.C.P. (2d) 206 (Gen. Div.), aff'd, 86 O.A.C. 385, 6 W.D.C.P. (2d) 237 (Gen. Div.), leave to appeal refused, 1996 CarswellOnt 38 (C.A.), 199 N.R. 400m (S.C.C.), the court found that the franchisor could not exercise the renewal provisions of the franchise agreement in bad faith.

The leading Québec case regarding the duty of good faith in contracts of adhesion, such as franchise agreements, is the case of *Supermarché A.R.G. Inc. v. Provigo Distribution Inc.*, [1995] R.J.Q. 464 (Sup. Ct.), rev'd (1997), J.E. 98-39, [1998] R.J.Q. 47 (C.A.). In that case, the franchisee operated four retail supermarkets under a series of agreements with the franchisor, Provigo. The agreements purported to give to the franchisee the benefit of the franchisor's purchasing power, and distribution system.

The franchisor, without consultation, introduced an everyday low-pricing concept into its own corporate store operations under the name Heritage, which competed with the operations of the franchisee. The supermarket business was in a very competitive state at the time. The franchisee's profits declined. The franchisor refused to address the situation in response to the franchisee's complaints.

The court held that the franchisor's unilateral changes in marketing strategy for its own stores, while requiring the franchisee to adhere to the franchise agreements, resulted in compensable losses to the franchisee. Punitive damages were not, however, awarded.

The contracts were silent regarding the franchisor's ability to compete with its franchisee. The court found that the franchisor's liability was only contractual, and that the remedies available to the franchisee could not exceed the damages resulting from the express and implied contractual obligations of the franchise agreement. The franchisor's change in strategy was not a civil wrong. The mere fact that the franchisor entered into competition with the franchisee, when there was no prohibition against doing so in the franchise agreements, was not illegal, and was not enough to make the franchisor liable for damages to the franchisee.

However, the franchisor failed to fulfill its obligations to give technical assistance to and to collaborate with its franchisee. The court found that it had a duty, in such a market situation, to work in concert with the franchisee and to supply it with the necessary marketing tools to minimize the impact of its financial prejudice. Instead, the franchisor was found to have used its expertise and information to improve the competitiveness of its own stores, while failing to give the support expected by the franchisee.

The franchisor was found to have abused its contractual rights in exercising its high level of control over marketing, supply and pricing, thereby rendering the franchisee unable to successfully compete with the franchisor's low price stores. Provigo had control over advertising, marketing, and the gross margins of the franchisee, as the exclusive wholesale supplier for 90% of the franchisee's store inventory.

The franchise agreements provided no territorial exclusivity to the franchisee. However, the franchisee was required to comply with the franchisor's advertising and marketing standards, and not to compete with Provigo. The franchisor was found to have been selling products in its Heritage stores for less than the wholesale prices being charged to the franchisee for the same products. The franchisor was also found to have been using the information it learned from approvals of the franchisee's proposed advertising, to allow its Heritage stores to counter the franchisee's promotions.

The Court of Appeal, in its interpretation of the franchise agreements, found that the obligations of the franchisor go beyond the express provisions of the franchise agreement, and derive from the nature of the agreement, custom, equity, and the law. While there is no general rule against competing with its franchisee, the franchisor was not operating in good faith. It was found to have targeted the franchisee in a way that deprived it of the advantages of being a franchisee of the franchisor. The court further found that while there is no prohibition against competing, the existence of the agreements between the parties limited the franchisor's rights (because of the duties the agreements imposed upon the franchisor). The court found that under the agreements, the parties should have reciprocal obligations. The court also found that it was a fundamental obligation of the franchisor to assist the franchisee technically and commercially and to collaborate with the franchisee in order to allow the franchisee to fully benefit from its franchise agreements. The franchisor had a duty of loyalty to its franchisee.

The following sets forth a summary of the key principles established in the *Provigo* case:

There is no fiduciary duty under the civil law of Québec.

Apart from the franchisor's obligations towards a franchisee as stipulated in the franchise agreement itself, the franchisor has the following additional legal obligations towards the franchisee:

(i) a loyalty obligation;
(ii) an obligation to provide the franchisee with technical and commercial support;
(iii) an obligation to act, at all times, in good faith towards the franchisee;
(iv) an obligation to collaborate with the franchisee; and
(v) an obligation to act towards the franchisee in such a way that the franchisee may benefit from the advantages of its franchise.

In the event that the franchisor competes in any way with the franchisee, the franchisor has the following additional legal obligations:

(i) unless the franchise agreement provides for some type of exclusivity in favour of the franchisee, the franchisor is not precluded per se from competing with the franchisee;
(ii) however, if the franchisor competes, in any way, with the franchisee, it must ensure that it still performs all of its legal obligations to the franchisee, including those provided in the franchise agreement and those described above;
(iii) in competing with the franchisee, the franchisor must take such steps as may be necessary to ensure that the franchisee can still benefit from the advantages of its franchise;
(iv) in competing with the franchisee, the franchisor should only do so in such a way as to minimize the impact of its competition on the franchisee; and
(v) the franchisor should assist the franchisee in repositioning itself, if necessary, or in being put in the best possible position to fight and counteract any competition, including the competition by the franchisor.

In making the above findings, the court was interpreting Article 1434 of the Civil Code of Québec, which reads as follows:

> 1434. A contract validly formed binds the parties who have entered into it not only as to what they have expressed in it but also as to what is incident to it according to its nature and in conformity with usage, equity or law.

In *Sirianni et al. v. Country Style Food Services Inc. et al.*, 2012 ONSC 881, the franchisor was held to have breached of the duty of fair dealing by deliberately concealing information from the franchisee regarding the length of the term of the lease, information that would have had an impact on the franchisee's decision to renew the franchise agreement.

Similarly, in *Salah v. Timothy's Coffees of the World Inc.*, 2010 ONCA 673, a franchisor was held to have breached the duty of fair dealing when it "actively misled" the franchisee about an opportunity to renew a lease at a mall location. The franchisor deliberately kept the franchisee in the dark about its intention to renew the lease albeit at another location within the same mall and the fact that it gave the opportunity to operate that business to someone else when it had a contractual obligation to give it to the plaintiff.

In *Fairview Donut Inc. v. TDL Group Corp.*, 2012 ONSC 1252, appeal dismissed, 2012 ONCA 867, a class proceeding commenced by franchisees of the Tim Hortons donut chain was dismissed on a motion for summary judgment on the grounds that the franchisor's changes to the franchise system were permitted by the franchise agreement and carried out in good faith.

The franchisees had complained that Tim Hortons' conversion from in-store baking to a central baking/distribution system called "Always Fresh," where goods were par-baked at a central bakery and then to be baked to completion in-store, increased costs to franchisees. They also complained that the cost of goods used to prepare the Lunch Menu were too high, with the result that they only broke even or lost money on the Lunch Menu.

The plaintiffs' argument that every new concept introduced by Tim Horton's had to be profitable was not accepted by the court. The court held that "the franchisor is entitled to consider the profitability and prosperity of this system as a whole":

> In order to keep the system healthy and competitive, the franchisor must be permitted to introduce new products, new methods of production or sale, new techniques or systems during the life of a franchise agreement. The franchisees have an expectation that this will be done. The franchise agreement contemplates this and allows this. It is done for the benefit of both the franchisor and the franchisee. It would not be commercially reasonable to require that the franchisor can only implement system-wide changes over the life of a particular franchise agreement if the proposed change is demonstrated to be an improvement that benefits that particular franchisee. Nor would it be commercially reasonable to require the franchisor to demonstrate that every such change will be a financial benefit for every franchisee.

The court held that the Always Fresh Conversion and the Lunch Menu were operational changes permitted by the franchise agreement. They neither took away legal rights nor imposed new legal obligations.

Franchisors generally include provisions in their franchise agreements that allow them to make system or operational changes in order to keep pace with changing consumer demands and competitive forces. Tim Hortons was no exception. Its franchise agreement and operations manual permitted it to make the changes it made to its system. Tim Hortons did not need to demonstrate that the changes it proposed would be necessarily profitable to its franchisees or that the proposed improvements would benefit a particular franchisee. It was not for franchisees or their experts to tell Tim Hortons how it should manage its franchise system. The evidence demonstrated that the franchisor had taken the interests of its franchisees into account in making these system changes.

This case is instructive as it illustrates that despite the robust protections of section 3 of the AWA franchisors still have room to make significant changes to their franchise system, which will affect the franchisees, without running afoul of the duty of fair dealing.

D. Damages for Breach of the Duty of Fair Dealing

Damages for breach of the duty of fair dealing need not be compensatory. The courts in Ontario have awarded general damages for breach of this duty as discussed in the damages section, above.

Damages for breach of the duty of fair dealing have generally been modest in the range of $25,000 to $50,000. See, for example, the *Sirianni* case ($25,000); *Burnett Management Inc. v. Cuts Fitness for Men*, [2012] O.J. No. 77 (S.C.J), $25,000; and the *Salah* case ($50,000). In *Canadian Tire Corp. v. Healy*, 2011 ONSC 4616 (S.C.J.), the court upheld an arbitrator's award of $250,000 for breach of the duty of fair dealing, which the arbitrator held was warranted because the franchisor gave its dealer projections relating to a project that it knew were questionable. Neither the arbitrator's decision nor the court's consideration of that decision provides any guidance as to how that figure was determined. The case is instructive, however, as it provides that the duty of fair dealing is a mutual one and that, in determining damages for breach of the duty of fair dealing, the trier of fact may take into account the conduct of the party seeking damages for breach of this duty. Here, the arbitrator reduced the damages that he would otherwise have awarded because of the dealer's own breach of the franchise agreement and the duty of fair dealing.

XIII. Injunctive Relief

Injunctions are equitable remedies that may be sought and granted on either a temporary or permanent basis, to either restrain a party from doing some act or, in less-frequent circumstances, to compel a party to do some act (also called a mandatory injunction). Injunctions are sought within a lawsuit or action already (or sometimes contemporaneously) commenced, and are not themselves the main proceeding. That being said, on a practical basis, the result of the injunction proceeding often determines the outcome of the overall proceeding (or whether it will be continued at all by the parties), and this is particularly so in a franchise dispute.

A. Types of Injunctions

A permanent injunction may be sought and granted as a part of the relief at trial. A temporary or interlocutory injunction is invariably sought, on an urgent basis, in order to provide temporary and immediate relief, pending and up to the time of trial.

In extreme circumstances, a party may apply for an "interim" injunction, on an ex parte basis, meaning that the application can be made to the court even without first serving notice of the application on the other party. These are rare and, if obtained, are often subject to challenge on the basis that the moving party did not make accurate or complete and full disclosure of all of the facts of the matter (even those contrary to their own interests or position), as they are required to do. More common is the "interlocutory" injunction sought on short but prior notice, which requires the applicant to first serve notice of the application on the other party before being heard.

B. Test for Injunction

The Supreme Court of Canada decision in *RJR-MacDonald Inc. v. Canada (A.G.)*, [1994] 1 S.C.R. 311; 1 D.L.R. (4th) 385 is often cited as setting forth the standard test that the moving party must meet before the court will grant an interlocutory injunction. The three factors are:

1. that there is a serious issue to be tried (or a strong prima facie case);
2. that the party moving for the injunction will suffer irreparable harm if the injunction is not granted; and
3. that the balance of convenience favours the granting of the injunction; in other words, the inconvenience to the moving party if the injunction is not granted is greater than the inconvenience to the responding party if it is granted.

A serious issue to be tried means that there is a triable issue, neither frivolous nor vexatious, and that there is no case to be made for summary judgment against the party seeking the injunction. The standard of review to be applied will likely depend on the consequence of granting the injunction. For example, in *Quizno's Canada Restaurant Corp. v. 1450987 Ontario Corp.* [2009] O.J. No. 1743 (S.C.J.), Justice Perell applied a higher standard of review, strong prima facie case, for a plaintiff franchisor seeking to close the operations of three franchises and restrain the franchisees from operating competing businesses. Since the interlocutory order would be tantamount to a final determination of the issues, the plaintiff had the additional burden of satisfying the court that it was clearly right on the merits. Justice Perell applied a comparatively lower standard of a serious issue to be tried, for a counter-motion by the franchisees to restrain the franchisor from disrupting the status quo pending trial.

Irreparable harm means that the party seeking the injunction could not be adequately compensated for the wrongs done or about to be done to it by an award of monetary damages. In *Paul Sadlon Motors Inc.,* 2011 ONSC 4432, a Chevrolet dealership franchisee brought a motion to enjoin General Motors, the franchisor, from allowing a rival Pontiac Buick GMC dealership to also sell Chevrolet vehicles. Justice Perell found that despite a loss of competitive advantage, the plaintiff franchisee would not suffer irreparable harm pending trial given that the plaintiff's actual market area remained unchanged and could thus continue to sell a competing product in the marketplace.

With respect to the balance of convenience, if the factors argued equally favour both sides, then the court can consider the merits of the case, to the extent that can be done based upon the facts before it, in order to see if it can determine who is more likely to win at trial. A court may also conflate its analysis of irreparable harm with the balance of convenience. For example, in *Paul Sadlon*, Justice Perell reiterated that the irreparable harm a franchisor would suffer if it were restrained in its ability to manage and plan its dealership network outweighed the plaintiff's "localized dispute." Although both parties would clearly suffer irreparable harm, it would at least be simpler to quantify part of the plaintiff franchisee's losses.

The court in *Home Instead, Inc. v. 244674 Ontario Inc.*, 2015 ONSC 7630, dealt with cross-motions, each for interlocutory injunctions. Justice F. L. Myers was satisfied that both parties in this case proved that in the absence of an injunction each would be likely to suffer irreparable harm that could not be compensated in damages. The court expressly agreed with *Quizno's Canada Restaurant Corp. v. 1450987* that, ". . .where it appears that a franchisee would not be able to satisfy a damages award against them and it appears that their breaches threaten the franchisor's goodwill, reputation, and implicate its responsibility to maintain the integrity of the chain, an award of damages will not fairly or adequately address those harms." The court also noted that in determining irreparable harm, the assessment looks more at the nature of the harm than the quantity. The court ultimately ruled in favour of the franchisor, relying on the proposition that courts are reluctant to force people to work together or to supervise a relationship.

Where a franchisee does not obey the terms of an injunction, he or she may be held in contempt of court. In *244674 Ontario Inc. v. Home Instead, Inc.*, 2015 ONSC 8004, soon after the court in the above-mentioned *Home Instead* case granted the interlocutory injunction in favour of the franchisors, the franchisors attained an order holding the franchisees in contempt of court after proving that the applicants intentionally committed acts that violated the letter and spirit of the order.

In addition, it should also be recognized that in certain cases when seeking injunctive relief based on the breach of a negative covenant, such as a non-competition provision of a franchise agreement, the tests of irreparable harm and balance of convenience may not need to be established. For example, in *Pet Valu Canada Inc. v. 1381114 Ontario Ltd.*, 2013 ONSC 5361, the Superior Court recognized that:

> [10] Where there is a clear breach of a non-competition provision which is a negative covenant, the elements of irreparable harm and balance of convenience are not required. The defendants are *prima facie* in breach of a non-competition clause, non-solicitation clause and other post-termination obligations, which are serious issues to be tried. Although I have found that irreparable harm and the balance of convenience need not be established, there is an abundance of evidence to satisfy these elements.

The awarding of an injunction must also not be contrary to public policy or the public interest, or else must be in furtherance of upholding public policy or the public interest. Upholding the general interests of the Canadian public is considered to be a matter of public policy, and as such, this is an overriding matter that the common-law courts of Canada will consider as a matter of course when considering whether or not to award an injunction. Restraining a party from performing an act, or requiring a party to perform an act, must thus not only be found to be appropriate in the circumstances as between the parties, but also not to otherwise offend the general public interest or public policy. The public policy or public interest issue does not often arise in the typical franchise injunction case, unless the matter deals with post-termination covenants against competition (as restraints of trade). The enforceability of such covenants is often greatly affected by public policy or public interest considerations.

Whether or not to grant an injunction, whether temporary or permanent, is within the overall discretion of the court. Indeed, some provinces may adopt their own particularity in respect of the degree of certainty required in order to grant an injunction. However, the natural tendency of the court is to maintain the status quo pending trial, as illustrated by the three tests a court will consider before an injunction will be granted.

C. Mandatory Injunctions

Where the application is for a mandatory order, namely an order to compel a party to do something, the tests become harder to meet. The threshold for the first test is immediately raised above the serious issue to be tried standard to that of a strong prima facie case favouring the moving party.

A mandatory order may be an order for specific performance, or an order for enforcement of a positive covenant. For example, in *Bark & Fitz Inc. v. 2139138,* 2010 ONSC 1793, a group of franchisees refused to sell a variety of the franchisor's core products. The franchisor submitted that the injunctive relief sought would not result in a positive act, but would instead prohibit a contractual breach in order to maintain the status quo. The court instead noted that the characterization of an order to comply with the provisions of a franchise agreement depends on the specific rights and obligations under it. In this case, the requirement to resume selling approved products constituted positive action on the part of the franchisees. The court framed the injunction as a step to restore a broken franchise relationship as opposed to the determination of the right to continue the franchise relationship altogether. The court also noted the possibility that such relief may require the ongoing supervision of the court. The relief was therefore considered a mandatory injunction. In *1460904 Ontario Inc. v. MDG Computers Canada Inc.,* 2006 CarswellOnt 6744, the court granted an injunction after the franchisee breached the terms of their franchise agreement by failing to assign their lease to the franchisor after termination. MDG, a manufacturer and reseller of computers and televisions, had a franchise agreement with 1460904. After a disputed invoice for advertising fees, the franchisee purported to terminate the agreement. They argued that the agreement was breached as per the AWA alleging non-disclosure and improper charging of expenses. They claimed that the agreement was repudiated because of a fundamental breach. MDG then purported to terminate the agreement on the basis of a failure to pay outstanding invoices for royalties, advertising and parts. As per the terms of the contract, a restrictive covenant included an assignment of the lease to MDG. Accordingly, MDG moved for an interim and interlocutory injunction on the basis that they would suffer irreparable harm should the lease not be assigned as this store's location had intangible earning power, In determining whether MDG was entitled to an assignment of the lease as per the franchise agreement, the Court considered the balance of the two parties interests, and ultimately held that the balance of convenience favours granting the requested relief to assign the lease to MDG.

D. Damage Undertakings

A party being awarded an interlocutory injunction will usually have to give an undertaking to the court as to damages. The undertaking is such that the party being granted the injunction undertakes to pay any damages suffered by the other party if the injunction is granted, and is later set aside. As a part of this process, the court may require the applicant party to post a bond or other security, such as the payment of money into court, to support its undertaking as to damages. Where a franchise agreement contains a clause stating that the franchisor can obtain injunctive relief without being required to post a bond or other security, such a clause will be given some weight by the court, though the imposition of the requirement to post a bond or other security upon the granting of an injunction is within the court's inherent jurisdiction. However, a common tactic used to attempt to defeat an injunction application is to argue that the moving party would not be able to satisfy such an undertaking due to its poor financial condition or lack of liquidity.

E. Equitable Factors

Because the injunction is an equitable remedy, one of the considerations of the court will be whether the moving party has come to court with "clean hands." Although not an injunction case, a franchise case in which this principle was cited by the court is the case of *Leader Window Fashions Ltd. v. Home Products Inc.*, (1993) 40 ACWS (3d) 708 (BCCA). The following is an excerpt from the judgment of the British Columbia Court of Appeal in that case:

> But, putting all of that aside, even if there may be circumstances in which it is open to this Court, and the court below, to relieve against a breach upon which cancellation has been founded, I do not think this is a proper case to do so. Equity has always insisted that those who come to it should come with clean hands. Here, in a commercial setting we have a plaintiff who has from time to time and many times been in breach of the contract by non-payment, non-delivery of documents on time and so on. I do not think a plaintiff in that position on the facts of this case should be given the benefit of the equitable jurisdiction if it exists.

A further consideration that flows out of the consideration of whether a party seeking relief from the court has clean hands is whether the party seeking the relief, either by way of an injunction application or at trial where an equitable remedy is being sought, is in a breach of its agreement. Franchisees who withhold their payments of royalties and advertising fund contributions or payments for products or supplies purchased, or who otherwise breach or repudiate their franchise agreements, are thus not helping themselves in the eyes of the court when they seek equitable relief, such as relief against their own termination. This is especially important to consider in light of the fact that a finding that a franchisor has fundamentally breached its (often relatively few) obligations under the franchise agreement is very hard to achieve for a franchisee. A finding by the court that the franchisor has fundamentally breached the franchise agreement would be required in order for the court to find that the franchisee is relieved of its obligations under the franchise agreement, as opposed to just having the right to sue for damages for a (non-fundamental) breach of contract by the franchisor.

F. Public Policy Issue

A franchise case that considered the issue of public policy or public interest was *We Care Health Services Inc. v. Barter,* 103 ACWS (3d) 1134; leave to appeal granted, [2001] OJ No 2029. The franchisee operated a nursing and healthcare business. The franchisee became unhappy with the performance of the franchisor, and alleged misrepresentations, fundamental breach, and bad faith. The franchisee took the position that its franchise agreement was terminated, transferred its business assets into another corporation, and began carrying on the same business outside of the franchise agreement. The franchisor sought an injunction, however the injunction was not granted. The court took the position that the franchisor had no means to care for the franchisee's patients, and declined to grant the injunction, because to restrain the franchisee from operating could compromise the ongoing care of the patients, who were totally dependent upon the franchisee for its nursing services. This decision was overturned on appeal. The franchise agreement in this case contained a provision whereby the franchisee acknowledged that any failure to comply with the agreement would cause the franchisor irreparable harm, not compensable by damages. Although the court acknowledged that there is debate among motions court judges as to what effect, if any, a contractual acknowledgment such as this should have on the granting of an injunction, it also noted that the motions judge did not address the issue in her reasons. Due to conflicting case law on an important issue, Justice Lally determined that a consideration of the issue by the Divisional Court would provide guidance and therefore granted the appeal.

In the more recent case of *1323257 Ontario Ltd. v. Hyundai Auto Canada Corp.*, 2009, 174 ACWS (3d) 830, a franchisee successfully enjoined the franchisor from terminating its Hyundai dealership agreement and from taking steps to develop a replacement dealership. Having already met the first test, the court contemplated the irreparable harm the franchisee would suffer. As part of the decision, the court noted that the franchisee would go out of business if an injunction would not be granted. The court stated, "Not only will the company lose the opportunity to earn a profit, but its 25 employees risk losing jobs at a time when it is common knowledge that the Canadian economy, particularly the automotive industry, is in real trouble." In this case, the court considered the irreparable harm to the franchisee's employees and the broader public policy issues surrounding the automotive industry at the time.

G. Recent Injunction Cases

In cases dealing with the termination of a franchise relationship it is important to consider whether the injunctive relief being sought is prohibitive or mandatory in nature, as this will influence the threshold under the first test. In *Chuang v. Toyota Canada Inc.*, 2007, 157 ACWS (3d) 1029, the defendant franchisor, Toyota Canada, terminated a letter of commitment between the plaintiff providing for the construction and owner of a Lexus dealership. The plaintiff brought an action for specific performance. The plaintiff sought an interlocutory injunction to enjoin the franchisor, from granting the dealership to any third party pending the outcome of trial. Since the facts concerning the letter of commitment were not in dispute, the court proceeded to analyze the agreement and found no legal basis for an award of specific performance, and therefore no serious issue to be tried. The court went on to apply the second and third test. With respect to irreparable harm, the court did not accept that the dealership's location was unique, and that damages could be quantified based on the dealership's future profitability. On the other hand, the franchisor would suffer irreparable harm if it was delayed in establishing a market share, where there were already a number of competitors in the area.

1323257 Ontario Ltd. (c.o.b. Hyundai of Thornhill) v. Hyundai Auto Canada Corp., mentioned above is a subsequent dealership case that was distinguished from *Chuang v. Toyota Canada*. The court similarly applied the lower threshold of "serious issue for trial" because the relief sought was to preserve the status quo of the dealership relationship pending trial. However, as opposed to *Chuang v. Toyota Canada*, the franchisee in the present case had already opened its doors for business. Consequently, the irreparable harm that would be suffered by the franchisee was much greater. Interestingly, the court also noted that in the event it erred in considering the appropriate standard under the first test, the franchisee had also met the strong prima facie case threshold applicable to mandatory injunctions.

In addition to *Bark & Fitz Inc. v. 2139138*, mentioned above, *Quizno's Canada Restaurant Corp. v. 1450987 Ontario Corp.* involves a situation in which the court awarded relief to enforce the terms of a restrictive covenant in the franchise agreement. In *Quizno's Canada Restaurant Corp.*, the franchisor was granted an interlocutory injunction to restrain three franchisees from operating competing businesses. The injunction was sought in connection with an action based on non-compliance with several of Quizno's promotions and a failure to implement a delivery service for orders placed over the phone. Without the court going as far as deciding the case on the merits, the franchisor satisfied the imposed higher standard of strong prima facie case. The first test was met in part based on the fact that the franchisees had already conceded to the breach of the covenant with respect to promotions and the delivery program. Further, the franchisor satisfied the second and third parts of the test by proving that if successful at trial, it was unlikely the franchisee would be able to satisfy a damages award and, more important, the irreparable harm that would be suffered by the franchisor would jeopardize the integrity of its entire national franchise system. The court emphasized the distinction between a breach of product standards (such as portioning) versus the much more serious breaches that went to the heart of the franchisor's marketing and operational systems.

This case followed a similar line of reasoning as *Quizno's Canada Restaurant Corp. v. David Davies* and *0703243 B.C. Ltd.* In *Quizno's v. Davies*, a franchisee refused to allow the franchisor to conduct an inspection of the restaurant in reaction to certain food cost rebates the franchisee believed he was entitled to. The court found in favour of the franchisor and granted an interlocutory injunction enforcing the termination of the franchise agreement, as well as restraining the franchisee from violating certain post-termination covenants. In its reasoning, the court noted:

> [22] In the franchise context, the trademark and system of a franchiser are its most valuable assets.
>
> [31] The right to inspections goes to the heart of Quizno's franchise system, as it is through inspections that Quizno's is able to maintain consistent quality and consumer confidence. The inspection process is vital to the integrity of its brand name.
>
> [32] . . . because without it Quizno's cannot maintain consistency amongst its stores, and Quizno's cannot have its franchisees picking and choosing what they will and will not agree to do.

XIV. Non-competition Covenants

Non-competition covenants are difficult to enforce in Canada, unless they have been properly drafted so as to be interpreted as being reasonable in all respects.

Generally speaking, the test of an enforceable non-competition covenant is that it is interpreted as being reasonable as between the parties, in reference to the public interest, and with respect to the circumstances in effect at the time the covenant is given and to those which are reasonably foreseeable as between the parties at that time. Non-competition covenants can be enforced for the protection of proprietary interests, such as goodwill, but they must be interpreted as having been drafted to be no broader, i.e. no more restrictive, than is necessary for the protection sought.

Reasonableness (and thus enforceability) is measured in respect of three elements: the geographical area; the time period; and the scope of the activities covered by the restriction.

The geography element usually requires a consideration of where the franchisee carries on business, where the franchisor carries on business, and, in many cases, the areas where expansion is targeted. One approach is to consider a certain radius around the location where the franchisee will operate, plus a certain radius around other franchise locations. The goal is to ensure the combination of these two locations do not overly restrain the franchisee from establishing a competing business.

The time period element relates to the length of time during which the restrictions on competition are to apply. There is also a time consideration involved in the geographical area of the covenant, in that the area or areas described must be considered reasonable at the time when the covenant is given, namely at the time the franchise agreement is entered into. Therefore, a finding of reasonableness in the interpretation of this element will require a consideration of the status quo as of the date of the franchise agreement, and may include a consideration of what was in the contemplation of the parties at the time the franchise agreement was entered into.

The scope of the activities covered by the restriction must also be interpreted as having been drafted to be no broader—i.e., no more restrictive—than is necessary for the protection sought. This will usually mean that the description of the restricted activity or business should be quite specific, in order to be found to match what the actual franchised business being carried on was, and not more general than that.

Practice Note

The interpretation and enforceability of non-competition covenants in Canada requires a consideration of three elements: geography, time period, and scope or description of the restricted business or activity.

A. Non-solicitation Provisions

Covenants restricting the solicitation of employees, contractors, suppliers, other franchisees, and customers may still be found to be enforceable, even if they have been more broadly drafted. The element of geographical area is less important for such provisions, as is the time period during which the restrictions on solicitations are to apply. It is important that the persons not to be solicited are readily ascertainable. The covenant against solicitation is usually based upon a recitation of the fact that the restrained party has acquired connections resulting from the activities performed by it in operating the franchised business, and that the covenant against solicitation is therefore for the protection of the goodwill and the business interests of the franchisor, and the other franchisees forming a part of the franchised system.

B. Chapter Note

This chapter is primarily concerned with the issues of interpretation and enforcement. The issue of drafting of non-competition covenants in franchise agreements is discussed elsewhere, in Chapter 3. However, in order to better understand the many and sometimes complex issues involved in the interpretation and enforcement of non-competition covenants in Canada, a few comments regarding how they have been drafted are useful here as well. Overall, the key is to not "overwrite" non-competition covenants because it may be read down at the enforcement stage.

With regard to some cases, this chapter also includes a lengthy commentary as drawn from the remarks of the court. Where the quotations are not of the decision or of the point for which the decision stands as support or precedent, the comments quoted are intended to illustrate what the court's approach is to interpretation and thus enforceability, as part of its decision-making process.

Practice Note

The enforcement in Canada of non-competition covenants found in many U.S.-drafted franchise agreements is often problematic. Specific attention is required to each issue of enforceability of these covenants in Canada at the drafting stage.

C. The Reasonableness Test

In determining whether a restrictive covenant against competition is enforceable, courts will consider whether the covenant is reasonable with reference to the interest of the parties concerned and the interests of the public at large. The general principles were set out by the Supreme Court of Canada in the leading case of *J.G. Collins Insurance Agencies Ltd. v. Elsley,* [1978] 2 S.C.R. 916. In that case, Justice Dickson stated the test as follows:

> [13] A covenant in restraint of trade is enforceable only if it is reasonable between the parties and with reference to the public interest. As in many of the cases which come before the courts, competing demands must be weighed. There is an important public interest in discouraging restraints on trade and maintaining free and open competition unencumbered by the fetters of restrictive covenants. On the other hand, the courts have been disinclined to restrict the right to contract, particularly when that right has been exercised by knowledgeable persons of equal bargaining power. In assessing the opposing interests, the word one finds repeated throughout the cases is the word "reasonable." The test of reasonableness can be applied, however, only in the peculiar circumstances of the particular case. Circumstances are of infinite variety. Other cases may help in enunciating broad general principles but are otherwise of little assistance.
>
> [14] It is important, I think, to resist the inclination to lift a restrictive covenant out of an employment agreement and examine it in a disembodied manner, as if it were some strange scientific specimen under microscopic scrutiny. The validity, or otherwise, of a restrictive covenant can be determined only upon an overall assessment of the clause, the agreement within which it is found and all of the surrounding circumstances.

Although *J.G. Collins* looked at restrictive covenants in an employment contract, the principles are applicable in the franchise context and are often cited by courts in franchise cases. Depending on the circumstances of each case, the standard applied by the court in assessing reasonableness may vary. Courts have found it appropriate in different cases to apply the more deferential standard applied in the sale of a business or the stricter standard applied in employment cases. For example, the Supreme Court, in *Shafron v. KRG Insurance Brokers (Western) Inc.* 2009 SCC 6, supports the use of restrictive covenants to further legitimate business objectives.

In *MacMillan Tucker Mackay v. Pyper,* 2009 BCSC 694, an employment case, the British Columbia Supreme Court distinguished franchise cases, suggesting that more deference should be given to the parties' freedom of contract in a franchise context where the former franchisee was "in a very real sense the face of the [franchisor]'s business" in the protected territory.

In *BMR Bath Master Reglazing Ltd. v. Watson* 2010 BCSC 1170, the British Columbia Supreme Court suggested a stricter standard was applicable. The court described franchise non-competition covenants as "a more drastic weapon enforceable only in exceptional circumstances, and limited in time and space, since they are attempts to keep a person out of business." The court found the facts of the case to be closer to that of a former employee than a sale of a business since the franchisee was not competing with his former franchise:

> [17] This case involves a franchise agreement which amongst other things attempts to prevent a former franchisee from competing against a current franchisee anywhere in the province. The facts of this case do not involve a former franchisee competing against the franchise he previously held. Mr. Watson is not competing in Kamloops. He is not in a position where he might take advantage of connections established in the Kamloops area for his own benefit and to the detriment of the current franchise there.
>
> [18] In my opinion, in these circumstances, the principles as they have been articulated in the context of employer/employee cases offer significant guidance to the resolution of the matter before me.

In *Invescor Restaurants Inc. v. 3574423 Canada Inc.*, 2012 ONCA 387, the court upheld a non-competition covenant which prohibited a franchisee from carrying on, within Canada, any business that was substantially similar to the operation of a restaurant that sold products similar to those of the franchisor. The court rejected the franchisee's assertion that the geographic scope was too broad. The franchisee failed to demonstrate that the covenant did not accord within the intention or reasonable expectation of the parties at the time of the execution of the franchise agreement. As to the reasonableness of the geographic covenant, the court stated:

> [91] First, the reasonableness of the geographic scope of the covenant must be considered against the background of the operation of the restrictive covenant. As described above, the covenant has a very limited reach for two general reasons. It does not extend to restaurants having a similar, even identical, décor to that of the Eaton Centre Restaurant. Further, it only operates if a competing restaurant sells most of the menu items offered by the Eaton Centre Restaurant prepared in accordance with recipes in the Manual. There is, therefore, no significant restriction on the ability of the Bouzikis Brothers to earn a livelihood by investing in other restaurants.

> [92] Second, as mentioned, the reasonableness of the covenant in section 16.2 must also be construed against the background of the intentions of the parties at the time of the negotiation and execution of the Franchise Agreement. While it did not have any franchisees outside of Quebec, the franchisor at the time, BRRI, had the intention of expanding beyond Montreal into other provinces. It would not be unreasonable in such circumstances for BRRI to seek to protect its market not just in Ontario but in the other major urban markets in Canada. The absence of evidence that the parties discussed expansion beyond the Ontario borders is not dispositive. The Mavromichalis Brothers were not obligated to discuss all of their plans or expectations with the Bouzikis Brothers at the time. There is also no evidence that the Bouzikis Brothers had any interest in establishing other restaurants in any other province in Canada.

It should be noted that in this case, the covenant in question operated only during the term of the franchise agreement. Consequently, the court held that as long as the franchisee was receiving the benefit of that agreement, it should not be able to undermine the value of the franchise unless special circumstances could be demonstrated. As such, *Invescor* may have limited precedential value for enforcing post-term covenants with a wider scope.

Invescor does, however, contain some potentially helpful comments on the reasonableness of covenants against competition in franchise agreements with respect to the "public policy" stage of the analysis. The court suggested that public policy will likely favour enforcement of non-compete provisions in franchise agreements, stating:

> [105] Precisely because there are numerous restaurants based on differing concepts, it is difficult to establish that it is unreasonable in respect of the public interest to enforce a non-competition covenant designed to protect any particular restaurant concept. This is not a situation in which the effect of the restrictive covenant is to perpetuate a monopoly contrary to the public interest. Conversely, in a fully competitive industry such as the restaurant industry which is characterized by limited barriers to entry, there is arguably some public benefit to upholding franchise agreements, both in order to allow a franchisor to enjoy the fruits of its efforts in developing a particular concept and to provide an opportunity to prospective franchisees who consider that an investment in a franchise of an operating chain with a recognized name, décor and menu reduces the franchisee's investment risk. (Emphasis Added)

The Court of Appeal in *MEDIchair LP v. DME Medequip Inc.*, 2016 ONCA 168, discussed reasonableness of a restrictive covenant contained in a franchise agreement when deciding to allow an appeal of a trial judge's finding that the restrictive covenant should be enforced. This case considered the issue of whether a franchisor was entitled to enforce the restrictive covenant when its evidence was that it had no intention of opening another franchise location within the protected area. Though the court agreed with *Imvestor* that the standard applied when addressing restrictive covenants is a "similar" business standard, the restrictive covenant in this case was ultimately not found to be reasonable in scope.

In assessing the reasonableness of the covenant for the purposes of protecting the legitimate or proprietary interest of the franchisor, the court's analysis focused mainly on whether there was a legitimate business interest in need of protection. However, the Court of Appeal took a moment to note that the level of scrutiny to be applied to a franchise agreement is the subject of recent ongoing debate; courts remain undecided about whether franchise agreements should garner a high level of scrutiny like that applied in the employment context or a lower level of scrutiny like that applied in the sale of business context. In this case, the court determined that, by not choosing to operate in the same city, the franchisors effectively acknowledged that it had no legitimate or proprietary interest to protect within the defined territorial scope of the covenant. While the clause would have been reasonable if the franchisor had wanted to continue to operate in the protected area, it would not be considered reasonable if it did not. Therefore, the covenant was held to be unreasonable in the circumstances of the particular franchise because the franchisor did not have a legitimate or proprietary interest to protect within the territorial scope of the covenant.

In the case of *Ergonic Resources Inc. v. Waker and Nascent Business Technology Ltd.* [(1982), 16 ACWS (2d) 54, the restrictive covenant contained in the franchise agreement read as follows:

> [9] You will not, directly or indirectly operate, be employed by, or involved as a shareholder, partner, director, officer or otherwise in or with any company or persons operating any retail business, or become similarly involved with any other franchising organization, that may be reasonably considered to deal in products or services that duplicate or complete with the products and services of the franchise system:
>
> (i) during the active period of this agreement this 'non-competing' requirement shall apply to any place in Canada or the U.S.;
> (ii) for a period of three (3) years following the expiration or termination of this agreement this 'non-competing' requirement shall apply to your current authorized location, and any other area in which we have granted a franchise.

The court held that a restrictive covenant that prohibited the defendant from competing with the plaintiff's operation in any area in which the plaintiff had granted a new franchise was presumptively overly broad, such that an injunction should not be granted, because it had the potential to apply to all the Province of Saskatchewan, all of Canada, or even wider areas. See also *Sask-Workwear Inc. Ollinik.* However, in both of these cases the business in question was clearly regional and the evidence did not suggest an intention that it be national or international in scope.

In contrast, in *Unisource Canada Inc. v. Network Paper & Packaging Ltd.*, 2000 BCSC 396, the vendor of a packaging company sold his business to Unisource and subsequently entered into an employment agreement as senior manager. The agreement contained a non-competition clause that applied to all the provinces and territories, as well as certain U.S. states. The broad nature of the covenant was out of concern that the vendor, which operated in British Columbia and some of the western U.S. states, might utilize his skills in establishing a competing business elsewhere. Although the court upheld geographic covenant as reasonable, the covenant restricting the types of business activities allowable was unreasonable. The court found the latter covenant restricted a variety of activities common to any business endeavour, even if it bore no resemblance to Unisource's business:

> [26] The defendants also submit that the covenant is too broad, in that it prohibits Davis from engaging in "any activities which are similar to the activities carried on by (Interpac 1992) at the time of acquisition by Unisource, or which compete with the business activities of Unisource at the time of cessation of employment. . ." The defendants submit that language is so broad that it would preclude a variety of acts common to any business, even if that business bore no resemblance to that of Interpac 1992 or Unisource, and did not compete with them, and even if those activities did not call for Davis' skill or experience. Counsel suggests the covenant is so broad that it would prohibit Davis from buying shares in a publicly traded company which competes with the business of Unisource, or from working for a company which is not a competitor of Unisource, but merely carries on "activity" (which is not defined) similar to an "activity" carried on by Unisource as at September 30th, 1994. She submits the effect of that is to prevent Davis from being gainfully employed, rather than to protect the proprietary interests of Unisource. I agree with that submission. It is one thing to prohibit Davis from performing activities "which compete with the business activities of Unisource" (as the covenant does). However, it is quite another to prohibit him from "any activities which are similar to the activities carried

on by the Company," especially when the term "activities" is not defined. That is broader than is necessary to protect the legitimate proprietary interest of Unisource.

In the case of *Kynas v. Zippy Print Franchise Ltd. et al.*, [1985] BCWLD 782, the franchise agreement contained a restrictive covenant covering "the printing business." The court found that description of the business to be too general. It found that the franchisor was actually in the "quick print business." The franchisor applied for an injunction to restrain the former franchisee from carrying on the "quick print business," but that was not what the restrictive covenant in the franchise agreement said. The court declined to grant the injunction, because the language of the contract relating to "the printing business" was found to be too broad.

D. Blue Pencil Doctrine

Canadian courts take a strict approach to enforcement. Generally, the courts will not rewrite a non-competition covenant to make it reasonable and enforceable. In some cases, a court may delete a section of a non-competition covenant, based upon a proper severance clause included in the franchise agreement and a finding of proper drafting, as long as the remainder of the non-competition covenant still makes sense in its interpretation. The rule against rewriting restrictive covenants has become known in Canadian jurisprudence as the "blue pencil doctrine."

Practice Note

In order for a severance to result in an enforceable restrictive covenant, there should be some separate and distinct covenants that can be severed, but not some parts of one and the same covenant, such as where alternatives are expressed.

The issue of severance and the "blue pencil doctrine" must be viewed through the lens of the decision of the Supreme Court of Canada in *Shafron v. KRG Insurance Brokers (Western) Inc.*, 2009 SCC 6. In *Shafron*, the owner of an insurance agency sold his business and continued to work as an employee for the purchaser. The vendor/employee signed a non-competition clause applicable to a geographic area referred to as the "Metropolitan City of Vancouver." The employee left his employment approximately 14 years later and began working for a competing agency. In finding the covenant ambiguous and therefore unenforceable, the Supreme Court held that severance, when permitted, takes two forms. A "notional" severance involves reading down a contractual provision so as to make it legal and enforceable, while blue-pencil severance denotes removing part of the contractual provision to render the remainder enforceable. Notional severance is not an appropriate mechanism to cure a defective restrictive covenant and blue-pencil severance may only be resorted to in rare cases where the part being removed is trivial and not part of the main purport of the restrictive covenant.

The Supreme Court reiterated Lambert J.A. in *Canadian American Financial Corp. (Canada) Ltd. v. King and Douglas W. King Marketing Corp.*, (1988) 13 ACWS (3d) 371, where the Court of Appeal considered a non-competition clause against conducting a similar business in Canada or Bermuda:

> [49] the courts will only [apply blue-pencil severance to] sever the covenant and expunge a part of it if the obligation that remains can fairly be said to be a sensible and reasonable obligation in itself and such that the parties would unquestionably have agreed to it without varying any other terms of the contract or otherwise changing the bargain. . . . It is in that context that reference is made in the cases severing and expunging merely trivial or technical parts of an invalid covenant, which are not part of the main purport of the clause, in order to make it valid.

Accordingly, blue-pencil severance is available only where there is evidence that the parties would have unquestionably agreed to remove words which would have the effect of changing the nature of the bargain.

The Supreme Court went on to explain:

> [50] Removal of the word "Metropolitan" would leave behind only "City of Vancouver." KRG Western, in its factum, stated that the "context makes it clear the parties intended the restricted area to cover not only the City of Vancouver, but also the suburbs immediately surrounding Vancouver" (para. 82). The Court of Appeal stated that the parties "clearly intended a geographic reach that included the City of Vancouver *and something more*" (para. 57 (emphasis added)). However, there is no evidence that the parties would have "unquestionably" agreed to remove the word "Metropolitan" "without varying any other terms of the contract or otherwise changing the bargain." Blue-pencil severance is therefore not applicable in this case.

With respect to the deference afforded in the franchise context, the court noted the following, relying on the Supreme Court in *J.G. Collins*:

> [18] It is important at this juncture to differentiate between a contract for the sale of a business and an employment contract.

> [21] The sale of a business often involves a payment to the vendor for goodwill. In consideration of the goodwill payment, the custom of the business being sold is intended to remain and reside with the purchaser. As Lord Ashbourne observed at p. 555 of *Nordenfelt:*
>
>> I think it is quite clear that the covenant must be taken as entered into in connection with the sale of the goodwill of the appellant's business, and that it was entered into with the plain and bona fide object of protecting that business.

And as stated by Justice Dickson (as he then was) in *J.G. Collins Insurance Agencies v. Elsley*, [1978] 2 S.C.R. 916 (S.C.C.), at p. 924:

> A person seeking to sell his business might find himself with an unsalable commodity if denied the right to assure the purchaser that he, the vendor, would not later enter into competition.
>
> [22] The same considerations will not apply in the employer/employee context . . .

Goodwill, reputation, and brand are essential elements of a franchise network. *Shafron* does support a strong policy argument to support the use restrictive covenants to further legitimate business objectives. However, regardless of the context, "blue-pencil" severance will generally only permit editing by way of deletion, and not redrafting.

Although pre-*Shafron,* the cases *Rapid-Med Plus Franchise Corp. v. Elliott,* (1992) 35 ACWS (3d) 96, and *TMI Turf Management Inc. v. R. De Noble Enterprise Ltd.,* 1994 CarswellBC 1150, both describe situations in which blue-pencil severance was not required for the purpose of restricting an overly broad geographic covenant.

In the case of *Rapid-Med Plus Franchise Corp. v. Elliott*, an interlocutory injunction had been granted, and was under appeal. The franchise agreement contained the following restrictive covenants:

> [4] (i) that neither would disclose the plaintiff's trade secrets, know-how or confidences to others;
>
> (ii) that, during the term of the agreement, neither would compete with the plaintiff's business anywhere; and
>
> (iii) that, for a period of three years from its termination, neither would compete with the plaintiff
>
> (a) within (the province of) Manitoba; or
>
> (b) within the exclusive territory of any other franchised dealer.

The following excerpts from the judgment are of interest:

> [13] In the present case, the restrictive covenant covers two distinct areas. The defendants Anna Elliott and the numbered company agreed that, on the termination of their agreement, they would not compete with the plaintiff either
>
> (a) in Manitoba; or
> (b) in the territory of any other franchise holder.
>
> [14] For the purpose of deciding this interlocutory appeal, I do not find it necessary to consider whether it was reasonable to restrict the activities of those defendants in both areas. The plaintiff says that, if the injunction presently covers an area wider than Manitoba, it has no objection to the injunction being amended so that it clearly applies to the activities of these defendants in this province only.
>
> [15] Such a limitation on the geographic scope of the injunction is only possible, of course, if the covenants not to compete in each of the two areas are severable. In my judgment, they are. Each area is separately defined in the contract and the covenant not to compete in it was included for a different reason. The covenant not to compete in the territories of other franchise holders was included to protect the plaintiff from the wrongful use of information which had been given to the defendants Anna Elliott and the numbered company to enable them to carry on the plaintiff's business in Manitoba. On the other hand, the covenant not to compete in the province of Manitoba was included to prevent these defendants from taking improper advantage of the close personal relationships which Anna Elliott might develop with the plaintiff's customers.

The Court of Appeal maintained the injunction; however, it was amended to make it clear that the non-competition covenant applied only in the Province of Manitoba. Enforceability of the covenant in Manitoba alone was aided by the fact that the different geographic areas were set forth simply, and in separate sub-paragraphs. The court also found that the distinction between a franchise and employment relationship made no difference in the context of the interlocutory injunction to enforce the non-compete provision in the agreement and opted to deal with the appeal on the basis that the defendant was an employee.

In *TMI Turf Management Inc. v. R. DeNoble Enterprise Ltd.,* 52 CPR (3d) 129; 1994 CanLII 146 (BCSC), the non-competition covenant was expressed as covering:

> [4] . . . any business the same as or similar to the lawn-care business of the Licensee within:

i) the licensed territory;
ii) the Province of Ontario;
iii) the provinces of Ontario and Quebec;
iv) Canada; and
v) Canada and the U.S.;

except pursuant to a license from the Licensor.

The licensed territory was a defined portion of southern Vancouver Island, British Columbia. In light of this small territory, the drafting of such a broad area of restriction into the non-competition covenant was unfortunate.

The franchise agreement also contained a separation (type of severance) clause, in which the franchisor sought enforcement of the restrictive covenant only with respect to the licensed territory. No request was made of the court to enforce the restrictive covenant with respect to the other geographic territories set out in the separate portions of the clause. This strategy of pleading only for enforcement in the licensed territory, together with the fortunate drafting style of the restrictive covenant, setting forth each of the geographic areas in a separate sub-clause, and the fortunate inclusion of the separation clause, allowed the judge to find this particular restriction, as pleaded, to be enforceable.

Practice Note

To enhance enforcement of only a portion of a restrictive covenant by pleading only for a geographically limited order, the whole covenant should be valid, while the remedy sought is limited to only the protection required in the particular circumstances.

In *Belron Canada Inc. v. TCG International Inc.*, 2009 BCSC 596, the plaintiff entered into an agreement to purchase an auto glass repair business, which also included the vendor's master franchisee business for proprietary glass repair technology. A non-competition agreement was executed, which contained a covenant restricting the vendor from engaging in a business that would be substantially the same or one that would compete with the purchaser's business anywhere in Canada. The vendor argued that the territorial scope of the covenant was overly broad because it covered Québec, a jurisdiction where the vendor did not operate a similar business at the time it entered into the sale. The court rejected the vendor's submission, and found legitimate business objectives for the purchaser to have imposed the Québec restraint. Factors that persuaded the court of the covenant's reasonableness are described as follows:

> [80] The Non-Competition Agreements contain a strongly worded provision acknowledging that the defendants have entered into such agree-

ments as "a material inducement to" Belron entering into the 2005 Agreement. That provision goes on to state that the parties agree that all of the restrictions in the Non-Competition Agreements are reasonable and valid. In particular, the defendants expressly acknowledge that the restrictions in terms of time, scope of activities and geography are reasonable and that they intend that such restrictions be enforced to the fullest extent.

Although explicit acknowledgment of the covenant does not in itself determine reasonableness, it appeared to be a factor. The court applied *Shafron*, in that the scrutiny imposed was less onerous because the restrictive covenant was between commercial arm's-length parties with relatively equal bargaining strength, in contrast to those negotiated between employer and employee.

In *Senos v. Pacesetter Performance Drilling Ltd.*, 2010 ABQB 533, the court was asked to interpret a non-competition clause in a shareholders' agreement. In obiter it was held that the particular provision gave the court jurisdiction to rewrite the clause so that it could, reduce the area of applicability, among other considerations. Justice Graesser noted the following:

> [63] In *Shafron*, however, there was no clause such as 17.3 as found in this agreement. I see no reason why the parties cannot expressly empower the court to blue pencil or read down a restriction that is otherwise unreasonable. *Shafron* is authority that the courts do not have the inherent power to do so, but does not suggest that the parties cannot agree to give the courts such powers.

In *Martin v. ConCreate USL Ltd. Partnership*, 2013 ONCA 72, the Court of Appeal considered the enforceability of a non-competition covenant in a sale of a national construction business. Although the Court of Appeal ultimately found the restrictive covenant at issue to be unenforceable due to an indefinite duration, the court agreed with Justice Perell (the application judge) that the non-compete provision's Canada-wide scope was reasonable because the parties envisaged that the scope of the business being sold was and would be national. As a framework for its analysis, the court noted that following:

> [51] If a covenant is ambiguous, in the sense that what is prohibited is not clear as to activity, time, or geography, it is not possible to demonstrate that it is reasonable. It is therefore unreasonable and unenforceable.
>
> [52] The law distinguishes between a restrictive covenant in connection with the sale of a business, and one between an employer and an employee. The former may be required to protect the goodwill sold to the

> purchaser, and does not usually involve the imbalance of power that exists between employer and employee. Accordingly, a less rigorous test is applied in determining the reasonableness of a restrictive covenant given in connection with the sale of a business.
>
> [53] Greater deference is given to the freedom of contract of "knowledgeable persons of equal bargaining power." Nevertheless, the broader restraints on trade justifiable in the context of a sale of a business must be reasonable within such a context. There is a strong public interest "in discouraging restraints on trade and, maintaining free and open competition unencumbered by the fetters of restrictive covenants.
>
> [54] The factors relevant in determining whether a restrictive covenant is reasonable are the same in the contexts of the sale of a business and an employment agreement: the geographic coverage of the covenant, the period of time that it is in effect and the extent of the activity prohibited. And, as the application judge noted, reasonableness is determined in light of the circumstances existing at the time that the covenant was made. Those circumstances include the reasonable expectations of the parties about the future activities and marketplace of the business.

Overall, non-competition provisions are unique because a fundamental aspect of any franchise system is the protection of its method of operation, goodwill, products, and services. Accordingly, franchise disputes likely fall somewhere on the spectrum in between the sale of a business and a relationship between employee and employer. However, since different policies and values are at play in a franchising context, case law must be analyzed within its proper context.

E. Privity and Proper Execution

Generally speaking, the principle of privity of contract will become important in the consideration of the franchise agreements and related documents by the courts for the purposes of the enforcement of restrictive covenants intended to protect the franchisor and franchise system from competition; unfair solicitations of employees, contractors, suppliers, franchisees, and customers; and improper use, disclosure, publication, or copying of trade secrets and proprietary confidential information.

The franchise agreement must not only contemplate who is to be restricted, but also include a mechanism for the franchise agreement, or a related document that contains the required non-competition covenant, to be signed by each such party. This requires proper paper-handling and administration by the franchisor, both at the outset and during the life of the contract when changes affecting the restricted parties occur. There is no general principle of Canadian law that would recognize the franchisor as having a third-party beneficial interest in these circumstances in order to allow the franchisor to enforce a restrictive covenant against a non-party to the franchise agreement.

A non-competition covenant in an agreement entered into between A and B, but which purports to limit C's ability to compete, will very likely be unenforceable by A (the franchisor) against C, where there is no privity of contract found between A and C. This is because C will not be found to have signed any agreement directly with A, agreeing to be bound by the restrictive covenant.

At best, such a clause may only be enforceable in the case of very special circumstances, or in the case of enforcing a damage claim against B for breach of contract committed by C, as only B (the franchisee) will be found to have contractually agreed with the franchisor that C will not compete. In such a case, the court will have to make a determination that B (the franchisee), as the signatory to the franchise agreement, has accepted the responsibility at law for the actions of C.

Getting all of the parties who are to be restricted to sign non-competition covenants, if not the franchise agreement itself, is somewhat like getting a full set of financial guarantees from all of the franchisee principals: while it may not be a desirable marketing tool, it is an essential enforcement tool.

These factors, coupled with the difficulties in enforcing restrictive covenants per se, make this a difficult area in respect of both signing and ongoing contract administration, requiring full consideration and proper procedures at all of the relevant stages of the life of the contract.

There are a multitude of Canadian franchise cases dealing with the enforceability of non-competition covenants. This chapter covers a few of them in the hopes of illustrating some of the finer points to keep in mind in the interpretation and enforcement of Canadian non-competition covenants.

In the case of *Bandag Inc.* and *Bandag Canada Ltd. v. Saint-Paul Bandag Inc., Robert Bernard (TRM) Limitee, Gerard Bernard, Jocelyn Bernard and Michelin Retread Technologies (Canada) Inc., Bandag Inc. v. St-Paul Bandag Inc.,* 2000 CanLII 19069 (QCCS), the existing franchise agreement had expired. A new franchise agreement was not signed; however, the parties continued doing business. A notice to terminate the business relationship was given.

The court characterized the relationship between the parties as being governed by a verbal agreement with an indefinite term, made up of their usual commercial practices. The court declined to grant an interlocutory injunction against termination, on the basis that the contract had already been terminated. The court stated that if the franchise agreement had been in force, it would have upheld the non-competition covenant (within the territory, for one year), as being reasonable.

The court went on to comment that it would also have upheld the non-competition covenant as against the shareholders and officers, even if they had not personally signed the agreement, because not doing so would facilitate the parties being able to do indirectly what they were prohibited from doing directly. This type of reasoning by the court reflects the civil law approach in Québec, rather than the common-law approach in the rest of Canada. This type of finding, if it had been made, would also have represented an example of those very special circumstances in which a court would enforce a non-competition covenant, even in the absence of a finding of privity of contract.

In *Second Cup v. Niranjan*, (2007) 39 BLR (4th) 73, the court considered whether a franchisee was bound by non-competition and confidentiality obligations set out in a franchise agreement following the expiration of that agreement. The franchisee opened a competing coffee shop approximately one month before the expiration of the franchise agreement. The franchisor brought a motion for an interlocutory injunction to restrain the franchisee.

In finding a strong prima facie case the court noted a profound deficiency in the franchise agreement: neither the franchisor nor the franchisee was able to produce a fully signed copy of the agreement (only a copy signed by the franchisee). During the negotiation of the agreement, the franchisor had insisted that it was not valid until signed by both parties. As a result, the court took a particularly critical position and found that without a fully executed agreement, the franchisee was not completely aware of the details of its non-competition obligations following the expiry of the agreement.

Although the franchisee was not bound by the restrictive covenants, the court did set out the following general principles:

> [17] The law recognizes that if the parties to an unsigned contract conduct themselves as if they were bound by that unsigned contract, they are subject to an implied or de facto contract on the unsigned contract's terms.
>
> [18] It is noteworthy, as well, that the *Arthur Wishart Act* (Franchise Disclosure) 2000, S.O. 2000 C.3 does not require that a franchise agreement be in writing . . . it was held that, by virtue of the continuing conduct of both parties, an implied franchise agreement could be interpreted to have existed after the expiry of the original agreement.
>
> [19] These principles would suggest that the conduct of the parties over a four-year period would bind them to the acceptance of the terms in the

> written document (although unsigned) to the extent that their conduct represented a clear assent to those terms. For example, the defendants having paid the royalty and advertising fees, as set out in the written document, could not contend at a later stage that those were not the terms of the arrangement. Nor could Second Cup, having conducted itself in such a way that Viji and the Company were their franchisees, resile and walk away from the arrangement alleging that it never did exist. However, those terms of the franchise agreement are not in issue in this case. What is in issue are the post-termination covenants and, specifically, the non-competition clause. There is nothing in the conduct of the parties which would suggest that they clearly assented to the precise terms of section 12 of the franchise agreement.

Although largely fact-driven, *Second Cup* may stand for a broader proposition that in situations where the scope of a post-term non-competition covenant is unclear or where the agreement containing such covenant is not signed by all parties, the parties may not be bound by the non-competition covenant.

In the case of *Bulk Barn Foods Limited v. Faber*, 2003 OJ No 5553, the franchisor had consented to a franchise agreement being assigned to a corporation on the condition that the shareholders, officers, and directors sign agreements with the franchisor undertaking to be bound by the non-competition covenant in the franchise agreement. The wife of the original individual franchisee was a shareholder, officer, and director of the new franchisee corporation, but this fact was deliberately concealed from the franchisor. The wife signed nothing with the franchisor and later set up a new business in competition after the franchise agreement had been terminated.

The judge ordered application of the non-competition covenant against her and her new business by way of an interlocutory injunction pending trial. The judge commented that she:

> [7]. . . must have known that she was affected by the franchise agreement and assignment and she should not now be forgiven for trying to circumvent her legal obligation to the plaintiff.

The judge felt that the wife ought to be viewed as if she had signed the undertaking she was obligated to sign, and that a refusal to enjoin her unlawful competition would severely injure the franchise system, cause irreparable harm, and that the balance of convenience favoured the franchisor.

Similarly, in *Pet Valu Canada Inc. v. 1381114 Ontario Ltd.*, 2013 ONSC 5361, a former franchisee arranged for her husband to incorporate a new company for the purpose of competing with the franchisor. The court issued an injunction against the former franchisee and the new company, on the basis that it had been formed to enable her to wrongfully compete against the franchisor. The court provided the following analysis:

> [8] While Mr. Fingarson was not a signatory to the franchise agreement, the evidence establishes that he incorporated 2347687 Ontario Limited for the purpose of assisting Ms. Martin to compete with the plaintiff when she had undertaken not to do so. It is plain that 2347687 Ontario Limited was incorporated by Mr. Fingarson to hide Ms. Martin's involvement. There is clear evidence that Ms. Martin is involved in the operation of Pet Stuff.

F. Internet Sales

Over the past few years the rise of e-commerce and other technological developments pose an interesting challenge to the formulation of traditional non-competition covenants. For example, how does one enforce or interpret such a clause where sales can happen anywhere in the world over the Internet? Does a geographic restriction apply to a website?

Although the courts have not commented on this issue specifically, the court in *Ensign Drilling Inc. v. Lundle*, 2007 ABQB 357, does comment on the issue of technology and enforcement of restrictive covenants.

In *Ensign Drilling*, the plaintiff company entered into a share purchase agreement for a drilling business with the defendant and signed a non-competition agreement. The geographic scope of the agreement extended to British Columbia, Alberta, Saskatchewan, and Manitoba, even though the plaintiff was engaged in operations only in southern Saskatchewan and southern Manitoba. The court found the geographic scope of the restraint reasonable for the drilling industry:

> [79] It is clear on the evidence that the drilling business is not a static one but rather a very mobile one. Drilling rigs are moved to a site, used until a well is drilled and then removed from that site to go elsewhere. Rigs move from site to site, field to field and sometimes (and there was evidence on this at trial) from province to province.

In particular, the court gave considerable deference to the actual agreement and also noted the following:

> [97] As Mr. Justice Dickson stated in *Elsley* the effect of a covenant in restraint of trade is not to be determined so much by previous judicial decisions but rather upon the circumstances of "infinite variety" surrounding every contract. Certainly depending upon the business in question, earlier decisions relating to geographic scope in particular will have less relevance in this era of cellular phones, fax, e-mail and the internet.

Practice Note

To be enforceable, a restrictive covenant, such as, and particularly in respect of, a non-competition covenant, must be:

A. certain, and
B. reasonable,
C. as between the actual parties to the agreement,
D. in the circumstances,
E. at the time the contract was entered into,
F. or as was within the contemplation of the parties at the time the contract was entered into,
G. such reasonableness being measured,
H. in each portion of the covenant,
I. as to:
   1. time,
   2. geographic scope, and
   3. the description of the business or activity which the covenanting party is restricted from,
J. so that the restraint is reasonably necessary to protect the interests of the party to whom the covenant is given,
K. but not more restrictive,
L. so as not to amount to an unreasonable restraint of trade or competition,
M. which would be against public policy and public interest[.]
N. or against the overall interests of the parties,
O. and thus not enforceable,
P. as it is written,
Q. bearing in mind that the courts will not modify the covenant as it is written,
R. but rather will either enforce it, or determine it to be unenforceable as it is written,
S. subject, in instances of proper drafting, to some severances,
T. which are contemplated by the contract as it is written, and
U. which are allowed for by the form in which the contract is written, and
V. which must still result in a readable and complete covenant being left in place,
W. which the court can find would have been agreed to by the parties,
X. at the time the contract was entered into, and
Y. without varying any of the other terms of the contract,
Z. and which the court will then consider to be enforceable.

XV. Alternative Dispute Resolution, Mediation, and Arbitration

A. Introduction

Mediation and arbitration are well developed and well recognized as alternative dispute resolution mechanisms throughout Canada. In general, alternative dispute resolution (ADR) is designed to encourage parties to resolve disputes based on compromise. The growing prevalence of ADR is a direct response to the inefficiencies, uncertainties, and expense of going to trial. The term encompasses processes such as negotiation, mediation, arbitration, mediation-arbitration, neutrals-party evaluation, and more. The ADR model endeavours to offer disputing parties an escape from rising legal fees, court backlogging, and the limited nature of judicial remedies. Given that the franchise relationship is one in which both parties generally wish to maintain an amicable business relationship in the future, franchise law would seem to be a fertile area for ADR.

Response to ADR in the context of franchise litigation, however, has remained somewhat tepid. It is still relatively rare to find a franchisor in Canada that obligates itself in the franchise agreement to resolve its disputes with its single-unit franchisees through some form of mandatory mediation or arbitration. The reasons, especially for the latter, are quite simple. Arbitrations have typically proven to be no less expensive than traditional litigation. Further, arbitration, and even sometimes mediation if it not concluded promptly, can often end up impeding a franchisor from achieving its goal of obtaining an injunction to enforce its rights upon termination.

B. Mediation

Provinces like British Columbia, Saskatchewan and Ontario have introduced some form of mandatory pre-trial mediation into the civil court process, meaning that mediation is or can be required after an action has been commenced, but before it reaches trial. This is now a mandatory part of the civil litigation process in Ontario in specified municipal jurisdictions. It is also a mandatory part of the civil litigation process in British Columbia, but the difference is that in British Columbia, the mediation process becomes mandatory only if one of the parties to the action requests it by way of delivering a notice to mediate. The Saskatchewan *Queen's Bench Act* compels mediation in civil proceedings before the Court of Queen's Bench. Both Alberta and Nova Scotia have legislation that contemplates use of mediation, though its implementation is not mandatory.

In New Brunswick, a regulation in the *Franchises Act* stipulates that mediation is mandatory if invoked by either party to the franchise agreement.

Noteworthy in Regulation 581/00 of the AWA is the requirement in section 5 that if an internal or external mediation or other ADR process is used by the franchisor in a dispute with a franchisee, the document is required to contain a description of the ADR process and the circumstances when the process may be invoked.

The *Code of Ethics* of the Canadian Franchise Association encourages mediation for its franchisor and franchisee members in Article 7, which reads as follows:

> A franchisor and its franchisees should make reasonable efforts to resolve complaints, grievances and disputes with each other through fair and reasonable direct communication and where reasonably appropriate under the circumstances, mediation or other alternative dispute resolution mechanisms.

Voluntary mediation is readily available in all major centres and most areas, as is arbitration, including through the alternative dispute resolution centres and service providers identified below. No federal organization equivalent to the American Arbitration Association has emerged. However, most major centres will have private mediation and arbitration service providers in place.

1. Private Mediation and Arbitration Services

In British Columbia, there is the British Columbia International Commercial Arbitration Centre, located in Vancouver. The centre is a not-for-profit organization established with the support of the governments of British Columbia and Canada. As such, it is probably the most officially recognized alternative dispute resolution service provision organization in Canada. Full information about this centre, including its rules of procedure, are available at its website, http://bcicac.com/. The website contains the centre's suggested model arbitration clause, and some commentary regarding additional matters to consider including therein. It reads as follows:

> All disputes arising out of or in connection with this contract, or in respect of any defined legal relationship associated therewith or derived therefrom, shall be referred to and finally resolved by arbitration under the rules of the British Columbia International Commercial Arbitration Centre.
>
> The appointing authority shall be the British Columbia International Commercial Arbitration Centre.

The case shall be administered by the British Columbia International Commercial Arbitration Centre in accordance with its Rules.

The place of arbitration shall be Vancouver, British Columbia, Canada.

In addition, there is the Canadian Commercial Arbitration Centre, with offices in Québec City and Montréal, Québec. This is a well-established centre, which is a private but a nonprofit organization. Extensive information regarding the Canadian Commercial Arbitration Centre, including its rules, is available on the centre's website. The centre's services are available in French or English, and its documentation is tri-lingual—English, French, and Spanish.

There are numerous other alternative dispute resolution service providers in operation privately throughout Canada. One example in Ontario is ADR Chambers International, located in Toronto, Ontario, the information pertaining to which is available on its website. ADR Chambers employs an extensive roster of dispute resolution experts, including nine former judges. The ADR firm conducted a staggering 25,000 mediations and arbitrations across Canada last year, illustrative of ADR's ongoing rise in popularity.

2. Arbitration

Most provinces have enacted arbitration legislation, and several provinces, including British Columbia and Ontario, have enacted two separate statutes, to apply to each of domestic and international arbitrations, respectively. The statutes contain a set of rules for the conduct of arbitration. They also provide for arbitral awards recognized by the court to be enforceable in the same manner as a judgment or order of the court.

It is customary in Canada for an arbitration clause in a franchise agreement to provide for the specific rules to be followed in the arbitration, as well as the forum, jurisdiction and language of the arbitration. Particularly in respect of the Province of Québec, it should be specified as to whether the arbitration is to be conducted in English or French.

The arbitration clause would also customarily provide that arbitration is final and binding as between the parties, and not subject to appeal. The parties can also specify that the award is to be confidential, however this confidentiality may be hampered somewhat by the disclosure requirements of both the Alberta and the Ontario franchise statutes.

Paragraphs 3 and 4 of schedule 1 of the Franchise Regulation to the Alberta Act provide specifically for disclosure of civil liabilities and administrative orders, as follows:

3 Civil Litigation and Liabilities

Provide details relating to the franchisor and its associates and to any of the directors, general partners and officers of the franchisor who have management responsibilities relating to the franchise on any finding of liability in a civil action or on any pending actions involving franchises or other businesses, involving misrepresentation, unfair or deceptive acts or practices and comparable actions.

4 Administrative Proceedings and Existing Orders
Provide details relating to the franchisor and its associates and to any of the directors, general partners and officers of the franchisor who have management responsibilities relating to the franchise on any currently effective injunctive or restrictive orders imposed by, or any pending administrative actions to be heard before, any public agency, whether in Alberta or outside Alberta, involving franchises or other businesses.

An arbitration award providing for a civil liability would probably have to be disclosed under these sections, when considered in combination with the general overall duty to disclose all material facts.

Paragraphs 4 and 5 of Part II of Regulation 581/00 to the AWA provide specifically for disclosure of civil liabilities and administrative orders or penalties, as follows:

A statement, including a description of details, indicating whether the franchisor, the franchisor's associate or a director, general partner or officer of the franchisor has been subject to an administrative order or penalty imposed under a law of any jurisdiction regulating franchises or business or if the person is the subject of any pending administrative actions to be heard under such a law.

5 A statement, including a description of details, indicating whether the franchisor, the franchisor's associate or a director, general partner or officer of the franchisor has been found liable in a civil action of misrepresentation, unfair or deceptive business practices or violating a law that regulates franchises or businesses, including a failure to provide proper disclosure to a franchisee, or if a civil action involving such allegations is pending against the person.

An arbitration award providing for a civil liability or penalty would probably have to be disclosed under these sections, when considered in combination with the general overall duty to disclose all material facts.

It is also to be noted that the provisions of the sections under the regulations to both statutes also require disclosure of pending actions. Arguably, this would similarly include pending arbitrations. Lastly, the arbitration clause will customarily provide that the award may be entered in any court having jurisdiction, and enforced in the same manner as an order of such court.

Some arbitration clauses refer specifically to the arbitration being conducted in accordance with the specific commercial arbitration or international commercial arbitration statute in effect in the relevant province, as applicable. Both Ontario and British Columbia have adopted the Model Law on International Commercial Arbitration, as adopted by the United Nations Commission on International Trade Law (the UNCITRAL Model Law). The Model Law has been made a schedule to the International Commercial Arbitration Act in each province, with some modifications and additions. These acts provide for the enforcement of foreign arbitral awards.

Canada is a signatory to the United Nations Convention on the Recognition and Enforcement of Foreign Arbitral Awards (otherwise known as the New York Convention), as evidenced by the passage of a federal statute known as the *United Nations Foreign Arbitral Awards Convention Act.* Each of the provinces has also passed their own legislation implementing the New York Convention.

The enforcement of a foreign arbitral award still requires that a legal action be commenced in a provincial court to obtain the enforcement order. This could conceivably allow a defence to be filed, although limited grounds are available, which would enable the subject party to challenge the jurisdiction and enforceability of the foreign arbitral award. This could have the result of requiring a trial on the merits of the award to be held prior to an enforcement order being granted.

A franchise case dealing with the enforcement of arbitral agreements is the case of *Ellis v. Subway Franchise Systems of Canada Ltd.,* (2000) 8 BLR (3d) 55.

In this case, the arbitration clause in the franchise agreement provided:

1. that the provincial arbitration legislation in force in the province where the shop is located shall apply to all claims arising out of the franchise agreement;
2. that any claim arising out of a breach of the franchise agreement shall be settled by arbitration in accordance with the commercial arbitration rules of the American Arbitration Association at a hearing to be held in Bridgeport, Connecticut; and
3. that judgment upon an award rendered by the arbitrator may be entered in any court having jurisdiction.

The franchisee was in default. The franchisor gave notice of default and the default was not cured. The franchisor filed its demand for arbitration with the American Arbitration Association. The franchisee sought a stay of the arbitration proceedings and an order that Ontario was the more appropriate forum for arbitration.

The franchisor responded with a motion for a permanent or temporary stay or dismissal of the franchisee's application, and a direction that the parties proceed with arbitration in Connecticut and under the terms of the franchise agreement. There was no evidence to support a claim of unconscionability and the franchisor prevailed, thereby enforcing the arbitration clause as agreed to by the parties in their franchise agreement. Whether the result would be the same today, in light of section 10 of the AWA, the section that precludes restricting jurisdiction or venue to a forum outside of Ontario, remains to be seen. This result in Ontario (and other provinces with franchise laws) would be open to question, at least with respect to claims otherwise enforceable in Ontario (or other provinces with franchise laws) under the franchise-specific statute.

Recent Developments

With ADR provisions becoming a requirement in certain jurisdictions, as described above with New Brunswick, parties are being forced to take notice. Gradually, the inclusion and utilization of ADR provisions has increased in Canada. A natural consequence of this fact is that Canadian courts have now had some opportunity to analyze the validity of such provisions.

In *MDG Kingston Inc. v. MDG Computers Canada Inc.*, 2008 ONCA 656 (MDG), the Ontario Court of Appeal considered whether an arbitration clause contained in a franchise agreement remained effective in the face of a notice of rescission. The franchisee was seeking to rescind, alleging that the franchisor failed to deliver a disclosure document required by s. 5 of the AWA. The court held that the fairly drafted arbitration clause was indeed valid and that the AWA does not change the "normal rules regarding arbitration clauses, including the arbitrator's authority to decide its own jurisdiction as well as the severability of an arbitration clause." In other words, the court held that neither the arbitration provision or the franchise agreement itself were invalid simply because the franchisee sought termination. The court directed the parties to arbitration and the matter remains ongoing.

Similarly, in *2162683 Ontario Inc. v. Flexsmart Inc.*, 2010 ONSC 6493, the Superior Court of Justice disagreed with a plaintiff franchisee's claim that an arbitration agreement was invalid due to the franchisor's failure to meet statutory disclosure obligations. As was held in MDG, the court stated that if there was some merit to the franchisee's other claims, grounded in misrepresentation, this would be a matter to be addressed during arbitration.

The approach in MDG was once again followed by the Ontario Court of Appeal in *Nazarinia Holdings Inc. v. 2049080 Ontario Inc.*, 2010 ONSC 1766; affirmed in 2010 ONCA 739; leave to appeal dismissed by the Supreme Court of Canada in 2010 CarswellOnt 10265. In this case, the court upheld the lower court's decision regarding the validity of an arbitration clause contained within a franchise agreement. It was held that an arbitration clause will be enforced where it "is very broad and provides a clear indication that the parties intended that their disputes, including disputes as to the validity of the franchise agreement itself, should be heard by an arbitrator and not by the courts." The court once again protected the validity of arbitration as a vehicle for the ultimate resolution of disagreements, stating that it would be within the jurisdiction of the arbitrator to determine whether the franchise agreement or any part thereof was invalid.

Finally, the Ontario Superior Court of Justice recently dealt with arbitration clauses in *1136845 Ontario Inc. v. Pillar to Post Inc.*, 2014 ONSC 7400, an important case for readers interested in understanding class action law in Canada as it relates to franchising. The court granted the defendant franchisor's motion to stay a proposed class action that had been brought by a group of franchisees, on the basis that class actions were precluded by the wording of the arbitration clause. The plaintiffs' argument that arbitration clauses contravened the AWA was dismissed, making it clear that the AWA does not confer exclusive jurisdiction on the courts to hear disputes, but rather, allows for parties to a franchise agreement to proceed with arbitration. The court further held that it was within the jurisdiction of the arbitrator, and not the courts, to decide whether the arbitration clause was itself enforceable. This decision effectively defeated the proposed class action. The case illustrates the importance of carefully considering the wording arbitration clauses at the drafting stage, and the utility of arbitration clauses in general, as such clauses may be decisive of potential litigation.

Practice Note

Particular care ought to be taken in drafting arbitration clauses in light of the decision in *Pillar to Post*, as such clauses may be decisive of disputes that arise between parties to a franchise agreement. Franchisors can be encouraged by this decision that well-worded arbitration clauses in franchise agreements will be enforced by Ontario courts.

3. Conclusion

There is a general trend for ADR-related issues to become more integral in franchise law disputes. From a franchisor perspective, ADR can result in cost and time saving, it can and usually does remain private and confidential, and could also restrict the ability of franchisees to participate in class actions. The processes are not without problems, though, and must be designed effectively to trigger the benefits it promises in theory.

Canada remains an arbitration-friendly jurisdiction, as evidenced by the court's attitude toward upholding the validity of arbitration clauses, if properly employed. As ADR continues to develop, franchisors and franchisees will need to continue exploring innovative dispute resolution practices as a strategy for avoiding the drawbacks of litigation.

XVI. Conclusion

The above discussions highlight the often significant differences between the provincial laws and jurisprudence approaches in Québec and the other nine common-law provinces of Canada.

Although the common-law provinces are considerably more similar in respect of their laws and approaches to the U.S. than is the case with Québec, the point must still be made that there are a multitude of subtle yet substantive and substantial differences that exist between the legal systems in place in Canada and those of the United States.

American franchisors and their counsel need to keep these differences in mind when franchising in Canada. The fact remains, however, that there are also substantial and significant similarities between Canada and the United States in the actual business of franchising.

CHAPTER 8

Acting for the Canadian Franchisee

Joseph Adler, Hoffer Adler LLP
Peter Viitre, Sotos LLP*

Contents

* The authors wish to acknowledge with gratitude Stephanie Chong of Hoffer Adler LLP who assisted in preparing the intellectual property related segments of the chapter.

I. Introduction

At the core of every commercial relationship is a bargain: one party agrees to perform a list of tasks and assumes a series of obligations in exchange for a defined set of benefits; the other does the same, but its tasks, obligations, and benefits will either reciprocate or dovetail with those of the first party. In a sense, they are like the two sides of a coin—different, yet complimentary——with the presence of each being required to create the value that the coin represents.

This general paradigm holds as true for franchise relationships as it does for any other complex commercial arrangement. The principal distinguishing characteristic of franchising, however, is that one party—the franchisor—typically establishes the parameters of the bargain that will form the basis for the relationship in a way that leaves little room for negotiation. In addition, the franchising model (at least at the unit-franchise level) invariably involves a significantly unbalanced relationship, wherein the franchisor possesses far more information and exerts much more bargaining power than its franchisees, thereby distinguishing this method of conducting business from many other commercial contexts, including in terms of the franchisee's ability to fully understand the opportunity, and then to negotiate its position.

A franchisee's analysis is often further complicated by the fact that its franchisor may choose not to contract directly with it, but rather, as was discussed in Chapter 1, to engage one or more Canadian national, regional, provincial or other master franchisees (masters) or area developers (area developers) to perform some or all of the franchisor's functions in the franchisee's particular jurisdiction or territory.

Given this complex and multifaceted context, the primary role of counsel in advising the prospective Canadian franchisee is essentially threefold. Counsel must: (a) help the franchisee understand the franchisor's system—both operationally (to the extent possible, recognizing that counsel should not represent him- or herself as having such operational expertise) and legally—and the part each party plays in it; (b) assist the franchisee in its investigation and assessment of the franchise opportunity being offered (i.e., its due diligence); and (c) help the franchisee to fully understand and, if possible, negotiate the terms of the franchise agreement and related documents with regard to the roles and responsibilities of each party under the system and the results of the franchisee's due diligence.

In this chapter, we will discuss these matters in greater depth, with a view to illustrating the framework of the franchisee's analysis of a U.S. or other foreign-based franchise opportunity, and some of the key considerations that should inform its decision whether to buy into that opportunity, and at what price.

A. Possible Structures and the Respective Roles of the Parties in Each

Generally speaking, in the franchising context, the franchisor's role (i.e., what it "brings to the table") is to provide the franchisee with:

- a strong and valuable brand under which to conduct its business;
- a tried and true business model that assures a reasonable level of profitability for each of the franchisor and franchisee;
- a set of standards, specifications and procedures that the franchisee will be required to follow, and that are consistently applied across the franchise system, in order to ensure a uniform and consistently high-quality image, customer offering, and experience;
- comprehensive initial and supplementary training and support (including marketing support) to instruct the franchisee on how to implement the franchisor's standards, specifications and procedures, in the hope of replicating the success of the franchisor and other franchisees in operating the business and in promoting that business within the franchisee's territory; and
- the possibility of purchasing services, products and other inputs on terms that are better than the franchisee could obtain by going into the market by itself—i.e., economies of scale.

In return, the franchisee is required to commit to:

- paying upfront and ongoing fees to the franchisor in exchange for the right to use the franchisor's marks and system, and for the support it provides in establishing and operating the business;
- (in most cases) devoting its full-time efforts and attention to operating the franchised business, which, in reality, typically entails investing far more time than a "full-time" job;
- operating the franchised business strictly in accordance with the franchisor's prescribed standards and procedures, and in accordance with all applicable law; and
- promoting the franchised business and system, including through local advertising and contributions to national and/or regional marketing funds, all strictly in accordance with the franchisor's standards and specifications regarding the use and display of its trademarks.

As noted, a foreign-based franchisor may, for its own reasons, choose to franchise its business in Canada either directly or through a Canadian master or area developer. How the franchisor chooses to proceed may have a significant impact on the franchisee, its ability to operate, its prospects for success, and thus its investment decision. For example, the master (and, to a lesser extent, the area developer) would act as the franchisor's "eyes and ears" in the applicable Canadian jurisdiction and would perform most, if not all, of the franchisor's functions enumerated above. As far as the unit franchisee is concerned, for most purposes, the master would *be* the franchisor. This sort of arrangement can be of considerable benefit to both franchisor and franchisee, alike. For the franchisor, it has the advantage of interposing a party with local knowledge and proximity to the territory between itself and the franchisee, thereby allowing the franchisor to effectively expand its reach—in terms of both supervision and assistance—beyond the borders of its own home jurisdiction. For the franchisee, the presence of a domestic master or area developer can provide valuable assurances that its support needs will be met in a more responsive manner and that there is a local entity against which it might obtain some form of recourse in the event of a breach.

On the other hand, just as the franchisor must consider what happens in the event that the master or area developer fails to do its job, the unit franchisee must also consider any added risks associated with being one step removed (both physically, in terms of geography or jurisdiction, and contractually) from the franchisor. For example, the franchisee may wish to seek some assurance that it will continue to be able to operate in the event that the master, for whatever reason, is removed from its relationship to the franchise system. In other words, the franchisee should seek some assurance that the franchisor will ultimately honor the franchisee's rights to continue to use the franchisor's marks and system if the relationship with the master is terminated, notwithstanding the lack of privity of contract between them in the first instance. Such assurances often take on the form of a comfort letter from the franchisor addressed directly to the franchisee.

Similarly, the master will, itself, usually want some assurance of its continuing ability to operate the franchise system in Canada in the event of any financial or other difficulties involving the franchisor. Again, either a comfort letter or commitment to continue to make the franchisor's marks and system available for use and sublicense by the master would typically be provided. In addition, the master will want to negotiate as much authority and flexibility as it can into the terms of its agreement(s) with the franchisor, including with respect to its rights and obligations to continue to both support and expand the system with or without the help of the franchisor, as is discussed in greater detail under Part IV, below.

B. Due Diligence

One of the main tasks of the franchisee and its counsel when determining whether the relationship is worth pursuing is to conduct in-depth due diligence on the franchisor and its system, which would include, at a high level:

- reviewing and considering the tasks and obligations that the franchisee will be expected to perform, and assessing the franchisee's ability to perform them, and
- assessing what the franchisor is promising to bring to the table and its ability to deliver those items over the life of the relationship.

In assessing what is being offered by the franchisor, the franchisee should examine such factors as: (a) the financial and operational health of the franchisor; (b) how well the franchisor's brand is known in the franchisee's territory and the franchisor's ability to validly license it to the franchisee and protect it from the claims of others; (c) the business terms being offered, including the amounts of money the franchisor is demanding in exchange for the opportunity and the assistance it is offering; and (d) the legal terms and conditions set out in the unit, area development or master franchise agreement and ancillary documentation that the franchisee is required to sign.

In terms of the franchisee's assessment of its own side of the transaction, the individual franchisee should consider carefully: (a) any particular skills, experience and interests he or she may have that are relevant to the type of business being considered; (b) his or her financial position and ability to obtain credit to finance the franchise acquisition and its ongoing operation; (c) his or her ability and desire to work long hours; and (d) his or her temperament and attitude towards working within a highly structured and closely controlled system, while maintaining a sense of entrepreneurialism.

In Canada, six provinces (namely, Alberta, British Columbia, Manitoba, New Brunswick, Ontario, and Prince Edward Island) have enacted franchise legislation designed to assist the franchisee in this exercise primarily by requiring the franchisor to prepare and deliver to the franchisee a franchise disclosure document (FDD) that contains all of the material information that the franchisee will require to make that assessment and decision. (British Columbia's *Franchises Act* was the most recent to be passed, effective February 1, 2017.) The details of what goes into an FDD and how to prepare it are discussed in detail in Chapter 6. From the perspective of advising the franchisee, however, counsel's task is threefold:

- to review the disclosure package and to factor the information contained in it into the franchisee's analysis of both the opportunity and his or her own aptitude for and interest in it;
- to consider the potential availability of remedies under applicable franchise legislation in the event that the FDD has not been prepared or delivered in accordance with the applicable disclosure laws; and
- to negotiate the terms and conditions of the franchise agreement and related documentation.

In addition to and in conjunction with the review of the FDD, the franchisee and their counsel should consult a number of other resources in order to complete their assessment of the franchisor and the franchise opportunity. Chief among these additional resources are other existing and former franchisees of the system in question. The franchisee should be advised to speak to as many of them as possible. While the list of questions the franchisee might ask is arguably endless, it should cover at least the following:

- What is the franchisor's general reputation for fairness and professionalism in its business dealings—is the franchisor generally reasonable to deal with, or is it generally adversarial and solely concerned with advancing its own interests?
- Were the startup and ongoing cost figures and financial performance representations, if any, provided by the franchisor, generally accurate?
- Do the franchisees feel that the costs of goods and services supplied by the franchisor and/or its approved suppliers are generally competitive, or are they above market price, and are deliveries of goods, and services provided by the franchisor or its suppliers generally on time?
- Do the franchisees generally feel that they are getting value from the franchisor's advertising programs or were the marketing and advertising funds and initiatives simply established to serve as yet another profit center for the franchisor?
- Does the franchisor provide sufficient training, operational assistance and other guidance and support to its franchisees?
- What is the franchisor's policy regarding such potentially contentious and expensive issues as required renovations, purchases of new equipment and other mandatory capital expenditures? Do franchisees think they are required to spend unreasonable sums of money or is the franchisor truly motivated to protect the goodwill of the system and trademarks by ensuring that all franchisees project a professional, clean, efficient and attractive image in the delivery of its products and/or services?
- Are franchisees profitable and does the franchisor's business model otherwise work?
- How tolerant is the franchisor of relatively minor breaches?
- How helpful or accommodating has the franchisor been toward franchisees who have sought to leave the system, for example, through buybacks or transfers?
- Is the franchisor generally responsive to franchisee concerns and complaints, or does it merely pay "lip service" to them? For example, is there a franchisee committee or advisory board that serves as a genuine platform to deal with such concerns?

The answers to these and other questions (preferably from varying and multiple sources) should give the franchisee a good idea as to the values, ethics and reasonableness of the franchisor and its overall approach to the franchise relationship; all of which will be critical to the franchisee's assessment of whether to enter into a long-term relationship with the franchisor.

In addition to speaking to current and former franchisees, the franchisee should also consult various publicly available resources, and conduct various searches, such as media, litigation and security searches, and commercial credit reports to help gauge the franchisor's financial wherewithal. Industry groups, such as the Canadian Franchise Association, may also have valuable information that may assist the franchisee in making a decision. The franchisee's professional advisors, including its legal counsel and financial advisors, should help the franchisee interpret the results of its research and to place them in the proper context of the franchise relationship.

II. Additional Risks and Benefits to Purchasing a Franchise from a Non-Canadian Franchisor vs. Buying into a Canadian-Based System

So far, the concerns described above can be said to apply to the consideration of any domestic franchise purchase. However, there are some additional factors to be considered in the purchase of a U.S.-based or other foreign-based franchise, each of which can have a significant impact on the franchisee's risk profile and the expected value to it of the business proposition.

A. How Well Does the Brand or Concept "Work" in Canada?

As was discussed in Chapter 4, and elsewhere, the heart of every franchise concept is its brand. In the case of a foreign-based franchise, the Canadian prospective franchisee must consider whether and to what extent the success, strength and value of the brand and concept in its home jurisdiction is a valid predictor of similar success, strength and value in Canada, particularly if it is considering becoming one of the first Canadian franchisees in the system. It should of course be noted that, in the case of an existing, mature foreign-based system with a history in one or multiple Canadian jurisdictions, these issues become commensurately less relevant, since the strength of the brand and concept will be self-evident, or at least as readily assessable as with any Canadian-based system.

The issue of how well the franchisor's brand and concept are capable of transplanting themselves into a foreign jurisdiction like Canada is one of great concern to the foreign franchisor, as was discussed at length in Chapter 1. The franchisor's willingness to adapt its concept and brand image, and even its customer offering, to its target jurisdiction is often one of the most significant considerations when determining whether or not to expand. From the franchisee's perspective, it is similarly important that the franchisor demonstrate a clear understanding of the cultural, religious, linguistic and political differences that exist between its home jurisdiction and the relevant Canadian province or region, and that it be willing to make any necessary changes in order to preserve and enhance the value of its brand in Canada, both for its own benefit and for that of its franchisees. Accordingly, the franchisee and its counsel will have to be keenly aware, themselves, of those factors that may impact the strength of the brand and concept in Canada, and incorporate those factors into their analysis of the franchise opportunity.

Moreover, the nature and extent of those cultural, legal and other distinctions (and hence the adaptations and modifications that may be called for in the expansion of a given franchise system into Canada) may well vary by province, region, municipality, or even neighborhood. So, too, must the advice given to franchisees in each such jurisdiction. Factors such as predominant food tastes and preferences, prevalent or legally mandated work, dining and shopping hours, common religious observances, and linguistic and cultural norms may vary quite dramatically from downtown Toronto, to a booming mineral resource town in Alberta or the Yukon, to a small Francophone community in eastern Québec, or to a fishing or logging village in one of the Maritime provinces. And it will, at least in part, be up to the franchisee to assess whether the community in which it operates will support one or more units of the type being considered and to consider the modifications that may be required in order to make it more palatable to the local customer base.

Again, a unit franchisee might derive some comfort here from the presence of a Canadian master or area developer, provided that (as is discussed in greater detail, below) the master or area developer has some ability to effect those changes itself. Conversely, when acting for the master or area developer, it will be of deep importance to ensure that the client has the ability to make the required modifications having regard both to the commercial, cultural and political realities that exist at the inception of the relationship, and to the fact that those realities, and hence the required modifications, may change over the course of the relationship.

Finally, there is the issue of cost and, in particular, who will bear the cost of implementing the changes and modifications that must be made in order to make the franchise concept viable in Canada. The franchisee should be advised to consider the franchisor's or master's/area developer's ability to mandate changes to the marks and system midstream and its ability to pass the costs of those changes down to the franchisee. From the franchisee's perspective, flexibility is often good, as discussed above, but it is even better if the franchisor, master, or area developer bears the costs.

B. How Well Does the Business Model "Work" on This Side of the Border?

As important as it is from the franchisee's perspective to assess how well the franchisor's brand and marks are, or will be, received in Canada, it is still more important for it and its advisors to assess the applicability and appropriateness of the franchisor's business model in light of the economic, political and other differences that exist between Canada (or the relevant province or region) and the franchisor's home jurisdiction.

One of the key differences between Canada and the United States, for example, lies in the cost of product and service inputs. For example, restaurant systems often run into difficulty when entering Canada due to the relatively higher cost of food ingredients, labor, and required government payments and statutory deductions. If a franchisor attempts to import its U.S. business model into Canada without first investigating these issues and modifying its key financial parameters accordingly, it may be setting itself up for failure. Similar concerns arise if the franchisor has not properly investigated and anticipated other market conditions, for example, related to demand for its products and services and the availability and pricing of goods and services that compete directly or indirectly with its core customer offering.

A key element of the franchisee's due diligence effort should therefore be focused on ensuring that the franchisor has in fact done its own homework and that each side's assumptions regarding expected costs, revenues and margins are both realistic and appropriate. One difficulty that arises, however, is that, like the FTC Rule and most states' franchise laws, the various Canadian franchise statutes make the provision of cost estimates and earnings projections optional and within the discretion of the franchisor, thus making the prospective franchisee's investigation of this issue more difficult. Once again, this concern is more acute, and the risk to the prospective franchisee is greater, in the case of a foreign-based franchise that is still in the early stages of its expansion into Canada than it would be with a system whose Canadian presence is more well-established.

In addition, in the same way that cultural differences across Canada may impact the strength of the franchisor's brand and appropriateness of its concept for use in Canada, the applicability and appropriateness of its business model may also be challenged by the stark economic (and, in some cases, political) differences that exist between Canada's various provinces and regions. A given customer offering, particularly at a specific price point, may be quite feasible in one part of Canada, while being prohibitively expensive or otherwise inaccessible to a large segment of the population in another.

Once again, the presence of an experienced master or area developer may provide some assurance that the above factors are properly accounted for in the franchise offering put to the prospective unit franchisee; if only because all of these factors similarly impact the revenues, costs and profitability of the master, and possibly the area developer, as well. However, this assurance is not ironclad and, in any event, only pushes the investigation up one level and into the hands of the master (or area developer) and its own Canadian counsel.

C. Legal Concerns

In addition to the branding and financial concerns described above, the prospective Canadian franchisee must also consider and address a number of legal issues with the help of local counsel.

1. Protection of Franchisor's IP

First, is the franchisor's IP protected in Canada and, if so, how well?

A Canadian prospective franchisee should conduct due diligence to determine to what extent a U.S. or foreign franchisor's intellectual property is protected in Canada. Intellectual property, in the context of a franchise system, most often refers to the trademark or trademarks (i.e., the names and logos used with the franchise) that are associated with the provision of certain franchised services. It can also refer to any patents for inventions that are being utilized during the provision of the franchised services, as well as trade secrets and copyrights.

The key factor to bear in mind is that IP rights are territorial. Thus, simply because the U.S. or foreign-based franchisor owns IP rights in the United States or some other foreign jurisdiction, does not necessarily mean that those same rights subsist in, or extend into, Canada.

2. Trademarks

In Canada, trademark rights arise from use, with enhanced rights being granted upon registration. Although many U.S. and other foreign brands are at least somewhat familiar to Canadian consumers, this does not mean that a U.S. trademark enjoys automatic protection north of the border.

To best assess the strength of a U.S. or other foreign-based franchisor's trademarks in Canada, comprehensive searches should be conducted. These searches assist in determining whether a third party has already filed an application to register an identical or confusingly similar trademark in Canada, whether a registration for such a mark has already issued in Canada, and whether a third party may be using a confusingly similar trademark without having filed an application to register it with the Canadian Intellectual Property Office (CIPO).

Potential barriers to the ability of a U.S. or foreign franchisor to the use of its trademark in Canada may arise if an identical or confusingly similar mark has previously been used by a third party in Canada (either with or without a corresponding registration), or if a third party has filed an application for an identical or confusingly similar mark, even if no such use has taken place. In either situation, steps should be taken to assess how significant a barrier the third-party trademark represents. It may, for example, be possible to take formal steps to oppose or otherwise object to the third-party use or pending application. It may also be possible to seek to invalidate a third-party registration. The mechanisms and strategies will vary depending on the precise situation.

Although the specifics will vary, it is important to note that the existence of third-party trademark rights could present a significant barrier to a potential franchisee being able to operate in Canada using the trademarks of the U.S. or foreign franchisor. In an extreme case, it may even be necessary for the potential Canadian franchisee to operate under trademarks that are wholly different from those used in the United States or in the other foreign jurisdiction(s) in which the franchisor is domiciled or operates.

Further, prospective Canadian franchisees should be sure to obtain trademark licensing rights from the correct legal entity that has the trademark rights being licensed, as U.S. or other foreign franchisors will not necessarily own the marks themselves. At times, therefore, it is recommended that the Canadian prospective franchisee seek and obtain a comfort letter directly from the trademark owner.

Finally, prospective Canadian franchisees should seek an indemnity from the U.S. or foreign-based franchisor to protect them in the event that they are required to substitute certain opposed or problematic trademarks and to make the required changes to their signage, trade dress, etc.

3. Patents

Patents are granted for new and useful inventions. A patent owner has the exclusive right to make, use and sell the subject matter claimed by the patent. Unlike a trademark, a patent must be registered before any enforceable rights will arise.

In a franchise system, patents may have been granted to the U.S. or foreign franchisor for anything the franchisor has developed that is unique and inventive for that system. For example, specific machinery used to manufacture a key component of the franchised services, and custom software applications, may be subject to patent protection.

However, patent protection is inherently territorial, so a U.S. or foreign patent provides no protection in Canada. A prospective Canadian franchisee should thus ensure that the U.S. or foreign franchisor has corresponding patents in Canada. If not, there is a risk that the use of any inventive technology in Canada could infringe a third party's Canadian patent. The scope of any such risk can be assessed through comprehensive Canadian patent searches, and evaluation of those searches by a qualified patent professional.

4. Trade Secrets

Trade secrets are often associated with recipes and other formulas. There is no specific statute that protects trade secrets in Canada. Rather, a prospective franchisee should assure itself that adequate steps are being taken by its franchisor in implementing the franchise system to keep any trade secrets from being revealed to the public. Of course, those steps will invariably also require a covenant of confidentiality from the franchisee itself; the expectation being that similar covenants are being obtained by the franchisor from all of its other franchisees and other relevant contractual counterparties, as well.

5. Copyright

Copyright protects various types of works, including artistic works and literary works. Copyright provides the owner with the exclusive right to produce or reproduce the work, or a substantial copy thereof. In a franchise system, copyright most often arises with respect to logos (which may be considered artistic works, and which may also function as trademarks), operating manuals and marketing collateral (including websites).

Although copyright arises automatically upon creation of the work, the person or entity who is deemed to be the first owner of copyright in that work varies depending on the circumstances. Thus, if website content was written by an employee of the franchisor within the scope of that person's employment, then the franchisor is deemed to be the owner of the copyright in the website content. If, however, the website content was developed by an independent contractor, the copyright in that content does not automatically belong to the franchisor, even if the franchisor paid the contractor for the work. What is needed is a written assignment of copyright, and the franchisee should attempt to satisfy itself that the franchisor has taken all necessary steps to protect itself from competing claims by its current and former employees, contractors and franchisees in respect of all relevant works that the franchisee would be using to operate the system in Canada.

6. Regulatory or Other Legal Barriers

In addition to intellectual property concerns, the prospective franchisee should also consider whether there are any regulatory or other legal barriers to conducting the franchised business in Canada that could impair the viability and value of the franchise it is buying. In particular, Canadian prospective and existing franchisees should be alert to the fact that if their franchisors are headquartered in the United States or in some other jurisdiction outside of Canada, their franchisors may not have a very good—much less, a full—understanding of the regulatory environment facing the applicable franchised businesses under consideration or then currently operating.

For example, franchisors interested in franchising in those Canadian provinces that impose franchise disclosure obligations are arguably required to be fully acquainted with the regulatory framework that their franchisees will face when operating their franchised businesses in those provinces. This is because such franchisors are required to provide disclosure of "every licence, registration, authorization or other permission the franchisee is required to obtain, under any applicable federal or provincial law or municipal by-law, to operate the franchise" (see Section 6(1)10 of Ontario's *Arthur Wishart Act (Franchise Disclosure), 2000*, for example). This disclosure obligation is often all too difficult for most non-Canadian based franchisors to fulfill given the rather expansive and unrealistic requirement to disclose "*every* licence, registration, authorization or other permission" [emphasis added], as there are simply too many such requirements to identify. Given the monumental task of meeting this disclosure requirement, many Canadian franchisors have adopted the practice of offering generic, rather than specific, disclosures in this regard.

Yet, even when franchisors do meet this onerous disclosure requirement, franchisees are only provided with an understanding of the regulatory environment for a very specific snapshot in time. That is, franchisees are only provided with a disclosure of "every licence, registration, authorization or other permission the franchisee is required to obtain" *as at the time of disclosure*. As laws and regulations are dynamic in nature and are constantly evolving over time, franchisees should be fully cognizant of their legal obligations under the laws of their jurisdiction. Though their U.S. or foreign franchisors may not face similar road blocks within their respective jurisdictions, Canadian franchisees may encounter difficulties in successfully operating their franchised businesses due to laws and regulations that are unique to their particular Canadian province or locality. In other words, franchisees should not assume that the successes and the experiences of U.S. and other foreign franchisees with their respective legal regimes and regulatory authorities will necessarily translate into similar successes and experiences in Canada.

Finally, while it is beyond the scope of this discussion to identify every piece of legislation that could impact a U.S. or other foreign franchisor's ability to expand into Canada, or that may contribute or inhibit a Canadian prospective franchisee's success in Canada, it is essential for such franchisors to identify some of the more critical pieces of legislation governing the industry in question, and for prospective franchisees to discuss them with their legal counsel and thus to conduct their own investigation into the legal and regulatory requirements that would be imposed upon their clients should they pursue the franchised opportunity under consideration. Relying solely on the franchisor's advice would be reckless and inadvisable even in the best of circumstances—i.e., even were both the franchisor and the franchisee were residents of the same jurisdiction—let alone where they are situated in different countries.

7. "Canadianization" and Translation of FDD and Operations Manual

Has the franchisor's FDD and operations manual been properly Canadianized and translated, where necessary?

In many respects, the failure of a franchisor to Canadianize its FDD and operations manual is more of an issue for the franchisor than it is for the franchisee. This is because the U.S. or other foreign franchisor's failure to Canadianize these documents may mean that it is not meeting its disclosure obligations. If a deficiency is deemed significant enough by a court of law, then the aggrieved franchisee will obtain certain powerful remedies, such as rescission of the franchise agreement. Prospective franchisees looking to launch their own franchises, however, are not looking for opportunities to initiate rescission claims, but are looking to succeed in their franchised businesses. In other words, though prospective franchisees may derive certain statutory benefits were they to remain silent in the light of certain of such deficiencies and not raise them with their franchisors, they would also be disadvantaged in some critical ways. That is, there are certain key provisions in franchise agreements and significant disclosures in disclosure documents that, if not Canadianized, will inevitably mislead prospective franchisees or cause them not to possess a fuller picture of the franchise offering. It is therefore highly recommended that prospective franchisees demand Canadianized versions of the documents from their U.S. or foreign franchisors, failing which, they should seriously reconsider investing in such franchise systems.

The exercise of Canadianizing a U.S. or other foreign FDD, and the legal issues imposed upon a U.S. or foreign franchisor in relation to this exercise, is more extensively dealt with in Chapter 5. From a Canadian prospective franchisee's perspective, it is important to understand the franchisor's corporate legal structure to confirm that the correct legal entity has provided the necessary disclosure and that the duly authorized directors and/or officers of the entity have fulfilled their statutory disclosure obligations in those provinces that currently have franchise disclosure legislation.

Often, U.S. and other foreign franchisors will Canadianize franchise agreements, but will fail to Canadianize their operations manuals. Failing to do so, however, may have serious legal consequences should the U.S. or foreign franchisor impose certain requirements upon its franchisees that are contrary to law and that will otherwise impede their franchisees' ability to operate their franchised businesses in Canada.

In the Province of Québec, moreover, U.S. or other foreign franchisors should translate their operations manuals into French, so that their franchisees can better understand their ongoing responsibilities. Though there is no legal requirement to translate the franchise agreements into French provided that the parties to the agreements agree in writing to the use of the English language, it is important to recognize that the vast majority of residents in Québec outside of the bilingual city of Montreal, almost exclusively speak French. As such, it may be prudent in certain circumstances to incur the cost of translating the franchise agreement and other agreements so as to ensure that the franchisees in that province fully understand their legal obligations.

D. The Impact of the Master on These Issues and Its Role in Managing or Supporting Them

Where a Canadian master or area developer is involved in the franchise offering, matters may become even further complicated for the prospective Canadian franchisee. This is because the prospective franchisee's negotiations and relationship may be adversely impacted by the interplay of two (i.e., the foreign franchisor and the master/area developer) and possibly more parties, both during the negotiations leading up to the execution of the franchise agreement and thereafter. For example, a master's ability to negotiate any of the terms and conditions of the franchise agreement may be restricted by its master franchise agreement. That is, master franchisees are often required to obtain their franchisors' consent to any amendments to the franchise agreement and, as such, any requested amendments made by the prospective franchisee may be refused by the franchisor, even where the master is agreeable to making the changes. Further, where another party such as a foreign franchisor is involved, a prospective franchisee should expect delays in consummating its negotiations with the master.

III. Common Relationship Flashpoints and Red Flags Arising Out of a Disclosure Document Review

Given the complexity of the franchise relationship and the decision of whether to acquire a particular franchise, it is extremely important that the prospective franchisee engage competent franchise counsel, as well as skilled business and financial advisors, to assist in reviewing the franchise disclosure document and related documents and to assist the franchisee in assessing the business opportunity.

It is crucial that the franchisee and its advisors review all available information thoroughly and ask lots of questions, not only of the franchisor, but also of current and former franchisees and other stakeholders in the business. There are many issues that can come up in the context of that review and it is important that they are discovered and addressed before any agreement is signed. Some of the new important issues are discussed below.

A. Franchisor Commitment to the Territory—Don't Become an Orphan

1. *Does the system have, or what is the franchisor's plan to achieve, "critical mass" in Canada?*

This is often, though not always, a critical question to ask when representing prospective franchisees of a U.S.-based or other foreign-based franchise system. This is because the presence of other franchisees in the territorial vicinity of the prospective franchisee could assist it in its efforts to build brand awareness for the offering in question. This issue may be more relevant and impactful for some franchisees than for others, depending on the industry, the level of existing brand awareness (due to cross-border travel, for example), the extent of the marketing support offered by the franchisor (or Canadian master or area developer), and the state of competition. In the worst case scenario, where a critical mass of franchisees is necessary to generate the required amount of interest in the product or service being offered, and it is not achieved within a certain timeframe, the lone franchisees may feel abandoned by their franchisor, alone in representing the brand to Canadians within their territories.

2. *How committed is the franchisor to expansion into Canada and to its Canadian franchisees?*

This question is inextricably linked to the previous one, as franchisors who are committed to expansion into Canada will often make a concerted effort to find more franchisees willing to service territories throughout Canada. Issues often arise when a U.S. or foreign franchisor behaves in a restrictive manner, rather than in a deliberate one, to develop territories throughout Canada. That is, where a franchisor decides to expand into Canada solely in response to an offer by a prospective Canadian franchisee to purchase a franchise (sometimes referred to as a "pull" expansion), such franchisor will likely not have developed as detailed and well-conceived a plan for expansion into Canada as it would if it had made the strategic decision to expand at its own initiative (sometimes referred to as a "push" expansion). Prospective franchisees should assure themselves that their franchisors are truly committed to expanding their franchise systems into Canada before investing in the purchase of a franchise. Clearly, however, this may be less of an issue where a Canadian master is appointed by the U.S. or foreign franchisor, as the Canadian master will presumably be focused exclusively on the Canadian expansion and will have developed a plan for doing so aggressively and profitably.

3. *How (and how well) is the franchisor or the master/area developer, if applicable, delivering its training and operational support to Canadian franchisees? How well-capitalized is the franchisor or the master/area developer—will it continue to be able to meet those obligations?*

The corollary of the foregoing analysis should include some examination and confirmation that the U.S. or foreign franchisor (or Canadian master franchisee) has tailored its training and support mechanisms for the Canadian landscape and that it has, and has dedicated, the required resources to carry out its training and support obligations. Important insights can be gleaned from a careful review of the franchisor's financial statements attached to the franchise disclosure document. These may indicate not only the profitability and financial condition of the franchisor, generally, but also provide information on the amount of money (both in absolute dollars and as a percentage of revenues), that the franchisor is spending to support the system (e.g., through advertising, training and back office support). In addition, if the franchisor is new, thinly capitalized or has had financial difficulties in the past, the notes to the financials, or even the risk warnings on the cover of the franchise disclosure document, can provide useful information and details, all of which the franchisee should discuss with its financial and business advisors when assessing the value and risk profile of the proposed franchise acquisition.

B. Marketing Funds and Other Pooled Resources

Franchise agreements typically require that franchisees contribute a certain fixed amount or percentage of their gross revenues into a marketing fund established and managed by their franchisors. Where a U.S. or foreign franchisor is involved, however, the term "national marketing fund" should raise a number of questions in the minds of prospective franchisees.

First, when referencing the term "national," is the franchisor looking to have its Canadian prospective franchisees make their marketing fund contributions toward a U.S.-based or foreign-based fund for purposes of financing marketing and advertising campaigns that are launched and operated in jurisdictions outside of Canada? If so, a Canadian prospective franchisee may not at all benefit from making such contributions and it should therefore request that the U.S. or foreign franchisor earmark such funds specifically for Canadian campaigns in a geographical area that encompasses the prospective franchisee's territory.

Second, though it may sound trite, it is also important to ensure that promotional literature, flyers, Internet advertising, and other marketing and advertising materials are directed to the specific target audience. Accordingly, Canadian prospective franchisees should confirm that their U.S. or foreign franchisors have Canadianized their marketing and advertising campaigns to tailor them to Canadian tastes and preferences.

Third, the foregoing analysis would apply not only to a national marketing fund, but also regional and local ones where such funds do not include the applicable Canadian territories, and will also be relevant to other circumstances where franchisees are required to pool their financial resources.

Finally, where a prospective franchisee is considering the purchase of a franchise from a master whose rights derive from a U.S. or foreign franchisor, it should confirm that the master, and not the U.S. or foreign franchisor, manages and controls the marketing fund and where the master does so manage and control the marketing fund, that the master is fully aware of local needs and preferences.

C. How to Deal with Disclosure Deficiencies

As was noted above, one of the key roles of the franchisee's counsel is to review the franchisor's FDD, not only for content, but for deficiencies (i.e., failures to comply with applicable franchise legislation). A detailed discussion of the sorts of deficiencies that will render an FDD invalid, and thus afford the franchisee an opportunity to rescind the franchise agreement and to claim its losses against the franchisor, is set forth in Chapter 6. The main issue for our present purposes is to consider how best to advise the prospective franchisee when such deficiencies become apparent to its counsel during the course of its review.

To a certain degree, this question may turn on the nature and scope of the deficiency. For example, the franchisee's approach to a delivery or timing deficiency (e.g., the FDD is disclosed by an impermissible means of delivery or is delivered after the franchisee has signed the franchise agreement or paid the franchisor a sum of money) may be quite different from its approach to a content deficiency (e.g., the FDD is missing certain material facts, such as the most recently completed fiscal year's financial statements). In either case, counsel must obviously inform the franchisee of the deficiency and of the remedies that potentially are available, ideally in the form of a written report or opinion. However, often the more interesting question is whether to alert the franchisor to the problem.

One may argue that the duty of fair dealing under the franchise legislation of the various Canadian provinces would require the franchisee to bring any material disclosure deficiency to the franchisor's attention. However, in the authors' view, the better argument is that, since the duty of fair dealing refers on its express terms to the "performance and enforcement" of the franchise agreement, it does not arise until after the FDD has been delivered and the franchise agreement has been signed.

The more practical issue that arises is that the sort of content deficiency that would give rise to a valid rescission claim generally (if not necessarily) involves the omission of material facts, which, by definition, are required for the franchisee to be able to make a fully informed decision about whether to buy the franchise. In other words, the franchisee is faced with a dilemma, in that there is a trade-off between: (a) telling the franchisor and possibly obtaining more valuable information on which to base the franchisee's purchase decision and (b) not telling the franchisor and thus holding the rescission claim in reserve in the event that the franchisee loses money during its first two years of operations. Indeed, not surprisingly, it is often the case that the more desirable or valuable the missing information is, the stronger the rescission claim based on its absence would be. Accordingly, how to proceed in a given situation is a matter of both professional judgment and commercial necessity.

In the case of a foreign-based franchisor it is also, at least in part, a question of how readily enforceable the possible rescission claim would be (see Part V, below, for a more detailed discussion of enforcement issues); with the franchisor's lack of assets and operations in Canada serving to reduce the expected value of the claim and thus suggesting that a relatively greater value be placed on the information to be gained from informing the franchisor and having the deficiency corrected.

IV. Negotiating Key Provisions of or Amendments to a Franchise or Multi-Unit Development Agreement

As with domestic franchises, it is often the case that there is very little opportunity to negotiate changes to the standard terms offered by a franchisor to its domestic franchisees. There are, however, a number of areas and circumstances in which the franchisor may be prepared to be flexible and/or where the franchisee may have additional leverage, including due to the heightened risk of international expansion and the additional legal or business responsibilities the franchisee may face.

A. Territory and Expansion Rights

Obtaining territorial rights is not always of primary concern to a Canadian prospective franchisee as their importance will often depend on the franchise system under consideration. Some franchise systems operate more seamlessly and effectively when their franchisees are not granted exclusive territories, for example, or other territorial rights. In such systems, franchisees may be permitted to offer their systems' products or services to any of their customers no matter where they are located in Canada and conversely, their franchisors may be entitled to situate new franchises even within a short distance from their existing franchisees. Franchisors of mature franchise systems are less likely to offer exclusive or other territorial rights, than are new or emerging franchisors. A franchise system that is mature in the franchisor's home country may still be new and relatively unknown in Canada, leading to a lengthier discussion about the need for an exclusive territory.

Where obtaining exclusive rights to a territory or other territorial rights is important to a prospective franchisee for it to have an opportunity to succeed, it should do its utmost to ensure that the U.S. or foreign franchisor is not permitted to easily eliminate or reduce the territorial exclusivity (e.g., on unreasonable grounds or by exempting various scenarios from the grant of exclusive rights to a territory through a broad "reservation of rights" clause). Canadian prospective franchisees should also be wary of provisions in their franchise agreements that permit their assignment to other franchisor entities or masters who have not explicitly assumed the obligations and liabilities of the U.S. or foreign franchisor.

Where exclusive territorial rights are important and where possible, a prospective Canadian franchisee may attempt to obtain a right to expand its pre-existing territory in the form of a right of first refusal or "right of first offer." U.S.

or foreign franchisors will typically be reluctant to accommodate such requests as they understandably wish to avoid scenarios where they are precluded from expanding their franchise systems in certain yet undeveloped territories. If amenable, however, a franchisee may be required to pay its franchisor certain monies that may be characterized as an area development or other expansion fee to obtain and retain such a privilege.

B. Development Schedules

Where a Canadian prospective franchisee is offered the right to open and operate more than one franchised unit, it is most often required to do so pursuant to a multi-unit development agreement. Such agreements typically will require that it open and continuously operate a certain number of units on an annual basis in accordance within a certain designated development schedule. In return for a franchisor's agreement not to develop the development territory, the franchisee is typically required to agree to certain material adverse consequences should it fail to meet the development schedule, such as a reduction of its territorial rights, the imposition of financial penalties and in the worst case scenario, termination of the multi-unit development agreement and/or franchise agreement. A franchisee seeking development rights should attempt to limit its franchisor's remedies, at a minimum by seeking extensions of time in which it could more likely meet its development requirements. Also, force majeure events should extend the development periods to accommodate the duration and the likely impact of the force majeure event. Finally, the area development agreement should be amended to relieve the franchisee from its failure to abide by the development schedule where its failure to do so is related to the franchisor's breach of the franchise or area development agreement.

C. Withholding Tax Issues

Whenever a Canadian resident franchisee makes a payment to a non-resident franchisor, the issue of withholding tax under the *Income Tax Act* (Canada) (the ITA) must be considered. Payments of franchise fees, royalties, and rent are among the types of payments that are generally subject to a 25% withholding tax on the gross amount (subject to any reduced rate established by way of a tax treaty between Canada and the franchisor's home country, such as the *Canada-United States Tax Convention (1980)*, which reduces the rate of withholding on royalties to 10%).

While a detailed discussion of withholding taxes is beyond the scope of this chapter, when advising the Canadian franchisee of a foreign-based system, counsel should advise the franchisee of its obligation to withhold from each payment to the franchisor, and to remit to the Canada Revenue Agency (CRA), the required amount of withholding tax within the time period mandated by the ITA. Specifically, the withheld amounts must be remitted to CRA on or before the 15th day of the month following the month in which the amount was paid to the non-resident. If the franchisee fails to do so or is more than seven days late then, in addition to charging the franchisee interest, CRA may assess a penalty equal to 10% of the amount required to be withheld, and if the franchisee receives more than one penalty in a calendar year for failure to remit or for late payment, CRA may assess a 20% penalty in respect of the second and subsequent failures if they were made knowingly or under circumstances of gross negligence.

Although it is the franchisee's responsibility to withhold and remit the tax, the franchisee is actually doing so on behalf of the franchisor. Accordingly, the franchise agreement will typically contain a positive obligation on the franchisee to withhold and remit the appropriate amounts in a timely fashion. Foreign franchisors will often require a gross-up of any payments required to be made by their Canadian franchisees so that the franchisors receive the full amount they would have been entitled to before payment of the applicable withholding taxes. Franchisees, however, typically will attempt to remove this requirement when negotiating this provision, especially where the franchisors are entitled to a domestic tax credit in their home country for any such withholding taxes paid.

This issue is of course not present for the unit franchisee where its franchise agreement is with a Canadian resident master. However, in that case, the withholding and remittance obligations simply move up a level and become the responsibility of the master, to be discharged by it when it makes its own payments, under its master franchise agreement, to the non-resident franchisor.

D. Conversion of Funds and Currency

On top of the risks that are already inherent in a franchise opportunity, foreign-based franchisors (at least those based in countries, such as the United States, that have a traditionally stable currency) often require payments under the franchise agreement to be made in their home currency. This places an element of foreign exchange risk on the franchisee and potentially makes its risk profile even less palatable than it would otherwise be (and less appealing than it might be in an equivalent Canadian-based system, or in a system where all payments are made to a domestic master). Obviously, there is always the possibility that the exchange rate can move in the franchisee's favour but, as noted, this issue usually comes up in circumstances where the franchisor's home currency is strong, and where the expected direction of the exchange rate over the term of the franchise is thus expected to be to the advantage of the franchisor.

It should be noted that the issue arises not only with respect to fees and royalties, but also on purchases of supplies and inventory to the extent that they are required to be purchased from the foreign franchisor or another (offshore) designated supplier.

Franchisee counsel should be sure to advise the franchisee to try to minimize this risk through all available measures, including by seeking amendments to the franchise agreement to allow for the sourcing of supplies and equipment from Canadian domestic sources. As discussed above, this may not be possible in respect of the purchase of specialized, proprietary products, but for most products, the franchisee should be permitted to source them locally, subject to the franchisor's reasonable approval to assure consistent quality.

E. Personal Liability: Guarantees and Indemnification

Personal liability will arise in various contexts of a franchise agreement involving a Canadian franchisee, including the following: (i) a personal guarantee; (ii) indemnities in favour of a franchisor; or (iii) where a principal of a franchisee is required to uphold certain of the obligations of a franchisee, including confidentiality obligations and restrictive covenants such as non-competition and non-solicitation obligations. Generally speaking, franchisors will require that the directing minds of a corporate franchisee be personally liable for the franchisee's covenants under a franchise agreement. Such directing minds may include any number and combination of directors, officers and shareholders of the franchisee. A franchisor will often demand that its franchisees provide guarantees to secure a promise to pay a monetary debt, such as continuing royalty payments, but they may also be required to secure non-monetary obligations under the franchise agreement and other agreements, such as the confidentiality obligations and restrictive covenants, and to support indemnification for any amounts owing by the franchisees to their franchisor and other assorted obligations of franchisees.

Many franchisors will refuse to waive the requirement of a personal guarantee, and few are willing to negotiate the terms and conditions of this requirement, which they see as being critical to managing their risk. Some franchisors, however, may be open to negotiating guarantees if they are operating a new or emerging franchise system, their franchisees are sophisticated investors, or they are otherwise motivated enough to do so. Though franchisors are generally reluctant to remove the guarantee in its entirety, many are inclined to negotiate a limit on the personal liability and on the kinds of obligations that are to be guaranteed by a guarantor.

Under a typical indemnification provision, a franchisee and its principals would be required to hold harmless their franchisor for losses or damages incurred by the franchisor as a result of the actions or omissions of the franchisee and its principals. Franchisors will often require that such parties agree to indemnify not only the franchisor, but also the franchisor's affiliates, and each of its and their shareholders, directors, officers, employees and agents. As with guarantees, though indemnification provisions are common in Canadian franchise agreements, and though franchisors are generally unwilling to remove them in their entirety, some franchisors are willing to consider negotiating the limit and scope of the indemnity provisions.

In the Province of Alberta, it is important to note that a personal guarantee will not be enforceable unless certain technical requirements are met. In particular, the Alberta's *Guarantees Acknowledgement Act*, R.S.A 2000, C G-11 (the GAA) requires that a guarantor acknowledge to a lawyer that he or she signed the guarantee, and that the guarantor sign a certain prescribed form in the lawyer's presence certifying that the guarantor was aware of and understood the contents of the guarantee. Until recently, the GAA required that the guarantor acknowledge that he or she signed the guarantee and then sign the prescribed form in front of a notary public and it further limited the amount that a notary public could charge for this service to a certain maximum fee. However, as of April 30, 2015, the GAA has been amended by requiring that only lawyers in good standing provide this service and by removing any maximum fee that could be charged. It is also important to note that the lawyer must be an active member of the Law Society of Alberta. Failure to abide by the requirements of the GAA has significant consequences, as doing so will nullify a guarantee that was signed in the Province of Alberta.

F. Restrictive Covenants: Non-competition and Non-solicitation

As in the United States and in other jurisdictions, a typical Canadian franchise agreement will likely contain restrictive covenants, such as non-competition and non-solicitation covenants. Generally, these covenants will apply to both the term of the franchise agreement and the period of time immediately following its expiration or termination.

1. Non-competition Covenants

While Canadian courts generally show a great deal of deference to freedom of contract, they are reluctant to enforce non-competition covenants against franchisees and ex-employees, for example, as such provisions are often seen as unduly restricting such persons or entities from earning a livelihood.

In assessing the enforceability of non-competition covenants, Canadian courts will only permit reasonable restrictions on trade. In determining the enforceability of a non-competition covenant, a Canadian court will generally consider the legitimate business interests of the franchisor and the system, and the level of protection required to protect these interests. In particular, in 2016 the

Ontario Court of Appeal ruled that a restrictive covenant may not be enforceable if it does not protect the legitimate interests of the party in whose favour it is granted. Therefore, there must be an actual legitimate interest to be protected within the geographical and temporal constraints of the covenant in question. In *MEDIchair LP v. DME Medequip Inc.*, 2016 ONCA 168, 2016 CarswellOnt 2700 (*MEDIchair*) at paragraphs 45–47, the Ontario Court of Appeal overturned a lower court's enforcement of a franchisor's restrictive covenant against an ex-franchisee because the franchisor did not intend to operate in the territory in question. As a result, the court ruled that the franchisor had no legitimate interest to be protected and, therefore, there was no reason to restrict the ex-franchisee's actions.

In general, if the restrictiveness of the covenant is unreasonable—in that it provides the franchisor with more protection than is necessary—the covenant may not be enforceable (*MEDIchair* at paras 38-40, 47-48). In order to determine the reasonableness of the covenant, the court will consider three factors:

(i) the geographical restriction covered by the covenant;
(ii) the length in months or years of the covenant; and
(iii) the scope of activity covered by the restriction.

Evaluating the reasonableness of the above factors involves considering both the franchisor's interests at the time the covenant is entered into (usually when the franchise agreement is executed) and the franchisor's interests that were reasonably foreseeable at the time the covenant was agreed upon. For example, when assessing the reasonableness of the geographical restriction of a covenant, Canadian courts will consider the reasonable mutual expectations of both parties at the time of making the contract (*Canadian American Financial Corp v King* (1989) 25 CPR 3d (315) at para 17). This means that if, at the time the franchisee signs a franchise agreement, it is aware that the franchisor reasonably expects to expand to a particular area, the franchisor may protect this area from competition by that particular franchisee, even though the franchisor does not have locations in that area at the time that they enter into the franchise agreement.

Generally, the more narrowly defined the non-competition covenant, the more likely a court will enforce the provision. If a covenant is applicable for too lengthy a period, the geographical area too far-reaching, or the definition of the competitive behaviour that is prohibited is deemed to be too broad in scope, a Canadian court is likely to strike out the entirety of the covenant and will refuse to apply a blue pencil rule (*Transport North American Express Inc. v. New Solutions Financial Corp.* [2004] 1 S.C.R. 249 at para 57). This is in contrast to U.S. courts, which are more likely to read down an overly restrictive non-competition covenant to render it enforceable.

Canadian courts are also unlikely to enforce a non-competition covenant that is longer than two years in duration. However, this is not an absolute rule; the court will determine the acceptable duration of the covenant by assessing the actual protection the franchisor and the system requires to recover from the departure of the franchisee from the system.

Finally, Canadian courts are more likely to enforce non-competition provisions in commercial contexts, such as the sale of a business, or in a franchising context, than in employment scenarios (*Ibid* at para 33). The Supreme Court of Canada has held that the criteria for determining the enforceability of restrictive covenants in a commercial contract is "less demanding" and that in a commercial context, "a restrictive covenant is lawful unless it can be established on a balance of probabilities that its scope is unreasonable" (*Payette v. Guay*, 2013 SCC 45, [2013] 3 S.C.R. 95 (S.C.C.) at para 58; *MEDIchair LP v. DME Medequip Inc.* (2015) 2015 CarswellOnt 10810 at paras 32-35).

2. Non-Solicitation Covenants

In contrast to non-competition covenants, non-solicitation covenants are more often and likely enforced by Canadian courts, because they are less restrictive on the departing party's ability to make a living (*Martin v. ConCreate USL Ltd. Partnership* (2012), 98 C.C.E.L. (3d) 177, 2012 CarswellOnt 3701, 2012 ONSC 1840 (Ont. S.C.J.) at para 5). The underlying rationale for the enforcement of non-solicitation covenants is that a franchisee only gained access to valuable business information and contacts because of its involvement in the franchise system.

To make a non-solicitation covenant more enforceable, a franchisor should clearly identify the parties that are not to be solicited. It is, however, less important to specify geographical restrictions and the duration of the non-solicitation covenant than it is with non-competition covenants.

The language of a restrictive covenant should be clear and unambiguous. However, Canadian courts may enforce non-solicitation provisions, even when they are ambiguous. In *Imvescor Restaurants Inc. v. 3574423 Canada Inc.*, the Ontario Court of Appeal ruled that it would only find a covenant so ambiguous as to be unenforceable if there was no intelligible meaning to the language used in the covenant. In addition, the language of the covenant could be supplemented by the franchise agreement in order to resolve ambiguity (*Imvescor Restaurants Inc. v. 3574423 Canada Inc.*, 2012 ONCA 387, 2012 CarswellOnt 7010 at paras 16-20).

The Ontario Superior Court of Justice has also ruled that where there is a clear breach of a restrictive covenant, the party seeking to enforce the covenant does not need to show "irreparable harm... unless special circumstances exist" as "the court will not give a contracting party a "'holiday' from a clear promise." (*Ontario Duct Cleaning Ltd. v. Wiles*, 2001 CarswellOnt 6190, [2001] O.J. No. 5150 at para 3). This means that the franchisor need not demonstrate that the former franchisee has actually caused significant damage to the system through solicitation in order to enforce the provision.

Finally, in the context of a master franchise agreement, for example, a franchisor may be unable to enforce a non-competition or non-solicitation provision against a subfranchisee if the franchisor is not a party to the franchise agreement between the master franchisee and the subfranchisee. To more readily and directly enforce a restrictive covenant, therefore, a franchisor may want to become a signatory to the restrictive covenant as well, to ensure that there is privity of contract in this regard between the franchisor and the subfranchisee. There are risks however in so doing, as the franchisor may then be exposed to potential liability insofar as it may be deemed to be a franchisor in the market.

V. Dispute Resolution and Enforcement Issues

One final area in which the franchisee faces a different risk profile with a foreign-based franchisor than it does with a Canadian franchisor is that of dispute resolution and enforcement issues. On the one hand, Canada's provincial franchise statutes provide some assistance by requiring at least some disputes to be adjudicated in the franchisee's home province and in accordance with that province's laws, but various practical issues and complexities persist, thereby making enforcement of a judgment against the franchisor more difficult.

A. Statutory Requirements

On the statutory side, Canadian franchise disclosure legislation prohibits any provision in a franchise agreement that would purport to restrict the application of the applicable provincial law or the jurisdiction or venue to a forum outside of the province and, in fact, renders such a provision void with respect to a claim otherwise enforceable under such legislation. In other words, at least as far as statute-based franchise claims are concerned, a franchisee whose franchise agreement is subject to the *Wishart Act* in the Province of Ontario, for example, has a right to have those claims adjudicated in Ontario under Ontario law.

Arguments are often made to the effect that non-statutory claims, such as claims for breach of contract, may be adjudicated in, and subject to the laws of, another jurisdiction, such as that of the franchisor's home territory. If this argument were to prevail, it could lead to bifurcated proceedings in multiple jurisdictions. While the matter is not settled in law, as a general matter, a franchisee operating in a Canadian province with franchise legislation should be able to insist on having its principal claims and remedies dealt with by its domestic counsel in its home jurisdiction.

It should be noted that, with very few specific exceptions (such as, for example, in respect of farm equipment dealers in Saskatchewan), Canada generally does not have the sorts of dealer protection laws that are present in other jurisdictions, including certain U.S. states. Accordingly, while Canada's disclosure provinces all impose a duty of good faith and fair dealing on all parties to a franchise agreement (as described in detail in Chapter 6), there are no specific protections for franchisees, such as mandated notice periods for termination or nonrenewal, beyond what may be required under common law in order to comply with the aforementioned duty.

B. Enforcement Issues

Even assuming that the franchisee is able to secure a hearing and judgment in its home province, that may not mean much if the franchisor has no assets in the jurisdiction and the franchisee is unable to enforce the judgment in the jurisdiction where those assets are located.

The first question franchisee counsel should ask (and help answer) is regarding the existence of franchisor's assets, if any, in the relevant Canadian province. As part of the franchisee's due diligence efforts, discussed above, counsel should perform local personal property security and related searches on the franchisor and its affiliates to determine what assets might be present and available to satisfy a potential judgment against the franchisor.

Secondly, even if the franchisor has assets in the jurisdiction (but more importantly if it does not, or the assets are already substantially encumbered), franchisee counsel should assess the ease or difficulty with which a judgment in the Canadian court could be enforced in the franchisor's home jurisdiction (or another jurisdiction in which the franchisor has significant assets). This analysis typically depends on a number of factors, including whether a treaty for the reciprocal enforcement of judgments exists between the franchisor's home jurisdiction and that in which the franchisee will be conducting its business.

Many jurisdictions' courts, including those of most of Canada's provinces and most U.S. states, will recognize and enforce (i.e., "domesticate") judgments obtained in other jurisdictions only if a new proceeding is commenced in their own local courts. In other words, the judgment creditor is required to sue on the judgment (again) in the judgment debtor's home jurisdiction. Although many such provinces and states provide that such a proceeding may be commenced in accordance with summary procedural rules, this is a second step that is not generally required if there is a reciprocal enforcement of judgments treaty in place between the two jurisdictions. Such a treaty would typically allow for the foreign judgment to be registered with the local court and enforced in the same fashion as one of its own judgments would be.

Accordingly, the procedure faced by Canadian franchisees attempting to enforce a judgment against a Canadian-based franchisor, which is based in another province or state with which the franchisee's home province has a reciprocal enforcement treaty, is considerably simpler than that faced by a Canadian franchisee attempting to enforce a judgment against a foreign-based franchisor in a non-treaty state. In essence, each province (i.e., each common-law province) has granted "full faith and credit" to each other province and to certain treaty states, thereby making enforcement as between franchisees and franchisors within and between those treaty jurisdictions somewhat simpler, and thus highlighting one further additional risk faced by franchisees who buy into franchise systems that are based in non-treaty jurisdictions.

That said, however, whether a treaty is in place or not, the Canadian franchisee (as judgment creditor) would still have to satisfy the local court that the judgment was properly obtained in the eyes of that local court as part of the domestication process. In attempting to enforce a Canadian judgment in a U.S. court, for example, the Canadian judgment creditor would have to demonstrate to the satisfaction of the U.S. court that the judgment debtor's (i.e., the franchisor's) due process rights were respected in obtaining the judgment.

Similarly, the judgment creditor might be faced with, and should be prepared to defend against, the argument that the judgment was based on a cause of action that would run afoul of public policy in the relevant U.S. state. Given the similarities between U.S. and Canadian common law, this is often not a major concern in enforcing a judgment based on a common law cause of action; it is somewhat more of a concern, however, when attempting to enforce a Québec civil law judgment or a judgment based upon a statutory right of action (although, historically, this has not been a major hurdle to Canadian franchisees in the enforcement of judgments based on claims under the *Wishart Act* or other similar provincial legislation).

In the result, even where the franchisor is based in a treaty jurisdiction whose laws are not dissimilar to those of the franchisee's Canadian home province, the franchisee's Canadian counsel should take care to advise the franchisee properly of the additional hurdles it may have to clear in order to enforce its rights against the foreign-based franchisor.

As a final consideration, however, here again the involvement of a Canadian master or area developer, with assets in the jurisdiction, may improve the franchisee's ability to enforce its franchise agreement. To the extent that the Canadian master or area developer would be the main party that will stand in privity to the franchisee, this may not only improve the franchisee's prospects from an operational standpoint, as described above, but may also provide an additional, local counterparty against whom to seek recourse if something goes wrong.

Appendix:
Provincial Franchise Laws in Canada
(as of April 2017)

Table of Concordance

Websites Listing Provincial Statutes

Alberta

a. Franchises Act, RSA 2000, c F-23 - http://canlii.ca/t/j8qr
   i. Franchises Regulation, Alta Reg 240/1995 - http://canlii.ca/t/52jdm
   ii. Franchises Act Exemption Regulation, Alta Reg 312/2000 - http://canlii.ca/t/52tv8

British Columbia

a. Franchises Act, SBC 2015, c 35 - http://canlii.ca/t/52w95
   i. Franchises Regulation, BC Reg 238/2016 - http://canlii.ca/t/52tv0

Manitoba

a. The Franchises Act, CCSM c F156 - http://canlii.ca/t/51wps
   i. Franchises Regulation, Man Reg 29/2012 - http://canlii.ca/t/lg6q

New Brunswick

a. Franchises Act, SNB 2014, c 111 - http://canlii.ca/t/52dnt
   i. Disclosure Document Regulation, NB Reg 2010-92 - http://canlii.ca/t/ktwg
   ii. Mediation Regulation, NB Reg 2010-93 - http://canlii.ca/t/ktwh

Ontario

a. Arthur Wishart Act (Franchise Disclosure), 2000, SO 2000, c 3 - http://canlii.ca/t/kq2q
   i. General, O Reg 581/00 - http://canlii.ca/t/52rm0

Prince Edward Island

a. Franchises Act, RSPEI 1988, c F-14.1 - http://canlii.ca/t/52kjm
i. Franchises Act Regulations, PEI Reg EC232/06 - http://canlii.ca/t/k485

TOPIC	PRINCE EDWARD ISLAND	NEW BRUNSWICK	ONTARIO	MANITOBA	BRITISH COLUMBIA	ALBERTA
Franchises Acts						
Title of Statute	***Franchises Act*, R.S.P.E.I. 1988, c. F-14.1**	***Franchises Act*, R.S.N.B. 2014, c. 111**	***Arthur Wishart Act (Franchise Disclosure)*, 2000, S.O. 2000, c. 3**	***The Franchises Act*, C.C.S.M., c. F156**	***Franchises Act*, S.B.C. 2015, c. 35**	***Franchises Act*, R.S.A. 2000, c. F-23**
	BE IT ENACTED by the Lieutenant Governor and the Legislative Assembly of the Province of Prince Edward Island as follows:			HER MAJESTY, by and with the advice and consent of the Legislative Assembly of Manitoba, enacts as follows:	HER MAJESTY, by and with the advice and consent of the Legislative Assembly of the Province of British Columbia, enacts as follows:	HER MAJESTY, by and with the advice and consent of the Legislative Assembly of Alberta, enacts as follows:
Definitions and Interpretation	**1.** (1) In this Act	**1**(1) The following definitions apply in this Act.	**1.** (1) In this Act,	**1**(1) The following definitions apply in this Act.	**1** (1) In this Act:	**1**(1) In this Act,
"Commission"		"Commission" means the Financial and Consumer Services Commission continued under the *Financial and Consumer Services Commission Act*. *(Commission)*				
"disclosure document"	(a) "disclosure document" means the disclosure document required by section 5;	"disclosure document" means the disclosure document required by section 5. *(document d'information)*	"disclosure document" means the disclosure document required by section 5; ("document d'information")	"disclosure document" means the disclosure document required by section 5. (« document d'information »)	"disclosure document" means a disclosure document required by section 5;	(a) "disclosure document" means a disclosure document required to be given under section 4 and includes any changes required to be given under section 4(4);
"former Act"						(b) "former Act" means the *Franchises Act*, RSA 1980 cF-17, as it read immediately before October 31, 1995;
"fractional franchise"						(c) "fractional franchise" means a franchise granted

TOPIC	PRINCE EDWARD ISLAND	NEW BRUNSWICK	ONTARIO	MANITOBA	BRITISH COLUMBIA	ALBERTA
Franchises Acts						
						to a person to sell goods or services within a business in which that person has an interest, the sales arising from which, as anticipated by the parties or that should be anticipated by the parties at the time the franchise is entered into, do not exceed, in relation to the total sales of the business, the percentage prescribed by the regulations;
"franchise"	(b) "franchise" means a right to engage in a business where the franchisee is required by contract or otherwise to make a payment or continuing payments, whether direct or indirect, or a commitment to make such payment or payments, to the franchisor or the franchisor's associate in the course of operating the business or as a condition of acquiring the franchise or commencing operations and,	"franchise" means a right to engage in a business in which the franchisee is required by contract or otherwise to make a payment or continuing payments, whether direct or indirect, or a commitment to make the payment or payments, to the franchisor or the franchisor's associate in the course of operating the business or as a condition of acquiring the franchise or commencing operations, and *(franchise)*	"franchise" means a right to engage in a business where the franchisee is required by contract or otherwise to make a payment or continuing payments, whether direct or indirect, or a commitment to make such payment or payments, to the franchisor, or the franchisor's associate, in the course of operating the business or as a condition of acquiring the franchise or commencing operations and,	"franchise" means a right to engage in a business in which the franchisee is required by contract or otherwise to make a payment or continuing payments (whether direct or indirect) or a commitment to make that payment or those payments to the franchisor or the franchisor's associate in the course of operating the business or as a condition of acquiring the franchise or commencing operations, and	"franchise" means a right to engage in a business in which a franchisee is required by contract or otherwise to make a payment or continuing payments, whether direct or indirect, or a commitment to make that payment or those payments, to a franchisor, or a franchisor's associate, in the course of operating the business or as a condition of acquiring the franchise or commencing operations, and	(d) "franchise" means a right to engage in a business (i) in which goods or services are sold or offered for sale or are distributed under a marketing or business plan prescribed in substantial part by the franchisor or its associate, (ii) that is substantially associated with a trademark, service mark, trade name, logotype or advertising of the franchisor or its associate or designating the franchisor or its associate, and (iii) that involves (A) a continuing
	(i) in which	(a) in which	(a) in which,	(a) in which	(a) in which	
	(A) the franchisor grants	(i) the franchisor grants	(i) the franchisor grants	(i) the franchisor grants	(i) the franchisor grants	

TOPIC	PRINCE EDWARD ISLAND	NEW BRUNSWICK	ONTARIO	MANITOBA	BRITISH COLUMBIA	ALBERTA
Franchises Acts						
	the franchisee the right to sell, offer for sale or distribute goods or services that are substantially associated with the franchisor's, or the franchisor's associate's, trade-mark, trade name, logo or advertising or other commercial symbol, and	the franchisee the right to sell, offer for sale or distribute goods or services that are substantially associated with the franchisor's, or the franchisor's associate's, trade-mark, trade name, logo or advertising or other commercial symbol, and	the franchisee the right to sell, offer for sale or distribute goods or services that are substantially associated with the franchisor's, or the franchisor's associate's, trade-mark, service mark, trade name, logo or advertising or other commercial symbol, and	the franchisee the right to sell, offer for sale or distribute goods or services that are substantially associated with the franchisor's, or the franchisor's associate's, trademark, trade name, logo or advertising, and	the franchisee the right to sell, offer for sale or distribute goods or services that are substantially associated with the franchisor's or the franchisor's associate's trademark, trade name, logo or advertising or other commercial symbol, and	financial obligation to the franchisor or its associate by the franchisee and significant continuing operational controls by the franchisor or its associate on the operations of the franchised business, or (B) the payment of a franchise fee, and includes a master franchise and a subfranchise;
	(B) the franchisor or the franchisor's associate exercises significant control over, or offers significant assistance in, the franchisee's method of operation, including building design and furnishings, locations, business organization, marketing techniques or training, or	(ii) the franchisor or the franchisor's associate exercises significant control over, or offers significant assistance in, the franchisee's method of operation, including building design and furnishings, locations, business organization, marketing techniques or training, or	(ii) the franchisor or the franchisor's associate exercises significant control over, or offers significant assistance in, the franchisee's method of operation, including building design and furnishings, locations, business organization, marketing techniques or training, or	(ii) the franchisor or the franchisor's associate exercises significant control over, or offers significant assistance in, the franchisee's method of operation under a business plan, including building design and furnishings, locations, business organization, marketing strategies or training; or	(ii) the franchisor or the franchisor's associate exercises significant control over, or offers significant assistance for, the franchisee's method of operation, including building design and furnishings, locations, business organization, marketing techniques or training, or	
	(ii) in which	(b) in which	(b) in which,	(b) in which	(b) in which	
	(A) the franchisor or the franchisor's associate grants the franchisee the representational or distribution rights, whether or not a trade-mark, trade name, logo or	(i) the franchisor or the franchisor's associate grants the franchisee the representational or distribution rights, whether or not a trademark, trade name, logo or	(i) the franchisor, or the franchisor's associate, grants the franchisee the representational or distribution rights, whether or not a trade-mark, service mark, trade name,	(i) the franchisor or the franchisor's associate grants the franchisee the representational or distribution rights — whether or not a trademark, trade name, logo or	(i) the franchisor or the franchisor's associate grants the franchisee the representational or distribution rights, whether or not a trademark, trade name, logo or	

TOPIC	PRINCE EDWARD ISLAND	NEW BRUNSWICK	ONTARIO	MANITOBA	BRITISH COLUMBIA	ALBERTA
			Franchises Acts			
	advertising or other commercial symbol is involved, to sell, offer for sale or distribute goods or services supplied by the franchisor or a supplier designated by the franchisor, and	advertising or other commercial symbol is involved, to sell, offer for sale or distribute goods or services supplied by the franchisor or a supplier designated by the franchisor, and	logo or advertising or other commercial symbol is involved, to sell, offer for sale or distribute goods or services supplied by the franchisor or a supplier designated by the franchisor, and	advertising is involved — to sell, offer for sale or distribute goods or services supplied by the franchisor or a supplier designated by the franchisor, and	advertising or other commercial symbol is involved, to sell, offer for sale or distribute goods or services supplied by the franchisor or a supplier designated by the franchisor, and	
	(B) the franchisor or the franchisor's associate or a third person designated by the franchisor, provides location assistance, including securing retail outlets or accounts for the goods or services to be sold, offered for sale or distributed or securing locations or sites for vending machines, display racks or other product sales displays used by the franchisee;	(ii) the franchisor or the franchisor's associate or a third person designated by the franchisor provides location assistance, including securing retail outlets or accounts for the goods or services to be sold, offered for sale or distributed or securing locations or sites for vending machines, display racks or other product sales displays used by the franchisee.	(ii) the franchisor, or the franchisor's associate, or a third person designated by the franchisor, provides location assistance, including securing retail outlets or accounts for the goods or services to be sold, offered for sale or distributed or securing locations or sites for vending machines, display racks or other product sales displays used by the franchisee; ("franchise")	(ii) the franchisor, the franchisor's associate or another person designated by the franchisor provides location assistance, including (A) securing retail outlets or customer accounts for the goods or services to be distributed, offered for sale or sold, or (B) securing locations or sites for vending machines, display racks or other product sales displays used by the franchisee; and includes a master franchise and a subfranchise. (« franchise »)	(ii) the franchisor or the franchisor's associate, or a third person designated by the franchisor, provides location assistance, including (A) securing retail outlets or accounts for the goods or services to be sold, offered for sale or distributed, or (B) securing locations or sites for vending machines, display racks or other product sales displays used by the franchisee;	
"franchise agreement"	(c) "franchise agreement" means any agreement that	"franchise agreement" means any agreement that relates to	"franchise agreement" means any agreement that relates to	"franchise agreement" means any agreement that relates to a	"franchise agreement" means any agreement that relates to	(e) "franchise agreement" means any agreement that

TOPIC	PRINCE EDWARD ISLAND	NEW BRUNSWICK	ONTARIO	MANITOBA	BRITISH COLUMBIA	ALBERTA
Franchises Acts						
	relates to a franchise between,	a franchise and is entered into between *(contrat de franchisage)*	a franchise between,	franchise between	a franchise and is entered into between	relates to a franchise between
	(i) a franchisor or franchisor's associate, and	(a) a franchisor or franchisor's associate, and	(a) a franchisor or franchisor's associate, and	(a) a franchisor or franchisor's associate; and	(a) a franchisor or franchisor's associate, and	(i) a franchisor or its associate, and
	(ii) a franchisee;	(b) a franchisee.	(b) a franchisee; ("contrat de franchisage")	(b) a franchisee. (« contrat de franchisage »)	(b) a franchisee;	(ii) a franchisee or prospective franchisee;
"franchised business"				"franchised business" means a business operating under a franchise agreement. (« entreprise franchisée »)		(h) "franchised business" means a business operating under a franchise agreement;
"franchise fee"						(f) "franchise fee" means a direct or indirect payment to purchase a franchise or to operate a franchised business, but does not include (i) a purchase of or an agreement to purchase a reasonable amount of goods at a reasonable bona fide wholesale price, (ii) a purchase of or an agreement to purchase a reasonable amount of services at a reasonable bona fide price, or (iii) a payment of a reasonable service charge to the issuer of a credit or debit card by an establishment

TOPIC	PRINCE EDWARD ISLAND	NEW BRUNSWICK	ONTARIO	MANITOBA	BRITISH COLUMBIA	ALBERTA
Franchises Acts						
						accepting the credit or debit card, as the case may be;
"franchisee"	(d) "franchisee" means a person to whom a franchise is granted and includes, (i) a subfranchisor with regard to that subfranchisor's relationship with a franchisor, and (ii) a subfranchisee with regard to that subfranchisee's relationship with a subfranchisor;	"franchisee" means a person to whom a franchise is granted and includes *(franchisé)* (a) a subfranchisor with regard to the subfranchisor's relationship with the franchisor, and (b) a subfranchisee with regard to the subfranchisee's relationship with the subfranchisor.	"franchisee" means a person to whom a franchise is granted and includes, (a) a subfranchisor with regard to that subfranchisor's relationship with a franchisor, and (b) a subfranchisee with regard to that subfranchisee's relationship with a subfranchisor; ("franchisé")	"franchisee" means a person to whom a franchise is granted and includes (a) a subfranchisor with regard to that subfranchisor's relationship with a franchisor; and (b) a subfranchisee with regard to that subfranchisee's relationship with a subfranchisor. (« franchisé »)	"franchisee" means a person to whom a franchise is granted, including (a) a subfranchisor with regard to that subfranchisor's relationship with a franchisor, and (b) a subfranchisee with regard to that subfranchisee's relationship with a subfranchisor;	(i) "franchisee" means a person to whom a franchise is granted and includes (i) a subfranchisor with regard to that subfranchisor's relationship with a franchisor, and (ii) a subfranchisee with regard to that subfranchisee's relationship with a subfranchisor;
"franchise system"	(e) "franchise system" includes,	"franchise system" includes *(système de franchise)*	"franchise system" includes,	"franchise system" includes	"franchise system" includes the following:	(g) "franchise system" includes
	(i) the marketing, marketing plan or business plan of the franchise,	(a) the marketing, marketing plan or business plan of the franchise,	(a) the marketing, marketing plan or business plan of the franchise,	(a) the franchise's business plan or marketing plan;	(a) the marketing, marketing plan or business plan of a franchise;	(i) the marketing or business plan of the franchise,
	(ii) the use of or association with a trade-mark, trade name, logo or advertising or other commercial symbol,	(b) the use of or association with a trade-mark, trade name, logo or advertising or other commercial symbol,	(b) the use of or association with a trade-mark, service mark, trade name, logo or advertising or other commercial symbol,	(b) the use of or association with a trademark, trade name, logo or advertising;	(b) the use of or association with a trademark, trade name, logo or advertising or other commercial symbol;	(ii) the use of or association with a trademark, service mark, trade name, logotype or advertising,
	(iii) the obligations of the franchisor and franchisee with regard to the operation of the business operated by the franchisee	(c) the obligations of the franchisor and franchisee with regard to the operation of the business operated by the franchisee under the	(c) the obligations of the franchisor and franchisee with regard to the operation of the business operated by the franchisee under the	(c) the obligations of the franchisor and franchisee with regard to the operation of the franchised business; and	(c) the obligations of a franchisor and franchisee with regard to the operation of the business operated by the franchisee under a	(iii) the obligations of the franchisor and franchisee with regard to the operation of the franchised business,

TOPIC	PRINCE EDWARD ISLAND	NEW BRUNSWICK	ONTARIO	MANITOBA	BRITISH COLUMBIA	ALBERTA
Franchises Acts						
	under the franchise agreement, and	franchise agreement, and	franchise agreement, and		franchise agreement;	and
	(iv) the goodwill associated with the franchise;	(d) the goodwill associated with the franchise.	(d) the goodwill associated with the franchise; ("système de franchise")	(d) the goodwill associated with the franchise. (« système de franchise »)	(d) the goodwill associated with the franchise;	(iv) the goodwill associated with the franchise;
"franchisor"	(f) "franchisor" means one or more persons who grant or offer to grant a franchise and includes a subfranchisor with regard to that subfranchisor's relationship with a subfranchisee;	"franchisor" means a person who grants or offers to grant a franchise and includes a subfranchisor with regard to the subfranchisor's relationship with the subfranchisee. *(franchiseur)*	"franchisor" means one or more persons who grant or offer to grant a franchise and includes a subfranchisor with regard to that subfranchisor's relationship with a subfranchisee; ("franchiseur")	"franchisor" means a person who grants or offers to grant a franchise and includes a subfranchisor with regard to that subfranchisor's relationship with a subfranchisee. (« franchiseur »)	"franchisor" means any person who grants or offers to grant a franchise, including a subfranchisor with regard to that subfranchisor's relationship with a subfranchisee;	(j) "franchisor" means one or more persons who grant a franchise and includes a subfranchisor with regard to its relationship with a subfranchisee;
"franchisor's associate"	(g) "franchisor's associate" means a person (i) who, directly or indirectly, (A) controls or is controlled by the franchisor, or (B) is controlled by another person who also controls, directly or indirectly, the franchisor, and	"franchisor's associate" means a person *(personne qui a un lien)* (a) who, directly or indirectly, (i) controls or is controlled by the franchisor, or (ii) is controlled by another person who also controls, directly or indirectly, the franchisor, and	"franchisor's associate" means a person, (a) who, directly or indirectly, (i) controls or is controlled by the franchisor, or (ii) is controlled by another person who also controls, directly or indirectly, the franchisor, and	"franchisor's associate" means a person (a) who, directly or indirectly, (i) controls the franchisor, (ii) is controlled by the franchisor, or (iii) is controlled by another person who also directly or indirectly controls the franchisor; and	"franchisor's associate" means a person (a) who, directly or indirectly, (i) controls or is controlled by a franchisor, or (ii) is controlled by another person who also controls, directly or indirectly, a franchisor, and	**NOTE: See section 1(2) below.**
	(ii) who, (A) is directly involved in the grant of the franchise, (I) by being involved in reviewing or approving the grant of the franchise, or	(b) who (i) is directly involved in the grant of the franchise (A) by being involved in reviewing or approving the grant of the franchise, or	(b) who, (i) is directly involved in the grant of the franchise, (A) by being involved in reviewing or approving the grant of the franchise, or	(b) who (i) is directly involved in the grant of the franchise (A) by being involved in reviewing or approving the grant, or (B) by making	(b) who (i) is directly involved in the grant of a franchise (A) by being involved in reviewing or approving the grant of the franchise, or	

TOPIC	PRINCE EDWARD ISLAND	NEW BRUNSWICK	ONTARIO	MANITOBA	BRITISH COLUMBIA	ALBERTA
Franchises Acts						
	(II) by making representations to the prospective franchisee on behalf of the franchisor for the purpose of granting the franchise, marketing the franchise or otherwise offering to grant the franchise, or (B) exercises significant operational control over the franchisee and to whom the franchisee has a continuing financial obligation in respect of the franchise;	(B) by making representations to the prospective franchisee on behalf of the franchisor for the purpose of granting the franchise, marketing the franchise or otherwise offering to grant the franchise, or (ii) exercises significant operational control over the franchisee and to whom the franchisee has a continuing financial obligation in respect of the franchise.	(B) by making representations to the prospective franchisee on behalf of the franchisor for the purpose of granting the franchise, marketing the franchise or otherwise offering to grant the franchise, or (ii) exercises significant operational control over the franchisee and to whom the franchisee has a continuing financial obligation in respect of the franchise; ("personne qui a un lien")	representations to the prospective franchisee on behalf of the franchisor for the purpose of granting the franchise, marketing the franchise or otherwise offering to grant the franchise, or (ii) exercises significant operational control over the franchisee and to whom the franchisee has a continuing financial obligation in respect of the franchise. (« personne qui a un lien »)	(B) by making representations to a prospective franchisee on behalf of the franchisor for the purpose of granting the franchise, marketing the franchise or otherwise offering to grant the franchise, or (ii) exercises significant operational control over a franchisee and to whom the franchisee has a continuing financial obligation in respect of a franchise;	
"franchisor's broker"	(h) "franchisor's broker" means a person, other than the franchisor, franchisor's associate or franchisee, who grants, markets or otherwise offers to grant a franchise, or who arranges for the grant of a franchise;	"franchisor's broker" means a person, other than the franchisee, franchisor or franchisor's associate, who, on behalf of the franchisor, grants, markets or otherwise offers to grant a franchise or who arranges for the grant of a franchise. *(courtier du franchiseur)*		"franchisor's broker" means a person — other than the franchisor, franchisor's associate or franchisee — who, on behalf of the franchisor, (a) grants, markets or otherwise offers to grant a franchise; or (b) arranges for the grant of a franchise. (« courtier du franchiseur »)	"franchisor's broker" means a person, other than a franchisee, franchisor or franchisor's associate, who grants, markets or otherwise offers to grant a franchise, or who arranges for the grant of a franchise;	
"grant"	(i) "grant", in respect of a franchise, includes the sale	"grant", in respect of a franchise, includes the sale or	"grant", in respect of a franchise, includes the sale or	"grant", in respect of a franchise, includes the sale or	"grant", in respect of a franchise, includes the	

TOPIC	PRINCE EDWARD ISLAND	NEW BRUNSWICK	ONTARIO	MANITOBA	BRITISH COLUMBIA	ALBERTA
Franchises Acts						
	or disposition of the franchise or of an interest in the franchise and, for such purposes, an interest in the franchise includes the ownership of shares in the corporation that owns the franchise;	disposition of the franchise or of an interest in the franchise and, for those purposes, an interest in the franchise includes the ownership of shares in the corporation that owns the franchise. *(concession)*	disposition of the franchise or of an interest in the franchise and, for such purposes, an interest in the franchise includes the ownership of shares in the corporation that owns the franchise; ("concession")	disposition of the franchise or of an interest in the franchise. (« concession »)	disposition of the franchise or of an interest in the franchise and, for this purpose, an interest in the franchise includes the ownership of shares in the corporation that owns the franchise;	
"interest in the franchise"				"interest in the franchise" includes the ownership of shares in the corporation that owns the franchise. (« intérêt dans la franchise »)		(k) "interest in a franchise" includes the ownership of shares in the corporation that owns the franchise;
"marketing or business plan"						(l) "marketing or business plan" means a plan or system that specifies a material aspect of conducting business, including, without limitation, any one or more of the following: (i) price specification, special pricing systems or discount plans; (ii) sales or display equipment or merchandising devices; (iii) equipment to be used to perform services; (iv) sales techniques; (v) promotional or advertising materials or co-operative advertising;

TOPIC	PRINCE EDWARD ISLAND	NEW BRUNSWICK	ONTARIO	MANITOBA	BRITISH COLUMBIA	ALBERTA
Franchises Acts						
						(vi) training relating to the promotion, operation or management of the business; (vii) operational, managerial, technical or financial guidelines or assistance.
"master franchise"	(j) "master franchise" means a franchise that is a right granted by a franchisor to a subfranchisor to grant or offer to grant franchises for the subfranchisor's own account;	"master franchise" means a franchise that is a right granted by a franchisor to a subfranchisor to grant or offer to grant franchises for the subfranchisor's own account. *(franchise maîtresse)*	"master franchise" means a franchise which is a right granted by a franchisor to a subfranchisor to grant or offer to grant franchises for the subfranchisor's own account; ("franchise maîtresse")	"master franchise" means a franchise that is a right granted by a franchisor to a subfranchisor to grant or offer to grant franchises for the subfranchisor's own account. (« franchise maîtresse »)	"master franchise" means a franchise that is a right granted, by a franchisor to a subfranchisor, to grant or offer to grant franchises for the subfranchisor's own account;	(m) "master franchise" means the right granted by a franchisor to a subfranchisor to sell or offer franchises for the subfranchisor's own account;
"material change"	(k) "material change" means a change, in the business, operations, capital or control of the franchisor or franchisor's associate or in the franchise or the franchise system, that would reasonably be expected to have a significant adverse effect on the value or price of the franchise to be granted or on the decision to acquire the franchise and includes a decision to implement such a change made by the board of directors of the franchisor or franchisor's associate or by senior management of the franchisor or franchisor's associate who	"material change" means a change, in the business, operations, capital or control of the franchisor or franchisor's associate or in the franchise or the franchise system, that would reasonably be expected to have a significant adverse effect on the value or price of the franchise to be granted or on the decision to acquire the franchise and includes a decision to implement such a change made by the board of directors of the franchisor or franchisor's associate or by senior management of the franchisor or franchisor's associate who believe that confirmation of the decision by the board of directors is	"material change" means a change in the business, operations, capital or control of the franchisor or franchisor's associate, a change in the franchise or the franchise system or a prescribed change, that would reasonably be expected to have a significant adverse effect on the value or price of the franchise to be granted or on the decision to acquire the franchise and includes a decision to implement such a change made by the board of directors of the franchisor or franchisor's associate or by senior management of the franchisor or franchisor's associate who believe that confirmation of the decision	"material change" means a change (a) in the business, operations, capital or control of the franchisor or franchisor's associate; or (b) in the franchise or the franchise system; that would reasonably be expected to have a significant adverse effect on the franchise's value or price to be granted or on the decision to acquire the franchise, and includes a decision to implement such a change made by the board of directors of the franchisor or franchisor's associate or	"material change" means a change in the business, operations, capital or control of the franchisor or franchisor's associate, or in the franchise or the franchise system, that would reasonably be expected to have a significant adverse effect on the value or price of the franchise to be granted or on the decision to acquire the franchise, including a decision to implement the change made by the board of directors of the franchisor or franchisor's associate or by senior management of the franchisor or franchisor's associate who believe that confirmation of the decision by the board of directors is	(n) "material change" means (i) a change in the business, operations, capital or control of the franchisor or its associate, or (ii) a change in the franchise system, that would reasonably be expected to have a significant adverse effect on the value or price of the franchise to be sold or the decision to purchase the franchise and includes a decision to implement the change made by the board of directors of the franchisor or its

TOPIC	PRINCE EDWARD ISLAND	NEW BRUNSWICK	ONTARIO	MANITOBA	BRITISH COLUMBIA	ALBERTA
			Franchises Acts			
	believe that confirmation of the decision by the board of directors is probable;	probable. *(changement important)*	by the board of directors is probable; ("changement important")	by senior management of the franchisor or franchisor's associate who believe that the decision's confirmation by the board of directors is probable. (« changement important »)	probable;	associate or by senior management of the franchisor or its associate who believe that confirmation of the decision by the board of directors is probable;
"material fact"	(l) "material fact" means any information, about the business, operations, capital or control of the franchisor or franchisor's associate or about the franchise or the franchise system, that would reasonably be expected to have a significant effect on the value or price of the franchise to be granted or the decision to acquire the franchise;	"material fact" means any information, about the business, operations, capital or control of the franchisor or franchisor's associate or about the franchise or the franchise system, that would reasonably be expected to have a significant effect on the value or price of the franchise to be granted or the decision to acquire the franchise. *(fait important)*	"material fact" includes any information about the business, operations, capital or control of the franchisor or franchisor's associate, or about the franchise system, that would reasonably be expected to have a significant effect on the value or price of the franchise to be granted or the decision to acquire the franchise; ("fait important")	"material fact" means any information about (a) the business, operations, capital or control of the franchisor or franchisor's associate; or (b) the franchise or the franchise system; that would reasonably be expected to have a significant effect on the franchise's value or price to be granted or the decision to acquire the franchise. (« fait important »)	"material fact" means any information about the business, operations, capital or control of the franchisor or franchisor's associate, or about the franchise or the franchise system, that would reasonably be expected to have a significant effect on the value or price of the franchise to be granted or on the decision to acquire the franchise;	(o) "material fact" means any information about the business, operations, capital or control of the franchisor or its associate, or about the franchise system, that would reasonably be expected to have a significant effect on the value or price of the franchise to be sold or the decision to purchase the franchise;
"Minister"	(m) "Minister" means the Minister of Justice and Public Safety and Attorney General;					(p) "Minister" means the Minister determined under section 16 of the *Government Organization Act* as the Minister responsible for this Act;
"misrepresentation"	(n) "misrepresentation" includes, (i) an untrue statement of a material fact, or (ii) an omission to state a material fact that is	"misrepresentation" includes *(assertion inexacte)* (a) an untrue statement of a material fact, or (b) an omission to state a material fact that is	"misrepresentation" includes, (a) an untrue statement of a material fact, or (b) an omission to state a material fact that is required to be stated or	"misrepresentation" includes (a) an untrue statement of a material fact; or (b) an omission to state a material fact that (i) is required to be	"misrepresentation" includes (a) an untrue statement of a material fact, or (b) an omission to state a material fact that is required to be stated or	(q) "misrepresentation" includes (i) an untrue statement of a material fact, (ii) an omission to state a material fact that is

TOPIC	PRINCE EDWARD ISLAND	NEW BRUNSWICK	ONTARIO	MANITOBA	BRITISH COLUMBIA	ALBERTA
			Franchises Acts			
	required to be stated or that is necessary to make a statement not misleading in light of the circumstances in which it was made;	required to be stated or that is necessary to make a statement not misleading in light of the circumstances in which it was made.	that is necessary to make a statement not misleading in the light of the circumstances in which it was made; ("présentation inexacte des faits")	stated, or (ii) is necessary to make a statement not misleading in light of the circumstances in which it was made. (« présentation inexacte des faits »)	that is necessary to make a statement not misleading in light of the circumstances in which it was made;	required to be stated, or (iii) an omission to state a material fact that needs to be stated in order for a statement not to be misleading;
"officer"				"officer" means (a) in relation to a corporation, a chief executive officer, president, vice-president, secretary, controller, treasurer or any other individual designated as an officer of the corporation by by-law or by resolution of the directors of the corporation; (b) any individual who performs functions or acts in a capacity similar to the functions or capacities referred to in clause (a); (c) in relation to any other entity, any individual designated as an officer of the entity by by-law, resolution of the members of the entity or otherwise. (« dirigeant »)		(r) "officer" means (i) the chair or vice-chair of the board of directors or the president, vice-president, secretary, assistant secretary, comptroller, assistant comptroller, treasurer, assistant treasurer or general manager of a corporation, (ii) any individual who performs functions or acts in a capacity similar to the functions or capacities referred to in subclause (i), or (iii) any individual designated as an officer of a corporation by bylaw or similar authority of the corporation;
"person"				"person" includes an individual, partnership, trustee and unincorporated association or		(s) "person" means an individual, partnership, corporation, unincorporated

TOPIC	PRINCE EDWARD ISLAND	NEW BRUNSWICK	ONTARIO	MANITOBA	BRITISH COLUMBIA	ALBERTA
			Franchises Acts			
				organization. (« personne »)		association, unincorporated organization, trustee, executor, administrator or other legal representative;
"prescribed"	(o) "prescribed" means prescribed by the regulations;	"prescribed" means prescribed by the regulations or, if the context requires, by the rules made by the Commission under the *Financial and Consumer Services Commission Act*. *(prescrit)*	"prescribed" means prescribed by regulations made under this Act; ("prescrit")	"prescribed" means prescribed by regulation under this Act.		
"prospective franchisee"	(p) "prospective franchisee" means a person who has indicated, directly or indirectly, to a franchisor or a franchisor's associate or broker an interest in entering into a franchise agreement, and a person whom a franchisor or a franchisor's associate or broker, directly or indirectly, invites to enter into a franchise agreement;	"prospective franchisee" means *(franchisé éventuel)* (a) a person who has indicated, directly or indirectly, to a franchisor, a franchisor's associate or a franchisor's broker an interest in entering into a franchise agreement, or (b) a person whom a franchisor, a franchisor's associate or a franchisor's broker, directly or indirectly, invites to enter into a franchise agreement.	"prospective franchisee" means a person who has indicated, directly or indirectly, to a franchisor or a franchisor's associate, agent or broker an interest in entering into a franchise agreement, and a person whom a franchisor or a franchisor's associate, agent or broker, directly or indirectly, invites to enter into a franchise agreement; ("franchisé éventuel")	"prospective franchisee" means a person (a) who has indicated, directly or indirectly, to a franchisor or a franchisor's associate or broker an interest in entering into a franchise agreement; or (b) whom a franchisor or a franchisor's associate or broker, directly or indirectly, invites to enter into a franchise agreement. (« franchisé éventuel »)	"prospective franchisee" means a person (a) who has indicated, directly or indirectly, to a franchisor, franchisor's associate or franchisor's broker an interest in entering into a franchise agreement, and (b) whom a franchisor, franchisor's associate or franchisor's broker invites, directly or indirectly, to enter into a franchise agreement;	
"sell"						(t) "sell" means a sale or a disposition of a franchise or an interest in a franchise;
"statement of material change"				"statement of material change" means the statement required by subsection 5(7). (« déclaration au sujet d'un		

TOPIC	PRINCE EDWARD ISLAND	NEW BRUNSWICK	ONTARIO	MANITOBA	BRITISH COLUMBIA	ALBERTA
			Franchises Acts			
				changement important »)		
"subfranchise"	(q) "subfranchise" means a franchise granted by a subfranchisor to a subfranchisee.	"subfranchise" means a franchise granted by a subfranchisor to a subfranchisee. *(sous-franchise)*	"subfranchise" means a franchise granted by a subfranchisor to a subfranchisee. ("sous-franchise")	"subfranchise" means a franchise granted by a subfranchisor to a subfranchisee. (« sous-franchise »)	"subfranchise" means a franchise granted by a subfranchisor to a subfranchisee.	(u) "subfranchise" means a franchise granted by a subfranchisor to a subfranchisee;
"subfranchisee"						(v) "subfranchisee" means a person to whom a subfranchise is granted by a subfranchisor;
"subfranchisor"						(w) "subfranchisor" means one or more persons who grant a subfranchise and includes a person to whom a master franchise is granted.
						1(2) A person is an associate of a franchisor if the person is directly involved in the granting of the franchise or if there are continuing financial obligations by the franchisee to that person and significant operational controls by that person on the franchisee and (a) the person controls the franchisor, (b) the person is controlled by the franchisor, or (c) the person and the franchisor are under the common control of another person.
Reference to "Act" includes Regulations				1(2) In this Act, a reference to "this Act" includes the		

TOPIC	PRINCE EDWARD SLAND	NEW BRUNSWICK	ONTARIO	MANITOBA	BRITISH COLUMBIA	ALBERTA
Franchises Acts						
				regulations under this Act.		
Master Franchise, Subfranchise	**1.** (2) A franchise includes a master franchise and a subfranchise.	**1**(2) A franchise includes a master franchise and a subfranchise.	**1.** (2) A franchise includes a master franchise and a subfranchise.		**1** (2) For the purposes of this Act, a reference to a franchise includes a master franchise and a subfranchise.	
Deemed Control / Corporation Controlled by Another Person	**1.** (3) A franchisee, franchisor or franchisor's associate that is a corporation shall be deemed to be controlled by another person or persons if,	**1**(3) A franchisee, franchisor or franchisor's associate that is a corporation shall be deemed to be controlled by another person or persons if	**1.** (3) A franchisee, franchisor or franchisor's associate which is a corporation shall be deemed to be controlled by another person or persons if,	**1**(3) A corporation is controlled by another person if	**1** (3) For the purposes of this Act, a franchisee, franchisor or franchisor's associate that is a corporation is deemed to be controlled by another person or persons, if	**1**(3) A corporation is controlled by another person if
	(a) voting securities of the franchisee or franchisor or franchisor's associate carrying more than 50 per cent of the votes for the election of directors are held, otherwise than by way of security only, by or for the benefit of the other person or persons; and	(a) voting securities of the franchisee or franchisor or franchisor's associate carrying more than 50% of the votes for the election of directors are held, otherwise than by way of security only, by or for the benefit of the other person or persons, and	(a) voting securities of the franchisee or franchisor or franchisor's associate carrying more than 50 per cent of the votes for the election of directors are held, otherwise than by way of security only, by or for the benefit of the other person or persons; and	(a) the corporation's voting securities carrying more than 50 percent of the votes for the election of directors are held — otherwise than by way of security only — by or for the benefit of the other person; and	(a) voting securities of the franchisee, franchisor or franchisor's associate carrying more than 50% of the votes for the election of directors are held, otherwise than by way of security only, by or for the benefit of the other person or persons, and	(a) the voting securities of the corporation carrying more than 50% of the votes that may be cast to elect directors are held, other than for the purpose of collateral for a debt, by or for the benefit of the other person, and
	(b) the votes carried by such securities are entitled, if exercised, to elect a majority of the board of directors of the franchisee or franchisor or franchisor's associate.	(b) the votes carried by the securities are entitled, if exercised, to elect a majority of the board of directors of the franchisee or franchisor or franchisor's associate.	(b) the votes carried by such securities are entitled, if exercised, to elect a majority of the board of directors of the franchisee or franchisor or franchisor's associate.	(b) the votes carried by those securities are entitled, if exercised, to elect a majority of the corporation's board of directors.	(b) the votes carried by the securities are entitled, if exercised, to elect a majority of the board of directors of the franchisee, franchisor or franchisor's associate.	(b) the votes carried by the securities referred to in clause (a) are sufficient, if exercised, to elect a majority of the board of directors of the corporation.
					1 (4) For the purposes of the definition of "franchise" in subsection (1), a reference to a payment or continuing payments, as described in that definition, does not include a	

TOPIC	PRINCE EDWARD ISLAND	NEW BRUNSWICK	ONTARIO	MANITOBA	BRITISH COLUMBIA	ALBERTA
Franchises Acts						
					payment made in respect of a purchase described in section 2 (3) (g).	
Purpose of the Act						**2** The purpose of this Act is (a) to assist prospective franchisees in making informed investment decisions by requiring the timely disclosure of necessary information, (b) to provide civil remedies to deal with breaches of this Act, and (c) to provide a means by which franchisors and franchisees will be able to govern themselves and promote fair dealing among themselves.
Crown	**2.** (4) This Act does not bind the Crown.	**2**(1) This Act binds the Crown.		**13** This Act binds the Crown.		
Application	**2.** (1) This Act applies with respect to, (a) a franchise agreement entered into on or after the coming into force of this section; (b) a renewal or extension of a franchise agreement described in clause (a) entered into on or after the coming into force of this section; and (c) a business operated under an agreement, renewal or	**2**(2) This Act applies with respect to (a) a franchise agreement entered into on or after February 1, 2011, if the business operated or to be operated by the franchisee under the agreement is partly or wholly in New Brunswick, and (b) a renewal or extension entered into on or after February 1, 2011 of a franchise agreement that	**2.** (1) This Act applies with respect to a franchise agreement entered into on or after the coming into force of this section, with respect to a renewal or extension of a franchise agreement entered into before or after the coming into force of this section and with respect to a business operated under such an agreement, renewal or extension if the business operated by the franchisee under the franchise agreement	**2**(1) This Act applies to (a) a franchise agreement entered into on or after the coming into force of this section, if the franchised business is operated, or is to be operated, partly or wholly in Manitoba; and (b) a renewal or extension of a franchise agreement If (i) the renewal or extension is entered into on or after the	**2** (1) This Act applies with respect to (a) a franchise agreement entered into on or after the coming into force of this section, and (b) a renewal or extension, entered into on or after the coming into force of this section, of a franchise agreement that was entered into before, on or after the coming into force of this section	**3**(1) This Act applies to the sale of a franchise made on or after November 1, 1995 (a) if the franchised business is to be operated either partly or wholly in Alberta, and (b) if the purchaser of the franchise is an Alberta resident or has a permanent establishment in Alberta for the purposes of the *Alberta Corporate Tax Act*.

TOPIC	PRINCE EDWARD ISLAND	NEW BRUNSWICK	ONTARIO	MANITOBA	BRITISH COLUMBIA	ALBERTA
Franchises Acts						
	extension described in clause (a) or (b), if the business operated by the franchisee under the franchise agreement or its renewal or extension is to be operated partly or wholly in Prince Edward Island.	was entered into before or after February 1, 2011, if the business operated or to be operated by the franchisee under the agreement is partly or wholly in New Brunswick.	or its renewal or extension is to be operated partly or wholly in Ontario.	coming into force of this section, (ii) the franchise agreement was entered into before, or is entered into after, the coming into force of this section, and (iii) the franchised business is operated, or is to be operated, partly or wholly in Manitoba.	if the business operated or to be operated by a franchisee under the franchise agreement is wholly or partly in British Columbia.	
Existing Franchise Agreements	**2.** (2) Sections 3 and 4, clause 5(7)(d) and sections 8, 10, 11, 12 and 13 apply with respect to a franchise agreement entered into before the coming into force of this section and with respect to a business operated under such agreement, if the business operated by the franchisee under the franchise agreement is operated or is to be operated partly or wholly in Prince Edward Island.	**2**(3) Sections 3 and 4, paragraph 5(8)(d) and sections 8, 10, 11, 12 and 13 apply with respect to a franchise agreement entered into before February 1, 2011, if the business operated or to be operated by the franchisee under the franchise agreement is partly or wholly in New Brunswick.	**2.** (2) Sections 3 and 4, clause 5 (7) (d) and sections 9, 11 and 12 apply with respect to a franchise agreement entered into before the coming into force of this section, and with respect to a business operated under such agreement, if the business operated by the franchisee under the franchise agreement is operated or is to be operated partly or wholly in Ontario.	**2**(2) Sections 3 and 4, clause 5(11)(d) and sections 9, 10, 11 and 12 apply to a franchise agreement entered into before the coming into force of this section, if the franchised business is operated partly or wholly in Manitoba.	**2** (2) Sections 3, 4, 5 (8) (d) and 10 to 13 apply with respect to a franchise agreement entered into before the coming into force of this section, if the business operated or to be operated by a franchisee under the franchise agreement is wholly or partly in British Columbia.	**3**(2) Sections 5(1)(d) and (f), 6, 7, 8, 11, 15, 20 and 21 apply to the sale of a franchise made before November 1, 1995 (a) if the franchised business is operating or is to be operated either partly or wholly in Alberta, and (b) if, on November 1, 1995, the franchisee is an Alberta resident or has a permanent establishment in Alberta for the purposes of the *Alberta Corporate Tax Act*.
Non-Application	**2.** (3) This Act does not apply to the following continuing commercial relationships or arrangements:	**2**(4) This Act does not apply to	**2.** (3) This Act does not apply to the following continuing commercial relationships or arrangements:	**2**(3) This Act does not apply to	**2** (3) This Act does not apply to the following:	
Employment	(a) employer-employee relationship;	(a) an employer-employee relationship,	1. Employer-employee relationship.	(a) the relationship between an employer and employee;	(a) an employer-employee relationship;	

TOPIC	PRINCE EDWARD ISLAND	NEW BRUNSWICK	ONTARIO	MANITOBA	BRITISH COLUMBIA	ALBERTA
			Franchises Acts			
Partnership	(b) partnership;	(b) a partnership,	2. Partnership.	(b) the relationship between partners under a partnership agreement where the partnership operates a franchised business;	(b) a partnership;	
Co-operative Organizations	(c) membership in, (i) an organization operated on a co-operative basis by and for independent retailers that,	(c) membership in (i) an organization operated on a cooperative basis by and for independent retailers that	3. Membership in a co-operative association, as prescribed.	(c) membership in an organization operated on a cooperative basis by and for independent retailers that	(c) a membership in (i) an organization, operated on a cooperative basis by and for independent retailers, that	
	(A) purchases or arranges the purchase of, on a non-exclusive basis, wholesale goods or services primarily for resale by its member retailers, and	(A) purchases or arranges the purchase of, on a non-exclusive basis, wholesale goods or services primarily for resale by its member retailers, and		(i) on a non-exclusive basis, purchases or arranges the purchase of wholesale goods or services primarily for resale by its member retailers, and	(A) purchases, or arranges for the purchase of, on a non-exclusive basis, wholesale goods or services primarily for resale by the organization's member retailers, and	
	(B) does not grant representational rights to or exercise significant operational control over its member retailers,	(B) does not grant representational rights to or exercise significant operational control over its member retailers,		(ii) does not grant representational rights to, or exercise significant operational control over, its member retailers;	(B) does not grant representational rights to or exercise significant operational control over the organization's member retailers,	
	(ii) a "cooperative corporation" as defined under subsection 136(2) of	(ii) a cooperative corporation as defined under subsection 136(2) of		(d) membership in a cooperative corporation as defined under subsection 136(2) of the *Income Tax*	(ii) a cooperative corporation, as defined in section 136 (2) of the *Income Tax*	

TOPIC	PRINCE EDWARD ISLAND	NEW BRUNSWICK	ONTARIO	MANITOBA	BRITISH COLUMBIA	ALBERTA
Franchises Acts						
Partnership	(b) partnership;	(b) a partnership,	2. Partnership.	(b) the relationship between partners under a partnership agreement where the partnership operates a franchised business;	(b) a partnership;	
Co-operative Organizations	(c) membership in, (i) an organization operated on a co-operative basis by and for independent retailers that,	(c) membership in (i) an organization operated on a cooperative basis by and for independent retailers that	3. Membership in a co-operative association, as prescribed.	(c) membership in an organization operated on a cooperative basis by and for independent retailers that	(c) a membership in (i) an organization, operated on a cooperative basis by and for independent retailers, that	
	(A) purchases or arranges the purchase of, on a non-exclusive basis, wholesale goods or services primarily for resale by its member retailers, and	(A) purchases or arranges the purchase of, on a non-exclusive basis, wholesale goods or services primarily for resale by its member retailers, and		(i) on a non-exclusive basis, purchases or arranges the purchase of wholesale goods or services primarily for resale by its member retailers, and	(A) purchases, or arranges for the purchase of, on a non-exclusive basis, wholesale goods or services primarily for resale by the organization's member retailers, and	
	(B) does not grant representational rights to or exercise significant operational control over its member retailers,	(B) does not grant representational rights to or exercise significant operational control over its member retailers,		(ii) does not grant representational rights to, or exercise significant operational control over, its member retailers;	(B) does not grant representational rights to or exercise significant operational control over the organization's member retailers,	
	(ii) a "cooperative corporation" as defined under subsection 136(2) of	(ii) a cooperative corporation as defined under subsection 136(2) of		(d) membership in a cooperative corporation as defined under subsection 136(2) of the *Income Tax*	(ii) a cooperative corporation, as defined in section 136 (2) of the *Income Tax*	

TOPIC	PRINCE EDWARD ISLAND	NEW BRUNSWICK	ONTARIO	MANITOBA	BRITISH COLUMBIA	ALBERTA
			Franchises Acts			
	or other commercial symbol where such license is the only one of its general nature and type to be granted in Canada by the licensor with respect to that trade-mark, trade name, logo or advertising or other commercial symbol;	or other commercial symbol if the licence is the only one of its general nature and type to be granted in Canada by the licensor with respect to that trademark, trade name, logo or advertising or other commercial symbol,	logo or advertising or other commercial symbol where such licence is the only one of its general nature and type to be granted by the licensor with respect to that trade-mark, service mark, trade name, logo or advertising or other commercial symbol.	licence is the only one of its general nature and type to be granted in Canada by the licensor with respect to that trademark, trade name or logo;	or other commercial symbol, if the licence is the only one of its general nature and type to be granted in Canada by the licensor with respect to the trademark, trade name, logo or advertising or other commercial symbol;	
Lease within Retailer's Premises			6. An arrangement arising out of a lease, licence or similar agreement whereby the franchisee leases space in the premises of another retailer and is not required or advised to buy the goods or services it sells from the retailer or an affiliate of the retailer.			
Oral Agreement	(f) a relationship or arrangement arising out of an oral agreement where there is no writing that evidences any material term or aspect of the relationship or arrangement;	(f) a relationship or arrangement arising out of an oral agreement if there is no writing that evidences any material term or aspect of the relationship or arrangement, or	7. A relationship or arrangement arising out of an oral agreement where there is no writing which evidences any material term or aspect of the relationship or arrangement.	(i) a relationship or arrangement arising out of an oral agreement in which there is no writing that evidences any material term or aspect of the relationship or arrangement; or	(f) a relationship or arrangement arising out of an oral agreement, if there is no writing that evidences any material term or aspect of the relationship or arrangement;	
Agreement with the Crown	(h) a service contract or franchise-like arrangement with the Crown or an agent of the Crown.		8. A service contract or franchise-like arrangement with the Crown or an agent of the Crown.			
Wholesale	(g) an arrangement arising	(g) an arrangement arising		(j) an arrangement arising out	(g) an arrangement arising	

TOPIC	PRINCE EDWARD ISLAND	NEW BRUNSWICK	ONTARIO	MANITOBA	BRITISH COLUMBIA	ALBERTA
Franchises Acts						
Arrangements	out of an agreement, (i) for the purchase and sale of a reasonable amount of goods at a reasonable wholesale price, or (ii) for the purchase of a reasonable amount of services at a reasonable price;	out of an agreement (i) for the purchase and sale of a reasonable amount of goods at a reasonable wholesale price, or (ii) for the purchase of a reasonable amount of services at a reasonable price.		of an agreement for (i) the purchase and sale of a reasonable amount of goods at a reasonable wholesale price, or (ii) the purchase of a reasonable amount of services at a reasonable price.	out of an agreement (i) for the purchase and sale of a reasonable amount of goods at a reasonable wholesale price, or (ii) for the purchase of a reasonable amount of services at a reasonable price.	
Fair Dealing	**3.** (1) Every franchise agreement imposes on each party a duty of fair dealing in the performance and enforcement of the agreement, including in the exercise of a right under the agreement.	**3**(1) Every franchise agreement imposes on each party a duty of fair dealing in the performance and enforcement of the franchise agreement.	**3.** (1) Every franchise agreement imposes on each party a duty of fair dealing in its performance and enforcement.	**3**(1) Every franchise agreement imposes on each party a duty of fair dealing in the performance and enforcement of the agreement.	**3** (1) Every franchise agreement imposes on each party a duty of fair dealing in the performance and enforcement of the franchise agreement, including in the exercise of a right under the franchise agreement.	**7** Every franchise agreement imposes on each party a duty of fair dealing in its performance and enforcement.
Right of Action	**3.** (2) A party to a franchise agreement has a right of action for damages against another party to the franchise agreement who breaches the duty of fair dealing.	**3**(2) A party to a franchise agreement has a right of action for damages against another party to the franchise agreement who breaches the duty of fair dealing.	**3.** (2) A party to a franchise agreement has a right of action for damages against another party to the franchise agreement who breaches the duty of fair dealing in the performance or enforcement of the franchise agreement.	**3**(2) A party to a franchise agreement has a right of action for damages against another party to the franchise agreement who breaches the duty of fair dealing.	**3** (2) A party to a franchise agreement has a right of action for damages against another party to the franchise agreement who breaches the duty of fair dealing.	
Interpretation	**3.** (3) For the purpose of this section, the duty of fair dealing includes the duty to act in good faith and in accordance with reasonable commercial standards.	**3**(3) For the purposes of this section, (a) the duty of fair dealing includes the duty to act in good faith and in accordance with reasonable commercial standards, and	**3.** (3) For the purpose of this section, the duty of fair dealing includes the duty to act in good faith and in accordance with reasonable commercial standards.	**3**(3) For the purpose of this section, (a) the duty of fair dealing includes the duty to act in good faith and in accordance with reasonable commercial standards; and	**3** (3) For the purposes of this section, the duty of fair dealing includes the duty to act in good faith and in accordance with reasonable commercial standards.	

TOPIC	PRINCE EDWARD ISLAND	NEW BRUNSWICK	ONTARIO	MANITOBA	BRITISH COLUMBIA	ALBERTA
Franchises Acts						
		(b) the performance and enforcement of the franchise agreement includes the exercise of a right under the agreement.		(b) the performance and enforcement of a franchise agreement includes the exercise of a right under the agreement.		
Right to Associate	**4.** (1) A franchisee may associate with other franchisees and may form or join an organization of franchisees.	**4**(1) A franchisee may associate with other franchisees and may form or join an organization of franchisees.	**4.** (1) A franchisee may associate with other franchisees and may form or join an organization of franchisees.	**4**(1) A franchisee may associate with other franchisees and may form or join an organization of franchisees.	**4** (1) A franchisee may associate with other franchisees and may form or join an organization of franchisees.	
Interfering with, Prohibiting or Restricting Association	**4.** (2) A franchisor and a franchisor's associate shall not interfere with, prohibit or restrict, by contract or otherwise, a franchisee from forming or joining an organization of franchisees or from associating with other franchisees.	**4**(2) A franchisor and a franchisor's associate shall not interfere with, prohibit or restrict, by contract or otherwise, a franchisee from forming or joining an organization of franchisees or from associating with other franchisees.	**4.** (2) A franchisor and a franchisor's associate shall not interfere with, prohibit or restrict, by contract or otherwise, a franchisee from forming or joining an organization of franchisees or from associating with other franchisees.	**4**(2) A franchisor or a franchisor's associate must not interfere with, prohibit or restrict — by contract or otherwise — a franchisee from forming or joining an organization of franchisees or from associating with other franchisees.	**4** (2) A franchisor and a franchisor's associate must not interfere with, prohibit or restrict, by contract or otherwise, a franchisee from associating with other franchisees, or from forming or joining an organization of franchisees.	**8**(1) A franchisor or its associate must not prohibit or restrict a franchisee from forming an organization of franchisees or from associating with other franchisees in any organization of franchisees.
Penalizing Franchisee Prohibited	**4.** (3) A franchisor and a franchisor's associate shall not, directly or indirectly, penalize, attempt to penalize or threaten to penalize a franchisee for exercising any right under this section.	**4**(3) A franchisor and a franchisor's associate shall not, directly or indirectly, penalize, attempt to penalize or threaten to penalize a franchisee for exercising any right under this section.	**4.** (3) A franchisor and franchisor's associate shall not, directly or indirectly, penalize, attempt to penalize or threaten to penalize a franchisee for exercising any right under this section.	**4**(3) A franchisor or a franchisor's associate must not — directly or indirectly — penalize, attempt to penalize or threaten to penalize a franchisee for exercising any right under this section.	**4** (3) A franchisor and a franchisor's associate must not, directly or indirectly, penalize, attempt to penalize or threaten to penalize a franchisee for associating with other franchisees, or for forming or joining an organization of franchisees.	**8**(2) A franchisor or its associate must not directly or indirectly penalize a franchisee for engaging in the activities described in subsection (1).
Provisions Void	**4.** (4) Any provision in a franchise agreement or other agreement relating to a franchise which purports to interfere with, prohibit or restrict a franchisee from exercising any right under this section is void.	**4**(4) A provision in a franchise agreement or other agreement relating to a franchise that purports to interfere with, prohibit or restrict a franchisee from exercising any right under this section is void.	**4.** (4) Any provision in a franchise agreement or other agreement relating to a franchise which purports to interfere with, prohibit or restrict a franchisee from exercising any right under this section is void.	**4**(4) Any provision in a franchise agreement or other agreement relating to a franchise that purports to interfere with, prohibit or restrict a franchisee from exercising any right under this section is void.	**4** (4) If a provision in a franchise agreement or other agreement relating to a franchise purports to interfere with, prohibit or restrict a franchisee from associating with other franchisees, or from forming or joining an organization of	

TOPIC	PRINCE EDWARD ISLAND	NEW BRUNSWICK	ONTARIO	MANITOBA	BRITISH COLUMBIA	ALBERTA
Franchises Acts						
					franchisees, the provision is void.	
Right of Action	**4.** (5) If a franchisor or a franchisor's associate contravenes this section, the franchisee has a right of action for damages against the franchisor or franchisor's associate, as the case may be.	**4**(5) If a franchisor or a franchisor's associate contravenes this section, the franchisee has a right of action for damages against the franchisor or franchisor's associate, as the case may be.	**4.** (5) If a franchisor or franchisor's associate contravenes this section, the franchisee has a right of action for damages against the franchisor or franchisor's associate, as the case may be.	**4**(5) The franchisee has a right of action for damages against a franchisor or franchisor's associate who contravenes this section.	**4** (5) If a franchisor or a franchisor's associate contravenes subsection (2) or (3), a franchisee has a right of action for damages against the franchisor or the franchisor's associate, as the case may be.	**11** If a franchisor or its associate contravenes section 8, the franchisee has a right of action for damages against the franchisor or its associate, as the case may be.
Franchisor's Obligation to Disclose	**5.** (1) A franchisor shall provide a prospective franchisee with a disclosure document and the prospective franchisee shall receive the disclosure document not less than 14 days before the earlier of,	**5**(1) A franchisor shall provide a prospective franchisee with a disclosure document, and the disclosure document shall be received by the prospective franchisee, not less than 14 days before the earlier of	**5.** (1) A franchisor shall provide a prospective franchisee with a disclosure document and the prospective franchisee shall receive the disclosure document not less than 14 days before the earlier of,	**5**(1) A franchisor must give every prospective franchisee a copy of the franchisor's disclosure document. **5**(2) The disclosure document must be received by the prospective franchisee at least 14 days before	**5** (1) A franchisor must provide a prospective franchisee with a disclosure document as set out in this section, and the prospective franchisee must have received the disclosure document at least 14 days before the earlier of	**4**(1) A franchisor must give every prospective franchisee a copy of the franchisor's disclosure document. **4**(2) The disclosure document must be received by the prospective franchisee at least 14 days before
	(a) the signing by the prospective franchisee of the franchise agreement or any other agreement relating to the franchise; and	(a) the signing by the prospective franchisee of the franchise agreement or any other agreement relating to the franchise, and	(a) the signing by the prospective franchisee of the franchise agreement or any other agreement relating to the franchise; and	(a) the signing of the franchise agreement or any other agreement relating to the franchise by the prospective franchisee; or	(a) the signing, by the prospective franchisee, of the franchise agreement or any other agreement relating to the franchise, and	(a) the signing by the prospective franchisee of any agreement relating to the franchise, or
	(b) the payment of any consideration by or on behalf of the prospective franchisee to the franchisor or franchisor's associate relating to the franchise.	(b) the payment by or on behalf of the prospective franchisee to the franchisor or franchisor's associate of any consideration relating to the franchise.	(b) the payment of any consideration by or on behalf of the prospective franchisee to the franchisor or franchisor's associate relating to the franchise.	(b) the payment of any consideration relating to the franchise by or on behalf of the prospective franchisee to the franchisor or franchisor's associate; whichever is earlier.	(b) the payment, by or on behalf of the prospective franchisee to the franchisor or the franchisor's associate, of any consideration relating to the franchise.	(b) the payment of any consideration by the prospective franchisee relating to the franchise, whichever is earlier.
Methods of Delivery	**5.** (2) A disclosure document may be delivered personally, by	**5**(2) A disclosure document may be delivered personally, by	**5.** (2) A disclosure document may be delivered personally, by	**5**(4) A disclosure document may be delivered personally or by	**5** (2) A disclosure document may be delivered personally, by	

TOPIC	PRINCE EDWARD ISLAND	NEW BRUNSWICK	ONTARIO	MANITOBA	BRITISH COLUMBIA	ALBERTA
			Franchises Acts			
	registered mail or by any other prescribed method.	registered mail or by any other prescribed method.	registered mail or by any other prescribed method.	registered mail, fax or any other prescribed method.	email or by any other prescribed method.	
One Document at One Time	**5.** (3) A disclosure document must be one document delivered as required under subsections (1) and (2) as one document at one time.	**5**(3) A disclosure document shall be one document delivered as required under subsections (1) and (2) as one document at one time.	**5.** (3) A disclosure document must be one document, delivered as required under subsections (1) and (2) as one document at one time.		**5** (3) A disclosure document must be delivered as one complete document and delivered at one time.	
Timing when Not Delivered as One Document				**5**(3) If the disclosure document is not delivered as one document, the requirement under subsection (2) is not met until the date of the delivery of the last document.		
Contents of Disclosure Document	**5.** (4) The disclosure document shall contain,	**5**(4) The disclosure document shall contain	**5.** (4) The disclosure document shall contain,	**5**(5) The disclosure document must contain	**5** (4) A disclosure document must contain the following:	**4**(3) A disclosure document must
						(a) comply with the requirements of the regulations,
	(a) all material facts, including material facts as prescribed;	**NOTE: See section 5(5) below.**	(a) all material facts, including material facts as prescribed;	(a) all material facts;	**NOTE: See section 5(5) below.**	
	(b) financial statements as prescribed;	(a) financial statements as prescribed,	(b) financial statements as prescribed;	(b) the prescribed financial statements;	(a) prescribed financial statements;	(c) contain financial statements, reports and other documents in accordance with the regulations.
	(c) copies of all proposed franchise agreements and other agreements relating to the franchise to be signed by the prospective franchisee;	(b) copies of all proposed franchise agreements and other agreements relating to the franchise to be signed by the prospective franchisee,	(c) copies of all proposed franchise agreements and other agreements relating to the franchise to be signed by the prospective franchisee;	(c) copies of all proposed franchise agreements and other agreements relating to the franchise to be signed by the prospective franchisee;	(b) copies of all proposed franchise agreements, and other agreements relating to the franchise, to be signed by a prospective franchisee;	(b) contain copies of all proposed franchise agreements, and
	(d) statements as prescribed	(c) statements, as prescribed,	(d) statements as prescribed	(d) the prescribed statements	(c) prescribed statements	

TOPIC	PRINCE EDWARD ISLAND	NEW BRUNSWICK	ONTARIO	MANITOBA	BRITISH COLUMBIA	ALBERTA
Franchises Acts						
	for the purposes of assisting the prospective franchisee in making informed investment decisions; and	that are for the purpose of assisting the prospective franchisee in making informed investment decisions,	for the purposes of assisting the prospective franchisee in making informed investment decisions; and	about making an informed investment decision;	that have the purpose of assisting a prospective franchisee to make informed investment decisions;	
	(e) other information and copies of documents as prescribed.	(d) other information as prescribed, and	(e) other information and copies of documents as prescribed.	(e) other prescribed information, statements, descriptions and certificates; and	(d) other prescribed information;	
		(e) copies of other documents as prescribed.		(f) copies of other prescribed documents.	(e) copies of other prescribed documents.	
		5(5) In addition to the statements, documents and information required by subsection (4), the disclosure document shall contain all material facts.			**5** (5) In addition to the statements, documents and information required by subsection (4), a disclosure document must include all material facts.	
Exception Regarding Requirement for Financial Statements		**5**(9) The Crown is not required to include the financial statements otherwise required by paragraph (4)(a) in its disclosure document.		**5**(15) The Crown is not required to include the financial statements otherwise required by clause (5)(b) in its disclosure document.	**5** (10) Subsection (4) (a) does not apply if the franchisor is the government of British Columbia.	
Disclosure re Mediation, Arbitration				**5**(6) If a franchise agreement provides that disputes may be referred to, or resolved by, mediation or arbitration, the disclosure document must include information about mediation procedures and arbitration proceedings, including		
				(a) the criteria and methods for selecting a mediator or arbitrator;		

TOPIC	PRINCE EDWARD ISLAND	NEW BRUNSWICK	ONTARIO	MANITOBA	BRITISH COLUMBIA	ALBERTA
			<u>**Franchises Acts**</u>			
				(b) the rules and procedures governing mediation and arbitration;		
				(c) any confidentiality obligations imposed on parties to the mediation or arbitration;		
				(d) the costs of mediation or arbitration proceedings or the method of calculating those costs; and		
				(e) any other prescribed information and statements.		
Material Change	**5.** (5) The franchisor shall provide the prospective franchisee with a written statement of any material change, and the franchisee shall receive such statement, as soon as practicable after the change has occurred and before the earlier of,	**5**(6) The franchisor shall provide the prospective franchisee with a written statement of any material change, and the statement shall be received by the prospective franchisee, as soon as practicable after the change has occurred and before the earlier of	**5.** (5) The franchisor shall provide the prospective franchisee with a written statement of any material change, and the franchisee must receive such statement, as soon as practicable after the change has occurred and before the earlier of,	**5**(7) The franchisor must give the prospective franchisee a written statement describing any material change. **5**(8) The statement of material change must be received by the prospective franchisee as soon as practicable after the change has occurred and before	**5** (6) A franchisor must provide a prospective franchisee with a written statement of any material change, and the prospective franchisee must receive the statement of material change as soon as practicable after the change has occurred and before the earlier of the following:	**4**(4) The franchisor must provide, in writing, to the prospective franchisee a description of any material change. **4**(5) The prospective franchisee must receive the description of the material change as soon as practicable after the change has occurred and before
	(a) the signing by the prospective franchisee of the franchise agreement or any other agreement relating to the franchise;	(a) the signing by the prospective franchisee of the franchise agreement or any other agreement relating to the franchise,	(a) the signing by the prospective franchisee of the franchise agreement or any other agreement relating to the franchise;	(a) the signing of the franchise agreement or any other agreement relating to the franchise by the prospective	(a) the signing, by the prospective franchisee, of a franchise agreement or any other agreement	(a) the signing by the prospective franchisee of any agreement relating to the franchise, or

TOPIC	PRINCE EDWARD ISLAND	NEW BRUNSWICK	ONTARIO	MANITOBA	BRITISH COLUMBIA	ALBERTA
Franchises Acts						
	and	and	and	franchisee; or	relating to a franchise;	
	(b) the payment of any consideration by or on behalf of the prospective franchisee to the franchisor or franchisor's associate relating to the franchise.	(b) the payment by or on behalf of the prospective franchisee to the franchisor or franchisor's associate of any consideration relating to the franchise.	(b) the payment of any consideration by or on behalf of the prospective franchisee to the franchisor or franchisor's associate relating to the franchise.	(b) the payment of any consideration relating to the franchise by or on behalf of the prospective franchisee to the franchisor or franchisor's associate; whichever is earlier.	(b) the payment, by or on behalf of the prospective franchisee to the franchisor or franchisor's associate, of any consideration relating to the franchise.	(b) the payment of any consideration by the prospective franchisee relating to the franchise, whichever is earlier.
Information to be Accurate, Clear, Concise	**5.** (6) All information in a disclosure document and a statement of material change shall be accurately, clearly and concisely set out.	5(7) All information in a disclosure document and a statement of material change shall be accurately, clearly and concisely set out.	**5.** (6) All information in a disclosure document and a statement of a material change shall be accurately, clearly and concisely set out.	5(9) The information in a disclosure document and statement of material change must be accurately, clearly and concisely set out.	5 (7) All information in a disclosure document and a statement of material change must be set out accurately, clearly and concisely.	
Substantial Compliance	**NOTE: See section 3(3) of *Franchise Act Regulations* (Prince Edward Island)**			5(10) A franchisor complies with this section	9 A disclosure document or a statement of material change complies with section 5 despite the presence of a defect in form, a technical irregularity or an error, if	**NOTE: See section 2(4) of *Franchises Regulation* (Alberta)**
				(a) if the franchisor's disclosure document substantially complies with this Act; and	(a) the defect in form, the technical irregularity or the error does not affect the substance of the disclosure document or the statement of material change, and	
				(b) even if the disclosure document contains a technical irregularity or mistake not affecting the substance of the document.	(b) the disclosure document or the statement of material change is substantially in compliance with this Act.	
Exemptions	**5.** (7) This section does not apply to,	5(8) This section does not apply to	**5.** (7) This section does not apply to,	5(11) This section does not apply to	5 (8) This section does not apply to the following:	5(1) The following are exempt from section 4:

TOPIC	PRINCE EDWARD ISLAND	NEW BRUNSWICK	ONTARIO	MANITOBA	BRITISH COLUMBIA	ALBERTA
Franchises Acts						
Grant by Franchisee	(a) the grant of a franchise by a franchisee if,	(a) the grant of a franchise by a franchisee if	(a) the grant of a franchise by a franchisee if,	(a) the grant of a franchise by a franchisee if	(a) the grant of a franchise by a franchisee, if	(a) the sale of a franchise by a franchisee if
	(i) the franchisee is not the franchisor, the franchisor's associate or a director, officer or employee of the franchisor or of the franchisor's associate,	(i) the franchisee is not the franchisor, the franchisor's associate or a director, officer or employee of the franchisor or of the franchisor's associate,	(i) the franchisee is not the franchisor, an associate of the franchisor or a director, officer or employee of the franchisor or of the franchisor's associate,	(i) the franchisee is not the franchisor or the franchisor's associate or a director, officer or employee of either of them,	(i) the franchisee is not the franchisor, the franchisor's associate or a director, officer or employee of the franchisor or of the franchisor's associate,	(i) the franchisee is not the franchisor or an associate of the franchisor or a director, officer or employee of the franchisor or its associate,
	(ii) the grant of the franchise is for the franchisee's own account,	(ii) the grant of the franchise is for the franchisee's own account,	(ii) the grant of the franchise is for the franchisee's own account,	(ii) the grant of the franchise is for the franchisee's own account,	(ii) the grant of the franchise is for the franchisee's own account,	(ii) the sale is for the franchisee's own account,
	(iii) in the case of a master franchise, the entire franchise is granted, and	(iii) in the case of a master franchise, the entire franchise is granted, and	(iii) in the case of a master franchise, the entire franchise is granted, and	(iii) in the case of a master franchise, the entire franchise is granted, and	(iii) in the case of a master franchise, the entire franchise is granted, and	(iii) in the case of a master franchise, the entire franchise is sold, and
	(iv) the grant of the franchise is not effected by or through the franchisor;	(iv) the grant of the franchise is not effected by or through the franchisor,	(iv) the grant of the franchise is not effected by or through the franchisor;	(iv) the grant of the franchise is not effected by or through the franchisor;	(iv) the grant of the franchise is not effected by or through the franchisor;	(iv) the sale is not effected by or through the franchisor;
Grant to Officer of Director of Franchisor	(b) the grant of a franchise to a person who has been an officer or director of the franchisor or of the franchisor's associate for at least six months immediately before the grant of the franchise, for that person's own account;	(b) the grant of a franchise to a person who has been an officer or director of the franchisor or of the franchisor's associate for at least 6 months immediately before the grant of the franchise, for that person's own account,	(b) the grant of a franchise to a person who has been an officer or director of the franchisor or of the franchisor's associate for at least six months, for that person's own account;	(b) the grant of a franchise to a person who has been an officer or director of the franchisor or franchisor's associate for at least six months immediately before the grant of the franchise for that person's own account;	(b) the grant of a franchise to a person who has been an officer or director of the franchisor or of the franchisor's associate for at least 6 months immediately before the grant of the franchise, for that person's own account;	(b) the sale of a franchise to a person who has been an officer or director of the franchisor or its associate for at least 6 months for that person's own account;

TOPIC	PRINCE EDWARD ISLAND	NEW BRUNSWICK	ONTARIO	MANITOBA	BRITISH COLUMBIA	ALBERTA
			Franchises Acts			
Grant of Additional Franchise to Existing Franchisee	(c) the grant of an additional franchise to an existing franchisee if that additional franchise is substantially the same as the existing franchise that the franchisee is operating and if there has been no material change since the existing franchise agreement or latest renewal or extension of the existing franchise agreement was entered into;	(c) the grant of an additional franchise to an existing franchisee if that additional franchise is substantially the same as the existing franchise that the franchisee is operating and if there has been no material change since the existing franchise agreement or most recent renewal or extension of the existing franchise agreement was entered into,	(c) the grant of an additional franchise to an existing franchisee if that additional franchise is substantially the same as the existing franchise that the franchisee is operating and if there has been no material change since the existing franchise agreement or latest renewal or extension of the existing franchise agreement was entered into;	(c) the grant of an additional franchise to an existing franchisee if (i) that additional franchise is substantially the same as the existing franchise that the franchisee is operating, and (ii) there has been no material change since the existing franchise agreement or its latest renewal or extension was entered into;	(c) the grant of an additional franchise to an existing franchisee, if (i) the additional franchise is substantially the same as the existing franchise that the franchisee is operating, and (ii) there has been no material change since the existing franchise agreement, or latest renewal or extension of the existing franchise agreement, was entered into;	(c) the sale of an additional franchise to an existing franchisee if that additional franchise is substantially the same as the existing franchise that the franchisee is operating;
Grant by Executor, Administrator, Sheriff, Receiver, Trustee, Trustee in Bankruptcy or Guardian	(d) the grant of a franchise by an executor, administrator, sheriff, receiver, trustee, trustee in bankruptcy or guardian on behalf of a person other than the franchisor or the estate of the franchisor;	(d) the grant of a franchise by an executor, administrator, sheriff, receiver, trustee, trustee in bankruptcy or guardian on behalf of a person other than the franchisor or the estate of the franchisor,	(d) the grant of a franchise by an executor, administrator, sheriff, receiver, trustee, trustee in bankruptcy or guardian on behalf of a person other than the franchisor or the estate of the franchisor;	(d) the grant of a franchise by an executor, administrator, sheriff, receiver, trustee, trustee in bankruptcy or guardian on behalf of a person other than the franchisor or the franchisor's estate;	(d) the grant of a franchise by an executor, administrator, sheriff, receiver, trustee, trustee in bankruptcy, liquidator or guardian on behalf of a person other than the franchisor or the estate of the franchisor;	(f) the sale of a franchise by an executor, administrator, sheriff, receiver, trustee, trustee in bankruptcy or guardian on behalf of a person other than the franchisor or the estate of the franchisor;
Grant of Fractional Franchise	(e) the grant of a franchise to a person to sell goods or services within a business in which that person has an interest, if the sales arising from those goods or services, as anticipated by the parties or that should be anticipated by the parties at the time	(e) the grant of a franchise to a person to sell goods or services within a business in which that person has an interest, if the sales arising from those goods or services, as anticipated by the parties or that should be anticipated by the parties at the time	(e) the grant of a franchise to a person to sell goods or services within a business in which that person has an interest if the sales arising from those goods or services, as anticipated by the parties or that should be anticipated by the parties at the time	(e) the grant of a franchise to a person to sell goods or services within a business in which that person has an interest if the sales arising from those goods or services — as anticipated by the parties or that should be anticipated by the parties	(e) the grant of a franchise to a person to sell goods or services within a business in which that person has an interest, if the sales arising from those goods or services, as anticipated by the parties or that should be anticipated by the parties at the time the	(h) the sale of a fractional franchise.

TOPIC	PRINCE EDWARD ISLAND	NEW BRUNSWICK	ONTARIO	MANITOBA	BRITISH COLUMBIA	ALBERTA
Franchises Acts						
	the franchise agreement is entered into, will not exceed 20 per cent of the total sales of the business during the first year of operation of the franchise;	the franchise agreement is entered into, will not exceed 20% of the total sales of the business during the first year of operation of the franchise,	the franchise agreement is entered into do not exceed, in relation to the total sales of the business, a prescribed percentage;	at the time the franchise agreement is entered into — will not exceed 20 percent of the business's total sales during the first year of the franchise's operation;	franchise agreement is entered into, will not exceed 20% of the total sales of the business during the first year of operation of the franchise;	
Renewal or Extension	(f) the renewal or extension of a franchise agreement where there has been no interruption in the operation of the business operated by the franchisee under the franchise agreement and there has been no material change since the franchise agreement or latest renewal or extension of the franchise agreement was entered into;	(f) the renewal or extension of a franchise agreement if there has been no interruption in the operation of the business operated by the franchisee under the franchise agreement and there has been no material change since the franchise agreement or most recent renewal or extension of the franchise agreement was entered into,	(f) the renewal or extension of a franchise agreement where there has been no interruption in the operation of the business operated by the franchisee under the franchise agreement and there has been no material change since the franchise agreement or latest renewal or extension of the franchise agreement was entered into;	(f) the renewal or extension of a franchise agreement if there has been (i) no interruption in the operation of the franchised business, and (ii) no material change since the franchise agreement or its latest renewal or extension was entered into;	(f) the renewal or extension of a franchise agreement, if there has been (i) no interruption in the operation of the business operated by the franchisee under the franchise agreement, and (ii) no material change since the franchise agreement, or the latest renewal or extension of the franchise agreement, was entered into;	(d) a renewal or extension of an existing franchise agreement;
Small Investment	(g) the grant of a franchise if the prospective franchisee is required to make a total annual investment to acquire and operate the franchise in an amount that does not exceed the prescribed amount;	(g) the grant of a franchise if the prospective franchisee is required to make a total annual investment to acquire and operate the franchise in an amount that does not exceed the prescribed amount,	(g) the grant of a franchise if, (i) the prospective franchisee is required to make a total annual investment to acquire and operate the franchise in an amount that does not exceed a prescribed amount,	(g) the grant of a franchise if the prospective franchisee is required to make a total annual investment to acquire and operate the franchise in an amount that does not exceed the prescribed amount;		(e) the sale of a franchise if the franchisee is required to make a total annual investment to acquire and operate the franchise in an amount that does not exceed the amount prescribed by the regulations.
Franchise Term Not Longer than One Year and No Non-Refundable	(h) the grant of a franchise if the franchise agreement is not valid for longer	(h) the grant of a franchise if the franchise agreement is not valid for longer	(ii) the franchise agreement is not valid for longer than one	(h) the grant of a franchise if (i) the franchise agreement is not valid	(g) the grant of a franchise, if the franchise agreement, including any renewal or	

TOPIC	PRINCE EDWARD ISLAND	NEW BRUNSWICK	ONTARIO	MANITOBA	BRITISH COLUMBIA	ALBERTA
Franchises Acts						
Fee	than one year and does not involve the payment of a nonrefundable fee and if the franchisor or franchisor's associate provides location assistance to the franchisee, including securing retail outlets or accounts for the goods or services to be sold, offered for sale or distributed or securing locations or sites for vending machines, display racks or other product sales displays used by the franchisee; or	than one year and does not involve the payment of a non-refundable fee and if the franchisor or franchisor's associate provides location assistance to the franchisee, including securing retail outlets or accounts for the goods or services to be sold, offered for sale or distributed or securing locations or sites for vending machines, display racks or other product sales displays used by the franchisee, or	year and does not involve the payment of a non-refundable franchise fee, or	for longer than one year and does not involve the payment of a non-refundable fee, and (ii) the franchisor or franchisor's associate provides location assistance to the franchisee, including (A) securing retail outlets or customer accounts for the goods or services to be distributed, offered for sale or sold, or (B) securing locations or sites for vending machines, display racks or other product sales displays used by the franchisee; or	extension of that franchise agreement, (i) is valid, or would be valid, for one year or less, and (ii) does not involve the payment of a non-refundable initial franchise fee, renewal fee or extension fee;	
Multilevel Marketing or Pyramid Selling	(i) the grant of a franchise if the franchisor is governed by section 55 of the *Competition Act* (Canada).	(i) the grant of a franchise if the franchisor is governed by section 55 of the *Competition Act* (Canada).	(iii) the franchisor is governed by section 55 of the *Competition Act* (Canada);	(i) the grant of a franchise if the franchisor is governed by section 55 of the *Competition Act* (Canada).	(h) the grant of a franchise, if section 55 of the *Competition Act* (Canada) applies to the franchisor;	
Large Investment			(h) the grant of a franchise where the prospective		(i) the grant of a franchise, if the prospective franchisee	

TOPIC	PRINCE EDWARD ISLAND	NEW BRUNSWICK	ONTARIO	MANITOBA	BRITISH COLUMBIA	ALBERTA
Franchises Acts						
			franchisee is investing in the acquisition and operation of the franchise, over a prescribed period, an amount greater than a prescribed amount.		is investing an amount greater than a prescribed amount in the acquisition of the franchise.	
Grant to Operate as Department or Division of Retail Establishment						(g) the sale of a right to a person to sell goods or services within or adjacent to a retail establishment as a department or division of the establishment, if the person is not required to purchase goods or services from the operator of the retail establishment;
Interpretation, Grant Effected by or Through Franchisor	**5.** (8) For the purpose of subclause (7)(a)(iv), a grant is not effected by or through a franchisor merely because	5(10) For the purposes of subparagraph (8)(a)(iv), a grant is not effected by or through a franchisor merely because	**5.** (8) For the purpose of subclause (7) (a) (iv), a grant is not effected by or through a franchisor merely because,	5(16) For the purpose of subclause (11)(a)(iv), a grant is not effected by or through a franchisor merely because	5 (9) For the purposes of subsection (8) (a) (iv), a grant is not effected by or through a franchisor merely because	5(2) For the purpose of subsection (1)(a)(iv), a sale is not effected by or through a franchisor merely because the franchisor
	(a) the franchisor has a right, exercisable on reasonable grounds, to approve or disapprove the grant; or	(a) the franchisor has a right, exercisable on reasonable grounds, to approve or disapprove the grant, or	(a) the franchisor has a right, exercisable on reasonable grounds, to approve or disapprove the grant; or	(a) the franchisor has a right — exercisable on reasonable grounds — to approve or disapprove the grant; or	(a) the franchisor has a right, exercisable on reasonable grounds, to approve or disapprove the grant, or	(a) has a reasonable right to approve or disapprove the sale, or
	(b) a fee must be paid to the franchisor in an amount set out in the franchise agreement or in an amount that does not exceed the reasonable actual costs incurred by	(b) a fee must be paid to the franchisor in an amount set out in the franchise agreement or in an amount that does not exceed the reasonable actual costs incurred by	(b) a transfer fee must be paid to the franchisor in an amount set out in the franchise agreement or in an amount that does not exceed the reasonable actual costs incurred by	(b) a fee must be paid to the franchisor (i) in an amount set out in the franchise agreement, or (ii) in an amount that	(b) a fee must be paid to the franchisor in an amount set out in a franchise agreement or in an amount that does not exceed the reasonable actual costs incurred by	(b) requires payment of a transfer fee (i) the specific amount of which is established in the franchise agreement, or

TOPIC	PRINCE EDWARD SLAND	NEW BRUNSWICK	ONTARIO	MANITOBA	BRITISH COLUMBIA	ALBERTA
			Franchises Acts			
	the franchisor to process the grant.	the franchisor to process the grant.	the franchisor to process the grant.	does not exceed the reasonable actual costs incurred by the franchisor to process the grant.	the franchisor to process the grant.	(ii) that does not exceed the reasonable actual costs incurred by the franchisor to process the transfer.
Interpretation, Franchise Agreement	**5.** (9) For the purposes of subsections (1) and (5), an agreement is not a franchise agreement or any other agreement relating to the franchise if the agreement only contains terms in respect of,	**5**(11) For the purposes of subsections (1) and (6), an agreement is not a franchise agreement or any other agreement relating to the franchise if the agreement only contains terms in respect of		**5**(12) For the purpose of clauses (2)(a) and (8)(a), an agreement is not a franchise agreement or any other agreement relating to the franchise if the agreement only contains terms about	**5** (11) For the purposes of subsections (1) and (6), an agreement is not a franchise agreement or any other agreement relating to a franchise, if the agreement only contains terms in respect of	**4**(7) For the purposes of subsections (2)(a) and (5)(a), an agreement that contains only terms and conditions relating to any one or more of the following is not a franchise agreement:
						(a) a fully refundable deposit;
	(a) keeping confidential or prohibiting the use of any information or material that may be provided to the prospective franchisee; or	(a) keeping confidential or prohibiting the use of any information or material that may be provided to the prospective franchisee, or		(a) keeping confidential, or prohibiting the use of, any information or material that may be provided to the prospective franchisee; or	(a) keeping confidential or prohibiting the use of any information or material that may be provided to a prospective franchisee, or	(b) the keeping confidential or prohibiting the use of any information or material that may be provided to the prospective franchisee;
	(b) designating a location, site or territory for a prospective franchisee.	(b) designating a location, site or territory for a prospective franchisee.		(b) designating a location, site or territory for a prospective franchisee.	(b) designating a location, site or territory for a prospective franchisee.	(c) the designation of a location or territory of the prospective franchised business.
Exception re Interpretation of Franchise Agreement	**5.** (10) Despite subsection (9), an agreement that only contains terms described in clause (9)(a) or (b) is a franchise agreement or any other agreement relating to the franchise for the purposes of	**5**(12) Despite subsection (11), an agreement that only contains terms described in paragraph (11)(a) or (b) is a franchise agreement or any other agreement relating to the franchise for the purposes of		**5**(13) Despite subsection (12), an agreement that contains only terms described in clause (12)(a) or (b) is a franchise agreement or any other agreement relating to the franchise for the purpose of	**5** (12) Despite subsection (11), an agreement that only contains terms described in paragraph (a) or (b) of that subsection is a franchise agreement or any other agreement relating to a	

TOPIC	PRINCE EDWARD ISLAND	NEW BRUNSWICK	ONTARIO	MANITOBA	BRITISH COLUMBIA	ALBERTA
Franchises Acts						
	subsections (1) and (5) if the agreement,	subsections (1) and (6) if the agreement		clauses (2)(a) and (8)(a) if the agreement	franchise for the purposes of subsections (1) and (6), if the agreement	
	(a) requires keeping confidential or prohibits the use of information,	(a) requires keeping confidential or prohibits the use of information		(a) requires keeping confidential or prohibits the use of information	(a) requires keeping confidential, or prohibits the use of, information	
	(i) that is or comes into the public domain without breaching the agreement,	(i) that is or comes into the public domain without breaching the agreement,		(i) that is or comes into the public domain without breaching the agreement,	(i) that is in or comes into the public domain without breaching the agreement,	
	(ii) that is disclosed to any person without breaching the agreement, or	(ii) that is disclosed to any person without breaching the agreement, or		(ii) that is disclosed to any person without breaching the agreement, or	(ii) that is disclosed to any person without breaching the agreement, or	
	(iii) that is disclosed with the consent of all the parties to the agreement; or	(iii) that is disclosed with the consent of all the parties to the agreement, or		(iii) that is disclosed with the consent of all the parties to the agreement; or	(iii) that is disclosed with the consent of all of the parties to the agreement, or	
	(b) prohibits the disclosure of information to an organization of franchisees, to other franchisees of the same franchise system or to a franchisee's professional advisors.	(b) prohibits the disclosure of information to an organization of franchisees, to other franchisees of the same franchise system or to a franchisee's professional advisors.		(b) prohibits the disclosure of information to an organization of franchisees, other franchisees of the same franchise system or a franchisee's professional advisors.	(b) prohibits the disclosure of information to an organization of franchisees, to other franchisees of the same franchise system or to a franchisee's professional advisors.	

TOPIC	PRINCE EDWARD ISLAND	NEW BRUNSWICK	ONTARIO	MANITOBA	BRITISH COLUMBIA	ALBERTA
			Franchises Acts			
Interpretation - Fully Refundable Deposit Not Included				**5**(14) For the purpose of clauses (2)(b) and (8)(b), the payment of any consideration relating to a franchise does not include the payment of a fully refundable deposit that (a) does not exceed the prescribed amount; (b) is refundable without any deductions; and (c) is given under an agreement that in no way binds the prospective franchisee to enter into any franchise agreement.	**5** (13) For the purposes of subsections (1) (b) and (6) (b), the payment of any consideration relating to a franchise does not include the payment of a deposit that (a) does not exceed an amount prescribed by regulation, (b) is refundable without any deductions, if a prospective franchisee does not enter into a franchise agreement, and (c) is given under an agreement with a franchisor concerning the deposit that does not obligate the prospective franchisee to enter into any franchise agreement.	**4**(6) For the purposes of subsections (2)(b) and (5)(b), the payment of any consideration relating to a franchise does not include the payment of a fully refundable deposit. **4**(8) For the purposes of this section, a fully refundable deposit is a deposit that does not exceed the amount prescribed by the regulations, that is refundable without any deductions and that is given under an agreement that in no way binds the prospective franchisee to enter into any franchise agreement.
Right of Rescission - 60 Day	**6.** (1) A franchisee may rescind the franchise agreement, without penalty or obligation, no later than 60 days after receiving the disclosure document, if the franchisor failed to provide the disclosure document or a statement of material change within the time required by section 5 or if the contents of the disclosure document did not meet the requirements of section 5.	**6**(1) A franchisee may rescind the franchise agreement, without penalty or obligation, no later than 60 days after receiving the disclosure document, if the franchisor failed to provide the disclosure document or a statement of material change within the time required by section 5 or if the contents of the disclosure document did not meet the requirements of section 5.	**6.** (1) A franchisee may rescind the franchise agreement, without penalty or obligation, no later than 60 days after receiving the disclosure document, if the franchisor failed to provide the disclosure document or a statement of material change within the time required by section 5 or if the contents of the disclosure document did not meet the requirements of section 5.	**6**(1) A franchisee may rescind the franchise agreement — without penalty or obligation — no later than 60 days after receiving the disclosure document if (a) the franchisor failed to provide the disclosure document or a statement of material change within the time required by section 5; or (b) the contents of the disclosure document did not meet the requirements of section 5.	**6** (1) A franchisee may rescind a franchise agreement, without penalty or obligation, within 60 days after receiving a disclosure document, if (a) a franchisor failed to provide the disclosure document or a statement of material change within the time required by section 5, or (b) the contents of the disclosure document did not meet the requirements of section 5.	**13** If a franchisor fails to give a prospective franchisee the disclosure document by the time referred to in section 4, the prospective franchisee may rescind all the franchise agreements by giving a notice of cancellation to the franchisor or its associate, as the case may be, (a) no later than 60 days after receiving the disclosure document, or

TOPIC	PRINCE EDWARD ISLAND	NEW BRUNSWICK	ONTARIO	MANITOBA	BRITISH COLUMBIA	ALBERTA
			Franchises Acts			
Right of Rescission - 2 Year	**6.** (2) A franchisee may rescind the franchise agreement, without penalty or obligation, no later than two years after entering into the franchise agreement if the franchisor never provided the disclosure document.	**6**(2) A franchisee may rescind the franchise agreement, without penalty or obligation, no later than 2 years after entering into the franchise agreement if the franchisor never provided the disclosure document.	**6.** (2) A franchisee may rescind the franchise agreement, without penalty or obligation, no later than two years after entering into the franchise agreement if the franchisor never provided the disclosure document.	**6**(2) A franchisee may rescind the franchise agreement — without penalty or obligation — no later than two years after entering into it if the franchisor never provided the disclosure document.	**6** (2) A franchisee may rescind a franchise agreement, without penalty or obligation, within 2 years after entering into the franchise agreement, if a franchisor never provided a disclosure document.	(b) no later than 2 years after the franchisee is granted the franchise, whichever occurs first.
Notice of Rescission/Cancellation	**6.** (3) Notice of rescission shall be in writing and shall be delivered to the franchisor, personally, by registered mail, by fax or by any other prescribed method, at the franchisor's address for service or to any other person designated for that purpose in the franchise agreement.	**6**(3) Notice of rescission shall be in writing and shall be delivered to the franchisor personally, by registered mail, by fax or by any other prescribed method, at the franchisor's address for service or to any other person designated for that purpose in the franchise agreement.	**6.** (3) Notice of rescission shall be in writing and shall be delivered to the franchisor, personally, by registered mail, by fax or by any other prescribed method, at the franchisor's address for service or to any other person designated for that purpose in the franchise agreement.	**6**(3) Notice of rescission must be in writing and must be delivered to the franchisor personally or by registered mail, fax or other prescribed method at the franchisor's address for service or to any other person designated for that purpose in the franchise agreement.	**6** (3) A notice of rescission must be in writing and delivered to a franchisor, personally or by any other prescribed method, at the franchisor's address for service or to any other person designated for that purpose in the franchise agreement.	
Effective Date of Rescission	**6.** (4) The notice of rescission is effective,	**6**(4) The notice of rescission is effective	**6.** (4) The notice of rescission is effective,	**6**(4) The notice of rescission is effective	**6** (4) A notice of rescission is effective,	
	(a) on the day it is delivered personally;	(a) on the day it is delivered personally,	(a) on the day it is delivered personally;	(a) on the day it is delivered personally;	(a) if delivered personally, on the day the notice is delivered, or	
	(b) on the fifth day after it was mailed;	(b) on the fifth day after it was mailed,	(b) on the fifth day after it was mailed;	(b) on the fifth day after it was mailed;		
	(c) on the day it is sent by fax, if sent before 5 p.m.;	(c) on the day it is sent by fax, if sent before 5 p.m.,	(c) on the day it is sent by fax, if sent before 5 p.m.;	(c) on the day it is sent by fax, if sent before 5:00 p.m.;		
	(d) on the day after it was sent by fax, if sent at or after 5 p.m.; or	(d) on the day after it was sent by fax, if sent at or after 5 p.m., or	(d) on the day after it was sent by fax, if sent at or after 5 p.m.;	(d) on the day after it was sent by fax, if sent at or after 5:00 p.m.; or		
	(e) on the day determined in accordance with the regulations, if sent by a	(e) on the day determined in accordance with the regulations, if delivered by	(e) on the day determined in accordance with the regulations, if sent by a	(e) on the day determined in accordance with the regulations, if sent by a	(b) if delivered by any other prescribed method of delivery, on the day	

TOPIC	PRINCE EDWARD ISLAND	NEW BRUNSWICK	ONTARIO	MANITOBA	BRITISH COLUMBIA	ALBERTA
			Franchises Acts			
	prescribed method of delivery.	a prescribed method.	prescribed method of delivery.	prescribed delivery method.	determined in accordance with the regulations.	
	6. (5) If the day described in clause (4)(b), (c) or (d) is a holiday, the notice of rescission is effective on the next day that is not a holiday.	**6**(5) If the day described in paragraph (4)(b), (c) or (d) is a holiday, the notice of rescission is effective on the next day that is not a holiday.	**6.** (5) If the day described in clause (4) (b), (c) or (d) is a holiday, the notice of rescission is effective on the next day that is not a holiday.			
						14(1) A notice of cancellation given under section 13 operates (a) to cancel the franchise agreements, or (b) in the case of an agreement that is an offer to purchase, to withdraw the offer to purchase.
Franchisor's Obligations on Rescission / Cancellation	**6.** (6) The franchisor or franchisor's associate, as the case may be, shall, within 60 days of the effective date of the rescission,	**6**(6) Within 60 days after the effective date of the rescission, the franchisor or franchisor's associate, as the case may be, shall	**6.** (6) The franchisor, or franchisor's associate, as the case may be, shall, within 60 days of the effective date of the rescission,	**6**(5) Within 60 days of the effective date of rescission, a franchisor or franchisor's associate must	**6** (5) A franchisor or franchisor's associate, as the case may be, must, within 60 days after the effective date of a rescission,	**14**(2) The franchisor or its associate, as the case may be, must, within 30 days after receiving a notice of cancellation under section 13, compensate the franchisee for any net losses that the franchisee has incurred in acquiring, setting up and operating the franchised business.
	(a) refund to the franchisee any money received from or on behalf of the franchisee, other than money for inventory, supplies or equipment;	(a) refund to the franchisee any money received from or on behalf of the franchisee, other than money for inventory, supplies or equipment,	(a) refund to the franchisee any money received from or on behalf of the franchisee, other than money for inventory, supplies or equipment;	(a) refund to the franchisee any money received from or on behalf of the franchisee, other than money for inventory, supplies or equipment;	(a) refund to a franchisee any money received from or on behalf of the franchisee, other than money for inventory, supplies or equipment,	
	(b) purchase from the franchisee any inventory that the franchisee had purchased pursuant to the franchise agreement and remaining at the effective date of rescission, at a price equal to the purchase price paid by the	(b) purchase from the franchisee the inventory that the franchisee had purchased under the franchise agreement and remaining at the effective date of rescission, at a price equal to the purchase price paid by the	(b) purchase from the franchisee any inventory that the franchisee had purchased pursuant to the franchise agreement and remaining at the effective date of rescission, at a price equal to the purchase	(b) purchase from the franchisee any inventory that the franchisee had purchased pursuant to the franchise agreement and remaining at the effective date of rescission at a price equal to the purchase price paid by the	(b) purchase from the franchisee any inventory that the franchisee had purchased under the franchise agreement and remaining on the effective date of rescission, at a price equal to the purchase price paid by the	

TOPIC	PRINCE EDWARD ISLAND	NEW BRUNSWICK	ONTARIO	MANITOBA	BRITISH COLUMBIA	ALBERTA
			Franchises Acts			
	franchisee;	franchisee,	price paid by the franchisee;	franchisee;	franchisee,	
	(c) purchase from the franchisee any supplies and equipment that the franchisee had purchased pursuant to the franchise agreement, at a price equal to the purchase price paid by the franchisee; and	(c) purchase from the franchisee the supplies and equipment that the franchisee had purchased under the franchise agreement, at a price equal to the purchase price paid by the franchisee, and	(c) purchase from the franchisee any supplies and equipment that the franchisee had purchased pursuant to the franchise agreement, at a price equal to the purchase price paid by the franchisee; and	(c) purchase from the franchisee any supplies and equipment that the franchisee had purchased pursuant to the franchise agreement at a price equal to the purchase price paid by the franchisee; and	(c) purchase from the franchisee any supplies and equipment that the franchisee had purchased under the franchise agreement at a price equal to the purchase price paid by the franchisee, and	
	(d) compensate the franchisee for any losses that the franchisee incurred in acquiring, setting up and operating the franchise, less the amounts set out in clauses (a) to (c).	(d) compensate the franchisee for the losses that the franchisee incurred in acquiring, setting up and operating the franchise, less the amounts set out in paragraphs (a) to (c).	(d) compensate the franchisee for any losses that the franchisee incurred in acquiring, setting up and operating the franchise, less the amounts set out in clauses (a) to (c).	(d) compensate the franchisee for any losses that the franchisee incurred in acquiring, setting up and operating the franchise, less the amounts set out in clauses (a) to (c).	(d) compensate the franchisee for any losses that the franchisee incurred in acquiring, setting up and operating the franchise, less the amounts set out in paragraphs (a) to (c).	
Other Remedies						**15** The rights of action conferred by this Act are in addition to and do not derogate from any other right the franchisee or franchisor may have at law.
Governing Law						**16** The law of Alberta applies to franchise agreements.
Damages for Misrepresentation, Failure to Disclose	**7.** (1) If a franchisee suffers a loss because of a misrepresentation contained in the disclosure document or in a statement of material change or as a result of the franchisor's failure to comply in any way with section 5, the franchisee	**7**(1) If a franchisee suffers a loss because of a misrepresentation contained in the disclosure document or in a statement of material change or as a result of the franchisor's failure to comply with section 5, the franchisee has a right of action	**7.** (1) If a franchisee suffers a loss because of a misrepresentation contained in the disclosure document or in a statement of a material change or as a result of the franchisor's failure to comply in any way with section 5, the franchisee	**7**(1) If a franchisee suffers a loss because of a misrepresentation contained in the disclosure document or a statement of material change or as a result of the franchisor's failure to comply in any way with section 5, the franchisee has a right of	**7** (1) If a franchisee suffers a loss because of a misrepresentation contained in a disclosure document or in a statement of material change, or as a result of a franchisor's failure to comply in any way with section 5, the franchisee	**9**(1) If a franchisee suffers a loss because of a misrepresentation contained in a disclosure document, the franchisee has a right of action for damages against any or all of the following:

TOPIC	PRINCE EDWARD ISLAND	NEW BRUNSWICK	ONTARIO	MANITOBA	BRITISH COLUMBIA	ALBERTA
Franchises Acts						
	has a right of action for damages against,	for damages against	has a right of action for damages against,	action for damages against	has a right of action for damages against the following:	
	(a) the franchisor;	(a) the franchisor,	(a) the franchisor;	(a) the franchisor;	(a) the franchisor;	(a) the franchisor;
			(b) the franchisor's agent;			
	(b) the franchisor's broker;	(b) the franchisor's broker,	(c) the franchisor's broker, being a person other than the franchisor, franchisor's associate, franchisor's agent or franchisee, who grants, markets or otherwise offers to grant a franchise, or who arranges for the grant of a franchise;	(c) the franchisor's broker; and	(b) the franchisor's broker;	
	(c) the franchisor's associate; and	(c) the franchisor's associate, and	(d) the franchisor's associate; and	(b) the franchisor's associate;	(c) the franchisor's associate;	
	(d) every person who signed the disclosure document or statement of material change.	(d) every person who signed the disclosure document or statement of material change.	(e) every person who signed the disclosure document or statement of material change.	(d) every person who signed the disclosure document or statement of material change.	(d) every person who signed the disclosure document or statement of material change.	(b) every person who signed the disclosure document.
Deemed Reliance on Misrepresentation	**7.** (2) If a disclosure document or statement of material change contains a misrepresentation, a franchisee who acquired a franchise to which the disclosure document or statement of material change relates shall be deemed to have relied on the misrepresentation.	**7**(2) If a disclosure document or statement of material change contains a misrepresentation, a franchisee who acquired a franchise to which the disclosure document or statement of material change relates shall be deemed to have relied on the misrepresentation.	**7.** (2) If a disclosure document or statement of material change contains a misrepresentation, a franchisee who acquired a franchise to which the disclosure document or statement of material change relates shall be deemed to have relied on the misrepresentation.	**7**(2) If a disclosure document or statement of material change contains a misrepresentation, a franchisee who acquired a franchise to which the document or statement relates is deemed to have relied on the misrepresentation.	**7** (2) Subject to section 8 (1), if a disclosure document or statement of material change contains a misrepresentation, a franchisee who acquired a franchise to which the disclosure document or statement of material change relates is conclusively deemed to have relied on the misrepresentation.	**9**(2) If a disclosure document contains a misrepresentation, a franchisee who purchases a franchise to which the disclosure document relates is deemed to have relied on the misrepresentation.
Deemed Reliance on	**7.** (3) If a franchisor failed to comply with section 5 with	**7**(3) If a franchisor failed to comply with section 5 with	**7.** (3) If a franchisor failed to comply with section 5 with	**7**(3) If a franchisor failed to comply with section 5 with	**7** (3) Subject to section 8 (1), if a franchisor failed to comply with	

TOPIC	PRINCE EDWARD ISLAND	NEW BRUNSWICK	ONTARIO	MANITOBA	BRITISH COLUMBIA	ALBERTA
			Franchises Acts			
Disclosure Document	respect to a statement of material change, a franchisee who acquired a franchise to which the material change relates shall be deemed to have relied on the information set out in the disclosure document.	respect to a statement of material change, a franchisee who acquired a franchise to which the material change relates shall be deemed to have relied on the information set out in the disclosure document.	respect to a statement of material change, a franchisee who acquired a franchise to which the material change relates shall be deemed to have relied on the information set out in the disclosure document.	respect to a statement of material change, a franchisee who acquired a franchise to which the material change relates is deemed to have relied on the information set out in the disclosure document.	section 5 with respect to a statement of material change, a franchisee who acquired a franchise to which the material change relates is conclusively deemed to have relied on the information set out in the disclosure document provided by the franchisor under section 5.	
Exceptions and Defences to Liability	**7.** (4) A person is not liable in an action under this section for misrepresentation if the person proves that the franchisee acquired the franchise with knowledge of the misrepresentation or of the material change, as the case may be.	**7**(4) A person is not liable in an action under this section for misrepresentation if the person proves that the franchisee acquired the franchise with knowledge of the misrepresentation or of the material change, as the case may be.	**7.** (4) A person is not liable in an action under this section for misrepresentation if the person proves that the franchisee acquired the franchise with knowledge of the misrepresentation or of the material change, as the case may be.	**7**(4) A person is not liable in an action for misrepresentation under this section if the person proves that the franchisee acquired the franchise with knowledge of the misrepresentation or material change.	**8** (1) A person is not liable in an action under section 7 (1) for misrepresentation, if the person proves that the franchisee acquired the franchise with actual knowledge of the misrepresentation or the material change.	**10**(1) A person is not liable in an action under Section 9 if the person proves that the franchisee purchased the franchise with knowledge of the misrepresentation.
Defences re Misrepresentation	**7.** (5) A person, other than a franchisor, is not liable in an action under this section for misrepresentation if the person proves,	**7**(5) A person, other than a franchisor, is not liable in an action under this section for misrepresentation if the person proves	**7.** (5) A person, other than a franchisor, is not liable in an action under this section for misrepresentation if the person proves,	**7**(5) A person — other than a franchisor — is not liable in an action for misrepresentation under this section if the person proves that	**8** (2) A person, other than a franchisor, is not liable in an action under section 7 (1) for misrepresentation, if the person proves any of the following:	**10**(2) A person other than the franchisor is not liable in an action under Section 9 if the person proves
Disclosure Document Given Without Knowledge or Consent	(a) that the disclosure document or statement of material change was given to the franchisee without the person's knowledge or consent and that, on becoming aware of its having been given, the person promptly gave written notice to the franchisee and the franchisor that it was given without that	(a) that the disclosure document or statement of material change was given to the franchisee without the person's knowledge or consent and that, on becoming aware of its having been given, the person promptly gave written notice to the franchisee and the franchisor that it was given without that	(a) that the disclosure document or statement of material change was given to the franchisee without the person's knowledge or consent and that, on becoming aware of its having been given, the person promptly gave written notice to the franchisee and the franchisor that it was given without that person's knowledge	(a) the disclosure document or statement of material change was given to the franchisee without the person's knowledge or consent and that, on becoming aware of its having been given, the person promptly gave written notice to the franchisee and the franchisor that it was given without that person's	(a) that the disclosure document or statement of material change was provided to the franchisee without that person's knowledge or consent and, on becoming aware that the disclosure document or statement of material change had been provided, that person promptly gave written notice to the franchisee	(a) that the disclosure document was given without the person's knowledge or consent and that on becoming aware of its having been given the person promptly gave notice as prescribed by the regulations that it was given without that person's knowledge and consent,

TOPIC	PRINCE EDWARD ISLAND	NEW BRUNSWICK	ONTARIO	MANITOBA	BRITISH COLUMBIA	ALBERTA
Franchises Acts						
	person's knowledge or consent;	person's knowledge or consent,	or consent;	knowledge or consent;	and the franchisor that the disclosure document or statement of material change had been provided without that person's knowledge or consent;	
Consent to Disclosure Document Withdrawn	(b) that, after the disclosure document or statement of material change was given to the franchisee and before the franchise was acquired by the franchisee, on becoming aware of any misrepresentation in the disclosure document or statement of material change, the person withdrew consent to it and gave written notice to the franchisee and the franchisor of the withdrawal and the reasons for it;	(b) that, after the disclosure document or statement of material change was given to the franchisee and before the franchise was acquired by the franchisee, on becoming aware of any misrepresentation in the disclosure document or statement of material change, the person withdrew consent to it and gave written notice to the franchisee and the franchisor of the withdrawal and the reasons for it,	(b) that, after the disclosure document or statement of material change was given to the franchisee and before the franchise was acquired by the franchisee, on becoming aware of any misrepresentation in the disclosure document or statement of material change, the person withdrew consent to it and gave written notice to the franchisee of the withdrawal and the reasons for it; or	(b) after the disclosure document or statement of material change was given to the franchisee and before the franchise was acquired by the franchisee, on becoming aware of any misrepresentation in the document or statement, the person withdrew consent to it and gave written notice of the withdrawal and the reasons for it to the franchisee and the franchisor;	(b) that, after the disclosure document or statement of material change was given to the franchisee and before the franchise was acquired by the franchisee, on becoming aware of any misrepresentation in the disclosure document or statement of material change, that person withdrew consent to it and gave written notice to the franchisee and the franchisor of the withdrawal of consent and the reasons for it;	(b) that, after the giving of the disclosure document and before the purchase of the franchise by the franchisee, on becoming aware of any misrepresentation in the disclosure document the person withdrew consent to it and gave notice as prescribed by the regulations of the withdrawal and the reasons for it,
Reliance on Expert	(c) that, with respect to any part of the disclosure document or statement of material change purporting to be made on the authority of an expert or purporting to be a copy of or an extract from a report, opinion or statement of an expert, the person had no reasonable grounds to believe and did not believe	(c) that, with respect to any part of the disclosure document or statement of material change purporting to be made on the authority of an expert or purporting to be a copy of or an extract from a report, opinion or statement of an expert, the person had no reasonable grounds to believe and did not	(c) that, with respect to any part of the disclosure document or statement of material change purporting to be made on the authority of an expert or purporting to be a copy of or an extract from a report, opinion or statement of an expert, the person had no reasonable grounds to believe and did not	(c) with respect to any part of the disclosure document or statement of material change purporting to be made on the authority of an expert or purporting to be a copy of or an extract from an expert's report, opinion or statement, the person had no reasonable grounds to believe and did not believe that	(c) that, with respect to any part of the disclosure document or statement of material change purporting to be made on the authority of an expert or purporting to be a copy of or an extract from a report, opinion or statement of an expert, that person had no reasonable grounds to believe, and did not	(c) that, with respect to any part of the disclosure document purporting to be made on the authority of an expert or purporting to be a copy of or an extract from a report, opinion or statement of an expert, the person had no reasonable grounds to believe and did not believe that

TOPIC	PRINCE EDWARD ISLAND	NEW BRUNSWICK	ONTARIO	MANITOBA	BRITISH COLUMBIA	ALBERTA
Franchises Acts						
	that,	believe that	believe that,		believe, that	
	(i) there had been a misrepresentation,	(i) there had been a misrepresentation,	(i) there had been a misrepresentation,	(i) there had been a misrepresentation,	(i) there had been a misrepresentation,	(i) there was a misrepresentation,
	(ii) the part of the disclosure document or statement of material change did not fairly represent the report, opinion or statement of the expert, or	(ii) the part of the disclosure document or statement of material change did not fairly represent the report, opinion or statement of the expert, or	(ii) the part of the disclosure document or statement of material change did not fairly represent the report, opinion or statement of the expert, or	(ii) the part of the document or statement did not fairly represent the expert's report, opinion or statement, or	(ii) the part of the disclosure document or statement of material change did not fairly represent the report, opinion or statement of the expert, or	(ii) the part of the disclosure document did not fairly represent the report, opinion or statement of the expert, or
	(iii) the part of the disclosure document or statement of material change was not a fair copy of or extract from the report, opinion or statement of the expert;	(iii) the part of the disclosure document or statement of material change was not a fair copy of or extract from the report, opinion or statement of the expert,	(iii) the part of the disclosure document or statement of material change was not a fair copy of or extract from the report, opinion or statement of the expert.	(iii) the part of the document or statement was not a fair copy of, or extract from, the expert's report, opinion or statement;	(iii) the part of the disclosure document or statement of material change was not a fair copy of or extract from the report, opinion or statement of the expert;	(iii) the part of the disclosure document was not a fair copy of or extract from the report, opinion or statement of the expert, or
Reliance on Statement of Public Official	(d) that, with respect to any part of the disclosure document or statement of material change purporting to be made on the authority of a statement in writing by a public official or purporting to be a copy of or an extract from a report, opinion or statement of a public official, the person had no reasonable grounds to believe and did not believe that,	(d) that, with respect to any part of the disclosure document or statement of material change purporting to be made on the authority of a statement in writing by a public official or purporting to be a copy of or an extract from a report, opinion or statement of a public official, the person had no reasonable grounds to believe and did not believe that		(d) with respect to any part of the disclosure document or statement of material change purporting to be made on the authority of a written statement by a public officer or purporting to be a copy of or an extract from a report, opinion or statement of a public officer, the person had no reasonable grounds to believe and did not believe that	(d) that, with respect to any part of the disclosure document or statement of material change purporting to be made on the authority of a statement in writing by a public official or purporting to be a copy of or an extract from a report, opinion or statement of a public official, that person had no reasonable grounds to believe, and did not believe, that	(d) that, with respect to a false statement purporting to be a statement made by an official person or contained in what purports to be a copy of or extract from a public official document,

TOPIC	PRINCE EDWARD ISLAND	NEW BRUNSWICK	ONTARIO	MANITOBA	BRITISH COLUMBIA	ALBERTA
			Franchises Acts			
	(i) there had been a misrepresentation,	(i) there had been a misrepresentation,		(i) there had been a misrepresentation,	(i) there had been a misrepresentation,	
	(ii) the part of the disclosure document or statement of material change did not fairly represent the report, opinion or statement of the public official, or	(ii) the part of the disclosure document or statement of material change did not fairly represent the report, opinion or statement of the public official, or		(ii) the part of the document or statement did not fairly represent the report, opinion or statement of the public officer, or	(ii) the part of the disclosure document or statement of material change did not fairly represent the report, opinion or statement of the public official, or	(i) it was a correct and fair representation of the statement or a copy of or extract from the document, and (ii) the person had reasonable grounds to believe and did believe that the statement was true.
	(iii) the part of the disclosure document or statement of material change was not a fair copy of or extract from the report, opinion or statement of the public official or	(iii) the part of the disclosure document or statement of material change was not a fair copy of or extract from the report, opinion or statement of the public official, or		(iii) the part of the document or statement was not a fair copy of, or extract from, the report, opinion or statement of the public officer; or	(iii) the part of the disclosure document or statement of material change was not a fair copy of or extract from the report, opinion or statement of the public official;	
Due Diligence	(e) that, with respect to any part of the disclosure document or statement of material change not purporting to be made on the authority of an expert or of a statement in writing by a public official and not purporting to be a copy of or an extract from a report, opinion or statement of an expert or public official, the person,	(e) that, with respect to any part of the disclosure document or statement of material change not purporting to be made on the authority of an expert or of a statement in writing by a public official and not purporting to be a copy of or an extract from a report, opinion or statement of an expert or public official, the person		(e) with respect to any part of the disclosure document or statement of material change not purporting to be made on the authority of an expert or of a public officer's written statement and not purporting to be a copy of or an extract from a report, opinion or statement of an expert or public officer, the person	(e) that, with respect to any part of the disclosure document or statement of material change not purporting to be made on the authority of an expert or of a statement in writing by a public official and not purporting to be a copy of or an extract from a report, opinion or statement of an expert or public official, that person	**10**(3) A person other than the franchisor is not liable in an action under section 9 with respect to any part of the disclosure document not purporting to be made on the authority of an expert and not purporting to be a copy of or an extract from a report, opinion or statement of an expert unless the person
	(i) conducted an investigation sufficient to provide reasonable grounds	(i) conducted an investigation sufficient to provide reasonable grounds for believing		(i) conducted an investigation sufficient to provide reasonable grounds for believing	(i) conducted an investigation sufficient to provide reasonable grounds	(a) did not conduct an investigation sufficient to provide reasonable grounds for believing that

TOPIC	PRINCE EDWARD ISLAND	NEW BRUNSWICK	ONTARIO	MANITOBA	BRITISH COLUMBIA	ALBERTA
Franchises Acts						
	for believing that there was no misrepresentation, and	that there was no misrepresentation, and		that there was no misrepresentation, and	for believing there was no misrepresentation, and	there was no misrepresentation, or
	(ii) believed there was no misrepresentation.	(ii) believed there was no misrepresentation.		(ii) believed there was no misrepresentation.	(ii) believed there was no misrepresentation.	(b) believed there was a misrepresentation.
Mandatory Dispute Resolution Process		**8**(1) A party to a franchise agreement who has a dispute with one or more other parties to the agreement may deliver to the party or parties with whom the party has a dispute a notice of dispute setting out				
		(a) the nature of the dispute, and				
		(b) the desired outcome of the dispute.				
		8(2) Within 15 days after delivery of the notice of dispute, the parties to the dispute shall attempt to resolve the dispute.				
		8(3) If the parties to the dispute fail to resolve the dispute under subsection (2), any party to the dispute, within 30 days after delivery of the notice of dispute but not before the expiry of the 15 days for resolving the dispute under subsection (2), may deliver a notice to mediate to all the parties to the franchise agreement.				

TOPIC	PRINCE EDWARD ISLAND	NEW BRUNSWICK	ONTARIO	MANITOBA	BRITISH COLUMBIA	ALBERTA
Franchises Acts						
		8(4) A notice of dispute or a notice to mediate may be delivered by a prescribed method.				
		8(5) Upon delivery of a notice to mediate under subsection (3), the parties to the dispute shall follow the rules set out in the regulations respecting mediation.				
		8(6) No person shall disclose or be compelled to disclose in a proceeding before a court, tribunal or arbitrator information acquired, an opinion disclosed or a document, offer or admission made in anticipation of, during or in connection with the mediation of a dispute under this section.				
		8(7) Subsection (6) does not apply to				
		(a) anything that the parties agree in writing may be disclosed,				
		(b) an agreement to mediate,				
		(c) a document respecting the costs of the mediation,				
		(d) a settlement agreement made in resolution of all or some of the issues in				

TOPIC	PRINCE EDWARD ISLAND	NEW BRUNSWICK	ONTARIO	MANITOBA	BRITISH COLUMBIA	ALBERTA
Franchises Acts						
		dispute, or				
		(e) any information that does not directly or indirectly identify the parties or the dispute and that is disclosed for research or statistical purposes only.				
		8(8) Subsection (6) does not apply to information disclosed to a court as permitted or required under the regulations.				
		8(9) Nothing in subsection (6) precludes a party from introducing into evidence in a proceeding before a court, tribunal or arbitrator information acquired, an opinion disclosed or a document, offer or admission made in anticipation of, during or in connection with the mediation that is otherwise producible or compellable in the proceeding.				
		8(10) Delivery of a notice of dispute or notice to mediate under this section does not preclude a party to a franchise agreement from taking another measure in relation to the subject matter of the dispute.				
Further Exemptions	**8.** (1) Upon application by a franchisor, and upon payment of the prescribed fee, the Minister may by order, if the		**13.** (1) REPEALED **13.** (2) If a franchisor meets the criteria prescribed for the purpose of this subsection, the			**6**(1) The Minister may by regulation, if the Minister, after consultation with the body designated under section 21(1),

TOPIC	PRINCE EDWARD ISLAND	NEW BRUNSWICK	ONTARIO	MANITOBA	BRITISH COLUMBIA	ALBERTA
Franchises Acts						
	Minister is satisfied that to do so would not be prejudicial to the public interest, exempt the franchisor from the requirement to include prescribed financial statements in a disclosure document, subject to the terms and conditions set out in the exempting order.		Lieutenant Governor in Council may, by regulation, exempt the franchisor from the requirement to include specified financial information in a disclosure document, subject to the terms and conditions set out in the exempting regulation.			is satisfied that to do so would not be prejudicial to the public interest, exempt (a) any person or class of persons, (b) any sale of a franchise or any class of sale of a franchise, or (c) any franchise or class of franchise from any or all provisions of this Act or the regulations, subject to any terms and conditions that the Minister considers appropriate.
			13. (3) A regulation made under this section may be general or specific in its application.			
			13. (4) A regulation made under this section may be revoked if the franchisor no longer meets the prescribed criteria or if the franchisor asks that the exemption be revoked.			
			13. (5) The *Statutory Powers Procedure Act* does not apply to a decision under this section to grant or to refuse to grant an exemption, to impose terms and conditions on an exemption or to revoke an exemption.			
			13. (6) REPEALED			
			13. (7) REPEALED			

TOPIC	PRINCE EDWARD ISLAND	NEW BRUNSWICK	ONTARIO	MANITOBA	BRITISH COLUMBIA	ALBERTA
			Franchises Acts			
	8. (2) An order made under subsection (1) may come into force on a date prior to the date on which the order is made.					**6**(2) A regulation under subsection (1) may come into force on a date prior to the date on which the regulation is made.
Joint and Several Liability	**9.** (1) All or any one or more of the parties to a franchise agreement who are found to be liable in an action under subsection 3(2) or who accept liability with respect to an action brought under that subsection are jointly and severally liable.	**9**(1) All or any one or more of the parties to a franchise agreement who are found to be liable in an action under subsection 3(2) or who accept liability with respect to an action brought under that subsection are jointly and severally liable.	**8.** (1) All or any one or more of the parties to a franchise agreement who are found to be liable in an action under subsection 3 (2) or who accept liability with respect to an action brought under that subsection are jointly and severally liable.	**8**(1) All or any one or more of the parties to a franchise agreement who are found to be liable in an action under subsection 3(2) (duty of fair dealing) or who accept liability with respect to an action brought under that subsection are jointly and severally liable.	**10** (1) If 2 or more parties to a franchise agreement are found to be liable in an action brought under section 3 (2), or accept liability with respect to an action brought under that section, they are jointly and severally liable.	**12** All or any one or more of the persons who are found to be liable in an action under this Act or who accept liability are jointly and severally liable.
Breach re Right to Associate	**9.** (2) All or any one or more of a franchisor or franchisor's associates who are found to be liable in an action under subsection 4(5) or who accept liability with respect to an action brought under that subsection are jointly and severally liable.	**9**(2) All or any one or more of the franchisor or franchisor's associates who are found to be liable in an action under subsection 4(5) or who accept liability with respect to an action brought under that subsection are jointly and severally liable.	**8.** (2) All or any one or more of a franchisor or franchisor's associates who are found to be liable in an action under subsection 4 (5) or who accept liability with respect to an action brought under that subsection are jointly and severally liable.	**8**(2) All or any one or more of a franchisor or franchisor's associates who are found to be liable in an action under subsection 4(5) (right to associate) or who accept liability with respect to an action brought under that subsection are jointly and severally liable.	**10** (2) If 2 or more franchisors or franchisor's associates are found to be liable in an action brought under section 4 (5), or accept liability with respect to an action brought under that section, they are jointly and severally liable.	
Breach re Misrepresentation, Failure to Disclose	**9.** (3) All or any one or more of the persons specified in subsection 7(1) who are found to be liable in an action under that subsection or who accept liability with respect to an action brought under that subsection are jointly and severally liable.	**9**(3) All or any one or more of the persons specified in subsection 7(1) who are found to be liable in an action under that subsection or who accept liability with respect to an action brought under that subsection are jointly and severally liable.	**8.** (3) All or any one or more of the persons specified in subsection 7(1) who are found to be liable in an action under that subsection or who accept liability with respect to an action brought under that subsection are jointly and severally liable.	**8**(3) All or any one or more of the persons specified in subsection 7(1) (misrepresentation, failure to disclose) who are found to be liable in an action under that subsection or who accept liability with respect to an action brought under that subsection are jointly and severally liable.	**10** (3) If 2 or more persons specified in section 7 (1) are found to be liable in an action brought under that section, or accept liability with respect to an action brought under that section, they are jointly and severally liable.	
No Derogation of Other	**10.** The rights conferred by or	**10** The rights conferred by or	**9.** The rights conferred by this	**9** The rights conferred by or	**11** (1) Subject to this section,	

TOPIC	PRINCE EDWARD ISLAND	NEW BRUNSWICK	ONTARIO	MANITOBA	BRITISH COLUMBIA	ALBERTA
Franchises Regulations						
	geographically closest to Prince Edward Island until information on 20 or all franchisees is provided.	type in Ontario, Quebec, Prince Edward Island, Nova Scotia or the State of Maine until information is provided on 20 or all the franchisees, whichever is the lesser number.		Saskatchewan or Alberta until information is provided on 20 or all the franchisees, whichever is the lesser number.		franchisee outlets outside Alberta, provide information on additional outlets that are geographically closest to Alberta until information on 20 outlets is provided. If the total number of franchisee outlets in operation in Alberta and outside Alberta is less than 20, information is only required for the total number of franchisee outlets in operation.
		1(3) If there are fewer than 20 franchisees described in subsection (1) in New Brunswick and the additional jurisdictions referred to in subsection (2), the list shall also include information on the franchisees that currently operate franchises of the same type elsewhere in Canada until information is provided on 20 or all the franchisees, whichever is the lesser number.		**25**(3) If there are fewer than 20 franchisees in Manitoba, Saskatchewan and Alberta, the list shall also include information on franchisees that operate franchises that are geographically closest to Manitoba until information on 20 or all franchisees is provided.		
		1(4) If there are fewer than 20 franchisees described in subsection (1) in Canada and the State of Maine, the list shall also include information on the franchisees that currently operate franchises of the same type elsewhere until information is provided on 20 or all the franchisees, whichever is				

TOPIC	PRINCE EDWARD ISLAND	NEW BRUNSWICK	ONTARIO	MANITOBA	BRITISH COLUMBIA	ALBERTA
			Franchises Acts			
		11(2) Subsection (1) does not apply to a claim if an action based on the claim was commenced before February 1, 2011.		**10**(2) Subsection (1) does not apply to a claim if an action based on the claim was commenced before the coming into force of this section.	**12** (3) Subsection (1) does not apply to a claim if an action based on the claim was commenced before the coming into force of this section.	
Rights Cannot Be Waived	**12.** Any purported waiver or release by a franchisee or a prospective franchisee of a right conferred by or under this Act or of an obligation or requirement imposed on a franchisor or franchisor's associate by or under this Act is void.	**12** A purported waiver or release by a franchisee or a prospective franchisee of a right conferred by or under this Act or of an obligation or requirement imposed on a franchisor or franchisor's associate by or under this Act is void.	**11.** Any purported waiver or release by a franchisee of a right given under this Act or of an obligation or requirement imposed on a franchisor or franchisor's associate by or under this Act is void.	**11** Any purported waiver or release by a franchisee or a prospective franchisee of a right conferred by or under this Act or of an obligation or requirement imposed on a franchisor or franchisor's associate by or under this Act is void.	**13** (1) Any purported waiver or release by a franchisee, or by a prospective franchisee, of a right conferred under this Act or of an obligation or requirement imposed on a franchisor or franchisor's associate under this Act is void.	**18** Any waiver or release by a franchisee of a right given by this Act or the regulations or of a requirement of this Act or the regulations is void.
					13 (2) Subsection (1) does not apply to a waiver or release by a franchisee, or by a prospective franchisee, made in accordance with a settlement of an action, claim or dispute.	
Burden of Proof	**13.** In any proceeding under this Act, the burden of proving an exemption or an exclusion from a requirement or provision is on the person claiming it.	**13** In a proceeding under this Act, the burden of proving an exemption or an exclusion from a requirement or provision is on the person claiming it.	**12.** In any proceeding under this Act, the burden of proving an exemption or an exclusion from a requirement or provision is on the person claiming it.	**12** In a proceeding under this Act, the burden of proving an exemption or an exclusion from a requirement or provision is on the person claiming it.	**14** In a proceeding under this Act, the burden of proving an exemption or exclusion from a requirement or provision is on the person claiming the exemption or exclusion.	**19** In any proceeding under this Act, the burden of proving (a) an exemption, or (b) an exclusion from a definition is on the person claiming it.
Offence Act (BC)					**15** Section 5 of the *Offence Act* does not apply to this Act or the regulations.	
Act Administered by Commission (NB)		**14** The Commission is responsible for the administration of this Act.				

TOPIC	PRINCE EDWARD ISLAND	NEW BRUNSWICK	ONTARIO	MANITOBA	BRITISH COLUMBIA	ALBERTA
Franchises Acts						
Regulations	**14.** (1) The Lieutenant Governor in Council may make regulations,	**15**(1) The Lieutenant-Governor in Council may make regulations	**14.** (1) The Lieutenant Governor in Council may make regulations,	**14**(1) The Lieutenant Governor in Council may make regulations	**16** (1) The Lieutenant Governor in Council may make regulations referred to in section 41 of the *Interpretation Act*. **16** (2) Without limiting subsection (1), the Lieutenant Governor in Council may make regulations as follows:	**20** The Lieutenant Governor in Council may make regulations
			(a) defining co-operative association for the purpose of paragraph 3 of subsection 2(3);			
			(b) prescribing types of changes that constitute a material change;			
	(a) prescribing material facts for the purpose of clause 5(4)(a);		(c) prescribing material facts for the purpose of clause 5(4)(a);			
	(b) prescribing the financial statements to be included in the disclosure document;	(a) prescribing and governing the financial statements to be contained in the disclosure document;	(d) prescribing the financial statements to be included in the disclosure document;	(a) prescribing and governing information, financial and other statements, costs, fees and payments, descriptions and certificates that must be disclosed under section 5, and respecting the form and manner in which the information is to be disclosed;	(c) prescribing and governing the financial statements to be contained in a disclosure document for the purposes of section 5(4)(a);	(c) respecting the preparation of financial statements and the reporting requirements for the financial statements;
	(c) prescribing statements for the purpose of clause 5(4)(d);	(b) prescribing statements for the purposes of paragraph 5(4)(c);	(e) prescribing statements for the purpose of clause 5(4)(d);		(d) prescribing statements, information and documents for the purposes of section 5(4)(c) to (e);	

TOPIC	PRINCE EDWARD ISLAND	NEW BRUNSWICK	ONTARIO	MANITOBA	BRITISH COLUMBIA	ALBERTA
Franchises Acts						
	(d) prescribing other information and copies of documents to be included in the disclosure document;	(c) prescribing other information and documents for the purposes of paragraphs 5(4)(d) and (e);	(f) prescribing other information and copies of documents to be included in the disclosure document;	**NOTE: See section 14(1)(a) above.**		(b) respecting the form and contents of financial statements, reports and other documents required to be contained in a disclosure document;
			(g) prescribing a percentage of sales for the purpose of clause 5(7)(e);			(h) prescribing the percentage for the purposes of section 1(1)(c);
	(e) prescribing an amount for the purpose of clause 5(7)(g);	(e) prescribing an amount for the purposes of paragraph 5(8)(g);	(h) prescribing an amount for the purpose of subclause 5(7)(g)(i);	(b) prescribing an amount for the purpose of clause 5(11)(g);	(e) prescribing an amount for the purposes of section 5(8)(i);	(i) prescribing the amount for the purposes of section 5(1)(e);
			(i) prescribing an amount and period of time for the purpose of clause 5(7)(h);			
	(f) prescribing methods of delivery for the purposes of subsections 5(2), 6(3) and 8(1) and (3), and prescribing rules surrounding the use of such methods, including the day on which a notice of rescission delivered by such methods is effective for the purpose of clause 6(4)(e);	(f) prescribing methods of delivery for the purposes of subsection 5(2), 6(3) or 8(4), and prescribing rules surrounding the use of such methods, including the day on which a notice of rescission delivered by any of those methods is effective for the purposes of paragraph 6(4)(e);	(j) prescribing methods of delivery for the purposes of subsections 5(2) and 6 (3), and prescribing rules surrounding the use of such methods, including the day on which a notice of rescission delivered by such methods is effective for the purpose of clause 6(4)(e);	(c) prescribing delivery methods for the purpose of subsections 5(4) and 6(3), and respecting rules surrounding the use of those methods, including the day on which a notice of rescission delivered by those methods is effective for the purpose of clause 6(4)(e);	(b) prescribing methods of delivery and rules with respect to the use of the methods of delivery for the purposes of section 5(2); (g) prescribing methods of delivery and rules with respect to the use of the methods of delivery for the purposes of section 6(3) and (4), including the day on which a notice of rescission delivered by	(e) respecting the notices required to be given under section 10(2)(a) and (b);

TOPIC	PRINCE EDWARD ISLAND	NEW BRUNSWICK	ONTARIO	MANITOBA	BRITISH COLUMBIA	ALBERTA
Franchises Acts						
					such methods is effective for the purposes of section 6(4)(b);	
	(g) providing for exemptions from the requirement to include prescribed financial statements in a disclosure document;	(j) respecting exemptions from a requirement of this Act or the regulations or a provision of this Act or the regulations;	(k) prescribing criteria for the purposes of subsections 13(1) and (2);		(a) exempting, with or without conditions, a person or class of persons completely or partially from the application of section 5;	(g) restricting any exemptions made under section 6;
	(i) respecting any matter that the Lieutenant Governor in Council considers necessary or advisable to carry out effectively the intent and purpose of this Act.	(m) respecting any matter that the Lieutenant-Governor in Council considers necessary or advisable to carry out the intent and purpose of this Act.	(l) respecting any matter that the Lieutenant Governor in Council considers necessary or advisable to carry out effectively the intent and purpose of this Act.	(f) respecting any matter the Lieutenant Governor in Council considers necessary or advisable to carry out the purpose of this Act.		(j) respecting any matter necessary or advisable to carry out the intent and purpose of this Act effectively.
		(d) respecting the form of a disclosure document;				(a) respecting the form and contents of disclosure documents and other matters relating to disclosure documents;
		(g) prescribing rules governing the informal resolution and mediation of a dispute for the purposes of section 8 and prescribing forms to be used in the mediation process;				
		(h) respecting the costs of the informal resolution and mediation of a dispute between parties to a franchise agreement;				

TOPIC	PRINCE EDWARD ISLAND	NEW BRUNSWICK	ONTARIO	MANITOBA	BRITISH COLUMBIA	ALBERTA
			Franchises Acts			
		(i) respecting the consequences of failing to comply with a provision of a regulation made under paragraph (g);				
		(k) prescribing forms and providing for their use;			(h) prescribing forms and providing for their use.	
	(h) prescribing fees for the purpose of section 8;					
				(d) governing the use of disclosure documents from other jurisdictions;		
				(e) prescribing any other matter required or authorized by this Act to be prescribed by regulation;		
					(f) prescribing a deposit amount for the purposes of section 5(13)(a);	(d) respecting refundable deposits referred to in section 4;
		(l) defining any word or expression used in but not defined in this Act;	(k.1) defining, for the purposes of this Act, any word or expression used in this Act that has not already been expressly defined in this Act;			(f) defining terms used in this Act that are not defined in this Act;
General or Specific	**14.** (2) A regulation made under subsection (1) may be general or specific in its application.	**15**(2) A regulation made under subsection (1) may be general or specific in its application.	**14.** (2) A regulation made under subsection (1) may be general or specific in its application.	**14**(2) A regulation made under subsection (1) may be general or specific in its application.	**16** (3) In making regulations under this Act, the Lieutenant Governor in Council may make different regulations for different circumstances, persons or things, or for different classes of	

TOPIC	PRINCE EDWARD ISLAND	NEW BRUNSWICK	ONTARIO	MANITOBA	BRITISH COLUMBIA	ALBERTA
Franchises Acts						
					circumstances, persons or things.	
Self-Government						**21**(1) The Lieutenant Governor in Council may designate one or more bodies to govern franchising and to promote fair dealing among franchisors and franchisees.
						21(2) A designated body must be a corporation and must in the opinion of the Lieutenant Governor in Council be capable of governing the persons involved in franchising and promoting fair dealing among franchisors and franchisees.
						21(3) The Lieutenant Governor in Council may make regulations
						(a) providing for the number of directors to be elected and on whose behalf they are to be elected;
						(b) respecting the powers, duties and functions of a designated body and the enforcement of any of its powers;
						(c) requiring franchisors and franchisees to be members of a designated body in order to sell franchises or operate franchised businesses in Alberta;

TOPIC	PRINCE EDWARD ISLAND	NEW BRUNSWICK	ONTARIO	MANITOBA	BRITISH COLUMBIA	ALBERTA
			Franchises Acts			
						(d) respecting bylaws that may be made by a designated body, including bylaws to ensure fair dealing between franchisors and franchisees;
						(e) authorizing a designated body to charge and collect fees;
						(f) respecting the termination of a designation under subsection (1);
						(g) respecting financial, policy or management audits of a designated body;
						(h) respecting any matter necessary or advisable to carry out the purposes of this section.
						21(4) A fee authorized under subsection (3)(e) may be levied only
						(a) to reimburse the cost of the designated body's administration and the exercise of the powers and performance of the duties and functions authorized under the regulations, and
						(b) in an amount and manner and on persons approved by the Minister.

TOPIC	PRINCE EDWARD ISLAND	NEW BRUNSWICK	ONTARIO	MANITOBA	BRITISH COLUMBIA	ALBERTA
Franchises Acts						
						21(5) A body designated under this section is not an agent of the Crown.
						21(6) If a body is designated under this section, the body may exercise its powers over and perform its duties and functions in regard to all franchisees and franchisors whether the franchise was granted before or after this Act came into force.
Transitional Provisions						**22**(1) Section 4(1) to (3) of this Act do not apply to the sale of a franchise if
						(a) before November 1, 1995 a franchise agreement has been entered into in respect of a franchise to which this Act applies, and one or more further franchise agreements are required to be entered into on or after November 1, 1995 to complete the sale of the franchise, and
						(b) a prospectus or statement of material facts has been given in compliance with the former Act with respect to that franchise.
						22(2) Despite the repeal of the former Act, Part 2 of the former Act, except sections 34 and 35, continues to apply in respect of

TOPIC	PRINCE EDWARD ISLAND	NEW BRUNSWICK	ONTARIO	MANITOBA	BRITISH COLUMBIA	ALBERTA
Franchises Acts						
						franchises to which that Act applied.
						22(3) Any proceeding, application or other matter commenced under the former Act and not completed on November 1, 1995 may be continued and completed

TOPIC	PRINCE EDWARD ISLAND	NEW BRUNSWICK	ONTARIO	MANITOBA	BRITISH COLUMBIA	ALBERTA
Franchises Acts						
						under the former Act.
						22(4) Exemptions under sections 2 and 3 of the former Act continue until they expire as stated in the orders giving the exemptions.
Public Consultation in Regulation Development				**14**(3) Except in circumstances that the minister appointed by the Lieutenant Governor in Council to administer this Act considers to be of an urgent nature, in the formation or substantive review of regulations made under this section, the minister must provide an opportunity for public consultation regarding the proposed regulation or amendment.		
C.C.S.M. Reference				**15** This Act may be referred to as chapter F156 of the *Continuing Consolidation of the Statutes of Manitoba*.		
Commencement		This Act was proclaimed and came into force February 9, 2015.	**15.** OMITTED (PROVIDES FOR COMING INTO FORCE PROVISIONS OF THIS ACT).	**16** This Act comes into force on a day to be fixed by proclamation. **NOTE: S.M. 2010, c. 13 was proclaimed in force October 1, 2012**	**17** This Act comes into force by regulation of the Lieutenant Governor in Council. **NOTE: As of the date of writing, this statute had not come into force.**	
Short title			**16.** OMITTED (PROVIDES FOR SHORT TITLE OF THIS ACT).			

TOPIC	PRINCE EDWARD ISLAND	NEW BRUNSWICK	ONTARIO	MANITOBA	BRITISH COLUMBIA	ALBERTA
Franchises Regulations						
	CHAPTER F-14.1 **FRANCHISES ACT REGULATIONS**	**NEW BRUNSWICK REGULATION 2010-92**	**Ontario Regulation 581/00 - General**	**THE FRANCHISES ACT** **(C.C.S.M. c. F156)** **Franchises Regulation** **Regulation 29/2012**	**NOTE: At the time of writing, the final version of the regulations under this Act had not been published.**	**ALBERTA REGULATION 240/95** **Franchises Act** **FRANCHISES REGULATION**
	Pursuant to section 14 of the Franchises Act R.S.P.E.I. 1988, Cap. F-14.1, Council made the following regulations:	Under section 14 of the Franchises Act, the Lieutenant-Governor in Council makes the following Regulation:				
Co-operative Associations			**1.** For the purpose of paragraph 3 of subsection 2 (3) of the Act, a co-operative association is defined as,			
			(a) an organization operated on a co-operative basis by and for independent retailers that,			
			(i) purchases or arranges the purchase of, on a non-exclusive basis, wholesale goods or services primarily for resale by its member retailers, and			
			(ii) does not grant representational rights or exercise significant operational control over its member retailers;			
			(b) a "co-operative corporation" as defined			

TOPIC	PRINCE EDWARD ISLAND	NEW BRUNSWICK	ONTARIO	MANITOBA	BRITISH COLUMBIA	ALBERTA
			Franchises Regulations			
			under subsection 136 (2) of the *Income Tax Act* (Canada) or would be a co-operative corporation as defined in that subsection, but for paragraph 136 (2) (c);			
			(c) an organization incorporated under the *Canada Cooperatives Act* (Canada); or			
			(d) an organization incorporated under the *Co-operative Corporations Act*.			
Citation		**1** This Regulation may be cited as the *Disclosure Document Regulation - Franchises Act*.				
Definitions and Interpretation	**1.** (1) In these regulations	**2**(1) The following definitions apply in this Regulation.		**1**(1) The following definitions apply in this regulation.		**1**(1) In this Regulation
"Act"	(a) "Act" means the *Franchises Act* R.S.P.E.I. 1988, Cap. F-14.1;	"Act" means the *Franchises Act*. (Loi)		"Act" means *The Franchises Act*. (« Loi »)		(a) "Act" means the *Franchises Act*, chapter F-17.1 of the Statutes of Alberta, 1995;
"affiliate"	(b) "affiliate" has the same meaning as in the *Canada Business Corporations Act* (Canada);	"affiliate" has the same meaning as in the *Canada Business Corporations Act* (Canada). groupe)				
"earnings projection"	(c) "earnings projection" includes any information given by or on behalf of the franchisor or	"earnings projection" includes any information given by or on behalf of the franchisor or franchisor's associate, directly		"earnings projection" includes any information given by or on behalf of the franchisor or the franchisor's associate, directly		

TOPIC	PRINCE EDWARD ISLAND	NEW BRUNSWICK	ONTARIO	MANITOBA	BRITISH COLUMBIA	ALBERTA
			Franchises Regulations			
	franchisor's associate, directly or indirectly, from which a specific level or range of actual or potential sales, costs, income, revenue or profits from franchises or businesses of the franchisor, franchisor's associates or affiliates of the franchisor of the same type as the franchise being offered can easily be ascertained.	or indirectly, from which a specific level or range of actual or potential sales, costs, income, revenue or profits from franchises or businesses of the franchisor, franchisor's associates or affiliates of the franchisor of the same type as the franchise being offered can easily be ascertained. (*prévisions des résultats*)		or indirectly, from which a specific level or range of actual or potential sales, costs, income, revenue or profits from franchises or businesses of the franchisor or the franchisor's associates of the same type as the franchise being offered can easily be ascertained. « prévisions des résultats »)		
"franchisor's agent"			**0.1** For the purposes of the Act, "franchisor's agent" means a sales agent of the franchisor who is engaged by the franchisor's broker and who is directly involved in the granting of a franchise.			
"franchisor outlet"						(b) "franchisor outlet" means an outlet owned (i) by the franchisor, (ii) by a corporation that controls the franchisor, (iii) by a corporation that is controlled by the franchisor, or (iv) by a corporation in common control with the franchisor

TOPIC	PRINCE EDWARD ISLAND	NEW BRUNSWICK	ONTARIO	MANITOBA	BRITISH COLUMBIA	ALBERTA
<u>Franchises Regulations</u>						
Words and Expressions Defined in the Act						**1**(2) Words and expressions defined in the Act have corresponding meanings in this Regulation.
Franchises of the Same Type	**1.** (2) In these regulations, a franchise or business is the same type as an existing franchise or as the franchise being offered if it is operated or to be operated under the same trade-mark, trade name, logo or advertising or other commercial symbol as that franchise.	**2**(2) For the purposes of this Regulation, a franchise is of the same type as another franchise or a business if they are operated or to be operated under the same trademark, trade name, logo or advertising or other commercial symbol.		**1**(2) For the purposes of this regulation, a franchise is of the same type as another franchise or a business if they are operated or are to be operated under the same trademark, trade name, logo or advertising.		
Methods of Delivery of Disclosure Document	**2.** For the purposes of subsection 5(2) of the Act, the prescribed methods of delivery are	**3**(1) For the purposes of subsection 5(2) of the Act, the following methods of delivery are prescribed:		**5**(1) For the purposes of subsection 5(4) of the Act, a disclosure document may be delivered		
Courier	(a) delivery by courier, if a written acknowledgment of receipt is received from the prospective franchisee; and	(a) delivery by prepaid courier, and	**NOTE: At the time of writing, the Ontario Ministry of Government and Consumer Services had proposed regulatory amendments to permit delivery of disclosure documents by prepaid courier in Ontario. However, the regulations had not yet been amended to implement that proposal.**	(a) by prepaid courier; or		
Electronic Delivery and Requirements	(b) delivery by electronic means or in machine-readable media, if	(b) delivery by electronic means, if the disclosure document	**NOTE: At the time of writing, the Ontario Ministry of Government and Consumer Services had proposed regulatory amendments to**	(b) by electronic means, if		

TOPIC	PRINCE EDWARD ISLAND	NEW BRUNSWICK	ONTARIO	MANITOBA	BRITISH COLUMBIA	ALBERTA
			Franchises Regulations			
			permit electronic delivery of disclosure documents in Ontario. However, the regulations had not yet been amended to implement that proposal.			
	(i) the disclosure document			(i) the disclosure document		
Single Integrated Document or File	(A) is delivered as a single, integrated, document or file,					
No Extraneous Content	(B) has no extraneous content beyond what is required or permitted by law, but which may include customary devices for manipulating electronic documents in machine readable form and tools or access to tools that may be necessary or convenient to enable the recipient to receive and view the disclosure document,					
Format Requirements	(D) is delivered in a form that	(i) is delivered in a form that enables the		(A) is delivered in a form that enables		

TOPIC	PRINCE EDWARD ISLAND	NEW BRUNSWICK	ONTARIO	MANITOBA	BRITISH COLUMBIA	ALBERTA
			Franchises Regulations			
	intrinsically enables the recipient to store, retrieve and print the disclosure document, and	recipient to view, store, retrieve and print the disclosure document, and		the recipient to retrieve and process the disclosure document, and		
No Links to External Content	(C) has no links to or from external documents or content	(ii) contains no links to or from external documents or content.		(B) contains no links to or from external documents or content, and		
Meets Requirements of Law	(E) conforms as to its content and format to the requirements of law,					
Franchisor Record	(ii) the franchisor keeps records of its electronic delivery of disclosure documents, and					
Written Acknowledgement from Franchisee	(iii) a written acknowledgment of receipt is received from the prospective franchisee.			(ii) a written acknowledgment of receipt is received from the prospective franchisee.		
Requirements When Electronic Disclosure Document Consists of Separate Electronic Files		**3**(2) If a disclosure document is delivered by electronic means and consists of separate electronic files, the disclosure document shall contain an index listing the following for each file:		**5**(2) If a disclosure document is delivered by electronic means and consists of separate electronic files, the disclosure document must contain an index for each file that sets out		

TOPIC	PRINCE EDWARD ISLAND	NEW BRUNSWICK	ONTARIO	MANITOBA	BRITISH COLUMBIA	ALBERTA
			Franchises Regulations			
		(a) the file name; and		(a) the file name; and		
		(b) if the file name is not sufficiently descriptive of the subject matter dealt with in the file, a statement of that subject matter.		(b) if the file name is not sufficiently descriptive of the subject matter dealt with in the file, a statement of that subject matter.		
Requirements When Disclosure Document Provided in Parts				**4** The following rules apply when a disclosure document is not delivered as one document:		
				(a) the risk warning statements required under section 3 must be provided first;		
				(b) all of the required information required in a Part of Schedule A must be provided together;		
				(c) the following statement must be printed prominently at the top or front of any document containing information that forms part of the disclosure document: THE FOLLOWING INFORMATION FORMS PART OF THE DISCLOSURE DOCUMENT REQUIRED TO BE PROVIDED UNDER *THE FRANCHISES ACT*.		
				(d) the certificate of		

TOPIC	PRINCE EDWARD ISLAND	NEW BRUNSWICK	ONTARIO	MANITOBA	BRITISH COLUMBIA	ALBERTA
			Franchises Regulations			
				franchisor must be included with the last part of the disclosure document provided by the franchisor.		
Contents of Disclosure Document	**3.** (1) Every disclosure document shall contain	**5** Every disclosure document shall contain		**2**(1) A disclosure document must contain the following:		**2**(1) A disclosure document must contain all material facts including material facts relating to the matters set out in Schedule 1
	(a) presented together at the beginning of the document, the risk warning statements set out in Part 1 of Schedule I;	(a) the risk warning statements set out in Part 1 of Schedule A,		(a) the risk warning statements required under section 3;		
	(b) the information pertaining to the franchisor described in Part 2 of Schedule I;	(b) the required information about the franchisor described in Part 2 of Schedule A,		(b) the required information about the franchisor specified in Part 1 of Schedule A;		
	(c) the information pertaining to the franchise described in Part 3 of Schedule I; and	(c) the required information about the franchise described in Part 3 of Schedule A, and		(c) the required information about the franchise specified in Part 2 of Schedule A;		
	(d) the lists of current and former franchisees described in Part 4 of Schedule I.	(d) the lists of franchisees and businesses described in Part 4 of Schedule A.		(d) the lists of franchisees and businesses specified in Part 3 of Schedule A;		
				(e) the financial statements required under section 7 or the statement under section 8.		

TOPIC	PRINCE EDWARD ISLAND	NEW BRUNSWICK	ONTARIO	MANITOBA	BRITISH COLUMBIA	ALBERTA
			<u>Franchises Regulations</u>			
Disclosure Documents Prepared for Other Jurisdictions	**3.** (2) A franchisor may use a document that is prepared and used to comply with the disclosure requirements under the franchise law of a jurisdiction outside Prince Edward Island as its disclosure document to be given to a franchisee, if the franchisor includes such supplementary information with that document as is necessary to comply with the disclosure requirements of the Act and these regulations.	**4** A franchisor may use as its disclosure document a document that is prepared and used to comply with the disclosure requirements under the franchise law of a jurisdiction outside New Brunswick if the franchisor includes such additional information with that document as is necessary to comply with the disclosure requirements of the Act and this Regulation.		2(2) A franchisor may use as its disclosure document a document that is prepared and used to comply with the disclosure requirements under the laws of another jurisdiction if the franchisor includes such additional information with that document as is necessary to comply with the disclosure requirements of the Act and this regulation.		2(2) A franchisor may use a document authorized under the franchise law of a jurisdiction outside Alberta as its disclosure document to be given to a franchisee, if supplementary information is included that sets out any material changes to the document from that jurisdiction so that it complies with the requirements of this Regulation.
Substantially Complete Disclosure Document	**3.** (3) A disclosure document is properly given for the purposes of section 6 of the Act if the document is substantially complete.			**NOTE: See Section 5(10) of *The Franchises Act* above.**	**NOTE: See Section 9 of the Franchises Act above.**	2(4) A disclosure document is properly given for the purposes of section 13 of the Act if the document is substantially complete.
Certificate of Franchisor (Disclosure Document)	**4.** (1) A Certificate of Franchisor in Form 1 of Schedule II shall be completed and attached to every disclosure document provided by a franchisor to a prospective franchisee. **NOTE: The Certificates of Franchisor in Forms 1 and 2 are not reproduced in this table but may be viewed online on the Government of Prince Edward Island website.**	6(1) Every disclosure document shall contain a completed Certificate of Franchisor in Form 1. **NOTE: The Certificate of Franchisor in Form 1 is not reproduced in this table but may be viewed online on the Government of New Brunswick website.**	**7.** (1) Every disclosure document shall include a certificate certifying that the document, (a) contains no untrue	2(3) A certificate of franchisor in Form 1 of Schedule B must be attached to the disclosure document. **NOTE: The Certificate of Franchisor in Form 1 is not reproduced in this table but may be viewed online on the Government of Manitoba website.**		2(3) A disclosure document, including any material changes made in respect of a disclosure document, must include a certificate set out in Schedule 2 that must be dated and must be signed **NOTE: The Certificate of Franchisor in Schedule 2 is not reproduced in this table but may be viewed online on the Government of Alberta website.**

TOPIC	PRINCE EDWARD ISLAND	NEW BRUNSWICK	ONTARIO	MANITOBA	BRITISH COLUMBIA	ALBERTA
Franchises Regulations						
			information, representations or statements; and			
			(b) includes every material fact, financial statement, statement and other information required by the Act and this Regulation.			
Signing and Dating Certificate of Franchisor	**4.** (3) A Certificate of Franchisor, in either Form 1 or Form 2 of Schedule II, shall be signed and dated,	**6**(2) A Certificate of Franchisor shall be signed and dated,	**7.** (2) A certificate referred to in subsection (1) shall be signed and dated by,	**2**(4) The certificate of franchisor must be signed and dated,		
Franchisor Not Incorporated	(a) in the case of a franchisor that is not incorporated, by the franchisor;	(a) in the case of a franchisor that is not incorporated, by the franchisor,	(a) in the case of a franchisor that is not incorporated, the franchisor;	(a) in the case of a franchisor that is not incorporated, by the franchisor;		(c) if the franchisor is not a corporation, by the franchisor
Franchisor has One Officer or Director	(b) in the case of a franchisor that is incorporated and has only one director or officer, by that person; or	(b) in the case of a franchisor that is incorporated and has only one director or officer, by that person, or	(b) in the case of a franchisor that is incorporated and has only one director or officer, by that person;	(b) in the case of a franchisor that is incorporated and has only one director or officer, by that person; or		(b) if the franchisor has only one director or officer, by that person, or
Franchisor has More than One Officer or Director	(c) in the case of a franchisor that is incorporated and has more than one officer or director, by at least two persons who are officers or directors.	(c) in the case of a franchisor that is incorporated and has more than one officer or director, by at least 2 persons who are officers or directors.	(c) in the case of a franchisor that is incorporated and has more than one officer or director, by at least two persons who are officers or directors.	(c) in the case of a franchisor that is incorporated and has more than one officer or director, by at least two persons who are officers or directors.		(a) by at least 2 officers or directors of the franchisor, or a combination of them totaling at least 2, if the franchisor has 2 or more directors or officers
Date of Disclosure Document						**2**(5) The date of a disclosure document is the date set out in the certificate referred to in subsection (3).

TOPIC	PRINCE EDWARD ISLAND	NEW BRUNSWICK	ONTARIO	MANITOBA	BRITISH COLUMBIA	ALBERTA
Franchises Regulations						
Methods of Delivery of Statement of Material Change				**6**(1) A statement of material change may be delivered by any method set out in subsection 5(4) of the Act or in subsection 5(1) of this regulation.		
Certificate of Franchisor (Statement of Material Change)	**4.** (2) A Certificate of Franchisor in Form 2 of Schedule II shall be completed and attached to every statement of material change provided by a franchisor to a prospective franchisee.			**6**(2) A certificate of franchisor in Form 2 of Schedule B must be attached to a statement of material change.		
Form of Statement of Material Change		**9**(1) A statement of material change to be provided under subsection 5(6) of the Act shall be in Form 2.				
Signing and Dating Statement of Material Change	**NOTE: See Section 4(3) above.**	**9**(2) A statement of material change shall be signed and dated,		**6**(3) Subsection 2(4) applies to a certificate of franchisor for a statement of material change.		
Franchisor Not Incorporated		(a) in the case of a franchisor that is not incorporated, by the franchisor,				
Franchisor has One Officer or Director		(b) in the case of a franchisor that is incorporated and has only one director or officer, by that person, or				
Franchisor has More than One Officer or Director		(c) in the case of a franchisor that is incorporated and has more than one officer or director, by at least 2 persons who are officers or directors.				

TOPIC	PRINCE EDWARD ISLAND	NEW BRUNSWICK	ONTARIO	MANITOBA	BRITISH COLUMBIA	ALBERTA
Franchises Regulations						
Financial Statements	**5.** (1) Subject to section 6 and to an exemption order made under subsection 8(1) of the Act, every disclosure document shall contain financial statements of the franchisor that are prepared in accordance with the generally accepted accounting principles of the jurisdiction in which the franchisor is based.	**7**(1) Subject to section 8, every disclosure document shall contain financial statements of the franchisor that are prepared in accordance with the generally accepted accounting principles of the jurisdiction in which the franchisor is based and that meet the other requirements of this section.	**3.** (1) Every disclosure document shall include,	**7**(1) Subject to section 8, a franchisor must include financial statements that meet the requirements of this section as part of the disclosure document.		**21** Financial statements must be included in the disclosure document and must comply with sections 2 and 3 of the Regulation.
				7(2) The financial statements of the franchisor must be prepared:		
Canadian Generally Accepted Accounting Principles				(a) in accordance with Canadian generally accepted accounting principles as set out in *The Canadian Institute of Chartered Accountants Handbook - Accounting*; or		**3**(1) Financial statements of the franchisor must be prepared in accordance with generally accepted accounting principles for the jurisdiction in which the franchisor is based.
Generally Accepted Accounting Principles of Franchisor's Jurisdiction plus Supplemental Information				(b) in accordance with generally accepted accounting principles of the jurisdiction in which the franchisor is based, if the statements are supplemented by information that sets out any changes necessary to make the presentation and content of such statements equivalent to those of clause (a).		

TOPIC	PRINCE EDWARD ISLAND	NEW BRUNSWICK	ONTARIO	MANITOBA	BRITISH COLUMBIA	ALBERTA
Franchises Regulations						
	5. (2) The financial statements must be either	**7**(2) The financial statements must be either		**7**(3) Subject to subsection (4), the financial statements must be either		**3**(2) Financial statements must be either
Audit	**5.** (2)(a) audited in accordance with the generally accepted auditing standards set out in the *Canadian Institute of Chartered Accountants Handbook*; or	**7**(2)(a) audited in accordance with the generally accepted auditing standards set out in the *Canadian Institute of Chartered Accountants Handbook*, or	(a) an audited financial statement for the most recently completed fiscal year of the franchisor's operations, prepared in accordance with generally accepted auditing standards that are at least equivalent to those set out in the *Canadian Institute of Chartered Accountants Handbook*;	(a) audited in accordance with Canadian generally accepted auditing standards set out in *The Canadian Institute of Chartered Accountants Handbook - Assurance*; or		(a) audited in accordance with Canadian generally accepted auditing standards, including the Canadian Standards on Quality Control and the Canadian Auditing Standards as set out in the CPA Canada Handbook published by the Chartered Professional Accountants of Canada, as amended from time to time, or
Review Engagement	**5.** (2)(b) reviewed in accordance with the review and reporting standards applicable to review engagements set out in the *Canadian Institute of Chartered Accountants Handbook*.	**7**(2)(b) reviewed in accordance with the review and reporting standards applicable to review engagements set out in the *Canadian Institute of Chartered Accountants Handbook*.	(b) a financial statement for the most recently completed fiscal year of the franchisor's operations, prepared in accordance with generally accepted accounting principles that are at least equivalent to the review and reporting standards applicable to review engagements set out in the *Canadian Institute of Chartered Accountants Handbook*; or	(b) reviewed in accordance with Canadian generally accepted standards for review engagements set out in *The Canadian Institute of Chartered Accountants Handbook - Assurance*.		(b) reviewed in accordance with Canadian generally accepted standards for review engagements, including the Canadian Standards on Quality Control and the Other Canadian Standards applicable to review engagement set out in the CPA Canada Handbook published by the Chartered Professional Accountants of Canada, as amended from time to time.
Auditing and Review Standards of Other	**5.** (3) The auditing standards and the review and reporting	**7**(3) The auditing standards and the review and reporting		**7**(4) The financial statements may be audited or reviewed in		**3**(3) The auditing standards and the review standards and

TOPIC	PRINCE EDWARD ISLAND	NEW BRUNSWICK	ONTARIO	MANITOBA	BRITISH COLUMBIA	ALBERTA
			Franchises Regulations			
Jurisdictions	standards of other jurisdictions that are at least equivalent to those referred to in subsection (2) are acceptable.	standards of other jurisdictions that are at least equivalent to those referred to in subsection (2) are acceptable.		accordance with the standards of the jurisdiction in which the franchisor is based if those standards are at least equivalent to those referred to in subsection (3).		reporting standards of other jurisdictions that are at least equivalent to subsection (2) are acceptable.
Most Recently Completed Fiscal Year	**5.** (4) The financial statements must be for the most recently completed fiscal year.	**7**(4) Subject to subsections (5) and (6), the financial statements must be for the most recently completed fiscal year.	**NOTE: See Sections 3(1)(a) and (b) above.**	**7**(5) Subject to subsections (6) and (7), the financial statements must be for the most recently completed fiscal year of the franchisor's operations.		**3**(4) The financial statements must be for the most recently completed fiscal year.
Financial Statements for Last Completed Fiscal Year Not Available	**5.** (5) Despite subsection (4), if 180 days have not yet passed since the end of the most recently completed fiscal year and financial statements have not been prepared and reported on for that fiscal year, the disclosure document shall contain the financial statements for the last completed fiscal year.	**7**(5) If 180 days have not yet passed since the end of the most recently completed fiscal year and the financial statements for that fiscal year have not been prepared and reported on, the disclosure document shall contain the financial statements for the previous fiscal year.	**3.** (2) Despite subsection (1), if 180 days have not yet passed since the end of the most recently completed fiscal year and a financial statement has not been prepared and reported for that year, the disclosure document shall include a financial statement for the previous fiscal year that is prepared in accordance with the requirements in clause (1) (a) or (b).	**7**(6) If 180 days have not yet passed since the end of the most recently completed fiscal year and the financial statements for that fiscal year have not been prepared and reported on, the disclosure document must contain the financial statements for the previous fiscal year.		**3**(5) If 180 days have not yet passed since the end of the most recently completed fiscal year and financial statements have not been prepared and reported on for that fiscal year, the financial statements for the previous fiscal year may be included.
Financial Statements for Initial Fiscal Year Not Available	**5.** (6) Despite subsection (4), if a franchisor has operated for less than one fiscal year or if 180 days have not yet passed since the end of the first fiscal year of operations and financial statements for that year have not been prepared and	**7**(6) If a franchisor has operated for less than one fiscal year or if 180 days have not yet passed since the end of the first fiscal year of operations and the financial statements for that fiscal year have not been prepared and reported on, the	**3.** (3) Despite subsection (1), if a franchisor has operated for less than one fiscal year or if 180 days have not yet passed since the end of the first fiscal year of operations and a financial statement for that year has not been prepared in accordance	**7**(7) If a franchisor has operated for less than one fiscal year or if 180 days have not yet passed since the end of the first fiscal year of operations and the financial statements for that fiscal year have not been prepared and reported on, the		**3**(6) If (a) the franchisor has not completed one fiscal year of operation, or (b) 180 days has not yet passed since the end of the first fiscal year of operation and financial

TOPIC	PRINCE EDWARD ISLAND	NEW BRUNSWICK	ONTARIO	MANITOBA	BRITISH COLUMBIA	ALBERTA
			Franchises Regulations			
	reported on for that fiscal year, the disclosure document shall contain the opening balance sheet for the franchisor.	disclosure document shall contain the opening balance sheet for the franchisor.	with the requirements in clause (1) (a) or (b), the disclosure document shall include the opening balance sheet for the franchisor.	disclosure document must contain the opening balance sheet for the franchisor.		statements have not been prepared and reported on for that fiscal year, the disclosure document must include the franchisor's opening balance sheet.
Exemption from Requirement to Include Financial Statements	**6.** A franchisor is exempt from the requirement in clause 5(4)(b) of the Act and section 5 of these regulations to include financial statements in a disclosure document if	**8**(1) A franchisor is exempt from the requirement in paragraph 5(4)(a) of the Act and subsection 7(1) of this Regulation to include financial statements in a disclosure document if the following conditions apply:	**11.** (1) Pursuant to subsection 13 (2) of the Act, a franchisor that meets the following criteria is exempt from the requirement to include the financial information described in clause 3 (1) (a) or (b) or subsection 3 (2) or (3) of this Regulation in a disclosure document, subject to the conditions set out in subsection (3):	**8**(1) A franchisor is not required to provide the financial statements required under section 7 if		**NOTE: See Alberta *Franchises Act Exemption Regulation* (below).**
Net Worth	(a) the franchisor has a net worth on a consolidated basis according to its most recent financial statements, which have been audited or for which a review engagement report has been prepared, which	(a) the franchisor has a net worth on a consolidated basis according to its most recent financial statements, which have been audited or for which a review engagement report has been prepared, which	1. The net worth of the franchisor on a consolidated basis according to its most recent financial statements that have been audited or for which a review engagement report has been prepared,	(a) the franchisor has a net worth on a consolidated basis according to its most recent financial statements, which have been audited or for which a review engagement report has been prepared, which		
	(i) is at least $2,000,000, or	(i) is at least $2,000,000, or	i. is at least $5,000,000, or	(i) is at least $5,000,000, or		
	(ii) is at least $1,000,000, if the franchisor is controlled by a corporation whose net worth on a	(ii) is at least $1,000,000, if the franchisor is controlled by a corporation whose net worth on a	ii. is at least $1,000,000, if the franchisor is controlled by a corporation whose net worth on a	(ii) is at least $1,000,000, if the franchisor is controlled by a corporation whose net worth on a		

TOPIC	PRINCE EDWARD ISLAND	NEW BRUNSWICK	ONTARIO	MANITOBA	BRITISH COLUMBIA	ALBERTA
Franchises Regulations						
	consolidated basis according to its most recent financial statements that have been audited or for which a review engagement report has been prepared is at least $2,000,000;	consolidated basis according to its most recent financial statements that have been audited or for which a review engagement report has been prepared is at least $2,000,000;	consolidated basis according to its most recent financial statements that have been audited or for which a review engagement report has been prepared is at least $5,000,000.	consolidated basis according to its most recent financial statements that have been audited or for which a review engagement report has been prepared is at least $5,000,000;		
Number of Franchisees	(b) the franchisor	(b) the franchisor	2. The franchisor,	(b) the franchisor		
	(i) has at least 25 franchisees engaging in business at all times in Canada in the five years immediately preceding the date of the disclosure document,	(i) has had at least 25 franchisees engaged in business in Canada at all times during the 5-year period immediately preceding the date of the disclosure document	i. in the five years immediately preceding the date of the disclosure document, has at least 25 franchisees engaging in business at all times in Canada,	(i) has had at least 25 franchisees engaged in business in Canada at all times during the five-year period immediately preceding the date of the disclosure document,		
	(ii) has fewer than 25 franchisees engaging in business at all times in Canada and has at least 25 franchisees engaging in business at all times in a single jurisdiction other than Canada in the five years immediately preceding the date of the disclosure document,	(ii) has had at least 25 franchisees engaged in business in a single jurisdiction other than Canada at all times during the 5-year period immediately preceding the date of the disclosure document,	ii. in the five years immediately preceding the date of the disclosure document, has fewer than 25 franchisees engaging in business at all times in Canada and has at least 25 franchisees engaging in business at all times in a single jurisdiction other than Canada,	(ii) has had at least 25 franchisees engaged in business in a single jurisdiction other than Canada at all times during the five-year period immediately preceding the date of the disclosure document,		
	(iii) does not meet the	(iii) is controlled by a	iii. does not meet the	(iii) is controlled by a		

TOPIC	PRINCE EDWARD ISLAND	NEW BRUNSWICK	ONTARIO	MANITOBA	BRITISH COLUMBIA	ALBERTA
Franchises Regulations						
	requirements of subclause (i) or (ii), but is controlled by a corporation that meets the requirements of subclause (i), or	corporation that meets the requirements of subparagraph (i),	requirements of subparagraph i or ii, but is controlled by a corporation that meets the requirements of subparagraph i, or	corporation that meets the requirements of subclause (i),		
	(iv) does not meet the requirements of subclause (i) or (ii), but is controlled by a corporation that meets the requirements of subclause (ii);	(iv) is controlled by a corporation that meets the requirements of subparagraph (ii),	iv. does not meet the requirements of subparagraph i or ii, but is controlled by a corporation that meets the requirements of subparagraph ii.	(iv) is controlled by a corporation that meets the requirements of subclause (ii),		
		(v) has had at least 25 franchisees engaged in business in Canada at all times during a portion of the 5-year period immediately preceding the date of the disclosure document and is controlled by a corporation that had at least 25 franchisees engaged in business in Canada at all times during the remainder of that 5-year period, or		(v) has had at least 25 franchisees engaged in business in Canada at all times during a portion of the five-year period immediately preceding the date of the disclosure document and is controlled by a corporation that had at least 25 franchisees engaged in business in Canada at all times during the remainder of that five-year period, or		
		(vi) has had at least 25 franchisees engaged		(vi) has had at least 25 franchisees engaged in		

TOPIC	PRINCE EDWARD SLAND	NEW BRUNSWICK	ONTARIO	MANITOBA	BRITISH COLUMBIA	ALBERTA
Franchises Regulations						
		in business in a single jurisdiction other than Canada at all times during a portion of the 5-year period immediately preceding the date of the disclosure document and is controlled by a corporation that had at least 25 franchisees engaged in business in that jurisdiction at all times during the remainder of that 5-year period;		business in a single jurisdiction other than Canada at all times during a portion of the five-year period immediately preceding the date of the disclosure document and is controlled by a corporation that had at least 25 franchisees engaged in business in that jurisdiction at all times during the remainder of that five-year period;		
Length of Time Engaged in Line of Business	(c) the franchisor	(c) the franchisor	3. The franchisor,	(c) the franchisor or a corporation controlling the franchisor		
	(i) has engaged in the line of business associated with the franchise continuously for not less than five years immediately preceding the date of the disclosure document, or	(i) has engaged in the line of business associated with the franchise continuously during the 5-year period immediately preceding the date of the disclosure document,	i. has engaged in the line of business associated with the franchise continuously for not less than five years immediately preceding the date of the disclosure document, or	(i) has engaged in the line of business associated with the franchise continuously during the five-year period immediately preceding the date of the disclosure document,		
	(ii) is controlled by a corporation that meets the requirements of subclause (i); and	(ii) is controlled by a corporation that meets the requirements of subparagraph (i), or	ii. is controlled by a corporation that meets the requirements of subparagraph i.	(ii) is controlled by a corporation that meets the requirements of subclause (i), or		

TOPIC	PRINCE EDWARD ISLAND	NEW BRUNSWICK	ONTARIO	MANITOBA	BRITISH COLUMBIA	ALBERTA
			Franchises Regulations			
		(iii) has engaged in the line of business associated with the franchise continuously during a portion of the 5-year period immediately preceding the date of the disclosure document and is controlled by a corporation that engaged continuously in that line of business during the remainder of that 5-year period; and		(iii) has engaged in the line of business associated with the franchise continuously during a portion of the five-year period immediately preceding the date of the disclosure document and is controlled by a corporation that engaged continuously in that line of business during the remainder of that five-year period; and		
Judgments, Orders and Awards Against Franchisor	(d) the franchisor, the franchisor's associates, and the directors, general partners and officers of the franchisor in the five years immediately preceding the date of the disclosure document,	(d) during the 5-year period immediately preceding the date of the disclosure document	4. In the five years immediately preceding the date of the disclosure document, the franchisor, the franchisor's associates, and the directors, general partners and officers of the franchisor,	(d) during the five-year period immediately preceding the date of the disclosure document,		
	(i) in the case of a franchisor described in subclause (b)(i) or (iii) have not had any judgment, order or award made in Canada against any of them relating to fraud, unfair or deceptive	(i) in the case of a franchisor described in subparagraph (b)(i) or (iii) or (v), the franchisor, the franchisor's associates and the directors, general partners and officers of the	i. in the case of a franchisor described in subparagraph 2 i or iii have not had any judgment, order or award made in Canada against any of them relating to fraud, unfair or deceptive	(i) in the case of a franchisor described in subclause (b)(i), (iii) or (v), the franchisor, the franchisor's associates and the directors, general partners and officers of the franchisor have not		

TOPIC	PRINCE EDWARD ISLAND	NEW BRUNSWICK	ONTARIO	MANITOBA	BRITISH COLUMBIA	ALBERTA
Franchises Regulations						
	practices, or a law regulating franchises including the Act, or	franchisor have not had any conviction, judgment, order or award relating to fraud or unfair or deceptive business practices made against any of them in Canada, and	practices, or a law regulating franchises, including the Act, or	had any conviction, judgment, order or award relating to fraud or unfair or deceptive business practices made against any of them in Canada, and		
	(ii) in the case of a franchisor described in subclause (b)(ii) or (iv) have not had any judgment, order or award in Canada or in the jurisdiction referred to in subclause (b)(ii) made against any of them relating to fraud, unfair or deceptive practices, or a law regulating franchises including the Act.	(ii) in the case of a franchisor described in subparagraph (b)(ii) or (iv) or (vi), the franchisor, the franchisor's associates and the directors, general partners and officers of the franchisor have not had any conviction, judgment, order or award relating to fraud or unfair or deceptive business practices made against any of them in Canada or in the jurisdiction referred to in subparagraph (b)(ii) or (vi).	ii. in the case of a franchisor described in subparagraph 2 ii or iv have not had any judgment, order or award made in Canada or in the jurisdiction referred to in subparagraph 2 ii against any of them relating to fraud, unfair or deceptive practices, or a law regulating franchises, including the Act.	(ii) in the case of a franchisor described in subclause (b)(ii), (iv) or (vi), the franchisor, the franchisor's associates and the directors, general partners and officers of the franchisor have not had any conviction, judgment, order or award relating to fraud or unfair or deceptive business practices made against any of them in Canada or in the jurisdiction referred to in subclause (b)(ii) or (vi).		
Disclosure if Exemption Claimed		**8**(2) If a franchisor relies on an exemption under subsection (1), the Certificate of Franchisor referred to in section 6 shall contain a statement that the franchisor meets the	**3**(1)(c) if a regulation has been made under subsection 13 (2) of the Act in respect of the franchisor, a declaration that the franchisor is exempt from the requirement to provide the	**8**(2) If a franchisor is not required to provide financial statements, the certificate of franchisor referred to in subsection 2(3) must include a statement that the franchisor		**21** If the franchisor does not include its financial statements in the disclosure document on the basis that it qualifies under a Ministerial exemption,

TOPIC	PRINCE EDWARD ISLAND	NEW BRUNSWICK	ONTARIO	MANITOBA	BRITISH COLUMBIA	ALBERTA
			Franchises Regulations			
		requirements of subsection (1) and is therefore not including financial statements in the disclosure document.	financial statement described in clause (a) or (b), and that the franchisor meets the criteria prescribed for the purpose of that exemption.	meets the requirements of this section and is not required to provide financial statements.		disclose this fact.
Financial Statement Standards for Determining Exemption			**11.** (2) Financial statements of a franchisor mentioned in paragraph 1 of subsection (1) shall,			
			(a) be prepared in accordance with generally accepted auditing standards that are at least equivalent to those set out in the Canadian Institute of Chartered Accountants Handbook, if the financial statements are audited; and			
			(b) be prepared in accordance with generally accepted accounting principles that are at least equivalent to the review and reporting standards applicable to review engagements set out in the Canadian Institute of Chartered Accountants Handbook, if a review engagement report has been prepared for the financial statements.			

TOPIC	PRINCE EDWARD ISLAND	NEW BRUNSWICK	ONTARIO	MANITOBA	BRITISH COLUMBIA	ALBERTA
			Franchises Regulations			
When Exemption Ceases to Be effective			**11.** (3) An exemption described in subsection (1) ceases to be effective if,			
			(a) the franchisor ceases to meet the exemption criteria set out in paragraph 1 of subsection (1);			
			(b) the franchisor no longer meets any of the following conditions:			
			(i) the franchisor has at least 25 franchisees engaging in business at all times in Canada,			
			(ii) the franchisor has fewer than 25 franchisees engaging in business at all times in Canada and has at least 25 franchisees engaging in business at all times in a single jurisdiction other than Canada,			
			(iii) the franchisor does not meet the conditions of subclause (i) or (ii), but is controlled by a corporation that meets the conditions of subclause (i), or			

TOPIC	PRINCE EDWARD ISLAND	NEW BRUNSWICK	ONTARIO	MANITOBA	BRITISH COLUMBIA	ALBERTA
			Franchises Regulations			
			(iv) the franchisor does not meet the conditions of subclause (i) or (ii), but is controlled by a corporation that meets the conditions of subclause (ii);			
			(c) the franchisor ceases to engage in the line of business associated with the franchise;			
			(d) in the case of a franchisor described in subparagraph 3 ii of subsection (1), the franchisor ceases to be controlled by a corporation that engages in the line of business associated with the franchise;			
			(e) in the case of a franchisor described in subparagraph 2 i or iii of subsection (1), a judgment, order or award relating to fraud, unfair or deceptive practices, or a law regulating franchises, including the Act, is made in Canada against any of the franchisor, the franchisor's associates, and the directors, general			

TOPIC	PRINCE EDWARD ISLAND	NEW BRUNSWICK	ONTARIO	MANITOBA	BRITISH COLUMBIA	ALBERTA
Franchises Regulations						
			partners and officers of the franchisor; or			
			(f) in the case of a franchisor described in subparagraph 2 ii or iv of subsection (1), a judgment, order or award relating to fraud, unfair or deceptive practices, or a law regulating franchises, including the Act, is made in Canada or in the single jurisdiction other than Canada referred to in subparagraph 2 ii of subsection (1) against any of the franchisor, the franchisor's associates, and the directors, general partners and officers of the franchisor.			
Prescribed Amount (Fully Refundable Deposit)				**11** For the purposes of subsection 5(14) of the Act, the prescribed amount is 20% of the initial franchise fee, to a maximum of $100,000.		**5** The maximum amount of a fully-refundable deposit referred to in section 4(8) of the Act is 20% of the initial franchise fee.
Prescribed Percentage (Fractional Franchise Exemption)			**8.** For the purposes of clause 5 (7) (e) of the Act, the prescribed percentage is 20 per cent.			**4** The percentage, for the purposes of the definition of "fractional franchise" in the Act, is 20%.
Prescribed Amount (Small Investment Exemption)	**7.** For the purposes of clause 5(7)(g) of the Act, the prescribed amount is $5,000.		**9.** For the purposes of subclause 5 (7) (g) (i) of the Act, the prescribed amount is $5,000.	**10** For the purposes of clause 5(11)(g) of the Act, the prescribed amount is $5,000.		**6**(1) The maximum total annual investment for the purposes of section 5(1)(e) of the Act is $5000

TOPIC	PRINCE EDWARD ISLAND	NEW BRUNSWICK	ONTARIO	MANITOBA	BRITISH COLUMBIA	ALBERTA
			Franchises Regulations			
						6(2) In calculating the total annual investment, the cost of acquiring pre-sold inventory or of purchasing reasonable quantities of inventory, if there is a reasonable buy-back policy for unsold inventory, is not to be included.
Prescribed Period and Prescribed Amount (Large Investment Exemption)			**10.** For the purposes of clause 5 (7) (h) of the Act, the prescribed period is one year and the prescribed amount is $5,000,000.			
Prescribed Fee to Apply for Ministerial Exemption	**8.** For the purposes of section 8 of the Act, the prescribed fee is $250.					
Notice of Misrepresentation						**7**(1) A notice under section 10 of the Act must be given to the franchisee and the franchisor.
						7(2) The person giving the notice must make all reasonable efforts to ensure that the notice is received by the franchisor and franchisee.
						7(3) The notice must be published in a daily newspaper having general circulation in Edmonton and in a daily newspaper having general circulation in Calgary.
						7(4) The notice must,

TOPIC	PRINCE EDWARD ISLAND	NEW BRUNSWICK	ONTARIO	MANITOBA	BRITISH COLUMBIA	ALBERTA
Franchises Regulations						
						(a) for the purpose of section 10(2)(a) of the Act, include a statement that the disclosure document was given without that person's consent, or
						(b) for the purpose of section 10(2)(b) of the Act, include a statement that the person has withdrawn his consent to the disclosure document and the reasons for doing so.
Method of Delivery of Notice of Rescission				**9**(1) For the purposes of subsection 6(3) of the Act, a notice of rescission may be delivered by prepaid courier.		
Effective Date of Notice of Rescission				**9**(2) For purposes of clause 6(4)(e) of the Act, a notice of rescission delivered by prepaid courier is effective when the notice of rescission is provided to the franchisor by the courier.		
Repeal						**8** The *Franchises Regulation* (Alta. Reg. 201/72) is repealed.
Expiry						**9** For the purpose of ensuring that this Regulation is reviewed for ongoing relevancy and necessity, with the option that it may be re-passed in its present or amended form following a review, this

TOPIC	PRINCE EDWARD ISLAND	NEW BRUNSWICK	ONTARIO	MANITOBA	BRITISH COLUMBIA	ALBERTA
			Franchises Regulations			
						Regulation expires on November 30, 2020.
Commencement		**11** This Regulation comes into force on February 1, 2011.	**12**. OMITTED (PROVIDES FOR COMING INTO FORCE OF PROVISIONS OF THIS REGULATION).	**12** This regulation comes into force on the same day that *The Franchises Act*, S.M. 2010, c. 13, comes into force.		**10** This Regulation comes into force on November 1, 1995.
DISCLOSURE DOCUMENT REQUIREMENTS						
Risk Warnings			**4.** For the purpose of clause 5 (4) (d) of the Act, every disclosure document shall include the following statements together in one section at the beginning of the document:	**3.** A disclosure document must contain the following statements at the beginning of the document:		
	1. A prospective franchisee should seek information on the franchisor and on the franchisor's business background, banking affairs, credit history and trade references.	1 A prospective franchisee should seek information on the franchisor and on the franchisor's business background, banking affairs, credit history and trade references.	1. A commercial credit report is a report which may include information on the franchisor's business background, banking information, credit history and trade references. Such reports may be obtained from private credit reporting companies and may provide information useful in making an investment decision.	1. A prospective franchisee should seek information on the franchisor and on the franchisor's business background, banking affairs, credit history and trade references.		
	2. A prospective franchisee should seek expert independent legal and financial advice in relation to franchising and the franchise agreement prior to entering into the franchise agreement.	2 A prospective franchisee should seek expert independent legal and financial advice in relation to franchising and the franchise agreement before entering into the franchise agreement.	2. Independent legal and financial advice in relation to the franchise agreement should be sought prior to entering into the franchise agreement.	2. A prospective franchisee should seek expert independent legal and financial advice in relation to franchising and the franchise agreement before entering into the franchise agreement.		

TOPIC	PRINCE EDWARD ISLAND	NEW BRUNSWICK	ONTARIO	MANITOBA	BRITISH COLUMBIA	ALBERTA
			Franchises Regulations			
	3. A prospective franchisee should contact current and previous franchisees prior to entering into the franchise agreement.	3 A prospective franchisee should contact current and previous franchisees before entering into the franchise agreement.	3. A prospective franchisee is strongly encouraged to contact any current or previous franchisees prior to entering into the franchise agreement.	3. A prospective franchisee should contact current and previous franchisees before entering into the franchise agreement.		
	4. Lists of current and previous franchisees and their contact information can be found in this disclosure document.	4 Lists of current and previous franchisees and their contact information can be found in this disclosure document.	4. The cost of goods and services acquired under the franchise agreement may not correspond to the lowest cost of the goods and services available in the marketplace.	4. Lists of current and previous franchisees and their contact information can be found in this disclosure document.		
Description of Franchisor's Business						**6** Describe the franchisor's business and the franchises to be offered in Alberta.
Required Information About the Franchisor			**2.** Every disclosure document shall include the following information:			
Business Background of the Franchisor	**1.**The business background of the franchisor, including	**1** The business background of the franchisor, including	1. The business background of the franchisor, including,	**1** The following information about the business background of the franchisor:		**1** Provide the following in a summary form:
	(a) the name of the franchisor;	(a) the name of the franchisor,	i. the name and address of the franchisor,	(a) the name of the franchisor;		(a) the name and address of the franchisor;
	(b) the name under which the franchisor is doing or intends to do business;	(b) the name under which the franchisor is doing or intends to do business,	ii. the name under which the franchisor engages in or intends to engage in business,	(b) the name under which the franchisor is doing or intends to do business;		(b) the name under which the franchisor does or intends to do business;
	(c) the franchisor's principal business address and, if the franchisor has an attorney for service in	(c) the franchisor's principal business address and, if the franchisor has an attorney for service in	iii. the principal business address of the franchisor and, if the franchisor's principal address is	(c) the franchisor's principal business address and, if the franchisor's principal business address is		(c) the principal business address of the franchisor and, if the franchisor has an attorney for service in

TOPIC	PRINCE EDWARD ISLAND	NEW BRUNSWICK	ONTARIO	MANITOBA	BRITISH COLUMBIA	ALBERTA
Franchises Regulations						
	Prince Edward Island, the name and address of that person;	New Brunswick, the name and address of that person,	outside Ontario, the name and address of a person authorized to accept service in Ontario on the franchisor's behalf,	outside Manitoba, the name and address of a person authorized to accept service in Manitoba on the franchisor's behalf;		Alberta, the name and address of that person;
	(d) the business form of the franchisor, whether corporate, partnership or otherwise;	(d) the business form of the franchisor, whether corporate, partnership or otherwise,	iv. the business form of the franchisor, including whether the franchisor is a sole proprietorship, partnership or corporation and, if incorporated, the jurisdiction where the franchisor is incorporated,	(d) the business form of the franchisor, whether corporate, partnership or otherwise, and if incorporated, the jurisdiction where the franchisor is incorporated;		(d) the business form of the franchisor;
	(e) if the franchisor is a subsidiary, the name and principal business address of the parent;	(e) if the franchisor is a subsidiary, the name and principal business address of the parent,	v. if the franchisor is a subsidiary, the name and principal address of the parent,	(e) if the franchisor is a subsidiary, the name and principal business address of the parent;		(e) the length of time the franchisor has conducted a business of the type to be operated by the franchisee;
	(f) the business experience of the franchisor, including the length of time the franchisor has operated a business of the same type as the franchise being offered, has granted franchises of that type or has granted any other type of franchise;	(f) the business experience of the franchisor, including the length of time the franchisor has operated a business of the same type as the franchise being offered, has granted franchises of that type or has granted any other type of franchise, and	vi. the length of time the franchisor has engaged in the line of business associated with the franchise,	(f) the length of time the franchisor has operated a business of the same type as the franchise being offered, has granted franchises of that type or has granted any other type of franchise;		(f) the length of time the franchisor has offered franchises for the same type of business as that to be operated by the franchisee;
			vii. the length of time the franchisor has offered franchises in the line of			

TOPIC	PRINCE EDWARD ISLAND	NEW BRUNSWICK	ONTARIO	MANITOBA	BRITISH COLUMBIA	ALBERTA
Franchises Regulations						
			business associated with the franchise, and			
	(g) if the franchisor has offered a different type of franchise from that being offered, a description of every such type of franchise, including for each type of franchise,	(g) if the franchisor has offered a franchise of a different type from that being offered, a description of every such type of franchise, including for each type of franchise,	viii. if the franchisor has offered a franchise in another line of business, a description of every franchise in each line of business, including for each franchise,	(g) if the franchisor has offered a franchise of a different type from that being offered, a description of every such type of franchise, including for each type of franchise		(g) whether the franchisor has offered franchises in other lines of business, including
						(i) a description of each other line of business,
	(i) the length of time the franchisor has offered the franchise to prospective franchisees, and	(i) the length of time the franchisor has offered the franchise to prospective franchisees, and	A. the length of time the franchisor has offered the franchise to prospective franchisees, and	(i) the length of time the franchisor has offered the franchise to prospective franchisees, and		(iii) the length of time the franchisor has offered franchises in other lines of business;
	(ii) the number of franchises granted in the five years immediately before the date of the disclosure document.	(ii) the number of franchises granted during the 5- year period immediately preceding the date of the disclosure document.	B. the number of franchises sold in the five years immediately preceding the date of the disclosure document.	(ii) the number of franchises granted during the five-year period immediately preceding the date of the disclosure document.		(ii) the number of franchises sold in the previous 5 years in each other line of business, and
Directors , General Partners and Officers	**2.** The business background of the directors, the general partners and the officers of the franchisor who will have day to day management responsibilities relating to the franchise, including	**2** The business background of the directors, the general partners and the officers of the franchisor, including	2. The business background of the directors, the general partners and the officers of the franchisor, including,	**2** The following information about the business background of the directors, the general partners and the officers of the franchisor:		(h) the names of the directors, general partners and officers of the franchisor who will have management responsibilities relating to the franchise. State each

TOPIC	PRINCE EDWARD ISLAND	NEW BRUNSWICK	ONTARIO	MANITOBA	BRITISH COLUMBIA	ALBERTA
			Franchises Regulations			
	(a) the name and current position of each person;	(a) the name and current position of each of them,	i. the name and current position of each person,	(a) the name and current position of each person;		person's principal occupation and employers during the 5 years preceding the date of the disclosure document. For the purposes of clause (h), the information need only be provided for those directors, general partners and officers of the franchisor who will have day to day management responsibilities relating to the franchise.
	(b) a brief description of the prior relevant business experience of each person;	(b) a brief description of the prior relevant business experience of each of them,	ii. a brief description of the prior relevant business experience of each person,	(b) a brief description of the prior relevant business experience of each person;		
	(c) the length of time each person has been engaged in business of the same type as the business of the franchise being offered; and	(c) the length of time each of them has been engaged in business of the same type as the franchise being offered, and	iii. the length of time each person has engaged in the line of business associated with the franchise, and	(c) the length of time each person has been engaged in business of the same type as the franchise being offered;		
	(d) the principal occupation and the employers of each person during the five years immediately before the date of the disclosure document.	(d) the principal occupation and the employers of each of them during the 5-year period immediately preceding the date of the disclosure document.	iv. the principal occupation and the employers of each person during the five years immediately preceding the date of the disclosure document.	(d) the principal occupation and the employers of each person during the five-year period immediately preceding the date of the disclosure document.		
Previous Convictions / Pending Charges	**3.** A statement indicating whether, during the ten years immediately before the date of the disclosure document, the franchisor, the franchisor's associate or a director, general partner or officer of the franchisor has been convicted of fraud, unfair or deceptive business practices or a violation of a law that regulates franchises, or if there is a charge pending against the person involving such a matter, and the details of any such conviction or charge.	3 A statement indicating whether, during the 5-year period immediately preceding the date of the disclosure document, the franchisor, the franchisor's associate or a director, a general partner or an officer of the franchisor was convicted of fraud, unfair or deceptive business practices or a violation of a law that regulates franchises, or if there is a charge pending against the person involving such a matter, and the details of any such conviction or charge.	3. A statement, including a description of details, indicating whether, during the ten years immediately preceding the date of the disclosure document, the franchisor, the franchisor's associate or a director, general partner or officer of the franchisor has been convicted of fraud, unfair or deceptive business practices, or a violation of a law that regulates franchises or business or if there is a charge pending against the person	**3** A statement indicating whether, during the 10-year period immediately preceding the date of the disclosure document, the franchisor, the franchisor's associate or a director, a general partner or an officer of the franchisor was convicted of fraud, unfair or deceptive business practices or a violation of a law that regulates franchises or business, or if there is a charge pending against the person involving such a matter, and the details of any such conviction or charge.		**2** Provide details on convictions for the previous 10 years relating to the franchisor and its associates and any of the directors, general partners and officers of the franchisor who have management responsibilities relating to the franchise

TOPIC	PRINCE EDWARD ISLAND	NEW BRUNSWICK	ONTARIO	MANITOBA	BRITISH COLUMBIA	ALBERTA
			Franchises Regulations			
			involving such a matter.			(a) for the commission of indictable offences (or equivalent in other jurisdictions, including pleading no contest to any offence) involving franchises or other businesses, and
						(b) for the commission of offences involving fraud, embezzlement, unfair or deceptive acts or practices or other comparable offences.
						Provide details relating to the franchisor and its associates and any of the directors, general partners and officers of the franchisor who have management responsibilities relating to the franchise on currently pending
						(a) indictable offences involving franchises or other businesses, and
						(b) offences involving fraud, embezzlement, unfair or deceptive acts or practices or other comparable offences.
Administrative Proceedings / Existing Orders	**4.** A statement indicating whether, during the ten years immediately before the date of	**4** A statement indicating whether, during the 5-year period immediately preceding	4. A statement, including a description of details, indicating whether the	**4** A statement indicating whether, during the 10-year period immediately preceding		**4** Provide details relating to the franchisor and its associates and to any of the directors,

TOPIC	PRINCE EDWARD ISLAND	NEW BRUNSWICK	ONTARIO	MANITOBA	BRITISH COLUMBIA	ALBERTA
			Franchises Regulations			
	the disclosure document, the franchisor, the franchisor's associate or a director, general partner or officer of the franchisor has been subject to an administrative order or penalty under a law that regulates franchises or if the person is the subject of any pending administrative actions to be heard under such a law, and the details of any such order, penalty or pending action.	the date of the disclosure document, the franchisor, the franchisor's associate or a director, a general partner or an officer of the franchisor was subject to an administrative order or penalty under a law that regulates franchises, or if the person is the subject of any pending administrative actions to be heard under such a law, and the details of any such order, penalty or pending action.	franchisor, the franchisor's associate or a director, general partner or officer of the franchisor has been subject to an administrative order or penalty imposed under a law of any jurisdiction regulating franchises or business or if the person is the subject of any pending administrative actions to be heard under such a law.	the date of the disclosure document, the franchisor, the franchisor's associate or a director, a general partner or an officer of the franchisor was subject to an administrative order or penalty under a law that regulates franchises or business, or if the person is the subject of any pending administrative actions to be heard under such a law, and the details of any such order, penalty or pending action.		general partners and officers of the franchisor who have management responsibilities relating to the franchise on any currently effective injunctive or restrictive orders imposed by, or any pending administrative actions to be heard before, any public agency, whether in Alberta or outside Alberta, involving franchises or other businesses.
Civil Litigation and Liabilities		**5** A statement indicating whether, during the 5-year period immediately preceding the date of the disclosure document, the franchisor, the franchisor's associate or a director, a general partner or an officer of the franchisor was found liable in a civil action for misrepresentation, engaging in unfair or deceptive business practices or violating a law that regulates franchises, including a failure to provide proper disclosure to a franchisee, or if a civil action involving such allegations is pending against the person, and the details of any such action or pending action.	5. A statement, including a description of details, indicating whether the franchisor, the franchisor's associate or a director, general partner or officer of the franchisor has been found liable in a civil action of misrepresentation, unfair or deceptive business practices or violating a law that regulates franchises or businesses, including a failure to provide proper disclosure to a franchisee, or if a civil action involving such allegations is pending against the person.	**5** A statement indicating whether, during the 10-year period immediately preceding the date of the disclosure document, the franchisor, the franchisor's associate or a director, a general partner or an officer of the franchisor was found liable in a civil action for misrepresentation, engaging in unfair or deceptive business practices or violating a law that regulates franchises or business, including a failure to provide proper disclosure to a franchisee, or if a civil action involving such allegations is pending against the person, and the details of any such action or pending action.		**3** Provide details relating to the franchisor and its associates and to any of the directors, general partners and officers of the franchisor who have management responsibilities relating to the franchise on any finding of liability in a civil action or on any pending actions involving franchises or other businesses, involving misrepresentation, unfair or deceptive acts or practices and comparable actions.
Bankruptcy	**6.** Details of any bankruptcy or insolvency proceedings,	**6** Details of any bankruptcy or insolvency proceedings,	6. Details of any bankruptcy or insolvency proceedings,	**6** Details of any bankruptcy or insolvency proceedings,		**5** Provide details of any bankruptcy or insolvency

TOPIC	PRINCE EDWARD ISLAND	NEW BRUNSWICK	ONTARIO	MANITOBA	BRITISH COLUMBIA	ALBERTA
			Franchises Regulations			
	voluntary or otherwise, any part of which took place during the six years immediately before the date of the disclosure document, in which the debtor is	voluntary or otherwise, any part of which took place during the 5-year period immediately preceding the date of the disclosure document, in which the debtor was	voluntary or otherwise, any part of which took place during the six years immediately preceding the date of the disclosure document, against any of the following persons as debtors:	voluntary or otherwise, any part of which took place during the six-year period immediately preceding the date of the disclosure document, in which the debtor was		proceedings, voluntary or otherwise, in the previous 6 years
	(a) the franchisor or the franchisor's associate;	(a) the franchisor or the franchisor's associate,	i. The franchisor or the franchisor's associate.	(a) the franchisor or the franchisor's associate;		(a) against the franchisor and its associates,
	(b) a corporation whose directors or officers include a current director, officer or general partner of the franchisor, or included such a person at a time when the bankruptcy or insolvency proceeding was taking place;	(b) a corporation whose directors or officers include a current director, officer or general partner of the franchisor, or included such a person at a time when the bankruptcy or insolvency proceeding was taking place,	ii. A corporation whose directors or officers include a current director, officer or general partner of the franchisor, or included such a person at a time when the bankruptcy or insolvency proceeding was taking place.	(b) a corporation whose directors or officers include a current director, officer or general partner of the franchisor, or included such a person at a time when the bankruptcy or insolvency proceeding was taking place;		(b) against a corporation, any of whose directors or officers are currently directors, general partners and officers of the franchisor who have management responsibilities relating to the franchise, and
	(c) a partnership whose general partners include a current director, officer or general partner of the franchisor, or included such a person at a time when the bankruptcy or insolvency proceeding was taking place; or	(c) a partnership whose general partners include a current director, officer or general partner of the franchisor, or included such a person at a time when the bankruptcy or insolvency proceeding was taking place, or	iii. A partnership whose general partners include a current director, officer or general partner of the franchisor, or included such a person at a time when the bankruptcy or insolvency proceeding was taking place.	(c) a partnership whose general partners include a current director, officer or general partner of the franchisor, or included such a person at a time when the bankruptcy or insolvency proceeding was taking place; or		(c) against a partnership whose general partners are currently directors, general partners and officers of the franchisor who have management responsibilities relating to the franchise.
	(d) a director, officer or general partner of the franchisor in his or her personal capacity.	(d) a director, an officer or a general partner of the franchisor in his or her personal capacity.	iv. A director, an officer or a general partner of the franchisor in their personal capacity.	(d) a director, an officer or a general partner of the franchisor in his or her personal capacity.		
Dispute Resolution	**16.** A description of any	**19** A description of any	**5.** (1) If an internal or external	**24**(1) A description of any		

TOPIC	PRINCE EDWARD ISLAND	NEW BRUNSWICK	ONTARIO	MANITOBA	BRITISH COLUMBIA	ALBERTA
			Franchises Regulations			
	restrictions or requirements imposed by the franchise agreement with respect to arbitration, mediation or other alternative dispute resolution process, including any requirements relating to the location or venue of such a process.	restrictions or requirements imposed by the franchise agreement with respect to arbitration, mediation or any other alternative dispute resolution process, including any requirements relating to the venue of such a process.	mediation or other alternative dispute resolution process is used by a franchisor in disputes with a franchisee, a disclosure document shall include, together with the statement referred to in subsection (2), a description of the mediation or other alternative dispute resolution process, and the circumstances when the process may be invoked. O. Reg.	restrictions or requirements imposed by the franchise agreement with respect to arbitration, mediation or any other alternative dispute resolution process, in addition to the information required by subsection 5(6) of the Act.		
			5. (2) Every disclosure document shall include the following statement: Mediation is a voluntary process to resolve disputes with the assistance of an independent third party. Any party may propose mediation or other dispute resolution process in regard to a dispute under the franchise agreement, and the process may be used to resolve the dispute if agreed to by all parties.	**24**(2) Every disclosure document shall include the following statement: Mediation is a voluntary process to resolve disputes with the assistance of an independent third party. Any party may propose mediation or other dispute resolution process in regard to a dispute under the franchise agreement, and the process may be used to resolve the dispute if agreed to by all parties.		
Required Information About the Franchise			**6.** For the purposes of clause 5 (4) (a) of the Act, every disclosure document shall include the following presented together in one part of the document:			
Costs of Establishing	**1.** A list of all of the franchisee's costs associated with the	**1** A list of all of the franchisee's costs associated with the	**1.** A list of all of the franchisee's costs associated with the	**7** A list of all of the franchisee's costs associated with the		**8** Provide details of the initial investment required by the

TOPIC	PRINCE EDWARD ISLAND	NEW BRUNSWICK	ONTARIO	MANITOBA	BRITISH COLUMBIA	ALBERTA
			Franchises Regulations			
the Franchise	establishment of the franchise, including	establishment of the franchise, including	establishment of the franchise, including,	establishment of the franchise, including		franchisee to start business operations.
Franchise Fees and Deposits	(a) the amount of any deposits or initial franchise fees, or the formula for determining the amount, whether the deposits or fees are refundable and if so, under what conditions;	(a) the amount of any deposits or initial franchise fees, or the formula for determining the amount, whether the deposits or fees are refundable and if so, under what conditions,	i. the amount of any deposits or franchise fees, whether the deposits or fees are refundable, and if so, under what conditions,	(a) the amount of any deposits or initial franchise fees, or the formula for determining the amount, whether the deposits or fees are refundable and if so, under what conditions;		**7** Disclose the initial franchise fee and state the conditions when this fee is refundable.
Estimate of Start-up Costs	(b) an estimate of the costs for inventory, supplies, leasehold improvements, fixtures, furnishings, equipment, signs, vehicles, leases, rentals, prepaid expenses and all other tangible or intangible property and an explanation of any assumptions underlying the estimate; and	(b) an estimate of the costs for inventory, supplies, leasehold improvements, fixtures, furnishings, equipment, signs, vehicles, leases, rentals, prepaid expenses and all other tangible or intangible property and an explanation of any assumptions underlying the estimate, and	ii. an estimate of the costs for inventory, leasehold improvements, equipment, leases, rentals and all other tangible and intangible property necessary to establish the franchise and an explanation of any assumptions underlying the estimate, and	(b) an estimate of the costs for inventory, supplies, leasehold improvements, fixtures, furnishings, equipment, signs, vehicles, leases, rentals, prepaid expenses and all other tangible or intangible property and an explanation of any assumptions underlying the estimate; and		
Other Costs of Establishing the Franchise	(c) any other costs associated with the establishment of the franchise not listed in (a) or (b), including any payment to the franchisor or franchisor's associate, whether direct or indirect, required by the franchise agreement, the nature and amount of the payment and when the payment is due.	(c) any other costs associated with the establishment of the franchise not listed in paragraph (a) or (b), including any payment to the franchisor or franchisor's associate, whether direct or indirect, required by the franchise agreement, the nature and amount of the payment and when the payment is due.	iii. any other costs associated with the establishment of the franchise not listed in subparagraph i or ii, including any payment to the franchisor, whether direct or indirect, required by the franchise agreement, the nature and amount of the payment, and when the payment is due.	(c) any other costs associated with the establishment of the franchise not listed in subsection (a) or (b), including any payment to the franchisor or the franchisor's associate, whether direct or indirect, required by the franchise agreement, the nature and amount of the payment and when the payment is due.		

TOPIC	PRINCE EDWARD ISLAND	NEW BRUNSWICK	ONTARIO	MANITOBA	BRITISH COLUMBIA	ALBERTA
Franchises Regulations						
Other Recurring or Isolated Fees	**2.** The nature and amount of any recurring or isolated fees or payments, other than those listed in item 1, that the franchisee must pay to the franchisor or franchisor's associate, whether directly or indirectly, or that the franchisor or franchisor's associate imposes or collects in whole or in part on behalf of a third party, whether directly or indirectly, except for payments required to be collected by law on behalf of a municipal, provincial or federal government or governmental agency.	**2** The nature and amount of any recurring or isolated fees or payments, other than those listed in section 1 of this Part, that the franchisee must pay to the franchisor or franchisor's associate, whether directly or indirectly, or that the franchisor or franchisor's associate imposes or collects in whole or in part on behalf of a third party, whether directly or indirectly, except for payments required to be collected by law on behalf of a municipal, provincial or federal government or governmental agency.		**8** The nature and amount of any recurring or isolated fees or payments, other than those listed in section 7, that the franchisee must pay to the franchisor or the franchisor's associate, whether directly or indirectly, or that the franchisor or the franchisor's associate imposes or collects in whole or in part on behalf of a third party, whether directly or indirectly, except for payments required to be collected by law on behalf of a municipal, provincial or federal government or governmental agency.		**7** Disclose other recurring or isolated fees or payments that the franchisee must pay to the franchisor or its associates or that the franchisor or its associates impose or collect in whole or in part on behalf of a third party. If any fee is refundable, state the conditions when each fee or payment is refundable.
Estimate of Working Capital						**10** If an estimate of working capital is provided, the information must (a) have a reasonable basis at the time it is made, and (b) include the material assumptions underlying its preparation and presentation. If an estimate of working capital is not provided, the disclosure document must include a statement that additional funds will be required to finance operations until a positive cash flow is produced.

TOPIC	PRINCE EDWARD ISLAND	NEW BRUNSWICK	ONTARIO	MANITOBA	BRITISH COLUMBIA	ALBERTA
			Franchises Regulations			
Guarantees and Security Interests	**3.** A description of the franchisor's policies and practices, if any, regarding guarantees and security interests required of franchisees.	**3** A description of the franchisor's policies and practices, if any, regarding guarantees and security interests required of franchisees.		**9** A description of the franchisor's policies and practices, if any, regarding guarantees and security interests required of franchisees.		
Estimate of Operating Costs	**4.** If an estimate of annual operating costs for the franchise or of operating costs for the franchise for another regular period is provided directly or indirectly, a statement specifying, (a) the assumptions and bases underlying the estimate; (b) that the assumptions and bases underlying the estimate are reasonable; and (c) where information that substantiates the estimate is available for inspection.	**4(1)** If an estimate of annual operating costs for the franchise or of operating costs for the franchise for another regular period is provided directly or indirectly, a statement specifying (a) the assumptions and bases underlying the estimate, (b) that the assumptions and bases underlying the estimate are reasonable, and (c) where information that substantiates the estimate is available for inspection.	**2.** If an estimate of annual operating costs for the franchise is provided, a statement specifying the basis for the estimate, the assumptions underlying the estimate and a location where information is available for inspection that substantiates the estimate.	**10(1)** If an estimate of annual operating costs for the franchise, or of operating costs for the franchise for another regular period, is provided, whether directly or indirectly, a statement specifying (a) the assumptions and bases underlying the estimate; and (b) where information that substantiates the estimate is available for inspection.		
Negative Disclosure Statement (Operating Costs)		**4(2)** If an estimate of annual operating costs for the franchise, or of operating costs for another regular period, is not provided, a statement to		**10(2)** If an estimate of annual operating costs for the franchise, or of operating costs for another regular period, is not provided, a statement to		

TOPIC	PRINCE EDWARD ISLAND	NEW BRUNSWICK	ONTARIO	MANITOBA	BRITISH COLUMBIA	ALBERTA
Franchises Regulations						
		that effect.		that effect.		
Earnings Projection/ Earnings Claim	**5.** If an earnings projection for the franchise is provided directly or indirectly, a statement specifying	**5(1)** If an earnings projection for the franchise is provided directly or indirectly, a statement specifying	**3.** If an earnings projection for the franchise is provided, a statement specifying the reasonable basis for the projection, the assumptions underlying the projection and a location where information is available for inspection that substantiates the projection.	**11**(1) If an earnings projection for the franchise is provided, whether directly or indirectly, a statement specifying		**16** If information is given or is to be given, by or on behalf of the franchisor or its associate, to a prospective franchisee from which a specific level or range of actual or potential sales, costs, income or profit from franchisee outlets or franchisor outlets can be easily ascertained, the information must
Reasonable Basis			**NOTE: See Section 3 above.**			(a) have a reasonable basis at the time it is made,
Assumptions and Bases	(a) the assumptions and bases underlying the projection, its preparation and presentation;	(a) the assumptions and bases underlying the projection, its preparation and its presentation,	**NOTE: See Section 3 above.**	(a) the assumptions and bases underlying the projection, its preparation and its presentation;		(b) include the material assumptions underlying its preparation and presentation, whether it is based on actual results of existing outlets and the percentage of outlets that meet or exceed each range of results, and
Reasonableness Statement	(b) that the assumptions and bases underlying the projection, its preparation and presentation are reasonable;	(b) that the assumptions and bases underlying the projection, its preparation and its presentation are reasonable,				
Period Covered	(c) the period covered by the projection;	(c) the period covered by the projection,				
Projection Based on Actual Results	(d) whether the projection is based on actual results of existing franchises or of	(d) whether the projection is based on actual results of existing franchises or of		(b) whether the projection is based on actual results of existing franchises or of		

TOPIC	PRINCE EDWARD ISLAND	NEW BRUNSWICK	ONTARIO	MANITOBA	BRITISH COLUMBIA	ALBERTA
Franchises Regulations						
	existing businesses of the franchisor, franchisor's associates or affiliates of the franchisor of the same type as the franchise being offered and, if so, the locations, areas, territories or markets of such franchises and businesses;	existing businesses of the franchisor, franchisor's associates or affiliates of the franchisor of the same type as the franchise being offered and, if so, the locations, areas, territories or markets of such franchises and businesses,		existing businesses of the franchisor or the franchisor's associates of the same type as the franchise being offered and, if so, the locations, areas, territories or markets of such franchises and businesses;		
Statement That Results May Differ	(e) if the projection is based on a business operated by the franchisor, franchisor's associate or affiliate of the franchisor, that the information may differ in respect of a franchise operated by a franchisee; and	(e) if the projection is based on a business operated by the franchisor, franchisor's associate or affiliate of the franchisor, that the information may differ in respect of a franchise operated by a franchisee, and		(c) if the projection is based on a business operated by the franchisor or the franchisor's associate, that the information may differ in respect of a franchise operated by a franchisee; and		**16** If information is given in respect of a franchisor outlet, the franchisor must state that the information may differ in respect of a franchise outlet.
Location of Information Substantiating the Projection	(f) where information that substantiates the projection is available for inspection.	(f) where information that substantiates the projection is available for inspection.	**NOTE: See Section 3 above.**	(d) where information that substantiates the projection is available for inspection.		(c) indicate the place where substantiating information is available for inspection by the franchisee.
Negative Disclosure Statement (Earnings Projection)		**5**(2) If an earnings projection for the franchise is not provided, a statement to that effect.		**11**(2) If an earnings projection for the franchise is not provided, a statement to that effect.		
Financing	**6.** The terms and conditions of any financing arrangements that the franchisor or franchisor's associate offers, directly or indirectly, to the franchisee.	**6** The terms and conditions of any financing arrangements that the franchisor or franchisor's associate offers, directly or indirectly, to the franchisee.	**4.** The terms and conditions of the financing arrangements that the franchisor or the franchisor's associate offers directly or indirectly to franchisees.	**12** The terms and conditions of any financing arrangements that the franchisor or the franchisor's associate offers, whether directly or indirectly, to the franchisee.		**9** Disclose the terms and conditions of each financing arrangement that the franchisor offers directly or indirectly to the franchisee.

TOPIC	PRINCE EDWARD ISLAND	NEW BRUNSWICK	ONTARIO	MANITOBA	BRITISH COLUMBIA	ALBERTA
			Franchises Regulations			
Training	**7.** A description of any training or other assistance offered to the franchisee by the franchisor or franchisor's associate, including where the training or other assistance will take place, whether the training or other assistance is mandatory or optional and, if it is mandatory, a statement specifying who bears the costs of the training or other assistance.	**7**(1) A description of any training or other assistance offered to the franchisee by the franchisor or franchisor's associate, including where the training or other assistance will take place, whether the training or other assistance is mandatory or optional and, if it is mandatory, a statement specifying who bears the costs of the training or other assistance.	**5.** A description of any training or other assistance offered to franchisees by the franchisor or the franchisor's associate, including whether the training is mandatory or optional, and if the training is mandatory, a statement specifying who bears the costs of the training.	**13**(1) A description of any training offered to the franchisee by the franchisor or the franchisor's associate, including where the training will take place if known at the date of disclosure, whether the training is mandatory or optional and, if it is mandatory, a statement specifying who bears the costs of the training.		
Negative Disclosure Statement (Training)		**7**(2) If training or other assistance is not offered to the franchisee by the franchisor or franchisor's associate, a statement to that effect.		**13**(2) If training is not offered to the franchisee by the franchisor or the franchisor's associate, a statement to that effect.		
Manuals		**8** If the franchisee will be required to operate in accordance with manuals provided by the franchisor, the table of contents of each manual or a statement specifying where in New Brunswick the manuals are available for inspection.		**14**(1) If the franchisee will be required to operate in accordance with manuals provided by the franchisor, the table of contents of each manual or a statement specifying where the manuals are available for inspection.		
Negative Disclosure Statement (Manuals)				**14**(2) If no manuals are provided to the franchisee, a statement to that effect.		
Advertising Fund	**8.** If the franchisee is required to contribute to an advertising, marketing, promotion or similar fund, a description of the fund,	**9** If the franchisee will be required to contribute to an advertising, marketing, promotion or similar fund, a	**6.** If the franchisee, as a condition of the franchise agreement, is required to contribute to an advertising	**15** If the franchisee will be required to contribute to an advertising, marketing, promotion or similar fund, a		

TOPIC	PRINCE EDWARD ISLAND	NEW BRUNSWICK	ONTARIO	MANITOBA	BRITISH COLUMBIA	ALBERTA
Franchises Regulations						
	and the amount or the basis of calculating the amount of the franchisee's required contribution.	statement describing the fund and specifying	fund,	statement describing the fund and specifying		
			i. a statement describing,			
Expenditure on Advertising – Last 2 Fiscal years		(b) the percentage of the fund that has been spent on national campaigns and local advertising in the 2 fiscal years immediately preceding the date of the disclosure document,	A. the percentage of the fund that has been spent on national campaigns and local advertising in the two fiscal years immediately preceding the date of the disclosure document, and	(b) the percentage of the fund that has been spent on national campaigns and local advertising in the two fiscal years immediately preceding the date of the disclosure document;		
Retention of Funds – Last 2 Fiscal years		(c) the percentage of the fund, other than the percentage referred to in paragraph (b), that has been retained by the franchisor, the franchisor's parent or the franchisor's associates in the 2 fiscal years immediately preceding the date of the disclosure document,	B. the percentage of the fund, other than the percentage described in sub-subparagraph A, that has been retained by the franchisor, the franchisor's parent or the franchisor's associate in the two fiscal years immediately preceding the date of the disclosure document,	(c) the percentage of the fund, other than the percentage referred to in subsection (b), that has been retained by the franchisor, the franchisor's parent or the franchisor's associates in the two fiscal years immediately preceding the date of the disclosure document;		
			ii. another statement describing,			
Projected	**NOTE: See Section 8 above.**	(a) the amount or the basis of	A. the projected amount	(a) the amount or the basis of		

TOPIC	PRINCE EDWARD ISLAND	NEW BRUNSWICK	ONTARIO	MANITOBA	BRITISH COLUMBIA	ALBERTA
Franchises Regulations						
Contribution		calculating the amount of the franchisee's required contribution,	of the contribution,	calculating the amount of the franchisee's required contribution;		
Projected Expenditure on Advertising – Current Fiscal Year		(d) a projection of the percentage of the fund to be spent on national or local advertising campaigns for the current fiscal year,	B. a projection of the percentage of the fund to be spent on national or local advertising campaigns for the current fiscal year, and	(d) a projection of the percentage of the fund to be spent on national or local advertising campaigns for the current fiscal year;		
Projected Retention of Funds – Current Fiscal Year		(e) a projection of the percentage of the fund to be retained by the franchisor, the franchisor's parent or the franchisor's associates in the current fiscal year, and	C. a projection of the percentage of the fund to be retained by the franchisor, the franchisor's parent or the franchisor's associate in the current fiscal year, and	(e) a projection of the percentage of the fund to be retained by the franchisor, the franchisor's parent or the franchisor's associates in the current fiscal year; and		
Reports on Activities of the Fund		(f) whether reports on advertising activities financed by the fund will be made available to the franchisee.	iii. an indication of whether reports on advertising activities financed by the fund will be made available to the franchisee.	(f) whether reports on advertising activities financed by the fund will be made available to the franchisee		
Purchase and Sale Restrictions	**9.** A description of any restrictions or requirements imposed by the franchise agreement with respect to	**10** A description of any restrictions or requirements imposed by the franchise agreement with respect to	**7.** A description of any restrictions or requirements imposed by the franchise agreement with respect to,	**16** A description of any restrictions or requirements imposed by the franchise agreement with respect to		**11** Disclose restrictions or conditions imposed by the franchisor or its associates
	(b) the goods and services the franchisee may sell; and	(b) the goods and services the franchisee may sell, and	ii. the goods and services the franchisee may sell, and	(b) the goods and services the franchisee may sell; and		(a) on the goods or services that the franchisee may sell, or

TOPIC	PRINCE EDWARD ISLAND	NEW BRUNSWICK	ONTARIO	MANITOBA	BRITISH COLUMBIA	ALBERTA
Franchises Regulations						
	(c) to whom or by what means the franchisee may sell goods or services.	(c) to whom or by what means the franchisee may sell goods or services.	iii. whom the franchisee may sell goods or services.	(c) to whom or by what means the franchisee may sell goods or services.		(b) that limit the customers to whom the franchisee may sell goods or services.
	(a) obligations to purchase or lease from the franchisor or franchisor's associate or from suppliers approved by the franchisor or franchisor's associate;	(a) obligations to purchase or lease from the franchisor or franchisor's associate or from suppliers approved by the franchisor or franchisor's associate,	i. obligations to purchase or lease from the franchisor, the franchisor's associate or suppliers approved by the franchisor or the franchisor's associate,	(a) obligations to purchase or lease from the franchisor or the franchisor's associate or from suppliers approved by the franchisor or franchisor's associate;		**11** Disclose franchisee obligations to purchase or lease from the franchisor or its associates or from suppliers approved by the franchisor or its associates or under the franchisor's or associate's specifications.
Rebates, Commissions, Payments or Other Benefits	**10.** A description of the franchisor's policies and practices, if any, regarding rebates, commissions, payment or other benefits, including	**11** A description of the franchisor's policies and practices regarding rebates, commissions, payments or other benefits, including	**8.** A description of the franchisor's policy, if any, regarding volume rebates, and whether or not the franchisor or the franchisor's associate receives a rebate, commission, payment or other benefit as a result of purchases of goods and services by a franchisee and, if so, whether rebates, commissions, payments or other benefits are shared with franchisees, either directly or indirectly.	**17** A description of the franchisor's policies and practices regarding rebates, commissions, payments or other benefits, including		**12** State whether or not there are any rebates or other benefits that the franchisor or its associates may receive or are receiving as a result of the purchase of goods or services by franchisees. Indicate if any of these rebates or benefits are shared with franchisees, either directly or indirectly.
	(a) the receipt, if any, by the franchisor or franchisor's associate of a rebate, commission, payment or other benefit as a result of purchases of goods and services by franchisees; and	(a) the receipt, if any, by the franchisor or franchisor's associate of a rebate, commission, payment or other benefit as a result of purchases of goods and services by franchisees, and		(a) the receipt, if any, by the franchisor or the franchisor's associate of a rebate, commission, payment or other benefit as a result of purchases of goods and services by franchisees; and		
	(b) whether rebates, commissions, payments or other benefits are shared with franchisees either directly or indirectly.	(b) whether rebates, commissions, payments or other benefits are shared with franchisees either directly or indirectly.		(b) whether rebates, commissions, payments or other benefits are shared with franchisees either directly or indirectly.		
Trademarks and Other Proprietary Rights	**13.** A description of the rights the franchisor or the franchisor's associate has to the	**15** A description of the rights the franchisor or the franchisor's associate has to the	**9.** A description of the rights the franchisor or the franchisor's associate has to the trade-mark,	**20** A description of the rights the franchisor or the franchisor's associate has to the		

TOPIC	PRINCE EDWARD ISLAND	NEW BRUNSWICK	ONTARIO	MANITOBA	BRITISH COLUMBIA	ALBERTA
			Franchises Regulations			
	trade-mark, trade name, logo or advertising or other commercial symbol associated with the franchise.	trade-mark, trade name, logo or advertising or other commercial symbol associated with the franchise and of any known or alleged material impediments to its use.	service mark, trade name, logo or advertising or other commercial symbol associated with the franchise.	trademark, trade name, logo or advertising associated with the franchise.		
Licences, Registrations, Authorizations and Other Permissions		**16**(1) A description of every licence, registration, authorization or other permission that the franchisee will be required to obtain under federal or provincial laws in order to sell or distribute the particular goods or services sold or distributed by the franchise.	**10.** A description of every licence, registration, authorization or other permission the franchisee is required to obtain, under any applicable federal or provincial law or municipal by-law, to operate the franchise.	**21**(1) A description of every licence, registration, authorization or other permission that the franchisee will be required to obtain under federal or provincial laws to operate the franchise.		
		16(2) A statement that, in addition to those identified in subsection (1), the franchisee may be required under other federal or provincial laws or under the by-laws of a municipal or other local authority to obtain licences, registrations, authorizations or other permissions to operate the franchise and that the franchisee should make inquiries to determine whether such licences, registrations, authorizations or other permissions are required.		**21**(2) A statement that, in addition to those identified in subsection (1), the franchisee may be required under other federal or provincial laws or under the by-laws of a municipal or other local authority to obtain licences, registrations, authorizations or other permissions to operate the franchise and that the franchisee should make inquiries to determine whether such licences, registrations, authorizations or other permissions are required.		
Personal Participation	**14.** A description of the extent to which the franchisee is required to participate personally and directly in the	**17** A description of the extent to which the franchisee will be required to participate personally and directly in the	**11.** A statement indicating whether the franchisee is required to participate personally and directly in the	**22** A description of the extent to which the franchisee will be required to participate personally and directly in the		**13** State whether or not the franchisor requires the franchisee to participate personally in the direct

TOPIC	PRINCE EDWARD ISLAND	NEW BRUNSWICK	ONTARIO	MANITOBA	BRITISH COLUMBIA	ALBERTA
Franchises Regulations						
	operation of the franchise or, if the franchisee is a corporation, partnership or other entity, the extent to which the principals of the corporation, partnership or other entity are so required.	operation of the franchise or, if the franchisee is a corporation, partnership or other entity, the extent to which the principals of the corporation, partnership or other entity are so required.	operation of the franchise or, if the franchisee is a corporation, whether the principals of the corporation are so required.	operation of the franchise or, if the franchisee is a corporation, partnership or other entity, the extent to which the principals of the corporation, partnership or other entity are so required.		operation of the franchise business.
Territory	**11.** A description of the franchisor's policies and practices, if any, regarding the granting of exclusive territory and, if the franchise agreement grants the franchisee rights to exclusive territory, a description of the franchisor's policy, if any, as to whether the continuation of the franchisee's rights to exclusive territory depends on the franchisee achieving a specific level of sales, market penetration, or other condition, and under what circumstances these rights might be altered.	**12**(1) A description of the franchisor's policies and practices regarding the granting of exclusive territory and, if the franchise agreement grants the franchisee rights to exclusive territory,		**18**(1) A description of the franchisor's policies and practices regarding the granting of exclusive territory and, if the franchise agreement grants the franchisee rights to exclusive territory,		
Description of Territory		(a) a description of the exclusive territory granted or of the manner in which and the person by whom the exclusive territory will be determined,	**12.** A description of any exclusive territory granted to the franchisee.	(a) a description of the exclusive territory granted or of the manner in which and the person by whom the exclusive territory will be determined;		**18** Describe any exclusive territory granted the franchisee.
Performance Levels to Maintain Territory	**NOTE: See section 11 above.**	(b) a description of the franchisor's policy, if any, as to whether the continuation of the franchisee's rights to the exclusive territory depends on the	**13.** If the franchise agreement grants the franchisee rights to exclusive territory, a description of the franchisor's policy, if any, as to whether the continuation of the franchisee's rights to exclusive territory depends on	(b) a description of the franchisor's policy, if any, as to whether the continuation of the franchisee's rights to the exclusive territory depends on the franchisee		**18** Disclose the franchisor's policy, if any, as to whether the continuation of the franchisee's territory depends on the achievement of a certain sales volume, market penetration or other contingency and under

TOPIC	PRINCE EDWARD ISLAND	NEW BRUNSWICK	ONTARIO	MANITOBA	BRITISH COLUMBIA	ALBERTA
Franchises Regulations						
		franchisee achieving a specific level of sales, market penetration, or other condition, and	the franchisee achieving a specific level of sales, market penetration, or other condition, and under what circumstances these rights may be altered.	achieving a specific level of sales, market penetration, or other condition;		what circumstances the franchisee's territory may be altered.
Circumstances in which Territory May be Altered	**NOTE: See section 11 above.**	(c) a description of the circumstances under which the franchisee's rights to the exclusive territory may be altered.	**NOTE: See section 13 above.**	(c) a description of the circumstances under which the franchisee's rights to the exclusive territory may be altered; and		
Reservations for Internet Sales and Other Sales by Franchisor Within Territory		**14** A description of the franchisor's policies and practices relating to Internet sales or other distance sales by a franchise, distributor, licensee or business described in section 13 of this Part.		(d) a description of any reservation of rights by the franchisor for Internet sales, telephone sales, catalogue sales or sales by other means.		
Negative Disclosure Statement (Territory)		**12**(2) If no exclusive territory is granted to the franchisee, a statement to that effect.		**18**(2) If no exclusive territory is granted to the franchisee, a statement to that effect.		
Proximity Policies or Practices	**12.** A description of the franchisor's policies and practices, if any, on the proximity between an existing franchise and	**13** A description of the franchisor's policies and practices on the proximity between an existing franchise and	**14.** A description of the franchisor's policy, if any, on the proximity between an existing franchise and,	**19** A description of the franchisor's policies and practices on the proximity between an existing franchise and		**18** Disclose the franchisor's policy, if any, as to how proximate to an existing franchisee outlet
Another Franchise	(a) another franchise of the franchisor or franchisor's associate of the same type as the existing franchise;	(a) another franchise of the franchisor or franchisor's associate of the same type as the existing franchise,	i. another franchise,	(a) another franchise of the franchisor or the franchisor's associate of the same type as the existing franchise;		(a) the franchisor may establish another franchise,

TOPIC	PRINCE EDWARD ISLAND	NEW BRUNSWICK	ONTARIO	MANITOBA	BRITISH COLUMBIA	ALBERTA
Franchises Regulations						
Franchisor Outlet						(b) a franchisor outlet may be established,
Other Distributor or Licensee Using Franchisor's Trademark	(b) any distributor or licensee using the franchisor's trade-mark, trade name, logo or advertising or other commercial symbol;	(b) any distributor or licensee using the franchisor's trade-mark, trade name, logo or advertising or other commercial symbol,	ii. any other distributor using the franchisor's trade-mark, service mark, trade name or logo or advertising or other commercial symbol,	(b) any distributor or licensee using the franchisor's trademark, trade name, logo or advertising;		(c) the franchisor may establish other methods of distribution using the franchisor's trademark, service mark, trade name or logotype,
Competing Franchisor Business Using Different Trademark	(c) a business operated by the franchisor, franchisor's associate or affiliate of the franchisor that distributes similar goods or services to those distributed by the existing franchise under a different trade-mark, trade name, logo or advertising or other commercial symbol; or	(c) a business operated by the franchisor, franchisor's associate or affiliate of the franchisor that distributes similar goods or services to those distributed by the existing franchise under a different trade-mark, trade name, logo or advertising or other commercial symbol, or	iii. a franchise owned or operated by the franchisor that distributes similar products or services under a different trade-mark, service mark, trade name or logo, and	(c) a business operated by the franchisor or the franchisor's associate that distributes similar goods or services to those distributed by the existing franchise under a different trademark, trade name, logo or advertising; or		(e) a franchisor outlet may be established that distributes similar products or services under a different trademark, service mark, trade name or logotype.
Competing Franchisor Franchise using Different Trademark	(d) a franchise of the franchisor, franchisor's associate or affiliate of the franchisor that distributes similar goods or services to those distributed by the existing franchise under a different trade-mark, trade name, logo or advertising or other commercial symbol.	(d) a franchise of the franchisor, franchisor's associate or affiliate of the franchisor that distributes similar goods or services to those distributed by the existing franchise under a different trade-mark, trade name, logo or advertising or other commercial symbol.	iv. a franchise granted by the franchisor that distributes similar products or services under a different trade-mark, service mark, trade name or logo.	(d) a franchise of the franchisor or the franchisor's associate that distributes similar goods or services to those distributed by the existing franchise under a different trademark, trade name, logo or advertising.		(d) the franchisor may establish other franchises that distribute similar products or services under a different trademark, service mark, trade name or logotype, and
List of Former Franchisees	**2.** A list of all franchisees of the franchisor, franchisor's	**2.** A list of all franchisees of the franchisor, franchisor's	**15.** The name, last known address and telephone number	**26** A list of all franchisees of the franchisor or the franchisor's		**15** Provide, with respect to any outlet operated under the same

TOPIC	PRINCE EDWARD ISLAND	NEW BRUNSWICK	ONTARIO	MANITOBA	BRITISH COLUMBIA	ALBERTA
			Franchises Regulations			
	associates or affiliates of the franchisor that operated a franchise in Prince Edward Island, New Brunswick or Nova Scotia of the same type as the franchise being offered that has been terminated, cancelled, not renewed or reacquired by the franchisor or otherwise left the system within the last fiscal year immediately preceding the date of the disclosure document, including the name, last known address and telephone number of each franchisee.	associates or affiliates of the franchisor that previously operated, in New Brunswick or in any other jurisdiction from which the franchisor draws the list of current franchisees required under section 1 of this Part, a franchise of the same type as the franchise being offered that has been terminated, cancelled, reacquired or not renewed by the franchisor or has otherwise left the franchise system within the fiscal year immediately preceding the date of the disclosure document, including the name, last known address and telephone number of each franchisee.	of each franchisee in Ontario who operated a franchise of the type being offered that has been terminated, cancelled, not renewed or reacquired by the franchisor or otherwise left the system within the last fiscal year immediately preceding the date of the disclosure document.	associates that previously operated, in Manitoba or in any other jurisdiction from which the franchisor draws the list of current franchisees required under section 25, a franchise of the same type as the franchise being offered that has been terminated, cancelled, reacquired or not renewed by the franchisor or has otherwise left the franchise system within the fiscal year immediately preceding the date of the disclosure document, including the name, last known address and telephone number of each franchisee.		trade name as the franchise being offered, the name, last known address and telephone number of every former franchisee in the total operating territory of the franchisor whose franchise has been terminated, cancelled, not renewed, reacquired by the franchisor or otherwise left the system within the previous fiscal year.
List of Closures and Reasons			**16.** For each closure of a franchise of the type being offered within the three fiscal years immediately preceding the date of the disclosure document, the reasons for the closure, including whether,			**15** Provide information about closures of franchisee outlets or franchisor outlets that operated under the same trade name as the franchise being offered, including the total number of franchises in the total operating territory of the franchisor within the previous 3 fiscal years that have
Termination			i. the franchisor or franchisor's associate terminated or cancelled the franchise agreement,			(a) been terminated or cancelled by the franchisor,
Not Renewed			ii. the franchisor or			(b) not been renewed by the

TOPIC	PRINCE EDWARD ISLAND	NEW BRUNSWICK	ONTARIO	MANITOBA	BRITISH COLUMBIA	ALBERTA
			Franchises Regulations			
			franchisor's associate refused to renew the franchise agreement, or			franchisor,
Reacquired						(c) been reacquired by the franchisor, or
Franchisee Refused Renewal			iii. the franchisee refused to renew the franchise agreement or otherwise left the franchise system.			
Otherwise Left the System			**NOTE: See Section 16. iii. Above.**			(d) otherwise left the system.
List of Current Franchisees	**1.** (1) A list of all franchisees of the franchisor, franchisor's associates, or affiliates of the franchisor, that currently operate franchises of the same type as the franchise being offered in Prince Edward Island, New Brunswick and Nova Scotia, including the name, business address and telephone number of the franchisee and the business address and telephone number of the franchise.	**1**(1) A list of all franchisees of the franchisor, franchisor's associates or affiliates of the franchisor that currently operate franchises in New Brunswick of the same type as the franchise being offered, including the name, business address and telephone number of each franchisee and the business address and telephone number of the franchise.	**17.** A list of the locations of all franchises in Ontario of the type being offered, including the business address, telephone number and name of the franchisee who operates the franchise and, if there are less than 20 franchises in Ontario, the list shall include those franchises which are geographically closest to Ontario, until information on 20 franchises is provided.	**25**(1) A list of all franchisees of the franchisor or the franchisor's associates that currently operate franchises in Manitoba of the same type as the franchise being offered, including the name, business address and telephone number of each franchisee.		**14** Provide the names, mailing addresses and phone numbers of all existing franchisees presently operating an outlet in Alberta under the same trade name as the franchise being offered and the addresses and phone numbers of those outlets.
	1. (2) If there are fewer than 20 franchisees in Prince Edward Island, New Brunswick and Nova Scotia, the list shall also include information on franchisees that operate franchises that are	**1**(2) If there are fewer than 20 franchisees described in subsection (1) in New Brunswick, the list shall also include information on the franchisees that currently operate franchises of the same		**25**(2) If there are fewer than 20 franchisees described in subsection (1) in Manitoba, the list shall also include information on the franchisees that currently operate franchises of the same type in		**14** If, with respect to franchisees operating outlets under the same trade name as the franchise being offered, there are less than 20 franchisee outlets in operation in Alberta and there are

TOPIC	PRINCE EDWARD ISLAND	NEW BRUNSWICK	ONTARIO	MANITOBA	BRITISH COLUMBIA	ALBERTA
Franchises Regulations						
	geographically closest to Prince Edward Island until information on 20 or all franchisees is provided.	type in Ontario, Quebec, Prince Edward Island, Nova Scotia or the State of Maine until information is provided on 20 or all the franchisees, whichever is the lesser number.		Saskatchewan or Alberta until information is provided on 20 or all the franchisees, whichever is the lesser number.		franchisee outlets outside Alberta, provide information on additional outlets that are geographically closest to Alberta until information on 20 outlets is provided. If the total number of franchisee outlets in operation in Alberta and outside Alberta is less than 20, information is only required for the total number of franchisee outlets in operation.
		1(3) If there are fewer than 20 franchisees described in subsection (1) in New Brunswick and the additional jurisdictions referred to in subsection (2), the list shall also include information on the franchisees that currently operate franchises of the same type elsewhere in Canada until information is provided on 20 or all the franchisees, whichever is the lesser number.		**25**(3) If there are fewer than 20 franchisees in Manitoba, Saskatchewan and Alberta, the list shall also include information on franchisees that operate franchises that are geographically closest to Manitoba until information on 20 or all franchisees is provided.		
		1(4) If there are fewer than 20 franchisees described in subsection (1) in Canada and the State of Maine, the list shall also include information on the franchisees that currently operate franchises of the same type elsewhere until information is provided on 20 or all the franchisees, whichever is				

TOPIC	PRINCE EDWARD ISLAND	NEW BRUNSWICK	ONTARIO	MANITOBA	BRITISH COLUMBIA	ALBERTA
			Franchises Regulations			
		the lesser number.				
List of Current Businesses/Franchisor Outlets		**3** A list of all businesses of the same type as the franchise being offered that the franchisor, franchisor's associates or affiliates of the franchisor currently operate in New Brunswick, including the name and business address of each business.		**27** A list of all businesses of the same type as the franchise being offered that the franchisor or the franchisor's associates currently operate in Manitoba, including the name and business address of each business.		**14** Provide the addresses and phone numbers of all existing franchisor outlets presently operating in Alberta under the same trade name as the franchise being offered.
Termination, Renewal and Transfer Provisions	**15.** A concise summary of all the provisions in the franchise agreement that deal with the termination of the agreement, the renewal of the agreement and the transfer of the franchise and a list of where these provisions are found in the agreement.	**18** A concise summary of all the provisions in the franchise agreement that deal with the termination of the agreement, the renewal of the agreement and the transfer of the franchise and a list of where these provisions are found in the agreement.	**18.** A description of all restrictions or conditions in the franchise agreement related to, i. the termination or renewal of the agreement, and ii. the transfer of the franchise.	**23** A concise summary of all the provisions in the franchise agreement that deal with the termination of the agreement, the renewal of the agreement and the transfer of the franchise.		**17** Disclose whether or not there are provisions in the franchise agreement that deal with renewal, termination and transfer of the franchise and, if so, where in the contract these provisions can be found.
Unilateral Amendments		**20**(1) If the franchisor has the right to unilaterally amend any terms or conditions of the franchise agreement, a statement to that effect.				
		20(2) The statement may identify the specific terms and conditions that are subject to unilateral amendment, but is not required to do so.				
Notice of Rescission and Effect of Cancellation						**19** Quote sections 13 and 14 of the Act.

TOPIC	PRINCE EDWARD ISLAND	NEW BRUNSWICK	ONTARIO	MANITOBA	BRITISH COLUMBIA	ALBERTA
Franchises Regulations						
Right of Action for Damages						**20** Quote section 9 of the Act.
						ALBERTA REGULATION 312/2000 **FRANCHISES ACT EXEMPTION REGULATION**
						1 A franchisor is not required to include financial statements in a disclosure document given to a prospective franchisee
						(a) if the franchisor has a net worth on a consolidated basis according to its most recent financial statements, which have been audited or for which a review engagement report has been prepared,
						(i) of not less than $5 000 000, or
						(ii) of not less than $1 000 000 if the franchisor is controlled by a corporation that meets the requirements of subclause (i), and
						(b) if the franchisor

TOPIC	PRINCE EDWARD ISLAND	NEW BRUNSWICK	ONTARIO	MANITOBA	BRITISH COLUMBIA	ALBERTA
Franchises Regulations						
						(i) has had at least 25 franchisees conducting business at all times in Canada during the 5-year period immediately preceding the date of the disclosure document,
						(ii) has conducted business that is the subject of the franchise continuously for not less than 5 years immediately preceding the date of the disclosure document, or
						(iii) is controlled by a corporation that meets the requirements of subclause (i) or (ii).
						1.1(1) The Collins Barrow National Cooperative Incorporated, registered under the *Canada Cooperatives Act*, is exempt from the disclosure requirements of section 4 of the Act.
						(2) Subsection (1) is deemed to have come into force on May 7, 2003.

TOPIC	PRINCE EDWARD ISLAND	NEW BRUNSWICK	ONTARIO	MANITOBA	BRITISH COLUMBIA	ALBERTA
			Franchises Regulations			
						2 The *Exemption Regulation* (AR 249/95) is repealed.
						3 For the purpose of ensuring that this Regulation is reviewed for ongoing relevancy and necessity, with the option that it may be repassed in its present or an amended form following a review, this Regulation expires on November 30, 2016.
		NEW BRUNSWICK REGULATION 2010-93				
		Under section 14 of the *Franchises Act*, the Lieutenant-Governor in Council makes the following Regulation:				
Citation		1 This Regulation may be cited as the *Mediation Regulation-Franchises Act*				
Definitions		2 The following definitions apply in this Regulation.				
"Act"		"Act" means the *Franchises Act*. (*Loi*)				
"mediation"		"mediation" means a process in which 2 or more parties meet and attempt to resolve issues in dispute between them with the				

TOPIC	PRINCE EDWARD ISLAND	NEW BRUNSWICK	ONTARIO	MANITOBA	BRITISH COLUMBIA	ALBERTA
			Franchises Regulations			
		assistance of a mediator. (*médiation*)				
"mediator"		"mediator" means a person who assists parties in resolving issues in dispute between them, but has no power to unilaterally resolve the dispute. (*médiateur*)				
"party"		"party" means a party to a franchise agreement who has a dispute with one or more other parties to the franchise agreement. (*partie*)				
Methods of Delivery		3(1) A notice of dispute under subsection 8(1) of the Act, a notice to mediate under subsection 8(3) of the Act and a notice declining mediation under section 4 of this Regulation may be delivered personally, by electronic means, by fax or by mail.				
		3(2) If mailed, the notice shall be deemed to be delivered on the fifth day after it was mailed.				
		3(3) If sent by electronic means or by fax, the notice shall be deemed to be delivered				
		(a) on the day it is sent, if sent before 5 p.m., or				
		(b) on the day after it was sent, if sent at or after 5				

TOPIC	PRINCE EDWARD ISLAND	NEW BRUNSWICK	ONTARIO	MANITOBA	BRITISH COLUMBIA	ALBERTA
			<u>Franchises Regulations</u>			
		p.m.				
Notice Declining Mediation		4 If a party to whom a notice to mediate is delivered under subsection 8(3) of the Act is of the opinion that the dispute is not suitable for mediation, the party may, within 7 days after that notice is delivered, deliver to the other party or parties a notice declining mediation that states the reasons why the party is of that opinion.				
Appointment of Mediator		5(1) If a notice to mediate is delivered under subsection 8(3) of the Act, the parties shall, unless a notice declining mediation is delivered under section 4, jointly appoint a mediator,				
		(a) if there are 4 or fewer parties, within 14 days after the notice to mediate was delivered, or				
		(b) if there are 5 or more parties, within 21 days after the notice to mediate was delivered.				
		5(2) If the parties fail to jointly appoint a mediator within the time required by subsection (1), each party may authorize a representative to agree on his or her behalf to the				

TOPIC	PRINCE EDWARD ISLAND	NEW BRUNSWICK	ONTARIO	MANITOBA	BRITISH COLUMBIA	ALBERTA
		Franchises Regulations				
		appointment of a mediator.				
Premediation Conference		6 A mediator may hold a premediation conference with the parties in order to consider organizational matters, including				
		(a) the identification of the issues that are to be addressed by the mediation,				
		(b) the exchange of information and documents before mediation, and				
		(c) scheduling and timing matters.				
Timing and Conduct of Mediation		7(1) Mediation of the dispute must begin within 45 days after a mediator is appointed under section 5, unless another date is specified by the mediator with the agreement of all the parties.				
		7(2) The mediator shall schedule the dates, times and locations of the mediation sessions.				
		7(3) The mediator shall conduct the mediation sessions in the manner he or she considers appropriate to assist the parties				

TOPIC	PRINCE EDWARD ISLAND	NEW BRUNSWICK	ONTARIO	MANITOBA	BRITISH COLUMBIA	ALBERTA
		Franchises Regulations				
		to reach a resolution of the dispute that is fair, timely and cost-effective.				
Representation of Party		8 A party may be represented at a premediation conference or a mediation session by counsel or by another person who				
		(a) is familiar with the relevant facts, and				
		(b) has full authority to settle the dispute on the party's behalf or is able to communicate promptly with the party or with another person who has full authority to settle the dispute on the party's behalf.				
Exchange of Information		9 Each party shall deliver to the mediator and the other parties a statement of facts and issues not less than 10 days before the first mediation session is scheduled to be held.				
Time Limits on Mediation		10(1) Subject to subsections (2) and (3), the mediator shall terminate the mediation, whether or not the issues are resolved, after 10 hours of mediation.				
		10(2) The mediator may terminate the mediation earlier if he or she is of the opinion				

TOPIC	PRINCE EDWARD ISLAND	NEW BRUNSWICK	ONTARIO	MANITOBA	BRITISH COLUMBIA	ALBERTA
			Franchises Regulations			
		that the mediation is not likely to be successful.				
		10(3) The mediator may extend the mediation, with the agreement of all the parties, if the mediator is of the opinion that the mediation is likely to be successful with the additional time.				
Conclusion of Mediation		11(1) A mediation is concluded when				
		(a) all the issues are resolved, or				
		(b) the mediator terminates the mediation before the issues are resolved.				
		11(2) When a mediation is concluded, the mediator shall complete a certificate of completed mediation and deliver a copy of it to each of the parties.				
Cost of the Mediation		12 The parties shall share the costs of the mediation equally unless the parties otherwise agree in writing.				
Forms		**NOTE: Forms 1-5, prescribed below, are not reproduced in this table but may be viewed online on the Government of New Brunswick website.**				

TOPIC	PRINCE EDWARD ISLAND	NEW BRUNSWICK	ONTARIO	MANITOBA	BRITISH COLUMBIA	ALBERTA
		Franchises Regulations				
		13(1) A notice of dispute under subsection 8(1) of the Act shall be in Form 1.				
		13(2) A notice to mediate under subsection 8(3) of the Act shall be in Form 2.				
		13(3) A notice declining mediation under section 4 shall be in Form 3.				
		13(4) A statement of facts and issues under section 9 shall be in Form 4.				
		13(5) A certificate of completed mediation under subsection 11(2) shall be in Form 5.				
Commencement		14 This Regulation comes into force on February 1, 2011.				

Table of Cases

Index

A

E

F

J

K

L

O

P

Q

U

V

W